Less managing. More teaching. Greater learning.

 INSTRUCTORS...

Would you like your **students** to show up for class **more prepared**?
(Let's face it, class is much more fun if everyone is engaged and prepared...)

Want ready-made application-level **interactive assignments,** student progress reporting, and auto-assignment grading? *(Less time grading means more time teaching...)*

Want an **instant view of student or class performance** relative to learning objectives? *(No more wondering if students understand...)*

Need to **collect data and generate reports** required for administration or accreditation? *(Say goodbye to manually tracking student learning outcomes...)*

Want to **record and post your lectures** for students to view online?

 With McGraw-Hill's *Connect*™ *Business Law*,

INSTRUCTORS GET:

- Interactive Applications – **book-specific interactive assignments** that require students to APPLY what they've learned.

- Simple **assignment management**, allowing you to spend more time teaching.

- **Auto-graded** assignments, quizzes, and tests.

- **Detailed Visual Reporting** where student and section results can be viewed and analyzed.

- Sophisticated **online testing** capability.

- A **filtering and reporting** function that allows you to easily assign and report on materials that are correlated to accreditation standards, learning outcomes, and Bloom's taxonomy.

- An easy-to-use **lecture capture** tool.

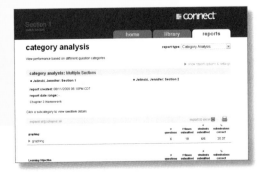

STUDENTS...

Want an online, **searchable version** of your textbook?

Wish your textbook could be **available online** while you're doing your assignments?

Connect™ Plus Business Law eBook

If you choose to use *Connect™ Plus Business Law*, you have an affordable and searchable online version of your book integrated with your other online tools.

Connect™ Plus Business Law eBook offers features like:

- Topic search
- Direct links from assignments
- Adjustable text size
- Jump to page number
- Print by section

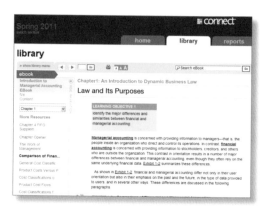

STUDENTS...

Want to get more **value** from your textbook purchase?

Think learning Business Law should be a bit more **interesting**?

Check out the STUDENT RESOURCES section under the *Connect™* Library tab.

Here you'll find a wealth of resources designed to help you achieve your goals in the course. You'll find things like **quizzes, PowerPoints, and Internet activities** to help you study. Every student has different needs, so explore the STUDENT RESOURCES to find the materials best suited to you.

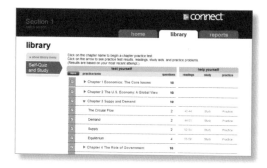

The Legal, Ethical, and Regulatory
Environment of Business in a Diverse Society

The Legal, Ethical, and Regulatory Environment of Business in a Diverse Society

Dawn D. Bennett-Alexander
University of Georgia

Linda F. Harrison
Nova Southeastern University

McGraw-Hill
Irwin

McGraw-Hill Irwin

THE LEGAL, ETHICAL, AND REGULATORY ENVIRONMENT OF BUSINESS IN A DIVERSE SOCIETY

1 2 3 4 5 6 7 8 9 0 QDB/QDB 1 0 9 8 7 6 5 4 3 2 1

ISBN 978-0-07-352492-4
MHID 0-07-352492-1

Vice president and editor-in-chief: *Brent Gordon*
Editorial director: *Paul Ducham*
Executive editor: *John Weimeister*
Executive director of development: *Ann Torbert*
Development editor: *Megan Richter*
Editorial coordinator: *Heather Darr*
Vice president and director of marketing: *Robin J. Zwettler*
Marketing director: *Amee Mosley*
Senior marketing manager: *Sarah Schuessler*
Marketing specialist: *Meredith Desmond*
Vice president of editing, design, and production: *Sesha Bolisetty*
Managing editor: *Lori Koetters*
Buyer II: *Kara Kudronowicz*
Interior and cover designer: *Pam Verros*
Media project manager: *Suresh Babu, Hurix Systems Pvt. Ltd.*
Cover credit: *Anne Alexis Bennett Alexander*
Typeface: *10/12 Times New Roman*
Compositor: *Aptara®, Inc.*
Printer: *Quad/Graphics*

Library of Congress Cataloging-in-Publication Data

Bennett-Alexander, Dawn.
    The legal, ethical, and regulatory environment of business in a diverse society / Dawn
D. Bennett-Alexander, Linda F. Harrison.
      p. cm.
    Includes index.
    ISBN-13: 978-0-07-352492-4 (alk. paper)
    ISBN-10: 0-07-352492-1 (alk. paper)
    1. Law—United States. 2. Businesspeople—United States—Handbooks, manuals, etc.
3. Business law—United States. I. Harrison, Linda F., 1950- II. Title.
KF390.B84B46 2012
346.7307—dc22

                                                                    2010041621

To Kelly Lowery (& crew) for her long ago foresight on the need for this text, and her trust in me to write it.
And to my incredible Ancestors. Thank you. For then, and for now.

–Dawn D. Bennett-Alexander

In loving memory of my mother, Carrie Irene Harrison.
To my siblings, each of whom nourishes me in a special way: my sisters Sharon and Charmaine and brothers Richard and Harold.
And last but most, to our father, Richard Harrison Jr.—the rock for us all.

–linda f. harrison

About the cover design: Acrylic on canvas, the art on the cover of this text was created by Anne Alexis Bennett Alexander, daughter of the authors. Anne Alexis is a teacher of English as a Second Language at Colorado Heights University in Denver and a graduate student in Counseling Psychology. Anne Alexis first sold her art to finance her first summer-long solo trip to Europe after graduating from the University of Georgia with degrees in Psychology and Criminal Justice, before going on to receive her Grande Diplome at Le Cordon Bleu Cooking School in Paris and London. She has sold many pieces around the country since. Fascinated by shapes, colors, and tactile mediums and surfaces for her work, Anne Alexis's art is unpredictable and allegorical and contains elements of realism, fantasy, fascinating shapes, and surprising three-dimensional elements such as shells, actual butterflies, and bees and odd surfaces such as ceiling tiles and wooden 2 x 4s. Anne Alexis believes art is a personal experience for the viewer and prefers viewers to bring themselves to her art and interpret it for what it means to them rather than shape meaning for them by even naming her pieces. Anne Alexis can be reached at annealexisba@gmail.com.

Dawn D. Bennett-Alexander

Dawn D. Bennett-Alexander, Esq., is a multi-award-winning associate professor of Employment Law and Legal Studies at the University of Georgia. Licensed to practice law in the District of Columbia and six federal jurisdictions, she has taught for nearly thirty years and co-authors with Laura Hartman the leading Employment Law text in the country, presently going into its seventh edition (*Employment Law for Business,* McGraw-Hill). Bennett-Alexander co-authored *The Legal, Ethical, and Regulatory Environment of Business,* an innovative legal environment textbook, with linda harrison (Southwestern) as well. Bennett-Alexander also wrote the first-ever sexual harassment entry for *Grolier Encyclopedia,* edited the comprehensive *Federal Employment Rights* for the National Employee Rights Institute, has contributed to several other texts and books, and has written many legal articles.

In addition to teaching, Bennett-Alexander is an internationally known diversity consultant who has written extensively on diversity issues, has conducted numerous diversity seminars over the past twenty-five years, and has been widely quoted in and been an information source for media such as *USAToday, Fortune* Magazine, and National Public Radio. Bennett-Alexander was a Senior Fulbright Fellow at the Ghana School of Law for 2000–2001. She has also taught in Austria, Budapest, Australia, New Zealand, Krakow and Prague. She has three daughters and one granddaughter (with another on the way!) to whom much of her work is dedicated.

Linda F. Harrison

Linda F. Harrison is associate dean for Critical Skills Programs and an associate professor of Law at Nova Southeastern University School of Law. She has taught law over twenty years in the areas of contracts, business entities, and antitrust and was a state prosecutor prior to that. She co-authored a legal environment of business text with Bennett-Alexander in 1995.

The world has changed. We are definitely not in Kansas anymore, Toto.

This is not your father and mother's business world you will be stepping into. Like law in general, the legal environment of business is not static. As society changes, laws change along with it, and the law as it relates to business must also change. For decades, the required course in law for business schools was composed mostly of contracts. Realizing the growing importance of government regulations on business, the AACSB, which sets accreditation standards for collegiate schools of business, believed the coverage of legal topics should be much broader, thus the required course in the Legal Environment of Business was born. Once merely an add-on mentioned only by professors who cared to do so, the incorporation of AACSB standards and ethics coverage is now standard material in Legal Environment courses. The authors of this new text believe that U.S. business is taking place in an increasingly diverse society that is not like the one in which previous generations may have operated. It is time to address this change.

A business person can no longer count on simply making a good product or hiring people who know how to perform a task. We live in a much more litigious society where every decision can result in a potential legal liability. Competition is so keen that every advantage must be capitalized upon to remain competitive. From setting up a business to financing it, hiring employees to making a product, advertising it and eventually shipping it, each and every step has legal, regulatory and, sometimes, diversity issues that can greatly impact the outcome. The point of being in business, for most people, is to make a profit—in fact, the more the better. But what is the purpose if you make a great product, but you lose time and money fighting a case brought by employees who believe they got sick from making the product because you did not tell them about a chemical they were using that could harm them? What sense does it make to race to make billions of dollars, only to lose it in a flash because of unethical and illegal choices you made in the process? (Does Enron come to mind?) Why spend the time, money, and energy to make the profits, only to have them taken away in a lawsuit by employees who allege you discriminated against them based on gender? (WalMart's pending suit for this is the largest in history.)

We are no longer the perceived "robber barons" creating vast wealth to the total exclusion of others' interests. Thanks to many things, including a vast public education system, omnipresent media second to none, instant communication, and information technology, we have developed into a country with a highly intelligent, involved, and informed population that expects to be treated with dignity and respect, even as we pursue profit. The country, through the growth and maturation process, as well as legislation, regulation, and experience, has come to a place where we understand that making money cannot be done while disregarding laws and people. Just as we have come to understand that we must "think green" in manufacturing, selling, advertising, and using our products so that we can protect the earth for future generations, we have also come to realize that being cognizant of the legal implications of our business decisions, the ethical implications of those decisions, and the diversity implications of those decisions are all a part of prudently considering the business decisions we make. Turns out, it's not quite "all about the Benjamins." How we get them matters as well.

This is the first legal environment text to take the diversity implications into consideration as a normal and necessary part of business decisions. It may seem like such a logical thing to do, given many of the situations we have seen recently in which not doing so has had dire consequences, but it has not yet been done until now. Whether it is actor Mel Gibson spewing out the n-word to his girlfriend during a phone conversation, or on a Jewish tirade as he was being arrested, without regard to the business implications it might have for his career or for the companies he was involved with and others invested in his career; or the Manhattan landlord who was said by Mayor Bloomberg to have lied to black apartment hunters about having apartments available in July 2010; or the lenders alleged to have steered perfectly qualified minorities to more expensive and risky subprime loans; or the recently struck down provision of the Arizona immigration law requiring officers to determine if those they stopped were legally in the U.S., diversity and ethics implications of everyday business decisions are all around us.

The goal for this text is to equip you for the legal, ethical, and diversity implications of the diverse business world you will move into, so that your decisions do not result in surprising, expensive, protracted, and embarrassing litigation that could have easily been avoided. We have no doubt that opening your eyes to these issues will greatly aid in that result.

The intentions of this book are to provide:

- A view of the legal environment of business from the broader perspective of not only the law and its theory, but also how it works in practice and the additional factors of ethics and diversity.

- Thorough incorporation of ethics and strategic ethical decision making.

- Thorough incorporation of diversity issues.

- An inviting, engaging, student-oriented approach to the subject matter.

- **Opening Scenarios** to allow you to preview the issues of the chapter in a familiar context.

- Active **Learning Objectives** that open the chapter and inform you of specific outcomes you should have after finishing the chapter, including icons throughout the chapter linked to the numbered objectives.

- **Take Away Boxes** to provide you with basic, bottom-line information you need from the chapter content.

- **Reality Check Boxes** to integrate the theoretical information for the chapter with real-life situations for application.

- **Diversity in the Law Boxes** to provide examples of how diversity impacts law and business and how it can be manifested in many different ways.

- Contemporary, engaging summarized **Cases** with a minimum of "legalese."

- End of chapter **Review Questions** to test your understanding of chapter topics.

- Comprehensive coverage of traditional legal environment subject matter.

- Extensive topic coverage allowing instructors to individually evaluate the chapters and topics to cover for their course; all topics are thorough and complete.

- Ethics queries throughout the chapters as well as an **Ethics Issue** challenge as part of the chapter-end material.

- Optional **Group Exercises** as part of the chapter-end material, which can be used by groups or by a single student to enhance learning.

You, as the students and the instructors, are our ultimate consumers and best judge of whether we have accomplished what we set out to do. We invite you to provide any feedback you think might be helpful in our quest. We sincerely want you to let us know what you think, and we promise that we don't just want kudos. We welcome any and all constructive criticism. Our goal is to have students step out into the world after gaining their business education, feeling that they are well prepared for the world they are stepping into. Based on the feedback we have received from them in growing numbers over recent years, diversity and ethics have become increasingly important parts of the landscape they must deal with. Please let us know if this has helped to address these issues for you. And we hope you have as much enjoyment reading the text as we did preparing it. Let us know! Really!!

Dawn D. Bennett-Alexander

Athens, GA

August 9, 2010

Send feedback to:

Dawn D. Bennett-Alexander   dawndba@uga.edu

linda f. harrison   harrisonlf@nsu.law.nova.edu

ACKNOWLEDGMENTS

The authors would like to honor and thank the following individuals, without whose assistance and support this text would never have been written: Editors Dana Woo and John Weimeister, Megan Richter, our Developmental Editor, Anne Alexis Bennett Alexander, artist extraordinaire for her incredible cover artwork, and Designer Pam Verros for her visuals.

Thank you also to our esteemed writing partner Laura Pincus Hartman who began this journey with us but had to withdraw early on due to unforeseen circumstances. You were missed, but we delight in the fact that we have other projects together!

Finally, for their contributions to text, we would like to thank the scholars who have reviewed this manuscript and offered extremely helpful feedback, including the following:

Robert W. Bing, *William Paterson University*
Russell Block, *San Diego State University*
Michael J. Costello, *University of Missouri–St. Louis*
Rebecca J. Davis, *University of Kentucky*
Roxane DeLaurell, *College of Charleston*
Pamela S. Evers, *University of North Carolina Wilmington*
Timothy J. Fogarty, *Case Western Reserve University*
Dr. John M. Garic, *University of Central Oklahoma*
John Gergacz, *University of Kansas*
Arlene Hibschweiler, *University at Buffalo*
Joseph W. Holland, *University of Wisconsin*
Dr. Jack E. Karns, *S.J.D., East Carolina University*

Ernest W. King, *University of Southern Mississippi*
Paul M. Klein, *Duquesne University*
Deborah S Kleiner, *St. John's University*
Tonia Hap Murphy, *University of Notre Dame*
Gail P. Petravick, *Bradley University*
Roger W. Reinsch, *Northeastern Illinois University*
Dr. Joanie Sompayrac, *University of Tennessee at Chattanooga*
Keith D. Swim, *Jr., Texas A&M University*
Kenneth R. Taurman, *Jr., Indiana University Southeast*
Dr. Leatha P. Ware, *Waubonsee Community College*
Stephen A. Yoder, *University of Alabama at Birmingham*

Dawn Bennett-Alexander: I'll bet you can't count the number of times you have read an author thanking lots of people even though it is only the author's name on the book. Well, the reason so many of them do it is because it's true. I am no exception. I sit at the computer and research and write, but I understand that not only am I standing on the shoulders of many who came before me, who never even dreamed of this, but really did, but also those in my life who make it possible for me to clear my mind and work from a place of comfort, understanding, insight, laughter, peace and clarity. Those include:

- *My esteemed co-author, linda f. harrison, who makes the task of writing so much more pleasant by making me laugh harder, louder and longer than anyone under the sun. I guess 31 years will do that;*

- My parents, Rev. William H. Bennett, Sr., and Anne Liles Bennett, who are no longer here with us, but remain a part of each breath we take and their lessons are forever a part of us;

- My daughters, Jenniffer Dawn Bennett Alexander Jones, Anne Alexis Bennett Alexander, and Tess Alexandra Bennett Harrison, who are the lights of my life and who truly understand and appreciate that being their Mama and hearing them laughing together is my favorite thing on earth;

- My granddaughter, Makayla Anne Jones for whom "Nana" is her favorite four-letter word, just as "Makayla" is my favorite 7-letter word;

- Edward Demont Jones, whom I love for being such a great son-in-law, husband to Jen and Dad to Makayla and Ed, Jr. who arrives in January 2011;

- My siblings, Brenda Bennett Watkins, Gale Bennett Pinson, and Rev. Dr. William H. Bennett, II, for being my biggest fan club and making me laugh so;

- My extended family of nieces, nephews, great-nieces and great-nephews, including the Harrison clan. You bring me so much joy, laughter and comfort;

- President Barack H. Obama and his voters, for giving each of us a chance to watch history happen in such a dramatic way. As a history buff, getting to watch history in the making was practically nirvana;

- My department chair, Dr. Robert Hoyt, for understanding what it means to take the heat so his faculty can just be left to do what they do best;

- My colleagues and adopters who have been so incredibly supportive and generous with their praise and feedback over the years;

- My students who never cease to amaze me with their new insights and willingness to "go there" and come out the better for having done so. Do we have fun or what?!!!

- The students and faculty who send us fan letters, which always humble us and which we *never* take for granted and always marvel that they took the time from their day to think of us and write and give their kudos;

- Attendees at consulting sessions over the years whose willing sharing of their experiences with me, both workplace and personal, have contributed so much to my own understanding of these issues and what to do about them;

- My assortment of cats, birds, fish, plants and music, which all make coming home so much more comforting and enjoyable.

Without each and every one of you, it would be immeasurably harder for me to be focused, and productive, and for that, I thank you more than words can say.

linda f. harrison: I would like to thank my co-author, Dawn D. Bennett-Alexander, whose gentle but persistent prodding always kept me on track. Thanks also to my girls, Jenniffer, Annie, and Tess for always being there for me and giving me love, laughter, and encouragement. A special thank you to Phyllis Kotey for tolerating an office door that was constantly closed throughout this process.

Appreciation goes to my research assistant, Gerald Donnini, J.D., expected 2011, Nova Southeastern University, for his assistance. Lastly, this journey was made immeasurably smoother by the able assistance and patience of our editor, Megan Richter. Thank you.

Text Organization

There are many, many ways to organize a textbook. As with our other texts, we have tried to keep what is familiar, yet give it a critical look to see what can be done to try to make things even more understandable and convenient for both students and faculty. Our text's coverage is traditional in terms of the usual coverage for a legal environment textbook, but we have tried to organize it in a way that makes logical sense. Of course, that varies from person to person and from instructor to instructor. Please feel free to use the text chapters in any way that makes sense for you. Do not feel committed to using the chapters in the order they are placed in the text if some other order is more to your liking.

Part One of the text explains background considerations and the infrastructure of law and the place ethics and diversity have in the law and the business world in general. Part One contains an introduction to the text and to the law, alternative dispute resolution, the court system, and administrative law as the basis for business regulations.

Part Two addresses the basic substantive considerations in the business environment, including contracts and sales, torts, real and personal property, business crimes, secured transactions, and bankruptcy.

Part Three is about the business itself including employment relationships formed in business and their considerations, as well as the financing of the business. It includes agency law, business organizations, the employment relationship, equal employment opportunity considerations, labor law, securities regulations, and antitrust laws.

Part Four includes other important business matters that form a part of the business landscape but may not necessarily be present in each and every business such as intellectual property, environmental law, and international law.

OPENING SCENARIOS

Based on real cases and situations, chapter opening scenarios introduce topics and material that illustrate the need for the concepts covered in the chapter in a way that puts them in an actual context the students can easily understand and relate to. Scenarios are then revisited throughout the chapter text as material pertinent to the opening scenario is discussed. When you encounter the opening scenario icon in the chapter body, you will find the discussion illustrated by a development of the opening scenario, and you may return to it to see if you can now articulate the correct way to solve the problem.

 Opening Scenario

Skycycle Bicycle Emporium has had several complaints filed against it with the Greater Business Bureau. Customers have complained about the quality of the goods and services at Skycycle. There have also been complaints from Skycycle's business suppliers that Skycycle is not honoring their agreements as they should. Cisnero, one of Skycycle owner Oscar's buddies, sees the storm brewing and thinks he can help. Cisnero suggests to Oscar that Cisnero set up a meeting between Oscar and each of the complainants. Cisnero says each complainant will be able to discuss his or her complaint with Oscar and Cisnero will try to broker a solution between the complainant and Oscar. Oscar says he has never heard of such a thing and cannot imagine that it would work. Should Oscar try Cisnero's suggestion?

Introduction and Background

When you think of legal disputes, you probably think of them being settled by a court. However, not every dispute will be litigated in court. In fact, most will not; and they need not be. In reality, the overwhelming majority of disputes are resolved without resort to costly court trials. Not only is litigation costly and time-consuming, but it simply is not necessary for the resolution of every disagreement or conflict. For some conflicts it would be like using a sledgehammer to kill a fly. Litigation is the heavy artillery of the conflict resolution arena and should be used most judiciously. Ideally it should be

Learning Objectives

After reading this chapter, you should be able to:

LO1   Define alternative dispute resolution

LO2   Explain how and why ADR is used in business

LO3   Identify the most popular types of ADR

LO4   Discuss the pros and cons of different types of ADR

LO5   Determine the appropriateness of different types of ADR for various disputes

LO6   Explain how administrative agencies have increasingly mandated ADR

LO7   Describe newly emerging ADR alternatives designed specifically for business

LO8   Evaluate ways that ADR can help business

 Opening Scenario

Skycycle Bicycle Emporium has had several complaints filed against it with the Greater Business Bureau. Customers have complained about the quality of the goods and services at Skycycle. There have also been complaints from Skycycle's business suppliers that Skycycle is not honoring their agreements as they should. Cisnero, one of Skycycle owner Oscar's buddies, sees the storm brewing and thinks he can help. Cisnero suggests to Oscar that Cisnero set up a meeting between Oscar and each of the complainants. Cisnero says each complainant will be able to discuss his or her complaint with Oscar and Cisnero will try to broker a solution between the complainant and Oscar. Oscar says he has never heard of such a thing and cannot imagine that it would work. Should Oscar try Cisnero's suggestion?

Introduction and Background

When you think of legal disputes, you probably think of them being settled by a court. However, not every dispute will be litigated in court. In fact, most will not; and they need not be. In reality, the overwhelming majority of disputes are resolved without resort to costly court trials. Not only is litigation costly and time-consuming, but it simply is not necessary for the resolution of every disagreement or conflict. For some conflicts it would be like using a sledgehammer to kill a fly. Litigation is the heavy artillery of

LEARNING OBJECTIVES

Active learning objectives are provided at the outset of each chapter that inform you of specific outcomes you should be able to achieve after finishing the chapter. The learning objectives are numbered and throughout the chapter you will see icons linked to the numbered objectives. The chapter-end review questions are also linked to the numbered learning objectives. Once you finish the chapter, go back to the learning objectives provided at the beginning of the chapter and test your chapter knowledge by seeing if you can do or know what the learning objective pointed you to accomplish. For example, can you explain what types of property exist? Can you discuss why ethics and diversity would be important business considerations? Can you list six types of intentional torts? If not, then you know precisely where to go to polish up your understanding of the chapter.

TAKE AWAY BOXES

Chapter content is provided in a larger context you need to be aware of as a business student. That is, you need not only rules, but also a context for them and to understand why such rules exist. Still, we provide you with basic, bottom-line information you need from the chapter content through the Take Away boxes.

The idea for the Take Aways came from our students, who often asked after we finished up a chapter concept lecture, "So what's the take away we need from this?" or "So, the take away from this is such and such?" At first we were taken aback that after all we had said in a lecture, this is what it came down to for them. But, as we thought about it, we realized it made sense, since they were coming to grips with what most likely was going to be tested on. Since it was such a common phenomenon, we decided that if our hundreds of students were asking this, they probably were not the only ones, and if that is the way students processed the material, perhaps it would help student understanding to present it that way. So, while we, of course, believe that everything we include in the chapters is important, you can use the Take Aways as a way to summarize the bottom-line need-to-know points of a given section. Thank your fellow students for this one!

TAKE AWAY 2-1

THREE MOST COMMON TYPES OF ALTERNATIVE DISPUTE RESOLUTION (ADR)

- Conciliation/Negotiation
- Mediation
- Arbitration

REALITY CHECK 2-1

10 REASONS TO USE ALTERNATIVE DISPUTE RESOLUTION

In this box you have an example of the Virginia Department of Veterans Affairs' attempt to have vets use ADR rather than litigation to resolve disputes. While some of the items are specifically tailored to the Virginia VA's issues, it gives you a concrete idea of the reasons for the push for ADR rather than protracted and expensive court litigation. Note that item 2 regarding services being free is not generally the case. The cost may be less than litigation, but it is generally not free.

1. ACCESSIBLE
   Alternative Dispute Resolution (ADR) can be requested at any time by any VA employee, manager or union official by contacting the local ADR coordinator or the Workplace ADR Program. A list of coordinators is located at http://vaww1.va.gov/adr/page.cfm?pg=86.
2. COST EFFECTIVE
   ADR services can be provided at no cost to the organization or employee.
3. FAIR AND NEUTRAL
   A facilitator or mediator is assigned to each case. These individuals have no vested interest in the dispute, can be objective, encourage active listening, promote understanding and generate options. When opinions begin to form and emotional responses surface, the parties can benefit from a third party's skills.
4. SAVES TIME AND MONEY
   On average, ADR can be requested, scheduled, and completed in 30 days. Other forums used to resolve disputes such as the grievance and EEO complaint process can take months, even years to reach an outcome.
5. STRUCTURED DIALOGUE
   Ineffective communication can cause workplace disputes. Facilitation and mediation are opportunities to improve communication through structured dialogue where conversations can be more meaningful and productive.

6. INCREASED KNOWLEDGE AND AWARENESS
   When lines of communication are opened or improved, all parties can gain new insights and more easily determine how to address the issues in dispute with an enhanced understanding of each other's concerns.
7. DESIGN YOUR OWN SOLUTION
   ADR outcomes are crafted by the parties. Through the exchange of information and ideas, you make choices on what is in your best interest. You determine if the dispute can be resolved and if not, parties can keep things from getting worse.
8. CONFIDENTIAL
   ADR typically involves the parties in dispute and their designated representatives, if any. An individual with authority to make decisions may also attend or be available to the parties if needed. Witnesses are not called and evidence is not produced. The facilitator is bound by strict confidentiality to keep anything shared in confidence unless otherwise permitted or required to disclose.
9. BETTER RELATIONSHIPS
   ADR is a professional way to deal with workplace disputes. Although disagreements will occur, how we choose to deal with them lays the foundation for our working relationships with others and how we serve our customers. Even if agreements cannot be reached, one can build a relationship of respect by trying to work things out instead of avoiding or doing nothing, and allowing the matter to escalate.
10. IT WORKS!
    More than half of all ADR requests end in resolution. A mutually acceptable settlement is reached, the scope of the issues is narrowed, or a pending action is withdrawn. In most cases, the parties leave having benefited from the process.

Source: Virginia Department of Veterans Affairs, Office of Resolution Management, http://www1.va.gov/adr/docs/adr_brochure.pdf.

REALITY CHECK BOXES

Sometimes there are current events or there is background information that is right on point with the substantive information we are presenting and which would be a great help to you to understand the important concept. The Reality Check boxes integrate such real-life information or situations for application into the theoretical content of the chapter. The Reality Checks often provide background or extended information on a topic discussed in the section, with the goal of having you understand the topic in more depth by providing a broader or deeper or more illustrative context.

DIVERSITY IN THE LAW BOXES

The legal environment in which business operates has increasingly included legal issues grounded in issues stemming from diversity. The Diversity in the Law boxes provide examples of how diversity impacts law and business and how it can be manifested in many different ways. The more ways you are exposed to this, the better. In that way, you will be much more likely to recognize potential trouble when you see it in the business world and can work to minimize any negative impact. No doubt some of the Diversity boxes will surprise you and also help you to understand the urgent need for addressing the issue of diversity in the business context as not only a means of avoiding potential liability, but also for creating better markets and more innovative and productive workplaces.

THE MISSISSIPPI STATE SOVEREIGNTY COMMISSION

The Mississippi State Sovereignty Commission was a state agency created two years after the *Brown v. Board of Education* case in which the U.S. Supreme Court outlawed racial segregation in public schools. The stated purpose of creating the agency was to "do and perform any and all acts deemed necessary and proper to protect the sovereignty of the state of Mississippi, and her sister states . . . from perceived encroachment thereon by the Federal Government or any branch, department or agency thereof." The agency was given extensive investigative powers, including subpoena power, had a budget, and had as ex-officio members granted a seat on the Commission purely because of their position, the governor as chairman, president of the Senate as vice-chairman, the attorney general and speaker of the House of Representatives. The Commission also had two members from the Senate appointed by president of the Senate and three members from the House of Representatives appointed by the Speaker. The agency had a director, a public relations director, clerical staff, and investigators.

Over the course of its life as an agency, the agency used investigators and paid informers to gather information on civil rights activity in the state. It worked to stop passage of the Civil Rights Act of 1964, created a speakers' bureau to travel nationwide to give Mississippi's version of segregation, created and distributed segregationist tracts, funded all-white Citizens' Councils created to retain segregation, and even provided funds to help get conservative (or scared) blacks to register to vote so that they would side with the segregationists. When the agency was made defunct in 1977, its records were ordered sealed, under penalty of law, for 50 years until 2027.

The Mississippi ACLU filed suit to have the records released because it alleged there was unauthorized surveillance of citizens. After a 21-year fight, the records were opened in 1998 and are now available in digital form online. They make fascinating reading. The records led to the discovery of the background surrounding the slaying of civil rights workers James Cheney, Michael Shwerner, and Andrew Goodman in 1964 for their civil rights work in trying to register voters in Mississippi and investigating a suspicious church fire. The information formed the basis for the Hollywood movie, "Mississippi Burning."

Source: Mississippi Department of Archives and History, http://mdah.state.ms.us/arrec/digital_archives/sovcom/scagencycasehistory.php.

CASE 2.1 Rodriguez de Quijas et al. v. Shearson/American Express

490 U.S. 477 (1989)

Facts: Even though a group of securities investors signed agreements requiring that account disputes be settled by binding arbitration, when their investments went bad, the investors brought suit in court alleging fraudulent and unauthorized transactions in violation of the Securities Act of 1933 and the Securities and Exchange Act of 1934. The U.S. Supreme Court held that the agreement to arbitrate securities claims was binding and the courts were not the only forum in which securities disputes are to be resolved.

Issue: Whether it is permissible for courts to allow legal claims to be resolved by arbitration rather than in a court of law.

Decision: Yes

Reasoning: Kennedy, J.: The Court's characterization of the arbitration process is pervaded by "the old judicial hostility to arbitration." That view has been steadily eroded over the years. The erosion intensified in our most recent decisions upholding agreements to arbitrate federal claims raised under the Securities Exchange Act of 1934, under the Racketeer Influenced and Corrupt Organizations (RICO) statutes, and under the antitrust laws. The shift in the Court's views is shown by the flat statement in *Mitusbishi Mostors Corp. v. Soler Chrysler-Plymouth, Inc.*, 473 US 614 (1985): "By agreeing to arbitrate a statutory claim, a party does not forgo the substantive rights afforded by the statute; it only submits to their resolution in an arbitral, rather than a judicial, forum." To the extent that [our decisions] rested on suspicion of arbitration as a method of weakening the protections afforded in the substantive law to would-be complainants, it has fallen far out of step with our current strong endorsement of the federal statutes favoring this method of resolving disputes.

There is nothing in the record before us, nor in the facts of which we can take judicial notice, to indicate that the arbitral system would not afford the plaintiff the rights to which he is entitled. AFFIRMED

CASES

Contemporary, engaging summarized cases have been chosen to illustrate legal points in a real context. They contain minimal legalese and avoid complicated, unnecessary court procedural matters and language. While using traditional standard cases, we also supplement these with contemporary cases involving people, concepts, issues, and entertainers with which you may be familiar. Our experience has been that students tend to think of law as dull, dry, and boring, but when they see the legal concepts at play in real life cases involving entertainers or public figures they know, they understand the human impact and excitement inherent in the law better, are more enthusiastic about learning, and have fun at the same time. Of course, we use such public-figure or celebrity cases only where they are helpful, and where they genuinely elucidate important legal concepts.

Understanding Cases—In reading the legal cases, you may come across some terms that may be unfamiliar to you. It is easy once you understand the terms. Court decisions are filed in books called "reporters." These are the set of tan books you often see behind lawyers in photos. Each state has its own reporters and there are reporters for various court levels and regions. Cases are found by using the case citation. You can now find most cases online simply by googling the case citation. Here is what the citation means. Case citation: 59 U.S. 367 (1972) means that the case can be found in volume 59 of the U.S. Supreme Court reporter at page 367, and the decision was issued by the court in 1972. Judge's name: Hockaway, J: means that Judge Hockaway wrote the opinion for the court. "CJ" means chief judge. Disposition: At the end of the case will be a decision to reverse or affirm. Reverse means a lower court case was overturned by a court of appeals. Affirm means that the decision of the lower court was left intact by the court of appeals. Remand means that the case was sent back to the lower court by the court of appeals for more work in light of the appellate court's decision. There is much more to legal research, but this should be enough to allow you to have a full understanding of what you are reading in this text.

CASE QUESTIONS

Cases are followed by case questions geared to getting you to think critically about what you have read rather than simply passively reading it and forgetting it or later regurgitating it on an exam. Judges are governed by precedent and legal expertise, but a part of their decisions are based on their own thoughts and judgment. We want to help you hone your critical thinking skills by using the case questions as a way of thinking beyond the case and using your own thought processes, along with what you have learned in the chapter, to extend your knowledge and sharpen your judgment. We often ask what you thought of the decision or some aspect of it. We do so because what you think matters. Yes, it is a case that has already been decided, but that does not make it sacrosanct. Someone, at some point, made a decision that led to this case going to court. That person could be you one day. We want you to begin right now to understand how to think through difficult and/or precarious facts and draw on your own knowledge, experience, and understanding of the law and legal issues to form an opinion and analysis of your own. This does not take the place of a qualified attorney, but it does give you some grounding in knowing when you need one and how to judge, at least on a basic level, the situation involved.

EXAMPLE ICONS

We have included many, many examples throughout the text in order to put legal concepts in context. Over the years, our students have told us that examples are important to help them understand concepts. Often, they will remember the concept by the example rather than the definition. Based on this, we have included an EXAMPLE icon by each example we use in the chapter discussion so that your attention is easily brought to it, your mind subconsciously gets ready to receive and process it, and you can easily find it again when you are flipping through pages to refresh your recollection.

UCC IN COLOR

In the "Contracts and Sales" chapter, you will find an awesome tool to help you. Contracts and Sales law is governed by at least two sources. We found that our students often forget this when addressing the subject matter. To keep it uppermost in your mind as you are reading, we have used a different color ink when addressing Uniform Commercial Code (UCC) concepts. We have no doubt that this will greatly assist you in keeping the two sets of rules straight in your mind as you read and study the material.

KEY TERMS

Each time a legal term is used for the first time and defined, it is bolded within the text. Each term is defined within its context, and can also be referenced in the Glossary at the end of the book. You may wonder why some terms are included, since you may already know them and think they are in general use. We would rather err on the side of too much rather than too little regarding important legal terms. Some terms may have a lay meaning that you may be familiar with, but also have a legal definition that you are not. The important terms in the chapter are also found listed at the end of the chapter.

CHAPTER SUMMARIES

Each chapter closes with a summary section, giving you a tool for reminding yourself of the highlights of the matters covered in the chapter and how they fit into the overall scheme of things in the business setting. Use this, along with the opening learning objectives, as an aide in retaining key chapter points.

REVIEW QUESTIONS

At the end of each chapter is a complete set of review questions incorporating chapter concepts. These questions help you nail down your understanding by applying the concepts discussed to practical situations. The format is varied and includes not only fact patterns to analyze and apply legal concepts to, but also true/false and multiple choice questions. Use these as tools to assess your understanding of chapter material reflected in the learning objectives.

ETHICS ISSUES

We mention ethical dilemmas and issues for you to think about throughout the chapter material. But the end of each chapter presents an ethical issue that goes into more depth. The goal is to allow you to not just regurgitate material, but apply it as well, to get to a deeper understanding of the chapter concepts. The issues are not designed to be easily resolved. That is why they are ethical issues. Whether or not your instructor chooses to use the activity, try it out yourself and see what you come up with. It will greatly aid you in learning to think through these matters so that when and if you face them later, you will be familiar with the territory and can better navigate it.

GROUP EXERCISES

At the end of each chapter, we have included optional group exercises that can be done to further facilitate your understanding of the chapter concepts. The group exercises put the issues into a real life context that helps facilitate understanding. The instructor may choose to have the students do the group exercises, or may not, but if the instructor does not do so, it does not stop you, as the student, from doing it on your own or in a group of your classmates. Some of the group exercises are interesting enough that whether the professor assigns them or not, you will want to do them on your own. For instance, what does it take to become a hot dog vendor in your city? Can you find online a case involving your favorite entertainer committing a tort or having one committed against him or her? What does your state law say about clean water standards? How do you copyright a song you wrote?

SUPPLEMENTS
Online Learning Center

With all of the possibilities that technology can offer, we've organized our Online Learning Center for ease of use for both instructor and student. Password-protected instructor materials can be found in the *Instructor Center,* including the Instructor's Manual, Testbank, PowerPoint presentations, and additional resources for classroom exercises. *You Be the Judge Online* (detailed below) is linked for accessibility and convenience. The *Student Center* offers opportunities for independent study, such as chapter quizzes and additional cases.

- **Instructor's Manual**   The Instructor's Manual, prepared by the authors, provides instructors with a hands-on approach to using this text in a classroom setting.
- **PowerPoints**   Created by Stella Sorovigas, Esq., of Grand Rapids Community College. Two sets of slides per chapter, to be used in-class or as an out-of-class supplement.
- **Test Bank**   The test bank contains approximately 100 true-false, multiple-choice, and essay questions per chapter. The test bank questions are also categorized by Bloom's taxonomy levels of learning and how they meet various AACSB objectives.
- **EZ Test**   A computerized version of the test bank is available, allowing the instructor to generate random tests and to add his or her own questions.
- **You Be the Judge Case Videos**   With these unscripted videos of typical business law case examples, students can watch as plaintiff and defendant present arguments before a real judge, explain their rationales, and hear the judge's verdict. Also available is the full set of You Be the Judge cases—this interactive DVD covers the full range of Legal Environment of Business topics and is formatted for easy use in personal computers. Students view background material in addition to hearing the courtroom argument, then must weigh in with their own rulings before hearing the judge's verdict. View the You Be the Judge demo at this book's Online Learning Center, and ask your sales representative how to package it with this book for a discount.

 MCGRAW-HILL *CONNECT BUSINESS LAW*

Less Managing. More Teaching. Greater Learning.

McGraw-Hill *Connect Business Law* is an online assignment and assessment solution that connects students with the tools and resources they'll need to achieve success.

McGraw-Hill *Connect Business Law* helps prepare students for their future by enabling faster learning, more efficient studying, and higher retention of knowledge.

McGraw-Hill *Connect Business Law* features

Connect Business Law offers a number of powerful tools and features to make managing assignments easier, so faculty can spend more time teaching. With *Connect Business Law*, students can engage with their course-work anytime and anywhere, making the learning process more accessible and efficient. *Connect Business Law* offers you the features described below.

Simple Assignment Management

With *Connect Business Law,* creating assignments is easier than ever, so you can spend more time teaching and less time managing. The assignment management function enables you to:

- Create and deliver assignments easily with selectable end-of-chapter questions and test bank items.
- Streamline lesson planning, student progress reporting, and assignment grading to make classroom management more efficient than ever.
- Go paperless with the eBook and online submission and grading of student assignments.

Smart Grading

When it comes to studying, time is precious. *Connect Business Law* helps students learn more efficiently by providing feedback and practice material when they need it, where they need it. When it comes to teaching, your time also is precious. The grading function enables you to:

- Have assignments scored automatically, giving students immediate feedback on their work and side-by-side comparisons with correct answers.
- Access and review each response; manually change grades or leave comments for students to review.
- Reinforce classroom concepts with practice tests and instant quizzes.

Instructor Library

The *Connect Business Law* Instructor Library is your repository for additional resources to improve student engagement in and out of class. You can select and use any asset that enhances your lecture. The *Connect Business Law* Instructor Library includes:

- *eBook*
- *PowerPoint files*
- *Videos*
- *Extra cases*

Student Study Center

The *Connect Business Law* Student Study Center is the place for students to access additional resources. The Student Study Center:

- Offers students quick access to lectures, practice materials, eBooks, and more.
- Provides instant practice material and study questions, easily accessible on the go.
- Gives students access to the Personalized Learning Plan described below.

Student Progress Tracking

Connect Business Law keeps instructors informed about how each student, section, and class is performing, allowing for more productive use of lecture and office hours. The progress-tracking function enables you to:

- View scored work immediately and track individual or group performance with assignment and grade reports.

- Access an instant view of student or class performance relative to learning objectives.
- Collect data and generate reports required by many accreditation organizations, such as AACSB.

Lecture capture

Increase the attention paid to lecture discussion by decreasing the attention paid to note taking. For an additional charge Lecture Capture offers new ways for students to focus on the in-class discussion, knowing they can revisit important topics later. Lecture Capture enables you to:

- Record and distribute your lecture with a click of button.
- Record and index PowerPoint presentations and anything shown on your computer so it is easily searchable, frame by frame.
- Offer access to lectures anytime and anywhere by computer, iPod, or mobile device.
- Increase intent listening and class participation by easing students' concerns about note-taking. Lecture Capture will make it more likely you will see students' faces, not the tops of their heads.

McGraw-Hill *Connect Plus Business Law*

McGraw-Hill reinvents the textbook learning experience for the modern student with *Connect Plus Business Law*. A seamless integration of an eBook and *Connect Business Law*, *Connect Plus Business Law* provides all of the Business Law features plus the following:

- An integrated eBook, allowing for anytime, anywhere access to the textbook.
- Dynamic links between the problems or questions you assign to your students and the location in the eBook where that problem or question is covered.
- A powerful search function to pinpoint and connect key concepts in a snap.

In short, *Connect Business Law* offers you and your students powerful tools and features that optimize your time and energies, enabling you to focus on course content, teaching, and student learning. *Connect Business Law* also offers a wealth of content resources for both instructors and students. This state-of-the-art, thoroughly tested system supports you in preparing students for the world that awaits.

For more information about Connect, go to **www.mcgrawhillconnect.com,** or contact your local McGraw-Hill sales representative.

TEGRITY CAMPUS: LECTURES 24/7

Tegrity Campus is a service that makes class time available 24/7 by automatically capturing every lecture in a searchable format for students to review when they study and complete assignments. With a simple one-click start-and-stop process, you capture all computer screens and corresponding audio. Students can replay any part of any class with easy-to-use browser-based viewing on a PC or Mac.

Educators know that the more students can see, hear, and experience class resources, the better they learn. In fact, studies prove it. With Tegrity Campus, students quickly recall key moments by using Tegrity Campus's unique search feature. This search helps students efficiently find what they need, when they need it, across an entire semester of class recordings. Help turn all your students' study time into learning moments immediately supported by your lecture.

To learn more about Tegrity watch a 2-minute Flash demo at **http://tegritycampus.mhhe.com.**

ASSURANCE OF LEARNING READY

Many educational institutions today are focused on the notion of *assurance of learning*, an important element of some accreditation standards. *The Legal, Ethical, and Regulatory Environment of Business in a Diverse Society* is designed specifically to support your assurance of learning initiatives with a simple, yet powerful solution.

Each test bank question for *The Legal, Ethical, and Regulatory Environment of Business in a Diverse Society* maps to a specific chapter learning outcome/objective listed in the text. You can use our test bank software, EZ Test and EZ Test Online, or in *Connect Business Law* to easily query for learning outcomes/objectives that directly relate to the learning objectives for your course. You can then use the reporting features of EZ Test to aggregate student results in similar fashion, making the collection and presentation of assurance of learning data simple and easy.

AACSB STATEMENT

The McGraw-Hill Companies is a proud corporate member of AACSB International. Understanding the importance and value of AACSB accreditation, *The Legal, Ethical, and Regulatory Environment of Business in a Diverse Society* 1e recognizes the curricula guidelines detailed in the AACSB standards for business accreditation by connecting selected questions in the text and the test bank to the six general knowledge and skill guidelines in the AACSB standards.

The statements contained in *The Legal, Ethical, and Regulatory Environment of Business in a Diverse Society* 1e are provided only as a guide for the users of this textbook. The AACSB leaves content coverage and assessment within the purview of individual schools, the mission of the school, and the faculty. While *The Legal, Ethical, and Regulatory Environment of Business in a Diverse Society* 1e and the teaching package make no claim of any specific AACSB qualification or evaluation, we have within *The Legal, Ethical, and Regulatory Environment of Business in a Diverse Society* 1e labeled selected questions according to the six general knowledge and skills areas.

MCGRAW-HILL CUSTOMER CARE CONTACT INFORMATION

At McGraw-Hill, we understand that getting the most from new technology can be challenging. That's why our services don't stop after you purchase our products. You can e-mail our Product Specialists 24 hours a day to get product-training online. Or you can search our knowledge bank of Frequently Asked Questions on our support website. For Customer Support, call **800-331-5094**, e-mail **hmsupport@mcgraw-hill.com**, or visit **www.mhhe.com/support**. One of our Technical Support Analysts will be able to assist you in a timely fashion.

TABLE OF CONTENTS

Voluntary Bankruptcy 218
What Is a Discharge in Bankruptcy? 218
Which Debts Are Discharged? 219

Chapter 7 Bankruptcy 219

Exemptions 223

Case 9.3 *Rousey v. Jacoway* 224

Chapter 11 Bankruptcy 225

Chapter 13 Bankruptcy 226

Servicemembers' Civil Relief Act 227

Summary 228

Review Questions 229

Ethics Issue 230

Group Exercise 230

Key Terms 231

PART 3

Business and Employment Regulation and Financing

10 Agency and Business Organizations 232

Introduction 233

Principals and Agents in the Commercial Context 233

Agent Defined 233
Principal Defined 234
Distinguishing Agency from Other Relationships 235
The Creation of Authority 235
Duties of Agents and Principals to Each Other and Third Parties 238
Ratification 243
Respondeat Superior 244

Case 10.1 *O'Connor v. Davis* 244

Termination of Authority 246

Forms of Business 246

Choosing a Business Form 247
Sole Proprietorships 247
General Partnerships 248

Case 10.2 *Wiggs v. Peedin* 248

The Uniform Partnership Act 249

Duties of Partners to Each Other 249
Limited Partnerships 250
Limited Liability Companies 251

Case 10.3 *In the Matter of Hausman* 252

Termination of a Partnership 253
Termination of a Limited Partnership 254
Termination of the Limited Liability Company 254

Corporations 255

Corporate Formation 256
Creating the Corporation 256
Promoter Liability 256
Corporate Structure 257
Corporate Attributes 257

Types of Corporations 259

Government-Owned Corporations 259
Public Corporations 259
Closely Held Corporations 260
Piercing the Corporate Veil 261
Profit and Not for Profit Corporations 261

Case 10.4 *Airlie Foundation v. IRS* 262

Professional Association 262
Domestic or Foreign Corporations 262

Corporate Governance 263

Duties of the Board of Directors and Officers 263
Duties of Controlling Shareholders 263
Government Regulation of Corporations 264

Corporate Dissolution 266

Summary 266

Review Questions 267

Ethics Issue 268

Group Exercise 268

Key Terms 268

11 The Employment Relationship and Equal Employment Opportunity 269

Introduction 270

What Is Title VII of the Civil Rights Act of 1964? 272

What Are the Discrimination Theories under Title VII? 274

Disparate Treatment 274
Disparate Impact 275

Case 11.1 *Bradley v. Pizzaco of Nebraska, Inc. d/b/a Domino's* 276

Is There More about Protected Categories under Title VII? 277

Race and Color 277
Gender 278

Case 11.2 *Price Waterhouse v. Hopkins* 279

Sexual Harassment 279
Pregnancy 282

Introduction to the Business and Ethics Environment in a Diverse Society

chapter

1

Learning Objectives

After reading this chapter, you should be able to:

LO1 Discuss what law is and what it is designed to do

LO2 Analyze the interplay between law, equity, morals, and justice

LO3 Recite four jurisprudential theories and decide which best reflects our law

LO4 Provide several sources of our law

LO5 Explain what common law is and where it came from

LO6 Distinguish between precedent and *stare decisis*

LO7 Explain the different classifications of law

LO8 Understand the various areas of law

LO9 Explain the role and importance of ethics in business

LO10 Discern how diversity may come into play in business and legal issues

 Opening Scenario

Makenna has just finished a 10-week financial planning course offered by the Finance Ministry of her church. Makenna believes she is now so well-versed in the subject that she can open her own business offering financial consulting services to the public. She obtains office space, creates a website, advertises in her local paper, and waits for clients to come. Is there anything else Makenna may need to be aware of before going into business?

Introduction: Why the Legal, Ethical, and Regulatory Environment in a Diverse Society?

In this chapter you will learn the background of the legal environment of business, how law and ethics relate to each other, and how the legal environment is impacted by a diverse American society.

In case you skipped the introduction to the textbook, you may be surprised at the informality of our discussion and that we use words like "you" and "we." As we noted in the introduction, we think you will more easily understand and digest what we are saying if we speak directly to you rather than using language that creates space between us. This does not take away from the importance, professionalism, or impact of what we say to you. Rather, we hope it will facilitate your understanding. In addition, examples will be given whenever they will help you understand the discussion. Examples will be highlighted by an icon in the text margin.

The purpose of this chapter is to introduce you to the concept of law in American society as a structure within which people and businesses operate, the different types of law our system recognizes, and how law relates to business, all in our rapidly changing diverse American society. We also introduce the broader aspects of the business environment: the regulatory environment of business, ethics in business, and diversity. This chapter provides a background and context for the rights and responsibilities that will be discussed throughout the text.

To get a brief overview of how the legal environment operates, let's take the relatively simple matter of Makenna starting her business as a financial consultant. Makenna has had an idea to open a financial planning business, found a place to conduct her business, and begun to operate her business. However, it is not quite that simple. In order to effectively do business, Makenna must determine the type of business organization that is best suited to her needs and create it according to state and local requirements. These needs include, among other things, Makenna's financial considerations, legal considerations, and the best means of protecting her business and personal assets in case she is sued. Is she going to incorporate? Will she be a sole practitioner? Does she want to create a limited liability company (LLC)? Does she want to have a partnership? As a financial planner, she must comply with regulations issued by the state and federal government that impact such matters as what she must do to qualify to offer her services to the public, what she can offer to clients who wish to use her services, what she must disclose to clients and the government, what taxes she must pay, and at what rate, and so on. In addition, Makenna must be aware of local ordinances that determine where she can conduct her business, hours of operation, parking concerns, type of building in which she can conduct business, licensing requirements for both her profession and her business or to have others occupy her premises for business purposes, and other relevant matters. Then once Makenna begins doing business, the law of contracts will govern the agreements she enters into with her clients and the agreements she enters into for the services and supplies she needs to conduct her business.

At this point you may think, "Well, of course setting up a *business* would involve a great many legal implications." But the law is more pervasive. Let's take a look at something as simple as downloading music for our iPods®, something millions of us do every day in a matter of seconds. Law governs everything from the contractual agreements which allowed the music to be there for us to purchase when we click on it, to the warning label which may be on the music we want to buy; from the agreement allowing the Internet service provider to be available for the download, to the art we view on the CD cover; and everything in between including the agreement to have the artist make the CD, the wages and hours of those who worked on the recording, the way in which we pay for purchases, the advertising used to persuade us to buy the music, copyright limitations on what we can do with the music, how the music provider finances its business, how it occupies its premises, what recourse is available if your downloaded music does not function correctly, and many other matters.

There is no such thing as a simple business transaction or even an entirely personal transaction. Even the simplest business transaction that we may even think of as personal takes place in a complex setting of laws and regulations of which a prudent business person must be aware.

Beyond matters of the law, there are always ethical considerations in every transaction. Sometimes these are starkly black and white. Bernard Madoff, former NASDAQ chairman, was sentenced in June 2009 to 150 years in prison after pleading guilty to charges that he purportedly conducted the largest Ponzi scheme swindle in the country's history and lost a reported $51 billion of his clients' assets.[1] Obviously, in addition to his unprecedented violations of law, it is an understatement to say there were serious lapses in his ethical judgment regarding investments (or lack thereof) he made for his clients. This *unethical* aspect of his schemes accounts for the horror with which he is widely regarded. But sometimes ethics come in shades of gray. There will be ethical implications for Makenna to consider when she must decide whether to convince a client to purchase a certain financial product or service which may be lucrative for her as the financial planner, but perhaps not as lucrative for her client, or when she contemplates whether to allow a client to buy into a financial product that looks good on paper but may prove too risky for the client's needs.

What appear to be purely business decisions can have diversity implications also. For our purposes, when we speak of diversity we are speaking of business operating in a society that is not homogeneous, but rather has multiple races, ethnicities, national origins, genders, ages, abilities, and gender identities that can impact business decisions. Since we are operating under American law, we address diversity issues in the context of American law, policy, and history. The country through its laws, businesses through their policies, and individuals through their social interactions try to be mindful of the credo that all are created equal in an effort to best use all of our country's inestimable resources and help the country live up to its founding vision. Sometimes it works, and as we will see, sometimes it does not.

We understand that you may wonder what diversity has to do with law since we are told that law is colorblind and the rules do not change based on the color of an individual's skin or the place where he or she was born. While the idea of equal justice under law is a nice thought, research consistently finds that there are many vestiges of our inequitable racial, cultural, gender, and socioeconomic past still very much with us that are expressed in many different ways in business decisions, both obvious as well as subtle. For instance, you may recall that in the wake of the recent drastic fall in the housing market, the National Association of Colored People (NAACP) filed suit against banking institutions and others when it was discovered that some institutions were actually targeting minority groups for loans that had a high probability of default, resulting in a disproportionate percentage of minority foreclosures and bankruptcies. In this debacle, both a lack of ethics and insensitivity to diversity issues came together to help create a business decision that could well result in legal liability for those involved, or at the very least, an embarrassing public relations disaster.

It may be hard to believe that a high school in Mississippi had its first racially integrated prom only in 2008, and then only because of Academy Award–winning actor Morgan Freeman's offer to pay for it (a proposal he began making in the 1990s).[2] As we get farther away from the time when segregation and racial discrimination, called **Jim Crow,** were the law, and now that openly treating others differently based on race or gender seems ancient history, we are less likely to believe discrimination occurs and more likely to believe it is only in the claimant's imagination ("playing the race card"). This failure to understand that discrimination is still happening is thought by some to be the "new racism." Failure to recognize that discrimination still exists means that it cannot be remedied. We think that making the determination to lend is purely based on

[1] Associated Press, July 19, 2009, http://www.msnbc.msn.com/id/31604191/ns/business-us_business/.

[2] See the HBO special "Prom Night in Mississippi"; and CNN, "Prom Night Reveals Racial Divides," January 21, 2009, http://www.cnn.com/ 2009/SHOWBIZ/Movies/01/21/mississippi.prom/.

financial data and has no room for treating customers differently based on skin color, ethnicity, or gender. Research indicates, however, that even with precisely the same financial data, blacks and Hispanics received loans with higher interest rates and less favorable terms.[3] Something other than an eye to financial statements accounted for banks and other lending institutions targeting minorities for risky loans that resulted in such a high rate of foreclosures for that group.

Why do we bring this issue with its associated pitfalls to your attention at the outset of our discussion? If biased decision making is a part of how business is sometimes done and such behavior results in legal liability, then we need to address it with those of you who will be in business and are required to learn about the legal and ethical environment in which businesses operate. Business decisions are not made in a vacuum. They very much reflect our likes, dislikes, prejudices, values and other attributes. If a factor we use can cause our decision to result in legal liability, we need to address it. Research indicates time after time that these factors do form a part of the business decision-making process, so they need to be a part of the discussion.

Another recent example of how diversity issues impact business occurred in June 2009, when the Valley Swim Club in Huntington Valley, Pennsylvania, a private club that advertised open membership, entered into an agreement with a local camp to allow a group of 65 young campers to join the club to swim one day a week, for which the camp paid the club more than $1900 in fees. When the campers got into the pool on their first visit, they reported that white parents immediately took their children out of the pool and made racial comments. Despite the fact that the camp had a membership agreement that allowed the campers to swim there, the pool attendant told the mostly black and Hispanic campers that minorities were not allowed in the club and they would have to leave. The next day the president of the swim club, John Deusler, suspended the swim club's agreement with the camp and told the camp director that her money would be returned, stating that "there was concern that a lot of kids would change the complexion . . . and the atmosphere of the club."[4] After a public uproar about the club's actions and Deusler's statement, Deusler said there was a misunderstanding and the statement was not about race.

Clearly the swim club's business decision to breach the contract with the camp has diversity implications. Given the nature of the outcry against the Valley Swim Club after the story was carried by the national media, including a planned investigation by Senator Arlen Specter and a lawsuit filed by the parents of four of the evicted children, it is probable that the Valley Swim Club wishes it had considered the diversity implications of the business decision it made to breach the contract, summarily evict the campers from the pool, cancel its contract with the camp, return the camp's money, and make the unfortunate statement it did about the campers not being allowed to attend the club. We believe that since these types of situations occur on a regular basis, they need to be addressed and we can do so in a way that makes better business decisions.

Returning once more to our opening scenario about Makenna and her new business, while you may think of the financial planner as simply someone who handles financial services in exchange for a fee, upon analyzing the situation more closely you quickly realize that financial consulting takes place in a much larger context that requires the financial planner to know much more than how to put together a financial plan. Each and every step of the process involves legal, regulatory, ethical, and at times, diversity considerations. In order to be fully prepared for today's business world, it is important to understand all aspects of business and its context rather than just the simple matter,

[3]Associated Press, "Study: Minorities Pay Higher Interest Rates on Auto Loans," May 8, 2007, http://origin.foxnews.com/story/
0,2933,270619,00.html; Eric Eckholm, "Black and Hispanic Home Buyers Pay Higher Interest on Mortgages Study Finds," *New York Times*,
June 1, 2006, http://www.nytimes.com/2006/06/01/us/01minorities.html.

[4]Karen Araiza, "Pool Boots Kids Who May Change the Complexion," NBC, July 9, 2009, http://www.nbcphiladelphia.com/news/local/
Pool-Boots-Kids-Who-Might-Change-the-Complexion.html.

for instance, of whether a contract made with a client will stand up in court if challenged. We want to provide you with tools to fully analyze business decisions before they turn into unnecessary legal problems and/or public relations nightmares.

Before we begin our journey into the business world, we must first establish a framework within which to operate. Before we begin to discuss different types of laws and specific laws, what business requires, and how such laws work, we will first discuss the law in general, that is, what law is, what law is designed to do, how it evolved, and how it operates as a system within which citizens and businesses must operate.

What is the basis of law? And what exactly *is* it? What are ethics? Do we really need to think about ethics? Why isn't the law enough? First we will take a look at law, then ethics, then see how diversity may impact business decisions.

Definition of Law

Law is a concept all of us have dealt with all of our lives, yet if asked to define it, most of us would probably hesitate and find it difficult to do so in a thoroughgoing way. Though we live with it every day, law can be hard to define. We have taken law so for granted it may be that we cannot readily think of how much it affects our lives (except perhaps when we run afoul of the law). However, law is the foundation of all of our business relationships and many of our personal ones. In fact, once we realize its impact, it may be difficult to think of anything in our lives that is *not* affected by law. This includes even the most personal areas of our lives.

Surely nothing is more personal than love. When we do something as intimate as gaze starry-eyed at our beloved, we are not thinking about law, but the law plays a large part in our personal relationships. Take the marriage covenant. Did you ever think about the fact that at one level marriage is simply a legal concept? As a legal concept it has nothing to do with love itself. The two often go hand in hand because in our society, if we love someone we may decide that we wish to "formalize" our feelings into the institution called marriage. The feelings are not based on law, but the institution itself is. Nowhere in any state's marriage statute does it require that the parties love each other in order to marry. Witness the fact that many people love, but do not marry, or marry but do not love. Neither violates the law. Once people enter into marriage, however, the law impinges on some of their personal decision making.

Then too, some love and cannot legally marry, for instance, people who are already married, are too closely related by blood, are of the same gender (except, presently, in Massachusetts, Connecticut, Iowa, Maine, and Vermont), or are too young, as in the case of Mary LaTourneau's 13-year-old boyfriend. Elementary school teacher Mary Kay LaTourneau, married with four children, had a relationship with, two babies by, and eventually married the student she had been having a relationship with since he was 13 years old and she 33. She went to prison for seven years for statutory rape, then married him (he was then 21) in 2005, nearly a year after her release from prison.

Until the U.S. Supreme Court's 1967 decision in *Loving v. Virginia*,[5] in many states it was illegal for African Americans to marry whites. In fact, it was a criminal act in Virginia when Mr. Loving, a white man, married a black woman. In refusing to set aside the conviction, the trial court judge in the case, Leon Bazile, said, "Almighty God created the races white, black, yellow, malay and red, and he placed them on separate continents. And but for the interference with his arrangement there would be no cause for such marriages. The fact that he separated the races shows that he did not intend for the races to mix."

---

[5]388 U.S. 1 (1967).

Regarding the intersection of the law and love, in a prepared statement to commemorate the 40th anniversary of the Supreme Court's *Loving* decision, on June 12, 2007, Ms. Loving, then a widow, stated:

> Surrounded as I am now by wonderful children and grandchildren, not a day goes by that I don't think of Richard and our love, our right to marry, and how much it meant to me to have that freedom to marry the person precious to me, even if others thought he was the "wrong kind of person" for me to marry. I believe all Americans, no matter their race, no matter their sex, no matter their sexual orientation, should have that same freedom to marry. Government has no business imposing some people's religious beliefs over others. Especially if it denies people's civil rights. I am still not a political person, but I am proud that Richard's and my name is on a court case that can help reinforce the love, the commitment, the fairness, and the family that so many people, black or white, young or old, gay or straight seek in life. I support the freedom to marry for all. That's what *Loving,* and loving, are all about.[6]

If the law plays such an important role in our personal lives you can imagine how central it must be to our business relationships.

Law has been defined in many different ways. For our purposes, **law** is a system of limitations upon our actions imposed by the government to ensure order, safety, predictability and control. We often think of law and justice as one and the same, but they do not always come together. As evidenced by the words chiseled into the marble of the West Pediment over the main steps of the U.S. Supreme Court, "Equal Justice Under Law," as a government we try for justice, or a balancing of the concerns in the case to the satisfaction of all, but if someone does not like the outcome, they will not believe justice has been done. Law may often reflect our **morals,** but law and morality, or ethics, are not the same. While law is our government's determination as to our limitations and rights, morality is our own personal view of what we believe is proper and how we should conduct ourselves.

Law can have many different underlying bases for its existence. How law is created and exists is the study of *jurisprudence.*

L03

Jurisprudence

Jurisprudence is the study of law, legal systems, and legal philosophy. Over the years judicial philosophers have developed many different approaches to explain law and its role in society. While each has been the focus of volumes of study, a brief overview of a few of the more popular theories follows.

NATURAL LAW

The theory underlying natural law is that there is a discoverable set of absolute right and wrong principles upon which our laws should be based. To the extent the laws reflect the natural law, that is, the laws of nature, or God, the laws are considered "good" ones. To the extent they do not, they are "bad."

EXAMPLE

A well-known example of natural law is the Declaration of Independence's statement that "We hold these truths to be self-evident, that all men are created equal, that they are endowed by their Creator with certain unalienable rights, that among these are life, liberty, and the pursuit of happiness." The statement specifically says that the truths are *self-evident*, and that *everyone* is endowed with certain *unalienable* rights. This is natural law at work. In the view of the signers of the Declaration, it was without question that this statement was true and all other laws were to flow from this natural law. Of course, the logical question is "Who determines what these natural laws are and

---

[6]http://www.freedomtomarry.org/pdfs/mildred_loving-statement.pdf.

how can we be sure?" Does the natural law change if the religion it may have been based on is no longer the only or predominant religion that exists in the country?

At the time the Declaration of Independence was written, the authors took for granted that natural law dictated that the "self-evident truths" applied only to men, not women. Not even all men were being referred to. Ironically, what was deemed to be "self-evident" and included everyone was actually limited only to white males, and this was considered the "natural order of things." As a compromise between having all humans in a state be counted for purposes of political representation and not counting slaves for these purposes, who were not considered people by some, the Constitution dictated that slaves be counted as three-fifths of a person. Later still, after the 13th Amendment to the Constitution abolished slavery in December 1865 after the Civil War ended, freed blacks were written and interpreted into our Constitution. Again, despite what had been written in the Declaration of Independence as the natural law to be followed, this turned out to be limited after all.

LEGAL POSITIVISM

This theory of jurisprudence is based on law as issued by a governing figure or sovereign. Here the law derives its status as law not from some natural order of things that dictates that things should be right and just and fair because it comes from the Creator, but rather from the fact that it has been enacted by the sovereign with the power to enforce his or her wishes. This law may or may not be just or fair. Of course, it can be problematic that there are no real guidelines for judging the law except that it came from the sovereign. It is this theory that could justify the restriction and eventual extermination of millions of Jews, Pentecostals, Gypsies, gays, blacks, and other "undesirables" during the Holocaust as ordered by Hitler, because he was, for all practical purposes, the sovereign. At the Nuremberg trials German officers prosecuted for their crimes routinely offered as their explanation that they did not do anything wrong, or should not be held responsible for their acts, because they were merely soldiers following the orders of their superior officers. Legal positivism would say that the soldiers were correct because the law they were carrying out was dictated by the sovereign and therefore had to be obeyed.

LEGAL REALISM

For legal realists, actual experience is the key to determining what law should be. What is actually done is important for them, rather than what the law says should be done. Some view the drawback to this theory as that it follows rather than leads. Legal realism does not establish law as a guideline to be followed, but rather would have law follow what people actually do. For legal realists, if the reality is that most people smoke marijuana, then it should be legalized, rather than deeming it illegal because it is viewed by some as immoral.

A well-known example perhaps reflecting legal realism was the repeal of Prohibition. It was virtually impossible to stop people from drinking alcohol even though its manufacture, sale, and transport were made illegal in 1929 by passage of the 18th Amendment to the U.S. Constitution, so the law was repealed 14 years later in 1933.

SOCIOLOGICAL THEORY

This theory of jurisprudence is based on the premise that society's ideas change over time and law should reflect a compromise between the changing, often conflicting, interests of society. For instance, African Americans experienced a change in status when public schools were desegregated by the U.S. Supreme Court's decision in *Brown v. Board of Education of Topeka, Kansas*[7] in 1954 and with the passage of the Civil Rights

---

[7]347 U.S. 483 (1954).

Act in 1964 prohibiting discrimination in employment, public accommodations, education and receipt of public funds on the basis of race, color, gender, religion or national origin. Both these legal landmarks were significant in moving America away from its discriminatory treatment of blacks and others and toward the equality set forth in the country's founding documents. The law thus wrestled with the competing interests of the Constitution's dictate that all are created equal and the fact that some in our society were still subject to Jim Crow 99 years after the Civil War ended slavery.

Women underwent a similar change in their status and rights when they were allowed to vote by Constitutional amendment in 1919 and were included (even though only as a means of trying to prevent the law from passing) in the Civil Rights Act in 1964. We are presently experiencing such a change with gays, lesbians, and transgendered individuals with Congressional consideration of legislation ending the "Don't Ask Don't Tell" policies in the military in 2010 and with the passage of new state and local laws extending them protection from employment and other discrimination, not to mention employer-generated protections.

In these instances, law has changed as societal ideas have changed, and the law has grown to encompass the new position society finds itself in. Compromises evolve among the competing interests of how we have treated certain groups of people and our constitutional dictate of equal justice. We see these competing interests reflected in the state of our laws all the time: Think about our use of fossil fuels and the competing interests of oil drillers and environmentalists; or our wish to avoid another financial meltdown like the country experienced in 2008, against our wish to have less government interference in business; or our wish to have less intrusive government competing with our wish to protect Americans from loss of life due to food contamination or not wearing seat belts.

Some think this sociological theory is not a good way to view law because it makes law too fluid and, some would say, "wishy washy." Keep in mind that our Constitution, which went into effect in 1789, is the oldest written continuous Constitution in existence. There have been many, many societal changes during its more than 200-year history, yet it is still a healthy and viable document from which all our laws flow, and to which they must adhere. If it were too inflexible, it would not have been able to withstand more than 200 years of societal changes. One of the things that makes this possible is the checks and balances built into the Constitution itself, discussed in the next section.

Whether we determine that our country's primary legal theory fits neatly into one category or another is not nearly as important as the fact that we have a framework for our laws that we respect and are able to live with as a society. Our laws are actually a mix of many different jurisprudential theories, depending on the times, the subject matter, and the interpretation, yet we still manage to have a fairly consistent and coherent approach to law. (See Take Away 1-1, "Theories of Jurisprudence.")

 TAKE AWAY 1-1

THEORIES OF JURISPRUDENCE

Natural Law: There is a discoverable set of absolute right and wrong principles upon which our laws should be based.
Legal Positivism: Law as issued by a governing figure or sovereign.
Legal Realism: Actual experience is the key to knowing what law is.
Sociological Theory: Society's ideas change over time and law should reflect a compromise between the changing, often conflicting, interests of society.

Sources of Law

Our laws come from several different sources. Our federal government is a **tripartite system** composed of three branches: the executive, the legislative, and the judicial. Our system is set up so that no one branch of government is more powerful than the others; they simply have different types of powers. The power and authority of the three branches are defined by the U.S. Constitution's first three articles. Each branch has its own primary powers, and also some of the powers that belong primarily to the other two branches. Allowing one branch of government to have some of the powers of the other is known as a system of **checks and balances** and ensures that government policies are not reached without the input of the other branches and ensures that power does not rest too heavily in one branch. The **legislative branch of government,** composed of Congress and the Senate, has primary responsibility for enacting laws in the areas over which the Constitution designated the federal government would have authority. The **judicial branch of government** is primarily responsible for interpreting the law by deciding cases in federal courts. The **executive branch of government** has the president as the chief executive and is responsible for executing the laws of the land.

While each branch has its own primary authority, each also has powers over the areas of the other two. For instance, the legislature has primary responsibility for enacting laws, but it also has responsibility for advising and giving consent for the chief executive's appointments, including appointing judges to the federal courts. As the judicial branch, the courts are primarily responsible for hearing cases and interpreting legislation, but they have the authority to declare unconstitutional laws passed by Congress, or acts done by the president as chief executive. In doing so, they use previously decided cases as **precedent** to which they must adhere under our system of *stare decisis* (look to the decision). The president, as chief executive, primarily executes the laws, but also has the right to nominate federal judges and others high level government executives, to issue executive orders and to veto bills Congress passes. (See Take Away 1-2, "The Tripartite System: Checks and Balances.")

All three branches of government have the authority to create agencies to which they delegate authority to carry out some aspect of their authority. The agencies are created by, and accountable to, the branch of government that created the agency. For instance, Congress created the Internal Revenue Service to carry out its Constitutional dictate under Article I, section 8 of the U.S. Constitution to lay and collect taxes. President Bush, as chief executive, created the Office of Homeland Security after 9/11 to address issues of domestic security (a year later Congress created the Department of Homeland Security). The Administrative Office of the United States Courts was established in 1939 to support the U.S. court system and its business, including the Judicial Conference.

The overarching source of law is the U.S. Constitution. It is the supreme law of the land and all laws must be consistent with the Constitution. States also have their own constitutions with which their state laws must be consistent, in addition to being consistent with the U.S. Constitution. Just as the U.S. Constitution addresses matters within the federal domain, state constitutions address matters within each state's domain. States also have tripartite systems, with the governor being the chief executive responsible for executing the laws of the state. State courts hear cases based on state law and state legislatures pass state laws.

Common law is also a large source of law to which we adhere. As the law that came over from England with the settlers, common law forms the basis of much of our law today.

There are also federal treaties entered into by the president and ratified by Congress, which must be complied with. Among other sources of law, the president has the authority to make executive orders that act much like the laws Congress passes. The

TAKE AWAY 1-2

THE TRIPARTITE SYSTEM: CHECKS AND BALANCES

Branch of Government	Checks and Balances
Legislative Primary Authority: Checks and Balances:	Enact laws * Judicial Branch has authority to interpret laws * Executive Branch has authority to request legislation; veto legislation
Judicial Primary Authority: Checks and Balances:	Interpret laws consistent with the Constitution * Legislative Branch has authority to pass laws to bring the court's interpretation of law in line with the views of the legislature; Senate must confirm judicial nominations made by the president * Executive Branch via the president as chief executive, has the authority to nominate federal judges
Executive Primary Authority: Checks and Balances:	Execute the laws of the land; can issue executive orders, nominate federal judges; nominate cabinet members; can request legislation * Legislative Branch has the authority to provide the president with advice and consent as to the president's judicial and other nominations * Judicial Branch has the authority to interpret executive orders or other presidential acts as unconstitutional

TAKE AWAY BOX 1-3

SOURCES OF LAW

U.S. and state constitutions
Treaties
Federal, state, and local legislation
Federal and state agency rules and regulations
Federal and state court decisions
Common law
Executive orders

agencies created by Congress within their authority have the **quasi-legislative power** if so provided in their **enabling statute** to create rules and regulations under which they operate. States also have agencies and legislatures and executive orders issued by governors. All of these are sources of law. The constitutions, both state and federal, legislation from state and federal legislatures as well as local jurisdictions, executive orders from the president and governors, rules and regulations promulgated by agencies, both state and federal, and case law issued by both state and federal courts, all form our laws to which we must adhere. (See Take Away 1-3, "Sources of Law.")

Classifications of Law

Laws fall into distinct categories. Law can be classified as civil or criminal, substantive or procedural, public or private, and legal or equitable. We will discuss each of these in turn.

CIVIL AND CRIMINAL LAW

You are probably most familiar with civil and criminal law. **Civil law** is generally the type of law that permits people to recover money damages for noncriminal actions which occur, such as car accidents, character defamation, or product liability. **Criminal law** addresses actions that violate criminal statutes and instead of granting money damages to the victim, generally result in punishment of the perpetrator. Examples of criminal law include laws relating to rape, murder, and robbery.

SUBSTANTIVE AND PROCEDURAL LAW

Substantive law provides rights and remedies and dictates what kinds of actions we can and cannot engage in. For example, laws regarding trade secrets would provide our financial planner, Makenna, with a right to keep her business secrets private, and she can sue for theft of trade secrets if someone intentionally takes her closely guarded client list and uses it for his or her own purposes.

Procedural law, on the other hand, provides rules and regulations for how to exercise the rights we are given by substantive law. That is, procedural law tells us how to proceed in enforcing substantive rights provided by law. Among other things, procedural rules govern matters such as the court in which Makenna must bring the trade secret case, the time by which the case must be brought or Makenna loses her right to sue, what motions can be filed in the case, what court costs must be paid to file the case or how long Makenna would have to file an appeal if she lost the case at trial, and so on. Substantive and procedural laws are quite different in what they do, but both are important types of law and provide order and predictability to our legal system.

PUBLIC AND PRIVATE LAW

Public law addresses areas such as criminal law and civil rights laws, which deal with people interacting with the government or the government's interest on behalf of its people. For instance, when a criminal law is violated, it is the government which brings the case on behalf of the people of the state or federal government in order to protect the interests of society. If Makenna stole money from her clients' accounts, she would be prosecuted for theft under criminal law statutes created to protect the public.

Private law focuses on areas like torts, contracts, or property law, all of which involve private parties' rights and interests rather than the interest of the government (though the government can be a party to a case involving private law). The private case is brought by the party interested in pursuing it rather than by the government. If Makenna sued someone who untruthfully said that she had defrauded clients, Makenna would use private law and the tort of defamation. If she wanted to pursue the matter, Makenna, not the state, would bring the case. If she did not wish to bring the case she would not be required to do so. Public cases, however, can proceed even if the party harmed does not wish for it to go forward since the government is bringing the case on behalf of the public rather than on behalf of the victim.

Public law may involve involuntary litigation and is brought by the state, while private law is voluntary on the part of the **plaintiff,** the party bringing the case, and will not be brought if plaintiff does not wish to do so. When someone is murdered or raped, the state, through its state attorney, makes a prosecutorial decision alone or with the help of the grand jury, as to whether to go forward with the case. The case can proceed whether or not the victim (or in the case of murder, the victim's family) wishes to go forward. The litigation is involuntary in the sense that it can proceed regardless of the wishes of the injured party. Of course, the case is not involuntary on the part of the **defendant** who is being prosecuted.

TAKE AWAY 1-4

PUBLIC LAW–PRIVATE LAW

Public Law	Private Law
Brought on behalf of public	Suit brought on behalf of harmed party
Suit can proceed if victim doesn't want it to	Suit does not proceed if harmed party says no
Often criminal case	Noncriminal case
Harmed party does not pay for suit	Harmed party bringing suit pays for suit

Not so with private law. In private law, the only way in which the case will go forward is if the injured party proceeds. If Makenna does not want to bring the defamation case, no cause of action will be filed. If it is to be filed, she is the one to do it, as it will not be brought by the state. (See Take Away 1-4, "Public Law–Private Law.")

LAW AND EQUITY

EXAMPLE

Equity stands outside the law to provide relief when legal remedies are not available. It is extralegal relief available when the law does not provide a legal remedy. For instance, if a homeowner wants to build a brick wall on her own property and it does not violate the zoning laws to do so, but building the wall would block the ocean view of her next door neighbor who built his house specifically for the ocean view, a court of equity might be able to help. Since no law has been violated, there is no basis for the neighbor to bring a case at law and obtain a legal remedy.

Equitable remedies are generally available when no law has been violated, but a party wishes to have relief. People's actions do not always fit into neat compartments;

TAKE AWAY 1-5

COMPARISON OF LAW AND EQUITY

Law	Equity
Generally a right to a jury trial	Generally no right to a jury trial
Money damages	Usually nonmonetary remedies
Law governs cases	Equitable principles/maxims govern cases
Stare decisis is used	Courts free to fashion unique remedy suited to facts
Need legal relief	Must allege remedy at law (legal relief) is insufficient

therefore courts of equity stand ready to look into offering relief when legal remedies are unavailing. Courts of law and equity were actually physically separate at one time in our history, but this is generally no longer the case. In most jurisdictions a judge may hear both legal and equitable claims in the same court. Jury trials are generally not permitted in equity cases since the Seventh Amendment to the U.S. Constitution provides the right to a jury in a noncriminal federal case in which at least $20 is at issue (state laws vary for state cases) and money is generally involved in legal claims but not equitable claims. However, if the claim is one of mixed law and equity, a jury trial may be allowed. (See Take Away 1-5, "Comparison of Law and Equity," and Take Away 1-6, "Classifications of Law.")

TAKE AWAY 1-6

CLASSIFICATIONS OF LAW

Civil and criminal
Substantive and procedural
Public and private
Legal and equitable

Areas of Law

L08

The law is divided into several distinct areas, each with separate considerations. Acts violating criminal law are called **crimes;** acts committed under civil law are called **torts.** Torts are noncontract violations of civil law. Under the broad concept of civil law, in addition to the torts, there are also the concepts of *property* and *contracts.* These two areas usually involve personal agreements of some kind between the parties, and violating the agreements do not result in violations of law, but rather breaches of contract. (See Take Away 1-7, "Civil Law Areas.")

CIVIL AND CRIMINAL LAW

Civil law and criminal laws are different in their purposes and effect. Criminal law is made to punish violators and deter further violations. Civil law is designed to make whole those who have suffered physical, monetary, property, or other injury at the hands of another. In certain types of civil cases punitive damages may be imposed in order to punish the liable party and act as a deterrent to others. Convictions under criminal law result in incarceration in jail or prison, perhaps, depending on the jurisdiction, restitution paid to the victims, and/or fines paid to the government. Tort liability generally results in financial liability on the part of the **tortfeasor** who committed the tort, with payment going to the party harmed.

As mentioned previously, criminal cases are brought (at times involuntarily on the part of the victim) by the state, while tort cases are voluntarily brought by the injured party. Crimes are divided into **felonies** and **misdemeanors,** with the latter being less serious and upon conviction resulting in jail time of less than a year.

Felonies are serious criminal offenses and convictions result in prison time of a year or more and loss of civil rights such as (in some states) voting and the right to possess firearms. Either felonies or misdemeanors may involve fines. Torts usually do not have the same type of degrees, though there

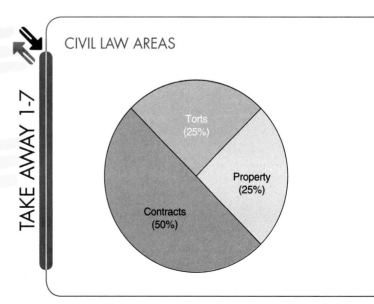

TAKE AWAY 1-7

CIVIL LAW AREAS

Torts (25%)
Property (25%)
Contracts (50%)

TAKE AWAY 1-8

COMPARISON OF CIVIL AND CRIMINAL LAW

Criminal Law	Civil Law
Intent is to punish	Intent is to make injured party whole
Perpetrator/criminal is violator	Tortfeasor/breaching party is violator
"Beyond reasonable doubt" burden of proof	"Preponderance of evidence" burden of proof
Results in conviction	Results in liability
Violator fined, incarcerated	Liable party pays damages
Case brought by state	Case brought by private party
Interest of society at stake	Interest of private party at stake
Felonies or misdemeanors	Usually no degrees of torts
Loss of civil rights if convicted	No loss of civil rights if liable
Possible restitution if convicted	Liability imposed if liable
Adversely impacts later job search	Generally no impact on job search
Generally must tell of criminal conviction	Need not tell of civil liability

may be gradations in the tort of negligence such as gross negligence or simple negligence, which generally impact the amount of damages awarded to the plaintiff, if any.

Though some states have victim restitution or reimbursement programs, in criminal cases the victim may receive no compensation for harm done, but rather may only see the perpetrator put behind bars. The injured party in a tort case generally receives money damages from the tortfeasor to compensate for the harm suffered or damage done to the plaintiff. Criminal cases are brought on behalf of the state to protect society. Tort cases are brought on behalf of a private party to protect that party's interest. (See Take Away 1-8, "Comparison of Civil and Criminal Law.")

TORT LAW

Just as there are many different types of crimes, there are also many different types of torts (discussed in detail in the torts chapter). They vary from state to state since this area was left to the states under the Constitution. Most torts are derived from the common law (discussed in the courts chapter) and, as such, are called *common law torts*. However, even where this is so, many of the torts have been codified into statutes, and new torts have been created by statute or judicial law.

Some typical common law torts include assault, battery, intentional infliction of emotional distress, fraud, negligent infliction of emotional distress, defamation, false imprisonment, invasion of privacy, and negligence. Business torts include disparagement; false advertising; trademark, patent, and copyright infringement; interference with contractual relations; and others. Each tort has its own requirements that must be met in order to impose liability on the tortfeasor, details of which will be discussed in the torts chapter.

The underlying basis for tort relief is that people have a right to be protected in their person, property, business, and reputation. If others cause injury to one or more of those protected interests, either intentionally or negligently, they must take legal responsibility for their actions if the acts result in harm to the innocent victim. The court will order the defendant tortfeasor to do so if such responsibility is found by a court. With business tortfeasors, there are additional considerations such as businesses generally being better positioned to pay for their torts and passing on the cost to consumers as a cost of doing business spread out over many people.

CONTRACTS

Civil law also includes the area of contracts. **Contracts** (discussed in more detail in the contracts chapter) are voluntary binding agreements people or businesses enter into in order to obtain something to which they are not otherwise entitled. For instance, if Makenna wishes to obtain office equipment, she would not be entitled to get it from the supplier simply because she wants it. Rather, she must negotiate with the equipment dealer to decide on the equipment to be purchased and the terms of the agreement between them for purchase of the equipment and provide the equipment seller with money (or something else of value agreed upon by both of them) in exchange for the equipment. Makenna would be entering into an agreement with the equipment seller to obtain equipment that she would not otherwise be entitled to receive in the absence of an agreement. The equipment dealer would be entering into a contract with Makenna to receive money to which he would not otherwise be entitled to receive from Makenna in the absence of the agreement. This agreement, if it meets all necessary requirements, is called a contract.

Failure of one of the parties to the contract to perform as agreed results in **breach of contract** for which money or other remedies may be granted by a court. When a person breaches a contract, he or she must be willing to pay the cost of doing so. Generally, when a breach of contract case is brought, the goal is to put the nonbreaching party in the position he or she would have been in had there been no breach.

PROPERTY

Property law is also an area in civil law. It governs acquiring title to either real or personal property, as well as rules for proper transfer of property, whether for purposes of sale, by will, by gift, as a **bailment,** or as an original owner (such as the right to wild game one has trapped or killed). It may or may not be governed by contract. For instance, a contract would govern a sale of property, but not a gift of property or the finding of lost property. A bailment is the legal relationship created when a person gives possession of property but not title to the property to another for a specific purpose, such as the owner of a car leaving the car—that is, giving over possession—to the car repair shop owner to have the car repaired, or leaving your cat, which is considered your personal property, with your friend to care for while you are out of town on vacation. Each of these property interests has its own laws that govern title and possession and will be discussed in more detail in the property chapter.

Again, while the areas of torts, contracts, and property have distinct subject matter, they all involve civil matters rather than criminal. Within the two large areas, civil and criminal, are virtually every cause of action which arises under our law.

Ethics and Ethical Decision Making

Ethics are subjective rules that exceed the law and guide how a business conducts itself with its employees, customers, suppliers, and others with which it does business. Will it consider profit above all? Will its employees' welfare be important? Does it care about how customers and others doing business with it are treated by the company? Studying business teaches you the information needed to carry on commerce and be successful using tried and true business concepts that have worked well over time. However, this is not all you need to know in order to make good business decisions any more than knowing the correct answers on the written portion of a driver's license exam gives you everything you need to be a good driver. Judgment, experience with various situations, common sense, and a certain outlook toward driving and your fellow man all go into your ultimately becoming a good driver. The same is true for business. We cannot simply teach you the rules about business without giving you tools to develop your ethical decision making so that your business decisions are ultimately good ones in every sense. We have seen what happens when this does not occur.

If you doubt this, just ask the 22,000 employees at Enron who lost their jobs, health insurance, and $2 billion in retirement funds when the company made what they thought were "good business decisions" (which were still questionable even in a pure business sense), but apparently gave little thought to the ethical implications of those decisions. As you well know, Enron is not the only company to have made such questionable decisions recently. It became clear to those who formulate business curricula in colleges of business, the Association to Advance Collegiate Schools of Business (AACSB), that business students needed more grounding in ethical decision making as an integral part of learning to make more effective business decisions. That is why you will no doubt have the issue of ethics arise in several of your business classes if not all of them.

More and more businesses and professions adopt ethical standards and guidelines on their own. There are many different underlying theories of ethics and most businesses that have adopted formal ethical standards have used all of them in some way or another. Except in limited circumstances to be discussed later, companies are free to develop and impose their formal ethical guidelines however and in any way they wish. But as the need for attention to business ethics has grown because of the public call for businesses to conduct their dealings with more honesty, openness, and accountability, codes of business ethics have become somewhat more uniform. For instance, most ethics codes include rules about giving or accepting consideration from those wishing to do business with the firm and about various typical conflicts of interests employees and company officials may face. More and more often the government is called upon to assist either the public harmed by businesses' unethical conduct or the businesses themselves (remember the acrimonious company bailouts in 2008 and 2009 due in part to issues the public considered unethical like paying executives huge bonuses while the company suffered). This government involvement also brings some uniformity to firms' codes of ethics.

On July 21, 2010, President Obama signed into law the Dodd-Frank Wall Street Reform and Consumer Protection Act (the Dodd-Frank Act). The Dodd-Frank Act is a sweeping legislative response to some of the more nefarious business practices that often stemmed from less than stellar ethical decision making by businesses and that ostensibly led to the financial downturn and bailouts of 2008 and 2009. In a good example of what can happen if a business makes legal, though ethically questionable, decisions, the 2,300-page law has been characterized as the most sweeping financial reform legislation since the collapse of Wall Street in 1929. The Sarbanes-Oxley Act of 2002, which we will discuss later in the text, was passed in the wake of the Enron, WorldCom, and other corporate investment disasters primarily to address the public accounting and independence issues that resulted in multibillion dollar losses in public companies.

As an example of the various underlying ways to look at ethical issues, consider the following famous scenario. It addresses the matter of how the decision should be made when a boat with seven people capsizes in the ocean and as the days go on without rescue it is clear that there is not enough food to sustain all of the survivors. Near starvation, with no more to eat, one of the survivors proposes that they consider killing and eating the sickest survivor who is near death. Not only will it provide a means of sustenance, but it will also mean fewer mouths to feed with the limited resources they have. Do they do what is best for the most people and kill off the sickest survivor to feed the rest so that they will not all die before rescue? Do they stand on principle and decide that killing is wrong no matter what the reason, so that they allow him to live even though it may mean they all die?

In considering this ethical dilemma you are basically given the choice between a **utilitarian approach,** where the ends justify the means and the choice is made to do what is the "greatest good" for the most people (the person will be killed and eaten because it will mean more people can live), and universalism's **categorical imperative,** under which everyone should act as they would want someone else to act in the situation (the Golden Rule your parents taught you of do unto others as you would have them do unto you) as long as the rule is one that can be considered universally good for, and applied to, everyone. Of course, no one would want to be chosen to die and be eaten by others, so under this theory, the survivor would not be killed even if it meant everyone else died. These are the two most widely held ethical theories, but there are others.

A business need not have only one theory that underlies its ethical decision making. It can choose whichever theory seems best under the particular circumstances. For some issues the business may wish to stand its ground no matter the consequences. In other matters, they may wish to do what seems best for the most people, such as in deciding to downsize the company rather than keeping everyone on and running the risk that the entire company will go under if the drastic belt-tightening is not done. The choice between the utilitarian approach and the universal categorical imperative could be faced when a company must decide between outsourcing its manufacturing to a country with cheaper labor or keeping its manufacturing in the United States. The former would allow its prices to be more competitive and thus allow it to sell more products. The latter would help loyal employees and also might help America rebound from its economic crisis, but might mean the firm would be less competitive because of higher manufacturing costs due to higher U.S. wages. It is up to the business how it wishes to consider the ethical aspects of these decisions, but every choice has consequences.

Every single decision a business makes can have ethical implications. How and what ethical standards a business implements and adheres to is up to the business, but the important thing is to be aware that all business decisions have ethical implications and to take those implications into consideration when making a decision so that there are as few as possible unnecessary negative or unexpected repercussions. Ethical dilemmas are always thorny, but not facing up to them may prove even thornier. Dealing with the impact on all stakeholders affected by a decision is easier when the matter has been given thought beforehand rather than addressing trouble after the fact in the midst of a maelstrom that could have been avoided.

Having a corporate culture that encourages ethical decision making from the top down and creating a climate in which employees accept this and govern themselves accordingly when conducting business for the organization goes a long way. But merely giving lip service to these ideals may be worse than having no ethical code at all.

Enron's unethical behavior cost thousands of employees their jobs and resulted in the collapse of Enron and its accountants, the firm Arthur Anderson, the oldest CPA firm in the U.S., which had previously enjoyed a stellar reputation, as well as the many, many businesses that relied on Enron and its employees for their business. Employees lost their jobs, pay, pensions, and benefits, including health insurance, which also greatly impacted health care professionals in the area, suppliers, and others who did business with Enron. Enron shareholders suffered greatly, as did the city of Houston, where the business operated. Could a sincere consideration of the ethical implications of their business decisions by Enron officials have saved Enron (and all others harmed) from all of this? No doubt it could have.

Keep in mind that among other things, there were four major Enron issues. First of all, they used the mark to market accounting system which allowed them to place on their accounting books the projected profits from a deal they signed today, but might not finish or begin to see profits from for 10 years. This allowed them to show profits where none existed, but which looked good to investors counting on those profits to make their investment decisions. Second, they set up hundreds of wholly owned off-shore corporations that allowed them to hide their losses so that they never showed up as Enron losses to investors. So, investors thought they were looking at a company that had lots of profits, and few losses, which looked great from an investment standpoint. Third, Enron employees arranged for "rolling blackouts" in California for long enough to create a panic so that when they agreed to sell electricity, they could do so at a greatly increased price in the deregulated electricity industry they had pushed for. Enron profits soared while consumers' utility bills more than doubled. Fourth, Enron also promised that the technology for its video on demand deal with Blockbuster would be ready by the end of the year, and when it was clear it would not be ready and Enron would have to make this announcement, higher-ups began selling off millions and millions of dollars of their stock, while other employees were urged by Enron executives to continue to purchase Enron stock because it would only continue to increase in value. One employee's 401(K) plan worth $348,000 before the fall, eventually sold for $1,200. No doubt you can see why so many Enron executives ended up with criminal sentences. Clearly, ethics had no place in their decision-making process.[8]

In imposing a 150-year sentence rather than the mere 12 years that Bernie Madoff's attorney suggested, District Judge Denny Chin said, "Here, the message must be sent that Mr. Madoff's crimes were extraordinarily evil and that this kind of irresponsible manipulation of the system is not merely a bloodless financial crime that takes place just on paper, but it is instead . . . one that takes a staggering human toll."[9] The point we are making should be obvious.

Throughout this text, we will call upon you to think not only about the legal implications of business decision making, but also the ethical implications. Our goal is not to choose your ethics for you, but to make you aware of the ethical dimension of business decisions and give you tools to make right ethical choices. What do you need to know to make an effective decision? What rules apply? Who are the stakeholders? What are their respective interests? What stands to be lost if a given decision is made? What stands to be gained? What is most important to the business? What is most important to its owners and its stakeholders? Are there ways to accomplish a particular goal with fewer harmful side effects? Being in the habit of asking such questions and answering them effectively will help you or any business person make more productive decisions.

L010

Diversity as a Business Imperative

While America has always been a nation of immigrants, its relationship to them, as well as who those immigrants are and what their expectations are when they arrive in the U.S., have changed over time. Today, business is taking place in an increasingly diverse

---

[8]See The *Smartest Guys in the Room: The Amazing Rise and Scandalous Fall of Enron,* by Bethany McLean and Peter Elkind (New York: The Penguin Group, 2003).

[9]Associated Press, July 19, 2009, http://www.msnbc.msn.com/id/31604191/ns/business-us_business/.

U.S. society quite different from the one in which previous generations have operated. In the 1990s, at the behest of the U.S. Department of Labor, the Hudson Institute released the "Workforce 2000 Report." The Report galvanized much of the business world when it reported that the country's present immigration experience was rivaled only by the mass immigrations of Europeans into the United States at the turn of the twentieth century. However, the present immigration influx will have a far more profound impact on American society, business, and the workplace than the previous one.

While the previous wave of immigration had been 90 percent European, with immigrants coming to America to seek a better life and wanting to assimilate, this wave of immigrants will be 90 percent Asian and Latin. While it may have been easier for Europeans, who looked like the predominantly white Americans, to fit in here, and because their reasons for coming to the U.S. included more of a wish to conform and assimilate, they were fairly quickly absorbed into their new culture. They had their troubles, to be sure (common signs posted in businesses said "No dogs or Irish allowed"). But over time they were thoroughly absorbed into the American fabric. However, the new wave of immigrants do not look like the mass of white Americans, they do not blend in as easily, and because they have often left their countries for different reasons than the earlier immigrants, and for other cultural reasons, they often come with a strong wish to maintain their ethnic identities, which may differ radically from majority of white Americans' whose roots were European. Fleeing their homes for political reasons, for instance, does not mean they want to leave their culture, music, language, food, religion, dress, or customs. Already having friends, family, or pockets of their culture here means that often they do not have to.

These newer immigrants want the opportunities America has to offer, but this does not mean that they do not have a profound and abiding feeling for the homelands they left behind under economic, religious, or political duress. In fact, America was the place that held out the promise of allowing them to be free to practice and express their culture while providing them the economic stability and physical safety they sought.

In a fairly short period of time, the American landscape has begun to change in fairly drastic ways. New immigrants have heightened expectations because of our law and economy emphasizing equal opportunity. Enforcement of antidiscrimination laws guaranteeing equal opportunities in employment, housing, education, public accommodations, and receipt of federal funds, particularly on the basis of national origin or religion, are well known to immigrants. The events of September 11, 2001, which caused an initial mistrust of certain groups of immigrants by some Americans (Equal Employment Opportunity Commission claims of discrimination and harassment against Middle Easterners rose by 50 percent), resulted in heightened visibility of those groups but also acted to galvanize them. Rather hearteningly, their expectations that their legal rights would be honored rebounded and rose. An ever-expanding economy that despite its recent woes remains strong and fairly easy to enter for those who come from outside the U.S. has been an enticement to immigrate here. So, the immigrants could come, participate in our economy to raise their standard of living and provide a better future for their children, and be protected by our laws while doing so. This has not so far meant the historical absorption of previous generations, however.

In addition to new immigrants coming into the U.S. and changing the business landscape, there are also the existing populations of African Americans, Hispanics, Asians, Native Americans and others who have struggled more and more successfully to be treated equally in this country. All of this has had a dramatic impact on American society, whether it is seeing more and different ethnicities in the workplace, in businesses we support, in our churches, libraries, stores, theaters or schools and universities, having more and different types of foods available to us at restaurants featuring foods from the new ethnicities, or seeing a wider array of new and different food and other products available to us when we shop. Today we see the directions on everything from a power tool at the hardware store to a bag of black beans at the grocery store written in English, Spanish, and French. More Hispanic and also African American radio and television stations and programming are appearing. In Atlanta recently, the branch of a national bank located in an area known to have a number of wealthy rap and hip-hop artists chose to reflect this robust culture in its décor, ambient music, and services. Banks and other businesses are doing the same thing in predominantly Hispanic areas. New and different music and movies available for public consumption have even resulted in new Grammy award categories.

Since the integration of these new (or old), vastly differing peoples and cultures into mainstream American life means their interfacing with the law and with the business world, it is imperative to address this new and interesting phenomenon in our discussion of the legal and business landscape. Failing to do so would mean leaving out an important part of what any business person should be aware of in order to be prepared to do business in the 21st century.

Recall the NAACP lawsuit we mentioned earlier. In March 2009 the NAACP filed suit in the federal district court in Los Angeles against Wells Fargo and HSBC, alleging that these businesses specifically targeted African Americans for subprime loans and steered them to such lenders even when their qualifications were exactly the same as white borrowers. At the time of this writing these allegations, though compelling anecdotal evidence, are not proven, but if true they are an example of the consequences of a business failing to take into consideration the obvious diversity implications, let alone the ethics of the situation. There are several such lawsuits pending in other jurisdictions.[10] Taking into account the ethical and diversity implications of a business decision can save a lot of trouble later. Not doing so is unethical and may be illegal, but it is also simply not good for business either.

None of us make decisions, even legal ones, in a vacuum. We view the world through our own individual lenses based on our gender, culture, race, ethnicity, religious beliefs, socioeconomic status, geography, family values, education, life experiences, and so on. Our decisions can reflect that. While we may intend for our decisions to be neutral, often they may not be completely so. All the more reason to be cognizant of ethical and diversity issues. Having our decisions impacted by these factors is not necessarily a bad thing. It simply must be kept in mind as a piece of our decision-making process.

Even the decisions of the highest court in the land reflect its own collective experiences, values, and beliefs. In fact, it has recently been taken to task for this by one of its own. After the *Ledbetter v. Goodyear Tire and Rubber Co. Inc.*[11] decision and the *Redding v. Stafford Unified School District*[12] oral arguments, U.S. Supreme Court Justice Ruth Bader Ginsburg made it clear that the high court needed more female justices because the decisions and oral argument comments of the male justices reflected that they were unaware of the realities of gender and its impact on the decisions and discussion in those cases.[13] In *Ledbetter* the Court held that a female manager who discovered she had been experiencing pay discrimination for virtually the whole 19 years she had been at her job was unable to successfully bring her discrimination lawsuit because the Court held that she should have brought it earlier even though there was virtually no way she could have done so. The Court's decision led to passage of the Lilly Ledbetter Fair Pay Act as the first piece of legislation signed into law by President Barack Obama. The Act allows such cases to be brought despite the passage of time,

---

[10]Associated Press, March 13, 2009, http://www.msnbc.msn.com/id/29678907/.

[11]550 U.S. 618, 2007 U.S. LEXIS 6295 (2007).

[12]2009 U.S. LEXIS 585 (January 16, 2009) (cert. granted) on appeal from the Ninth Circuit, 531 F.3d 1071; 2008 U.S. App. LEXIS 14756 (9th Cir. 2008).

[13]Joan Biscupic, *USAToday,* May 5, 2009, http://www.usatoday.com/news/washington/judicial/2009-05-05-ruthginsburg_N.htm.

determining that the statute of limitations begins to run anew each time a discriminatory paycheck is issued. In Justice Ginsburg's dissent in *Ledbetter*, she believed the Court's decision denied the reality of a solo female manager's precarious position in the workplace, since she would certainly have been ridiculed had she complained about her pay, particularly since she was usually the only female manager and in addition there was a workplace rule prohibiting discussions about salaries.

In the *Redding* oral arguments, Justice Ginsburg believed that the male justices minimized the lasting humiliation and trauma suffered by a 13-year-old girl who was strip searched by school officials looking for Ibuprofen. Ginsburg said it was clear that the members of the Court had never experienced being a 13-year-old female.

As we write this, Justice Ginsburg's comment may well have found quarter, as President Obama nominated 16-year veteran federal appellate court judge Sonia Sotomayor for the U.S. Supreme Court vacancy created by the resignation of Justice David H. Souter, and Sotomayor has been confirmed. As the heated debate raged about the nominee who would be the first Hispanic on the high court, you may recall the many comments made about whether Sotomayor could be "objective" as a jurist. Even though she has been reputed to be the nominee with the most judicial experience in the last 70 years of the Court,[14] her objectivity has been called into question since she is a Latina—even to the point of calling her a racist.[15] In August 2010, U.S. Solicitor General Elena Kagan was President Obama's second appointment to the high court and only the fourth female to sit on the U.S. Supreme Court in its history. If you watched the Senate hearings you had a chance to see the very things we are saying about diversity as a major issue of our times being played out at the highest levels of our government. The same sorts of issues arose in the consideration of Senator Barack Obama and Senator Hillary Clinton as the first serious African American and female contenders for the U.S. presidency. While we tend not to think of a candidate's objectivity and ability to make unbiased decisions when such high positions are sought or held by those we are used to seeing in power, it apparently becomes a political issue when someone "different than we are used to" is involved.

As a society, largely because of the cultural changes alluded to above, we are just now seriously realizing the implications of how much our own experience and world view impact decisions we make, how we see life and its challenges, and how our past (whether as a business, an individual, or a nation) can impact everything from educational opportunities to the way we conduct business, from who is hired to what food is available in a workplace cafeteria. If I watch my mother fight insurance companies for coverage while dying of cancer (as Obama did), as a legislator, or president, I will no doubt fight to alleviate such suffering for others. To that extent, my personal experience is impacting my agenda as a legislator. That need not be a bad thing, clearly. It may be that some senators genuinely feared what Judge Sotomayor would bring to the high court because of her experiences as a Latina. Such recent political events underscore the importance of understanding that our business and legal decisions are not confined to objective, quantifiable factors.

What this text strives to do as you study it is to open your eyes to ethical and diversity issues so, where applicable, they become a relevant part of your business decision-making process, just as legal considerations are. Our aim is to teach you the legal, regulatory, and ethical implications of business decisions in the context of diversity, as business cannot be divorced from the reality of the world in which we live. We of course do not tell you how you must think about such issues on a personal level, as you are able to hold whatever opinions you wish. Rather, we make you aware of how your business decisions may be impacted by issues you might not otherwise have considered. Remember the swim club discussed earlier; the point was to point out the public

[14]Nico Pitney, "Sonia Sotomayor, Supreme Court Nominee: All You Need to Know," May 27, 2009, http://www.huffingtonpost.com/2009/05/01/sonia-sotomayor-supreme-c_n_194470.html.

[15]Jake P. Tapper, ABC News White House Correspondent, "Gingrich Calls Sotomayor 'Racist,'" May 27, 2009, http://blogs.abcnews.com/politicalpunch/2009/05/gingrich-calls.html.

relations, legal, and other implications of their decision. We want you to consider these factors as a routine part of your business decision making since the reality is that they will have an impact.

Diversity considerations will be included in the text's discussion only as they arise. Not every legal issue has aspects related to diversity. We will provide you with our best judgment as to when and how these issues may arise as legitimate business considerations based on the myriad of legal cases and business situations that may serve as precedent. Note that diversity considerations are not a matter of "political correctness" or "jumping on the diversity bandwagon." The diverse makeup of the United States of the 21st century is not a fad. Not taking the new reality into consideration may result in inefficiency, lower productivity, lost opportunities, and unnecessary litigation and ill will. Our increasing diversity in America is an important reality that must be addressed in constructive, productive ways if we—and you—are to remain at the forefront of the business world.

Summary

The legal, ethical, and regulatory structure within which business operates is broad and far-reaching, with diverse constituencies that must be considered. This environment impacts in some way or another virtually every business decision we make. Knowing the background of our business life and the structure within which we make legal and business decisions gives us a better idea of the factors at play in our business decisions so we may make better and more effective choices in business matters.

The legal structure within which we make business decisions includes the various jurisprudential theories of law, our sources of law, including the U.S. Constitution and its many business-related provisions, treaties, the common law, statutes, executive orders and judicial decisions. Law is divided into criminal and civil law, with the latter being divided into torts, contracts, and property. Further, law may be public or private, substantive or procedural.

The ethical environment goes hand in hand with the legal and regulatory structure for business. We have come to realize that we can no longer make business decisions while considering only the legal or regulatory requirements and their implications. Just as important is that business decisions be made ethically. It makes little sense for a business to make lots of money for its shareholders, only to lose it all because of disastrous ethical lapses.

Where appropriate, we must also consider the diversity implications that may have a serious impact on our business decisions. Sometimes diversity may have no relevance at all, while at other times it may have a profound impact. Learning to become aware of the new reality of cultural diversity in our country and taking the related issues into account as needed will make for better, more informed, and more efficient and sensible business decisions. Keep this in mind as you explore the remaining chapters.

One final note: We take the information, examples, and business scenarios we present to you from real life and use them to teach you how to confront similar situations or avoid similar mistakes in your business dealings. Nothing in this text should be taken as informed by any antibusiness attitude—in fact, just the opposite. We want businesses (and you) to do as well and be as successful as they (and you) can be without wasting time and money by making unnecessary, avoidable mistakes that cause loss of income and embarrassment. The standard of living in the United States is one of the highest in the world due in large part to our unparalleled, though admittedly imperfect, system of the rule of law and the environment it creates for our businesses to be innovative, to be courageous, and to flourish. Part of the job of this text is to point out certain flaws in decision making as a lesson to you in how to avoid such mistakes and continue to make American businesses even better in our unique social and legal enviroment.

Review Questions

1. Define law. LO1

2. List and explain three theories of jurisprudence. LO3

3. All but which of the following is an attribute of criminal law? LO3, 8

   a. punishment

   b. make-whole relief

   c. involuntary litigation

   d. public law

4. _____ law provides rights and remedies, while _____ law provides a method for pursuing those rights. LO7, 8

5. Jettie Robinson was rear-ended by Bunn Liles at a busy intersection. At the time of the accident, Bunn was driving a delivery truck for Ratliff Shipping, Inc. Jettie decides to sue for the damages she sustained. Of the broad classifications of law covered in the chapter, discuss what kind of case Jettie's attorney would likely bring, against whom, and why. LO8

6. Srabanti tells Brett that if he breaches his contract with her it will be a tort. Is Srabanti correct? LO7, 8

7. Hitler's heinous actions during the Holocaust are an example of what legal theory? LO3

8. Prohibition is an example of what legal theory? LO3

9. List five differences between civil and criminal law. LO8

10. Reginald's shirt was shredded when it was cleaned at the dry cleaner. Reginald wants to sue the owner of the cleaning establishment in small claims court, so Reginald accesses the court website where he finds that the filing cost will be $35 and he has two years in which to bring his cause of action. The site also tells him how to notify the owner of the dry cleaning establishment that he is being sued. These types of rules are _____ law. LO7

Ethics Issue

Zircon, Inc., a mouthwash and toothpaste manufacturer in the U.S., discovers during a routine shipment laboratory spot check that a shipment of its mouthwash manufactured in a country outside the U.S. contains a chemical that is not a part of its normal formula. The international manufacturer says that the compound is not harmful and it made the substitution in order to meet the contract deadline when it became clear that the agreed upon ingredient would not be available in time. The compound is only present in microscopic amounts and is not harmful to users. However, the ingredients listed on the mouthwash bottle and packaging still have the original ingredient listed and do not include the substitution.

Zircon understands that it has a cause of action for breach of contract against the company it contracted to manufacture the product, but it is in a quandary as to what to do about the substitution. It would be extremely costly and time-consuming to order that the labels on the bottles and boxes be changed, or for the formula to be changed back to the original in the mouthwash. Consumers will not be harmed by the substitution and no one will likely know except appropriate company personnel. Think about what you consider the relevant issues Zircon must consider in determining the ethics of what it should do about this situation.

Group Exercise

Have each group choose a current article from a newspaper, magazine, or the Internet. The article can be about virtually anything. Have the group discuss the different aspects of law that they see in the article, using as many of the chapter topics as possible and telling how the aspect of the article they have chosen relates to the topic they have connected it to.

The students can even extrapolate on the article's legal implications. For instance, in an article on the Rose Bowl winner, students may discuss who could be sued if a fan was hurt during the game, whether the game rules are public or private "law," what recourse would there be if a star player decided to quit just before the game, and so forth.

Key Terms

www.mhhe.com/bennett-alexanderLE1e

Alternative Dispute Resolution

Learning Objectives

After reading this chapter, you should be able to:

L01   Define alternative dispute resolution

L02   Explain how and why ADR is used in business

L03   Identify the most popular types of ADR

L04   Discuss the pros and cons of different types of ADR

L05   Determine the appropriateness of different types of ADR for various disputes

L06   Explain how administrative agencies have increasingly mandated ADR

L07   Describe newly emerging ADR alternatives designed specifically for business

L08   Evaluate ways that ADR can help business

 ## Opening Scenario

Skycycle Bicycle Emporium has had several complaints filed against it with the Greater Business Bureau. Customers have complained about the quality of the goods and services at Skycycle. There have also been complaints from Skycycle's business suppliers that Skycycle is not honoring their agreements as they should. Cisnero, one of Skycycle owner Oscar's buddies, sees the storm brewing and thinks he can help. Cisnero suggests to Oscar that Cisnero set up a meeting between Oscar and each of the complainants. Cisnero says each complainant will be able to discuss his or her complaint with Oscar and Cisnero will try to broker a solution between the complainant and Oscar. Oscar says he has never heard of such a thing and cannot imagine that it would work. Should Oscar try Cisnero's suggestion?

Introduction and Background   **L01**

When you think of legal disputes, you probably think of them being settled by a court. However, not every dispute will be litigated in court. In fact, most will not; and they need not be. In reality, the overwhelming majority of disputes are resolved without resort to costly court trials. Not only is litigation costly and time-consuming, but it simply is not necessary for the resolution of every disagreement or conflict. For some conflicts it would be like using a sledgehammer to kill a fly. Litigation is the heavy artillery of the conflict resolution arena and should be used most judiciously. Ideally it should be

10 REASONS TO USE ALTERNATIVE DISPUTE RESOLUTION

In this box you have an example of the Virginia Department of Veterans Affairs' attempt to have vets use ADR rather than litigation to resolve disputes. While some of the items are specifically tailored to the Virginia VA's issues, it gives you a concrete idea of the reasons for the push for ADR rather than protracted and expensive court litigation. Note that item 2 regarding services being free is not generally the case. The cost may be less than litigation, but it is generally not free.

1. **ACCESSIBLE**
   Alternative Dispute Resolution (ADR) can be requested at any time by any VA employee, manager or union official by contacting the local ADR coordinator or the Workplace ADR Program. A list of coordinators is located at http://vaww1.va.gov/adr/page.cfm?pg=86.
2. **COST EFFECTIVE**
   ADR services can be provided at no cost to the organization or employee.
3. **FAIR AND NEUTRAL**
   A facilitator or mediator is assigned to each case. These individuals have no vested interest in the dispute, can be objective, encourage active listening, promote understanding and generate options. When opinions begin to form and emotional responses surface, the parties can benefit from a third party's skills.
4. **SAVES TIME AND MONEY**
   On average, ADR can be requested, scheduled, and completed in 30 days. Other forums used to resolve disputes such as the grievance and EEO complaint process can take months, even years to reach an outcome.
5. **STRUCTURED DIALOGUE**
   Ineffective communication can cause workplace disputes. Facilitation and mediation are opportunities to improve communication through structured dialogue where conversations can be more meaningful and productive.
6. **INCREASED KNOWLEDGE AND AWARENESS**
   When lines of communication are opened or improved, all parties can gain new insights and more easily determine how to address the issues in dispute with an enhanced understanding of each other's concerns.
7. **DESIGN YOUR OWN SOLUTION**
   ADR outcomes are crafted by the parties. Through the exchange of information and ideas, you make choices on what is in your best interest. You determine if the dispute can be resolved and if not, parties can keep things from getting worse.
8. **CONFIDENTIAL**
   ADR typically involves the parties in dispute and their designated representatives, if any. An individual with authority to make decisions may also attend or be available to the parties if needed. Witnesses are not called and evidence is not produced. The facilitator is bound by strict confidentiality to keep anything shared in confidence unless otherwise permitted or required to disclose.
9. **BETTER RELATIONSHIPS**
   ADR is a professional way to deal with workplace disputes. Although disagreements will occur, how we choose to deal with them lays the foundation for our working relationships with others and how we serve our customers. Even if agreements cannot be reached, one can build a relationship of respect by trying to work things out instead of avoiding or doing nothing, and allowing the matter to escalate.
10. **IT WORKS!**
    More than half of all ADR requests end in resolution. A mutually acceptable settlement is reached, the scope of the issues is narrowed, or a pending action is withdrawn. In most cases, the parties leave having benefited from the process.

Source: Virginia Department of Veterans Affairs, Office of Resolution Management, http://www1.va.gov/adr/docs/adr_brochure.pdf.

used only as a means of last resort. That is why we have placed our discussion of alternatives to litigation before our chapter on the court system. For those conflicts which do not need litigation, there are several alternatives. Together, these mechanisms have come to be known as **alternative dispute resolution** or **ADR.**

Our becoming a more litigious society has had a tremendous impact on the options available when we have a dispute. The immediate issue was that the startling increase in lawsuits greatly clogged the court system. Litigants could languish for years while waiting to get on a busy court's calendar. Litigation was virtually the only recourse for those with disputes, and that route was time-consuming and expensive.

The primary reason the courts were clogged was that for years lawyers and judges had been hostile to the idea of parties to a dispute disposing of the dispute in any way other than litigation. The legal establishment believed parties might lose important protections provided by litigation. The more cynical view was that lawyers believed ADR would diminish their ability to make the money they may have been accustomed to. However, the more litigious our society became and the more cases there were, the more frustration there was at legitimate litigation being held up because of a court system congested with so many less compelling disputes.

To a large extent, the only alternatives to litigation that existed were arbitration and mediation. To put it simplistically, arbitration was primarily utilized by unions and later the securities industry, and mediation was for baseball disputes. This is intentionally simplistic, but it was clear that the limited use of alternatives was not optimal, and something needed to be done.

The growing concern over overcrowded court systems finally overcame judges' and lawyers' objections to alternatives to litigation. In the past 20 years or so ADR has experienced an explosion in popularity. The old standbys of **conciliation, mediation,** and **arbitration** have been joined by a spate of new and innovative approaches to resolving disputes in far shorter time for far less money when compared to litigation. Things have changed to the point that federal agencies are now mandated to engage in ADR and many court systems have court-annexed ADR as an initial means of resolving appropriate disputes that lend themselves to such an alternative. Such a procedure would have been unheard of before. (See Reality Check 2-1, "10 Reasons to Use Alternative Dispute Resolution.")

Despite its advantages, ADR has not always been favored. In fact, as previously mentioned, at one time courts were downright hostile to the idea. However, logic and convenience eventually won out. In the *Rodriguez* case (Case 2.1), the Supreme Court discusses its change of heart.

CASE 2.1 Rodriguez de Quijas et al. v. Shearson/ American Express

490 U.S. 477 (1989)

Facts: Even though a group of securities investors signed agreements requiring that account disputes be settled by binding arbitration, when their investments went bad, the investors brought suit in court alleging fraudulent and unauthorized transactions in violation of the Securities Act of 1933 and the Securities and Exchange Act of 1934. The U.S. Supreme Court held that the agreement to arbitrate securities claims was binding and the courts were not the only forum in which securities disputes are to be resolved.

Issue: Whether it is permissible for courts to allow legal claims to be resolved by arbitration rather than in a court of law.

Decision: Yes

Reasoning: Kennedy, J.: The Court's characterization of the arbitration process is pervaded by "the old judicial hostility to arbitration." That view has been steadily eroded over the years. The erosion intensified in our most recent decisions upholding agreements to arbitrate federal claims raised under the Securities Exchange Act of 1934, under the Racketeer Influenced and Corrupt Organizations (RICO) statutes, and under the antitrust laws. The shift in the Court's views is shown by the flat statement in *Mitusbishi Mostors Corp. v. Soler Chrysler-Plymouth, Inc.*, 473 US 614 (1985): "By agreeing to arbitrate a statutory claim, a party does not forgo the substantive rights afforded by the statute; it only submits to their resolution in an arbitral, rather than a judicial, forum." To the extent that [our decisions] rested on suspicion of arbitration as a method of weakening the protections afforded in the substantive law to would-be complainants, it has fallen far out of step with our current strong endorsement of the federal statutes favoring this method of resolving disputes.

There is nothing in the record before us, nor in the facts of which we can take judicial notice, to indicate that the arbitral system would not afford the plaintiff the rights to which he is entitled. AFFIRMED

1. Do you agree with the court that "by agreeing to arbitrate a statutory claim, a party does not forgo the substantive rights afforded by the statute; it only submits to their resolution in an arbitral, rather than a judicial, forum"? Why or why not?

2. If arbitration awards can only be reviewed by a court for reasons such as fraud or collusion on the part of the arbitrator, unconstitutionality, and so on, aren't the courts virtually foreclosed to the parties? Discuss.

3. Are you surprised that the Court would rethink its previously hostile position on arbitration and now decide to endorse arbitration?

Types of Alternative Dispute Resolution

Unless the state or local law in a given jurisdiction has a prescribed means by which ADR must be pursued, it is very flexible and the mechanisms need not be used in any particular order, though they tend to lend themselves to a natural logic. In fact, because of its flexibility, some have come to call ADR "appropriate dispute resolution." Because they offer considerable cost-saving to the court and parties, time saving, and privacy, they should be pursued before litigation. We will explore some of those alternatives to litigation and see what they have to offer and how they can be of help in the business world. First we will take a look at the three most prevalent approaches, then some more and newer innovations. (See Take Away 2-1, "Three Most Common Types of ADR.")

WHAT IS CONCILIATION AND HOW IS IT DONE?

It may seem too obvious to even discuss, but the very first thing a party with a conflict should do is to attempt conciliation, also called negotiation, with the other party to the dispute. It is the easiest, cheapest thing to do, and if it is successful, nothing else need be done and the conflict ends at this point. Conciliation is important enough that it has been written into some statutes. For instance, under the statutory scheme of Title VII of the Civil Rights Act of 1964 and its administrative regulations, by law the parties must first attempt to conciliate claims of employment discrimination before proceeding further.

As simplistic as it may sound, conciliation simply involves the parties talking to each other about their dispute, either orally or in writing, in an effort to reach a resolution of the conflict. Conciliation costs nothing and nothing is lost if the parties do not reach a satisfactory resolution. It is surprising how many people caught up in the frustration, anger, or high emotion of their situation skip this step and go directly to litigation. Many times they find after filing suit that the matter could have been handled without legal intervention at all. Again, if conciliation does not work, the parties can move on to the next logical step, mediation, and nothing is lost.

TAKE AWAY 2-1

THREE MOST COMMON TYPES OF ALTERNATIVE DISPUTE RESOLUTION (ADR)

- Conciliation/Negotiation
- Mediation
- Arbitration

MUST I MEDIATE AND HOW IS IT DONE?

Like conciliation or negotiation, mediation of a conflict may not be required, but can be quite advantageous. Conciliation is between the parties to the conflict without the intervention of a disinterested third party, but mediation brings an outsider into the conflict for the first time. The purpose of the third party is for the outsider to try to facilitate the parties' reaching a resolution on their own. Have you ever had a conflict with one of your parents and your other parent talks to each of you separately and tries to get you to see the other's side of things or to look at things a different way in order to resolve the conflict? This is mediation.

Mediation is most useful when the parties wish to maintain an ongoing relationship but simply need help resolving the present conflict. You can see how important that would be in the business context with parties that need to continue to deal with each other. However, the parties may be so angry or frustrated about the dispute that talking to each other is virtually useless and may even result in an escalation of the conflict. There are other reasons that dealing with each other may not be as fruitful as the parties would like. One party may fear the other, be intimidated, may be jealous, or feel there is too much of some power or other differential that makes dealing with the other directly a bad idea.

A third party outsider may well be able to make headway where the parties themselves were not able to. In union negotiations, often the parties become so angry with each other, perceiving the other side to be recalcitrant and unwilling to be open to effective discussion of a given point, that it is more productive to allow a mediator to go back and forth between the parties, speaking to each, to get them to focus on the real issues and reach an agreement.

For instance, let's say Skycycle from our opening scenario has a disagreement over the terms of an agreement with the national distributor of the specialty tires it needs for its business. If this is the best place from which they can purchase the necessary tires and Skycycle and the distributor are essentially locked in this relationship together, they need to be able to preserve their relationship, yet still resolve their dispute. Rather than resort to the adversarial path of litigation, which rarely preserves the relationship between the parties, they are prime candidates for mediation.

In mediation, a third party is brought into the conflict to try to assist the parties themselves in resolving it. For instance, suppose you have a conflict with your roommate over her having guys stay overnight in the apartment you two share. You two become so angry over the conflict that you can barely tolerate being around each other (we've heard this one a lot from our students!). But you want to remain roommates. A mutual friend may talk to each of you and get you to come to some understanding rather than the two of you getting angrier and angrier and the situation escalating to the point where one of you moves out. Your mutual friend has mediated the situation in order to save the relationship between you and your roommate.

Federal Mediation and Conciliation Service

Mediation can be as informal as getting a mutual friend both you and your roommate trust to mediate the conflict by talking to you two and trying to help you work things out. There are no formal requirements for who can mediate disputes, but there are formal structures in place for those who wish to take advantage of them. For instance, professional baseball teams routinely call on the **Federal Mediation and Conciliation Service (FMCS)** for assistance in resolving their contract disputes.

FMCS is a government agency that can be used by parties to conduct mediation of a dispute. The agency maintains a roster of mediators who have agreed to mediate disputes for FMCS. Parties seeking the services of a federal mediator notify FMCS and either request a mediator they both know and trust or request a list of names of mediators available to call upon. The list also has the mediators' backgrounds, previous mediations they have conducted, and other pertinent information that can be used by the parties to evaluate the mediator's suitability for their purposes. Each party strikes names from the list until they decide on one that is mutually satisfactory. Arrangements are then made for the mediator to meet with the parties and try to help them resolve the conflict.

There are also now many private mediation organizations also, as well as attorneys offering mediation ADR as part of their services. Under state rules and regulations, the mediators usually have been certified to act as mediators by taking courses to learn how to best deal with parties attempting to resolve conflict. These rules and regulations vary from state to state and may be quite different from one place to another.

Most often the mediator engages in a type of "shuttle diplomacy" wherein the mediator goes back and forth between the two parties and listens to their concerns and tries to find a way for each to get what he or she wants from the situation. The mediator can "hear" the parties' concerns better than they can hear each other because the mediator is not involved in the dispute and does not evaluate information with an eye toward trying to gain an advantage, keeping from being embarrassed, saving face, or appearing weak. The result is that the mediator can generally get the parties to reach an agreement with each other even though they were initially so angry that they may not have even wanted to be in the same room together.

LO6

AGENCY- AND COURT-ANNEXED ADR

In an attempt to lighten their caseloads, relieve court docket congestion, decrease the wait for court dates for litigants, decrease the cost of dispute resolution, and to reserve the courts only for those matters which actually need court disposition, some courts have instituted some form of an ADR program attached to the court itself. The programs vary from jurisdiction to jurisdiction, but most screen the cases filed with the court and call for at least a request that parties first attempt to mediate certain types of cases as an extension of the court's jurisdiction. In many court schemes the use of **court-annexed ADR** is optional. In most, parties still retain the option of proceeding to court if they are not satisfied with the ADR result. The courts generally limit the ADR option to cases that involve only certain subject matter, certain issues, or specified monetary amounts. (See Reality Check 2-2, "Michigan's Court-Annexed ADR Brochure Excerpt.")

State and federal agencies have also increased their support for mediation, up to, and including, mandating it for claims filed. The Equal Employment Opportunity

Commission (EEOC), the federal agency that enforces the Civil Rights Act of 1964 prohibiting discrimination on the basis of race, color, gender, religion or national origin in employment, education, public accommodations, and the receipt of federal funds, recently instituted mandatory mediation of all suitable claims filed with the agency.

In addition, in an effort to more quickly and efficiently handle claims filed with the agency and address its chronic backlog, EEOC has instituted innovative programs such as its **Universal Agreements to Mediate (UAMs)** and **Referral Back programs** for mediation. UAMs are agreements the EEOC makes with employers locally, regionally, or nationally, under which the employer has an identified contact point with EEOC for scheduling the mediation of claims filed by employees with EEOC. Referral Back programs allow EEOC, with the permission of the employee filing the claim with EEOC, to hold off on proceeding with the claim filed by the employee with EEOC and instead refer it back to the employer for handling by the employer's own internal EEOC-approved mediation program.

Beginning with its adoption of a policy statement on ADR in 1995, then to its development of a framework for ADR in 1998, and to its full implementation of ADR in 1999, EEOC has fully embraced ADR for resolving claims and continues to explore new innovations like the UAMs and Referral Back programs begun in 2002 and 2003. According to EEOC, from 1999 through 2003, over 52,400 mediations were held and more than 35,100 charges (69%) successfully resolved in an average of 85 days. In Reality Check 2-3, you get to see the actual court order issued by the U.S. Court of Appeals for the Federal Circuit in October 2005, establishing a pilot program for confidential, risk-free, voluntary mediation of claims even at the appellate court level. Since EEOC had a history of a chronic backlog, you can imagine how relieved EEOC must have been when it already had an ADR plan in place once claims filed with them increased so dramatically in the recent economic downturn.

There are definite advantages to the use of mediation which any astute business person should explore and utilize when disputes arise. However, if mediation between the parties is not satisfactory to the parties in terms of resolving the dispute, they may then proceed to the next most frequent ADR mechanism, arbitration.

ARBITRATION

Arbitration also involves the intervention of a disinterested third party into a dispute, but the purpose and method are quite different. In mediation the disinterested third party attempts to get the parties to reach a resolution of their conflict on their own. In arbitration, the role of the third party is to listen to the concerns and evidence of both parties and impose a decision, much like a judge does. The parties will not be resolving their own conflict, but instead they contractually agree between themselves to have a resolution imposed by an outsider to the conflict. Arbitrators can be found who specialize in certain areas, such as securities disputes, marital conflicts, environmental disputes, business disputes, sports conflicts, and so on.

Arbitration may be **binding** or **nonbinding.** If the arbitration is binding, the parties agree to abide by the decision (called an **award**) reached by the arbitrator, thus ending the dispute. If it is nonbinding arbitration, a party not satisfied with the arbitrator's decision can proceed to litigation to resolve the dispute. You might wonder why a party would agree to nonbinding arbitration and what the difference is between nonbinding arbitration and mediation. Remember that mediation is an attempt to have the parties reach their own agreement with the assistance of a disinterested third party. Arbitration, on the other hand, involves the disinterested third party hearing the dispute much like a judge would do and rendering a decision for the parties. Thus, the mediation resolution arises from the parties, while an arbitration award is imposed by the disinterested third

FEDERAL CIRCUIT COURT ORDER INSTITUTING A PILOT PROGRAM FOR ADR

United States Court of Appeals for the Federal Circuit

Order Establishing Appellate Mediation Pilot Program

Before MICHEL, Chief Judge, NEWMAN, MAYER, LOURIE, CLEVENGER, RADER, SCHALL, BRYSON, GAJARSA, LINN, DYK, and PROST, Circuit Judges.
PER CURIAM.

ORDER

It is ORDERED, by the court en banc.

(1)   The court is establishing an appellate mediation pilot program that will be monitored by a three-judge committee appointed by the chief judge. The program will be administered by the Circuit Mediation Officer, who is a member of the Office of the Clerk and Circuit Executive. The program is set forth in the Appellate Mediation Pilot Program Guidelines, available from the clerk's office and the court's web site. The purpose of the program is to help the parties achieve settlement.

(2)   The Circuit Mediation Officer will select cases for mediation and refer them to outside mediators. Participation in the Pilot program is voluntary. The court will select mediators from a list compiled by the Federal Circuit Bar Association. The mediators will not be in active practice. The mediators will serve without compensation. The court will reimburse mediators for minor out-of-pocket expenses.

(3)   Cases will be selected for mediation as early as possible in the appellate process and in no event after a case has been heard or submitted to a merits panel.

(4)   The content of mediation discussions and proceedings is confidential as explained in the Appellate Mediation Pilot Program Guidelines. The Circuit Mediation Officer will not communicate with the judges about the content of any particular mediation, but may discuss the overall effectiveness of the Appellate Mediation Pilot Program with the court. The outside mediators will protect the confidentiality of all proceedings and are prohibited from complying with subpoenas or other requests for information. The limited exceptions are that statistical data and other summary data may be disclosed by the Circuit Mediation Officer in connection with the court's evaluation of the Appellate Mediation Pilot Program, and there may be public disclosure by counsel or the parties if all counsel and parties involved in a particular mediation agree in writing and the mediator consents.

(5)   If, following mediation in a case, settlement is reached, then the agreement must be in writing. The appellant or parties must file a motion to dismiss or other appropriate motion. If settlement is not achieved, then the case will proceed as if mediation had not been initiated.

(6)   The effective date for the Appellate Mediation Pilot Program is October 3, 2005.

(7)   The Program may be altered, expanded, or discontinued at any time by direction of the court.

FOR THE COURT

AUG - 1 2005
Date

Jan Horbaly
Clerk

FILED
U.S. COURT OF APPEALS FOR
THE FEDERAL CIRCUIT

AUG - 1 2005

JAN HORBALY
CLERK

party. A party may be interested in having a disinterested third party come up with a solution, but they may not feel so strongly that they wish to be bound. In such cases, nonbinding arbitration gives them the opportunity to take a chance on having a viable solution, but if it is not satisfactory, they are not bound to it.

In binding arbitration, the arbitrator's award is virtually final, and can be reviewed only by a court of law for reasons involving unconstitutionality, abuse, collusion, or fraud in the arbitrator's decision and like bases attacking the validity of the award itself. However, parties who simply do not like the award cannot decide to use the courts as another chance to resolve the dispute. As you saw in the earlier *Shearson* case, if they have contractually agreed to be bound by the arbitrator's decision, the courts take this agreement seriously. Arbitrators' awards can therefore be even more powerful than those of a court that is subject to review by higher courts on appeal. This is interesting considering there is generally no requirement that an arbitrator be a lawyer or have any legal training, or that their awards be consistent as with the concept of *stare decisis* and precedent as in legal cases.

Binding arbitration agreements are often found in documents that a party may not even be aware contains such provisions. For instance, they frequently are included in employment agreements or consumer purchase agreements. They are almost always included in international commercial transactions as a way of avoiding international litigation. Since many, if not most, of us do not read many of the documents we agree to (did you actually read the 52-page agreement the last time you logged onto iTunes to download music?), these arbitration agreements often come as an unwelcome surprise. The June 1, 2010, issue of *The Village Voice* carried the story of an employee who alleges she was terminated from her position as a banker at Citibank in Manhattan because her managers found her figure too distracting.[1] Due to an arbitration clause in her employment contract, she will not be able to take the matter to court, but must submit it to arbitration. One of the downsides of arbitration can be that if an arbitrator is routinely used by a particular company for its disputes, arbitration awards may favor the business and reflect a wish for the arbitrator to keep being chosen as an arbitrator for the company.

While binding arbitration awards are subject to only very limited review by a court of law by a dissatisfied party, parties can, however, contract to have their arbitration award review be broader than the limited review generally provided. In the *Cable Connection* case (Case 2.2), that is exactly what the parties did, and it was upheld by the court.

While there is some type of court-annexed ADR in all states,[2] in more than 20 state and federal districts, court-annexed arbitration programs have been adopted to help ease court dockets. Under most of the statutes, cases which are filed for litigation are reviewed for arbitration potential. If they fit the profile, for instance, of involving less than a certain amount of money or being a certain subject matter, the judge to whom the case is assigned refers the case to arbitration. Most systems have a roster of arbitrators, many times attorneys, who hear the cases and render an award. Under most schemes, parties must participate in the court-annexed arbitration, but the award is nonbinding and a party may proceed with litigation if he or she demands a trial within a certain time after the arbitrator's award.

The American Arbitration Association, the largest arbitration organization in the U.S., maintains a roster of over 7,000 arbitrators which anyone can use to choose an arbitrator for a dispute. Arbitrators on the roster have been vetted by AAA and meet certain requirements, such as experience with arbitrating a certain number of disputes. Much as with mediators, at the client's request the AAA will send to the parties a list of potential arbitrators to decide the dispute. Each party views the list and strikes persons

EXAMPLE

---

[1] Elizabeth Dwoskin, "Is This Woman Too Hot to Be a Banker?" *The Village Voice*, June 1, 2010, http://www.villagevoice.com/2010-06-01/news/is-this-woman-too-hot-to-work-in-a-bank/1.

[2] The National Center for State Courts maintains a website with links to find help in your own state: http://www.ncsconline.org/WC/Publications/ADR/.

CASE 2.2 Cable Connection, Inc. v. DirectTV, Inc.

44 Cal4th 1344; 2008 Cal. LEXIS 10354 (S. Ct. Cal. 2008)

Facts: The parties entered into an agreement which included terms for arbitration of disputes. The arbitration agreement stated that the right to judicial review would include a broader range of issues than the general law limiting review of arbitration decisions to issues like fraud, collusion, or awards that were arbitrary, capricious or unconstitutional.

Issue: Whether an agreement to arbitrate can include a provision expanding the usual limited basis for judicial review.

Decision: Yes

Reasoning: Corrigan, J.: This case presents a question regarding arbitration agreements. May the parties structure their agreement to allow for judicial review of legal error in the arbitration award? The United States Supreme Court has held that the Federal Arbitration Act (FAA) does not permit the parties to expand the scope of review by agreement. However, the high court went on to say that federal law does not preclude "more searching review based on authority outside the [federal] statute," including "state statutory or common law." The California Legislature "adopt[ed] the position taken in case law . . . that is, 'that in the absence of some limiting clause in the arbitration agreement, the merits of the award, either on questions of fact or of law, may not be reviewed except as provided in the statute.' "

We adhere to our holding recognizing that contractual limitations may alter the usual scope of review. The California rule is that the parties may obtain judicial review of the merits by express agreement. There is a statutory as well as a contractual basis for this rule; one of the grounds for review of an arbitration award is that "[t]he arbitrators exceeded their powers." Here, the parties agreed that "[t]he arbitrators shall not have the power to commit errors of law or legal reasoning, and the award may be vacated or corrected on appeal to a court of competent jurisdiction for any such error." This contract provision is enforceable under state law, and we reverse the contrary ruling of the Court of Appeal.

CASE QUESTIONS

1. Does the court's decision make sense, given what you know about arbitration?
2. Why do you think the U.S. Supreme Court would not allow parties to broaden the scope of arbitration award review?
3. Given what you know about the purpose of ADR, does it seem consistent for parties not to be able to decide on the scope of their judicial review? Explain.

they do not want until agreement is finally reached. The matters of scheduling the arbitration hearing and paying for the arbitrator's services are arranged with the arbitrator directly by the parties. The cost of the arbitrator's fees is usually split equally between the parties by prior agreement. AAA handles about 55,000 commercial arbitrations per year, but they arbitrate all types of disputes. U.S. Arbitration and Mediation also offers ADR services. Note that while mediation and arbitration tend to be less expensive than litigation, they are not free, and, in fact, can be quite costly, depending on the nature of the dispute and the parties and issues involved.

It is also possible for arbitrators to sit to hear conflicts in panels of three or more, rather than sitting alone. Generally panels comprise an odd number of arbitrators so that the decision will not be evenly split and therefore will not result in a tied decision. When there is more than one arbitrator, generally the majority rules. While arbitration proceedings are like trials in that both parties present evidence and witnesses supportive of their claims, the rules are generally more relaxed and the structure less formal than in court. For instance, the hearing can be held anywhere the parties decide, rather than in a courtroom, and the rules of evidence adhered to in a court of law where a jury usually decides the case are not necessary in an arbitration hearing where only the arbitrator makes the determination so there is not the issue of a jury not knowing what is important as evidence.

Collective bargaining agreements between labor unions and employers commonly contain a provision for binding arbitration requiring that contract disputes will be handled by an arbitrator rather than a court. This is **labor arbitration.** This permits the parties to the collective bargaining agreement to dispose of disagreements arising under the contract without resort to the time-consuming method of litigating every disagreement. You can imagine how burdensome that would be for an employer. Rather than having to go to court for every single complaint an employee has, it serves both the employer and the employee to have an easy, quick, inexpensive means of resolving disputes.

Commercial arbitration addresses virtually all disputes to be arbitrated other than labor. It includes employer/employee disputes where no union or collective bargaining agreement is in effect.

The **Federal Arbitration Act** applies to commercial agreements that affect interstate commerce and make the arbitrator's awards in such cases legally enforceable. State laws make other arbitrator's awards (those not affecting interstate commerce) enforceable, though states vary in their commitment to ADR. In addition, some specific statutes contain arbitration provisions. For instance, there is a Securities and Exchange Commission rule that securities disputes be handled by arbitration if possible.

Some states have done the same thing with disputes between customers and car manufacturers. The Better Business Bureau has an automobile arbitration program which allows car owners to negotiate with manufacturers free of charge and receive a decision within 10 days. If the owner does not like the decision he or she is not bound, though the automobile manufacturer is.

Other Alternatives

L08

In addition to the mechanisms described above, parties may also use any of several other alternatives developed in recent years which may be appropriate for their dispute. (See Take Away 2-2, "Other Alternatives.") Some employers also use **ombudspeople** to try to avoid disputes. Such a person would generally have wide-ranging authority to have potential disputes brought to them for investigation and resolution.

Mock Trials

An attorney may wish to use this to determine how a jury might react to his or her case. The attorney assembles a mock jury made up of ordinary citizens, presents the case as if in court, then requests them to make a decision. Hearing the decision and questioning the "jury" about their deliberations can be very instructive for the attorney in deciding how best to proceed with the case and whether to seek a path other than litigation.

Minitrials

Minitrials are used for business cases and are presented to top business executives rather than ordinary citizens. Lawyers for both sides assemble a panel of a neutral advisors and high-ranking business executives with settlement authority from each business. Agreements vary, but generally the parties look at the problem as one of a business nature rather than a legal nature, then go into settlement negotiations afterwards, incorporating what the results of the minitrial have disclosed. There have been instances in which large, complex cases have been settled quickly after a minitrial, whereas litigation may have dragged on for years.

TAKE AWAY 2-2

OTHER ALTERNATIVES

Mock Trials
Mini Trials
Summary Jury Trial
Regulatory Negotiation

Regulatory Negotiation

This mechanism is used by administrative agencies wishing to avoid protracted litigation with interested groups over regulations which the agency wants to issue. The agency meets with these groups before formally proposing the regulations, often with a third party such as a mediator present, and attempts to negotiate the provisions of the regulations. In this way there is less likelihood of a challenge once the regulations are promulgated. For instance, the Environmental Protection Agency has used this mechanism for air and water quality regulations to be imposed.

Summary Jury Trial

Some jurisdictions provide for summary jury trials after cases have been filed if the case will require a great deal of time for trial and is unlikely to be settled by negotiation. Without telling them that their decision is not binding, a small (about 6 people) jury is chosen just as a regular jury would be, the case is presented in summary fashion by the parties, and the jury renders a verdict. Based on the jury's input, the parties are urged to negotiate a settlement if it is appropriate.

Summary

Alternative dispute resolution has become an important aspect of resolving conflicts and a necessary adjunct to litigation. With rising attorney fees, court costs, witness fees, and other expenses associated with litigation, it is appropriate that these mechanisms continue to grow in popularity. In addition to the traditional ADR mechanisms of conciliation, mediation, and arbitration, new and innovative alternatives have arisen in recent years to more quickly and efficiently resolve disputes without resort to litigation. It is in a business person's best interest to keep ADR in mind when disputes arise.

Review Questions

1. Antwon, who owns a large investment firm, is having a dispute with Tyrell, the owner of the company that makes the computer software Antwon's employees use to make their market predictions. The dispute has gone on for several weeks but the parties have been unable to come to a satisfactory solution. Antwon and Tyrell wish to maintain their working relationship with each other, as it is mutually beneficial, and they would like to resolve this conflict and move on with their other business concerns. With these facts, what is most likely the best way of resolving the dispute and why? LO7

2. Zhaio Ping is involved in an arbitration that has been heard by a five-member arbitration panel. When the arbitration panel hands down its award, Zhaio learns that two of the panel members did not agree with the award and instead favored an award more favorable to Zhaio. Can Zhaio use as the basis for appealing the award the fact that two of the arbitrators did not agree with it? Explain. LO3

3. The Music Review Board, an agency charged with monitoring decency in music broadcast on the airwaves, is contemplating issuing regulations requiring advisories to be placed on music to inform potential buyers of the level of violence, sex and adult language contained in a compact disc of music. The Music Review Board anticipates that there will be a long, involved dispute between the Board, the music industry, and many of the artists whose music will be affected, resulting in years of court litigation by artists challenging the regulations. As legal advisor to the Music Review Board, what would you advise them to do to minimize resistance by the music industry as they contemplate these regulations? LO6

4. When Megan dropped her silk blouse off at Saloum's cleaners, she had no idea that when

she picked it up, it would be a different color than when she left it, and would have holes in the bottom and buttons missing. Megan immediately informs Saloum that she is not paying for the dry cleaning and wants money for a new silk blouse. Saloum demands the money for the cleaning and refuses to pay for a new blouse. When their discussions become quite heated and the issue is not resolved, Rousley, a well-trusted neighbor to them both, happens to enter the cleaners and offers to help them with the dispute. What has Rousley offered to do? If Megan and Saloum agree to let Rousley help and eventually Rousley makes a suggestion that neither Megan nor Saloum is happy with, what can Megan and/or Saloum do about their respective claims? LO3

5. If Amir has a dispute with Chad, explain why Amir should not immediately take it to court? LO2

6. Bradley files a negligence case in court because he was rear-ended by Cheryl and the insurance companies refused to pay the entire repair bill. After filing the suit, Bradley receives a letter from the court recommending that he participate in court-annexed mediation for his claim because it will save him time and money. Bradley refuses because he says he wants his day in court and he will not have it if he goes to mediation. Is Bradley correct? Explain. LO6

7. Sheldon Industries had a lot on the line. Its recent industrial accident had seriously damaged not only plant employees and the plant itself, but also Sheldon's reputation. The company is being sued for millions of dollars. It has doubts about whether its witnesses will be believed and come across as down to earth and appealing to a jury. They are also a bit shaky about how their theory of the case will be accepted by a jury. With so much riding on the line, Sheldon Industries would like to have some idea of what might happen with its case. What should they do? LO7

8. In conciliation, a disinterested third party hears the dispute and tries to get the parties to come to a mutually satisfactory agreement. True or False?

Ethics Issue

Fernandina works as a receptionist in the office of a local mediation service. One day a client, a storeowner with whom the mediation service does a considerable amount of business, comes in to take part in a mediation between the client and a customer who has a dispute with the storeowner about an expensive item the customer purchased. The mediation service's code of ethics says that the mediation service is to render all services in a way that treats each dispute as objectively as possible, and it precludes them hearing disputes involving businesses or individuals with whom the mediators have a personal relationship. When the customer shows up, Fernandina realizes that the customer is the same person with whom the mediator is having a clandestine extramarital affair. Under the firm's code of ethics, anyone who knows of a conflict of interest is responsible for making the conflict known and adhering to the code. It becomes clear to Fernandina that the mediator is planning to mediate the dispute. Fernandina is afraid of losing her job if she tells, and afraid of losing it if she does not tell and the firm finds out she knew. Think this ethical dilemma through and decide what Fernandina should do.

Group Exercise

Ask around and see if anyone you know has a dispute going on. Nothing serious, just roommate troubles, or a light dispute with a significant other, or even a sibling's dispute with a parent. See if you can assist them by trying to mediate the dispute. In doing so, you want to gather all the pertinent facts from each of them, then see if you can discuss it with each of them and try to find a solution that will work for resolving the issue. No yelling or even raising your voice, no dictating what should be done. Just try your hand at trying to reach a solution.

Key Terms

www.mhhe.com/bennett-alexanderLE1e

The Court System and Legal Process

Learning Objectives

After reading this chapter, you should be able to:

L01 Explain the constitutional basis of the U.S. court systems

L02 Discuss how the courts are organized

L03 Describe the role of the federal courts

L04 Explain the process of selecting federal judges

L05 Describe the process by which a court gains jurisdiction over people and matters

L06 Discuss the use of precedent by courts

L07 Discuss the process for bringing a civil case through the court system

L08 Describe the remedies available to grant relief to aggrieved parties

Opening Scenario

Damian Jones is the owner of an Internet-based company, Stretchrite, that manufactures and sells exercise equipment. His primary product has been a thigh-strengthening device, Squeeze Knees, that is supposed to be used by placing the item between the knees and bringing the knees together in repetition so that the outer and inner thighs can become stronger. The equipment uses two pieces of rubber to create the tension so that the device "snaps back" into the open position after being squeezed shut. Within the past three months, Damian has been sued in 12 states by consumers who claim the rubber pieces have "popped" in mid-use, causing injury to various parts of their body. Damian's manufacturing plant is located in Georgia, the company is incorporated just over the Georgia border in Florida, and that is where the operators sit who take the orders over the phone and the Internet. The lawsuits require Damian to answer in every jurisdiction to the complaints filed by these consumers. Damian consults you for advice. What should he do? Does he have to be in all 12 states to answer to these complaints? Can you get them dismissed if Damian has never been to these states and has not done business there? Does it matter that these sales have happened over the Internet or the phone? Can the consumers sue wherever they are? Can Damian make them come to Florida to sue him?

Introduction

Courts. Where would we be without them? Try to imagine life or our system of government without a means of resolving disputes in court. It is very difficult to even imagine. As we discussed in the previous chapter, courts are not the only means of resolving disputes; however, when those alternatives are unavailing, the court system is there. Our legal system is designed as an adversarial system in which parties representing separate and opposing interests are vigorous advocates for their clients, which is believed to sharpen the issues for debate and represent the most effective pursuit of interests. In pursuit of this approach, the law provides strict protection of attorney-client privilege that protects communications between the two.

As established by the framers of the U.S. Constitution in 1787, the judicial branch of government involves the administration of justice at every level, from the Supreme Court to the local magistrate. Central to any level of court is the 14th Amendment's admonition that "No state shall . . . deprive any person of life, liberty or property, without due process of law; nor deny to any person within its jurisdiction the equal protection of the laws." This chapter will introduce you to the role of the courts and the system of justice as it operates in the United States.

LO1 Constitutional Basis for the Court System

Article III, Section I, of the U.S. Constitution gives Congress the power to create "one supreme Court, and . . . such inferior Courts" as Congress deems necessary. Because the United States has a federal system of government and each state has its system of government, the U.S. has two different court systems. Each state has its own courts to enforce that state's law, and in addition the federal government has courts throughout the country to enforce federal law. The U.S. Constitution allocates certain responsibilities to the federal government and reserves the rest to the states. State court systems tend to be organized as needed by the state, while the federal courts operate the same way throughout the nation. Congress has created the U.S. Supreme Court, 12 Courts of Appeal, two **specialized courts,** and numerous District Courts located throughout the United States. Federal courts also have the authority to review decisions from some administrative agencies. State constitutions establish and grant power to state courts.

In addition to Article III courts, Congress has the power to create legislative courts under Article I. Such legislative courts are the Tax Court, the Court of International Trade, and the Claims Court. In a legislative court, Congress has power to remove judges, whereas in an Article III court, appointments are for a lifetime. Take Away 3-1 ("The United States Court System") illustrates the courts divisions.

LO2 How Courts Are Organized

Both the federal and state courts are hierarchical. At the lowest level are trial courts, which have fact-finding as their primary function. These are the courts with which people are most familiar and you have probably seen examples on television or in the movies. At the trial court level, a jury generally hears the evidence (although a judge may sit without a jury if none is requested or allowed), and the court then enters a judgment. These courts, whether federal or state, are courts of **original jurisdiction,** that is, they are empowered to hear the case for the first time. In the opening scenario, the lawsuits that have been filed against Damian and his company are filed in courts that have original jurisdiction. Original jurisdiction differs from appellate jurisdiction

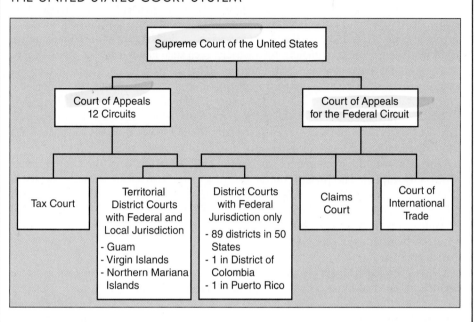

THE UNITED STATES COURT SYSTEM

Supreme Court of the United States

Court of Appeals
12 Circuits

Court of Appeals
for the Federal Circuit

Tax Court

Territorial
District Courts
with Federal and
Local Jurisdiction

- Guam
- Virgin Islands
- Northern Mariana
  Islands

District Courts
with Federal
Jurisdiction only

- 89 districts in 50
  States
- 1 in District of
  Colombia
- 1 in Puerto Rico

Claims
Court

Court of
International
Trade

Most of the courts in the federal court system are constitutional courts; the exceptions—the Tax Court, the Court of International Trade, and the Claims Court—are legislative courts. Constitutional courts decide the constitutionality of federal, state, and local laws and regulations. The Supreme Court makes final decisions regarding constitutionality and is the highest court of appeals in the country. Although this court hears some cases never tried before, the bulk of the work of the nine Supreme Court justices is made up of appeals from lower courts.

Source: http://encarta.msn.com/media_461543420/U_S_Federal_Court_Circuits.html.

in that the court has the right to hear the case for the first time rather than on review from a lower court.

At the next level are the intermediate courts of appeal, that is, courts between trial courts and the Supreme Court that have appellate jurisdiction. These courts hear the majority of **appeals** to decide whether the trial court applied the correct law and whether there was sufficient evidence to support the verdict. Unlike trial courts, the intermediate court does not conduct trials. There are no witnesses, and decisions are based solely on the record created by the trial court and the written **legal briefs** and **oral arguments** of the attorneys. If Damian were to prevail in one of the lawsuits filed against him, the losing party could file an appeal, alleging errors of law or wrongful findings of fact.

At the highest level are the state supreme courts and the Supreme Court of the United States. The primary focus of the supreme courts is to make final interpretations of law and to be the final authority on legal interpretations. The supreme courts hear only cases that involve issues of great public importance or cases in which different court divisions have applied conflicting laws. Like the intermediate courts, they do not hear evidence, but instead rely on the record as well as attorneys' written legal briefs and oral arguments.

Federal Courts

Unlike the state court systems, discussed later, the federal court system is uniform throughout the country. In the federal court system, a case is heard initially in a general trial court, the **United States District Court,** which is the court of original jurisdiction in the federal system. **Federal district courts** have the authority to hear most questions involving federal law and have the power to review the decisions of some administrative agencies. There are approximately 100 districts; each state has at least one district court, and some states have several. Cases are tried before a single judge. Cases that are not heard in the district courts are heard in one of several specialized courts, such as the United States Tax Court or the United States Court of Claims. Reality Check 3-1, "Federal Court Snapshot for 2009," illustrates how many cases are heard by U.S. District Courts and Courts of Appeal. Diversity in the Law 3-1 ("Does This Mean We Don't Discriminate?") looks at just one type of claim brought in civil court.

Appeals from the decisions of the district courts are heard by the United States **Courts of Appeal.** The **jurisdictional** area of a Court of Appeals is called a **circuit.** There are 13 circuit Courts of Appeal: 12 covering geographic areas (the First through Eleventh and the D.C. Circuit) and one Federal Circuit Court of Appeal. The Federal Circuit Court of Appeal, created in 1982, has appellate jurisdiction over the U.S. Court of International Trade, U.S. Claims Court, the Court of Veterans' Appeals and patent appeals.

The highest federal court is the United States Supreme Court, and it is the final appellate court. Each case that comes before the Supreme Court is heard by all nine justices. Each year the Supreme Court receives more than 5000 requests for review, also called **writs of certiorari.** Of the approximately 160 cases the Supreme Court actually hears, about two-thirds are

REALITY CHECK 3-1

FEDERAL COURT SNAPSHOT FOR 2009

In 2009 there were 57,740 appeals filed in the U.S. Courts of Appeal; 19,211 were civil trials, 13,710 were criminal, 8,570 were administrative, and 16,249 were prisoner cases. There were 60,508 appeals terminated; 30,160 on the merits of the case and 28,029 on a procedural basis.

The District Court statistics are even more staggering. In 2009, there were 363,774 cases filed in district court, an increase of 3.9 percent over 2008. That averages approximately 537 cases per judge—408 civil and 97 criminal felony cases. Each judge in the federal district court system presided at over 20 trials in 2009. Statistics show that the average time from filing to disposition for a civil case to be disposed was 8.9 months. If the case went to trial, the length of time increased from 8.9 to 25.3 months. Overall, there were 35,824 cases over three years old.

Of the civil cases filed, the breakdown by type is:

Social Security	13,622
Pers Inj/Prod Liab	58,335
Prisoner petitions	52,304
Forfeitures	3,677
Real Property	5,998
Labor Suits	17,719
Contracts	35,634
Other Torts	19,758
Civil Rights	33,761
Antitrust	812
All other	26,412

Source: http://www.uscourts.gov/viewer.aspx?doc=/cgi-bin/cmsd2009.pl.

appeals from the U.S. Courts of Appeals, and about one-third is from state courts.

FEDERAL JUDGES

Justices of the Supreme Court, judges of the courts of appeals and the district courts, and judges of the Court of International Trade, are appointed under Article III of the Constitution by the President of the United States with the advice and consent of the Senate. Article III judges are appointed for life, and they can be removed only through the impeachment process. Although there are no special qualifications to become a judge of these courts, those who are nominated are typically significantly accomplished attorneys from the private or government sectors, judges in state courts, magistrate judges or bankruptcy judges, or law professors. The judiciary plays no role in the nomination or confirmation process. In Reality Check 3-2 ("When You Are in Line for a Lifetime Appointment Every Case Is Scrutinized"), it's difficult to imagine having your professional life reviewed before receiving a vote of approval from the Senate.

DIVERSITY IN THE LAW 3-1

DOES THIS MEAN WE DON'T DISCRIMINATE?

Some statistics for civil rights claims based on race, age, sex, or national origin involving employment, welfare, housing, voting, or other civil rights discrimination issues follow, covering civil rights claims litigated in federal district courts from 1990 to 2006.

- Civil rights filings doubled in U.S. district courts from 1990 (18,922 filings) to 1997 (43,278 filings) and subsequently stabilized until 2003. From 2003 through 2006, the number of civil rights cases filed in U.S. district courts declined by 20 percent.
- During the period from 1990 through 2006, the percentage of civil rights cases concluded by trial declined from 8 percent to 3 percent.
- From 2000 to 2006 plaintiffs won just under a third of civil rights trials on average, and the median damage awards for plaintiffs who won in civil rights trials ranged from $114,000 to $154,500.

Source: BJN, http://www.ojp.usdoj.gov/bjs/abstract/crcusdc06.htm.

FEDERAL SUBJECT MATTER JURISDICTION

A federal court cannot hear a case unless it has jurisdiction over the subject matter of the case. If a case is filed in a federal court, and the court lacks subject matter jurisdiction, the case will be removed from the federal court and sent to a state court to be heard. Only certain types of cases can be heard in federal court.

Jurisdiction of federal courts exists in **federal question** cases and in cases with **diversity of citizenship** of the parties. A case may also arise in federal court if it has **concurrent jurisdiction** with a state court.

Whenever a case is based on federal law, a federal treaty, or the federal Constitution, it raises a federal question. The federal courts also have jurisdiction in all matters, other than divorce, in which the parties are citizens of different states, citizens of a state and the government of a different state, or between a state or its citizens and a foreign government or its citizens (diversity of citizenship). The amount in controversy must be at least $75,000. Even if the parties meet the diversity requirements, if the dispute does not reach $75,000 the case will be heard in state court. Federal courts' diversity jurisdiction helps to ensure fairness by avoiding the state court's potential bias in favor of the state's citizen.

The citizenship of a corporation may be in two states—the state of incorporation and the state where the corporation does business. In that case, no citizen of either of those states is diverse from the corporation for citizenship purposes. A citizen would have to come from a state different from either state in order for his or her case to be heard in federal court. For example, in the opening scenario, if one of the 12 lawsuits filed against Damian is filed by a citizen of Georgia or Florida in a federal court located in either of those states, the court would dismiss the lawsuit in that court and remove it to a state court because Damian's company is incorporated in Florida and its plant is located in Georgia. Thus, neither citizen would have diversity of citizenship to satisfy the federal requirements.

WHEN YOU ARE IN LINE FOR A LIFETIME APPOINTMENT EVERY CASE IS SCRUTINIZED

On May 26, 2009, President Barack Obama nominated Justice Sonia Sotomayor to the U.S. Supreme Court, replacing Justice David Souter. With an Ivy League undergraduate and law school education and the most judicial experience of any justice appointed to the Court in the past hundred years, Sotomayor's confirmation was still not an easy one. Though she was confirmed on August 6, 2009, and sworn in on August 8, 2009, as the 111th Justice, first Hispanic, and third woman nominated to the court, she underwent intense and, at times, acrimonious scrutiny during the confirmation process. Despite six years as a federal trial judge and eleven as a federal appellate judge (in addition to time as a New York prosecutor and a private corporate attorney), every word of every decision Sotomayor had ever issued was analyzed for an indication of the type of justice she might become.

Justice Sotomayor graduated summa cum laude from Princeton University in 1976 and received her J.D. from Yale Law School in 1979. In 1991, Sotomayor was nominated by George H. W. Bush to a seat on the U.S. District Court for the Southern District of New York; she was confirmed by unanimous Senate consent. She was the first Hispanic and youngest federal judge in New York State. It was while on the District Court bench that she issued the preliminary injunction against major league baseball in the case of *Silverman v. Major League Baseball Player Relations Committee, Inc.* Her preliminary injunction prevented major league baseball from unilaterally implementing a new collective bargaining agreement and using replacement players, ending the 232-day baseball strike in 1994.

In 1997 Sotomayor was nominated by then-President Bill Clinton to a seat on the U.S. Court of Appeals for the Second Circuit. Although she was ultimately confirmed, it was a contentious 16-month-long delay in which her Puerto Rican heritage was scrutinized. Her confirmation was also held up in retaliation for a procedural delay orchestrated by the Democrats for an earlier Senate challenge to a confirmation that the Republicans wanted.

During her Senate confirmation for the Supreme Court appointment Sotomayor was questioned about all of her controversial cases, but none as much as *Ricci v. DeStefano*. In that case, Sotomayor, as part of a three-judge panel, upheld a trial court's ruling which rejected a reverse discrimination claim by white firefighters in the city of New Haven, Connecticut. It was alleged that the city violated the rights of the firefighters when they discarded an officer's promotion examination in which minority candidates scored disproportionately low.

In affirming the trial court's ruling, the panel issued a brief, unsigned order rather than issuing an order of their own. Four months later, the panel withdrew the summary order and wrote a full opinion, still affirming the trial court.

The problem seemed to be in the way it was handled rather than in the decision itself, although there has been controversy over that as well. It seems that some question the use of a summary order when the precedent was not clear; others place less blame on her because it was a panel of three who agreed to issue the order. The case was appealed to the U.S. Supreme Court, and in the midst of her confirmation process, the Court overturned the Second Circuit's ruling.

Every decision she made during her career as a jurist was scrutinized by her supporters and detractors. We will have to see whether the extensive vetting process provided any indication of what Justice Sotomayor's U.S. Supreme Court rulings will be.

Source: Seth Stern, "Discrimination Case Could Pose Problems for Sotomayor," *YahooNews,* May 27, 2009, http://news.yahoo.com/s/cq/20090527/pl_cq_politics/politics3126035.

EXAMPLE

Federal courts may have concurrent jurisdiction with state courts in some matters. In cases in which there is concurrent jurisdiction, both the state court and the federal court can hear the case. Cases such as those in which a crime under state law is committed on federal property or certain offenses involving Indian tribal members invoke concurrent jurisdiction. Such cases can be brought in either state or federal court. Whichever court actually exercises jurisdiction first will have it exclusively. For example, suppose Ken commits bank robbery—a federal offense and state offense. Ken can be tried in state or federal court, and there will generally be an agreement between the two prosecution offices as to which agency will take jurisdiction.

In a federal question case, a federal court decides issues according to federal law and the court is bound by the law of the appellate federal courts. In diversity of citizenship cases, the court is bound by the legislation and case law of the highest court of that state. In a diversity of citizenship case, it applies the law of the state where it sits, if that state proves to have the most significant relationship to the parties involved.

TAKE AWAY 3-2

THE FEDERAL COURT SYSTEM

Court of Final Appeals	United States Supreme Court
Courts of Intermediate Appeals	U.S. Court of Appeals U.S. Court of Appeals for the Federal Circuit
Courts of Original Jurisdiction	U.S. District Courts U.S. Tax Court U.S. Claims Court U.S. Court of International Trade

Cases in which federal law provides for the **exclusive jurisdiction** of federal courts are heard in federal court. For example, cases involving bankruptcy, patent and copyright law, federal criminal law, maritime claims, and claims arising under the Securities and Exchange Act, are heard in federal court because the federal court is said to have the exclusive jurisdiction to decide those cases. In some cases the Supreme Court has original jurisdiction under Article III, Section 2, of the U.S. Constitution. One area of original jurisdiction for the Supreme Court is in cases involving disputes among states. For example, in 1995, the Supreme Court was asked to resolve a dispute between Louisiana and Mississippi involving the boundary of a seven-mile stretch of the Mississippi River.[1] Take Away 3-2, The "Federal Court System," outlines and three levels of federal courts.

EXAMPLE

EXAMPLE

L05

FEDERAL PERSONAL JURISDICTION

What happens when a lawsuit is filed against someone who does not live in the state or within the jurisdiction of the court? The court lacks jurisdiction over nonresidents unless the nonresident is subject to a long-arm statute. A **long-arm statute** is a state law that grants federal courts the power to extend jurisdiction over an out-of-state person if that person has sufficient **minimum contacts,** i.e., personal or business contacts with the state in which the court sits. A long-arm statute will reach an out-of-state defendant if "(1) the defendant has purposefully availed himself or herself of the benefits of the state so as to reasonably foresee being haled into court in that state; (2) that the forum state has sufficient interest in the dispute; and (3) that hauling the defendant into court does not offend notions of fair play and substantial justice."[2] If the party has purposefully availed itself of the resources or protection of the state, then the court will extend the long-arm statute and find the person to be within its jurisdiction. For example, a Delaware corporation whose principle place of business was New Mexico was sued in New Mexico state court by an employee who had been transferred from New Mexico to Colorado, where he had been working for over one year. He had a New Mexico driver's license, bank account, a home, and intended to return there. The court found that there was diversity of citizenship because even though he intended to return to New Mexico that was just a "floating idea"; he had in fact resided in Colorado for a year and the case should be in federal court.[3]

EXAMPLE

[1] *Louisiana v. Mississippi,* 516 U.S. 22 (1995).

[2] *International Shoe Co. v. Washington,* 326 U.S. 310 (1945).

[3] *Chaara v. Intel Corp,* 245 Fed. Appx. 784 (10th Cir. 2007).

EXAMPLE

Personal jurisdiction issues arise whenever a business conducts transactions across state lines. Internet cases raise several issues regarding personal jurisdiction because of the omnipresence of the website. A website may be viewed anywhere, and its products sold worldwide, just like Damian's business in our opening scenario, where his operators took orders for his product from anyone who had access to his website and placed an order. Courts must decide in which jurisdiction disputes can be raised. In *California v. Caddy* (Case 3.1), the court was faced with determining how far California's long-

CASE 3.1 California v. Caddy

453 F.3d 1151 (9th Cir. 2006)

Facts: Michael Caddy runs a small bed and breakfast restaurant located in Southern England. Caddy's restaurant is located on a cliff overlooking the pebbly beaches of England. Given its location there is no surprise that Caddy named his restaurant "Pebble Beach." Caddy advertises for his establishment on his website www.pebblebeach-uk.com, which includes information, menus, and wine lists. The Pebble Beach Golf Club and Resort is a well-known golf course and resort located in California. The resort has used "Pebble Beach" as its name for some 50 years and has an established website located at www.pebblebeach.com. In 2003, the golf club sued Caddy under international infringement and charged dilution of the "Pebble Beach" mark. Caddy contends he cannot be sued in California because all of his acts took place in England. He has only been to California once, has no stores in California, and no employees there. Pebble Beach contends, however, that he has a website that can be reached by citizens of California and has committed tortious acts against a California company. The lower court dismissed the complaint filed against him on the ground that the court lacked personal jurisdiction over him. Pebble Beach appealed.

Issue: Did the long-arm statute of California allow the federal court to have personal jurisdiction over Caddy?

Decision: No.

Reasoning: When a defendant moves to dismiss for lack of personal jurisdiction, the plaintiff bears the burden of demonstrating that the court has jurisdiction over the defendant. The general rule is that personal jurisdiction over a defendant is proper if it is permitted by a long-arm statute and if the exercise of that jurisdiction does not violate federal due process. Here, both the California long-arm statute and Rule 4(k)(2)—what is often referred to as the federal long-arm statute—require compliance with due process requirements. For due process to be satisfied, a defendant, if not present in the forum, must have "minimum contacts" with the forum state such that the assertion of jurisdiction does not offend traditional notions of fair play and substantial justice. This "minimum contacts" test is satisfied when,

1. the defendant has performed some act or consummated some transaction within the forum or otherwise purposefully availed himself of the privileges of conducting activities in the forum,
2. the claim arises out of or results from the defendant's forum-related activities, and
3. the exercise of jurisdiction is reasonable.

If any of the three requirements is not satisfied, jurisdiction in the forum would deprive the defendant of due process of law. Here, Pebble Beach's arguments fail under the first prong. Accordingly, we need not address whether the claim arose out of or resulted from Caddy's forum-related activities or whether an exercise of jurisdiction is reasonable. Under the first prong of the "minimum contacts" test, Pebble Beach has the burden of establishing that Caddy "has performed some act or consummated some transaction within the forum or otherwise purposefully availed himself of the privileges of conducting activities in the forum." Thus, in order to satisfy the first prong of the "minimum contacts" test, Pebble Beach must establish either that Caddy (1) purposefully availed himself of the privilege of conducting activities in California, or the United States as a whole, or (2) that he purposefully directed its activities toward one of those two forums.

Pebble Beach fails to identify any conduct by Caddy that took place in California or in the United States that adequately supports the availment concept. Evidence of availment is typically action taking place in the forum that invokes the benefits and protections of the laws in the forum. Evidence of direction generally consists of action taking place outside the forum that is directed at the forum. All of Caddy's action identified by Pebble Beach is action taking place outside the forum. We conclude that Caddy's actions were not expressly aimed at California. The only acts identified by Pebble Beach as being directed at

California are the website and the use of the name "Pebble Beach" in the domain name. These acts were not aimed at California and, regardless of foreseeable effect, are insufficient to establish jurisdiction.

CASE QUESTIONS

1. What was lacking in the suit that did not allow the court to have jurisdiction?

2. What is the benefit derived from the long-arm statute? What primary purpose does it serve?
3. How has the Internet complicated use of the long-arm statute? Does the test that the court applied adequately work for this type of issue?

arm statute reached. Take Away 3-3, "Personal v. Subject Matter Jurisdiction," explains ways to distinguish between the two types of jurisdiction.

LIMITATIONS OF FEDERAL COURTS

Federal jurisdiction is limited by several requirements. First, every case must present a **case or controversy.** Second, the case must be **ripe** for decision. Third, a plaintiff must have **standing** to sue, that is, the plaintiff must be directly concerned by the case. In Damian's case in our opening scenario, each plaintiff was injured by the device manufactured and sold by Damian's company, and thus, each case was ripe for decision and each plaintiff had standing to sue.

The case or controversy requirement requires that every case represent an actual, not hypothetical, issue. Courts do not issue advisory opinions. The issues of ripeness and standing are related. Ripeness refers to the readiness for litigation. A case is not ready, or ripe, if it rests upon future, contingent events that may occur or may never occur. Standing is the ability of a plaintiff to convince the court that he has sufficient connection to the law challenged, or that he has been harmed by an action so that he is the proper party to bring the suit. If the court finds that a person has not yet been harmed, or there is an insufficient connection of the plaintiff to the law challenged, the court will dismiss the case for lack of standing. If an issue is not ripe or a plaintiff does not have

TAKE AWAY 3-3

PERSONAL V. SUBJECT MATTER JURISDICTION

What's the difference between personal and subject matter jurisdiction?

Personal Jurisdiction	Subject Matter Jurisdiction
Jurisdiction over the person regardless of their location	Court's authority over the subject of the legal question involved in the case
Can be waived or stipulated to by the parties	Cannot be waived or stipulated to by the parties
Asks the question "In which court can I sue the defendant?" Or "In which court can I be sued?"	Asks the question "Does this court have the power to hear this case?" Or "Does another court have exclusive authority over the subject of my suit?"

standing, then the issue is an *abstract* question, and the case does not provide the necessary case or controversy to allow the court to hear it. For example, let us suppose that a developer wishes to construct a building on land owned by your neighbors and he asks the city to take the property by eminent domain and give it to him for that purpose. You agree that it is unfair to your neighbors for their property to be taken and you wish to join the lawsuit filed by your neighbors as a show of support. You cannot join the lawsuit because it is not your land and you stand to lose nothing if the city condemns your neighbor's property. You lack standing to sue.

In addition, federal courts do not consider **political questions.** The definition of what constitutes a political question changes with time and circumstance. For example, questions related to the inner workings of the legislature and the executive branches, once deemed to be political questions, have been subject to **judicial review.**

For example, in Powell v. McCormack,[4] members of the House of Representatives refused to allow Adam Clayton Powell, a black legislator who had been elected to the House of Representatives' 90th Congress, to take his seat in Congress after he was elected. Powell was under investigation for improperly using Congressional funds for his personal use and the Congress did not want to seat him until the investigation was completed. Essentially, the argument advanced by the defendants was that the question of whether a member was seated or not is solely within the discretion of the House and is not subject to review by the judiciary, because it represents a political question. The court disagreed, stating that the qualifications are stated in the Constitution, the interpretation of which was a judicial function, and therefore the case was subject to the Court's review. Absent a showing by the House that he was not constitutionally qualified, Powell had to be seated. In Reality Check 3-3 ("The Travails of Roland Burris"), the Senate did not want to seat Burris for a completely different reason than in the case of Congressman Powell.

REALITY CHECK 3-3

THE TRAVAILS OF ROLAND BURRIS

Since Reconstruction in this country, there have been only four blacks in the U.S. Senate: Ed Brooke, Republican from Massachusetts; Carol Moseley Braun (the only woman), Democrat from Illinois; Barack Obama, Democrat from Illinois; and the man appointed to replace him in the Senate, Roland Burris, Democrat from Illinois. The careers of few senators, black or white, have been shorter or more circuitous and controversial than that of Roland Burris.

Burris's nomination to the Senate was made by then-Governor Rod Blagojevich, who had just been arrested for trying to sell the seat vacated by the election of Barack Obama as President of the United States. Because Blagojevich's authority to appoint a replacement was being questioned, the Senate took the position that Burris would not be seated as a Senator until his certificate of appointment was signed by Illinois Secretary of State Jesse White, who was refusing to sign the certificate. Signing the certificate is usually a perfunctory event, not one that would prevent a seating in the Senate. In addition, the Secretary of State has no authority to withhold his signature as long as it can be shown that the candidate is qualified. No one was questioning Burris's qualifications. Clearly, the issue was not the certificate, but whether Burris was one of the people who Blagojevich had tried to sell the seat to. Burris, upon being questioned about his contact with the Blagojevich camp, adamantly denied having spoken to him or contacting him about the seat. Burris denied doing anything improper to gain the appointment and was eventually seated.

Within weeks, Burris admitted that he had in fact had fund-raising conversations with Blagojevich while seeking the Senate seat from him. Facing a perjury probe in Illinois and an ethics investigation in D.C., he then tried to explain himself amid calls by both parties for his resignation.

Within a few months of his appointment, Burris announced that he would not run for election to the seat when his appointment expired, citing the high cost of raising money for a campaign, thus ending his ignominious career in the U.S. Senate. When his term is up, he will be replaced.

Sources: Ray Long, John Chase, and Monique Garcia, "Burris' Senate-seat Story Changes Again," *Chicago Tribune.com,* http://www.chicagotribune.com/news/local/chi-burris-18-feb18,0,6205161.story; and Deanna Belladini and Christopher Wells, "Roland Burris Confirms: No Senate Run in 2010, Says It's About Money," *The Huffington Post,* July 10, 2009, http://www.huffingtonpost.com/2009/07/10/roland-burris-confirms-no_n_229671.html.

---

[4]395 U.S. 486 (1969).

State Courts

State courts are patterned after the federal hierarchy, but states are free to construct their state court system as they choose in order to accommodate their needs. Thus, all states have a judicial hierarchy that consists of two or more levels of courts; but the courts are given different designations that vary from state to state. Courts of **general jurisdiction** have the power to review decisions of the courts of limited jurisdiction and of original jurisdiction over claims arising under state law. They are sometimes called district courts, circuit courts, superior courts, courts of common pleas, or, in New York for example, the Supreme Court. State courts may also have courts of general jurisdiction that are used to handle special areas of the law such as domestic relations courts, family courts, probate courts, or surrogate courts. Take Away 3-4 ("The Florida Court Structure") shows the levels of court in one state court system. Reality Check 3-4 ("Texas State Court Judges") demonstrates how many judges are in a state system.

TAKE AWAY 3-4

THE FLORIDA COURT STRUCTURE

State High Court	Court(s) of Last Resort Supreme Court
Intermediate Court	Intermediate Appellate Court(s) District Courts of Appeal
Trial Court	Court(s) of General Jurisdiction Circuit Court Court(s) of Limited Jurisdiction County Court

Source: http://wlwatch.westlaw.com/aca/west/statecrtorg.htm#FL.

REALITY CHECK 3-4

TEXAS STATE COURT JUDGES

To get an idea of how many state court judges it takes to run a state court system, let's take a look at one of the largest state court systems: Texas. In this system alone, there are a total of 3326 judges to take care of the Texas caseload. It breaks down like this.

Name of Court	Jurisdiction	# Cts. /# Judges
Supreme Court: Civil and Juvenile	Final Appellate Jurisdiction	1/9
Supreme Court: Criminal	Final Appellate Jurisdiction	1/9
Courts of Appeal	Intermediate appeals from trial courts	14/80
District Courts	State Trial Courts General and Special Jurisdiction	453/453
County-Level Courts	Trials of Limited Jurisdiction	503/503
Justice Courts	Local Trial Courts of Limited Jurisdiction	822/822
Municipal Courts	Local Courts of Limited Jurisdiction	915/1,490

Of course, not all states have nearly the territory or population to cover, so there are not this many judges in those states. Some do not even have an intermediate court. What is your state court structure and how many judges does it take to run it?

Source: http://www.courts.state.tx.us/.

WHAT'S GOING ON IN THE CIVIL CASES IN THE STATES?

In 2005 there were an estimated 26,950 tort, contract, and real property trials in state courts of general jurisdiction nationwide. During 2005, juries decided 68 percent (18,404) of the nearly 27,000 civil trial cases disposed of by state courts of general jurisdiction nationwide. During 2005, judges decided 32 percent (8543) of the nearly 27,000 civil trials disposed of by state courts of general jurisdiction nationwide. (The 2005 statistics are the latest available.)

Source: Bureau of Justice Statistics, http://www.ojp.usdoj.gov/bjs/courts.htm.

Courts of **limited jurisdiction** are those courts that fall within some specialized trial court. Specialized courts might include a Court of Claims to hear suits against the state government, a Probate Court to adjudicate questions involving wills and inheritances, a Family Court to settle matters of support and child custody, a Juvenile Court to determine whether minors have committed crimes or are otherwise in need of special supervision, a Small Claims Court to decide (perhaps without lawyers) disputes where the value at stake is not large, a Magistrate's Court to try some misdemeanors and other offenses, and a Housing Court to resolve litigation between landlords and tenants. Sometimes these functions are merged. For example, a Small Claims Court might not be a separate court, but instead a Small Claims

EXAMPLE

Division of a court of general jurisdiction. In Reality Check 3-5 ("What's Going On in the Civil Cases in the States?") it is easy to see why judges complain about the backlog of cases. That's a lot of cases to try in one year.

About two-thirds of the states have intermediate courts of appeal which sit between the court of general jurisdiction and the final appellate court. These courts hear appeals from the state courts of general jurisdiction. Because of their heavy workload, many are divided into specific divisions, such as a criminal division and civil division. In some states, such as Pennsylvania and Maryland, the intermediate court is divided geographically into districts. Reality Check 3-6 ("Doing 'Katrina Time' in New Orleans") discusses a hard time in our history and what happens when the court system breaks down.

DOING "KATRINA TIME" IN NEW ORLEANS

Imagine being a prisoner in the New Orleans jail the night Katrina hit. No evacuation plan, no emergency plan, no plan for what to do. Not only that, but after the city found itself nearly completely destroyed, there was no court system left for you to redress the wrongs that occurred. That is, if you were still there. Many prisoners were sent, after the fact, to other cities while New Orleans figured out what to do. So what happened to the court system?

For approximately two months following Katrina, New Orleans had no court system in place. The city courts weren't working, the court of appeals was closed, and even the Supreme Court relocated to Baton Rouge.

When the local courts did get up and running at a temporary center, there were no records to be found anywhere. The bond hearings proceeded without records, and often without attorneys, because they had been displaced, too, by the storm. The first nonjury trial after Katrina to take place in New Orleans did not occur until March 31, 2006—seven months after Katrina hit.

And what about the prisoners? "Katrina time" refers to the time between the end of a prisoner's sentence and the time he was released from custody, which was often extended because the prisons didn't know what to do with prisoners that had no records of time served or sentences imposed. After writs of *habeas corpus* were filed on their behalf, many of them were released, but not before their constitutional rights were run over roughshod. (A writ of ***habeas corpus*** asks the court to have a hearing to ensure that a party's imprisonment is not illegal.)

Source: Phyllis Kotey, "Judging under Disaster," in *Hurricane Katrina: America's Unnatural Disaster,* Jeremy Levitt and Matthew Whittaker, eds. (University of Nebraska Press, 2009).

Final appellate jurisdiction, whether states have two or three levels, is the state supreme court. Such courts review the decision of the state trial courts and the courts of appeal; they are the final arbiters of the state's constitutional, statutory, and common law. Reality Check 3-7 ("Appeal Rate for State Civil Trials") discusses the number of appeals that are handled by the courts.

State courts possess general jurisdiction to hear most matters, except when exclusive jurisdiction is in effect. That is, their jurisdiction extends to all personal issues and to all subject matters. They are limited, however, to cases in which the issue is one properly before the state courts. For example, the court dismissed a case in which the plaintiffs brought suit in the Wyoming state court for a case based on the Telecommunications Act of 1966.[5] The court pointed out that the statute itself limited the resolution of its disputes to federal court, giving it exclusive jurisdiction. The court dismissed the case. Take Away 3-5, "The State Court System," details the levels of state courts.

EXAMPLE

REALITY CHECK 3-7

APPEAL RATE FOR STATE CIVIL TRIALS

From 2001 to 2006, only about 15 percent of state civil trials were appealed. The appeals were taken in 11 percent of all tort trials, 21 percent of all contract trials, and 24 percent of all property trials. Plaintiffs and defendants filed in nearly equal rates. Of the cases appealed, only 57 percent were actually decided on the merits; 43 percent were dismissed or withdrawn. Of those decided on the merits, two-thirds were affirmed, and one-third reversed or modified. Of those cases that found for the plaintiffs at trial, 42 percent were reversed on appeal, while only 21 percent of trial decisions were reversed for defendants. Finally, of the cases that went to an intermediate level of appeal, 218 were appealed to a court of last resort. Of those 218, 25 were granted a review.

Source: U.S. Department of Justice, "Approximately 15 Percent of State Civil Trials Are Appealed," June 6, 2006, http://www.ojp.usdoj.gov/newsroom/pressreleases/2006/BJS07062006.htm.

TAKE AWAY 3-5

THE STATE COURT SYSTEM

State Supreme Court

Court of final resort. Some states call it the Court of Appeals, Supreme Court, or Supreme Court of Appeals.

Intermediate Appellate Courts

Currently 37 of the 50 states have intermediate appellate courts, which constitute an intermediate appellate tribunal between the trial court and the court of final resort. A majority of cases are decided finally by these appellate courts. Other states have appeals to the state supreme court as a matter of right.

Superior Courts

Highest trial court with general jurisdiction. Some states call it the Circuit Court, District Court of Common Pleas, or in New York State, the Supreme Court. May have specialized branches like probate and family court.

County Court of Limited Jurisdiction

These courts, sometimes called Common Pleas or District Courts, have limited jurisdiction in both civil and criminal cases.

Municipal Court

In some cities, it is customary to have less important cases tried by both civil and criminal municipal magistrates.

---

[5]*Union Telephone Co. v. Wyoming Public Service Comm.*, 142 P.3d 678 (Wy. 2006).

L06

Using Case Precedent

The United States has a common law legal system. Under common law, great weight is given to prior judicial opinions (called **precedents**) on the meaning of the law, which in many cases are binding upon other courts addressing the same or similar issues.[6]

The principle of ***stare decisis***, which means to stand by things decided, is what gives a precedent its strength. *Stare decisis* encourages courts to follow their own prior decisions, and it requires lower courts to follow decisions of higher courts in the same jurisdiction. The principle of *stare decisis,* however, applies only to the **holding** of the previous case. In Damian's case in our opening scenario, if there are earlier cases in the same jurisdiction which have decided the issues in either Damian's or the plaintiffs' favor, and the facts are substantially similar, those precedent cases will be persuasive in deciding Damian's cases.

Judicial reasoning that is unnecessary to a decision, called *obiter dictum,* or just *dictum,* has no binding effect on later courts. For example, suppose a case is before the court on the question of whether the court has jurisdiction to hear the case. In the opinion written by the court, the court holds that the court lacks jurisdiction to hear the case because there is no diversity of citizenship because both parties legally reside in the same state. That is the holding of the case, and that's the rule that will have precedential value for the next case. However, suppose the court goes on to expound on what the court's ruling would be on the issue if it did have jurisdiction. This part of the opinion would be *dictum* because the court does not need to decide the merits of the case to rule on the jurisdiction issue.

The use of precedent is basically reasoning by analogy. There are three steps in using the analogy.[7] First, find the similarity in the two cases. Second, announce what the rule of law was in the first case. Third, apply the rule of law announced in the first case to the next case. Through this method, the rule of law announced that resolved the original case is cited over and over again as being relevant to a similar case.

The question, of course, is, what is a similar case? Is it just a factually similar case? Is it similar because it implicates the same underlying values? Cases that are deemed not to be similar are said to be distinguishable from the first case. To apply a case by analogy is to find that there is a sufficient similarity to apply the rule of the earlier case to this case. When we distinguish a case it means that a necessary condition for applying the first case is not there, or is lacking. In easy cases, courts may apply or distinguish prior cases on factual grounds, i.e., because the facts of the first case are similar to the facts of the second case. In most cases, it is clear whether the facts of the cases are similar. But in difficult cases, the factual similarity is not clear. For example, when technological or social change occurs, it becomes difficult to reason by analogy. The U.S. Supreme Court was faced with just such an issue in the case of *Sony Corp. v. Universal Studios.*[8] In this 1984 decision, the court was asked to determine whether videotaping entire television shows for the purpose of time-shifting (that is what the court called taping a show and watching it later) constitutes copyright infringement. The film companies sued Sony because Sony had developed Betamax, a competitor of VHS, which had the capability of allowing the taping of television shows. The film companies argued that Sony contributed to copyright infringement by marketing these machines that were capable of infringing uses. Looking at the precedent provided by

---

[6]This is in contrast to the civil law system in which legal opinions by the court are viewed as advisory opinions about the meaning of law. Civil law systems are prevalent in Europe.

[7]This process of reasoning was first stated by Edward Levi, *An Introduction to Legal Reasoning,* 1-2 (1948).

[8]464 U.S. 417 (1984).

case law and the copyright statute, the court recognized that prior cases allowed fair use (an exception to copyright infringement) for purposes such as criticism, comment, news reporting, teaching, scholarship, research, or other uses found in the cases. But the precedent only allowed fair use when the use resulted in some added benefit to the public beyond that produced by the original work. Here, there was no added benefit other than to the private individual in allowing time-shifting. In a narrow 5-4 decision, the Court ultimately held that a device that allows for private, noncommercial time-shifting in the home is noninfringing, even though there is the potential for infringement. Aren't we glad?

What happens when a case has no precedent in the jurisdiction to which the court can look to resolve the issue? In that case, called, a **case of first impression,** the courts will either look at a closely analogous case in its jurisdiction or look to other jurisdictions that have decided the issue to see what has been done by them. After looking at either of these sources, the court can choose to follow either the analogous precedent, or the precedent of another jurisdiction. In the *Schembre* case (Case 3.2), the court did the latter.

CASE 3.2 Schembre v. Mid-America Transplant Ass'n.

135 S.W.3d (Mo. App. 2004)

Facts: Mr. Schembre suffered a heart attack in 1998. His wife, the appellant, arrived at the hospital shortly after, and was told he could not be resuscitated. Later, the hospital staff explained to the family that Mr. Schembre did not meet the criteria for donation of organs, but could donate eyes, bones, or tissue from his body if they wished. Mrs. Schembre refused adamantly to donate organs but did allow donation of Mr. Schembre's corneas. Mrs. Schembre also agreed to donate bone marrow from Mr. Schembre's leg, because the hospital staff explained to her that similar to the cornea donation, the procedure would be minimally invasive. The family signed the consent form and the hospital removed the tissue. At the funeral the family learned the hospital actually removed the entire eyeballs. In addition, it was learned that the hospital removed the entire leg bones. Mrs. Schembre and her children brought suit against the hospital and MTS for damages. The Defendants moved for and were granted summary judgment at trial which was GRANTED. Appellants appeal.

Issue: How is the court to rule when there is no governing precedent?

Holding: The court often looks to other jurisdictions to see how they handled similar matters.

Reasoning: This is a case of first impression in Missouri; therefore, the court must examine cases from other jurisdictions addressing the issue. The law in Missouri says, "a person who acts without negligence and in good faith and in accord with the terms of this act or with anatomical gift laws of another state or foreign country is not liable for damages in a civil action or subject to prosecution in any criminal proceeding for his act." In this instance MTS must prove they acted in good faith in removing the tissue. The court then looked to New York and Florida for the definition of good faith in an organ donation context. They discovered in New York, good faith is "an honest belief, the absence of malice and the absence of design or to seek an unconscionable advantage." Further, other jurisdictions have adopted the above analysis. Under this analysis, MTS did not prove they acted in good faith and this case must go to trial.

CASE QUESTIONS

1. Why would a court choose to look at other jurisdictions for guidance when there's no precedent in their jurisdiction?
2. What would happen if a court disagreed with the out-of-state court's decision? Are they bound by it?
3. Shouldn't most cases be of first impression? Why would a litigant choose to bring a case where the law already exists? Wouldn't they be bound by the precedent?

L07

Getting through the Civil Court System: Civil Procedure

Civil cases are governed by civil procedure rules and criminal cases by criminal procedure rules. In this section we will discuss civil cases. Every court has a set of rules that govern how cases brought in the court are filed. In the federal system, these are the Federal Rules of Civil Procedure. Every state court has corresponding rules. The rules are designed to provide all the relevant participants in the suit information such as where to file the case, to whom to give notice of the suit, how the pleadings must look and to whom they must be given, how many copies of each pleading, and the time deadlines for filing court documents. Failure to comply with the rules can result in sanctions being filed against either the lawyer handling the case or the client. Sanctions can include monetary penalties for rule violations, and can result in dismissal of the case for more serious violations or infractions. Thus, every lawyer practicing in federal or state court who handles civil cases must familiarize themselves with the rules of civil procedure. In our opening scenario the plaintiffs who filed in federal courts used the Federal Rules of Civil Procedure to govern the filing of the cases. If any cases were filed in state court, those plaintiffs used the state's rules of civil procedure to guide their filings.

EXAMPLE

INITIATING A LAWSUIT

While people have the right to bring cases on their own, without the assistance of an attorney, our chapter assumes an attorney is present representing the interests of the parties. As you can see just from our discussion of the rules of civil or criminal procedure, there is a lot of information involved in a lawsuit of which the average person would not be aware. If the litigant truly believes he or she has a viable case, it would only make sense to engage an attorney to represent his or her interests rather than have the suit dismissed for procedural reasons.

A CIVIL CASE

A civil lawsuit is a means of seeking redress for a wrong that has occurred. Lawsuits are subject to procedural rules, and there are rules for both civil and criminal procedure. Both federal and state courts have rules that govern procedure. Federal rules are uniform in all federal jurisdictions. States are free to fashion their own rules, so state rules differ from state to state. Rules may vary but are all designed to allow litigation to proceed in an orderly fashion and to give notice to all parties involved of the steps each party and the court are taking during the pendency of the suit.

Aside from the actual event causing the dispute, a civil case usually begins when a client contacts a lawyer about some matter that needs resolution. A party may have had a lawsuit filed naming him as a defendant, or the party may wish to begin a lawsuit of his or her own. If the lawyer decides to take the case, a **retainer** is usually signed by the party, which formally retains the services of the lawyer, and that party becomes the lawyer's client. In some cases, a **contingency fee arrangement** may be made. Unlike the regular fee arrangement whereby the client simply pays the attorney the agreed upon amount at the agreed upon time, a contingency agreement requires little or no money from the client, but instead the client pays only if he or she wins the case. The amount of a contingency fee is generally arrived at by a formula in which the amount is unspecified because it is a percentage of the award, whether by settlement or verdict. For example in a personal injury case, a contingency fee might be 40 percent of the jury award, if a trial is necessary. The more difficult it is to establish liability, the higher the

EXAMPLE

contingency fee. Reality Check 3-8 ("Not All Contingency Fees Are Desirable") shows why in some cases, contingency fees do not work well as a means of payment and are discouraged or made illegal.

The attorney then investigates the matter and advises her or his client of all the options available at that point. Options may include settlement, filing the case in a court, or pursuing pretrial alternative dispute resolution methods discussed in the previous chapter. If a settlement can be reached at this point, then the matter is ended. If not, then the attorney will file formal documents with the court to begin the lawsuit. Of course, the quicker and less complicated manner in which the agreement can be reached, generally the less expensive and time consuming the legal process is. Since it can be so expensive and time consuming, litigation is not a desirable option, but it can turn out to be the only solution available if all else fails.

FILING A LAWSUIT

The Pleadings

Pleadings are documents filed by the parties to outline the most critical facts that they intend to prove at trial. Usually pleadings consist of a complaint, summons, answer, reply, and motions. In a civil lawsuit, a party seeks damages, usually monetary, for harm suffered as a result of another's wrongdoing. There might be several legal bases for the lawsuit, called **causes of action.** Once the pleadings are filed, the person who consulted the lawyer and who filed the initial pleading is called the **plaintiff** (or in some cases the petitioner or claimant), and the person who is sued is called the **defendant** (or, in some cases, the respondent). In the opening scenario, Damian is the Defendant in each of the cases filed, and the party filing the lawsuit is the Plaintiff. Courts' powers are not unlimited. Whether a court can hear and decide a case brought before it depends on whether the court has jurisdiction, or authority, over the dispute. In Take Away 3-6, "Sample Complaint," a complaint has been filed in federal court against Damian Jones, the business owner in the opening scenario.

EXAMPLE

A lawsuit typically begins with the filing of a **complaint** by the plaintiff. A complaint is the document that states the court's jurisdiction to hear the case, alleges the facts, and asks for the relief being sought. Upon filing the complaint, the court will issue a **summons** to the defendant, who is the party named in the complaint who has allegedly caused harm to the plaintiff. It notifies the defendant that a lawsuit has been filed against him or her, and brings the defendant under the jurisdiction of the court. The defendant files an **answer** to the complaint, which admits or denies the allegations in the complaint. If the defendant believes that the plaintiff is also or instead the one at fault, the defendant can file a **counterclaim** against the plaintiff. A counterclaim alleges that rather than or in addition to the harm the defendant may have caused the plaintiff, the plaintiff has instead or also harmed the defendant. In other words, if a counterclaim is filed, each party is suing the other. For example, if a lender sues a borrower for nonpayment of a debt, the borrower can counterclaim that the lender used fraud to obtain the loan.

EXAMPLE

SAMPLE COMPLAINT

**United States District Court for
the District of Arizona**

Jenny Terry, Plaintiff	No. _____
v.	Civil Action
Damian Jones, d/b/a Stretchrite	JURY TRIAL DEMANDED

COMPLAINT

Plaintiff Jenny Terry complains of the Defendant Damian Jones, d/b/a Stretchrite, as follows:

1. Jurisdiction in this case is based on diversity of citizenship and the amount in controversy. Plaintiff is a citizen of the state of Arizona. The amount in controversy exceeds, exclusive of interest and costs, the sum of seventy-five thousand ($75,000) dollars.
2. On September 30, 2009, at approximately 2:00 pm, plaintiff Jenny Terry was using a device known as Squeeze Knees (the device). During her use, the device malfunctioned, causing serious injury to Plaintiff.
3. Upon inspection of the device, it was observed that the rubber used in the device had torn into two pieces, causing the device to become airborne, striking Plaintiff in the face and neck.
4. As a result of the direct and proximate result of Damian Jones' d/b/a Stretchrite negligence, Plaintiff injured her face, eyes, nose, and mouth and other bodily parts, received other physical injuries, suffered physical and mental pain and suffering, incurred medical expenses, lost income, and will incur further medical expenses and lost income in the future.

WHEREFORE, Plaintiff Jenny Terry demands judgment against Defendant Damian Jones d/b/a Stretchrite for the sum of $100,000, with interest and costs.

Dated: January 2, 2010

Anne Johnson

Anne Johnson

Attorney for Plaintiff

123 Main Street

Phoenix, AZ 85001

PLAINTIFF DEMANDS TRIAL BY JURY

A **cross-claim** can be filed against a party on the same side of the suit as the defendant. For example, a buyer refuses to pay for items shipped to him because when they arrived, they were damaged. The manufacturer of the item sues both the buyer and the trucking company that shipped the items for his money. The buyer, in his answer to the manufacturer's suit, can cross-claim against the trucking company, claiming that the trucking company caused the damage, and thus, should be responsible to the manufacturer for the money owed for the items.

In addition to filing an answer, the defendant may assert an **affirmative defense.** An affirmative defense states that even if all the allegations made by the plaintiff are true, there is a defense to the allegation, and the plaintiff should lose. For example, self-defense is an affirmative defense to a charge of battery. Therefore, if plaintiff sues defendant for battery, alleging that the defendant hit him, the defendant can, in turn, allege the affirmative defense of self-defense, alleging that the reason he hit plaintiff was because plaintiff pulled a gun on him and he thought he was in danger from plaintiff and only hit plaintiff in an effort to defend himself.

During these proceedings, either side may **motion** the court. A motion is a request for the trial court to take an action requested by the **moving party** (the party filing the motion). Each party will have an opportunity to be heard, and after the hearing, the trial court will make a decision. One typical motion filed is a motion to dismiss, in which case the defendant asks the court to dismiss the case filed against her because of lack of evidence, lack of jurisdiction, or because the facts alleged are insufficient to support a claim against her. If the court grants the motion to dismiss, it ends the litigation, unless there is an appeal.

If a defendant raises new allegations in an answer, the plaintiff may file a **reply.** A reply admits or denies the new facts alleged by defendant. Once the complaint has been answered and counterclaims, cross-claims, motions, or replies have been filed or heard, any facts that remain in dispute form the subject of the litigation. These documents, taken together, are called the pleadings.

Pretrial

Pretrial is the period before trial but after the pleadings, in which the parties use discovery procedures to investigate their case. The rules of **discovery** attempt to remove trial by ambush by eliminating any surprises in the evidence. Discovery makes it possible for both sides of a lawsuit to be informed about witnesses and evidence that will be presented. Discovery also helps reveal whether a defense exists that may either lead to dismissal of the case, thereby saving time and expense, or may lead to a settlement. Discovery can also lead to information that can strengthen a case.

Keep in mind that when a party decides to bring a case, they know very little other information. Discovery allows them to find out more and this may result in the plaintiff feeling justified in bringing the case, or, on the other hand, realizing that they do not have a viable case. In the opening scenario, Damian has no idea what happened to bring on the claims that have been filed. Was the device being used properly? Was there a manufacturing defect that he will be responsible for? Were the instructions printed improperly? Were the rubber tensions that Damian purchased from his supplier damaged or defective, allowing him to sue the supplier? Was each injury caused by the same problem? On the other hand, Jenny has no idea that there are other complaints that have been filed alleging the same defect in the product. During the discovery stage, more is learned about what actually occurred to cause the accident. Based on findings during the discovery stage, it can impact not only the parties' decision of whether to move forward with the case, but also how best to proceed if they decide to do so. There are several discovery tools available.

A **deposition** is a statement made by a witness under oath outside of court while being questioned (also known as examined) by both parties to the litigation. Depositions are taken in order to probe a witness's memory about facts known to the witness while memory is still fresh. Such depositions can be used by a witness to refresh memory at trial, and discrepancies between a witness's deposition testimony and trial testimony can be used to discredit or **impeach** a witness. For example, if a plaintiff in her deposition claims that she suffered certain injuries to her head, neck and face, and then at trial alleged that she also suffered injuries to her back and spine, the deposition would be used to impeach, or call into question, her testimony at trial about her injuries.

Interrogatories are written questions submitted to an opposing party, and, like depositions, the answers must be sworn to under oath. Note that in depositions those involved in the deposition are together in a live proceeding, while interrogatories are conducted in writing.

A **request for production of documents,** tangible items, or entry to property for inspection is a discovery tool whereby documents and other relevant evidence in the possession of one party may be freely examined by the other party. In the opening scenario, it would be expected that medical records from the plaintiff would be requested, and any bills related to those records.

Upon motion, an opposing party can request that a party submit to a medical examination by a doctor chosen by the opposing party. Such examinations can be physical or psychological.

Electronically Stored Information (ESI)

The Federal Rules of Civil Procedure were amended in 2006 to include rules regarding discovery of electronic records. While some business owners feared that every e-mail and electronic document would now have to be retained and produced in litigation, this is not what is required of the electronic discovery rules. The rules do require a responding party to produce **electronically stored information (ESI)** that is *relevant* and *reasonably accessible*. Generally, the responding party need not restore relatively inaccessible information. However, parties must automatically disclose electronically stored information (ESI) that it may use to support its claims or defenses. Reality Check 3-9 ("The Scope of Electronically Stored Information") is a reminder of why we have to be careful when we use the social networks. It may have unintended consequences for the unwary.

Further, the electronic discovery rules provide that opposing parties may serve on each other requests to produce electronically stored information in a specified form, or,

REALITY CHECK 3-9

THE SCOPE OF ELECTRONICALLY STORED INFORMATION

Most people have no idea how much they are being watched and monitored electronically. And most are contributing to it just by doing everyday activities. More people are using Facebook, MySpace, Twitter, and other social networks than ever before. The amount of information contained on those sites, even after you close your account, can reveal a lot of information about you—information that others can access.

Investigators, divorce attorneys, prosecutors, and employers are finding information, photos, and videos online which can become evidence in their cases. For employers, it can simply mean you're not hired. Some employers now ask potential hires to log into their Facebook or MySpace accounts while in the interview. They're looking for anything that can enhance, or destroy, your integrity.

Most of what gets posted becomes permanent. Photos contain embedded information that acts much like a GPS. It can tell where the photo was taken and can reveal the serial number of your camera. So you have to be careful what you do or you might leave a trail right to you.

Source: Chris Wheelock, "A Growing Trend: Social Media as Legal Evidence," *West Michigan Business,* July 29, 2009, http://www.mlive.com/business/westmichigan/index.ssf/2009/07/a_growing_trend_social_media_a.html.

ATTORNEY-CLIENT CONFIDENTIALITY CAN BE BREACHED BY FAILURE TO FOLLOW RULES

When discovery is demanded during litigation, it's understood that documents that contain confidences between an attorney and client are not discoverable. However, as one company found out the hard way, it's not always easy to protect such information.

Target Corporation was ordered to turn over numerous e-mail communications it sought to protect under the attorney-client privilege, not because the communications were not confidential and otherwise subject to protection, but because the court found that Target did not comply with Federal Rule of Civil Procedure 26(b)(5). That rule requires all communications that a litigant deems subject to the privilege to be listed in a privilege log. The log must describe the nature of the documents, communications, or things not produced or disclosed in a way that will enable the other party to assess the applicability of the privilege. It also must be expressly stated. The court ruled that Target's privilege log was wholly inadequate, in that it gave the categories of information, but did not list the factual details. The court found that Target simply cut and pasted the subject line of each email into the log, and in some cases only revealed the final e-mail in the string, which the court ruled was inadequate. In addition, in order to remain privileged, the information must not be revealed to third parties not involved in the litigation. Here, the court found that the e-mails were forwarded to unknown employees, mainly because they were linked to regular business mails. Thus, Target's confidential attorney-client communications were ordered revealed to the opposition.

Sources: http://www.rumberger.com/?t=11&la=657&format=xml, July 31, 2007; *Muro v. Target Corporation,* 2007 U.S. Dist. Lexis 41442 (June 7, 2007).

---

if no form is specified, in a form that is reasonably usable. While parties will not be sanctioned for failing to provide ESI that is lost as a result of the routine, good faith operation of their electronic information system, businesses should ensure that they maintain a policy regarding retention and destruction of electronic documents which includes a suspension of destruction of documents in response to litigation or dispute. As technology advances, the law catches up; so it is critical that decision makers use their ethical judgment in determining what constitutes a "good faith" effort. What is considered "good faith" today (such as mere suspension of the destruction of documents) might be behind the times tomorrow (perhaps it will be commonplace to do much more to retrieve destroyed documents). In Reality Check 3-10, "Attorney-Client Confidentiality Can Be Breached by Failure to Follow Rules," it's easy to see how a firm can be sloppy with its e-mail and other electronic documents, especially given the ease with which these documents can be and are created.

Statutes of Limitation

The law places limits on the length of time that a potential plaintiff can wait to file a lawsuit. Each state legislature decides the maximum length of time a potential plaintiff may wait before bringing a lawsuit, which usually varies depending on the type of claim asserted. These laws governing the time frame for filing lawsuits are collectively referred to as **statutes of limitation.** What if there were no limits on time to file a lawsuit? Evidence would be lost, witnesses would forget what they know, or perhaps be hard to find altogether. Therefore, statutes of limitation helps to ensure that a claim arising from a plaintiff's alleged injury or loss will be resolved in a timely and fair manner. Suppose, for instance, that a plaintiff in Damian's case was injured while using the device five years before filing a lawsuit against him. It is likely that the lawsuit would be barred by the statute of limitation. If a claim is brought after the time frame dictated in the applicable statute of limitations, it is considered "time barred." Reality Check 3-11 ("Time's Up!") deals with a case in which the court refused to extend the time limits for filing a medical malpractice action.

EXAMPLE

TIME'S UP!

In 1995, plaintiff suffered a reaction to a drug during medical treatment. Four years later, when being treated for another matter, she told the health care provider that she was allergic to that drug. She was prescribed another drug that contained the same ingredient as the first drug and suffered another reaction to it. Four years later, she sued the health care provider for medical malpractice for prescribing the second drug. The defendants moved to have the case dismissed. The trial court refused to dismiss the case.

On appeal the court reversed. It ruled that she should have known of her injury and the alleged malpractice

sooner. Generally, the period of limitation for starting a malpractice action is two years. However, a medical malpractice action is considered timely after the general period of limitation has expired if it is commenced within six months of when the plaintiff discovers or should have discovered through the exercise of reasonable diligence that an injury occurred. Plaintiff sued the drug maker in 2000; there is no reason she should have waited until 2003 to bring suit against the health care provider that prescribed the medicine.

Source: Bonucci v. Michigan State Univ. Board of Trustees, 2006 WL 782269 (Ct. App. Mich., 2006).

LITIGATION AS A MEANS OF DISPUTE RESOLUTION

Assuming that all pretrial dispute resolution has failed, parties may resolve their conflicts by going to trial. A trial has two purposes: to decide what the law of the case is and to decide what the facts of the case are. Generally, a judge decides the legal issues, and the jury is the trier of fact. Sometimes the judge is the trier of fact and decides the applicable law as well. If a plaintiff asks for and receives a **bench trial,** i.e., a trial before a judge without a jury, then the judge hears the facts and decides the verdict applying the law.

CONSULTANTS TO THE STARS

Some have doctorates and others psychiatric degrees. They are self-styled juror consultants, hired to help convict or get their defendant off the hook. They worked for O.J. Simpson in his first trial, Jason Williams' acquittal in his murder trial; they worked to help convict Martha Stewart. They would have been employed in Kobe Bryant's trial, had it gone that far. They are jury consultants, and they have become as much a part of the attorney team as the lawyers have.

Claiming to be just keen observers of the obvious, consultants are sought after in all high-profile trials for what they can do with the jury and for the witnesses. They claim to be able to read people quickly, claim to know which jurors to eliminate just by looking at their shoes, and judge people on whom they name as their favorite person. Whether it's believable or not, both the defense and the prosecution have lined up in high profile cases to take their advice.

Although their fees can run into the hundreds of thousands of dollars, some lawyers are not convinced that they do anything other than give the lawyers who lose a person to blame.

Source: Tricia McDermott, "The Jury Consultants," *48 Hours,* June 2, 2004, http://www.cbsnews.com/stories/2004/06/02/48hours/main620794.shtml.

JURY AND NONJURY TRIAL

Jury selection, also called **voir dire** (which literally means "to see what one says" or "to speak the truth"), is the process by which the triers of fact—the jurors—are chosen. The purpose of the process is to seat a fair and impartial jury that will listen to the case with an open mind and determine the facts accordingly.

If a party is entitled to a trial by jury, generally that right can be waived by the parties. If they so waive, then the trial judge conducts a bench trial.

If a jury is not waived, jury selection proceeds. Challenges to a juror can be made for cause or by using **peremptory strikes.** A **challenge for cause** is made when, as a matter of law, a juror cannot sit on the jury because that juror cannot be impartial. For example, a juror may be stricken for cause by being related to or having close acquaintance with a person who is an integral part of the trial, such as a witness, the judge, or an attorney. Reality Check 3-12, "Consultant to the Stars," shows how much of a cottage industry has grown up

EXAMPLE

around jury selection and whom to strike from the jury.

A peremptory strike is generally used when the potential juror does not fit the profile of jurors who the attorney feels would most benefit the client. For example, in a trial involving a landlord/tenant dispute, the attorney for the landlord would want to strike any tenants on the jury who might be sympathetic to the tenant's case. An attorney could remove such jurors by using a peremptory strike. Reality Check 3-13, "Juror Misconduct Overturns Trial Verdict," explores the question of what happens when jurors lie.

Unlike challenges for cause, peremptory strikes are limited in number. Also unlike challenges for cause, peremptory strikes can be used for any reason, subject to constitutional limitations. No reason has to be disclosed when using a peremptory strike, unless it is subject to a constitutional challenge, such as race-based strikes, found unlawful in *Batson v. Kentucky*,[9] or gender-based strikes, found unlawful in *J.E.B. v. Alabama*.[10] Some discussion continues over whether the use of preemptory challenges should still be allowed, as illustrated in Reality Check 3-14, "Peremptory Challenges: Should the Court Allow Them at All?"

REALITY CHECK 3-13

JUROR MISCONDUCT OVERTURNS TRIAL VERDICT

Lance Bean was convicted of killing Donald Sanders and was serving a 45-year sentence. However, he now will have another day in court because of a juror who went too far and a judge who didn't declare a mistrial as a result of it.

One of the jurors in the case told the other jurors that he had visited the crime scene. In addition, he spoke to some of the prosecution's witnesses in clear violation of the rules. Rather than declare a mistrial, the judge simply substituted another juror for this one in the deliberation phase. On appeal, the court reversed on the error made by the judge in not declaring a mistrial and starting all over again.

Source: Associated Press, *NJ.com*, "Appeals Court Grants Camden Man Another Trial in '03 Shooting," May 15, 2009, http://www.nj.com/news/index.ssf/2009/05/appeals_court_grants_camden_ma.html.

REALITY CHECK 3-14

PEREMPTORY CHALLENGES: SHOULD THE COURT ALLOW THEM AT ALL?

The use of peremptory challenges is constantly debated in legal circles, despite their long tradition in the legal system. The challenges are based on two different perceptions. On the one hand, opponents of the use of peremptory challenges argue that eliminating them would create greater efficiency in the system. It would reduce the number of jurors that need to be called to duty to select a particular panel, eliminate the need for jury consultants who specialize in which jurors are optimal for each case, and eliminate the need for "Batson" hearings—hearings that are held when one party alleges a constitutional challenge to the use of the peremptory strikes. Critics also argue that it dilutes the jury's ability to correct misperceptions held by jurors of a different background. For example, a minority on the jury might give a different view of the evidence, while eliminating minorities leaves the jury without that corrected view. They also hold that challenges are often based on stereotypes, which is inconsistent with ideals. Lastly, they argue that elimination of jurors based on these stereotypes leaves those jurors with a negative view of the jury system, which often makes them feel like they would not be treated fairly.

Proponents of the system argue that peremptory challenges have been successful at getting impartial juries in the past and they will continue to do so. They also argue that placing the rights of the juror to serve above the defendant's right to challenge impartial jurors is not the right balance. They argue that eliminating peremptory strikes will add to jury deliberations because there will be less understanding between the jurors. Attorneys will ask fewer questions because they will not want to antagonize existing jurors.

The use of peremptory challenges may in the future be limited to the point where the exceptions for when you cannot strike might overcome the opportunities when you can. Challenges have been upheld for striking on the basis of race and gender, but thus far courts have refused to extend it on the basis of generalizations based on religion, national origin, disability, or occupation. Perhaps all group-based challenges will be eliminated one day.

Source: Patricia Henley, "Improving the Jury System: Peremptory Challenges," Public Law Research Institute, http://w3.uchastings.edu/plri/spr96tex/juryper.html.

---

[9]476 U.S. 79 (1976).
[10]114 S. Ct. 1419 (1994).

TRIAL

After the jury is sworn in, the trial begins. A trial consists of several parts, all interrelated. First, the lawyers have the opportunity to make an **opening statement.** Opening statements are narratives that present each side's theory of the case to the jury. After both sides have given their opening statement (though the defendant may reserve his opening statement until the beginning of the defendant's case), the plaintiff presents the plaintiff's side of the case by calling witnesses and introducing evidence into the trial. When a plaintiff's witness testifies for the plaintiff, the questions and answers are called **direct examination.** After such direct examination, the witness is tendered to the defense, and the question and answers then given are called **cross-examination.** Rebuttal testimony may be provided on redirect examination or re-cross-examination. After all the witnesses have testified and the evidence has been admitted for the plaintiffs, the defense presents its side of the case, using the same format and procedure as for the plaintiff.

Once all of the evidence has been presented, both sides (generally, the plaintiff goes first) have the opportunity to present to the jurors their **closing argument,** which is a summary of the evidence and the law. It is during closing argument that the lawyers will try to persuade jurors that the evidence admitted during the trial and the law given to them by the judge during the jury instructions will require them to reach a verdict for their respective client.

In most civil cases, the burden of proof required is a **preponderance of the evidence.** This means that the jury feels the evidence shows that the defendant more likely than not did act as alleged by plaintiff. In more serious cases, the burden of proof on the plaintiff is, instead, **clear and convincing evidence** to show that the events occurred as alleged. The heavier burden is imposed because of the more serious nature of an offense.

APPEAL

The party against whom a **judgment** has been entered may move to have the judgment set aside. The two most common devices to achieve this are the **judgment notwithstanding the verdict (JNOV)** and a **motion for a new trial.** Generally a JNOV must be filed within a few days after judgment has been entered, and it asks that the judgment be set aside. It is rare that a judge will grant a JNOV; but it is granted if the weight of the evidence is overwhelmingly contrary to the jury's verdict.

Generally, a motion for a new trial also must be filed within days of the entry of judgment. Typically, this motion alleges procedure errors (e.g., improper argument by opposing counsel, improperly admitted or excluded evidence, or prejudicial jury instructions), a verdict contrary to law, excessive or inadequate damages, or other grounds.

If neither motion is successful, the losing party may choose to **appeal** the decision. The party seeking the appeal is known as the **appellant** (or petitioner), and the party who must defend against the appeal is the **appellee** (or defendant).

The rules for an appeal generally require the appellant to file with the court that will hear the appeal a notice of appeal within a specific time limit after the court enters the judgment on the trial verdict. After giving notice of the appeal to the appellate court and to the appellee, the appellant must comply with appellate court rules, which generally require the filing of a brief. A brief is a written document outlining the points of error that the appellant alleges were made in the trial, along with whatever exhibits are relevant. Once a copy of the appellant's brief has been filed with the court and a copy served to the appellee, the appellee then responds by filing an answer brief, which argues that the trial court was correct and that the verdict should stand.

The appellate court, in addition to reading the briefs in the case, may wish to hear the arguments and ask questions of the lawyers. This process, known as oral (or appellate)

TAKE AWAY 3-7

PHASES OF A CIVIL TRIAL

Pleadings	Complaint, Summons, Answer, Reply, and Motions
Pretrial	Discovery, Depositions, Interrogatories, Request for Production of Documents,
Trial	Voir Dire, Peremptory Strikes, Challenge for Cause , Opening Statement, Direct Examination, Cross Examination, Closing Argument, Judgment, Judgment Notwithstanding the Verdict, Motion for New Trial
Appeal	Appellate Brief, Oral Argument, Final Decision

argument, is usually requested by all appellants, but is granted in only a few cases the court deems to be significant in some way. If granted, each party is given a specific time period (usually no more than 30 minutes) in which to present arguments and respond to questions from the justices.

Unlike at trial, the justices, as many appellate judges are called, do not render their opinion about the case immediately following oral arguments. Instead, they consider the case among themselves for as long as it takes to reach a decision, and sometime in the future the parties are notified of that decision. If the decision comes from a court of last resort, or the highest court that can hear the case (for example, the state supreme court), then that decision is the final decision. If the court is an intermediate court, the losing party may choose to appeal the decision to the highest court. If so, then the appellate process begins again. Take Away 3-7, "Phases of a Trial," discusses the phases of a civil trial.

Criminal Trial

Once a criminal case proceeds to trial, the trial is conducted in much the same manner as a civil suit, with the primary distinction being at the conclusion of the trial, when the defendant is judged either not guilty (acquitted) or guilty. The burden of proof in a criminal trial is guilt **beyond a reasonable doubt.** That is, to convict a defendant, a jury must be convinced beyond all reasonable doubt that the evidence shows the defendant committed the crime as charged.

Occasionally, a jury is unable to reach a verdict, and that results in a mistrial, or **hung jury,** in which case the government has the opportunity to retry the case. If a jury renders a verdict of guilty, then the defendant can appeal to a higher court. If the jury acquits the defendant, then the government generally does not have the right to appeal; nor can it retry the case. The doctrine of **double jeopardy** prevents the government from retrying a defendant on the same charges twice, and the doctrine is protected by the Fifth Amendment of the Constitution.

In addition to those constitutional protections, a defendant has the right to other constitutional protections, including the right to a speedy trial, the right to face one's accuser, and the right to know of any evidence tending to point to the defendant's innocence (exculpatory evidence).

Remember the attorney-client privilege we mentioned earlier and how inviolate it is? You can imagine how it would seem even more so when an attorney is dealing with a defendant who may have engaged in illegal activity. The fear is that clients will not be honest with their attorneys if they know that at some point the attorney may violate the privilege and disclose the client's confidential information. In most cases the privilege remains in place even after the client dies. An interesting ethical dilemma is presented when an attorney violates the privilege to keep an innocent person from going to prison because the attorney knows his client committed the crime. This is not usually a sufficient basis for violating the privilege. For one attorney who broke the privilege after his client died, "it seemed to me at that point ethically permissible and morally imperative that I spill the beans"[11] in order to free a prisoner who the client told the attorney 22 years before did not commit the double homicide but had now served 22 years for it. The judge before whom the attorney testified about the situation reported the attorney to the bar association for breaching the privilege. States vary as to whether and when the privilege can be breached, but violating the privilege is not taken lightly and can cost an attorney his or her career. Does this make ethical sense to you? Who are the stakeholders? What are the various interests, including the client, the attorney, and society at large? How do you balance letting an innocent person go to prison for 22 years with the inviolability of the privilege?

The vast majority of criminal appeals are initiated by defendants unhappy with the results of their case and hoping that the appellate court will make a more favorable decision. All 50 states provide some form of appeal or review of criminal convictions. Indigent defendants (those who cannot afford counsel) are entitled to appointed counsel for the first appeal. Few appeals are initiated by the prosecutor, because of the problem of double jeopardy.

L08

Remedies

There are two basic types of **remedies** for a civil wrong: legal remedies and equitable remedies. In law, a party is entitled to monetary damages. In equity, a party is entitled to nonmonetary relief because sometimes money simply will not suffice.

LEGAL DAMAGES

Damages are awarded as compensation to a party for any loss or harm sustained due to the misconduct of another. The primary purpose of awarding compensation is to place the injured party in the same position that party would have occupied if the wrong had not occurred. In addition to compensatory damages, two other categories of money damages exist: punitive damages and nominal damages.

Compensatory damages are intended to pay for the actual harm caused to the injured party. What a party is entitled to be compensated for depends on the type of action that is brought. For example, in an action for breach of contract, compensatory damages are for the actual loss suffered because of the defendant's breach of (noncompliance with) the contract. In a tort action, however, compensatory damages are intended to cover a wider variety of injuries, such as pain and suffering, physical and mental impairment, emotional distress, medical expenses, loss of enjoyment of life, or injury to reputation, in addition to the actual physical loss suffered by the injured party. In the Complaint (see again Take Away 3-6) filed in the lawsuit against Damian's company, the Plaintiff, Jenny Terry, alleged damages for pain and suffering caused by her injuries.

EXAMPLE

EXAMPLE

---

[11]Adam Liptak, "When Law Prevents Righting a Wrong," *New York Times,* May 4, 2008, http://www.nytimes.com/2008/05/04/ weekinreview/04liptak.html?_r=2&pagewanted=1.

Injuries that are caused by a defendant indirectly may also be recovered under compensatory damages. Such indirect damages are called **consequential damages** and are limited to injuries that are a natural and probable consequence of the defendant's acts, of which the defendant was aware. A defendant is not required to pay avoidable or speculative damages, or damages as a result of unforeseen events.

Punitive damages have as their purpose both punishment and deterrence. They are damages over and above what is necessary to make the party whole. Punitive damages are intended to reflect society's reaction to the harm inflicted by the defendant. In order to recover punitive damages a party must first prove entitlement to compensatory damages, or in some jurisdictions, nominal damages.

A party's financial condition is irrelevant to a claim of compensatory damages; but it is relevant to an award of punitive damages. Punitive damages must be significant enough to punish the defendant, but should not be so excessive as to ruin him or her. Punitive damages are generally not available in contract actions, unless specifically authorized by statute.

Damages are assessed by the trier of fact: the jury or the judge in a nonjury trial. Although appellate courts are reluctant to interfere with a jury's determination of punitive awards, the verdict can be amended or set aside if it (1) resulted from a mistake of fact or law; (2) was grossly excessive or inadequate; (3) was against the weight of the evidence; (4) shocks the conscious of the court; or (5) was motivated by bias, passion, or prejudice.

Nominal damages may be awarded when a legal right has been injured or if fault has been shown, but plaintiff has failed to prove that any actual loss occurred as a result of that fault. Nominal damages are damages in name only, and are a trivial or inconsiderate sum, typically $1.

Why would a party seek damages where no actual injury exists? As stated by the court in *Cottone v. Cristiano*,[12] "Whenever any cognizable right of a person is violated, though there be no substantial injury nor general nor consequential damages, the law requires that the right be declared and affirmed and disapproval of its violation significantly voiced through the form of an award of nominal damages." Even though we are generally only talking about minimal amounts of money being awarded in nominal damage cases, does it seem ethical to you to award such damages if it has been shown that the party suffered no harm?

EXAMPLE

LIQUIDATED DAMAGES

Liquidated damages (sometimes called *stipulated damages*) are used in contract law to specify the predetermined amount of damages for which a defendant will be liable in case of breach of contract. A liquidated damage provision anticipates a breach and sets the amount to be recovered before any party breaches and represents the estimate of the extent of probable damages. Liquidated damages provisions may not be "punitive," i.e., they may not be so out of proportion to the anticipated injury that its very design is to prevent the breach. If the court determines that the liquidated damage provision is punitive, then it can invalidate the provision and make its own assessment of damages. Liquidated damage provisions are often found in real estate contracts, where amount is set by the seller if the buyer breaches, usually set at the down payment amount, and the amount is set by the buyer if the seller breaches, usually some predetermined amount. Take Away 3-8 ("Restatement 2d of Contracts: Liquidated Damages and Penalties") displays the exact language courts have adopted.

---

[12]156 N.Y S. 2d 115 (Civ. Ct. 1956).

TAKE AWAY 3-8

RESTATEMENT 2D OF CONTRACTS
§ 339. LIQUIDATED DAMAGES AND PENALTIES

(1) An agreement, made in advance of breach, fixing the damages therefor, is not enforceable as a contract and does not affect the damages recoverable for the breach, unless
(a) the amount so fixed is a reasonable forecast of just compensation for the harm that is caused by the breach, and
(b) the harm that is caused by the breach is one that is incapable or very difficult of accurate estimation.

Source: Restatement of Contracts 2d.

EXAMPLE

For example, Brutus, an actor, is hired by the Roxy Theater to perform 40 times over the summer in exchange for $200 per performance. The contract states that if either party breaches in any way, the breaching party must pay $5000 as liquidated damages. Brutus breaches by failing to give the last three performances and the theater tries to enforce the liquidated damages provision. The theater's attempt to enforce will probably fail because it does not appear to represent a proportional compensation for Brutus's breach. Although the amount need not be exact, the liquidated damage amount cannot be so much in excess of actual damages suffered by the nonbreaching party until it acts as punitive damages, for punitive damages are generally not allowed in contract actions. In *Barrie School* (Case 3.3) a school successfully enforced a liquidated damages clause for the entire year's tuition even though the student was withdrawn before the school year ever began. The parents argued that the school had a duty to **mitigate damages,** that is, to work to make the damages less even though they agreed to a liquidated damages clause.

EQUITABLE REMEDIES

An equitable remedy will be awarded only when a monetary remedy will not resolve the dispute. In fact, if the party's remedies at law are sufficient, equitable relief cannot be granted. **Equitable remedies** take the form of court orders, called **decrees,** to do or refrain from doing something specific. Three common types of decrees are **specific performance, injunction,** and **accounting.**

Specific performance is a decree ordering a party to specifically perform the obligations of a contract. As a general rule, specific performance is ordered only in cases involving the sale of unique or one-of-a-kind goods. For example, Glenda contracts to sell Bobbi 1000 bushels of wheat at $4.00 per bushel. On the date set for delivery, Glenda does not perform as agreed. Assuming there is a market for wheat, Bobbi can purchase wheat to replace that anticipated by the contract with Glenda and the damage will be the difference between what she would have paid Glenda under the contract and what she had to pay in the market. However, what if Glenda contracted to sell Bobbi "The Nude" by Picasso for $250,000? If Glenda breaches the contract, a suit for specific performance should be successful. A decree of specific performance would require Glenda to sell the painting to Bobbi for $250,000 because no amount of money awarded to Bobbi would compensate her for Glenda's breach. There is no way in which Bobbi could buy another original of the painting since there is only one and thus no marketplace for "The Nude." In addition to

CASE 3.3 Barrie School v. Patch

933 A.2d 382 (Md. 2007)

Facts: Petitioner, The Barrie School, is a private, non-profit Montessori school located in Silver Spring, Maryland. Respondents, Andrew and Pamela Patch, are parents who enrolled their daughter, Christiana, in The Barrie School for the 2004–2005 academic year. The Patches entered into a re-enrollment agreement with The Barrie School that contained a specific deadline for cancelling the Agreement. The Agreement stated that if respondents withdrew their child from The Barrie School after a specific date, respondents would pay tuition for the entire academic year as liquidated damages. The Agreement provided for a $1000.00 nonrefundable deposit and payment of the remaining tuition balance of $13,490.00 in two installments. The Agreement contained an escape clause that allowed for unilateral cancellation, provided that the head of the school received written notice by certified letter before May 31, 2004. Under §3 of the Agreement, respondents were obligated to pay the full tuition if they failed to meet the May 31, 2004 deadline for withdrawal. Section 3 of the Agreement provided as follows:

"I understand that unless the Student is withdrawn by written notice given by certified letter, return receipt requested, and received by the Head of School prior to May 31, 2004, I am liable for and agree to pay the entire year's charges for the academic year, including expenses, as later defined, incurred by the School for collection. Withdrawal, dismissal, absences or illness of Student during the year do not release me from any portion of this obligation."

The Patches did not cancel the Agreement on or before May 31, 2004. On July 14, 2004, forty-four days after the withdrawal deadline noted in §3 of the Agreement, the Patches sent a cancellation notice via facsimile to the Barrie School's admissions office and demanded a refund of their initial deposit. Respondents refused to pay any of the remaining tuition balance to the school and enrolled Christiana in another school. In their notice of intent to defend, respondents claimed that the Agreement had been procured by fraud, that it was a contract of adhesion, that the damages constituted a penalty, that The Barrie School had a duty to mitigate any damages, and that the Agreement was unenforceable because it violated public policy and Maryland's anti-competition laws. Respondents also filed a counterclaim, seeking the return of their $1000.00 deposit, interest, and attorney's fees. The trial court held it was a valid liquidated damages provision, as the exact amount of damages associated with losing one child for the school year would be impossible to know. However, the court found that the failure of the Barrie School to mitigate its damages was fatal to its case.

Issue: Whether a nonbreaching party has a duty to mitigate their damages where the parties agree to a valid liquidated damages sum in the event of a breach?

Decision: No.

Reasoning: Respondents do not appear to controvert petitioner's argument that there exists a liquidated damages clause in the Agreement. Rather, respondents argue that the general law of contracts, i.e., the general duty to mitigate damages in the event of a breach, applies to a contract containing a liquidated damages provision. Maryland courts will uphold a liquidated damages clause as valid, and not a penalty, if it satisfies two primary requirements. First, the clause must provide a fair estimate of potential damages at the time the parties entered into the contract. Second, the damages must have been incapable of estimation, or very difficult to estimate, at the time of contracting. In this case, the lower courts found correctly that §3 of the Agreement was a valid liquidated damages clause and not a penalty. Respondents argue that there exists a duty to mitigate damages even in the face of a valid liquidated damages clause. Respondents would have us hold that there is such a duty because parties to a contract are required usually to minimize loss in the event of breach. Liquidated damages differ fundamentally from mitigation of damages. While mitigation is part of a court's determination of actual damages that have resulted from a breach of contract, liquidated damages clauses are the remedy the parties to a contract have determined to be proper in the event of breach. Where the parties to a contract have included a reasonable sum that stipulates damages in the event of breach, that sum replaces any determination of actual loss.

CASE QUESTIONS

1. The school board argues it cannot anticipate the amount of damages if the child does not attend school for the year. Is that accurate? Wouldn't it be the cost of tuition?

2. The court held that the duty to mitigate does not apply here because the damages have already been established. If the court did entertain mitigation for cases like this, the school here would not have received anything because they were overenrolled for that year. Do you think that motivated the court to rule the way it did?

3. Do you think the school got a windfall here? Explain.

TAKE AWAY 3-9

REMEDIES

Legal Damages	Compensatory, Consequential, Punitive, Nominal
Liquidated Damages	Pre-Determined Damages for Breach
Equitable Remedies	Decrees, Specific Performance, Injunctions, Accounting, Temporary Restraining Order, Permanent Injunction

unique goods, specific performance is most often ordered in real property cases because of the belief that each piece of real estate is unique from all others.

An injunction is a court order to do or stop doing a particular thing. When an injunction is issued, it generally enjoins, (i.e., prevents) a party from continuing to do a harmful act, such as pollute or create noise. A **mandatory injunction** is a court order requiring an affirmative act, such as providing a zoning ordinance.

Injunctions are issued in three phases. First, a **temporary restraining order** may be issued. This is an extraordinary measure issued by a judge without notice to the other party, and it is of very limited duration (usually a few days). Next, a **preliminary injunction** halts the harmful act temporarily after both sides have an opportunity to be heard and the complaining party has established both likelihood of success on the merits and that there will be irreparable harm if the injunction is not ordered. If, after a full trial, the harm is held to exist, a **permanent injunction** may be ordered by the court.

EXAMPLE

EXAMPLE

In cases involving funds held in trust, the court may order an accounting, which requires the defendant to account for use of the monies in question. For example, a court can demand an accounting from a court-appointed guardian of a trust account which will require the guardian to account for all the money spent that belongs to the trust. A partner in a partnership can also seek an accounting of partnership assets if he or she thinks another partner is misapplying the funds, or when a partner withdraws from the partnership and wants the partnership assets split. You may recall that in 2008, Rev. Bernice King and Martin Luther King III filed suit against their third sibling, Dexter King, administrator of the estate of their father, Rev. Dr. Martin Luther King, Jr., asking the court to order an accounting of their father's estate. The suit was filed after Dexter King allegedly refused to turn over documents, contracts, or financial information to the other siblings so they could see the state of their father's estate.[13] Since over 10,000 of their father's papers had been sold to the city of Atlanta for $32 million, you can imagine why they would be concerned about not having any idea what was happening with the estate. Take Away 3-9, "Remedies," discusses the remedies available to an injured party.

---

[13]"Martin Luther King, Jr. Family Estate in Dispute," July 12, 2008, http://articles.latimes.com/2008/jul/12/nation/na-mlk12.

Summary

The court system is an important part of the tripartite system of government in the United States. It operates on the state and federal level, with the federal level being authorized by the U.S. Constitution. Divided into specialized and general courts, the system covers all the litigation needs of the citizens of the country. The courts are open to anyone who qualifies with a ripe issue who has a case or controversy in dispute.

Federal courts are divided geographically and have district courts, courts of appeal and the U.S. Supreme Court. States courts follow a similar jurisdictional plan but may not have an intermediate court if not needed. Federal courts have jurisdiction to hear cases between parties who have diversity of citizenship, or whose controversy exceeds $75,000. Courts use the doctrine of *stare decisis* when deciding cases. They use a body of precedent to ensure that their opinions are rendered fairly to each side.

The rules of civil procedure govern how a case proceeds through the court system. The rules of criminal procedure govern the criminal trial. Each system pursues its own agenda; the civil system is used to bring cases in which a private wrong is addressed and results in monetary damages or nonmonetary relief such as injunction. The criminal system is designed to address public harms to society and results in punishment in the form of prison or fines or both.

Review Questions

1. Rita has sued Acme Co., a manufacturer of hair dryers, for damages resulting from her purchase of an Acme hair dryer ("Acme 2000"). The hair dryer caught on fire as she used it. The litigation has moved to the "discovery" phase. Outline discovery requests that Acme Co. might serve on Rita. Identify examples of discovery requests that Rita might serve on Acme Co. What steps could Acme Co. take to prepare for Rita's discovery requests? LO7

2. Stanley Young, the warden at the Wallens Ridge State Prison in Virginia, filed a complaint in the U.S. District Court in West Virginia against the *New Haven Advocate* and the *Hartford Courant,* two Connecticut-based newspapers, and their individual editors and writers, alleging defamation. Both newspapers maintain websites, in which it published stories which made statements regarding Wallens Ridge and Warden Young. The defendants asked the trial court to dismiss the case as it lacked personal jurisdiction over them, but the judge disagreed. On appeal, the Fourth Circuit of Appeals reversed, holding that the federal trial court erred, noting that the newspapers did not aim to target Virginia readers in posting articles on its website.[14]

   Write a statement in support of the defendants' motion to dismiss. Write a statement against it. What additional facts will the judge need to decide whether the defendants' motion should be granted or denied?[15] LO6

3. How do discovery rules help achieve justice? How might the discovery process be improved? LO7

4. Chad, a train engineer, is on duty when a train he is operating is involved in an accident that kills several people. The passengers sue the railroad company, alleging that Chad operated the train negligently, thereby causing the accident, because he was under the influence of an illegal drug. In deciding the case, the court will likely impose what standard upon the jury hearing the case?

5. During the voir dire for a civil case involving computer software infringement, Rachel, the

---

[14]"4th Circuit Rules in Internet Jurisdiction Case," citing *Young v. New Haven Advocate* (4th Cir. 2002), http://www.techlawjournal.com/topstories/2002/20021213.asp.

[15]Adapted from "4th Circuit Rules in Internet Jurisdiction Case," citing *Young v. New Haven Advocate* (4th Cir. 2002), http://www.techlawjournal.com/topstories/2002/20021213.asp.

attorney for the software company, tries to strike from the jury anyone who has ever used a computer because she thinks such persons would be predisposed to think that copying software is no big deal because virtually everyone does it. Rachel's attempts to strike prospective jurors will likely be on the basis of what type of strikes? Will she likely be successful in striking all the computer users from the jury? LO7

6. Ralph is riding in his automobile when Becky runs into his car, causing him severe injury. Ralph is from Georgia and Becky is from Florida. Ralph sues Becky for $115,000 in federal court. Becky argues that the federal court lacks jurisdiction. Who is correct and why? LO5

7. Barton alleged that he had a contract with Ace Motor Company to purchase a car and that Ace sold the car to someone else. Barton was able to purchase an identical car at Bowers Motor Co. for the same price he was to purchase it from Ace. Barton argues that since Ace breached the contract with him, he is entitled to compensatory damages. Barton is awarded $1 in damages. Is he correct about the compensatory damages? Explain. LO8

8. Dawn takes her great-great-grandmother's sewing machine, which has been in her family for over 100 years, to Charlie's Sew'n Vac Repair for servicing. When Dawn returns to pick up the sewing machine, she is told that it has been sold. Charlie offers to pay Dawn the price of a similar machine. She refuses the offer. Explain Dawn's alternatives for relief. LO8

9. Kadisha was raped one night by a clothing store employee while she was trying on clothes just before the store closed. Kadisha wants two things: money for her injuries and that the perpetrator be punished for what he did. Kadisha's friend Regine tells her that if she wants to receive compensation for her injuries, she should allow the case to be prosecuted, and as part of the decision, if the perpetrator is found guilty, he will have to pay her. Is Regine's advice good advice? Explain. LO6

10. Jim entered into a contract with Luis for Luis to build Jim his dream house. In the contract was a liquidated damages provision that gave Jim $1000 per day for every day that Luis was delayed, for whatever reason. A hurricane struck, destroying the house which was one-half completed and on schedule. Jim sued Luis at the expiration of the time for completion, claiming any reason included hurricanes, and he owed him $1000 for every day he was delayed. What is the court likely to do to Jim's demand of $1000 per day? LO8

Ethics Issue

Anyone charged with a crime is entitled to legal representation. Largely, this job falls to a public defender, either state or federal, who is generally overworked and unable to give the attention to the case that he or she should. Because of the caseload, many cases are pled that maybe should not be. But then there's another side of the issue—public defenders that do not seem to care about their clients.

Take the case of Mychal Bell, a member of the Jena Six. The Jena Six were so named because their case occurred in Jena, Louisiana (in 2007). There had been a racially charged atmosphere at the school where the Jena Six and those involved with them attended. There were accusations back and forth, but the arrests of the six black youths, ages 17 and 18, followed a battery committed on a white boy which allegedly occurred after at least two nooses were found hanging from a tree frequented by white students the day after a black student sat under the tree with the principal's permission.[16] Tensions grew after the white students who allegedly hung the nooses were given what some considered light discipline involving in-school suspension. When matters escalated and an altercation ensued and a white male student was involved in a fight with several black male students, the black students were arrested.

Mychal Bell, age 17, was charged as an adult. The white prosecutor who handled the case charged Bell with aggravated battery—a charge that required the use of a deadly weapon. The prosecutor alleged that the sneakers Bell wore when he kicked the victim were the deadly weapons. At trial, Bell was represented by a

---

[16]This case drew national attention and captured the media for over a year while the case worked its way through the courts. For a full story see Tom Mangold, "Racism Goes on Trial Again in America's Deep South," *The Observer,* May 20, 2007, http://www.guardian.co.uk/world/2007/may/20/usa.theobserver.

white public defender. Despite witnesses who would testify that Bell was not involved, Bell's public defender urged Bell to take a plea. Bell refused. During trial, Bell's public defender rested his case without calling a single witness or offering any evidence on Bell's behalf. Even though the jury pool consisted of 50 venire, none was black. Bell's public defender never challenged the venire. The jury found Bell guilty. Facing 22 years in prison, Bell secured a new set of attorneys privately hired on his behalf. Eventually his case was resolved on time served on other unrelated charges.

The question is, what made the difference in the case? Do you think most lawyers would have challenged an all-white jury in a jurisdiction that was 10 percent black? Do you think most lawyers would have put on a case for their client where there were willing witnesses to challenge the prosecution's witnesses? What makes the difference? Where do ethics come into play? If lawyers are bound by their code of professional ethics, do you think the prosecutor and public defender abided by them here? What is the impact of such an occurrence on the defendant as well as on society viewing the situation? Should the judge viewing this situation step in? Would it be ethical to do so? Who are the stakeholders and what are their issues? Does this appear to be equal justice under law as promised by the U.S. Constitution?

Group Exercise

If you can, attend a trial in your jurisdiction, federal or state. If you cannot attend an actual trial, view one on TV or in a movie. What did you learn in this chapter that you see in action in the courtroom?

Key Terms

accounting 66

affirmative defense 57

answer 55

appeal 41

appellant 62

appellee 62

bench trial 60

beyond a reasonable doubt 63

case or controversy 47

case of first impression 53

cause of action 55

challenge 60

challenge for cause 60

circuit 42

clear and convincing evidence 62

closing argument 62

compensatory damages 64

complaint 55

concurrent jurisdiction 43

consequential damages 65

contingency fee arrangement 54

counterclaim 55

court of Appeal 42

cross-claim 57

cross-examination 62

decree 66

defendant 55

deposition 57

direct examination 62

discovery 57

diversity of citizenship jurisdiction 43

double jeopardy 63

electronically stored information (ESI) 58

equitable remedies 66

exclusive jurisdiction 45

federal district court 42

federal question jurisdiction 43

general jurisdiction 49

habeas corpus 50

holding 52

hung jury 63

impeach 58

injunction 66

interrogatories 58

judgment 62

judgment notwithstanding verdict 62

judicial review 48

jurisdiction 40

legal brief 41

limited jurisdiction 50

liquidated damages 65

long-arm statute 45

mandatory injunction 68

minimum contacts 45

mitigate damages 66

motion 57

motion for a new trial 62

moving party 57

nominal damages 65

opening statement 62

oral arguments 41

original jurisdiction 40

peremptory strikes 60

permanent injunction 68

plaintiff 55

www.mhhe.com/bennett-alexanderLE1e

Administrative Law

Learning Objectives

After reading this chapter, you should be able to:

L01 Explain what administrative law is

L02 Analyze the role of administrative law in business

L03 Identify ways that diversity is important for administrative law

L04 Explain how administrative agencies are created

L05 Describe the powers of administrative agencies

L06 Explain the Administrative Procedures Act and what it is designed to do

L07 Evaluate how administrative law interfaces with courts

L08 Define the constitutional limitations of administrative law

 Opening Scenario

Matthew is known for his great empanadas. After losing his job and not being able to find one for several months, Matthew decides to make money the only way he can think of. Each morning Matthew loads up his car with homemade empanadas and heads off to construction sites in town. After several days of doing a booming business, Matthew receives a citation and a notice to appear before the local boards of health and licensing. Why?

Introduction

In this chapter we will discuss administrative law created by government agencies. You will learn why and how such agencies are created, what they do, how what they do relates to law and the legal environment of business and why this is such a critical aspect of law of which any business must be thoroughly aware.

In our opening scenario, Matthew could have avoided his citation if he had been aware of the administrative agencies' regulations relating to his serving food to the public, operating a business without a license, operating a business without a premises in which to do so, and so on.

Administrative law is the area of law that addresses federal and state government agencies and their role in carrying out their delegated authority. Agencies are created by the government to conduct business on its behalf. For instance, the Constitution gives Congress the authority to lay and collect taxes. Congress passes laws determining at

EEOC ENABLING STATUTE

The Equal Employment Opportunity Commission (EEOC) is the agency created by Congress to enforce the Civil Rights Act of 1964 that, among other things, prohibits workplace discrimination on the basis of race, color, gender, religion and national origin. Later, age, disability and pregnancy were determined by Congress to be additional prohibited bases of employment discrimination. Here, you see excerpts from the original enabling statute that created the agency. Notice that there are provisions for how the agency is to be structured, what it has the power to do, whether it can go to court, whether it can issue rules and regulations, and even where it is to be located.

An Act . . . to establish a Commission on Equal Employment Opportunity, and for other purposes.

Be it enacted by the Senate and House of Representatives of the United States of America in Congress assembled, That this Act may be cited as the "Civil Rights Act of 1964."

. . .

DISCRIMINATION BECAUSE OF RACE, COLOR, RELIGION, SEX, OR NATIONAL ORIGIN

SEC. 703. (a) It shall be an unlawful employment practice for an employer—

(1) to fail or refuse to hire or to discharge any individual, or otherwise to discriminate against any individual with respect to his compensation, terms, conditions, or privileges of employment, because of such individual's race, color, religion, sex, or national origin; or

(2) to limit, segregate, or classify his employees in any way which would deprive or tend to deprive any individual of employment opportunities or otherwise adversely affect his status as an employee, because of such individual's race, color, religion, sex, or national origin.

. . .

EQUAL EMPLOYMENT OPPORTUNITY COMMISSION

SEC. 705. (a) There is hereby created a Commission to be known as the Equal Employment Opportunity Commission, which shall be composed of five members, not more than three of whom shall be members of the same political party, who shall be appointed by the President by and with the advice and consent of the Senate. One of the original members shall be appointed for a term of one year, one for a term of two years, one for a term of three years, one for a term of four years, and one for a term of five years, beginning from the date of enactment of this title, but their successors shall be appointed for terms of five years each, except that any individual chosen to fill a vacancy shall be appointed only for the unexpired term of the member whom he shall succeed. The President shall designate one member to serve as Chairman of the Commission, and one member to serve as Vice Chairman. The Chairman shall be responsible on behalf of the Commission for the administrative operations of the Commission, and shall appoint, in accordance with the civil service laws, such officers, agents, attorneys, and employees as it deems necessary to assist it in the performance of its functions and to fix their compensation in accordance with the Classification Act of 1949, as amended. The Vice Chairman shall act as Chairman in the absence or disability of the Chairman or in the event of a vacancy in that office.

(b) A vacancy in the Commission shall not impair the right of the remaining members to exercise all the powers of the Commission and three members thereof shall constitute a quorum.

what rate we are to be taxed ("laying" taxes) but is too busy making laws to deal with collecting these taxes. It needs a helper, so it created an agency called the Internal Revenue Service (IRS) to do this task.

In undertaking to do the task of collecting taxes, among other things, the IRS needs rules as to how to conduct its business, needs to have an organized way of collecting taxes, and needs some means of dealing with disputes that may arise between the agency and taxpayers who disagree with an IRS tax determination. Knowing this, Congress gave the IRS the authority to create or acquire what it needs in order to carry out the task it was created to do.

(c) The Commission shall have an official seal which shall be judicially noticed.

(d) The Commission shall at the close of each fiscal year report to the Congress and to the President concerning the action it has taken; the names, salaries, and duties of all individuals in its employ and the moneys it has disbursed; and shall make such further reports on the cause of and means of eliminating discrimination and such recommendations for further legislation as may appear desirable.

...

(f) The principal office of the Commission shall be in or near the District of Columbia, but it may meet or exercise any or all its powers at any other place. The Commission may establish such regional or State offices as it deems necessary to accomplish the purpose of this title.

(g) The Commission shall have power—

(1) to cooperate with and, with their consent, utilize regional, State, local, and other agencies, both public and private, and individuals;

(2) to pay to witnesses whose depositions are taken or who are summoned before the Commission or any of its agents the same witness and mileage fees as are paid to witnesses in the courts of the United States;

(3) to furnish to persons subject to this title such technical assistance as they may request to further their compliance with this title or an order issued thereunder;

...

(f) Each United States district court and each United States court of a place subject to the jurisdiction of the United States shall have jurisdiction of actions brought under this title.

...

INVESTIGATORY POWERS

SEC. 710. (a) For the purposes of any investigation of a charge filed under the authority contained in section 706, the Commission shall have authority to examine witnesses under oath and to require the production of documentary evidence relevant or material to the charge under investigation.

...

RULES AND REGULATIONS

SEC. 713. (a) The Commission shall have authority from time to time to issue, amend, or rescind suitable procedural regulations to carry out the provisions of this title. Regulations issued under this section shall be in conformity with the standards and limitations of the Administrative Procedure Act.

...

Approved July 2, 1964.

Source: (Pub. L. 88-352), http://www.eeoc.gov/eeoc/history/35th/thelaw/civil_rights_act.html.

As we mentioned in Chapter 1's discussion on the sources of law, agencies are generally created by way of enabling statutes. These statutes set forth the purpose of the agency, the authority by which the agency is created, the powers of the agency, the overall structure of the agency, how it will be governed, and what powers it is granted to carry out its mission including whether it has quasi-legislative and/or judicial power and whether its decisions can be appealed to a court of law. (See Reality Check 4-1, "EEOC Enabling Statute.")

Agencies' rules about carrying on their business is accomplished through **administrative rules** and **regulations.** The general law governing how federal agencies must

EEOC ADMINISTRATIVE RULES AND REGULATION EXCERPTS

In the following excerpts you can see for yourself the regulations setting forth the procedures for EEOC handling its subject area. In particular, these regulations address the matter of how to file a charge of discrimination with the EEOC.

TITLE 29—LABOR
CHAPTER XIV—EQUAL EMPLOYMENT OPPORTUNITY COMMISSION
PART 1601—PROCEDURAL REGULATIONS

Subpart B—Procedure for the Prevention of Unlawful Employment Practices

Sec. 1601.8 Where to make a charge.

A charge may be made in person or by mail at any office of the Commission or with any designated representative of the Commission. The addresses of the Commission's offices appear in Sec. 1610.4.

. . .

Sec. 1601.9 Form of charge.

A charge shall be in writing and signed and shall be verified.

. . .

Sec. 1601.12 Contents of charge; amendment of charge.

(a) Each charge should contain the following:

   (1) The full name, address and telephone number of the person making the charge . . . ;
   (2) The full name and address of the person against whom the charge is made, if known (hereinafter referred to as the respondent);
   (3) A clear and concise statement of the facts, including pertinent dates, constituting the alleged unlawful employment practices . . . ;
   (4) If known, the approximate number of employees of the respondent employer or the approximate number of members of the respondent labor organization, as the case may be; and
   (5) A statement disclosing whether proceedings involving the alleged unlawful employment practice have been commenced before a State or local agency charged with the enforcement of fair employment practice laws and, if so, the date of such commencement and the name of the agency.
(b) Notwithstanding the provisions of paragraph (a) of this section, a charge is sufficient when the Commission receives from the person making the charge a written statement sufficiently precise to identify the parties, and to describe generally the action or practices complained of. A charge may be amended to cure technical defects or omissions, including failure to verify the charge, or to clarify and amplify allegations made therein. Such amendments and amendments alleging additional acts which constitute unlawful employment practices related to or growing out of the subject matter of the original charge will relate back to the date the charge was first received. A charge that has been so amended shall not be required to be redeferred.

Source: 29CFR1601, http://edocket.access.gpo.gov/cfr_2009/julqtr/29cfr1601.12.htm.

conduct business is set forth in the **Administrative Procedures Act.** States generally have such laws also. Each federal agency's own internal rules and regulations are set forth in its administrative regulations published in the **Code of Federal Regulations** (CFR). States have similar administrative schemes. From here on in the chapter, know that while we will address administrative law in the federal context, state administrative law works much the same way. (See Reality Check 4-2, "EEOC Administrative Rules and Regulation Excerpts.")

In addition, the IRS has a compilation of substantive rules and regulations related to collecting taxes and how its regulations are to be interpreted (which many of you may already be more familiar with than you would like from your tax or accounting classes). This is known as the Tax Regulations, or "Tax Regs." As you may know, these regulations are extremely comprehensive, detailed, and extensive. All of this together is IRS's administrative law.

These general categories of (1) the law regulating agencies, (2) the agency's internal regulations for conducting business, and (3) the rules and regulations regarding the specific subject matter of the agency comprise the subject matter of administrative law.

LO2

Since administrative agencies promulgate rules and regulations pursuant to delegations of authority from the governmental entities, their rules and regulations must be complied with just as laws passed by the legislature must be. Since many of those regulations impact business, a knowledge of administrative law is quite important for anyone in business. For instance, since a Federal Trade Commission regulation requires that funeral directors provide prospective clients with a written list of prices for each item of their services from caskets to embalming fluid, then the funeral director must provide such information or be subject to the penalty imposed for violation of the regulation.

EXAMPLE

As you can see, then, from this brief look at IRS, EEOC, and FTC, since there are so many administrative agencies, each with its own rules and procedures and regulations, agencies are a considerable source of law about which a discerning business person needs to know as much as possible in order to be in compliance with whatever agencies' rules and regulations apply to their business. (See Reality Check 4-3, "Selected Administrative Agencies Impacting Business.")

In recent years, as you are no doubt aware, many of the nation's agencies have been tasked with divesting society of the vestiges of historical discrimination and encouraging practices reflecting our country's diversity. Of course, since administrative agencies and their personnel operate in the real world like the rest of us and are a part of society like we are, you may not be surprised to learn how enmeshed in diversity issues they have been in the sense of being part and parcel of the history leading up to the present. Whether it is the U.S. Department of Agriculture admitting its long-standing discrimination, which resulted in the loss of thousands of black farms over the years and entering into the largest settlement in U.S. history for discrimination against black farmers, or the Bureau of Indian Affairs admitting to wrong-doing in administering Native American lands, or the Mississippi Sovereignty Commission owing its existence to being a state-funded agency whose mission was to keep segregation legal, we will see that even something as seemingly dry as administrative law can be full of human drama relevant to diversity issues.

LO3

Creating Administrative Agencies

LO4

As we first mentioned in Chapter 1 while discussing sources of the law, enabling statutes are laws passed by Congress (or state legislatures) delegating some of the legislature's authority to an entity created by the statute. That entity is called an administrative

SELECTED ADMINISTRATIVE AGENCIES IMPACTING BUSINESS

Below is a noncomprehensive list of federal agencies and some of laws they enforce that directly impact business.

Agency	Business Impact
Securities & Exchange Commission	Regulates securities issued by business
Federal Trade Commission	Enforces laws regulating unfair trade practices and unfair competition by business
EEOC	Enforces law prohibiting employers with 15 or more employees from discriminating in the workplace on the basis of race, color, religion, gender, national origin, age, and disability
Occupational Safety & Health Administration	Enforces safe workplace laws
Wage & Hour Division	Enforces minimum wage, overtime, and child labor laws
National Labor Relations Board	Enforces law permitting collective bargaining by employees (unions)
Environmental Protection Agency	Enforces air and water pollution laws
Food & Drug Administration	Enforces safe food and drug laws
U.S. Department of Agriculture	Enforces food safety laws

agency, as we have said. The president can also create executive agencies by executive order, for example the Environmental Protection Agency, the CIA, and the FBI.

The causes leading to creation of administrative agencies often arise from some sort of agitation by the public. Consumer activist and perennial presidential candidate Ralph Nader and his Public Interest Research Group (PIRG) pushed for regulation of, among other things, the auto and food industries. In 1966, this resulted in Congress establishing the National Highway Traffic Safety Administration. Rachel Carson, noted ecologist, was instrumental in making the public aware of the need for regulating the quality of our air and water. We now have the Environmental Protection Agency. Dr. Martin Luther King, Jr., and (now) Rep. John Lewis of Georgia were instrumental in pushing for legal protection against race discrimination resulting in creation of the EEOC. Sometimes the precipitating event is a national tragedy demanding action. The horrors of September 11, 2001, led to President George W. Bush's creation of the Department of Homeland Security after Congress passed the Homeland Security Act of 2002.

The administrative agency does not stand alone and has no authority other than that which Congress delegates to it. The agency operates only under a delegation of authority and, thus, is responsible to its delegator for its actions. It is much like a parent giving a EXAMPLE babysitter authority to care for his children while he is at work. The babysitter is not the parent of the children and is only authorized to do what the parent wishes to have the babysitter do in the parent's absence. While we know that agencies can be formed by presidents, governors, state legislators, federal legislators and others, for simplicity's sake we will discuss the delegator as being Congress.

Congress oversees the delegation of authority by monitoring the agency and making sure it is acting within its delegated authority. No doubt you have heard of Congressional oversight hearings. It is Congress's chance to take a close look at the work that is being done pursuant to its delegation and under its authority and to make sure the agency has adequate funding to accomplish its mission, is not going astray of its mission, and has the authority and tools it needs to be able to effectively do what it was designed to do.

You may also have heard news stories of Congress and an agency being at odds during such oversight hearings. That is because, once created, agencies often take on a life of their own and may wish to operate in ways Congress did not intend. Since the authority delegated to the agency has been granted to Congress pursuant to the Constitution, however, Congress is the one to determine what the agency should and should not do.

In our babysitter example, not only could the babysitter not take the children out of EXAMPLE state on a trip to Disney World without the parent's authority, but also, when the parent gets home from work the parent has a right to know what has taken place in his absence. The administrative agency does not exist apart from Congress and is only in existence to carry out Congress's wishes. Congress has a right to check and make sure this is happening through conducting oversight hearings.

Delegating Administrative Powers

The powers that an agency is given in the enabling statute depends on what the agency is created to do. Sometimes an agency does not need a good deal of authority because it is created merely for overseeing, monitoring, or providing education or investigation in a given area. Other times an agency may need more extensive powers to carry out its mission. Such powers could include the power to promulgate regulations, hold hearing on disputes involving those regulations, or issue subpoenas for documents or access to facilities. When Congress delegates parts of its power and creates agencies through enabling statutes, it also determines what powers the agency will need to accomplish its mission and grants the agency the necessary powers in the enabling statute.

For instance, in the case of the IRS, it has the power both to issue regulations regarding the collection of taxes and to hold hearings regarding disputes over tax collection. It issues tax regulations, and if a taxpayer has a dispute over, say, a nonallowable deduction, the taxpayer can go before an IRS **administrative law judge** to dispute the deduction and have IRS render a decision. See Diversity in the Law 4-1, "The Mississippi State Sovereignty Commission," for a very interesting look at how a state government created an agency to which it granted very broad powers to accomplish a most unusual function. Two years after the U.S. Supreme Court outlawed public school segregation in the United States, Mississippi created an agency whose mission was to protect any further encroachment upon southern states' longtime policy of legal racial segregation.

QUASI-LEGISLATIVE AUTHORITY

L05

Under Article III of the Constitution the primary role of Congress is to enact laws. This power to enact laws rests solely with Congress and may not be delegated to another

THE MISSISSIPPI STATE SOVEREIGNTY COMMISSION

The Mississippi State Sovereignty Commission was a state agency created two years after the *Brown v. Board of Education* case in which the U.S. Supreme Court outlawed racial segregation in public schools. The stated purpose of creating the agency was to "do and perform any and all acts deemed necessary and proper to protect the sovereignty of the state of Mississippi, and her sister states . . . from perceived encroachment thereon by the Federal Government or any branch, department or agency thereof." The agency was given extensive investigative powers, including subpoena power, had a budget, and had as ex-officio members granted a seat on the Commission purely because of their position, the governor as chairman, president of the Senate as vice-chairman, the attorney general and speaker of the House of Representatives. The Commission also had two members from the Senate appointed by president of the Senate and three members from the House of Representatives appointed by the Speaker. The agency had a director, a public relations director, clerical staff, and investigators.

Over the course of its life as an agency, the agency used investigators and paid informers to gather information on civil rights activity in the state. It worked to stop passage of the Civil Rights Act of 1964, created a speakers' bureau to travel nationwide to give Mississippi's version of segregation, created and distributed segregationist tracts, funded all-white Citizens' Councils created to retain segregation, and even provided funds to help get conservative (or scared) blacks to register to vote so that they would side with the segregationists. When the agency was made defunct in 1977, its records were ordered sealed, under penalty of law, for 50 years until 2027.

The Mississippi ACLU filed suit to have the records released because it alleged there was unauthorized surveillance of citizens. After a 21-year fight, the records were opened in 1998 and are now available in digital form online. They make fascinating reading. The records led to the discovery of the background surrounding the slaying of civil rights workers James Cheney, Michael Shwerner, and Andrew Goodman in 1964 for their civil rights work in trying to register voters in Mississippi and investigating a suspicious church fire. The information formed the basis for the Hollywood movie, "Mississippi Burning."

Source: Mississippi Department of Archives and History, http://mdah.state.ms.us/arrec/digital_archives/sovcom/scagencycasehistory.php.

body. If Congress grants an agency the authority to issue regulations, the agency is said to have *quasi*-**legislative** authority. The term quasi means "like" or "as if." The agency can use its quasi-legislative authority to promulgate rules and regulations within the area over which it is granted authority. See Reality Check 4-4, "Title IX," for the statutory language granting such authority to the Department of Education's Office of Civil Rights for effectuating Title IX of the Equal Opportunity in Education Act that prohibits, among other things, gender discrimination in school sports.

The fact that the rule or regulation is promulgated under quasi-legislative power does not make the regulation any less effective as a dictate that must be followed much like law. The agency rules and regulations, while not actual legislative or statutory law, are similar to it and for all practical purposes carry the same weight in the sense that violation of a regulation carries legal consequences.

L06

An important aspect of the regulatory power of administrative agencies is receiving input from affected constituents about rules and regulations proposed by the agency. The Administrative Procedures Act sets forth certain requirements with which federal administrative agencies must comply in order to ensure that the agency's rules and regulations can withstand judicial scrutiny if challenged in court as unconstitutional.

L07

The federal government is constitutionally required by the Fifth Amendment (and states by the Fourteenth) to provide **due process of law** if there is the possibility of depriving a citizen of a right. Administrative agencies are acting on behalf of the government, therefore without due process citizens cannot be deprived of rights to which they would otherwise be entitled when dealing with the government.

At a minimum, due process involves notice and an opportunity to be heard. The purpose of the APA is to ensure that those affected by the rules and regulations of administrative agencies are provided with such notice and opportunity to be heard before rules or regulations are passed by the agency that may adversely impact their interests. If an agency does not adhere to the APA requirements regarding appropriate notice and an opportunity to be heard, the agency's decisions can be nullified as unconstitutional by a court of law. Notice and opportunity to be heard does not mean that the administrative

TITLE IX

In this box you get to see the language that created the delegation of authority from Congress to have Title IX effectuated through granting the authority to issue regulations. You probably know Title IX as the law that prohibits discrimination in sports on the basis of gender for schools receiving federal funds. The law, named for its principal sponsor, Rep. Patsy Mink, did not actually mention sports, but that is the primary context in which we now know the law.

P.L. 92-318, Approved June 23, 1972 (86 Stat. 235)

Education Amendments of 1972

* * * * * * *

TITLE IX—PATSY TAKEMOTO MINK

EQUAL OPPORTUNITY IN EDUCATION ACT

SEX DISCRIMINATION PROHIBITED

FEDERAL ADMINISTRATIVE ENFORCEMENT

Sec. 902. [20 U.S.C. 1682]

Each Federal department and agency which is empowered to extend Federal financial assistance to any education program or activity, by way of grant, loan, or contract other than a contract of insurance or guaranty, *is authorized* and directed *to effectuate the provisions of section 901* with respect to such program or activity *by issuing rules, regulations, or orders* of general applicability which shall be consistent with achievement of the objectives of the statute authorizing the financial assistance in connection with which the action is taken. . . . [italics added]

agency cannot do what it thinks best. Rather, it means that the agency will not unconstitutionally be operating in the dark to the disadvantage of those who may be adversely affected by its actions.

For instance, when the Federal Trade Commission decided to address the issue of unfair trade practices in the funeral industry, it was required under the APA to publish in the **Federal Register** a **notice of proposed rulemaking** about the issue, publish the proposed rules (notice), request input from members of the industry (opportunity to be heard), and consider that input before deciding on final rules. (See Reality Check 4-5, "Federal Trade Commission Funeral Regulations.") The notice must be appropriate to the action being taken by the agency. The more the public stands to lose, the more notice and opportunity to be heard is provided. For instance, less notice may be appropriate if an agency is only exploring whether it should issue regulations rather than if the notice is to inform an individual or business that they have violated an agency regulation and a citation issued. In the American Airlines Case 4.1, the airline argued that it did not receive sufficient notice of an agency's informal adjudication. The court held the agency's notice to be sufficient under the circumstances. See if you agree.

Even though the FTC regulations in Reality Check 4-5 primarily address notifying consumers of prices for services, you can see how funeral directors who had not heretofore been conducting business the way the rules now require (virtually all of them) were upset when these regulations were imposed on their industry. The rules were issued

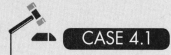

CASE 4.1 American Airlines, Inc. v. Department of Transportation

202 F.3d 788 (5th Cir. 2000)

Facts: The Department of Transportation issued a declaratory order after it held an informal adjudication which it had notified the parties would take place and provided them an opportunity for them to comment on the issues at hand. The airline challenged the declaratory order on the basis that, among other things, it violated the Administrative Procedure Act by failing to provide them with sufficient notice.

Issue: Whether it was sufficient notice of an informal agency adjudication for an agency to provide the parties with an order detailing the issues to be reviewed and allowing submission of written comment.

Decision: Yes

Reasoning: Garza, J.: While the APA does not expressly require notice in informal adjudication, courts have inferred a requirement that there be "some sort of procedures for

notice [and] comment . . . as a necessary means of carrying out our responsibility for a thorough and searching review [of agency action]." Here, DOT issued an order in which it specified the legal issues on which it would rule, allowed the parties to submit comments on these issues, and extended the comment period at the request of several parties. It then ruled on precisely the issues that it identified. We find that DOT's actions satisfied the minimum procedural notice requirements. We AFFIRM DOT's orders.

CASE QUESTIONS

1. Does it seem that there was sufficient due process here? Explain.
2. Would you have thought an adjudication, even informal, would mean a hearing at which the parties could present evidence?
3. Does this outcome surprise you? Explain.

after hearings indicated that bereaved families were being taken advantage of at their most vulnerable time, while making arrangements after the death of a loved one, and the regulations were an attempt to at least provide them with notice about services being offered by their funeral director.

We provided you with Reality Check 4-5 about the funeral business for several reasons: (1) We want you to see what actual administrative regulatory language looks like; (2) we want you to see how intricately the regulatory process affects business and understand why it is so important for a business to be aware of the regulatory process and know how to be informed and interface with it; (3) we want to demonstrate to you how intimately administrative regulations can impact our lives; and (4) we want you to understand what a business can miss by not regularly reading the Federal Register or belonging to an organization that provides information about the industry in which the business operates.

The Federal Register is the "official daily publication for rules, proposed rules, and notices of Federal agencies and organizations, as well as executive orders and other presidential documents,"[1] loaded with all sorts of information that we as business people are responsible for knowing (which constitutes proper statutory notice) but about which many of us are clueless.

QUASI-JUDICIAL AUTHORITY

An agency may also be granted **quasi-judicial** authority in its enabling statute and have the power to hear and decide disputes involving agency regulations. These

---

[1]From the Federal Register website, http://www.gpoaccess.gov/fr/index.html.

agency decisions also become quasi-judicial law binding on the agency in its future decisions. For instance if our mortician is cited for unfair or deceptive practices for violation of the FTC regulation requiring that he provide certain information about service costs to prospective clients, the mortician will be allowed an opportunity to contest the citation in proceedings before the FTC, usually before an administrative law judge. Under FTC regulations, if the mortician is not satisfied with the determination, he can proceed to the next step of the agency's review process. Like most court systems, this is generally a three-level process, ending in review by those who head the administrative agency.

In our opening scenario about Matthew and his empanadas, the agency that has given Matthew a citation and requested him to appear clearly must have some measure of quasi-judicial authority since he has the right to an opportunity to be heard. Matthew has evidently violated rules and regulations that he apparently did not know existed involving the serving of food for commercial purposes. This is why it is so important for those in business to check for administrative regulations before beginning their business. It can save much time and trouble to check to see if there are regulations which a business must be aware of and conform to, before starting up.

Many businesses address this issue by belonging to trade organizations composed of those in the same business or industry. The trade organization generally monitors relevant agencies for actions impacting the organization's members and notifies them when issues arise. The organization also serves the important function of organizing itself and its members to respond to pending agency actions. They may even have lobbyists who lobby legislators or agency personnel on their behalf. Some familiar trade associations are the American Bar Association, the American Medical Association, the American Manufacturing Association, and so on. Unions may also serve a similar function for their members, notifying them and rallying them around issues important to the union's members. You saw this phenomenon in action when the Health Care legislation was being considered in Congress in 2010. Trade and professional organizations of all types related to the medical and related fields rushed to comment on what the proposed legislation would mean to their business.

JUDICIAL REVIEW

In most cases, enabling statutes that grant an agency the authority to hear and decide agency disputes will also provide for **judicial review** of those decisions. That is, the law will grant the agency authority to have courts hear and decide cases arising from agency decisions once the litigant **exhausts administrative remedies** as set forth under the agency's regulations. Exhaustion means the claimant has done all he or she can do within the agency's regulatory structure and is still not satisfied with the outcome and wishes to take the matter to a court of law. The enabling statute will set forth the court in which the agency's final administrative decision may be pursued (i.e., federal court) and at what level of court it will be permitted to be heard (i.e., district court level or appellate court level). In our opening scenario example, if Matthew responds to the agency citation hearing and does not like the outcome, he may be able to seek judicial review of the decision in a court after exhausting his administrative remedies, depending on the agency's regulations.

Some enabling statutes permit courts to have only **limited review** of administrative decisions upon judicial review. That is, the administrative agency's final decision may only be reviewed at the appellate level by a court of appeals. Such a review is limited to the reviewing court ensuring that the agency's decision is not unconstitutional, not in violation of its legislatively granted authority, and not fraudulent, arbitrary, capricious or otherwise not in accordance with law. If the

FEDERAL TRADE COMMISSION FUNERAL REGULATIONS

Title 16: Commercial Practices

PART 453—FUNERAL INDUSTRY PRACTICES

Authority: 15 U.S.C. 57a(a); 15 U.S.C. 46(g); 5 U.S.C. 552.

Source: 59 FR 1611, Jan. 11, 1994, unless otherwise noted.

§ 453.2 Price disclosures.

(a) *Unfair or deceptive acts or practices.* In selling or offering to sell funeral goods or funeral services to the public, it is an unfair or deceptive act or practice for a funeral provider to fail to furnish accurate price information disclosing the cost to the purchaser for each of the specific funeral goods and funeral services used in connection with the disposition of deceased human bodies, including at least the price of embalming, transportation of remains, use of facilities, caskets, outer burial containers, immediate burials, or direct cremations, to persons inquiring about the purchase of funerals. Any funeral provider who complies with the preventive requirements in paragraph (b) of this section is not engaged in the unfair or deceptive acts or practices defined here.

(b) *Preventive requirements.* To prevent these unfair or deceptive acts or practices, as well as the unfair or deceptive acts or practices defined in §453.4(b)(1), funeral providers must:

(1) *Telephone price disclosure.* Tell persons who ask by telephone about the funeral provider's offerings or prices any accurate information from the price lists described in paragraphs (b)(2) through (4) of this section and any other readily available information that reasonably answers the question.

(2) *Casket price list.* (i) Give a printed or typewritten price list to people who inquire in person about the offerings or prices of caskets or alternative containers. The funeral provider must offer the list upon beginning discussion of, but in any event before showing caskets. The list must contain at least the retail prices of all caskets and alternative containers offered which do not require special ordering, enough information to identify each, and the effective date for the price list. In lieu of a written list, other formats, such as notebooks, brochures, or charts may be used if they contain the same information as would the printed or typewritten list, and display it in a clear and conspicuous manner. Provided, however, that funeral providers do not have to make a casket price list available if the funeral providers place on the general price list, specified in paragraph (b)(4) of this section, the information required by this paragraph.

(ii) Place on the list, however produced, the name of the funeral provider's place of business and a caption describing the list as a "casket price list."

(3) *Outer burial container price list.* (i) Give a printed or typewritten price list to persons who inquire in person about outer burial container offerings or prices. The funeral provider must offer the list upon beginning discussion of, but in any event before showing the containers. The list must contain at least the retail prices of all outer burial containers offered which do not require special ordering, enough information to identify each container, and the effective date for the prices listed. In lieu of a written list, the funeral provider may use other formats, such as notebooks, brochures, or charts, if they contain the same information as the printed or typewritten list, and display it in a clear and conspicuous manner. Provided, however, that funeral providers do not have to make an outer burial container price list available if the funeral providers place on the general price list, specified in paragraph (b)(4) of this section, the information required by this paragraph.

(ii) Place on the list, however produced, the name of the funeral provider's place of business and a caption describing the list as an "outer burial container price list."

(4) *General price list.* (i)(A) Give a printed or typewritten price list for retention to persons who inquire in person about the funeral goods, funeral services or prices of funeral goods or services offered by the funeral provider. The funeral provider must give the list upon beginning discussion of any of the following:

(*1*) The prices of funeral goods or funeral services;

(*2*) The overall type of funeral service or disposition; or

(*3*) Specific funeral goods or funeral services offered by the funeral provider.

(B) The requirement in paragraph (b)(4)(i)(A) of this section applies whether the discussion takes place in the funeral home or elsewhere. Provided, however, that when the deceased is removed for transportation to the funeral home, an in-person request at that time for authorization to embalm, required by §453.5(a)(2), does not, by itself, trigger the requirement to offer the general price list if the provider in seeking prior embalming approval discloses that embalming is not required by law except in certain special cases, if any. Any other discussion during that time about prices or the selection of funeral goods or services triggers the requirement under paragraph (b)(4)(i)(A) of this section to give consumers a general price list.

(C) The list required in paragraph (b)(4)(i)(A) of this section must contain at least the following information:

(*1*) The name, address, and telephone number of the funeral provider's place of business;

(*2*) A caption describing the list as a "general price list"; and

(*3*) The effective date for the price list;

(ii) Include on the price list, in any order, the retail prices (expressed either as the flat fee, or as the price per hour, mile or other unit of computation) and the other information specified below for at least each of the following items, if offered for sale:

(A) Forwarding of remains to another funeral home, together with a list of the services provided for any quoted price;

(B) Receiving remains from another funeral home, together with a list of the services provided for any quoted price;

(C) The price range for the direct cremations offered by the funeral provider, together with:

(1) A separate price for a direct cremation where the purchaser provides the container;

(2) Separate prices for each direct cremation offered including an alternative container; and

(3) A description of the services and container (where applicable), included in each price;

(D) The price range for the immediate burials offered by the funeral provider, together with:

(1) A separate price for an immediate burial where the purchaser provides the casket;

(2) Separate prices for each immediate burial offered including a casket or alternative container; and

(3) A description of the services and container (where applicable) included in that price;

(E) Transfer of remains to funeral home;

(F) Embalming;

(G) Other preparation of the body;

(H) Use of facilities and staff for viewing;

(I) Use of facilities and staff for funeral ceremony;

(J) Use of facilities and staff for memorial service;

(K) Use of equipment and staff for graveside service;

(L) Hearse; and

(M) Limousine.

(iii) Include on the price list, in any order, the following information:

(A) Either of the following:

(1) The price range for the caskets offered by the funeral provider, together with the statement: "A complete price list will be provided at the funeral home."; or

(2) The prices of individual caskets, disclosed in the manner specified by paragraph (b)(2)(i) of this section; and

(B) Either of the following:

(1) The price range for the outer burial containers offered by the funeral provider, together with the statement: "A complete price list will be provided at the funeral home."; or

(2) The prices of individual outer burial containers, disclosed in the manner specified by paragraph (b)(3)(i) of this section; and

(C) Either of the following:

(1) The price for the basic services of funeral director and staff, together with a list of the principal basic services provided for any quoted price and, if the charge cannot be declined by the purchaser, the statement: "This fee for our basic services will be added to the total cost of the funeral arrangements you select. (This fee is already included in our charges for direct cremations, immediate burials, and forwarding or receiving remains.)". If the charge cannot be declined by the purchaser, the quoted price shall include all charges for the recovery of unallocated funeral provider overhead, and funeral providers may include in the required disclosure the phrase "and overhead" after the word "services"; or

(2) The following statement: "Please note that a fee of (specify dollar amount) for the use of our basic services is included in the price of our caskets. This same fee shall be added to the total cost of your funeral arrangements if you provide the casket. Our services include (specify)." The fee shall include all charges for the recovery of unallocated funeral provider overhead, and funeral providers may include in the required disclosure the phrase "and overhead" after the word "services." The statement must be placed on the general price list together with the casket price range, required by paragraph (b)(4)(iii)(A)(1) of this section, or together with the prices of individual caskets, required by (b)(4)(iii)(A)(2) of this section.

(iv) The services fee permitted by §453.2(b)(4)(iii)(C)(1) or (C)(2) is the only funeral provider fee for services, facilities or unallocated overhead permitted by this part to be non-declinable, unless otherwise required by law.

(5) *Statement of funeral goods and services selected.* (i) Give an itemized written statement for retention to each person who arranges a funeral or other disposition of human remains, at the conclusion of the discussion of arrangements. The statement must list at least the following information:

(A) The funeral goods and funeral services selected by that person and the prices to be paid for each of them;

(B) Specifically itemized cash advance items. (These prices must be given to the extent then known or reasonably ascertainable. If the prices are not known or reasonably ascertainable, a good faith estimate shall be given and a written statement of the actual charges shall be provided before the final bill is paid.); and

(C) The total cost of the goods and services selected.

(ii) The information required by this paragraph (b)(5) may be included on any contract, statement, or other document which the funeral provider would otherwise provide at the conclusion of discussion of arrangements.

(6) *Other pricing methods.* Funeral providers may give persons any other price information, in any other format, in addition to that required by §453.2(b)(2), (3), and (4) so long as the statement required by §453.2(b)(5) is given when required by the rule.

CASE 4.2 Miami Nation of Indians of
Indiana v. Babbit

979 F. Supp. 771; 1996 U.S. Dist. LEXIS 21644 (N.D. IN. 1996)

Facts: The Miami Nation Native Americans sought recognition by the U.S. government of status as an Indian tribe so that they could deal with the government as government-to-government. The Miami Nation petitioned for recognition with the U.S. Department of the Interior in 1980 and the petition for recognition was rejected in 1990. In seeking judicial review of the Department's decision to deny recognition, the Nation wished to have the entire administrative record used to deny recognition submitted for review, including notes, comments, drafts, logs and internal directives. The Department refused to include certain requested items and the Miami Nation sought judicial review of the agency's decision to refuse to include certain items into the administrative record.

Issue: Whether an administrative record used to review an agency decision is subject to judicial review.

Decision: Yes

Reasoning: Robert L. Miller, Jr., J.: Under the Administrative Procedures Act ("APA"), the court ultimately reviews the agency's action in this case to determine if it was "arbitrary, capricious, an abuse of discretion, or otherwise not in accordance with law." The APA directs that "in making the foregoing determination, the court shall review the whole record or those parts of it cited by a party." The parties dispute whether the agency has produced the "whole record."

Generally, judicial review of agency action is limited to review of the administrative record. In the present case, it appears that the exhibits attached to the federal defendants' motion do not comprise the entire administrative record. Further, it would be improper for this court to allow the federal defendants to determine unilaterally what shall constitute the administrative record and thereby limit the scope of the court's inquiry. For that reason, plaintiffs are entitled to discover any materials, including internal memoranda, guidelines, or hearing transcripts, that are necessary to complete the administrative record. Motion GRANTED IN PART.

CASE QUESTIONS

1. Do you understand why an agency might not wish to include all the documents it used to make a decision?

2. Do you think it makes sense for someone who had an agency decide against him or her to wish to see all the information that was used to make the decision?

3. Do you agree with the court that the decision as to what constitutes the administrative record should not be left solely to the administrative agency? Explain.

administrative agency's decision is none of these, then the agency's decision stands. In the *Miami Nation of Indians of Indiana* Case 4.2, the court used this standard to review an agency decision to withhold certain documents from the administrative record on appeal.

A statute may instead grant a reviewing court ***de novo* review** of an administrative agency's decision. Since ***de novo*** means "like new," this review is much broader. *De novo* judicial review allows the administrative decision to be brought to court at the trial court level where the parties begin litigation all over again as if there has not already been an agency decision. This trial court decision can then be appealed up through the various appellate levels of the court system if it complies with applicable procedural requirements. In Reality Check 4-6, you can see the judicial review provision of the Title IX statute we discussed previously.

ENFORCEMENT OF ADMINISTRATIVE AGENCY ORDERS

If an administrative agency issues a final order in an adjudication, the order will have full force and effect only if the order is enforced by a court of law. Remember that the Constitution rests judicial authority in the courts and an agency performing quasi-judicial

TITLE IX

P.L. 92-318, Approved June 23, 1972 (86 Stat. 235)

Education Amendments of 1972

* * * * * * *

TITLE IX—PATSY TAKEMOTO MINK

EQUAL OPPORTUNITY IN EDUCATION ACT

SEX DISCRIMINATION PROHIBITED

JUDICIAL REVIEW

Sec. 903. [20 U.S.C. 1683]

Any department or agency action taken pursuant to section 1002 shall be subject to such judicial review as may otherwise be provided by law for similar action taken by such department or agency on other grounds. In the case of action, not otherwise subject to judicial review, terminating or refusing to grant or to continue financial assistance upon a finding of failure to comply with any requirement imposed pursuant to section 902, any person aggrieved (including any State or political subdivision thereof and any agency of either) may obtain judicial review of such action in accordance with chapter 7 of title 5, United States Code, and such action shall not be deemed committed to unreviewable agency discretion within the meaning of section 701 of that title. [italics provided]

functions does not constitutionally have the final say to enforce its order since it is not a court of law. The effect of this move is to take the issue out of the purview of the agency, with its limited authority, and give it the full force and effect of law as issued by a more comprehensive court of law. But take a look at Reality Check 4-7 to see what happens when the agency itself is sued.

Administrative Regulations and Business

L03

Since many state, federal, and local regulations involve business matters, it is extremely important for those in business to know how administrative agencies work and how to provide input into the agencies' regulatory processes. Administrative agencies routinely promulgate rules and regulations affecting business. Under the Administrative Procedures Act, these regulations generally must undergo a period of seeking input from those likely to be affected by the regulation. Different types of rules and regulations have different levels of input, ranging from writing letters in response to the proposed rule or regulation, to testifying at full administrative hearings held on the proposed rules or regulations. Being aware of the agency's existing and proposed rules and regulations is imperative if they relate to an individual's business.

Business owners' participation in the administrative process in whatever way that is permitted by the administrative agency is very important. An agency may propose rules

BUREAU OF INDIAN AFFAIRS SUED FOR MISHANDLING TRUST RECORDS

The Bureau of Indian Affairs is a federal agency under the U.S. Department of the Interior. The mission of the BIA "is to enhance the quality of life, to promote economic opportunity, and to carry out the responsibility to protect and improve the trust assets of American Indians, Indian tribes and Alaska Natives." Part of the responsibilities of the BIA is to manage Indian trust accounts which are set up to administer 66 million acres of land held in trust for Native Americans, including Alaska natives. For several years now, the BIA has been involved in a legal battle with Native American tribes who sued the BIA for $100 billion, alleging that the BIA has terribly mishandled the trust accounts, resulting in significant loss of revenue for the Native Americans while masses of Native Americans languish on reservations in grinding poverty. It was alleged that, among other things, there were dozens of years of money not being collected by BIA from companies for pumping oil and gas on reservation land, losing Native Americans billions of dollars in revenue, money belonging to individuals and tribes being deposited into slush funds with phony names, and fraud, theft and embezzlement by federal personnel on Indian reservations, with little prosecution. BIA has admitted to mishandling trust accounts and over 70 government reports have reported on it over the years. There are nearly 100 cases pending, but one of the largest, *Cobell v. Salazar,* 573 F.3d 808 (D.C. Cir. 2009) was settled for $3.4 billion in December 2009 after 14 years of litigation. Congress and the court must still sign off on the settlement. On May 28, 2010, the House voted to pay the money. On July 22, 2010, the Senate voted to remove the payment provision from a funding bill for the war in the Middle East, so the payment for both the Native Americans as well as the black farmers under the USDA settlement mentioned earlier and included in the same funding legislation remained unpaid. On August 5, 2010, the Senate, for the seventh time, refused to fund the court-ordered settlement by failing to pass several unanimous consent measures. The other cases are still ongoing.

Does this sound to you like the BIA or USDA agencies were doing the jobs they were created to do? Given what you now know about administrative law, how do you think they managed to get away with it? What steps could be taken to correct the situation? What do you think of the ethics of the U.S. government entering into a settlement with groups and promising to pay out funds that it then does not pay them? Think about the relevant stakeholders and their interests. Be expansive. Rather than thinking about just the parties involved, think about the message this sends to others about the government and how sound its word is, or foreign governments seeing the federal government's treatment of its established legal obligations. Where would this money come from? How do private citizens who cannot pay a judgment or settlement manage? Should it be different for the government? Does it matter that these are two groups that have a long history of being the objects of discrimination and ill treatment? Do you think the outcome would be different if the groups were someone else, say, a group of bankers or a group of Texas oil well owners? What would make the difference, if any?

Sources: http://www.doi.gov/bia/; Dwyer Arce, "U.S. Senate Fails to Approve Minority Farmer Settlement, *Jurist,* August 6, 2010, http://jurist.org/paperchase/2010/08/us-senate-fails-to-approve-minority-farmer-settlement.php; Charles D. Ellison, "Shirley Sherrod, Black Farmers and the 2010 Racial World Cup," *The Huffington Post,* August 9, 2010, http://www.huffingtonpost.com/charles-d-ellison/shirley-sherrod-black-far_b_658392.html; Melody L. McCoy, "Tribal Trust Funds Accounting and Mismanagement Litigation," http://www.law.ku.edu/academics/triballaw/pdfs/McCoy_CLE.pdf; Charlie Savage, "U.S. Will Settle Indian Lawsuit for $3.4 Billion," *New York Times,* December 8, 2009, http://www.nytimes.com/2009/12/09/us/09tribes.html?_r=1&scp=2&sq=charlie%20savage&st=cse; and Shannon Dininny, "Mistrust Remains, Landowners Wonder if Conclusion Is Real after $3.4B Indian Trust Settlement," *Political News,* May 29, 2010, http://blog.taragana.com/politics/2010/05/29/mistrust-remains-landowners-wonder-if-conclusion-is-real-after-34b-indian-trust-settlement-40051/.

that would virtually wipe out an individual's business. Being able to provide input to the agency about the impact the proposed regulation would have on the business is an important aspect of protecting the business. It is important for the business owner to have a means of having his or her business interests heard and represented. Ordinarily it is our elected representatives who pass laws and we express our views to our legislators and hope they vote accordingly. With administrative rules and regulations it is the administrative agency that determines the final regulation. The agency personnel are not elected officials and thus are not accountable to the public in the same way elected officials are. This is, in part, why the APA is so important. It protects the public by ensuring that agency proceedings and actions are public so that input into the process by those whose interests may be affected can occur.

It can seem overwhelming for a business owner, especially a small business owner, to keep up with new rules and regulations that so many administrative agencies promulgate. Again, one of the primary reasons for belonging to a trade association is that the associations have people whose sole job it is to keep abreast of the legislative

THE ADMINISTRATIVE PROCESS IN ACTION

Ronald Kantor doesn't have high-minded ideas about the environment. To him, clean means green—as in dollars.

Kantor is owner of Leather-Rich Inc., in Oconomowoc, Wisconsin, a dry-cleaning business that specializes in leather. He opened a new plant in a 29,000-square-foot building, equipped with the latest machinery to clean clothing without spewing chemicals into the air, water, or soil.

Regulations by states and the Environmental Protection Agency covering proper use and disposal of dry-cleaning fluids have tightened, as concern about the environment has increased. In some states, dry cleaners have been sued because of solvent leaks or air pollution.

"The laws were changing to meet the needs of society," he says. "I felt that if I were to put into a business real money—and we're talking a couple million dollars—I had to do things to protect my investment. We can't sell our business or even pass it on to our children without the worry that the business will be sued for past transgressions."

To avoid such problems, Kantor hired an environmental lawyer, worked with a builder and a manufacturer, and came up with "a plant that's built for the future."

Starting from the ground and working up, Kantor had the floor dug out to a depth of three feet, then put down a heavy plastic liner, covered it with sand, and laid pipes over it. The liner is there to protect the soil and groundwater in the event a pipe breaks and spills chemicals. "This plant sits on an aquifer," Kantor says. "We had to protect the water."

Eight dry-cleaning machines use a "dry-to-dry" system in which all the solvents used are encapsulated within the machinery, cooled, and extracted from garments before they're removed. "The whole dry-cleaning machine is completely enclosed," Kantor says. "No stacks release fumes to the atmosphere." Other machinery removes volatile gases from the water, so that whatever goes into the sewer system is clean. "Our neighbors, their children, our customers can all rest assured we're doing everything we can," he says.

But it's expensive. The sad truth, he says, is "there are trade-offs. The environmental things we're talking about cost money."

Source: © 1994, *USA Today*. Reprinted with permission.

and regulatory interests of their members. The dues paid to such an association are well worth it if paying them results in keeping the business owner abreast of important legal and regulatory changes that may seriously impact the owner's business interests.

Reality Check 4-8, "The Administrative Process in Action," is an example of how agency regulations impact something as commonplace as a dry-cleaning business.

Summary

In this chapter we have discussed the purpose and structure of administrative agencies, what they can and cannot do, how business interests are impacted by administrative rules and regulations, and how businesses can interface with such agencies to make sure their interests are taken into account when the agency creates rules and regulations impacting business. In addition, we also saw how administrative agencies are subject to the same types of diversity considerations in carrying out their missions as the rest of business and society.

Review Questions

1. Andrea operates a commercial shrimping business. Andrea is cited and fined for failure to have certain safety equipment on board her vessel in violation of a federal regulation. Andrea opposes the citation, stating that it is a denial of due process to cite her for violating the regulation since she was unaware of the existence of the regulation and the regulation operated a hardship on her shrimping business. Will Andrea's argument be likely to prevail? LO6

2. Administrative rules and regulations are the same as laws. True or False? Explain. LO5

3. When Simeon decided to bake his fancy cakes for special occasions and sell them to select customers, Simeon's friend Sam tells Simeon that Simeon

cannot do this without using a commercial baking facility. What should Simeon do? LO3

4. Due process requires that an agency must hold hearings and allow interested persons to testify before the agency can promulgate rules or regulations. True or False? LO7

5. When an agency decision is reviewed by a court, *de novo* review means the reviewing court can only review the agency's decision to determine if it is

   a. arbitrary

   b. capricious

   c. not in accordance with law

   d. all of the above

   e. none of the above

6. Wayne is issued a citation by an agency for something he says he did not do. He had a hearing before an administrative law judge who determined that Wayne did the act and the citation was justified. Wayne, angry, goes to his lawyer and tells him to take the matter to court. Will the attorney do so? Explain.

Ethics Issue

After the April 2010 explosion of the Deep Water Horizon oil rig in the Gulf of Mexico, it became apparent that the oil companies were too cozy with the Minerals Management Service agency responsible for regulating the industry, including the MMS personnel accepting gifts from oil industry friends, trips to the Peach Bowl, hunting and fishing vacations, skeet shooting, and crawfish boils. One MMS employee was conducting an inspection for a company while negotiating a job with the company. MMS inspectors allowed company personnel to fill out their own inspection reports in pencil, then MMS inspectors would write on top of the pencil in ink. Discuss the ethics of an administrative agency engaging in such a relationship with those the agency regulated.

Group Exercise

Choose an area you would like to know something about. See if you can find administrative rules and regulations about that issue. You might want to use the list below to spur your thinking. After looking into your area, decide if you find any surprises.

The recording industry
CD lyric warning labels
Food sanitation in restaurants
Food sanitation in manufacturing
Establishing colleges
Starting a business
Becoming a minister
Becoming a lawyer
Becoming a nurse
Becoming a real estate agent
Water restrictions

Car emission standards
Having a neighborhood block party
Owning a domesticated animal
Owning a wild animal
Getting a commercial driver's license
Becoming a beautician, barber or cosmetician
Getting a restaurant liquor license
Acquiring a handicap sticker for a car
Starting a day care center
Home schooling

Key Terms

Contracts and Sales

Learning Objectives

After reading this chapter, you should be able to:

L01 List the two sources of contract law

L02 Define a contract and what it is designed to do

L03 Explain the difference between the various classifications of contracts

L04 Describe the remedies available for breach of contract

L05 Explain the requirements for a valid contract

L06 Define mutual assent and know what comprises it

L07 List and explain at least five bases for termination of offers

L08 Distinguish between acceptance under the UCC and the Restatement

L09 Explain what is and is not sufficient consideration to support a contract

L010 Discuss the various ways parties can lack capacity to contract

L011 List several bases for contracts lacking legality and the impact of such

L012 Distinguish between the Statute of Frauds and the Parol Evidence Rule

L013 Distinguish between assignment and delegation of contracts

L014 Explain whether one not a party to a contact can still benefit therefrom

L015 Analyze conditions impact contract performance

Opening Scenario

Ed offered to sell his car to Mike for $1500. Mike came over to Ed's house with his mechanic brother to look over the car. The two looked over the car and drove it around for hours. Mike finally decided to buy the car and asked Ed if he would take $1000 for the car. Ed said no, only $1500, and Mike gave Ed the $1500. Two days later, Mike calls Ed and angrily tells him that the car's engine is giving him trouble. Mike demands that Ed give him at least $500 of the money back and says that if he doesn't get it, "he knows where Ed lives and he has friends." Must Ed return the $500 to Mike? Does either have a sufficient basis for a breach of contract action?

Introduction and Overview

Entered into any good contracts lately? You would not be able to be in this class or even at your school without entering into one. In fact, you would not even be able to have this book in your hands if not for a contract. Any time we have someone perform a service for us (unless it is a gift or favor) or we buy things, a contract is formed. So while you may think you haven't entered into a contract lately, it's a pretty good bet that you have. You did so when you took your clothes to the cleaners, got your hair cut or styled, purchased your groceries, ordered a drink at the club last weekend, arranged for your cable TV, filled your gas tank at the local pump, picked up food at the drive-thru, or paid your tuition. If you went to a restaurant and ordered a burger and fries and the meal was brought to you on a plate, still frozen, and the server handed you a check, requested payment, and said brightly, "Have a nice day!," you would quickly realize that you had a contract that included a set of expectations about what the meal would be. Further, you would expect that if those expectations were not met because the food was not cooked, you would not have to pay.

In this chapter we will learn what it takes to enter into legally enforceable agreements, how to create them, how to avoid problems with them, and what to do when contracts must be enforced because they have been breached. You will also see how diversity issues can come into play when dealing with something as seemingly objective as contracts. You were introduced to this in Chapter 1 when reading about blacks being targeted for sub-prime loans that often resulted in foreclosure of their homes. Of course, since contracts are based on promises to perform, usually in exchange for money, ethical issues obviously arise when one person or one corporation or business wants to take advantage of another.

LO2

As we discussed briefly in Chapter 1 regarding areas of law, a contract is a voluntary promise between two or more parties for which the law will provide a remedy for nonperformance. Now you can better understand why in Chapter 1, the Valley Swim Club evicting the black and Hispanic campers from the club after a contract was made and the camp paid its $1950 membership fee was not a legally smart thing to do, aside from any ethical or diversity considerations. The club's returning the money to the camp director and telling her that the camp's membership was revoked was a breach of contract.

You can see how important contracts are to business. Business owners must purchase goods and services and provide goods or services to others and be paid for them as a source of business revenue. They need to have a means of ensuring that when they make agreements to receive or to render goods or services, then there will be a way to obtain redress if the promise is not kept. The way in which they address it is through the law of contracts. Without contracts we would have no way to make sure that what we have agreed to with someone will, in fact, occur and if it does not we will be compensated.

Think about how basic and important contracts are to our lives and to business and then realize that it took an act of Congress to allow African Americans the right to contract. (See Diversity in the Law 5-1, "Giving Blacks the Right to Contract.") The law that allowed them to have access to the courts (which they did not have before) also gave them the same right to contract "as enjoyed by white citizens." Women also had only a limited right to contract at one point in our history and it had to be accomplished through a husband, father, or male guardian.

But there are still indications that the right to contract and what goes into the contract and its performance can be quite different. You may have heard the news stories of the insurance companies that admitted that for decades they routinely charged African Americans more than whites for the same life insurance without any actuarial basis. (See Diversity in the Law 5-2, "Racial Discrimination in Insurance Contracts.") Companies obtained these contracts by selling the burial policies door-to-door to poor blacks (including your author's grandparents) by impressing upon them the importance of not burdening their families at death, yet the policies often cost far more in premiums than the payout benefits of the contract. According to government and company accounts, well-respected insurance companies like Metropolitan Life of New York (MetLife) built their businesses largely using this practice of racially discriminatory insurance contracts. At its height there were 155 million policies worth $40 billion.

RACIAL DISCRIMINATION IN INSURANCE CONTRACTS

Beginning in the 1980s, burial policies, also known as industrial policies, began to come under scrutiny. Brought to the United States from England (where they had been used to provide burial insurance for low-wage industry workers) shortly after the end of the Civil War, insurance companies sent thousands of insurance agents out door to door to sell these policies mostly to poor blacks. When the policies began, race discrimination was a part of American life, and blacks were routinely charged up to one-third more in premiums simply because they were black and the belief was that simply being black led to a lower life expectancy. The practice, however, continued even after it was well-known that it was not race, but poverty and other factors that accounted for differences in life expectancy. The race-based policies accounted for some of the largest insurance companies we know today. At its zenith in 1955, these policies accounted for about $40 billion in insurance revenue from 155 million policies. According to the U.S. Federal Trade Commission, some large insurance company giants, including Metropolitan Life, built their business on such policies.

Between 2000 and 2004, alone, 16 major cases were settled for more than $556 million, involving 14.8 million policies sold by 90 insurance companies between 1900 and the 1980s. Many of the people owning policies never received the benefits they paid for, and many others paid far more in premiums than they received in benefits. Mario Parcella, an attorney for policyholders, said that this did not necessarily break the law, but "it's part and parcel of what we consider a scheme to take advantage of African Americans." The cases are still ongoing.

Source: Jeff Donn, The Associated Press, "After Century of Overcharging Blacks, Insurance Industry Faces Suits," http://www.usatoday.com/news/nation/2004-10-10-insurance-suits_x.htm.

Does this seem like equality of contract to you? What about the ethics of the discriminatory contracts entered into with poor blacks, those who could least afford to be taken advantage of? Can you think of how the company must have justified this from an ethical standpoint?

As you can imagine, ethical issues arise a good deal in contracts. Whether it amounts to actual fraud or not, many of the ethical issues involve parties to the contract alleging they did not agree to something that they may have agreed to, particularly if the contract is not in writing. But even if it is, there is still plenty of room for ethical considerations. When you click on the "agree" button when registering at a website on the Internet, did you really read the pages and pages of the agreement you are signing? If the website owner knows that no one reads this, is it ethical to use this contract to govern disputes between the parties? Can the same be said of a car purchase or car rental agreement or even a video rental agreement which is handed to you while others are waiting in line, with instructions for you to "sign by the X"? We could be signing away our lives and never even know it because the vast majority of us do not read these agreements. What if you had paid hundreds of dollars for tickets to Michael Jackson's final concert tour and only after he died, you discovered that the online agreement said that your money would not be returned in such an event? Whether these provisions could be enforced is another matter, but there is definitely room in the making of contracts for more attention to ethics. Of course, personal responsibility is a significant factor also and it is not up to the business providing the contract to also make individuals carefully read it.

The purpose of contracts is to secure some good or performance we would not otherwise be entitled to. To do this, we enter into contracts with others, as a way of promising we will perform or give the thing of value in exchange for what we agree is payment. If one of the parties does not perform as promised, then that party has **breached** the contract. For instance, in the spring of 2009, a lawsuit was filed in federal court against Envision EMI by students who entered into a contract with the company to receive a trip to the inauguration of president-elect Barack Obama, including tickets to the inauguration, the parade, and a black-tie inaugural ball. After some of the students worked hard to raise the $2400 to $2600 for the trip, not including transportation, clothing rental/purchase or food, they alleged that they had no tickets to the inauguration or parade, were abandoned on the bus at their destination in DC, and that the inaugural ball was not an official one but rather was a "glorified prom."[1] Clearly, these students did not get what they thought they agreed to. If it is found that what they alleged is true, the company would have breached the contract and would be liable to the students for damages. The law will allow recovery for the breach by generally requiring the breaching party to put the nonbreaching party in the position the nonbreaching party would have been in had there been no breach. Here the unprecedented historic event could not be recaptured as a remedy for the students, but they could at least have their money returned.

In order to be able to recover for breach of contract, the parties to the contract must meet the requirements of a **valid contract** or none will exist to serve as a basis for breach. The contract must have (1) legal subject matter, (2) capacity of the parties to enter into contracts, (3) the exchange of consideration or something of agreed value between them, and (4) **mutual assent** between the parties, i.e., true agreement between the parties as to the contract's terms.

Legality refers to the subject matter of the contract being legal. Generally, if it is illegal to do an act, then it is illegal to contract to have the act done. For instance, gambling contracts in states where gambling is illegal or agreements to commit a crime lack legality.

Capacity ensures that those who enter into agreements understand the nature and effect of their agreements. Therefore, those under the legal age of contracting (generally 18), those who are intoxicated or otherwise under the influence of mind-altering drugs, or those who are mentally incompetent lack capacity.

Consideration ensures that parties to the contract actually bind themselves to the agreement by exchanging an agreed-upon legal detriment, that is, the parties agree to do something they do not have to do, or agree to **forbear** from doing something they could do if they want to. In contracting to buy a car, you agree to exchange money you otherwise would not have to give the dealer in exchange for title and possession of a car the dealer would not otherwise have to give you.

Mutual assent is agreement between the parties as to the contract's terms and their intent to actually enter into a contract rather than just inquiring or joking with each other. It consists of the offeror extending an offer and the offeree accepting the offer.

We will go into more detail about each of these requirements in the sections below. Before we do, however, it is important to discuss that the law of contract is derived from two sources which must constantly be kept in mind.

---

[1]Associated Press, "Students Sue over Inauguration Letdown: Say They Were Left out in Cold even though They Paid Full Costs," May 13, 2009, http://www.msnbc.msn.com/id/30727265.

Sources of Contract Law

There are two sets of laws that govern contracts: the common law or Restatement of Contracts, and the Uniform Commercial Code (UCC). We will explain why this is the case.

Each state has its own common law of contracts that governs how contracts are made and enforced in its state. You can imagine how unwieldy this would be when interstate commerce is such an integral part of our lives. In any given home or business you find goods from virtually all 50 states brought there by a contract of some sort. Rather than know the law in each state, states' contract laws have been distilled into a compilation called the **Restatement of Contracts.**

The Restatement is a compilation of the most common approaches to states' common law of contracts, but is not, in and of itself, law. States can adopt the Restatement in whole, or in part, or even modify, as they see fit. A state adopting the Restatement brings a measure of consistency to the various state laws governing contracts and makes it easier to deal with the interstate nature of business transactions. Since most contract law in the Restatement arises from the common law, the terms "common law of contracts," or "common law" tend to be used interchangeably with contract law contained in the Restatement.

The other source of contract law is the **Uniform Commercial Code, or UCC.** Article 2 of the UCC addresses contracts for the sale of **goods,** defined as **tangible,** movable, personal property. Since Article 2 of the UCC deals with buying and selling goods (rather than all possible types of contracts) it is a discrete and predictable relationship that lends itself to uniformity.

The Restatement and the UCC, which have been adopted in some form by all states, together cover all contract actions, with contracts for the sale of goods addressed by the UCC, while contracts involving land, services or intangibles are addressed by the Restatement or common law. Much of the Restatement law is consistent with the UCC rules, but there are some areas where the two differ. Our discussion will address the common law of contracts, except where there are UCC rules of which you should be aware. Keep in mind that it can be frustrating on an exam to answer a question using UCC rules when you should be using common law rules. To help you keep the differences in mind we have printed UCC information in a different color ink so that the differences will be brought to your attention as you read. Memory Tip: "If it's blue (the ink), think U (CC)!" "If it's blue, think U!"

Classification of Contracts

It is important to know some of the classifications of contracts because they form the basis for much of how contracts are discussed. We will introduce you to the classifications now and they will be discussed in greater detail shortly. (See "Take Away 5-1, "Classifications of Contracts")

VALID, VOID, VOIDABLE, UNENFORCEABLE

As stated above, a valid contract is one which meets each of the four requirements discussed above, i.e., mutual assent, consideration, legality, and capacity. If all of these things are present, the contract is said to be valid. We will discuss these issues briefly here in the context of categories, but a more in-depth discussion of each will come later in the chapter.

If a contract meets these requirements, but is required to be in writing and is not (discussed later), or part of an agreement reached orally before or at the time of contracting is not included in the final written agreement (whether or not the agreement was *required* to be in writing), then the contract will be **unenforceable.**

If a contract meets the requirements, except one or both of the parties was not of legal age, or there was **fraud in the inducement** (discussed later) as the basis for a party to enter the contract, then the contract is **voidable.**

If the contract does not have legal subject matter or there was **fraud in the execution** (discussed later), in entering into the agreement, then the contract does not actually exist at all. This is called a **void** contract—an oxymoron, since a void contract is not actually a contract at all. Void contracts have no legal force and effect and therefore cannot be enforced when the nonbreaching party sues for breach of contract. Of course, both types of fraud are unethical, but they are also the basis for altering the agreement.

EXECUTORY, EXECUTED

If the terms of a contract have been fully performed, it is known as an **executed contract.** When the terms of the contract have not yet been performed, it is known as an **executory contract.** It is possible to have a contract that is partially executed, in that some, but not all of it, has been performed. For instance, if Sinduja takes out a school loan at the bank, the bank's duty is executed since it has given Sinduja the money. Sinduja's duties are executory, since she must repay, generally on a monthly basis. When Sinduja completes the repayment, the contract will be executed on her part as well.

EXAMPLE

UNILATERAL, BILATERAL

Remember that a contract is a set of promises for which the law will recognize a remedy for nonperformance. If one party promises to do an act if the other party *does* something, it is a **unilateral contract.** If one party promises to do something if the other *promises* to do something, it is a **bilateral contract.** Thus, a promise in exchange for an act is a unilateral contract; a promise in exchange for a promise is a bilateral contract. If it is not clear from the language whether the contract is unilateral or bilateral, treat it as bilateral. However, the law will recognize unilateral contracts if the parties so intend. Always pay close attention to any information in quotation marks when trying to determine if it is one or the other.

EXAMPLE

For example, Jan says to Pedro, "I promise to give you $400 if you drive my car to Malibu from San Francisco." Since Jan rquested the act of driving the car, this creates a unilateral contract when the car reaches Malibu, and Jan must pay Pedro.

If, instead, Jan said to Pedro, "I promise to give you $400 if you promise to drive my car to Malibu from San Francisco," Jan requested from Pedro a return promise and it creates a bilateral contract when Pedro accepts the offer by agreeing.

This difference between the two becomes quite important if Jan takes back his promise and decides not to have Pedro make the trip. If Jan had made a unilateral offer and before Pedro accepted by driving the car to San Francisco Jan takes back the offer, there would be no contract upon which Pedro could sue for breach when Jan fails to perform as promised.

If, instead, Jan's offer is for a bilateral contract, a contract was formed as soon as Pedro agreed to Jan's offer so there is no longer an offer for Jan to take back. There is a contract Jan must perform and failure of Jan to do so gives rise to breach.

EXPRESS, IMPLIED IN FACT, AND IMPLIED IN LAW CONTRACTS

This categorization addresses how contracts are created by the parties. Contracts can be express, implied in fact, or implied in law.

If the parties to the contract actually discuss the contract and reach agreement, then it is an **express contract.** Express contracts may be either written or oral. If they do not commit the contract to writing, it is still an express contract. Again, as we will see later, some contracts are required to be in writing in order to be enforced, but the writing rule affects enforcement of the contract, not its creation.

The vast majority of contracts are actually contracts **implied in fact.** A contract implied in fact is created when the parties enter into the agreement by their actions rather than because they have actually discussed the matter.

For instance, an implied in fact contract is formed if you are sitting in a bar drinking club soda and signal the bartender and point to your glass. In that setting your actions are understood to mean the bartender is to give you another club soda and you will pay, so she does and you are bound. The two of you have not actually discussed a contract in the usual sense, but your actions indicate one has been formed.

Similarly, in neither of these cases have the parties actually discussed entering into a contract, and they certainly have not committed anything to writing, yet it is a contract implied in fact.

Contracts implied in law, also known as **quasi contracts,** are not really contracts at all. Rather, they are an obligation imposed by law upon an individual who receives a benefit under circumstances in which they would ordinarily be required to pay but no agreement to pay exists. The law prevents the party receiving the benefit from being **unjustly enriched** at the expense of the party who provided the benefit by imposing upon the recipient a duty to pay to the party who performed the service the reasonable value of the benefit received by the recipient. In a way, the law builds on ethics here. The law understands that it would be unethical for a person who receives something of benefit, under circumstances in which they would ordinarily expect to pay, to not pay and be able to hide behind the fact that there was no agreement, so it imposes liability under such circumstances.

For instance, a doctor is driving along and sees someone lying in the road injured and unconscious. The doctor takes the patient to the nearest hospital, administers the necessary medical attention and later sends the patient a bill for services rendered. There is no contract since there was no mutual assent because the injured party was unconscious and unable to communicate. However, the patient would ordinarily expect that if he received needed medical services, he would have to pay for them. A contract is implied in law and the patient must pay. The law believes it is not fair to let the injured party who received much needed medical care be absolved of paying for the services by simply saying "I never agreed to anything, so there is no contract and I don't have to pay." To keep the doctor from going away empty-handed, the law requires the patient to pay the doctor at least reasonable value for the services rendered. This is recovery in **quantum meruit.** The doctor may not get to charge her normal contract price, but at least does not go away empty handed. The patient is not required to pay the usual contract amount, but only the reasonable value of what was received.

Remedies

LO4

If a party does not perform the contract as agreed, the nonbreaching party is generally entitled to remedies for breach. As previously mentioned in the introductory chapter, these remedies can take the form of legal remedies or equitable remedies. The goal in breach of contract actions is to put the nonbreaching party in the position he or she would have been in had there been no breach. Several kinds of remedies can be used together in order to make the nonbreaching party whole. Money damages may be the most likely way to make the nonbreaching party whole, but if not, then equitable remedies may be used, as appropriate. Punitive damages are generally not awarded in breach of contract actions. However, if the breach was malicious, fraudulent, or

TAKE AWAY 5-1

CLASSIFICATIONS OF CONTRACTS

- Valid, Void, Voidable, Unenforceable
- Executory, Executed
- Unilateral, Bilateral
- Express, Implied in Fact, Implied in Law/quasi contract

CASE 5.1 Stambovsky v. Ackley

169 A.2d 254, 572 NYS2d 672 (Sup. Ct. NY, App. Div. 1991)

Facts: After purchasing a home, the buyer discovered that the home was widely reputed to be haunted with poltergeists. The seller knew of the ghostly activity and had even promoted the house as such for publicity, but did not tell this to the buyer, who did not live in the area and had not heard. When the buyer found out, he brought an action to have the court rescind the purchase agreement and grant restitution.

Issue: Whether failure of a seller to tell a buyer of a house that the house reputedly had poltergeists is sufficient basis for the buyer to be able to **rescind** the agreement to buy and receive **restitution** of money buyer gave the seller.

Decision: Yes

Reasoning: Rubin, J.: The doctrine of caveat emptor [buyer beware] requires that a buyer act prudently to assess the fitness and value of his purchase and operates to bar the purchaser who fails to exercise due care from seeking the equitable remedy of rescission. Here, however, the purchaser is not a member of the local community, and the record indicates he met his obligation to conduct an inspection of the premises and a search of available public records with respect to the title. The most meticulous inspection and search would not reveal the presence of poltergeists at the premises or unearth the property's ghoulish reputation in the community. Therefore there is no sound policy reason to deny the purchaser relief for failing to discover a state of affairs that the most prudent purchaser would not be expected to even contemplate. Nondisclosure, under these circumstances constitutes a basis for rescission as a matter of equity. REVERSED.

CASE QUESTIONS

1. Do you think it was appropriate to return the buyer's money? Why or why not?
2. The court held the house was haunted as a matter of law, meaning there could be no proof offered to the contrary. Do you think the court was correct in so holding? Explain.
3. Can you understand why sometimes a remedy at law is insufficient? Discuss.

connected with a tort, they may be awarded. In the *Stambovsky* case (Case 5.1), the court was faced with granting an equitable remedy in a very unusual case: the purchased house was reputed to be haunted.

Requirements for a Valid Contract

A valid contract is a bundle of rights surrounding an agreement. Making sure we have our complete bundle of rights for validity is important because if we do not and the contract is breached, we may not be able to have the breach remedied. The four requirements of validity are mutual assent, capacity, consideration, and legality. (See Take Away 5-2, "Requirements for Valid and Enforceable Contract.") In order for our bundle to be complete, we must also give attention to any writing requirements that address the enforceability of our agreement.

MUTUAL ASSENT

Mutual assent is the combination of a valid offer by an **offeror** who extends the offer, with an acceptance of the offer by the **offeree,** to whom the offer is extended.

Offer

An offer is the proposal by the offeror that will create a contract upon acceptance by the offeree. In order for an offer to be sufficient to create a contract by its acceptance, it must meet certain requirements.

Requirements In order to be sufficient to create a contract, the offer must contain (1) definiteness of terms, (2) intent, and (3) communication. All three requirements must be met in order to have an effective offer.

Definiteness of terms ensures that the parties understand exactly what is being offered. Anything the parties wish to have as part of the contract should be included in the offer. For the UCC, that means, at a minimum, quantity, quality, and price. If other terms are left out, it is not fatal because they can be filled in by UCC provisions. For instance, if there is no term for where delivery will take place, under the UCC delivery will take place at the seller's place of business, or if none, the seller's home. This process of using UCC provisions to fill in terms left out of an offer is called **gap filling.** For non-UCC contracts, all pertinent terms of the offer should be included, as the Restatement historically has not permitted gap filling as the UCC does although Section 34 of the Restatement has recently adopted an approach similar to the UCC regarding gap filling.

Intent ensures that the offeror intended to actually make an offer and was not merely exploring, joking, or angry or in the midst of great excitement. Generally courts look to the *objective intent* actually manifested by the offeror to determine intent, rather than the *subjective intent* of what was in his or her head. What an offeror *says or does* is considered in determining intent, *not* what he or she was *thinking*. If an offeror appears to be serious in making an offer, then it matters little that in the offeror's mind it was only a joke.

Communication of the offer must be made to the offeree by the offeror or the offeror's agent. It is not sufficient for the offeree to simply hear about the offer and respond to it.

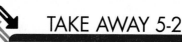

REQUIREMENTS FOR VALID AND ENFORCEABLE CONTRACT

The first four items below are the requirements for a valid contract. As a practical matter however, validity does not mean a good deal if the contract cannot be enforced in a court of law, so we have also provided the considerations regarding enforceability.

Validity

- Mutual assent (offer and acceptance)
- Consideration
- Legality
- Capacity

Enforceability

- Compliance with the Statute of Frauds *when necessary*
- Compliance with the Parol Evidence Rule *when necessary*

Termination of Offers

In order for an offer to create a contract upon acceptance by the offeree, the offer must still be alive and viable when accepted by the offeree. There are several factors that can affect the viability of the offer. If one of the factors is present, the offer is terminated and is no longer in existence when the offeree attempts to accept it; therefore no contract is created. If the offer has been terminated by one of the factors below, when the offeree accepts the offer she is accepting nothing and does not create a contract that can then be enforced by suing for breach. (See Take Away 5-3 "Factors Terminating an Offer.")

Destruction of the Subject Matter The subject matter of the contract is destroyed through no fault of the parties. In our opening scenario, if Ed's car is struck by lightning and destroyed after Ed makes the offer to Mike, but before Mike accepts, Ed's offer to Mike is terminated and no longer exists.

Death or Incapacity The death or incapacity of either party immediately terminates the offer. Jung sends Tamiko a letter offering to sell her his antique coin collection. Tamiko calls to accept but learns that Jung died the day before. The offer was terminated when Jung died and is no longer outstanding when Tamiko calls and attempts to accept.

Rejection If the offeree declines to accept the offer, the offer is terminated. Brad offers to buy Donna's drum set. Donna tells Brad she doesn't want to sell. Donna has rejected Brad's offer.

FACTORS TERMINATING AN OFFER

The seven factors which will terminate an offer form the pneumonic DDRRIIL. The first letter of each of the factors is used to form the word. Keep in mind that the offer has been made by the offeror and one of these factors occurs before it is accepted by the offeree. Memory Tip: To remind yourself of these items, think "Termination? You know the DDRRIIL!"

Death of either party
Destruction of the subject matter
Revocation by the offeror
Rejection by the offeree
Incapacity of either party
Illegality of the subject matter
Lapse of stated or reasonable time

EXAMPLE

If the offer is under the Restatement and the offeree changes the terms of the offer in any way, it is considered to be a **counteroffer** which terminates the original offer and creates a new offer by the old offeree who now becomes the offeror. June offers to sell a parcel of land to Seth, as is. Seth says he will purchase the land if June will repair the fence. Seth has given June a counteroffer and it terminates June's original offer. However, Seth's counteroffer becomes an offer to June which she can accept or reject, as she is now an offeree and Seth has become the offeror. Under the UCC a change in the offer by offeree will only be considered a counteroffer if the offeree intends it to be so. It will not be presumed to be a counteroffer terminating the original offer as is the case under the Restatement.

EXAMPLE

Revocation The offeror takes back the offer before it is accepted. Renee offers to purchase Leslie's house. Before Leslie gives Renee an answer, Renee takes the offer back. The offer is now terminated and no longer exists for Leslie to accept.

The general rule is that an offer can be revoked by an offeror any time prior to acceptance by the offeree unless it meets one of the three exceptions. The exceptions are:

1. Option contract. Since an offeror can revoke the offer any time prior to acceptance by the offeree, the offeree may wish to pay the offeror to keep the offer open. An **option contract** is a contractual agreement, complete with consideration, that the offeror will hold the offer open for the offeree for an agreed upon period of time. The offeror cannot revoke the offer during the period of the option. An option contract only buys the offeree time to accept or reject the offer and does not mean the offeree must accept. The consideration the offeree pays for the option is not a part of the contract price, but rather the option is a separate contract addressing only the offer being kept open while offeree thinks about it or makes arrangements. The consideration given for the option is not a "down payment" unless the offeror makes it so. If the offeree decides not to accept the offer, the consideration for the option need not be returned to the offeree. Grayson offers to sell his car to Jack for $750. Jack wants to accept but is not sure he can get the money from his parents. Jack gives Grayson $50 to keep the offer open for two days. Grayson will not be able to revoke the offer during that two-day period or sell the car to anyone else. If, within the two days, Jack decides not to buy the car, nothing further need be done and Grayson keeps the $50 option price. If, instead, Jack decides to purchase the car, he would owe Grayson $750, as the option consideration is not a

EXAMPLE

part of the purchase price for the car, but is a separate contract to simply hold the offer open.

2. Unilateral offer upon which performance has begun. Unilateral offers are accepted and create contracts by the offeree completely performing the act requested by the offeror. Since the general rule is that an offer can be revoked any time prior to acceptance, it would be theoretically possible for offeree to begin performance of a unilateral offer, and in the middle of performing, the offeror revokes the offer. Since the offeree has not yet accepted by completing performance of the requested act, the offer can be revoked. However, the law provides that if the offeree substantially begins performance, the offeror's power to revoke is suspended until the performance is finished or the time has come for the performance to be completed, even if it is not. Jason says to Josh, "I offer to pay you $100 if you climb up the flag pole." Josh begins to climb and when he gets three-quarters of the way up, Jason yells up, "Stop! I take back my offer!" Josh hasn't climbed to the top of the flagpole yet, so he hasn't actually accepted Jason's unilateral offer. However, because he has substantially performed, Jason would not be able to take the offer back. Josh would be allowed to finish performing, at which time a contract is formed if he has performed as agreed.

3. **Merchant's firm offer.** This is a UCC concept. A **merchant** is one who deals in goods of the kind involved in the contract. If a merchant gives written, signed assurances that an offer will be held open for a specified period of time (not to exceed 90 days), then even without consideration to hold the offer open (as is needed with an option contract), the offer cannot be revoked by the offeror. Christopher, a dress manufacturer, sends to Kristy, a dress retailer, a letter, the pertinent part of which reads: "I offer to ship you 200 red silk shantung dresses for $50 each. Offer good for ten days from receipt." Three days later Christopher gets an offer from Quincy for Quincy to immediately purchase the same dresses from Christopher for $75 each. Christopher would not be able to sell the dresses to Quincy. Since Christopher is a merchant and sent Kristy a signed writing that gave assurances that the offer would be held open for ten days, it took away Christopher's power to revoke the offer to Kristy during that period.

Incapacity If either of the parties becomes incapacitated while the offer is pending then the offer is terminated and has no legal significance. Daisuke (DICE-kay), a famous portrait artist, offers to paint Brian's portrait. Before Brian can accept, Daisuke suffers a stroke and his arms are paralyzed. The offer from Daisuke to Brian is terminated.

Illegality If an offer is made but before it can be accepted the subject matter of the offer becomes illegal, the offer is terminated. Sherry, a liquor distiller, makes an offer to Beth, owner of Beth's Bar, to sell Beth 6 cases of cognac, 7 cases of Cristal, and 30 cases of beer. Before Beth accepts the offer the county makes it illegal to sell liquor to bars. Sherry's offer to Beth would immediately be terminated. Beth would not be able to successfully sue Sherry for refusing to deliver the liquor.

Lapse of Stated or Reasonable Time If the offeror specifies a time within which the offer must be accepted, it must be accepted within that time or the offer is terminated. Under the UCC, if no time is specified in the offer, then the law will impose a reasonable time based on the circumstances. At the end of that time, if the offer is not accepted, the offer lapses and is no longer an outstanding offer that can be accepted to create a contract.

Acceptance

General Under the Restatement's **mirror image rule,** the offeree's acceptance of an offer must be unequivocal and be a mirror image of the offer. If it is not, and any terms

TAKE AWAY 5-4

EFFECTIVE DATES OF ACTIONS

Unless otherwise agreed by the parties, the following actions are effective as noted:

Offer—Effective when received by the offeree
Acceptance—Effective when sent if properly done.
     If not properly done, effective when received by offeror
Acceptance after a prior rejection—first response to reach offeror is effective
Rejection—Effective when received by offeror
Revocation—Effective when received by the offeree

are changed by the offeree, it is considered to be a counteroffer which terminates the offer. Acceptance must be by the intended offeree or the offeree's agent or no contract is created. An offeror can make the terms of acceptance whatever he or she wants them to be. The offeror has complete control over the offer and how it is to be accepted. If the offeror says that acceptance must be at midnight in front of the double-barrel cannon in the town square, with the football linebacker-offeree wearing green fishnet stockings and a polka dot dress, then that is how the offer must be accepted. If the linebacker wants the contract, he must accept the offer as the offeror specified. Under the UCC, for the most part, any means of acceptance reasonable under the circumstances is effective as an acceptance that creates a contract, although the offeror can still dictate the terms of the offer.

Type of Acceptance Acceptance can be direct or indirect. Direct acceptance occurs when the offeree communicates to the offeror his wish to enter into the contract. Indirect acceptance is the offeror doing some act consistent with acceptance, such as sending a check for the amount of the offer within the time specified.

Unless otherwise agreed, an acceptance is effective when it is sent if it is sent correctly. (See Take Away 5-4 "Effective Dates of Actions") This is the **mailbox rule or deposited acceptance rule.** That is, if the offeror specified how acceptance must be made (postal mail, e-mail, mail, phone, FAX, and so on) then it is effective as soon as it is sent that way, even though something may happen to delay it reaching the offeror or it is lost altogether. A contract is still created because the contract was created when the acceptance was sent.

EXAMPLE

Martin receives an offer from Coretta to purchase a painting called "The Dream." Coretta specifies that if Martin accepts her offer he is to fax his acceptance within three days of receipt. Martin does so, but the fax is never received by Coretta. The contract for the painting was formed when Martin faxed the acceptance, so regardless of Coretta not receiving the fax, there is a contract between Martin and Coretta.

Students always ask, "But how can you prove you sent it?!" There is no magic. It must be proved by whatever means are available. There can be the offeree's testimony that he or she sent it, testimony of any witnesses who saw it being sent, a photocopy offeree made, a copy of the e-mail, or the printout from the fax machine indicating the fax went through successfully. All would be helpful. Just know that the issue of proof is separate from the issue of law. The acceptance is effective when sent the correct way. It's up to the party to prove to the court's satisfaction that acceptance was sent. Keep in mind that the mailbox rule only applies when the parties have not agreed otherwise. Trouble can be avoided by the offeror simply requiring that the acceptance will not be effective until received.

Acceptance after a Prior Rejection When the offeree initially rejects an offer, then later accepts it, it is deemed an **acceptance after a prior rejection.** In such a case, acceptance is *not* effective when sent. Rather, the first communication to reach the offeror is effective. The acceptance is effective to create a contract only if it reaches the offeror before the rejection. If the rejection reaches the offeror first, the rejection is effective and the offer is terminated. Jackie writes to Carmine offering to sell her boat to him for $6000. Carmine doesn't have the money so he writes Jackie back and rejects the offer. The next day Carmine hits the lottery for $75,000. He calls Jackie and tells her he accepts her offer. She has not yet received his letter rejecting the offer. Since the acceptance reached Jackie before the rejection, the acceptance is effective and a contract is formed.

EXAMPLE

Silence Generally, silence by the offeree after being given an offer does not constitute acceptance. The offeror cannot make offeree's silence to an offer an acceptance by saying, for instance, "If I don't hear from you by 12:00, we have a contract." If the parties have a contract, previous relationship, or history making silence an acceptance, then silence will operate as acceptance.

Acceptance under the UCC Acceptance under the UCC is a bit more relaxed than under the Restatement. Since the transactions are always sales, the parties understand what is involved and what the general course of conduct is. However, there are some rather cumbersome rules that govern the transaction. They make sense when you think about them, but if you are anything like the thousands of students we have had over the past 20+ years, you may find yourself feeling frustrated at trying to put it all together. Relax and try to think about it as a transaction you are involved in rather than just a set of rules you have to memorize. If it helps, imagine you are a snowboard retailer who buys boards from manufacturers all the time and sells them to snowboarders every day of the week. Try to think about the transactions from that point of view. Just try to walk your way through it. Once you get the picture in your head the rules makes perfect sense.

Acceptance with Varied Terms Under the UCC an acceptance that makes changes to the offer is only considered a counteroffer if the offeree so intends. Otherwise, the offeree is said to have given the offeror an **acceptance with varied terms.** Unlike a counteroffer, an acceptance with varied terms does *not* have the effect of terminating the original offer. XYZ Corp. sends an offer to ABC Corp. to sell ABC Corp. 10,000 wind-power blades at $60 per blade, deliverable two weeks from acceptance. ABC Corp. writes back that it accepts the offer but needs the blades in a week and a half. In its acceptance, ABC has changed the terms of XYZ's offer from two weeks to one and a half weeks. This change, in and of itself, does not terminate XYZ's offer as a counteroffer.

EXAMPLE

Go slow here—it sounds complicated, but it really isn't. If the acceptance with varied terms is **definite** and **seasonable** (explained shortly) and acceptance is not conditioned on the offeror's acceptance of the offeree's varied terms (remember that it is the *offeror* who has complete control over the offer, not the offeree), then there is a contract between the parties on terms of the original offer. The varied terms that were different from the original offer will be considered as **proposals for addition to the contract** that must be negotiated into the contract in order to become a part of it. If varied terms are not negotiated in by the parties the contract is for the offeror's original offer. Before you start feeling sorry for the offeree who is now stuck with a contract he does not want, keep in mind that if the offeree wanted terms other than those the offeror proposed, the offeree should have simply rejected the offeror's offer and given the offeror an offer instead. But once he gave a definite and seasonable acceptance that was unconditional, a contract was formed on the original terms of the offer and the offeree is bound.

If the acceptance is not definite or seasonable, then there is no acceptance and no contract. Seasonable means the offer was accepted within the time set out by the offeror, or if none is given, then a reasonable time based upon the circumstances. Definiteness addresses the overall impression that the offer is being accepted rather than rejected.

For instance, in our wind blade example, since the offer is for the sale of blades and the blades are a good, this agreement is governed by the UCC. Since it is within the UCC, the offeree's changing the delivery date from two weeks to a week and a half is not automatically considered a counteroffer simply because the acceptance is not a mirror image of the offer, but has instead been changed in some way. Rather, it would be considered an acceptance with varied terms since ABC accepted immediately, and the acceptance was seasonable, even though it changed a term of the original offer. ABC's acceptance is definite because it expresses a wish to enter into the contract even though they changed the time for delivery. XYZ Corp. and ABC Corp therefore have a contract for the blades and they will be delivered in two weeks unless XYZ Corp. agrees to a week and a half.

Our experience over the years has been that students tend to get caught up in thinking the offeree is now legally bound to something he may not want and they do not understand why the law would impose such an agreement upon someone. Keep in mind that the offeree had every right to reject the offer if it did not reflect terms he wanted. However, once he did not and instead gave a definite and seasonable acceptance, a contract was formed. Also keep in mind the requirement is that there be a definite acceptance that is unconditional. The offeree is not being forced into anything, as he has given a definite acceptance to the offer that is not conditioned on the offeror accepting the offeree's changed terms. Does that make you feel better?

Varied Terms between Merchants OK, this is going to get a bit hairier, but again, just take it slowly and get the picture in your head. It makes perfect sense when you do. If the varied terms are between (meaning both buyer and seller) merchants (those who deal in goods of the kind), then the rule about acceptance with varied terms is somewhat different. The UCC presumes that merchants understand and know the landscape they are dealing with in buying and selling goods, so they can deal with each other in sort of a shortcut way. The shortcuts are created by the UCC making certain presumptions about what the parties intend to do based on how commerce usually operates. The course of the parties' dealings and the usage of trade give a measure of predictability to the transactions that allows the UCC to do this. However, even with this, there is ample opportunity for the merchants to opt out and not use the shortcuts so they do not end up with a contract they do not want.

If the varied terms are *different,* in that they change what is actually in the offer to something else (you say you accept the offer but you want a car, not a truck), then it is like the above rule, in that there will be a contract if there is a definite and seasonable acceptance, and the varied terms will have to be negotiated into the contract or the original offer stands.

If, instead, the offeree's varied terms are *additional* in that the different terms leave what is in the original offer, but add something to it (yes you want the car in the offer but you also want a car stereo to go with it), then the varied terms *automatically* become a part of the contract *unless:*

1. the offer is expressly limited to its terms (the offeror indicates in the offer that he is unwilling to consider any other terms)
2. the offeror objects to the different terms within ten days of receiving them (offeree gives the additional terms and offeror says no), or
3. the newly proposed terms materially alter the original offer (you want the car in the offer and 6 other cars too).

TAKE AWAY 5-5

ACCEPTANCE UNDER THE UCC

Use this information to work your way through acceptance with varied terms under the UCC. You should be very comfortable with the situation after you study this box.

Under the UCC, the offeror gives an offer to the offeree and the offeree has several choices, each of which has consequences.

The offeree can:

- accept the offer as is: contract formed
- reject the offer: no contract formed
- accept the offer with conditions: no contract formed
- accept the offer late: no contract formed
- accept the offer but vary the terms; this leads to two queries:

  1. *Is there a contract?*
     no definite acceptance, unseasonable acceptance, conditional acceptance (any of the three): no contract formed
     definite, seasonable, unconditional acceptance: contract formed
  2. *What are the contract terms?*
     Query: are the varied terms *different* or *additional*?
     A. If the varied terms are *different* from the original offer terms the *contract will be the offeror's terms* and the varied terms will be considered proposals for addition to the contract that must be negotiated into the contract in order to become a part of it.
     B If the varied terms are *additional* to the original offer terms, then two queries:
        Is the offer for additional terms *between two nonmerchants, a merchant and a nonmerchant or between two non-merchants?* In either case, the terms of the contract will be the same as the rule for different terms above: the contract *will be on the offeror's terms* with the additional terms considered proposals for addition to the contract that must be negotiated in to become a part of the contract.
        Is the offer for additional terms *between two merchants?* If so, the varied terms will *automatically become a part of the contract unless* one of three things is present, in which case the "different" rule above is used:
        1. The offer is limited to its terms initially by the offeror.
        2. The offeror objects to the additional terms within 10 days of receiving them from the offeree.
        3. The additional terms substantially alter the offeror's offer.

If any of these three exceptions occurs, then the first rule above applies and the varied terms are treated as proposals for addition to the contract that must be negotiated in to become a part of it. If this all seems as clear as mud to you, then read over it again, slowly, thinking about the parties involved, and it will make perfect sense. Trust us. (But also take a look at Take Away 5-5 "Acceptance under the UCC.")

Genuineness of Assent Closely aligned with this matter of how acceptance is accomplished is the issue of whether the agreement between the parties is, in fact, voluntary and legitimate. Oftentimes it may appear so, but it is not so in actuality. For instance, a seller's name may appear on a deed to property, yet it was only there because the buyer had a gun to the seller's head and made her sign the deed. It looks like a perfectly good title to property, but upon investigation, there are serious issues as to whether it is a voluntary agreement as the law requires. Other challenges to mutual assent follow (also see Take Away 5-6, "Challenges to Mutual Assent"):

EXAMPLE

TAKE AWAY 5-6

CHALLENGES TO MUTUAL ASSENT

- Duress
- Undue influence
- Mutual mistake
- Unilateral mistake
- Mutual ignorance
- Unconscionability
- Fraud in the inducement
- Fraud in the execution

Duress is exerting pressure through threats or use of physical force, economic disadvantage, exposure of private matters, etc., to get a party to enter into a contract. The contract is voidable by the party experiencing the duress. If threat of deadly force is used (gun, knife, etc.) to obtain assent the contract is void. For instance, Toby's signature conveying his property to Shelby is obtained by Shelby threatening to start false rumors about Toby and Matthew having a relationship.

EXAMPLE

Undue influence is a rebuttable presumption that arises when it is shown that:

a. the person accused of exerting undue influence had a dominant relationship with the other party to the contract;

b. the unduly influenced party is shown to be in a subservient position to the accused;

c. there was opportunity for the dominant party to exert undue influence over the subservient party; and

d. there is a contract which appears to give an unreasonable advantage to the dominant party.

If the presumption is not rebutted by the dominant party the subservient party will be able to avoid performance under the contract. Dominant-subservient relationships include doctor and patient, priest and parishioner, attorney and client, parent and child, and so on. An 87-year-old ill, bedridden patient who lives alone and is in constant pain signs over the deed to her $650,000 house to her doctor, who is the only one who comes to visit her on a regular basis and provides her pain medication. The deed conveys the property to the doctor for $2500. The contract deeding the house is voidable at the option of the patient. Note that the doctor may not actually have exerted undue influence upon the patient. However, since the circumstances are such that it is highly unlikely that a $650,000 piece of property would be sold for $2500, and the patient is vulnerable and dependent upon the doctor, it sets up a rebuttable presumption of undue influence. The doctor can then rebut the presumption by showing it is not true, in which case the sale to him would be upheld. As you can see here, with a dominant and subservient relationship between the parties, the situation is ripe for unethical behavior, particularly when there is something of value at stake.

EXAMPLE

Mutual mistake is when both parties think they are agreeing to something, when, in fact, neither has the same thing in mind. Shawnee agrees to provide massage therapy to Pam for six months. Shawnee thought the agreement was for Swedish massage. Pam thought it was for deep tissue massage. Deep tissue massage costs twice as much as Swedish massage and Shawnee refuses to honor the agreement. Pam and Shawnee have experienced a mutual mistake and the contract may be rescinded. The parties never actually had a meeting of the minds for mutual assent, so rescinding the agreement makes sense.

EXAMPLE

If a mistake is made by only one party to the contract, or **unilateral mistake,** and the other knows of the mistake, the court will not allow the innocent party to be taken advantage of. The contract will be on the terms both were aware of. Domino's Pizza Company developed an online ad for free pizza during the bank bailout in 2008. The promotion was actually never approved before it was posted, but when the word "bailout" was typed into search engines, the promotion coupon came up.

EXAMPLE

Word spread quickly that the company was giving away free pizzas. Eleven thousand medium pizzas were given away before the ad was removed. The company made a unilateral mistake in that it inadvertently offered the ad on its website, but web surfers seeing the ad had no reason to believe the ad was not legitimate so the coupons were honored.[2]

Mutual ignorance applies when both parties are aware that they do not know all they need to know before contracting, and they contract anyway. Both are bound by the contract even though things turn out differently than the parties thought they would. Of course, again, if one party has superior knowledge, she will not be able to use it to disadvantage the other. While shopping for office furniture at a second-hand store, Garrett comes across an interesting painting. The store owner says she doesn't know who the artist is. Neither does Garrett. Garrett purchases the painting for $5. Garrett later discovers the painting is an original Vivaldi worth $2.5 million. The store owner would not be able to rescind the agreement and reclaim the painting. Both parties did not know the artist and both knew they did not know and decided to contract about the painting anyway. If Garrett had been aware of the value of the painting and knew the store owner was not aware of its value, then the court would rescind the agreement and not allow Garrett to keep the painting.

Unconscionability is primarily a UCC concept. Undue influence or duress has not been exerted over a party to the contract in the traditional sense but there is a disadvantage involved in the contract that prevents courts from enforcing it. Sherman sells gourmet cookware door-to-door. Sherman calls on Mr. Pringle, 67, who lives alone on a fixed income in an efficiency apartment. Sherman does a great presentation and contracts to sell Mr. Pringle a set of the cookware under a contract in which Mr. Pringle will pay $25 per month, for a total price of $465, including interest. The actual value of the cookware is about $37. Courts would most likely not allow this contract to be enforced against Mr. Pringle. Courts do not generally protect parties to a contract from being unwise in their agreement, but here the situation is more than that. Due to Mr. Pringle's age, living situation (alone, efficiency apartment), and fixed income, it is likely that he was simply caught up in a good sales job and bit off more than he could chew (no pun intended). It should be noted that some courts have taken the concept of unconscionability out of the UCC and applied it to other, non-UCC contracts. Notice that there need be no actual allegation of wrongdoing by the one benefiting by the contract, but only that the outcome seems so unethical and unbalanced that the court is not comfortable in enforcing the contract.

Fraud is intentionally making untrue statements to a person in order to get him or her to enter into an agreement. As mentioned earlier, there are two kinds of fraud: fraud in the execution and fraud in the inducement. In fraud in the execution, the person being defrauded knows he or she is signing something, but does not know it is a contract. For instance, Jane told Grandma that Grandma was signing a birthday card for her son. In fact, it is the deed to Grandma's house. The court would not allow the deed to be effective to convey the property. With fraud in the inducement, the one being defrauded actually knows he or she is entering into a contract, but has been told untruths about significant parts of the contract that form the basis of the bargain. The court will allow the defrauded party to either avoid the agreement altogether, or go through with it, but receive damages for the difference between what he or she thought he or she was getting, and what he or

[2]Associated Press, "Mamma Mia! Goof Cost Domino's 11,000 Pizzas: Stumbled-upon Online 'Bailout' Promotion Turns into Pizza-palooza," April 2, 2009, http://www.msnbc.msn.com/id/30013159/.

she actually received. In this instance, Grandma knows she is signing over the deed to her house, but her daughter Jane told her it is because the house has been sold for $600,000, when, in fact, the house has not been sold and Jane is the one to whom the deed was signed.

In our opening scenario, Ed does not have to give the money back to Mike for the car that is now not performing. Mike is essentially alleging that Ed fraudulently induced him to purchase a car that later did not perform as Ed promised. However, Ed allowed Mike full access to the car all day, Mike drove the car around, and Mike had his mechanic brother inspect the car. There is no evidence of fraud in the inducement on Ed's part, and therefore there is no basis upon which Mike should have his money returned.

CONSIDERATION

Consideration is the thing of value exchanged between the parties to a contract. If there is no consideration between the parties, there is no valid and binding contract. Consideration is often defined as "bargained for legal detriment exchanged between the parties." For instance, if you buy a car the seller's consideration is title and possession to the car, and the buyer's consideration is the price of the automobile. That is, the seller gives the buyer the car's title and possession and the buyer gives the seller the price of the car.

The law does not deal with the value of consideration unless fraud is involved. Since contracts are voluntary agreements and parties are presumed to know and understand what they are agreeing to, the law is not concerned with the personal subjective matter of what value a party places on a the subject matter of a contract. The parties can agree to consideration of as little or as much as they want. If you want to pay a million dollars for a car that means a lot to you but may be worthless on the market, the consideration is legally sound. If the parties agree that buyer will pay $1000 for a house worth $300,000, the consideration is legally sufficient as long as no fraud is involved. So, when we speak of the adequacy of consideration we do not mean the monetary or market value, but rather the legal sufficiency of the consideration.

Adequate Consideration

Consideration is often money on one side of the contract (for instance, you pay money to buy a new computer), but it need not be. Consideration can be anything the parties decide it is. It is, however, required that to qualify as adequate consideration to create a binding contract, the party giving it must suffer a legal detriment and the party receiving it receives a legal benefit.

A **legal detriment** is a party doing something they do not have to do, or not doing something they could do if they wanted to. Not doing something you can do if you want to do is called *forbearance*. The legal detriment could be giving someone money you have no legal obligation to give in the absence of an agreement. It could just as well be promising to clean someone's garage, repair their car, cook for them, give them a plane ride, or anything legal that the parties decide. Forbearance is agreeing *not* to do something a party would otherwise have a legal right to do, for instance, promising not to smoke or drink between ages 21 and 25. A **legal benefit** is a party gaining something to which he or she would not otherwise be entitled in the absence of an agreement.

Note that the terms "detriment" and "benefit" do not have their usual lay meanings. Usually you think of a detriment as a disadvantage or negative, and a benefit as an advantage or positive. The term "legal" in front of both limits their meaning to the contractual context of gaining or losing something because one has agreed to do so by contract. As such, something may actually be a benefit but is considered to be a legal detriment for contracting purposes.

If your employer promises to pay you a bonus if you do not smoke while you work for her, this is an actual benefit to your lungs and general health since you will not be subject to the ill effects of smoking. However, you have a legal right to smoke if you want to (thought we hope you don't), and in giving this right away to your employer under contract you suffer a legal detriment.

You also gained a legal benefit because you will receive money you would not otherwise be entitled to receive. Your employer seems to gain nothing by having you abstain from smoking but actually receives a legal benefit since she is gaining something she would not be entitled to in the absence of the agreement (your not smoking when you have a legal right to do so). She also suffers a legal detriment in that she is paying you money she would not otherwise have to pay in the absence of the agreement with you.

Some kinds of consideration do not qualify as adequate consideration to create a binding contract because they lack one of the requirements of the three-pronged definition above. That is, they are not bargained for, are not a legal detriment, or are not exchanged between the parties. If the consideration is lacking, then no contract is formed. When a party sues for breach of contract he or she will lose because there is no contract to enforce since it lacks the essential element of adequate consideration.

Sometimes it is easy to determine the consideration in a contract, as in our car example above. But other times determining the consideration is not quite so easy and can seem confusing. To help you determine what is being used as consideration in an agreement, put the agreement in what we will call our "consideration sentence": "In exchange for ___, I will give you/do ___." In our car example, the sentence would say, "In exchange for title and possession of the car, I will give you $15,000." You can easily see what is being given as consideration when it otherwise may seem confusing.

Inadequate Consideration

Sometimes parties make agreements to exchange something that is to act as consideration for the agreement, and it does not meet the legal requirements for the reasons we spoke of above. Following are a few that fit into that category. Again, because they are not sufficient as consideration, there is no contract, so when the nonbreaching party sues for breach of contract, he or she will lose. (See Take Away 5-7 "Not Adequate as Consideration.")

Past Consideration Past consideration is not adequate consideration to support a promise, therefore, it will not create a contract. Past consideration is something that has already taken place. Since it has already taken place, the bargaining element is not met and the past consideration is not adequate to support a promise.

While she is away from home, Brenda's dog, Butch, who jumped the fence and is roaming the neighborhood, is almost hit by a truck. However, Naomi, a neighbor, rescues Butch. When Brenda hears of the rescue, she is so grateful that she tells Naomi, "Thank you so much for rescuing Butch. I really owe you one. In fact, come by my house tomorrow after work. It is my payday and I'll give you a $50 reward." Naomi comes over the next evening and Brenda, irritated with Butch for chewing her new shoes, refuses to pay Naomi the $50. If Naomi sues Brenda for breach of contract, who wins?

Brenda wins. Even though Brenda promised Naomi the reward, the promise is not supported by adequate consideration since the consideration was promised for an event that had already taken place. Butch had already been rescued when Brenda made the promise. If we put the agreement in our consideration

TAKE AWAY 5-7

NOT ADEQUATE AS CONSIDERATION

The following are not adequate consideration to support a promise and create a contract:

- gratuitous promises
- past consideration
- pre-existing legal or contractual obligation
- moral obligation
- illusory promise

sentence, the agreement is "In consideration of you rescuing my dog, I will give you $50." Since the rescue had already taken place, it is past consideration and fails as consideration sufficient to create a binding contract.

EXAMPLE

Moral Obligation If a promise is based only upon a moral obligation, it will not be adequate consideration to support the promise and create a contract. Yinka owns a company. Venis, one of Yinka's oldest and most trusted employees, is injured on the job. Yinka knows Venis well and knows that she is putting three kids through college as a single mom. Yinka believes the worker's compensation payments Venis is entitled to for five months will not be sufficient to meet her obligations. Yinka tells Venis that he will pay her $5000 a month for the period of her worker's comp entitlement. Yinka makes the payments for two months, then stops when the company experiences a financial setback. Venis sues Yinka for breach of contract for failure to pay the additional three months. Venis loses. If you put this in our "consideration sentence" it would read: "In consideration of the feeling I have for you as a valued employee and what you are trying to do with your family and knowing the worker's comp income is insufficient, I promise to give you $500 per month while you receive worker's comp benefits." Yinka had no legal obligation to give Venis anything since she was collecting worker's comp. He only felt a moral obligation to help her. This is not adequate as consideration to create a binding contract so Venis loses the breach of contract action.

Pre-existing Legal or Contractual Obligation If the act that forms the basis of the contract is based on a **pre-existing legal or contractual obligation,** then it will not be adequate consideration to support a contract. The pre-existing obligation may be based on law or contract. Legal obligations arise from laws requiring a party to do a certain act or forbear from doing an act, while contractual obligations arise from contractual obligations already in existence.

EXAMPLE

Craig hires Lee as a computer programmer for a year. Lee's work is quite good and in six months Jeff, Craig's competitor, hears about Lee and begins to woo Lee away to work for Jeff. Craig tells Lee that if Lee stays with Craig's company for the term of Lee's contract, Craig will pay Lee a bonus of $2500 at the end of the year. Lee agrees and stays. At the end of the year Craig refuses to pay Lee the bonus. Lee sues Craig for breach of contract. As much as you will hate this, Lee loses.

After teaching thousands of students, we know you think it isn't fair that Craig promised Lee the bonus, didn't give it to her, and the court sides with Craig. But let's go back to our "consideration sentence." Our sentence would read: "In consideration of your fulfilling your already-existing contract to work for me for a year, I will give you $2500." Since Lee promises to do something she was already contractually obligated to do, she suffers no legal detriment and thus the consideration is inadequate to support the contract. When you think about how unfair this seems (as our students always do) since Craig promised the bonus to Lee, don't forget to think about the promise Lee had already made to Craig that Lee would stay for the year for the agreed upon salary.

Gratuitous Promises Gratuitous promises will also not act as good consideration to support a contract. A gratuitous promise is a promise to give someone a gift. A gift is a unilateral transaction going from one party to the other, not an exchange between the parties as consideration must be. If Linda promise to give Tess a party for Tess's 21st birthday, but then later decides not to do so, Tess cannot successfully sue Linda for breach of contract. Using our "consideration sentence," the agreement would be: "In consideration of the fact that you're turning 21, I will give you a party." This is a one-way deal. Linda is giving Tess something but Tess is not agreeing to give Linda anything in exchange. The law says no consideration supports Linda's promise to give Tess the party and since it is merely a gratuitous promise, it is not good consideration to support a contract.

EXAMPLE

However, if Tess moves in reliance on Linda's promise, and based on the promise, contracts with a florist, band, caterer, hotel, party store and dressmaker, putting down payments on all contracts to secure performance, then she will be able to get back from Linda what she has paid out in reliance on Linda's promise. **Promissory estoppel** is an equitable concept and can be thought of as rather a "substitute" for consideration that sometimes can be used where actual consideration is not present and injustice would otherwise result. Tess would be able to recover what she paid out, but no more. She cannot enforce the contract because there is no contract since there is no consideration. But the court will not allow Tess to be left holding the bag if she made the arrangements only because she justifiably relied on Linda's promise and Linda had reason to know Tess would rely on it. Since Linda set up this situation and Tess relied on Linda's promise to her detriment by spending money she would not have otherwise spent for the promised party, the court will stop Linda from using lack of consideration as a defense to a breach of contract action by Tess. Again we have a sort of forced ethics involved in the court's position here in that the court is imposing upon a person who makes a promise under circumstances they should know the other party would take seriously liability for the promise since it would be inequitable and unethical otherwise.

EXAMPLE

Illusory Promise An illusory promise looks like someone is making a commitment to an agreement, but upon closer inspection, they are not. Rose, an aromatherapist, says to Peter, owner of Smells So Good Oil Co., "I will purchase all the oil I want from you for the next six months." Four months later Rose has purchased no oil. When Peter inquires about it, Rose tells him she has no plans to do so. Peter sues Rose for breach of contract. Peter loses. The parties seemed to have a contract for Rose to buy oil from Peter for six months, but under the wording of the agreement, Rose only says she will buy the oil if she wants it. Under the agreement Rose is never required to purchase the oil. It looked like a promise to buy the oil, but it is not and the illusory promise is not enforceable as good consideration. It would be a different case entirely if Rose agreed to buy all the oil she needed for six months and she actually needed oil and did not buy it from Smells So Good.

EXAMPLE

CAPACITY

LO10

Capacity addresses whether parties entering into a contract have the minimal age or mental ability to comprehend what they have done by agreeing to be bound. Since contracts are voluntary agreements entered into by parties, it is important to ensure that the parties understand what they are doing. Did you know that the law did not give women the capacity to contract for a large part of our country's history? Women could not own property in their names and property that belonged to them was in the name of their husband or father or other male figure. If a married woman's parents died and left their estate to her, it was her husband who received the property and could do with it as he wished. Until the 1970s, married women could not have credit without their husband's signature. The Equal Credit Opportunity Act of 1974 changed that. The ECOA prohibits credit discrimination on the basis of race, color, gender, religion, national origin and age (above the age of contracting) though we have seen that such things still exist.

In addressing capacity, the law has "three Is." That is, it protects three groups in particular regarding capacity: *I*nfants, *I*ntoxicants and *I*ncompetents. Memory tip: "Capacity has three eyes" or "Infants are incompetent when they are intoxicated."

Infants

This is what the law calls those under the legal age for contracting in the state—generally 18. Parties must be very careful when dealing with minors. The law of contract is set up to protect them, and if an adult is not careful, he or she can get left holding the bag. If a party is below the legal age for contracting, his or her contracts are voidable at their option and only their option. They may **disaffirm,** or get out of, the contract any time before reaching the age of majority, or within a short time thereafter (time depends on the circumstances). If they do not wish to disaffirm the contract, they can **ratify** it by continuing the contract after reaching the age of majority, in which case the contract will be binding.

Disaffirmance and ratification can be accomplished directly or indirectly. In direct disaffirmance the minor tells the other party that she no longer wishes to be a part of the contract. Indirect disaffirmance is the minor doing something at odds with continuing the contract, such as no longer making payments on a car loan. Ratification can be direct or indirect also. That is, upon reaching the age of majority or within a short time thereafter the minor can tell the other party he wishes to continue the contract or simply engage in behavior consistent with doing so (such as continuing the car payments after reaching age 18).

In most states when a minor disaffirms a contract he has the right to the full return of whatever he gave the other party. His only responsibility is to give back whatever is left of what he received, regardless of its condition. If the car is wrecked, he gives back a wrecked car and receives whatever he has thus far paid. If the minor contracts for **necessaries** (generally defined as food, clothing or shelter) then decides to disaffirm, she can do so, but the other party is entitled to receive reasonable value for whatever he or she provided the minor. The law's position is that someone providing a minor with necessaries should not be left uncompensated if the minor disaffirms. As with recovery for contracts implied in law, recovery for extending necessaries to minors under a contract is in quantum meruit, so it is not necessarily the contract price or market value the minor must pay, but rather, the reasonable value of the necessaries received.

Incompetents

The law requires that the parties to a contract be able to know and understand what they are doing by entering into the contract. If a party suffers from a mental impairment that would prevent this, then he or she can disaffirm the contract and use the defense of incompetency if sued by the nonbreaching party. The incompetent party need not be declared incompetent by a court. In fact, if she is, the contract is void, rather than voidable. The incompetent party need only show she was incapable of understanding the nature and extent of her actions at the time she contracted. If, however, she ratifies the contract during a lucid moment the contract will be fully enforceable. How one shows that the contracting party was having a lucid moment is a matter of factual proof. Only the incompetent has a right to disaffirm the contract, and if the contract is for necessaries, the incompetent party can be made to pay reasonable value as discussed above.

Intoxicants

This includes those whose mental faculties are voluntarily or involuntarily temporarily impaired because of drugs, alcohol, or some other mind-altering substance. Intoxicants lack capacity to enter into contracts and can disaffirm them if made. They can also ratify upon becoming sober and the contract becomes enforceable. They too are responsible for the reasonable value of necessaries provided to them.

As you can see by the way the law protects those who lack capacity, the approach is that if a party lacks capacity, the other party may engage in unethical behavior and take advantage of the situation, so the law provides the a measure of protection. To a large extent, the law has not really caught up to the much more sophisticated party under 18 who legally lacks capacity to contract, but is sophisticated enough to know they are protected, so he or she takes advantage of the law. This is, of course, unethical, but it is not illegal, so liability does not generally attach.

LEGALITY

LO11

The last of our four requirements for a valid contract is legality. In order for a contract to be legal, what it proposes to do must be legal. If it is not, the contract is void.

Generally, anything that is illegal to do is illegal to contract to do or have done. When one sues the other for breach of contract due to nonperformance of an illegal contract, the court generally leaves the parties where it finds them. It does not enforce the agreement because to do so would encourage parties to continue making illegal agreements.

The law of contracts singles out certain kinds of contracts, such as those for illegally high interest rates on noncorporate loans (usury), gambling, and unlicensed professionals as illustrative of this. For instance, if a lawyer is unlicensed and performs legal services for a client, the lawyer would not be able to collect the fee for services from the client because it is illegal to contract to perform legal services if one is not a lawyer. The law closes the courts to the unlicensed lawyer, so that he will be less likely to engage in unlicensed practice if he knows he cannot sue on contracts for his services.

EXAMPLE

DIVERSITY IN THE LAW 5-3

RESTRICTIVE COVENANTS IN 2010?!

In 2005, some University of Washington students, working with the Seattle Civil Rights and Labor History Project, compiled an online database homeowners can use to see if their property is subject to a racially restrictive covenant. Their work led to the Washington legislature passing a law making it easier for homeowner associations to get rid of such restrictions. Senate Bill 6169, passed in 2006, was the direct result of the work the students did in uncovering Seattle's racial past.

Many Seattle housing subdivisions, including the one built by Bill Boeing, of Boeing airplane manufacturing fame, contained provisions much like this:

"No person or persons of Asiatic, African or Negro blood, lineage, or extraction shall be permitted to occupy a portion of said property . . .", or "No person other than one of the White Race shall be permitted to occupy any portion of any lot in said plat or of any building at any time thereon, except a domestic servant actually employed by a White occupant of such building," or "No part of said property hereby conveyed shall ever be used or occupied by any Hebrew or by any person of the Ethiopian, Malay or any Asiatic Race . . . excepting only employees in the domestic service on the premises of persons qualified hereunder as occupants and users and residing on the premises."

Though racial restrictive covenants have been illegal since 1968, they still operate informally to keep certain areas all-white. These covenants existed in virtually all areas of the country and were instrumental in creating the housing patterns we still see today, as they restricted the places where blacks, Jews, Asians, and others could live. Despite the fact that you may think that if anyone has enough money they can live anywhere they want, many of the covenants are still in operation today. An August 10, 2010 *USA Today* article reported that many of the covenants are still on the books and in Cape St. Clair, Maryland, where the covenant states that "At no time shall any lot or any part thereof be sold, leased, transferred to or permitted to be occupied by any Negro, Chinaman, Japanese, or person of Negro, Chinese or Japanese descent," the home improvement association has been trying to get rid of it, but need an 85% vote of the association to do so. They do not yet have it. Some members of the community say that although they find the provision offensive, it is a part of the community's history and worth preserving.

Do you think this is a sufficient reason for prohibiting these groups from living in this area? What "worth" do you think they are speaking of? What do you think the ethical implications are for the situation? Should the state step in and do something about it if the townspeople are not willing to? Who are the stakeholders and what are their interests? What would you do if you were white and wanted to live there without the covenant?

Sources: Greg Latshaw, "Racism Shadows Property Covenants," *USA Today*, http://www.usatoday.com/news/nation/2010-08-03-racistcovenants03_ST_N.htm?csp=usat.me Lornet Turnbull, "Homeowners Find Records Still Hold Blot of Racism," *The Seattle Times*, June 3, 2005, http://seattletimes.nwsource.com/html/localnews/2002297312_covenants03m.html; and James N. Gregory, "Stain of Racism Still Haunts Seattle Neighborhoods," *The Seattle Times*, April 6, 2006, http://seattletimes.nwsource.com/html/opinion/2002913362_jamesgregory06.html.

Courts also will not enforce agreements that may not actually be illegal, but are considered to violate public policy, that is, agreements that go against the court's determination as to the underlying policy exhibited by statutes or closely held beliefs of which the court takes notice. Public policy was at issue when courts were called upon to uphold restrictive covenants in real estate contracts. These covenants at one point routinely included in property deeds prohibited property from being conveyed to nonwhites and Jews. Courts eventually refused to uphold such covenants as against public policy, but they still exist, including the one in a home former President George W. Bush sold in 1995 restricting ownership to whites. (See Diversity in the Law 5-3, "Restrictive Covenants in 2010?!")

In the *Calvert* case (Case 5.2), the California court was called upon to determine if surrogate mother agreements, in which one woman agrees to bear a child for another, violated public policy.

CASE 5.2 Johnson v. Calvert

5 Cal. 4th 84; 871 P2d 776 (1993)

Facts: A married couple wanted a child, but the wife had undergone a hysterectomy. The couple entered into an agreement with a woman who contracted to carry a fetus comprised of the couple's sperm and egg to birth in exchange for $10,000. After relations deteriorated between the couple and the surrogate during the pregnancy, the couple went to court seeking to be declared the legal parents of the unborn child. The surrogate mother filed to be declared the mother. In deciding the matter, the court had to make a determination as to the legitimacy of the contract between the parties. The court decided the contract did not violate public policy.

Issue: Whether an agreement for a woman to carry in her body a fetus that is the product of someone else's sperm and egg, in exchange for money, violates public policy and thus is not a legal contract?

Decision: No

Reasoning: Panelli, J.: The surrogacy contract does not violate public policy. The parties voluntarily agreed to participate in *in vitro* fertilization and related medical procedures before the child was conceived; at the time when Anna [the surrogate mother] entered into the contract, therefore, she was not vulnerable to financial inducements to part with her own expected offspring. Anna was not the genetic mother of the child. The payments to Anna under the contract were meant to compensate her for her services in gestating the fetus and undergoing labor, rather than giving up "parental" rights to the child.

Anna and some commentators have expressed concern that surrogacy contracts tend to exploit or dehumanize women, especially women of lower economic status. Although common sense suggests that women of lesser means serve as surrogacy mothers more often than do wealthy women, there has been no proof that surrogacy contracts exploit poor women to any greater degree than economic necessity in general exploits them by inducing them to accept lower-paid or otherwise undesirable employment.

The argument that a woman cannot knowingly and intelligently agree to gestate and deliver a baby for intending parents carries overtones of the reasoning that for centuries prevented women from attaining equal economic rights and professional status under the law. To resurrect this view is both to foreclose a personal and economic choice on the part of the surrogate mother, and to deny intending parents what may be their only means of procreating a child of their own genes. Judgment of the Court of appeals is Affirmed.

CASE QUESTIONS

1. Do you agree with the court that surrogacy contracts do not violate public policy? Discuss.
2. Does the court's comment about the exploitation of women make sense to you? Explain.
3. What factors should the court consider in determining if contracts are void as against public policy?

Enforceability of Contracts

While not a requirement for validity, there is another requirement in the bundle of rights for contracts to be fully effective: enforceability. After all, what good is a valid contract if it cannot be enforced by a court of law?

STATUTE OF FRAUDS

There is no requirement that a contract be written to be valid; however, under the **Statute of Frauds,** certain types of contracts thought to lend themselves to "faulty memories" must be in writing in order to be enforced in court. If a contract is one of those required to be written under the Statute of Frauds, it is referred to as being "within the Statute." (See Take Away 5-8, "Contracts Within the Statute of Frauds: MY LEGS") Oral contracts about these matters are legal, and may be valid, but they simply cannot be enforced in a court of law because they are not in writing. If the contract is not in writing as required by the Statute of Frauds, check to see if there are facts supporting an exception to the Statute that applies to make the contract enforceable even though no writing is present. Do not use an exception to the writing requirement until and unless you are certain that no sufficient writing exists. The following are contracts that are within the Statute of Frauds and thus required to be in writing.

Contracts Made in Consideration of Marriage

As unromantic as it may sound, if parties agree to certain promises as a prerequisite to marriage ("If you marry me, I'll give you $10,000") then the agreement is only enforceable if it is in writing.

Contracts Incapable of Being Performed within a Year from the Time They Are Made

These must be in writing to be enforceable. The time starts to run when the contract is made, *not* when it is to be performed. Whether it is capable of being performed is not a function of the substantive performance itself, but rather, what the agreement language says about the *time* of performance. Look at what we will call the "time language" to determine if the contract is capable of being performed within a year from the time it

 TAKE AWAY 5-8

CONTRACTS WITHIN THE STATUTE OF FRAUDS: MY LEGS

There are only six contracts mentioned as being within the Statute of Frauds and therefore need a writing to be enforceable. However, since some of the contracts have parts to them, they can sometimes seem like a lot to remember. Try using the MEMORY TIP: MY LEGS. As always, if you think of a better one, by all means let us know.

 Marriage (contracts made in consideration of marriage)
Year (Contracts incapable of being performed within a year from the time they are made)
Land (Contracts for an interest in land)
Executor (Executor's promise to be personally liable for decedent's debts)
Goods (Contracts for the sale of goods of $500 or more)
Surety (Contract of a surety to be bound for the debts of debtor if debtor does not pay)

was made. Do not be concerned with the time period itself, but rather, what the agreement says about the time.

EXAMPLE

For instance, if the agreement is that "Jenny will come work for XYZ Corporation for two years," then the contract is incapable of being performed within a year and must be in writing to be enforced. Under the "time language" the contract is to be performed for a two-year period. If Jenny leaves before two years, the contract is breached. If the contract is not in writing, XYZ Corporation would not be able to successfully sue Jenny for breach even if she left before two years because under the Statute of Frauds since the contract is incapable of being performed within a year from the time it was made it is required to be in writing and is not, so it is unenforceable.

EXAMPLE

However, if the agreement is that Jenny is to work for XYZ Corporation "for up to two years," then the contract is capable of being performed within a year from the time it was made and need not be in writing to be enforced. The "time language" says that Jenny has up to two years, not that she must stay for two years. If Jenny leaves in six months she will not have breached the contract because by its language the contract was capable of being performed in less than a year from the time it was made. If an issue arose about the contract, XYZ (or Jenny) would be able to take the case to court to have it enforced even though the agreement was not in writing. The agreement was not required to be in writing under the Statute of Frauds because by its time language it was capable of being performed within a year from the time it was made.

Contracts for an Interest in Land

These must be in writing to be enforceable. This includes leases of over a year, sales of real estate, mortgages and any other interests in land. If the agreement is not in writing but the buyer moves onto the property, makes improvements and pays part of the purchase price, the law will allow the agreement to be enforced even without the writing. This is the **part performance exception.**

Agreements for an Executor to Be Personally Bound

An executor is the individual appointed in a will to take charge of the decedent's estate. Agreements in which an executor agrees to be personally bound to pay the decedent's debts must be in writing to be enforceable. Under the terms of Ann's will, Bill is the executor of Ann's estate. At the repast following the funeral Bill tells one of Ann's creditors that if the assets of Ann's estate are insufficient to pay the debt to the creditor, that Bill will make good on the debt himself out of deference to Ann and Bill's friendship. Ann's assets are not sufficient to pay the creditor. Bill refuses to pay the creditor as promised. The creditor sues Bill. Bill wins. Since this is the promise of an executor to be personally liable for the decedent's debt, the Statute of Frauds requires the promise to be in writing to be enforceable. Since the promise is not in writing the creditor cannot successfully take the matter to court.

EXAMPLE

Goods of $500 or More

Contracts for the sale of goods of $500 or more must be in writing to be enforceable. This is a UCC rule. If the goods involved cost $499.99 or less there need not be a writing. If it is $500 or more, a writing is required. There are four exceptions to the rule:

    a. *Specially manufactured goods upon which performance has begun* This applies where specially manufactured goods of $500 or more have been ordered orally, for instance, by phone. If the maker has begun to make them and the buyer backs out of the deal the law will permit the seller to recover on this oral contract for $500 or more even though it should have been in writing. For instance, Anita places a $650 catalog order by phone with OfficeSupply for business

EXAMPLE

stationery, pencils, pens, cards and magnets, all with her business logo. After the printer begins to fill the order, Anita cancels. The oral contract for more than $500 will be enforced anyway since the contract was for specially manufactured goods (personalized items) and the printer has begun performance on the contract.

b. *Part performance* If one of the parties partially performs the contract, then the contract will be enforceable to the extent it was performed. For example, Viji places a phone order for 100 new brooms, 100 new mops, 100 new dustpans, and 100 new vacuum cleaners, for a total of $525. Half of the order was delivered and Viji accepted it, but refused to go through with the rest of the contract. Since the contract was for over $500, it was required to be in writing for the seller to be able to sue Viji for breach of contract. It was not in writing. However, Viji accepted half the goods. She must now pay for the goods she accepted but the contract for the other half is still unenforceable since the contract is only enforceable to the amount partially performed.

If the contract cannot be divided because of its nature, it will be enforceable in its entirety. David orally orders a new $650 television set for his employee lounge. He sends a $50 down payment. David then backs out of the contract. The contract for the television set would be enforceable by the seller.

c. *Admissions in court documents* Sometimes parties to an oral contract will admit in court documents that they entered into a contract, but because they know oral contracts of $500 or more must be in writing to be enforceable, they believe they have a defense. Or they may agree that they had a contract, but they allege it is for a lesser amount than asserted. If in the court documents they admit to the contract, then they are liable for the amount to which they admitted. However, they are responsible for no more than they admitted.

d. *Written confirmation between merchants* This is a merchants-only rule under the UCC. That is, it applies to contracts where both parties to the contracts are merchants. If a merchant orally contracts to buy goods of $500 or more and the seller sends the buyer a written confirmation after the oral agreement, the written confirmation will bind both of the merchants unless the buyer merchant objects to the terms of the written confirmation within 10 days of receiving it. This generally covers situations in which the parties agree orally, but the written confirmation differs from the oral agreement in some way. The merchant receiving the written confirmation has a duty to look at it and make sure it accurately reflects the oral agreement, or she will be bound.

Suretyship Agreements

Suretyship is the legal relationship formed when someone agrees to pay another's debt if the debtor does not pay. The surety agreement is essentially, "Give the debtor the money and if the debtor does not pay, I will." It is a secondary promise in the sense that the debtor is actually the one who incurs the debt. This is perfectly legal, as you well know if your parents did this so you could purchase a car or borrow your tuition. You probably know it as co-signing a loan. The co-signor is acting as a surety for the borrower's loan. If the surety's promise to pay is to be enforced in court when the debtor doesn't pay and the creditor wants to look to the surety for payment, the suretyship agreement must be in writing.

However, if the real purpose of the promise is to benefit the surety (the one making the promise to pay if the primary debtor does not), then under the **main purpose doctrine,** the promise is enforceable even though oral. For instance, Brittany is having an office building built. Sam, the electrician working on the building, tells Brittany that Sam cannot finish Brittany's work because she cannot get the rest of the electrical supplies she needs from the electrical supplier because of a dispute between Sam and the supplier. Until Sam finishes the job, no other work can proceed on the building. Brittany goes to the supplier and asks the supplier to give Sam what she needs to finish and if Sam does not pay him then Brittany will. This really isn't a promise being made for Sam's benefit, but rather for Brittany's and it need not be in writing to be enforced. Therefore, though technically Brittany is a surety the law will allow Brittany's promise to be enforceable though not in writing because the promise to the electrical supplier is really for Brittany's own benefit so the work can continue on her building. This is different from a true co-signor.

If instead of "give it to him and if he doesn't pay I will," the promise is instead "give it to him and I'll pay," then a writing is not required. This is what happens, for instance, when you send flowers to someone. You order flowers from the florist but they are for someone else, not you. You are agreeing to pay for the flowers yourself though they will not go to you but to someone else. This is a primary promise, not a secondary one, and since it is not a surety agreement, it need not be in writing to be enforced.

THE WRITING REQUIREMENT

We usually think of a contract as a long, formal written document but that is not what the Statute of Frauds requires. There must simply be something in writing, signed by the party who is being sued, evidencing the material terms of the agreement. If it is in more than one writing that must be read together to understand the contract, the parts must be able to relate the pieces together without explanation. It is conceivable that a cancelled check is a sufficient writing for Statute of Fraud purposes.

Let's say Tracy enters into an oral contract to purchase a parcel of land for a new office building. Tracy pays half the price by check, and then the seller breached the contract and refused to sell the land to Tracy. Tracy sues the seller for breach and the seller defends by pleading that the contract for the sale of land was required to be in writing under the Statute of Frauds but was not, thus rendering it unenforceable. Tracy has the cancelled check made out to the seller as the payee, Tracy's name as drawer of the check who is purchasing the land, the amount of half the price, the signature of the buyer on the back as an endorsement from when she cashed the check, and a memo notation on left front bottom of the check that it was "1/2 the payment for Plot 40, Plat 63, Clarke County, GA." It is therefore clear that there was an agreement for Tracy to purchase a specific piece of legally described land from the seller, for which she paid the seller half the price. The seller's signature (the party to be charged, i.e., the party being sued) is on the back of the check as an endorsement, and the date of the transaction is there. This writing would be sufficient for Statute of Frauds purposes, though it is not a written contract, per se.

PAROL EVIDENCE RULE

The Parol Evidence Rule provides that if there is a valid, written, integrated contract between the parties, then evidence of prior or contemporaneous agreements will not be permitted to vary or alter its terms. In other words, if the parties to a contract commit the contract to writing as the sole agreement between them, but do not include in it some point they agreed on orally before signing the contract, then the point is lost. Contracts are to be enforced as written. It does not require that certain types of contracts be in writing as the Statute of Frauds does. Rather, it requires that *if* the parties decide to commit their contract to writing and it is the sole evidence of their agreement, then everything they wanted to include in the written contract be there.

Larry enters into an oral agreement with Mark to purchase a piece of equipment for $400, to be delivered at Larry's warehouse. Before Mark and Larry sign the written agreement Larry realizes it does not contain the delivery provision. Larry mentions it to Mark. Mark replies "Don't worry. I know where it's going and I'll be the one making the delivery." They sign the contract without the delivery provision.

Later, the equipment is not delivered and Mark says it is at his warehouse waiting for Larry to come and get it. Larry sues for breach of contract, alleging Mark did not deliver the equipment as agreed. The written contract, however, had no provision saying Mark would deliver it to Larry. Since this provision is not included in the written contract and it was agreed to before the contract was signed, Larry will not be able to introduce evidence in court showing he made such an agreement with Mark. Only the terms of the written contract will be enforced and that does not say seller is to deliver, so Larry loses. If you have a written contract, make sure to include everything!

Contracts Involving Third Parties

L013

Until now we have talked only about the offeror and the offeree being involved in the contract. However, there is the possibility that others will be involved at some point. In such cases, the issue is whether the third party has any rights in the contract, either to sue for breach or to demand performance. The answer to these questions depends on the type of relationship the third party has to the contract. The ways in which a third party can be involved in a contract are by assignment or as third party beneficiaries.

ASSIGNMENT

EXAMPLE

Once a contract is formed, there are rights and benefits on both sides. If Ketan contracts to dispose of hazardous waste for Heather, Ketan has the right to receive payment and the obligation to dispose of the waste. Heather has the right to have the waste disposed of, and the obligation to pay. If either side decides to allow someone else to receive their benefit in the contract, it is accomplished by an **assignment.** If the duties are given to a third party to perform, it is called a **delegation.** The word assignment is used in a dual sense. It means giving one's rights in a contract over to a third party not originally involved in the contract, and, more generically, the relationship which transfers the rights and duties in a contract to someone else not originally a party to the contract.

PARTIES TO ASSIGNMENTS

The language of assignments can seem a bit confusing since you are probably not used to hearing it. Let's give you the terms for the parties right up front. The party who assigns their right is an **assignor.** The one to whom such rights are assigned is an **assignee.** The one who owes a duty to perform is the **obligor.** The one to whom performance is owed is the **obligee.** The one who delegates his or her duties is the **delegator.** The one to whom such duties are delegated is the **delegatee.** (See Take Away 5-9, "Assignment of Contract," to see the relationship formed when this occurs.)

Either party to a contract can assign his or her rights to a third party and generally can do so without the permission of the original obligor in the contract. The obligor, who was to perform for the original party, must now perform, instead, for the assignee. Virtually any contract may be assigned as long as the contract is not too personal or does not substantially change the obligation of the obligor. The obligor who must now perform for the assignee may not refuse to perform simply because the assignee was not originally a party to the contract. However, if the obligation is too personal, or if assigning the contract changes the obligor's duties under the contract to make performance more burdensome, the obligor can refuse to perform.

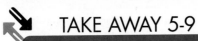

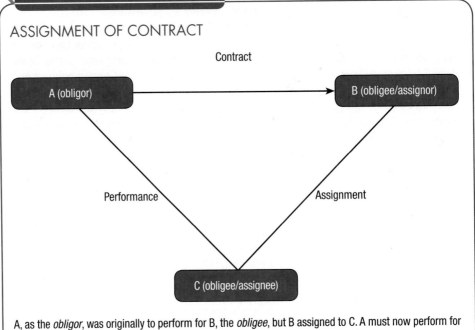

ASSIGNMENT OF CONTRACT

A, as the *obligor*, was originally to perform for B, the *obligee*, but B assigned to C. A must now perform for C rather than A.

EXAMPLE

Sangrae, owner of Kleen N' Brite Janitorial Services, contracts to clean Jay's office building. Jay later assigns his rights in the contract to Paul, so that Sangrae must now clean Paul's office building rather than Jay's. If the two buildings are substantially the same, Sangrae cannot refuse to perform for Paul under the assigned contract. However, if Jay's building is 240,000 square feet, and Paul's building is 560,000 square feet, Sangrae's duties under the contract with Paul would be substantially different than they were under the contract with Jay. If Sangrae refused to clean Paul's building, she would not be liable for breach.

There are no formalities to assigning a contract and no consideration is necessary. However, if no consideration is given and the assignor chooses to take back the assignment, the assignee has no recourse. The assignment is an agreement between the assignor and assignee, but it is not considered to be a contract between them. Instead, when an assignment is made, the assignor makes certain implied warranties. If these warranties are breached, the assignee can sue for breach of warranty. The warranties are mainly that the assignor has the right to assign under the contract and will not do anything to interfere with the assignee's right to receive performance under the contract. Other than the warranties, the assignee who gives no consideration for an assignment has no rights if the assignor wishes to rescind the assignment.

When a contract is assigned, the assignee steps into the shoes of the assignor and is in the same position the assignor was under the contract. The assignee is subject to any defenses to nonperformance which the obligor has against the assignor. Under an assignment the assignee gets no greater rights in the contract than the original party/assignor had.

EXAMPLE

For instance, in our previous example, if the buildings were comparable and Jay assigned his rights to Paul, but Jay had not paid for the office cleaning as agreed under the contract, then Sangrae would not have to perform for Paul, the assignee. Paul would have to sue Jay for breach of warranty for engaging in activity (nonpayment of the contract price) which adversely impacted Paul's rights under the assignment (since the price was not paid, Paul could not get his building cleaned). If Sangrae does not clean Paul's building and Paul sues Sangrae for breach of contract for her refusal to do so, Sangrae can use the defense of nonperformance by Jay, which is good against Paul's breach of contract action.

An assignable contract need not have the permission of the obligor to be assigned, but notice should be given to the obligor by the assignee or assignor as soon as possible after assignment so that the obligor will not perform for the original party/assignor. While the obligor's permission is not necessary for a valid assignment, if the obligor gives permission, so that now all three parties agree to the assignment, it is called a **novation**. A novation takes the assignor out of the contract altogether and substitutes the assignee in the assignor's place. The assignor no longer has any part in the contract. This can be very important since an assignment does not otherwise relieve the assignor of any contractual responsibilities. Without a novation, if the obligor did not perform for the assignee, the assignee could look to the assignor for performance. If there is a novation, however, the assignor is totally out of the picture. (See Law in the News 5-1, "Car Customers' Big Assignment Surprise Backfire.")

Delegations cannot be made without the permission of the other party to the contract if the contract is based on the personal reputation or skills of the delegator. For instance, The White House contracts to have President Obama's official portrait painted by a famous portrait artist who is known around the world for his skill and life-like portraiture. He gets too busy to do the portrait and delegates his duties under the contract to another artist as a delegatee. The White House can refuse performance by the delegatee since the contract is too personal to be delegated.

EXAMPLE

THIRD PARTY BENEFICIARY CONTRACTS

LO14

Unlike assignments, which have third parties enter the contract only after the contract is created, **third party beneficiary contracts** include third parties in the contract from the

LAW IN THE NEWS 5-1

CAR CUSTOMERS' BIG ASSIGNMENT SURPRISE BACKFIRE

As if the country's economic woes were not bad enough, another financial surprise took place that has left car buyers more than a bit perturbed. A good number of car buyers trade in their present car when buying a new one order to make their payments more affordable. The trade-in is basically an assignment by the customer of their contract rights in the vehicle being traded in. The agreement is generally that the car dealer will take the traded-in vehicle, pay off the balance to the original seller who sold the customer the car, and the dealer will re-sell the car as a used car.

Well, imagine trading in your old car, buying a new one, only to receive notice that the dealer to whom you assigned the rights in your car is now going out of business and has not paid off the trade-in as promised and has left you to take care of it. This happened to quite a few customers during the recent car industry downturn when car manufacturers cut back so substantially on their dealerships, and because consumers were buying so few cars, many dealerships went under. Between the car dealers having a rough time of it because of higher gas prices, the economy tanking, and the car industry bailout fiasco, it was all some of them could do to stay afloat. One of the obligations they were unable to meet was paying off the cars that had been traded in to them under contract assignments.

Since the assignment of a contract does not relieve the original party to the contract unless there is novation, customers who had traded in their cars were not the least bit happy to have the trade-in bounce back and the customer now had two car notes to contend with!

Source: Don Thompson, Associated Press, "Car Dealers Shock Buyers with Unpaid Liens," March 4, 2009, http://gotplates.wordpress.com/2009/03/04/some-dealers-are-not-paying-off-the-trade-insbe-careful-when-you-make-a-dealer-trade/.

outset. By design, the contract is between the offeror and offeree, but it is for the benefit of the third party beneficiary. Third party beneficiaries have rights in the contract from the time it was made and their rights cannot be abridged without their consent.

EXAMPLE

As we discussed earlier, a very simple, but familiar, example of a third party beneficiary contract is having the florist deliver flowers to someone. Kenyatta decides to send flowers to Blake on the occasion of their first anniversary in business. Kenyatta calls the florist and orders the flowers, but the flowers are not to be sent to her, but rather, to Blake. From the outset and by design, the contract is between the Kenyatta and the florist, for the benefit of Blake.

The contract between Kenyatta and the florist is one with which you are already familiar. It is just a regular contract, with the regular contract remedies if something should go wrong. However, with the third party contract aspect, the question often arises as to what rights Blake, who was not involved in making the contract, has if something goes wrong with the performance he is to receive, such as the flowers do not arrive, or they arrive wilted and dead. Does Blake have the right to sue the florist since he was not involved in the contract? The answer is yes. Blake is a third party beneficiary and has the right to sue the florist for breach of contract if something goes wrong with the flowers.

EXAMPLE

The other question is who else can Blake sue if something goes wrong? Can he also sue Kenyatta? This depends on what the relationship is between Kenyatta and Blake relative to the flowers. If the flowers are a gift, then Kenyatta is a **donor** and Blake is a **donee beneficiary.** A donor is someone who gives a gift and a donee is one who receives a gift from the donor. Since there is no contract between the two, and a gift is a gratuitous promise not supported by consideration, there is no basis for a donee to sue a donor. Thus, Blake could not sue Kenyatta if the flowers were a gift. Blake could only sue the florist.

EXAMPLE

If, instead of sending the flowers to Blake for their company's anniversary, Kenyatta was sending the flowers to Blake to repay a debt between the two based on a previous obligation, Kenyatta would be the debtor and Blake would be the creditor. Since a creditor can sue a debtor for nonpayment of a debt, Blake would be able to sue Kenyatta if the flowers arrived dead. If Kenyatta was sending the flowers to Blake to repay a debt, Blake is a **third party creditor beneficiary.** If something goes wrong with the flowers, Blake can sue the florist who was contractually obligated to provide fresh flowers to Blake, or Kenyatta, who owed him a debt and did not repay it. Blake would not be able to recover twice for the same debt.

Whether Blake was a donee beneficiary or a creditor beneficiary, he has rights in the third party beneficiary contract because he is an **intended beneficiary.** However, there are times when a third party may benefit from a contract, but the benefit was unintentional. The company that provides the florist with gas for his delivery trucks benefits by the florist having flowers to deliver. However, the gas station owner would only be an unintended beneficiary, and thus have no right to sue on the contract if Kenyatta decided not to have the flowers delivered after all. **Unintended beneficiaries** have no right to enforce a contract as a third party beneficiary.

EXAMPLE

LO15

Contract Performance

A party to a contract is generally supposed to perform the contract as soon as his or her duty to perform arises. We are used to thinking of that duty as immediate. However, it need not be. A contract can be set up so that there are conditions that must occur. If the duty to perform has a **condition precedent** to performance, then the duty to perform does not rise until the condition has been met. The condition being met precedes the party's performance. For instance, Calvin and Iris agree that Iris will wash and detail Calvin's car on Saturday for $75 if it is a pretty sunny day. If it rains on Saturday Iris has no responsibility to wash and detail Calvin's car. If it a sunny day, Iris must do so. Saturday being a sunny day is a condition precedent to Iris's duty to perform for Calvin.

EXAMPLE

If the condition is a **condition subsequent,** then performance is due until and unless the condition is met. For instance, Joaquin deeds a piece of property to his alma mater, The University of New Mexico, "only so long as the land is used for purposes of teaching the business curriculum." The University would be able to keep the property unless the condition of not using it for business education purposes is met. If the university began using the property for something other than business education purposes, the land would revert back to Joaquin.

EXAMPLE

Most conditions are **concurrent conditions.** That is, the performance by both parties takes place at the same time. When you go to the store to buy groceries for cash, you pay for the groceries and the store gives you the groceries immediately. The delivery of the groceries and the payment of the grocery bill are both done at the same time and are thus concurrent conditions. Unless a party makes arrangements to the contrary, conditions are usually concurrent. In order to bring a cause of action for breach, a party would be required to have attempted to perform as per the contract and the other party did not perform as agreed.

EXAMPLE

Summary

Whew! That was a long chapter! Contracts are an important part of both our business and personal lives. In this chapter we have discussed what is required in order to have a valid enforceable contract, what to do if contracts are breached, how third parties come into contracts, which contracts must be in writing to be enforced, and how parties to a contract must perform in order to avoid liability. In addition to the requirements for valid contracts, we have also seen how easy it is for unethical behavior to take place when making contracts and what to be aware of in particular aspects of contracting. Following these rules closely will greatly lessen the possibility of legal problems in this area.

Review Questions

1. On July 1, 2010, Andre, a computer engineer, orally contracts with UGA Construction Company to provide computer support services for innovations UGA wishes to institute. Under the contract, Andre is to provide the services to UGA from January 2, 2011 to September 1, 2011. Andre begins work as scheduled, but is terminated by UGA without explanation on April 11, 2011. When Andre sues UGA Construction Company for breach of contract, UGA's defense is that the contact is not enforceable because it is oral. Is this a good defense? Explain. LO12

2. Linda O. organizes an office betting pool at her workplace for the NCAA Basketball Tournament. Gambling is illegal in the state.

Everyone contributes $25, winner take all. When Chris wins the pool, Linda refuses to give Chris the money that Chris won, well over $1200. When Chris sues Linda for breach of contract to collect her money, Chris loses. Explain. LO11

3. The agreement between Chris and Linda is LO3
   a. void.
   b. voidable.
   c. valid.
   d. unconscionable.

4. In agreements of this sort, when a party sues for breach of contact, the court will _____ _____. LO4

5. On March 4, Gloria calls Sheffield, Inc., and inquires about cleaning services for her office building. Kim Sung gives Gloria an offer over the phone and says he will send the contract over for her to sign. When Gloria receives the contract on March 6, she immediately signs it and puts it in the mail. A few hours later Gloria finds out she can have the work done elsewhere for cheaper, and faxes a rejection to Sheffield. Sheffield receives the signed contract on March 12. As per the contract, Sheffield employees show up on March 15 to clean Gloria's office building. Gloria refuses to let them enter the premises, and says there is no contract between Gloria and Sheffield because she rejected it. If Sheffield sues Gloria for breach of contract, who wins, and why? LO7

6. Weinstein, Inc., orders four Lear jets from Johnson Aerospace Co., for an agreed price of $295,000 per jet. The contract for the purchase of the jets is 10 pages long, with complete specifications as to instrumentality, capacity, interior decor, etc. When Weinstein gets ready to sign the contracts, it notices that the color for the cloth on one jet's seats is "#301, Meadow Green." The color is supposed to be "#306 Forest Green." Weinstein calls Johnson and discusses the matter and signs the contracts after Johnson said the seats would be "Forest Green." Satisfied that the seats would be the correct color, Weinstein signs the contracts as is, and does not note the change on the contract. When the jets are delivered, the seats are "Meadow Green" not Forest Green." When Weinstein sues Johnson, what happens? LO12

7. Archie has been trying to get a contract to handle a very large, very prestigious account. Unbeknownst to him, his friend Ku mentioned him to the owner of the company he was trying to deal with. Archie later receives a call from the owner of the company asking if Archie could take on the account, which Archie agrees to do.

When Archie calls Ku to tell him the good news, Ku tells Archie of his conversation with the owner. Archie tells Ku that he is so thankful for what Ku did, he wants to give $50,000 to Ku's favorite charity. When Ku later calls to give Archie the name of the charity, Archie says he has decided not to give the money. When Ku sues Archie for breach of contract, who wins and why? LO9

8. A promise for a promise is a LO3
   a. unilateral contract.
   b. bilateral contract.
   c. executed contract.
   d. voidable contract.

9. When Jekyll goes to paint Hyde's house at the time agreed, Hyde refuses to allow Jekyll in to do the painting. If Hyde sues Jekyll for breach of contract for failure to paint his house, Jekyll can likely successfully defend on the basis of _____. LO15

10. Sarafina enters into a contract with The Biceps Store weight training facility to use their facility for one year. After five months, Sarafina feels she has become too muscular and no longer wishes to train. Sarafina assigns her rights in the contract to Alice. When Alice comes to The Biceps Store to train, they refuse to allow her to do so, saying they did not enter into a contract with her. What are Alice's rights, if any? LO13

11. Mariko is having a house built. After the specifications for the house have been provided to the contractor, the contract has been signed and the contractor has begun to build the house, Mariko demands that the contractor add beneath her bedroom floor heating coils to heat the floor and floor lights which will light her path to the bathroom during the night. These additions were not in the original agreement. The contractor refuses. Is this a breach of contract? Why or why not? Does Mariko have any recourse? Explain. LO4

Ethics Issue

Early in the chapter we alluded to an ethical aspect of contracts by imagining you were a ticketholder to a Michael Jackson concert at the time of his death. The Final Tour is announced, tickets go on sale, the shows immediately sell out, and then Michael Jackson dies quite suddenly two weeks before the tour is to begin. Aside from any legal contractual issues, discuss the ethical considerations for what to do about refunding the tickets. That is, even if the agreement that ticketholders (generally unknowingly) entered into said their money would not be refunded in such an event, discuss the ethics of the situation. Who are the stakeholders? Think of as many as you possibly can. What are the issues involved? What does the tour promoter stand to lose with each scenario? What does it stand to gain? Where do law and ethics interface here in such an unprecedented occurrence (not just the death of a performer, but one of Michael Jackson's unparalleled stature)? Does sentiment enter into the picture under the circumstances? In what way? Should it? How would you determine the best ethical position to take about refunding the money?

Group Exercise

Have each group decide on some type of agreement they would like to enter into. After the decision is made, have two groups come together and negotiate one group's contract. The group then meets with another group and has that group negotiate its contract.

Each group will have met with one group to negotiate their own contract, and one to negotiate the contract of another group. How does it work out? Were all matters in the contract carefully considered? Were the parties willing to compromise if necessary?

Key Terms

Torts

Learning Objectives

After reading this chapter, you should be able to:

L01   Define what torts are and who commits them

L02   Recite the different categories of torts

L03   Discuss the underlying basis for the different categories of torts

L04   Discuss responsibility a business owner has for torts committed by employees

L05   Define strict liability and give its defense

L06   Explain negligence actions and list the requirements and their defenses

L07   List the intentional torts and give the requirements for each as well as defenses

L08   Determine appropriate ethical considerations regarding torts

 ## Opening Scenario

Shema owns an art business called Shema's Art Works. Shema receives a commission to paint a mural on the side of a building downtown. Three of Shema's employees are painting the mural on the building when the scaffold they erected to do the project falls and injures a passerby. Is Shema legally liable for the injuries to the passerby?

Introduction and Background: What Torts are, Who Commits Them, and the Categories of Torts

In this chapter you will learn about personal and business liability for civil wrongs that may occur and defenses that may be used to avoid tort liability.

L01

As we discussed briefly in the introductory chapter, torts are civil wrongs—violations of law that are civil rather than criminal in nature. The plaintiff sues to receive compensation for losses suffered by the tort being committed against him or her. In this chapter, we will learn what actions are available to individuals and to business owners for torts against the person, property, or business. We will also discuss business owner liability for torts that are committed by those who work for the business owner. Learning about torts will also help you know what to do to to avoid or lessen possible liability for tortious activity in business.

Ethical considerations are numerous in the tort area, and are often quite gray. Even the decision as to whether to sue for a perceived wrong can be an ethical decision. Should parents sue a school when their child is disciplined at school for items placed on MySpace or Facebook? Should an individual who buys a dog like the one she saw on a movie sue when the dog turns out not to be like the movie animal (an issue that comes up each time a movie is released with a cute/funny/ smart/cuddly animal featured)? Should bloggers and website owners be held liable for posting what turns out to be defamatory comments written by third parties? Should one set of parents sue another set of parents who served alcohol to the underaged children of the first parents in the home of the second? Should lawyers who sign up to go surfing at an American Bar Association meeting in Hawaii sue the ABA if they are injured while surfing? All of these are actual cases so it is clear that as a society we have come to expect tort law to compensate for virtually every perceived injury we may encounter. Thus, often when we see or hear news of someone suing, we think it was unethical for them to do so. This chapter will explore the torts for which the law allows recovery, and those it does not, and some of the ethical issues involved in tort law.

LO1 LO2 LO3

There are three large categories of torts, based on the intent of the tortfeasor. If the tortfeasor intended to do the act that resulted in the harm to the victim, it is an intentional tort. If the tortfeasor did not intend to do the act, and instead the act was the result of the tortfeasor's failure to meet a required standard of care to prevent an unreasonable risk of harm to others, it is negligence. If the tortfeasor engaged in activity that a statute classifies as one that is so dangerous that the tortfeasor must be responsible for virtually all the harm that arises as a result of engaging in the activity, the offense is one of strict liability. There are torts that arise when businesses manufacture or sell products placed in the stream of commerce as well. These are product liability cases and are thought of as a type of negligence action rather than an intentional tort.

Business Owner Liability for Torts Committed by Employees: Vicarious Liability and Respondeat Superior

LO4

Generally speaking, everyone is responsible for the torts he or she commits. However, an important part of torts committed in the business setting is the concept of **respondeat superior.** Respondeat superior involves **vicarious liability** which is liability imposed upon someone who did not actually commit the tort. Under this theory the law imposes upon a business owner liability for torts committed by an employee working for the business owner if the tort was committed within the scope of the employee's employment. For instance, in the opening scenario if Shema were sued, she would be held liable if her employees had not put the scaffolding together correctly and it resulted in the accident. The employees are liable for the torts they committed also, but generally it is the employer who has the deeper pockets,(known as the **deep pockets theory**) allowing the victim to recover more money for his or her injuries. Both are named in the lawsuit, but it is the employer who generally pays.

EXAMPLE

"Within the scope of employment" generally refers to an employee engaging in any activity reasonably within the realm of what would ordinarily be expected to be performed by an employee on the job (see Diversity in the Law 6-1, "Torts Even in War"). For instance, in the opening scenario, assembling the scaffolding would be within the scope of Shema's employees' employment.

EXAMPLE

TORTS EVEN IN WAR

Among interesting attempts to impose "vicarious liability," the issue of who is to be held responsible has arisen in some rather unusual circumstances, including torts that arose in the context of war.

In a much publicized case involving treatment of prisoners of war at the infamous Abu Ghraib prison in Iraq, seven Iraqis who allege that they or their husbands were detained by the U.S. military at Abu Ghraib sued private contractors who provided interpreters and interrogators to the U.S. military in Iraq, asserting tort claims including assault, battery, false imprisonment, intentional infliction of emotional distress, and negligence. Plaintiffs, Muslims, allege that defendants and/or their agents tortured one or more of them by, among other things, holding (what turned out to be an unloaded) gun to the head of one of them and pulling the trigger, beating them, urinating on them, electrocuting one of them, gouging out an eye, threatening to attack them with dogs, depriving them of food and water, forcing them to be naked for prolonged periods, subjecting them to long periods of cold, excessive noise, and loud music, photographing them while naked, forcing them to witness the abuse of other prisoners including rape, sexual abuse, beatings and attack by dogs, forcing one of them to wear women's underwear on his head, having women soldiers order one of them to take off his clothes, then beating him when he refused, forbidding them to pray, and falsely telling one of them his family members had been killed. *Ibrahim v. Titan Corporation* (391 F. Supp 2d 10; 2005 U.S. Dist. LEXIS 22814 [DCDC 2005]).

In a similar case, eleven Indonesian citizens filed suit against Exxon, for various torts, alleging that during an ongoing conflict between the Indonesian government and Achenese rebels, Exxon attempted to protect and secure its liquid natural gas extraction pipeline and liquification facility in Arun, Indonesia, by contracting with a unit of the Indonesian national army to provide security for the pipeline. Exxon allegedly made decisions about where to build bases, hired mercenaries to train security troops, and provided logistical support. Plaintiffs allege that because of this, Exxon is an aider and abettor or the proximate cause of the alleged misconduct of the soldiers through genocide, torture, crimes against humanity, kidnapping, murder, and sexual violence. *John Doe v. Exxon Mobil Corporation*, 393 F. Supp. 2d 20 (DDC 2005).

In *Abiola v. Gen. Abdusalami Abubakar,* 2005 U.S. Dist. LEXIS 27831 (N.D. IL, E Div. 2005), Nigerian nationals sued a Nigerian general they alleged committed grave human rights abuses while a member of the military regime that ruled Nigeria from 1993–1999.

In each case the courts allowed the cases to proceed over the objection of the defendants. You may wish to consider the ethical implications of vicarious liability. No matter how much training an individual might have, employers can only control so much in terms of the actions of their employees. Is it fair and just to hold employers to this level of accountability for these allegedly wrongful actions? Where might you draw a line? Keeping in mind that the Abu Ghraib situation was post-9/11, what impact do you think the national origin, ethnicity, or religion of the prisoners had on the decision as to who ended up there? Do you think a prisoner should be able to make a valid claim that he was wrongfully detained simply because he was Middle Eastern, Muslim, and fit the profile of a terrorist? Even though an employer can provide training to employees regarding how to conduct themselves, if the employee is working for the employer, doesn't the employer have the ultimate power to terminate employees who do not act in accordance with the employer's dictates?

In Reality Check 6-1 (see p. 129), "Liability? You Make the Call . . . ," several actual situations are presented for you to decide if the employer should be held vicariously liable for an employee's actions through respondeat superior.

Now that you understand how a business owner can be held liable for the torts of his or her employees committed within the scope of employment (see Take Away 6-1, "Vicarious Liability"), we can discuss the torts themselves.

 L07

What are Intentional Torts?

Intentional torts are civil wrongs which occur because the tortfeasor does an intentional act that results in harm to the victim. The intentional act required depends on the type of intentional tort committed. Unlike negligence, which is a single, self-contained tort, there are many different kinds of intentional torts, each with its own requirements.

LIABILITY? YOU MAKE THE CALL . . .

The following scenarios are from recent newspaper reports. Make the determination as to whether you think the employer would be or should be liable for the acts committed by the employee. In doing so, consider the ethical implications of your answer and under which ethical theory you believe that the employer should be held accountable for the acts of another.

a. Two grocery store employees, who saw a customer slap her son in the face while in the store, called the police. The police came into the store, handcuffed the mother, and charged her with felony cruelty to children. The charges were later dropped because of the prosecutor's inability to prove the mother caused the boy excessive pain as required by the statute. If the mother sues the grocery store and employees for defamation, should the store be held vicariously liable for the actions of its two employees?

b. A high school teacher provided 15 cases of beer to a group of eight teen-agers for a spring break trip to Florida. One of the students was killed when he was struck by a car while walking along a road near the beach in Florida. The autopsy found his blood-alcohol content at the time was 0.13 percent. This was higher than the state's legal presumption of intoxication. If the parents of the deceased teen sue the school system for the wrongful death of their child because of the teacher's actions, should the school be held liable?

c. After setting up a hidden video camera to discover why the coffee "tasted funny," the videotape revealed a worker, who had previously been feuding with co-workers, urinating in a workplace coffee pot. If an employee who drank from the coffee pot becomes ill and sues the employer, should the employer be held liable?

d. A black employee is subjected to a barrage of racial epithets culminating in a white co-worker placing a noose around the black employee's neck in the company bathroom and choking him while calling him a monkey and the N-word. Managers knew about the harassment but did nothing about it. Should the employer be held liable?

The torts vary widely, but the one thing they have in common is that the tortfeasor committed an intentional act which resulted in harm to the plaintiff. Intentional torts may be against a person, against a business, or against property.

In order to hold a tortfeasor liable for an intentional tort, the plaintiff must show that the act required for the tort was committed, and that it was intentional rather than an accident. Unlike negligence, in which injury is required, with intentional torts whether injury must be shown depends upon the type of tort involved. Some require a showing of injury, some do not.

EXAMPLE

The intent required to be shown is the intent to do the act that results in the harm rather than an intent to harm. This is an extremely important distinction. Suppose Jack throws a bowling ball at Jill because Jack is angry with Jill and wants to hurt Jill. Rather than hit Jill, the ball hits Humpty Dumpty and causes him to fall off the wall. Humpty Dumpty sues Jack for the intentional tort of battery. Since Jack intentionally threw the bowling ball, it is an intentional tort. Throwing the bowling ball is an intentional act that resulted in the harm to Humpty. While Jack did not intend to hit Humpty, this does not matter, since it is the intent to do the act that resulted in harm that is required, not the intent to do harm.

EXAMPLE

If, on the other hand, Jack had accidentally slipped while carrying the bowling ball and the ball flew out of his hand and hit Humpty, there is no intent to do the act that resulted in the harm, and this would not be an intentional tort and Humpty could not recover.

Intentional torts can be committed by individuals personally, or in the business setting, creating vicarious liability for the business owner through respondeat superior.

TAKE AWAY 6-1

VICARIOUS LIABILITY

An employer is vicariously liable under the theory of respondeat superior for the torts of his or her employees committed within the scope of employment. This usually does not include crimes unless the employer directed the employee to commit the crime.

The common intentional torts are given in an overview in Take Away 6-2, "Selected Intentional Torts." We will discuss them in the following sections, one by one. The torts against property will be discussed in detail in Chapter 7, "Property."

L07

The intentional torts will be defined individually, with each requirement listed so that you will be sure to include each requirement in your analysis of whether the tort has been committed. Each requirement must be met in order for the tort to occur.

BATTERY

L07

Battery is the intentional, unpermitted, or offensive touching of the body of another.

Intentional—The intent necessary is the intent to do the act that results in the touching, not an intent to touch or to do harm. The intent to harm may be present, but it is not necessary for the intentional tort of battery. A Boy Scout helping a "little old lady" across the street who does not wish to be helped across the street has no intent to harm her, but if she does not want to be touched and he is intentionally doing so, then it is a battery. The battery lies in the violation of the victim's bodily integrity. The law gives us the general right not to be touched without our permission.

EXAMPLE

Unpermitted or offensive—The touching must be nonconsensual. It is possible for the victim to have initially given consent, but for the consent to be exceeded. For instance, a group of friends playing a game of touch football would not be giving consent to being brutally sacked and injured. That type of touching exceeds the permission given to make touch football contact. (See Reality Check, 6-2 "Even an NFL Player Can Exceed Permission.") Some measure of consent is also implied, for instance, when you get into a crowded elevator or on a crowded bus. You expect to be touched in the normal jostling of a crowded bus or elevator, but not to be "felt up" in a sexual way by a fellow passenger. The harm required need not be harmful, such as a slap or kick. How harmful the touch is goes to the measure of damages that can be recovered by plaintiff, not whether the tort of battery has been committed.

EXAMPLE

Touching—There must be contact with the victim's body. Note that in an assault, discussed next, touching is not required. Assault only requires putting someone in fear or apprehension of an immediate bodily touching. With battery, actual contact is necessary. The touching may be accomplished by something used by the tortfeasor to accomplish the unpermitted touching, such as a baseball bat used by the tortfeasor to beat the victim, or even drugs or poison used by the tortfeasor to poison the victim (see Reality Check 6-3, "Cosby and Drug No Laughing Matter").

Of another's body—The touching must be of the victim's body, not the victim's property. Courts have permitted the tort of battery when what was being touched was not the actual body of the victim, but rather, something closely attached to it like a cane, hat or even gloves. In one case, the tort was permitted when a plate was snatched out of the hands of an African American man standing in line at a buffet who was told that the restaurant did not serve blacks.

 EXAMPLE

ASSAULT

Assault is intentionally putting another in fear or apprehension of an immediate unwanted or offensive bodily touching.

Intentionally—Again, this is an intent to do the act that resulted in the harm, not an intent to do harm, i.e., if I pointed a toy pistol at you and it frightened you because you thought it was real, the fact that I did not mean to frighten you is irrelevant. The important issue is whether I intentionally pointed the gun at you. Intentionally (rather than by accident) pointing the gun at you is what resulted in the harm.

Putting another—The act must be toward a person, not an animal or property. Directing acts toward property constitutes another tort, but not assault.

In fear and/or apprehension—The victim need not be deathly afraid; simply not wanting the event to occur is sufficient, i.e., a toddler running toward you to give you a hug with muddy hands with you dressed in a new outfit would cause you apprehension because you do not want to be touched with muddy hands, though you are not afraid of the child in terms of fear. Note, too, that while some assaults are threats, not all threats are assaults. In order to be an assault a statement need not be considered a threat as we generally think of threats in terms of intent to do bodily harm. For instance, the toddler intentionally running toward you for a hug with muddy hands would not ordinarily be thought of as a threat, yet it fits the definition of an assault. The toddler is doing the intentional act of running toward you and your new outfit with muddy hands, which puts you in apprehension of an immediate bodily touching you do not want to occur. Also, a threat can be negated by its own language and therefore not meet this requirement of an assault, i.e., "if you weren't wearing glasses I would smack your face." It sounds like a threat, but if the victim is wearing glasses the threat is negated because by the terms of the statement, the victim will not be slapped.

Of an immediate—It must appear that the unwanted act is imminent. "I'll beat you up when you come to class tomorrow" is not sufficiently immediate, since it is to take place tomorrow. Again, notice that it appears to be a threat, but it does not constitute an assault because it does not meet the immediacy requirement.

Harmful or offensive—The touching that seems imminent need not actually be something harmful like a punch or kick or cut. It may instead be something the victim reasonably considers to be offensive. That can include being touched by someone the victim has not given permission to do so, including a tortfeasor exceeding consent that is initially given.

EXAMPLE

EXAMPLE

EXAMPLE

EXAMPLE

Bodily—The touching expected must be the touching of the victim's body, not the victim's property. Making gestures as if to hit the victim's new car with a sledgehammer would not fit the definition of assault because the expected touching would be of the victim's property, not the victim's body.

Touching—The imminent touch need not be a hit or slap, but it must, in fact, be perceived as being some type of contact with the victim of the tort. The touching may be accomplished by the tortfeasor using something to accomplish the imminent touching, such as a knife, bat, or gun.

Note that an assault is a completed act. It is not an attempted battery. This cause of action lies for the victim's mental integrity. The fact that the tortfeasor did an intentional act that put another in fear or apprehension of an immediate bodily touching is sufficient. The touching itself need not occur for the tort of assault to be committed. When Janine, a customer who comes to the counter to return an expensive sweater, draws a gun on the counter attendant who refuses to allow the return, this would constitute an assault even though no touching occurred.

There are also criminal versions of assault and battery, and in fact, this is what you may be more familiar with through movies, books and television shows. At the very least, criminal assault and battery cases require *mens rea,* or criminal intent. No such intent is required in a civil case. The facts in a particular case may or may not allow both civil and criminal causes of action arising from the same facts. However, the disposition in one is not generally binding on the other. The prosecutor in a criminal case may not have enough evidence to prove her criminal case of assault and battery beyond a reasonable doubt, but the proof may be more than sufficient to impose liability in a civil case where the burden of proof is only a preponderance of the evidence. You may recall that in the case involving O.J. Simpson being accused of the murder of his ex-wife Nicole Simpson and her friend Ron Brown, Simpson was acquitted of murder charges, but found liable in the civil claim for wrongful death. As we saw in the chapter on the court system, the two burdens of proof are quite different and can lead to different outcomes stemming from the same facts. The tort may not be sufficient for a criminal case; however, punitive damages may be recovered in appropriate circumstances.

FALSE IMPRISONMENT

Intentionally confining someone to a space from which there is no viable means of egress is **false imprisonment.**

Intentionally—Again, the intent is to do the act that results in the harm, not the intent to harm. If the false imprisonment is accidental rather than intentional, this requirement is not met. For instance, Mickey, a waiter at a fast-food restaurant, accidentally brushes past the door of the restaurant's walk-in freezer and unknowingly locks an employee in the freezer. Since the act of shutting the door was accidental rather than intentional, the intentional tort of false imprisonment has not occurred.

Confining someone—Again, locking up someone's pet or other property is not sufficient for this tort. It must be a person.

In a space—The space need not be small, such as a closet or walk-in freezer, but generally the space must be confined. In some situations, however, it may be possible that the space is not confined in the usual sense, but the threat of consequences for leaving is so dire that it may as well be (see Reality Check 6-4, "False Imprisonment for Ten Years?!").

From which there is no viable means of egress—The space can be locked or there can be some other means which makes it so the victim cannot leave the premises. For instance, if the door is open, but an electrical zapping system attached to the

REALITY CHECK 6-4

FALSE IMPRISONMENT FOR TEN YEARS?!

For ten years, Randolph Dial, a convicted murderer who escaped from an Oklahoma prison, kept Bobbi Parker, wife of the deputy warden, with him as a hostage and posed them as a married couple. It is believed that Dial originally took Parker at knifepoint. Dial said he warned Parker that if she tried to escape he would hurt her family. An employer who saw the two together during the time Parker was allegedly a hostage said he saw Dial slap and beat Parker, with no hint of romance between them. Dial was finally captured by the FBI in April 2005.

Aside from any criminal charges, Parker would likely have a viable claim for false imprisonment if she can prove these facts. Even though she was not locked in a room, the violence toward her and serious threat to her family, with ample reason to think it would be carried out, could suffice as no viable means of escape.

Dial died in prison in June 2007. Parker was scheduled to stand trial on August 9, 2010, for helping Dial escape.

Sources: "Escapee Says He Held Woman Captive for Decade," Associated Press, April 8, 2005, http://www.msnbc.msn.com/id/7387510/; "Kidnapped Warden's Wife Found, Alive—Living with Captor," *The Herald Mail*, April 7, 2005, http://www.herald-mail.com/forums/index.php?showtopic=1399; Manny Gamalo, "Killer, Dial, 62, Dies in Prison," *Tulsa World*, June 14, 2009, http://www.accessmylibrary.com/article-1G1-164955917/killer-dial-62-dies.html; "Bobbie Parker Trial Set for August 9, 2010," *Mangum Star*, http://mangumstarnews.net/view/full_story/6983598/article-Bobbie-Parker-Trial-Set-For--August-9--2010: "The Oklahoman, Bob Doucette, Sept. 15, 2010, "Bobbi Parker Trial Postponed, http://newsok.com/bobbi-parker-trial-postponed/article/3495437.

entrance would electrocute the victim if he or she went out the unlocked door, then there is no viable means of egress from the confines of the room.

The cause of action of false imprisonment is probably most often used in cases involving shoplifting allegations by someone who is wrongfully accused of shoplifting and held for questioning by the store and later sues the store for false imprisonment. Aside from any criminal issues involved, the courts have permitted the use of the **shopkeeper's rule** to protect storeowners.

Under the shopkeeper's rule, a shopkeeper is given a conditional privilege to detain a suspected shoplifter even if it turns out he or she is innocent, if the shopkeeper conducts the detention in the correct way. If the shopkeeper is later sued for false imprisonment, the shopkeeper may use this conditional privilege as a defense. The conditions of the privilege are that the shopkeeper:

Have a reasonable suspicion of theft—A reasonable suspicion of theft can be based on any number of factors including seeing the customer place something in his or her pocket or bag, the customer looking around furtively or suspiciously, the customer wearing inappropriate clothing, such as a big coat in hot summer weather, or very large clothing on a small person, and other similar factors (see Diversity in the Law 6-2, "SWB/H, or Shopping While Black/Hispanic: Is Race or Ethnicity Alone Enough for Reasonable Suspicion?").

Detain the suspect for a reasonable amount of time—What is considered a reasonable amount of time can vary depending on the circumstances. If the shopkeeper is short of help and the suspect is detained for six hours before someone can question her, this may be reasonable. To detain the suspect for six hours when the staff could easily have quickly investigated and taken care of the matter may be unreasonable.

Treat the suspect in a reasonable way during detention—No sitting the suspect under a spotlight in a darkened room and firing questions in a staccato voice or beating the suspected shoplifter with a rubber hose is allowed. Seriously, aside from whatever criminal or law enforcement considerations are involved, the shopkeeper may only use reasonable force to pursue and question a suspect. Two big, strong linebacker-looking department store security guards approach a frail elderly customer and accuse him of stealing a necktie. The customer says he has not done so, and the guards roughly handle him, raise their voices to him in front of other customers, and drag him through the store

SWB/H, OR SHOPPING WHILE BLACK/HISPANIC: IS RACE OR ETHNICITY ALONE ENOUGH FOR REASONABLE SUSPICION?

In a great (though unfortunate) example of how messages we have received in operating in the world can impact various groups' interaction with the law, we often have students working in retail who tell us they have been told by their managers to keep a very close eye on, and even follow around the store, African American or Hispanic customers who walk into the establishment. This is what African Americans and Hispanics call "SWB/H" or "shopping while black/Hispanic." These customers have done nothing suspicious, but they are followed around a store or are closely watched by store personnel who obviously suspect they will steal. In other places, it is other groups who are treated this way, such as Native Americans in the Southwest. Perhaps because someone of that group may have stolen from the storeowner at some point, or even because the storeowner simply believes the group to be less honest or trustworthy in general, everyone in the group becomes suspect and is treated as a potential shoplifter.

Membership in a certain racial or ethnic group, alone, does not suffice to meet the reasonable suspicion requirement of the shopkeeper's rule. In order to meet the condition of the privilege, there must be more than simply the suspect belonging to a particular racial or ethnic group. If the customer behaves in suspicious ways such as those mentioned above (i.e., wearing seasonally inappropriate clothing capable of hiding items, looking around furtively, moving a product toward his or her pocket, and so forth), this is considered suspicious. Simply walking into the store and being a member of a particular racial or ethnic group is not.

You may wish to check your own "messages" you have received in your lifetime about various groups before making workplace decisions that could unnecessarily adversely impact certain groups and lead to legal issues.

EXAMPLE

to the office, only to find no tie, and the elderly customer in the throes of a heart attack. Since the treatment of the suspect was unreasonable under the circumstances, when the gentleman sues for false imprisonment, he wins. The shopkeeper lost the **conditional or qualified privilege** of the shopkeeper's rule by not complying with the reasonable detention requirement of the conditional privilege.

If all three conditions are met, when the shopkeeper is sued for false imprisonment by a shopper suspected of shoplifting who turned out to be innocent of the crime, then the shopkeeper will not be held liable. However, all of the conditions must be met in order for the rule to provide the shopkeeper with protection.

DEFAMATION   L07

Intentionally making untrue statements about an individual in the presence of another or communicated to a third party that has the effect of lessening the individual's reputation in the community is **defamation.**

Intentionally making—If the statement is made accidentally, the requisite intent is not present.

Untrue—In order for a statement to be actionable, it must be untrue. Truth is an **absolute defense** to the tort of defamation. A true statement may constitute a privacy or other tort, but it is not defamation.

Statements—The untrue statements must be presented as fact, not opinion. Facts are an expression of what is or is not. Opinion is one's personal feeling or belief about someone or something. Only statements of fact are actionable as defamation.

About an individual—Again, making negative statements about an individual's property, animals or business is not actionable as defamation. It must be about a person. If it is about a business, it may constitute the tort of disparagement, but not defamation.

To a third person—The statement must be said in the presence of, or conveyed to, someone other than the person making the statement and the person the statement is about. This requirement is called **publication.** If the third person is a private secretary or other such close agent of the tortfeasor, the third person requirement is not met.

Which lessens the individual's reputation in the community—The statement must be one which a reasonable person would consider negative enough that she would think less of the person about whom the statement was made. It is a community standard that varies from community to community. What may adversely impact one's reputation in Fargo, North Dakota, may not have the same impact in Los Angeles, California.

Everyone is entitled to maintain the integrity of his or her reputation. Defamation can be accomplished through either **slander** or **libel.** Slander involves spoken statements while libel involves written or widely broadcast (such as on TV or radio) statements. Libel is generally thought of as more serious since the impact may be larger because of the written word being more permanent than a spoken statement. However, when many people hear the spoken statement, such as in a TV show, the impact can be as great (see Reality Check 6-5, "New Technology, New Issues: Websites and Defamation"). In Case 6.1, KISS lead singer Gene Simmons was sued for defamation by his former girlfriend for a depiction of her as a promiscuous woman in a VH-1 production.

Privileges

When appropriate, privileges are available to the defendant in defamation cases. For instance, legislators on the floor of the legislature have an absolute privilege, as do individuals testifying in court. The law takes the position that some situations are so important that those speaking should not have to worry about whether they will be sued for defamation. The privilege for court testimony only extends to protecting against actions for defamation based on the testimony. The privilege protects the speaker from defamation claims but it does not prevent a witness who knowingly lied under oath from being prosecuted for perjury.

News Media

Since the primary mission of the news media is informing the public, the media has more latitude when it comes to being sued for defamation. In order to show the

---

CASE 6.1 Ward v. Klein

Index No. 100231-05 (S. Ct. NY, Pt. 24 Nov. 2005)

Facts: Gene Simmons, leader of the rock band KISS, was sued by his former girlfriend of three years for, among other things, defamation when a 2004 VH1 "rockumentary" entitled "When KISS Ruled the World," without her knowledge or permission, used her photo in connection with a segment of the video in which the group's promiscuous sex lives were revealed. The girlfriend alleged she and Simmons began a three-year monogamous relationship before KISS was formed and picturing her the way the documentary did was defamatory in that it made her seem promiscuous. Plaintiff's photograph was shown a number of times during the documentary, mostly during a segment highlighting Simmons's sexual proclivities in which Simmons boasts of his sexual prowess and his ability to sleep with any woman he wanted. At the beginning of the segment, the caption "24 Hour Whore" appears on the screen followed shortly by a photograph of plaintiff with Simmons. Simmons exclaims: "I was a 24 hour whore. All I ever thought about was sex." Simmons then lists some of the casual sexual encounters he shared with women, such as a hotel maid who came to clean the room and a nurse in his doctor's office. During one part of the segment, Simmons comments: "There wasn't a girl that was off limits, and I enjoyed every one of them." Plaintiff's photograph is briefly shown at or about the same time as Simmons's remarks. A narrator then states: "These guys were wild," and again plaintiff's photograph flashes across the screen. The complaint alleges that at another point in the documentary, a narrator comments: "Everywhere [Simmons] went he found a woman and it didn't matter who they were, what size, shape or anything, he'd find a woman and disappear with her." At a later point in the program, a photograph of plaintiff is purportedly shown while a narrator comments about KISS's increasing commercialization: "It was no longer bagging

every groupie in sight." Simmons requested that the court dismiss the claims for lack of a cause of action.

Issue: Whether airing on national television a documentary containing the repeated use of a rock star's ex-girlfriend's picture without her permission, with sexual commentary about the star's casual encounters with many women, is defamatory.

Decision: Yes, this is defamatory.

Reasoning: Richter, J.: Although it is true that the documentary never mentions plaintiff by name, or otherwise identifies her, the use of her photographs during the "24 Hour Whore" segment could certainly lead a reasonable person to conclude that she was one of those women with whom Simmons had a casual sexual liaison. Simmons's motion to dismiss the causes of action for defamation is denied.

CASE QUESTIONS

1. Do you agree with the court's decision? Do you believe the outcome would have been different if the genders were reversed? Should it? Explain.

2. Do you think anyone takes "rockumentaries" seriously enough for someone like a former girlfriend to sue over it? Explain. Does it matter? What if only a handful of people believed the statements? In your opinion would that be sufficient for fair damages?

3. How would a court determine whether being seen this way with a rock star would lower a plaintiff's reputation in the community when being with a rock star may be construed as a positive thing? Explain. Was it ethical for Simmons to do what he did? Discuss.

---

necessary intent for defamation against the media, plaintiff must show not just that the information was untrue, but that the media outlet published the untrue information with malice, that is, knowing it was untrue, or in reckless disregard of the truth or falsity of the information. This is particularly true when the defamation involves a public figure (see Reality Check 6-6, "College Football Coaches and Strippers Don't Mix").

Former Employers

One of the most frequent types of defamation cases involve ex-employees suing their former employers for statements made while the employee's references were being checked. Fear of such suits is why many employers refuse to provide the prospective employer with anything other than the meager information of whether the ex-employee worked for the employer and the dates of that employment. Fearing defamation suits from their former employees, employers refuse to say more. But imagine the ethical dilemma when employers are discussing the ex-employee with colleagues in a similar industry. They lose credibility if they are not honest about a particularly challenging employee, but are subject to potential liability if they say too much. Some cases might even involve an employee with a history of violence or sexual harassment, about whom a prior employer would very much like to warn the prospective employer. To respond to this difficult ethical dilemma, most states have provided employers with a conditional privilege that permits them to offer prospective employers with substantive information about the ex-employee.

The conditions are that the information must be provided on the basis of a legitimate business request (usually requested on business stationery) in the course of business, not be intentionally false, and be provided in a businesslike manner. The intent of disclosing the information must be to respond to a business inquiry, rather than to retaliate or seek vengeance on the former employee and cause trouble for him or her, or simply to gossip. Cocktail chitchat or over-the-back-fence gossip about an ex-employee by a former employer to a prospective employee does not come within the conditional privilege. If the information is provided consistent with the conditions of the privilege, then even if the ex-employee sues the former employer for defamation, the former employer will have a legitimate defense and will not be held liable (see Reality Check 6-7, "Limits to Personal Information in Hiring").

INTENTIONAL INFLICTION OF EMOTIONAL DISTRESS

L07

Intentional infliction of emotional distress is intentionally doing an outrageous act that goes outside all bounds of common decency and causes the victim severe emotional distress.

Intentionally—Means what it says, that is, the act is not accidental.

Doing an outrageous act—This is a local standard based on the place where the act took place. There is no actual definition of what the act must be, since it is such a localized standard, but it should be an act that others would reasonably think was outrageous. In fact, another name for this tort is "outrageous conduct."

Toward another—Again, the act must be toward another person, not toward property.

Which goes beyond all bounds of common decency—Acts which cause mere embarrassment, or are simply in bad taste, are not sufficient.

And causes the victim severe emotional distress—Again, mere embarrassment or anger resulting from the act is not enough. Since no physical damage is required for this tort and it would otherwise be easy to fake, courts have a high threshold for determining whether the victim has suffered severe emotional distress. The rule of thumb is generally that the act is so ridiculously outrageous that any reasonable person would suffer

EXAMPLE

LIMITS TO PERSONAL INFORMATION IN HIRING

What limits should be placed on the grounds upon which employment can be denied to a job applicant? Federal law prohibits denying someone a job on the basis of race, color, religion, ethnicity, gender, age, and disability. The law generally allows denial of a job on the basis of drug use. Like employment at will which will be discussed in the employment chapter, the burden of proof lies with the job applicant to demonstrate that the denial was based on a prohibited category, otherwise employers need no reason to deny someone a job. Suppose a business wanted to insure not only a drug-free workplace, but also an alcohol-free workplace. Would a business have the ethical right to deny a job, or dismiss an employee, for discovering that an employee was drinking alcohol or smoking off the job? Among other things, courts have been asked to decide the legitimacy of dismissals for cigarette smoking, political beliefs, interracial marriages, and for having an abortion. Discovering such information in making inquiries about a prospective employee has served as the basis for not hiring applicants. Which of these do you think is legitimate grounds for not hiring or for dismissal?

Many businesses have also used personality tests and psychological profiling to evaluate potential employees. Such tests ask many personal questions, including some that concern an applicant's sex life. Do you believe a business has an ethical right to deny employment to someone on the basis of the results of a personality test (unless the test indicates dangerous or violent proclivities, or otherwise antisocial behavior)? These tests can be quite costly, so the presumption is that a business would not spend the revenue to gather this information if it did not think it was helpful. Make the case for use of such information.

What are some of the questions or concerns you might raise in trying to answer the above challenge and what would you suggest a business do to respond to them?

- What are the key facts relevant to your response?
- What are the ethical issues involved in peer spying in the workplace?
- Who are the stakeholders?
- What alternatives would you suggest to business in gathering information, and what alternatives exist for employers who wish to gather information about employees surreptitiously?
- How do the alternatives compare?
- How do the alternatives affect the stakeholders?

severe emotional distress if such an act was directed at him or her. The plaitiff need not have had a nervous breakdown or have seen a psychiatrist or such.

Unlike the other torts we have discussed, this tort was not recognized at common law, but only fairly recently, in legal terms. As you can see, it is loose in its definition; but courts leave it to juries to handle it the way they do obscenity: they know it when they see it. Since this tort can so easily be misused, it is not found by courts as much as many of the more common common law torts. However, it is generally added along with other torts when a plaintiff is suing for something that has upsetting dimensions, such as an unlawful termination, defamation, or in some cases, even breach of contract. Some of the really interesting cases have arisen in the area of debt collection. There are specific rules about collecting debts and how it is to be accomplished under the Fair Debt Collection Practices Act, but debt collectors often go outside these rules and perform outrageous acts in order to get recalcitrant debtors to pay up.

EXAMPLE

For instance, Jeff, a debt collector, is frustrated at being given the runaround by a delinquent debtor. He cannot locate the debtor and in an effort to do so, calls the debtor's mother. Jeff pretends to be an emergency room doctor and tells the debtor's mother that the debtor's child has been in a serious accident and the hospital needs the debtor's phone number in order to notify him. The grandmother, distraught about the news of her grandchild, gives Jeff the number. She later discovers this was only a trick to allow the debt collector to locate her son, the delinquent debtor.

LO7

INVASION OF PRIVACY

Invasion of privacy actually includes four different torts. What each has in common is that there is an expectation of privacy that has been violated by the tortfeasor. The way in which the privacy is violated forms the differences in the privacy causes of action.

LO7 Intrusion upon Seclusion

Intrusion upon seclusion is intentionally intruding into a space someone has a right to consider private, for instance, sneaking into your boyfriend's house to see if he has another girl there with him. It can also include wiretapping, taking unwanted photos of someone in a private place, intrusive telephoning, and other

EXAMPLE such activity. Media frenzies were created when, for instance, a German newspaper published nude photos of Britain's Prince Charles in a bathroom drying off after a bath, or then-Princess Fergie having her toes sucked by a paramour poolside, with her young daughter playing nearby—while Fergie was still married to Prince Andrew. The pictures had been taken with powerful telephoto lenses while the targets were in private places. Reality Check 6-8 ("Restroom Videos??!!") reports on a restaurant owner's troubles in this area.

REALITY CHECK 6-8

RESTROOM VIDEOS??!!

The owner of a Georgia pizzeria was sentenced to six months in a detention center—with the balance of a 10-year sentence to be served on probation—for videotaping women using a restaurant bathroom.

Stephen DeLoach, of Doraville, GA, was arrested as he entered Mazzio's Pizza carrying videotapes used to record the women through a small camera installed behind a hole in the restroom ceiling, almost directly above a toilet stall. The camera was connected to a video recorder in a restaurant office.

Two of DeLoach's victims—both former employees—made statements. "We were raped of our dignity," one of the women said. "I'm just ill about the whole situation. It's not fair."

The other victim said she has developed a fear of being watched in restrooms. "I look on the ceilings, I look behind the toilet," she said. "What happened is disgraceful, disgusting."

DeLoach said, "I had a sexual problem and I didn't recognize it. I never meant to hurt anybody."

LO7 Appropriation of Name or Likeness

Using someone's name or photo, usually in an advertisement, without his or her permission is the tort **appropriation of name or likeness.** The name or photo may be used with permission, but not if permission has not been provided. For instance, Jimmy Choo shoes are some of the most expensive and beautiful women's shoes in the world. But the shoes are not made by Jimmy Choo, nor is Jimmy Choo the owner of the company. Tamara Mellon is the president and founder of Jimmy Choo's shoes. Jimmy Choo is a shoe designer Ms. Mellon worked with while employed at a magazine. Choo designed and made beautiful shoes by hand. Ms. Mellon eventually decided to go into the shoe business and chose the name Jimmy Choo for her business. In order to do that, she had to have the permission of Jimmy Choo or he would have been able (had they been in the U.S. rather than in London, where they are) to sue Ms. Mellon for appropriation of name or likeness for using his name without his permission to do so. In the KISS case earlier in the chapter, one of the claims the former girlfriend sued for was appropriation of name or likeness for the use of her photos in connection with the rockumentary, without her permission. The court held, however, that since this was a documentary rather than a commercial enterprise, it would not allow her claim.

EXAMPLE

False Light

The intentional act of publishing something that puts another in an unfavorable or untruthful light, though it is true, is the tort **false light.** For instance, do you know who Kevin Clash is? We'd be surprised if you did. Mr. Clash is the highest paid puppeteer in the world. He is the real live human being behind the Muppet, Elmo, the most financially successful puppet in history. Yep, bright red sweet little funny Elmo from TV. Suppose Mr. Clash's photo is on the front page of the newspaper under a large headline that reads "Local caught selling drugs!" Mr. Clash happens to be a tall, broad-shouldered African American male. However, the caption under his photo reads "Voice of Elmo finally revealed for first time on Oprah Winfrey show." In our

LO7

EXAMPLE

HIGH SCHOOL STUDENT SUES OVER YEARBOOK PHOTO

A basketball player at a New Jersey high school sued the high school and nine students on the yearbook staff for invasion of privacy and intentional infliction of emotional distress for putting in the yearbook a picture of him taken from a low angle, shooting a basketball on a day when he wore boxers rather than an athletic supporter. The student's genitals were partly visible, so when the yearbook was distributed to seniors, the photo "touched off a buzz." The student asked the principal to halt further distribution and recall the books already distributed, but nothing was done until the student "went home in shame" and brought his parents back. Seniors were asked to return their yearbooks and the picture was cut out of every copy except a few that were not returned. The case was dismissed and the dismissal affirmed by an appellate court because of lack of evidence of psychological harm.

Bennett v. Board of Education, Freehold Regional High School Dist., Mon-L-4700-03 (May 16, 2006).

scenario the headline actually refers to a story on the right-hand column of the page. But to anyone seeing the paper, because of the placement of the photo under the large headline, it appears that Mr. Clash has been caught selling drugs. Both the stories were true, but the way they were placed in the newspaper would have put Mr. Clash in a false light, which is actionable.

Publication of Private Facts

L07

The last privacy action is **publication of private facts.** This involves the tortfeasor widely disseminating information about someone which, though true, is highly private and need not be publicized. In a classic case, a store **EXAMPLE** owner was owed money by a doctor for a long time and the doctor had not paid. The store owner put a sign in his store window saying that the doctor was a deadbeat. It was not defamation since the statement was true, yet it was private information which others had no right or need to know. The doctor was able to successfully sue the store owner for publication of private facts. (See Reality Check 6-9, "High School Student Sues over Yearbook Photo.")

INTENTIONAL TORTS AGAINST PROPERTY

The intentional torts against property are trespass to land, trespass to personal property, and conversion. We will discuss these in Chapter 7, "Property."

INTENTIONAL TORTS AGAINST BUSINESS

L07

EXAMPLE

Many of the common law torts we have discussed can be used for business-related litigation. As we have seen, for instance, a negligence action may be brought against a business owner if her truck driver accidentally runs into another vehicle while making a delivery. However, over the years, several torts specifically related to the business setting have been developed. (See the overview in Take Away 6-3, "Selected Business Torts.") Business-related torts include disparagement, interference with contractual or business relations, palming off, theft of trade secrets, and infringement of trademarks, trade names, patents, and copyrights. The infringement torts are only briefly mentioned here, but will be discussed in greater detail in the chapter on intellectual property.

Disparagement

L07

EXAMPLE

Disparagement, also known as **injurious falsehood,** is intentionally making false statements about the quality or ownership of someone's goods. It can be thought of as a sort of defamation against a business rather than an individual. If a terminated employee stands outside the restaurant from which he was fired and falsely tells approaching customers that the restaurant uses horsemeat in its hamburgers rather than beef, the restaurant owner can successfully sue the ex-employee for disparagement if she can show she did

TAKE AWAY 6-3

SELECTED BUSINESS TORTS

Disparagement—Intentionally misrepresenting the quality or title of another's goods or services. For example, Benjamin, a restaurant owner, falsely tells others that his competitor, Jake, is using inferior food products in his restaurant's offerings. EXAMPLE

Interference with contractual or business relations—Intentionally doing an act that interferes with the contractual relations between parties to a contract, generally resulting in causing one of the parties not to perform as agreed. For example, Kwan tells her competitor's creditor that the competitor cannot pay his bills and the creditor decides not to extend further credit to the competitor as planned. The competitor has a cause of action against Kwan for interference with contractual relations. EXAMPLE

Palming off—Sometimes known as *passing off*, seller sells products as one brand, when it is actually another, generally inferior, brand. For instance, Brad sells XYZ clothing as the more well-known ABC brand. Brad is "palming off" goods on unsuspecting buyers who think they are buying and paying for the better ABC clothing. EXAMPLE

Theft of trade secrets—If a business owner has business secrets such as a particular recipe, method of manufacturing, or list of customers, which are kept closely guarded and are not public information even within the company, and these are taken by the tortfeasor without the business owner's permission, it is theft of trade secrets. For example, Hola! Cola painstakingly takes precautions to keep its soft drink recipe secret from everyone, including employees who manufacture the drink. Manuel steals the recipe and opens a competing soft drink company using Hola!'s recipe. The makers of Hola! Cola would have a cause of action against Manuel for theft of trade secrets and can recover the profits Manuel made using the recipe. EXAMPLE

Infringements of trademark, trade name; Patent infringement; Copyright infringement—See Chapter 15, "Intellectual Property."

not use horsemeat and that she was injured or otherwise damaged by the ex-employee's untrue statements.

Intentional Interference with Contractual Relations

An individual can use this tort when someone intentionally interferes with either an existing or a prospective contract the individual has with another. For instance, Annie, owner of Good Stuff Restaurant, has a contract with Good Earth Organic Groceries for Good Earth to daily provide Annie with the organic fruits and vegetables she needs for her restaurant. Tim, owner of Totally Tim's Fare Restaurant, is jealous of Annie's success. He knows that her vegetable and fruit dishes are a big part of her success. Tim falsely tells Shaniqua, owner of Good Earth Organic Groceries, that Annie's restaurant is not doing as well as it appears to be and that Annie is falling behind with her creditors. Because of this, Shaniqua requires Annie to pay for each delivery as it is delivered, rather than at the end of the month as required by Annie's contract with Good Earth. This puts a financial strain on Annie. Annie has a cause of action against Tim for intentional interference with contractual relations and can use as her measure of damages any harm that resulted from Tim's interference with Annie's contract with Good Earth. EXAMPLE

Theft of Trade Secrets

If a business owner has a particular way of doing things that makes the business unique or special, including recipes, client lists, formulas, business contacts, and so on and actively works to keep that information secret, the owner can sue someone L07

KEEPING COKE SECRET?

In 2006, an administrative assistant to the Coca-Cola Company's global brand director was accused of stealing confidential documents and a sample of a new Coke product and, along with two others, of trying to sell the items to PepsiCo, Coca-Cola's competitor. The corporate espionage case caused quite a stir as companies around the country scrambled to develop or reassert policies regarding their trade secrets. To its ethical credit, Pepsi reported the situation to authorities after being approached by the sellers and they were caught and criminally prosecuted.

What legal and ethical duties and responsibilities did Pepsi have in this situation? What fundamental principles may have been implicated here? How might the standards of universalism be particularly appropriate in this case?

who steals that information and uses it or sells it to someone else. In order for the claim to be successful, the business owner must show that she actually did keep the matter secret and it was not general knowledge. This tort is often used in situations where an employee leaves a business and takes information which he then uses for his own purposes, financial gain, or economic advantage (see Reality Check 6-10, "Keeping Coke Secret?").

Palming Off `L07`

In **palming off** someone passes off their competitor's goods as their own so that buyers think they are buying one thing, when in fact, they are buying another. Usually what the purchaser buys is of inferior quality or at least not the brand or quality they thought they were purchasing. This tort is often committed in conjunction with trademark infringement, but need not be.

Patent, Trademark and Copyright Infringement

Patent, trademark and copyright infringement are discussed in Chapter 15, "Intellectual Property."

`L07`

What are the Defenses to Intentional Torts?

Even if a tortfeasor engages in tortious activity, he or she may be able to defend his or her actions and thus avoid liability. With intentional torts there is no liability if the tortfeasor can show that

- `EXAMPLE` There was *no intent* to do the act which resulted in the harm (i.e., it was an accident). For instance, if Sophie drives into Marisa's car because Sophie's brakes failed through no fault of her own and she lost control of her car, Sophie will not be liable to Marisa for trespass to personal property.
- `EXAMPLE` The victim gave **consent** to the activity. For instance, there is no liability for the intentional tort of invasion of privacy by appropriation of name or likeness if Charmaine gives Sharon permission to use Charmaine's photo in a book Sharon publishes.
- `EXAMPLE` The tort was committed in **defense of self or others.** For instance if Jacinto sues Melinda for battery, alleging Melinda hit him, but Melinda can show that she hit Jacinto because Jacinto was attacking her husband, Jim, and Melinda was only trying to protect Jim, then Melinda would be relieved of liability for battery.

`L06`

What is a Negligence Action?

- `EXAMPLE` A woman plunged 60 feet to her death when the safety harness on the carnival ride she was on became too loose.
- The nation's largest bullet-proof vest manufacturer recalls nearly 100,000 vests when its tests indicate the fabric used in the vests could suddenly degrade and cause a dramatic loss in the vests' ability to stop bullets.
- A school is blamed in the death of an 11-year-old student who suffered from severe asthma because the school district did not have enough personnel to have a nurse at

every school, resulting in a $9 million award for the family (later reduced by the judge to $2.23 million).

- Five children, ages 10–17, die while on a church picnic when they are caught in the swift current of a state park river known for dangerous currents, but no signs were posted.
- An Illinois man sues Kraft Foods, Inc., claiming he found a rodent tooth in a package of Planters peanuts.
- The family of a Walmart worker killed during the mad rush of shoppers coming into the "Black Friday" sale for bargains the day after Thanksgiving sues the store for the death, alleging the store knew how dangerous Black Friday crowds could be, specifically created advertising with deep discounts that they had reason to know would cause the frenzy, and failed to have sufficient security on hand.
- Airplane black box recordings indicate that a pilot, whose plane crashed killing all aboard, did so, in part, because of ice accumulation on the wings and because the pilot did not have enough flight experience to fly in the weather conditions present.

All of these events occurred recently. All are based, in some way, on claims of **negligence.** All of these incidents are examples of ways in which businesses can be held liable and required to pay out large sums of money for failing to meet the necessary standard of care in providing their services.

Recovery for foreseeable unintentional or accidental injuries is addressed through negligence (often called *personal injury*) actions. When a tortfeasor fails to meet a standard of reasonable care appropriate for the circumstances and another is forseeably subjected to an unreasonable risk of harm and is injured as a result, the tortfeasor can be sued by the injured party for negligence. Generally, the standard for judging the behavior of the tortfeasor is one of a reasonable person under the particular circumstances. We are all held to a standard of acting like a reasonable person under the circumstances and conducting ourselves in such a way that we do not present a reasonably forseeable unreasonable risk of harm to others. Rather than a one-size-fits-all approach, it is a standard that takes the specifics of the situation into consideration in determining what is reasonable. If a 12-year-old commits a tort, the court holds him to the standard of a reasonable 12-year-old and what a reasonable 12-year-old would be likely to know and do. If a house is on fire, we are required to act as someone involved in an emergency, not someone who is not, and so on.

This can become quite important in a situation where, for instance, a short person is sued for negligence for not setting off a fire alarm to notify occupants that a building is on fire. If the person was too short to reach the fire alarm and there was no means of lifting himself to the height of the alarm, then he did not act unreasonably in failing to turn on the alarm. If the tortfeasor acted as a reasonable person under the circumstances there is no liability. If not, the court imposes liability for negligence.

L06 NEGLIGENCE REQUIREMENTS

In order for negligence liability to attach to the tortfeasor, plaintiffs must prove four requirements: duty, breach of duty, actual and proximate cause, and damages. (See Take Away 6-4, "Negligence Requirements.") In our chapter-opening scenario where Shema's workers' scaffolding fell, in order to recover, the injured passerby must show that (1) the workers had a duty to build the

EXAMPLE

TAKE AWAY 6-4

NEGLIGENCE REQUIREMENTS

Negligence is doing an act (or not doing an act you should do) that results in a failure to meet a standard of reasonable care owed to a person resulting in harm to the person or his or her property. Negligence requires:

- a duty
- breach of duty
- actual and proximate cause
- damages

scaffold in such a way that it would not come apart and cause injury to others; (2) the workers breached the duty by building the unsafe scaffold which fell when used; (3) the reason for the injury was the workers' failure to build the scaffold so that it would not come apart and present an unreasonable risk of harm to others; and (4) the passerby was injured.

If these requirements are proved, then the passerby can recover for the injuries sustained as a result of Shema's employees' failure to meet the standard of reasonable care under the circumstances. Shema and the employees would be liable for negligence.

Duty

EXAMPLE

Under the law, in general each person has a duty to conduct him- or herself in a way that does not present a forseeable unreasonable risk of harm to others. The duty can be imposed by statute or reason. If the duty is imposed by statute and the statute is violated, it is **negligence per se.** Anytown, USA, has a local ordinance prohibiting motor vehicles from proceeding through a red light. Kim drives through a red light and hits Mohammed, a pedestrian who is crossing the street. This is negligence per se since there is an ordinance prohibiting the motorist from doing the act that resulted in the harm to the pedestrian (running the red light).

EXAMPLE

The duty owed can also be imposed by law based on a relationship or activity: a parent has a responsibility to a child, a doctor to a patient, a babysitter to his or her charge, and so forth. The law may also impose a duty when a person is performing a certain act, such as driving a car or operating machinery. However, the law does not impose a general duty on each of us toward others. Heather, a great swimmer, is at the beach and sees a child drowning. Heather does nothing and the child drowns. While, as a society, we would prefer that Heather assist the child, the law imposes no duty on Heather to rescue the child. The parents would not be able to bring a successful action for negligence against Heather because Heather has no relationship to the child and thus no legal duty. On the other hand, if the child's parents did precisely what Heather did, negligence would attach since the law imposes a duty upon a parent to a child to protect the child from forseeable harm. There would also be negligence if Heather was a lifeguard on duty at the time and she did not attempt to rescue the child, as the lifeguard has a contractual duty to help those in distress in the water.

Breach of Duty

EXAMPLE

Breach of duty is violating a duty the tortfeasor owes to the injured party. The breach of duty may arise either from doing an act that should not be done because it presents an unreasonable risk of harm to another (such as speeding on the highway in rainy conditions), or failing to do an act that would be expected to be done under the circumstances in order to prevent an unreasonable risk of harm to another (such as a lifeguard failing to provide assistance to the drowning swimmer).

Actual and Proximate Cause

EXAMPLE

Actual cause is the tortfeasor's actions resulting in harm to the injured party. But for the act by the tortfeasor, the plaintiff would not have been harmed. In addition, there must be proximate cause in order to impose liability upon the tortfeasor. The basis of liability for negligence is to make us more circumspect in dealing with others so we do not cause them harm. **Proximate cause** is a legal mechanism used to allow legal responsibility only for consequences of our actions if the consequences were forseeable. If we can foresee that our conduct would present an unreasonable risk of harm to others and we engage in the conduct anyway, we are held responsible for the harm that results. For instance, we should not drink and drive because we realize that to do so presents an unreasonable risk of harm to others who may be on the roads with us (or to ourselves!).

However, the consequences from our actions are not always foreseeable. Proximate cause is the means the law uses to cut off responsibility for the consequences of our actions so that we are not responsible for every single act that flowed from our breach of duty but only those that are foreseeable and that we should have contemplated and thus prevented. While the tortfeasor's act may have been the actual cause of harm to a victim, it may not be the proximate or legal cause because the law cuts off liability past the point where it is foreseeable. Sound confusing? See if the following example helps.

EXAMPLE

Jesse is washing department store display windows for a client. Ordinarily he puts caution signs around a site where he is working to warn people to be careful of the slippery surface, but he forgets to do so this time. Deke comes by and slips in the soapy water, falls, and is injured. As Deke is slipping, he grabs onto Gale, a passerby, to try to steady himself. Gale, carrying Leslie, a toddler, falls and is injured also. Leslie tumbles out of Gale's arms and in a panic, runs into the street and is hit by a car. Richard, a pedestrian across the street, has a heart attack when he sees Leslie being hit by the car. When Richard collapses he falls against an art shop wall. Reneé, browsing inside the shop, is injured when Richard's fall causes a painting Reneé is standing near to fall on her head.

Convoluted enough for you? Let's see if we can determine where liability lies and who can recover. The actual cause of everyone's injuries is Jesse's negligence in not putting up a sign to warn pedestrians. Because Jesse did not do so, Deke slipped and began a chain of events directly causing the final injury of Richard's heart attack and Reneé's head injury in the art shop across the street. But for Jesse's failure, none of this would have happened.

But the law will likely not hold Jesse liable for all of the injuries even though his negligence was the actual cause that began this chain of events. Negligence is designed to keep us from creating reasonably foreseeable unreasonable risks of harm to others. Some of what occurred here was not a foreseeable consequence of Jesse failing to post the caution sign so the law will not hold Jesse liable even though his failure was the actual case of injuries.

What should we include as a foreseeable consequence here? Steve slipping? Gale falling? Leslie falling? Leslie being hit by a car? Richard's heart attack? Reneé being hit on the head by a picture on the wall in an art shop?

You would probably think that Steve's and Gale's injuries were pretty foreseeable harm which would be likely to result from Jesse failing to put up adequate warning signs. However, you probably think that Richard's heart attack from seeing the toddler run into the street and the subsequent head injury of Reneé due to Richard's fall are not the kinds of foreseeable consequences the law had in mind when it holds Jesse responsible for not adequately warning pedestrians of the slippery surface.

If you thought this, you are correct. Though Jesse's actions were the actual cause of all the injuries, they were not the proximate or legal cause of the injuries to Richard and Reneé because those were not the kind of harms reasonably foreseeable from a failure to warn pedestrians about the slippery surface.

It is not enough that a plaintiff was harmed. In the famous case of *Palsgraf v. Long Island Central Railroad*,[1] the court said that "proof of negligence in the air so

EXAMPLE

---

[1]162 N.E. 99 (N.Y. 1928).

LIABILITY FOR "MARCH MADNESS" DRINKING?

In a 2005 *USA Today* editorial, Sandy Grady, who wrote a sports column in Philadelphia from 1957–1972, argues that the intense beer ads during the televising of the college basketball playoffs (one survey said the 2003 tournament aired 395 beer commercials), commonly referred to as "March Madness," is hypocritical when the primary audience is college students and there are 1400 alcohol-related campus deaths per year. At the same time colleges preach responsibility, Grady says, they take the millions of dollars from television rights made by glamorizing beer. Beer companies spend $52 million a year on college TV sports, $21 million of it on beer ads during March Madness, and colleges say they cannot operate without that income for scholarships and other things. Grady says the other things include fat coaching salaries and fancy weight rooms. According to Grady, Tom Osborne, the ex–Nebraska football coach of 25 years who is now a U.S. Congressman, has tried to pass a nonbinding resolution urging colleges to ban beer ads, but 380 of the 435 House members get an average of $11,650 in donations from the alcohol industry, so the measure has not been successful. "If aspirin were killing college students, how long do you think chancellors and presidents would allow ads for aspirin during telecasts?"

- Can a legitimate argument be made that the college drinking deaths are a foreseeable consequence of beer company advertising? Is the connection too remote for proximate cause?
- Who are the primary stakeholders who would be impacted by the advertising campaigns during March Madness?
- To whom do the advertisers (and spirits industry) owe a primary legal responsibility? To whom do the advertisers (and spirits industry) owe a primary ethical responsibility? Are these stakeholders different?
- Can you frame an ethical argument to the spirits industry that they should reduce their advertising to this market?
- Given these statistics, why do you think little or nothing has been done to address this issue?

Source: USA Today, March 14, 2005, p. 19A.

to speak, will not do. [Plaintiff] must show that the act as to him has possibilities of danger . . . so apparent as to be protected against the doing of it though the harm was unintended." In *Palsgraf*, a passenger running to catch a train with a package under his arm was pulled onto the moving train by a railroad employee. In the process the package fell. The package contained fireworks that exploded and caused freight scales on the train platform to fall on Ms. Palsgraf, causing injury. She sued, and won even though the jury found that the harm could not have been anticipated with the negligent act of the railroad employee. On appeal, the court reversed and held that there could be no recovery because the harm to Ms. Palsgraf was not foreseeable.

Proximate cause is the means by which the law will cut off the liability for which a tortfeasor will be responsible when the liability becomes too remote and thus unforeseeable. It is also the law's way of encouraging us to think ahead and consider the reasonably foreseeable consequences of our choices. In other words, the law is trying to find a balance between our actions and harm to others (see Reality Checks 6-11, "Liability for 'March Madness' Drinking?" and 6-12, "Just When You Thought You'd Heard It All . . . ").

Damages

In order to make out a claim for negligence, it is not enough that there be a duty, breach of duty, and proximate cause. There must also be injury caused by the breach of duty. If a car is accidentally rear-ended by another vehicle, but there is no damage to the hit car or the driver of the hit car, then even though the tortfeasor may have presented an unreasonable risk of harm to the victim, if there is no damage, there is no cause of action for negligence.

WHAT ARE THE DEFENSES TO NEGLIGENCE?

L06

Aside from showing that plaintiff did not prove that the requirements of negligence existed in this case, it is possible for a tortfeasor to defend against a negligence suit by showing that the plaintiff either

- Voluntarily assumed the risk (**assumption of the risk**) by knowing of the risk presented by the tortfeasor's negligence and continuing to act anyway.
- Contributed to the injury by doing a negligent act him- or herself (**contributory negligence**), including **comparative negligence.**

In both these defenses the tortfeasor does not deny the act took place or that plaintiff was harmed, but instead alleges he is not responsible because other legally cognizable factors were at play that relieve him of liability.

Voluntary Assumption of the Risk

L06

When the injured party had reason to know that there was the possibility of harm from defendant's negligence and decided to do an act anyway, the defendant can avoid liability by using the defense of voluntary assumption of the risk. In our opening scenario with Shema the mural painter and the falling scaffolding, Shema's employees building the scaffolding in such a way that it was likely to fall was certainly negligent. However, suppose a passerby saw that the scaffold looked shaky and walked under it anyway. Doing so would mean the passerby voluntarily assumed the risk of walking under scaffolding that looked unsafe to walk under. The passerby saw the risk and decided to undertake the risk by walking under the scaffolding rather than around it. Passerby's voluntary assumption of the risk would relieve Shema of liability for negligence.

EXAMPLE

Similarly, baseball fans have sued baseball park owners when they were injured by balls hitting them while they attended games. When they are harmed by the ball and sue for damages, the owner defends against the action by alleging that signs were posted in the area warning of the possibility of injury from balls, so plaintiff knew of the potential risk and the plaintiff voluntarily assumed the risk of sitting in the area. This relieves the park owners of liability (see Reality Check 6-13, "Sports and Voluntary Assumption of the Risk"). A karate student sued the karate school for having received a broken nose

EXAMPLE

EXAMPLE

REALITY CHECK 6-13

SPORTS AND VOLUNTARY ASSUMPTION OF THE RISK

In two recent cases involving sports, courts in New York and Hawaii have considered the voluntary assumption of the risk doctrine and ruled against claimants.

In Hawaii, when a golfer was hit in the eye by a stray golf ball, the Hawaii Supreme Court ruled that a golfer whose ball goes astray and hits and injures another golfer is not liable for the injury because golfers voluntarily assume the risk that not all golf balls are going to go where they are aimed.

In New York, Nicole Ziegelmeyer, who won a silver medal in the 1992 Olympics and bronze in 1994 for ice skating, was training for the 1998 Nagano games when she suffered a spinal injury after crashing into the fiberglass boards surrounding a rink in Lake Placid, NY, on which the pads were not properly anchored. A New York appellate panel ruled against Ziegelmeyer, finding that she voluntarily assumed the risk of injury by choosing to skate even though the pads on the fiberglass boards were not property anchored.

Sources: Yoneda v. Tom, No. 26271 (Hawaii, April 28, 2006); Ziegelmeyer v. United States Olympic Committee, 28 AD3d 1019 (NY 3d Dept. 2006).

during karate practice. The trial court dismissed the suit, holding that the karate student voluntarily assumed the risk of such injury by taking the sparring classes knowing that injury was a distinct possibility. In fact, the court went on to say that, as a seasoned karate practitioner, the student knew the inherent risk of injury, up to, and including, death.[2] In the *Konesky* case (Case 6.2), the court discusses voluntary assumption of the risk as well as foreseeability.

Contributory Negligence

The defense of contributory negligence is appropriate for a defendant to use when the plaintiff suing for negligence performed a negligent act him- or herself, in addition to the negligence of the tortfeasor. In our opening scenario example, let us say that the contributory negligence occurred when a passerby walked under the shaky scaffolding while drunk and accidentally stumbled into the scaffolding causing it to fall. Even though Shema's employees were negligent in erecting shaky scaffolding, this would be outweighed by the fact that the passerby was drunk and stumbled into the scaffolding and it fell and injured him. This would relieve Shema of responsibility for her employees' negligence in building the shaky scaffolding.

If either of the voluntary assumption of the risk defense or the contributory negligence defense were shown, it would be an effective defense to the negligence action brought by passerby and would prevent him or her from recovering from Shema for the injuries.

The contributory negligence theory has been steadily eroded over the years by legislatures, leaving only a minority of states using the theory. In its place is the less drastic theory of comparative negligence.

Comparative Negligence

Since a finding that passerby was contributorily negligent would relieve Shema of all liability under contributory negligence even though she may have some responsibility because the scaffold was not put together correctly, many states have passed comparative negligence statutes. If both plaintiff and defendant are negligent, the comparative negligence theory allots to each of the parties his or her proportionate share of the negligence and deducts from the total plaintiff would have received, the value of plaintiff's negligence. In jurisdictions with such statutes, when Shema shows that the plaintiff was contributorily negligent, it does not erase Shema's liability altogether. Rather, plaintiff can show that his or her negligence accounted for only a certain percentage of the harm, and thus, the rest of it should be Shema's responsibility.

For instance, if the jury decided that passerby was to receive $100,000 for his injuries and it was found that passerby was responsible for 30 percent of the injury because of his own negligence in bumping into Shema's scaffolding and causing it to fall, his recovery would be $100,000 minus 30 percent of $100,000 ($30,000) or $70,000.

[2]*Martezian v. Empire State Karate,* 04-1064 (NY 2006).

CASE 6.2 Konesky v. Wood County Agricultural Society

164 Ohio App. 3d 839 (OH Ct. App., 6th App. Dist. 2005)

Facts: Eighty-two-year-old Rose Konesky was standing outside of the harness race track at the Wood County Fair in a grassy area well away from an opening in the fence surrounding the track, loading horse grooming equipment into her truck, when one of the horses in the race threw its rider and ran through the opening, trampling and injuring her. In 1974, a runaway horse ran through the same opening, striking and injuring a bystander who was outside the track. Fair officials then instituted precautions to ensure the future safety of fair patrons, but these efforts diminished over time. The absence of a barrier during harness races at the fair was contrary to the longstanding and strong recommendations of the fair commission and, further, was at odds with the practice of various other county fairs.

Issue: Whether the race track owner was liable for Mrs. Konesky's injuries caused by the runaway horse if the owner was on notice that the injury could occur since it had happened before?

Decision: Yes.

Reasoning: Skow, J.: In applying the doctrine of primary assumption of the risk to sports and recreational activities in particular, the Supreme Court of Ohio has held: "where individuals engage in recreational or sports activities, they assume the ordinary risks of the activity and cannot recover for any injury unless it can be shown that the other participant's actions were either 'reckless' or 'intentional.' Underlying the doctrine is the notion that some risks are so inherent in an activity that the risks cannot be eliminated.

The types of risks that are covered under the doctrine are those that are the foreseeable and customary risks of the sport or recreational activity. In addition, "only those risks *directly associated* with the activity in question are within the scope of primary assumption of the risk." To be covered under the doctrine, the risk must be one that is so inherent to the sport or activity that it cannot be eliminated.

We find that the risk of being trampled by a runaway horse that has come off of a racetrack through a negligently placed or permitted gap in the surrounding fence is not an inherent risk of horse racing. Therefore, the doctrine of primary assumption of the risk is inapplicable herein. We further find that a reasonable jury could conclude in this case that appellees breached their duty of ordinary care to appellants by allowing the gate through which the runaway horse emerged to remain open, thereby creating an unreasonable danger that someone located outside of the racetrack would be trampled. Reversed and remanded.

CASE QUESTIONS

1. Do you agree with the court's decision? Explain.
2. Do you think it made a difference that there had been a similar event before? Explain.
3. Do you think the age of the plaintiff played any part in the court's decision? Should it? Explain.

If the jurisdiction in which the case is brought has no comparative negligence statute and the plaintiff was found to be contributorily negligent, plaintiff would recover nothing. Some statutes restrict plaintiff's coverage such that he will not be able to recover anything if the amount of liability attributable to him is over 50 percent since the plaintiff's negligence would then outweigh that of the defendant.

What is Strict Liability?

L05

Strict liability is responsibility imposed on tortfeasors for engaging in activity deemed by statute to be so dangerous until the tortfeasors must take responsibility for all harm that arises therefrom, even if the tortfeasor was as careful as possible. The tort is about the dangerous nature of the activity rather than the intent or actions of the tortfeasor. The activities included in strict liability are determined by statute and include acts such as blasting explosives or the keeping of wild animals (whether an animal is wild is dictated by state law), but it can include other things as the state determines. Once the victim proves that the activity was a strict liability offense and that the victim was injured by the activity, liability attaches to the tortfeasor. At the municipal park's annual Fourth of July fireworks display one of the fireworks misfires and goes into the crowd, injuring Whitney. Whitney sues the fireworks company and the company defends by saying it did everything possible to prevent the fireworks from misfiring. Whitney wins. The state statute includes the use of fireworks in its strict liability offenses. Since the company engaged in an activity that is within the strict liability statute, the fact that it was careful does not matter. What matters is that it engaged in the activity and Whitney was injured.

In strict liability, the tortfeasor has virtually no defense if sued by the injured party. The only defense to a strict liability offense is that the victim knew of the danger and voluntarily assumed the risk of being harmed. As you saw above, this is called voluntary assumption of the risk. Jillian sees the prominent blasting warning signs posted on the fence enclosing a site where a building is being blown up to make way for a new stadium. Jillian wants to see the building collapse, so she goes onto the site anyway and is injured during the blast. When Jillian sues the demolition company for her injuries, she loses. Blasting is a strict liability offense, but the company can show that Jillian voluntarily assumed the risk of injury and the company is therefore not liable to her.

 ## What is Product Liability?

Product liability is the name given to a group of several different legal bases including negligence, breach of warranty, and strict liability, for imposing liability on product makers and distributors for harm caused to people and property by defective, unreasonably dangerous products. When manufacturers and distributors place goods in the stream of commerce and those goods are defective and malfunction causing harm because of some act on the part of those who produce the goods, the possibility of harm is enormous because the goods are offered to the public at large and a great many people can be adversely affected. Liability can be so severe that the business goes bankrupt. For this reason, these actions are generally handled differently and they are called product liability cases. Not only does the state have an interest in protecting its population from harm by defective goods placed in the stream of commerce, but the federal government does as well. As a result, there are laws from each protecting the public, of which the prudent business owner must be aware.

NEGLIGENCE AND STRICT LIABILITY

The negligence we discussed earlier can be the basis for product liability actions in several ways. The good manufactured or sold by the tortfeasor can be designed in a way that makes it defective and likely to cause harm when used in the normal way. This is known as a **design defect,** for instance, the Ford Pinto car whose gas tank was placed in the car in such a way that it made it easy to cause explosions when the car was tapped lightly as often occurs in driving.

Negligence can instead occur when a product is designed just fine but there is negligence in the manufacturing process causing a **manufacturing defect** that makes the defective item unreasonably dangerous when used in the normal way (think of a mishap during the manufacturing of your curling iron such that the wiring in the curling iron caused it to explode when heated to the normal curling temperature because the plastic wire cover was frayed. Ouch!). Most product liability statutes hold manufacturers and distributors strictly liable for harm caused by their defectively manufactured products.

Negligence can also occur from a manufacturer's **failure to warn or adequately warn** consumers of known dangers about the product (think about all the warnings on your bathroom cleaner container), or **failure to adequately package** goods (imagine bleach in a thin glass bottle) so that the consumer is protected from foreseeable harm.

The Restatement (Third) of Torts, which operates much like the Restatement of Contracts discussed in the Contracts chapter except as it relates to torts, has been adopted in some form in all states. It allows recovery for harm to persons or property arising from a defect in the goods.[3] It applies different standards of liability, depending on which type of negligence occurs. In cases of manufacturing defects, if someone engages in selling or otherwise distributes products that are defective because the product "departs from its intended design," strict liability attaches. Regardless of how carefully the defective product was made, if it is defective because of a manufacturing defect, liability attaches for the harm the product does.

In design defect and failure to warn cases, rather than a strict liability standard, the standard applied is one of reasonableness or a regular negligence standard. A product is defectively designed when the harm could have been reduced or avoided by use of a reasonable alternative design and not doing so makes the product unreasonably safe. For failure to warn, a product is defective when its inadequate warning or failure to warn could have been avoided or reduced by a reasonable warning by the manufacturer or seller. In these two latter situations a seller or distributor can at least argue that the harm occurred because to avoid it would mean an unreasonable burden. Not so with manufacturing defects, because the seller is strictly liable for the harm arising from the defective goods. Of course, if a product is misused (you stick the curling iron in drinks to warm them) or the user voluntarily assumed the risk of using the defective product, (you saw the curling iron sparking and smoking, but used it anyway), it is a defense to strict liability. The negligence defenses discussed earlier apply in product liability cases using a reasonableness standard.

WARRANTIES

It is also possible for an individual harmed by a good to recover for his or her injuries by way of promises imposed upon the seller automatically because of the sale of goods under the Uniform Commercial Code (UCC) discussed in the contracts chapter. When an individual sells a good to a buyer, aside from any **express warranties** (warranties are absolute promises) that the seller explicitly makes to the buyer, the sale also carries **implied warranties** that the goods will be of at least average quality for such goods (**warranty of merchantability**), or they will be fit for the particular purpose for which they are sold if the buyer tells the seller the purpose and the seller provides the goods in response (**warranty of fitness for particular purpose**). If the buyer is harmed by goods that do not perform as promised, buyer can recover from the seller for breach of warranty.

Though the warranty is based on the contract of sale between the parties, the UCC did away with the concept of **privity of contract** that required there be a contract between the injured party and the seller. You can see the problem that would create if, for

---

[3]American Law Institute's Restatement (Third) of Contracts, Section 402A.

instance, you were injured by a gift you received for your birthday. The contract to purchase the good was between the one who gave you the gift and the seller, not between you and the seller. Under warranty provisions, this relationship is no longer necessary and the action can be brought by parties other than the buyer harmed by the goods.

In addition, the federal **Magnuson-Moss Warranty Act** allows recovery for harm that arises if the goods do not perform as warranted. The law does not require a manufacturer to provide a warranty, but if one is given, there are certain requirements that must be met in order for the warranty to protect the manufacturer.

Summary

Torts are civil wrongs for which businesses and individuals may sue to receive compensation for injuries. Sometimes the question of whether to sue can pose challenging ethical dilemmas. Negligence requires tortfeasors to pay for failing to meet the standard of care necessary to avoid foreseeable and unnecessary risk of harm to others, though the question of foreseeability can also be somewhat vexing. The law strikes a balance in order to encourage accountability while ensuring that one is not held liable for *every* resulting consequence of one's action. A host of intentional torts are available for intentional acts interfering with the right of others in their person and property. Business torts exist for the protection of business interests. The law of torts exists to compensate the injured party for the harm done by the tortfeasor and plays an important part in the legal environment of business. Tort law ensures that rights and duties are legally protected through this system of redress so that a system of trust and reliance can develop in business and other interpersonal relationships. Business owners should ensure that they, as well as their employees, do not engage in activity that might cause injury to the person, property, or economic interest of others.

Review Questions

1. Roscoe erects a home-size golf driving range in his backyard, complete with a 10 X 10 foot mesh screen to prevent the balls from going too far. One day while practicing his swing, one of the balls goes over the screen and crashes through the window of his nextdoor neighbor's office, injuring his neighbor E. J, and a client in E. J.'s office at the time. When Roscoe is sued by E. J. and the client, what will it likely be for, and what will Roscoe's response likely be? LO7

2. As Cindy Ho is walking to work one day, she sees that Botticelli's Glassworks workers are putting in place a plate glass window in Puck's Deli. The rope they are using to help lift the glass does not seem very strong to Cindy, but she does not want to be late for work, and hurries through the workers, underneath the glass, rather than around it. The rope breaks, the glass falls, and Cindy is injured. Will Cindy be able to recover from Botticelli's Glassworks? Discuss. LO4, 6

3. A basketball-sized chunk of Vermont marble fell from the U.S. Supreme Court building's molding façade just as a group of people waiting in line in front of the Court to go in and hear arguments entered the building. The chunk fell directly in the middle of the path of entry up to the Court. The marble façade had been inspected two years earlier and no indication of problems found. Those who had been waiting outside the building were very upset when they heard of the

falling marble. If one of them filed a lawsuit for assault, is he likely to win? (Based on Associated Press article, November 29, 2005). LO6

4. Jamil sues Jose for battery and intentional infliction of emotional distress because Jamil's Volkswagen Beetle was crushed by Jose's Hummer as Jamil watched from inside the barber shop where his hair was being trimmed. Does Jamil recover? Explain. LO7

5. While Matthew is asleep on the bus that is taking employees on a company picnic, Maria, whom Matthew barely knows, kisses him. Matthew finds this out after he awakens upon arrival and the other employees tease him about it. If Matthew wanted to bring an action against Maria, it would likely be for LO7

   a. assault.
   b. battery.
   c. intrusion upon seclusion.
   d. intentional infliction of emotional distress.

6. Ceilia, who is pregnant, comes into the Athletic Outlet sporting goods store to find a left-handed catcher's mitt for her daughter Tess. While in the store, Ceilia is approached by two store personnel who grab her arms and loudly tell her to give them the basketball they say she has hidden under her clothing. Ceilia denies the allegation and the employees drag her to the back of the store where she is detained for three hours. Eventually they discover that Ceilia's stomach is not a basketball, but, rather, a baby. Celia is pregnant. What likely happens if Ceilia sues for false imprisonment? LO4, 7

7. Jeanie Undies, Inc., is an innovator in women's lingerie. Jeanie's is coming out with a brand new line of bras that miraculously enhance women's natural bodies. Jeanie's ex-boyfriend is furious that Jeanie has been so successful. He obtains a job at the plant manufacturing the new item and manages to put into the thread used to make the product a chemical that will cause the wearer itch, burn, and blister wherever the thread touches their body. Hundreds of thousands of the new bras are sold in Jeanie's Undies, Inc.'s huge product rollout. The company is immediately deluged with angry complaints. When customers sue, what will be their likely theory? What standard will be used by the court? LO4, 6, 7

8. Robert, owner of Robert's Inc., one of Cory's Window Washers' commercial customers, is not satisfied with the cleaning his building's windows has received. He complains to Ruby, the crew leader responsible for the building. The discussion becomes heated and Ruby ends up punching Robert in the face. When Robert sues Cory for the injuries he received, Cory defends by saying that he was not involved in the dispute and is therefore not responsible. Is this a good defense? Explain. LO4, 7

9. What is another name for injurious falsehood? LO7

10. Manuel opens up a new business, Delightful Donuts! because of his secret recipe. Delightful Donuts! is an instant hit because of its light, delicious, melt-in-your-mouth delicacies. Because he doesn't want anyone else to know his recipe, Manuel comes into the shop every morning before the other employees and makes up the dough for the day. One morning Deborah, an employee of Delightful Donuts! sneaks in and watches while Manuel makes the dough. A few weeks later Deborah quits working for Manuel and opens her own donut shop on the other side of town. Deborah's recipe is the one Manuel uses for his donuts. Is there anything Manuel can do? Explain. LO7

11. Aimee, a 24-year-old grad student in town for a convention, walks into a bar and is hit by a flaming rum drink which a man at a table tossed over his shoulder as she passed by. Aimee falls to the floor and shouts "I'm on fire! I'm on fire!" as the flames on her arm spread to her back, hip and hair. The five men at the table, including a doctor and a lawyer, do not deny that one of them lit the 151-proof Bacardi rum, but each denied either throwing the drink or seeing who did. Aimee, who suffered second and third degree burns and has permanent scarring, sues the five men. The bar has requested the court to keep the bar out of Aimee's lawsuit since the server who served the drinks said she did not light them, as it would violate bar policy. However, the server allegedly did not attempt to stop the men from lighting the drink. Will the bar likely be kept out of a negligence suit? (*Atlanta Journal & Constitution*, September 18, 2004) LO4, 6

Ethics Issue

On Donald Trump's personal blog, "Carolyn,"[4] about Carolyn Kepcher, Donald Trump's former apprentice on his *Apprentice* show, Trump wrote that Ms. Kepcher was terminated because "she loved her fame and she loved her celebrity on *The Apprentice* and it was affecting her work. She wasn't doing her job like she used to or was capable of doing." Mr. Trump told Ms. Kepcher, "in the nicest way possible, … Get a new job." He did not say "you're fired." He replaced Ms. Kepcher with his daughter, Ivanka Trump. Was it ethical of Trump to broadcast this type of information to the general public? Compare the information found in each week's *People* magazine, or *Us Weekly*. Is there a difference? Does it matter that the sources in those publications are journalists and here it is the original decision maker publicizing the basis of the decision? Does it matter that Ms. Kepcher voluntarily sought a position in the public eye? If so, what personal information would then be acceptable for Mr. Trump to share about Ms. Kepcher and what information would you consider too personal to be shared? Where should we, as a society, draw our legal and ethical lines? For instance, what about the extensive media coverage of speculation about Michael Jackson's reputed drug use immediately after his death? Any ethical issues there? Is it the same as the Trump situation? If not, why?

Group Exercise

Have each person in the room relate to the class a tort that they have either been involved with or know of (whether or not a case was brought). See if the class can make out the requirements for the case.

Key Terms

absolute privilege 135

appropriation of name or likeness 139

assault 131

assumption of the risk 147

battery 130

comparative negligence 147

consent 142

contributory negligence 147

deep pockets theory 127

defamation 134

design defect 150

disparagement 140

express warranty 151

failure to adequately package goods 151

failure to adequately warn 151

false imprisonment 132

false light 139

implied warranty 151

injurious falsehood 140

intentional infliction of emotional distress 137

intentional interference with contractual relations 141

intentional tort 140

intrusion upon seclusion 139

invasion of privacy 138

libel 135

Magnuson-Moss Warranty Act 152

manufacturing defect 150

negligence 143

negligence per se 144

palming off 142

privity of contract 151

product liability 150

proximate cause 144

publication 134

publication of private facts 140

qualified privilege 134

respondeat superior 127

self-defense 142

shopkeeper's rule 133

slander 135

theft of trade secrets 141

voluntary assumption of the risk 147

warranty of fitness for a particular purpose 151

warranty of merchantability 151

---

[4]Donald Trump, "Carolyn," September 10, 2006, http://www.trumpuniversity.com/blog/index.cfm?blogpost_id=713.

Property, Real and Personal

Learning Objectives

After reading this chapter, you should be able to:

LO1 List and define the types of property the law recognizes

LO2 Explain how different types of property can be transferred

LO3 Distinguish the various property estates the law recognizes

LO4 Give the pros and cons of different types of property estates

LO5 Explain the different ways property can be held

LO6 Distinguish between lost, abandoned, and mislaid property

LO7 Analyze whether personal property has been the subject of trespass or conversion

LO8 Discuss some ways in which ethics and diversity has impacted property issues

Opening Scenario

While on a hunting trip with some of her co-workers and other professional acquaintances on property owned by her employer, Clarice stumbles over what she thinks is a stump as she goes to claim her catch. As it turns out, Clarice did not stumble over a stump. She stumbled over a plastic-lined canvas bag near the stump. Upon inspection, Clarice finds the debris-covered bag contains a very expensive camera in a case, a pair of very expensive earphones, and a top-of-the-line laptop. Can Clarice keep what she found?

Introduction and Background: The Role of Property in Business and Law

In this chapter we will discuss the various types of property recognized at law and the way in which law recognizes interests in property, as well as property being held and conveyed to others.

In some ways the United States is fairly unique among other countries of the world as relates to its system of property. It was important enough to include in our Constitution and, in many ways, virtually all of our important legal rights come from our concept of property. It has been both the boon as well as the bane of our existence. For Americans, property is the foundation upon which virtually everything else exists. It undergirds our legal system, our social system, and our government.

LO8

It is no happenstance that along with marriage come certain property rights such as married couples holding property they own as tenants by the entirety, or the right to receive half of all property acquired during the marriage in community property states. Much of our legal system involves conflicts around property: who has a right to it, who can be excluded, how it can be held, what can be done on it, to it, over it, or with it, what happens if someone without rights takes it, and so on. It is no accident that, traditionally, those who owned the most property were also the most powerful. Property gives us status and the more property we have, the more status and wealth we tend to have.

Property has been much impacted by our perceptions of diversity as well. At one point we thought it was acceptable—even divinely ordained—for us to live out the concept of Manifest Destiny and take away property from Native Americans who had lived for tens of thousands of years on land we wanted for the expansion of our new country, and we did what it took to get it, including forced removal, hunting their primary food source, bison, to near extinction, and trying our best to assimilate them into American culture, including sending their children away to boarding schools to "civilize" them. Even though treaties we made with them were based on our virtually unassailable American contractual principles, treaties meant little as we decided that we wanted more and more of Native Americans' land and simply abandoned the treaties. Eventually, Native Americans were consigned to small reservations, often hundreds of miles from their traditional homeland, and with little regard for how they would fare.

Interestingly enough, our belief that Native Americans should accept our view of property, as reflected in the Allotment (or Dawes) Act of 1887, ended up being their undoing and led to our owning even more. We tried to use property as a social organizer. The idea behind the law was that if each individual Native American family had a plot of land, they would be more likely to care for it and use it to become an assimilated, productive member of our society and less likely to engage in acts harmful to settlers. The theory was that individual private property ownership meant that the communal approach so important to Native American culture, governance and society would disappear and they would meld into American culture by adopting our values of the positive attributes arising from individual ownership of property.

Since this approach to property went directly against the Native American concept of communal property ownership, it is no surprise that the result was that in the 47 years of the law's existence, Native Americans lost over 90 million acres, or two-thirds of their land, and 90,000 of them became landless, and, for the most part, dependent upon the federal government for subsistence. Someone who gives something, then takes it away, is called by the negative and offensive term "Indian giver," when the reality is that it was our government that continuously made treaties with Native Americans granting them some of the land on which they had lived for thousands of years, then ignored the treaties and took the land. (See Diversity in the Law 7-1, "Not Just Ancient

History.") This is not a denigration of our country. It simply is what it is. When we knew better, we did better. But ignoring what happened and acting as if our concept of property rights is purely based on law simply does not reflect reality.

In another example of how much property undergirds our history and our approach to law, even though we were a country founded on the bedrock principles of individual freedom, our concept of property told us that it was permissible for us to own other human beings and to engage in the barter and trade of them. So, while ordinarily the idea of owning a human being would be an anathema to Americans' idea of freedom and property, when we wanted to make the land we confiscated from Native Americans more productive and thus needed a cheap and plentiful source of labor, Africans were taken from their homeland and brought here to the U.S. to help build the fledgling country into the powerhouse it is today. This group was virtually barred from participating in the strong land base that formed the foundation of later fortunes that have been the basis of much of the wealth that the country has enjoyed. The U.S. Constitution itself was the battleground for this issue with slaveholding colonies in the Continental Congress winning the fight and allowing the 150+-year old institution to continue to exist under the new Constitution despite the Declaration of Independence statement that "all men are created equal."

The issue of reparations for African Americans held in bondage for 246 years and unable to enjoy the property interest in even their own ability to work and produce also rears its head from time to time, with the idea being that the use of them as property for the benefit of others deprived them of the ability to participate in their own creation of wealth. In Congress's apology for slavery of July 29, 2008, it alluded to the lingering impact of slavery and its 110-year aftermath of Jim Crow or legalized segregation on today's population, as represented by African Americans' "long term loss of income and opportunity." (See Diversity in the Law 7-2, "Impact of Property Struggles Still Lingers.") Keep in mind, too, the property issues we discussed in the contracts chapter relating to the concept of limiting the right to property ownership to exclude blacks, Hispanics, Asians, and others through restrictive covenants and the ethics of such provisions.

In this chapter we will explore the concept of property and its role in business. We will consider the various ways property can be held, how it can be transferred, and how it can best be protected. In our legal system, property is divided into real property and personal property, including intellectual property discussed in detail in the intellectual property chapter. Personal property is further divided broadly into tangible and intangible property. We will discuss each in turn.

LO1

What Is Real Property and Why Do We Care?

Real property is land and anything permanently attached to it such as houses, trees, fences, and so on. Our law recognizes property rights in land as far down as we can go, and as far up as is feasible (recognizing that, for instance, airplanes need to be able to fly across land unimpeded by property claims). Our law considers property to be important, but it considers real property as of truly unique significance. Even though one plot of land may look much like another, our law considers each piece of real property unique and its owner has a right to claim it to the exclusion of all others. Property rights include what interest a person holds in the real property, as well as how that interest is held. Does the person own it? Rent it? Have it only for a lifetime but then it goes to someone designated by someone other than the owner of it? Does the party hold it alone? Along with others? If so, if one dies does the remaining property go to the other owners or can the interest of the decedent be passed to his or her designees?

IMPACT OF PROPERTY STRUGGLES STILL LINGERS

The following House Resolution apologizing for slavery was is-sued on July 29, 2008. You may well wonder what it is doing in a property chapter in a book about the legal environment of business. If you look closely at the resolution, you will see the many ways in which the House of Representatives noted the impact today of slavery so long ago, and much of what they note has to do with property: it is clear in the subtext who was owned, what ownership meant to being able to amass wealth, leave a financial legacy, qualify for jobs in order to purchase property, obtain education to be able to amass property, and so on. It took a long time to get to the point where the U.S. House of Representatives was willing to issue an apology. The Senate did so a year later. Virginia, where the first Africans landed in 1619, apologized, as did North Carolina, Alabama, Florida, Maryland, Connecticut, and New Jersey. In recognizing the lin-gering effects of slavery, the Resolution again acknowledges that the importance of control over oneself is the most impor-tant source of property rights our country offers.

H. Res. 194
In the House of Representatives, U.S.,
July 29, 2008.

Whereas millions of Africans and their descendants were enslaved in the United States and the 13 American colonies from 1619 through 1865;

Whereas slavery in America resembled no other form of involuntary servitude known in history, as Africans were cap-tured and sold at auction like inanimate objects or animals;

Whereas Africans forced into slavery were brutalized, hu-miliated, dehumanized, and subjected to the indignity of be-ing stripped of their names and heritage;

Whereas enslaved families were torn apart after having been sold separately from one another;

Whereas the system of slavery and the visceral racism against persons of African descent upon which it depended became entrenched in the Nation's social fabric;

Whereas slavery was not officially abolished until the passage of the 13th Amendment to the United States Constitution in 1865 after the end of the Civil War;

Whereas after emancipation from 246 years of slavery, African-Americans soon saw the fleeting political, social, and economic gains they made during Reconstruction eviscerated by virulent racism, lynchings, disenfranchisement, Black Codes, and racial segregation laws that imposed a rigid system of of-ficially sanctioned racial segregation in virtually all areas of life;

Whereas the system of de jure racial segregation known as "Jim Crow," which arose in certain parts of the Nation following the Civil War to create separate and unequal societies for whites and African-Americans, was a direct result of the racism against persons of African descent engendered by slavery;

Whereas a century after the official end of slavery in America, Federal action was required during the 1960s to elim-inate the dejure and defacto system of Jim Crow throughout parts of the Nation, though its vestiges still linger to this day;

Whereas African-Americans continue to suffer from the complex interplay between slavery and Jim Crow—long after both systems were formally abolished—through enormous damage and loss, both tangible and intangible, including the loss of human dignity, the frustration of careers and profes-sional lives, and the long-term loss of income and opportunity;

Whereas the story of the enslavement and de jure segre-gation of African-Americans and the dehumanizing atrocities committed against them should not be purged from or mini-mized in the telling of American history;

Whereas on July 8, 2003, during a trip to Goree Island, Senegal, a former slave port, President George W. Bush ac-knowledged slavery's continuing legacy in American life and the need to confront that legacy when he stated that slavery "was . . . one of the greatest crimes of history. . . . The racial bigotry fed by slavery did not end with slavery or with segre-gation. And many of the issues that still trouble America have roots in the bitter experience of other times. But however long the journey, our destiny is set: liberty and justice for all";

Whereas President Bill Clinton also acknowledged the deep-seated problems caused by the continuing legacy of racism against African-Americans that began with slavery when he initiated a national dialogue about race;

Whereas a genuine apology is an important and neces-sary first step in the process of racial reconciliation;

Whereas an apology for centuries of brutal dehumaniza-tion and injustices cannot erase the past, but confession of the wrongs committed can speed racial healing and recon-ciliation and help Americans confront the ghosts of their past;

Whereas the legislature of the Commonwealth of Virginia has recently taken the lead in adopting a resolution officially expressing appropriate remorse for slavery and other State legislatures have adopted or are considering similar resolu-tions; and

Whereas it is important for this country, which legally rec-ognized slavery through its Constitution and its laws, to make a formal apology for slavery and for its successor, Jim Crow, so that it can move forward and seek reconciliation, justice, and harmony for all of its citizens: Now, therefore, be it

Resolved, That the House of Representatives—

1. acknowledges that slavery is incompatible with the basic founding principles recognized in the Declaration of Independence that all men are created equal;
2. acknowledges the fundamental injustice, cruelty, brutality, and inhumanity of slavery and Jim Crow;
3. apologizes to African-Americans on behalf of the people of the United States, for the wrongs commit-ted against them and their ancestors who suffered under slavery and Jim Crow; and
4. expresses its commitment to rectify the lingering con-sequences of the misdeeds committed against African-Americans under slavery and Jim Crow and to stop the occurrence of human rights violations in the future.

Source: H. Res. 194, July 29, 2008, http://thomas.loc.gov/cgi-bin/ query/D?c110:2:./temp/~c110f4cfLp.

Each of these situations has a different legal position and each has different legal repercussions.

TAKE AWAY 7-1

PROPERTY ESTATES RECOGNIZED BY LAW

- Fee simple
- Life estate
- Estate for years
- Remainder
- Reversion
- Tenant

 L03
L04
WHAT REAL PROPERTY INTERESTS DOES THE LAW RECOGNIZE?

One of the most important questions about real property is the nature of the property interest that is held. It determines what the owner can do with the property regarding his or her possession of it. There are several different types of interests, called **estates** or **interests,** recognized at law (see Take Away 7-1, "Property Estates Recognized by Law").

Fee Simple

A **fee simple** interest in real estate is the most rights our law recognizes in property. The owner of a fee simple interest has the most ownership rights in that he or she owns his or her land, particularly if it is owned solely by him or her, outright, forever and ever, and is only constrained in its use by law. Ownership of property is evidenced by a **deed,** which is a legal document that gives **title** to the property to the owner. Legal constraints include zoning laws, restrictions contained in the deed, as well as the government's right to **eminent domain.** Eminent domain is the government's right to take property for government use while providing the owner with fair market value for the taking. It includes everything from allowing utility lines or sidewalks to be installed, to a full taking to replace a taken house with a government parking lot. However, other than the government's limitations on ownership, the holder of a fee simple owns the land outright forever and can do with it as he or she wishes, including selling it, willing it, giving it as a gift, extracting minerals, leasing mineral rights, using it as collateral or renting it. However, as you can see from Reality Check 7-1, "Eminent Domain for Nothing?!" the government's rights to your property can be considerable.

EXAMPLE

It is also possible for someone to come into ownership of real property by means of **adverse possession.** When an individual possesses another's land openly, notoriously, and treats it as his or her own for a period set forth in a statute (usually 21 years) and the true owner makes no claim, the individual can petition the court to have title transferred into his or her name and become the owner of the property. The idea is that property is so important in our system, that if an owner does not deal with it for the statutory period and an adverse possessor takes care of it without hiding that fact from the owner, that adverse possessor should be able to own it. Most statutes will allow the statutory period to be tolled or stopped for a period if the owner can show that there is a good reason that he or she did not deal with the property (for instance they were in a coma for 25 years).

Life Estate

A **life estate** is an interest in land that is only good for the life of the **life tenant** who holds the interest. Now you can see why we mentioned owning the property forever when we discussed fee simple. A life estate is quite different, in that the holder of a life estate does not own the property forever and cannot do with it as he or she pleases. The life tenant only owns the land during the measuring life (which may be that of the life tenant or someone else), and after the death of the measuring life, the land goes back either to the grantor of the life tenancy or whoever else he or she interest designates. For instance, a mother can execute a deed as a **grantor** giving a life interest to her daughter, the **grantee,** with the land to go to the mother's church after the daughter dies. As you

EXAMPLE

EMINENT DOMAIN FOR NOTHING?!

Generally, in eminent domain, the government has been allowed to take private property for public use under the "Takings Clause" of the Fifth Amendment to the U.S. Constitution. In 2005, however, the U.S. Supreme Court rendered a decision that sent shudders down the spines of virtually anyone who owned real property in the U.S. In *Kelo v. City of New London*, 545 U.S. 469 (2005), the high court held that the government's power of eminent domain included the right to require a private property owner to convey the property to another private property owner (rather than to the government) for purposes of economic development. Ms. Kelo's home, and others, were taken by eminent domain by the city as part of a proposed private redevelopment plan after Pfizer announced it was moving a research facility to the city. In the Court's view, the benefit to the community of economic development qualified as a public use under the Takings Clause. The proposal projected 3,169 new jobs and 1.2 million dollars in annual tax revenue for the city. The Court held that increasing tax revenues, creating jobs and revitalizing an area, even if it is not blighted, was sufficient public use. Public reaction against the decision was very strong, and in the wake of the holding, President Bush issued an executive order (which had limited effect since eminent domain is exercised by states) and over 40 states passed some type of law restricting the power of eminent domain to take property for private economic development. As it turned out, Pfizer, the main business that would anchor the new redevelopment, decided to move its business elsewhere and the plan did not materialize.

The other side of this issue is that allowing a city to use eminent domain powers for partnerships with private industry can encourage much needed new growth and revitalization for cities, resulting in the increased jobs and tax revenues alluded to above. However, when it comes to their homes, Americans find it difficult to look at the big picture and sacrifice their homes for the greater good promised.

How should a government decide such issues? What are the relevant considerations? Who are the stakeholders? What are the ethical considerations a government should use in making such determinations? At what point should homeowners think past themselves and instead think of the greater good for the town? Is this even a fair question, given how important property is in our legal system?

Source: Kelo v. City of New London, 545 U.S. 469 (2005); Eric Tucker, "Pfizer Move New Blow to Conn. City in Land Fight," *Newsday*, November 16, 2009, http://www.newsday.com/business/pfizer-move-a-new-blow-to-conn-city-in-land-fight-1.1591865; Avi Salzman, "Holdout Ends, Letting a City Seize Property in Connecticut," *New York Times*, July 1, 2006, http://www.nytimes.com/2006/07/01/nyregion/01eminent.html?_r=2&adxnnl=1&oref=slogin&adxnnlx=1276704055-bZaE1EYnFWQwTveS+ZOkRQ; *Executive Order: Protecting the Property Rights of the American People*, June 23, 2006, http://georgewbush-whitehouse.archives.gov/news/releases/2006/06/20060623-10.html.

can see, the daughter only gets the property for her lifetime. Because she is limited in what she owns, she does not have the right to will the property to someone else because her interest terminates as soon as she dies, which is when a will becomes effective. As a life tenant, the daughter can give the property away, or sell it if she wishes, but the grantee only receives the interest that the life tenant had, so upon the life tenant's death the property would still have to go to the mother's church. Often, life tenancies are given by a spouse in a will, so that the surviving spouse will always have a place to live. However, upon the death of the spouse, the property will often then go the couple's children in fee simple. The measuring life need not be that of the life tenant. For instance, the grantor can deed the property to Jane, for the life of John, and when John dies, the land goes to the grantor's alma mater.

While possessing the property during his or her lifetime, the life tenant cannot do anything that would undermine the interests of those taking after the life estate. The life tenant may carry on such usual and ordinary activities as are generally done on the property, but cannot attempt to deplete the resources of the property as if he or she was the only one to be considered. If the life tenant takes more than his or her share, those who have an interest in the property after the life estate can bring an action to stop the life tenant, and even to have any excess value held in trust until their interest is realized.

Estate for Years

The grantor can have the transferee hold the land for a period less than the grantee's life. In such a case, it is called an **estate for years.** It operates much like a life estate, in that the grantee only has the land for the period for which it is granted and cannot sell it or will it away to the exclusion of the remaining interest in the property.

Remainder

If the grantor of land orders that the land will go to a third party (i.e., not the grantor or grantee/life tenant) after the life estate is over, then the third party receives a remainder interest. Of course, because it is a remainder interest, it means that someone has an interest ahead of the remainder, so the remainder cannot have the property as soon as the grantor conveys the interest. The first (and there can be more) interest holders must have their interest first, then the remainder takes the property. The remainder can transfer his or her remainder interest, but it will not take effect until the remainder interest is actualized.

Reversion

If, rather that have the interest after the life estate go to a third party, the grantor dictates that the interest is to return to the grantor, this is a reversion. That is, the interest in the land reverts back to the grantor. Generally, the one with a reversionary interest takes the property as a fee simple, but the grantor can do otherwise if he or she wishes, in which case the grantee with the reversionary interest would have to use the property consistent with that interest.

Tenant

The owner of property may not wish to give complete title and control of the property over to another even for a period. The landowner/**landlord** can instead rent the property out for a period of time and the one to whom the property is rented is known as a **tenant.** This is something with which many of you will be quite familiar. Title and ownership to the property do not pass to the tenant; only possession does. The tenant cannot sell or otherwise convey the property to another. The most the tenant can do, and this is generally if the landlord agrees, is to **sublease** the premises to another for part of the lease term. The tenant would still be liable for the rent, however, unless the landlord agreed otherwise and gave a novation which we discussed in the contracts chapter. This is what occurs when, for instance, a student leases an apartment but is on a semester abroad and allows someone to take over the lease while they are away. The **sublessee** is only renting the property for part of the student/tenant's lease period, and the student/lessee is still responsible to the landlord for the rent even though someone else is subleasing the apartment. This will sound familiar, as this is an assignment, as we discussed in the contracts chapter, with the sublessee being assigned the tenant's right to occupy the premises.

EXAMPLE

You will be happy to know that along with a lease of a premises in most jurisdictions comes an **implied warranty of habitability.** Aside from the lease, the warranty requires that a landlord provide premises that are safe and at least reasonably habitable. Tenants often use this breach of implied warranty as the basis of claims (often in the form of withholding rent) against a landlord for failure of the landlord to maintain appliances, lighting in common areas, safety hazards, and other items that may not be covered explicitly in the lease but are expected in a rental. In Reality Check 7-2 we give you a lease agreement for a furnished house, which many of you may have, but have probably not read. This is just a sample lease but gives you a chance to take a good look at some of the things you may have signed off on in your own lease. See if you can find language related to the warranty of habitability provision or the subleasing provision.

LEASE AGREEMENT FOR FURNISHED HOUSE

This Agreement is made and entered in this _____ day of _____, 20_____, between _____, hereinafter referred to as "Landlord" and _____, hereinafter referred to as "Tenant."

WHEREAS, Landlord desires to lease to Tenant and Tenant desires to lease from Landlord the premises generally described as _____, it is herein agreed as follows:

1. Landlord hereby leases to Tenant, the furnished premises described above for a term of _____ beginning _____ and ending _____, at a monthly rate of _____.

2. The described premises are leased furnished, to include all furnishings enumerated on the List of Furnishings, which is a part of this lease, signed by both parties and dated.

3. Tenant agrees to pay the rent herein provided subject to the terms and conditions set forth herein.

4. Rent shall be payable in equal monthly installments on the _____ day of each month, to the address of Landlord as stated above or at such other address as Landlord may, from time to time, require.

5. Tenant shall pay for all electricity, water, fuel oil and gas during the term of this lease and any extension or renewal thereof.

6. Landlord covenants that the leased premises are, to the best of his knowledge, clean, safe, sound and healthful and that there exists no violation of any applicable housing code, law or regulation of which he is aware.

7. Tenant agrees to comply with all sanitary laws, ordinances and rules affecting the cleanliness, occupancy and preservation of the premises during the term of this lease.

8. Tenant shall use the leased premises exclusively for a private residence for occupancy by no more than _____ persons, unless otherwise specified herein, and Tenant shall not make any alterations to the house, outbuildings or grounds without written consent of Landlord.

9. Tenant shall keep the premises in good order and repair and shall advise Landlord or Landlord's agent of any needed repairs or maintenance reasonably expected to cost $ _____ or more.

10. Tenant agrees to take good care of the furniture, carpets, draperies, appliances and other household goods, and the personal effects of Landlord, and further agrees that he will deliver up same to Landlord in good condition at the end of the term of this lease, normal wear and tear expected.

11. Tenant shall repair or replace, at Tenant's expense, all loss or damage to any of the listed furniture, carpets, draperies, appliances and other household goods, and personal effects of Landlord, whenever such damage or loss shall have resulted from Tenant's misuse, waste or neglect of said furnishings and personal effects of Landlord.

12. Tenant shall cause to be made, at Tenant's expense, all required repairs to heating and air-conditioning apparatus, electric and gas fixtures and plumbing work whenever such damage shall have resulted from misuse, waste or neglect of Tenant, it being understood that Landlord is to have same in good order and repair when giving possession.

13. Tenant shall not keep or have in or on the leased house, outbuildings or grounds any article or thing of a dangerous, flammable or explosive nature that might be pronounced "hazardous" or "extra hazardous" by any responsible insurance company.

14. Tenant shall give prompt notice to Landlord or his agent of any dangerous, defective, unsafe or emergency condition in or on the leased premises, said notice being by any suitable means. Landlord or his agent shall repair and correct said conditions promptly upon receiving notice thereof from Tenant.

15. Landlord covenants that the Tenant and Tenant's family shall have, hold and enjoy the leased premises for the term of this lease, subject to the conditions set forth herein.

16. Tenant covenants that he shall not commit nor permit a nuisance in or upon the premises, that he shall not maliciously or by reason of gross negligence damage the house, outbuildings or grounds, and that he shall not engage, nor permit any member of his family to engage in conduct so as to interfere substantially with the comfort and safety of residents of adjacent buildings.

17. Tenant agrees to place a security deposit with Landlord in the amount of $ _____, to be used by Landlord at the termination of this lease for the cost of replacing or repairing damage, if any, to the house, outbuildings, grounds, furnishings or personal effects of Landlord resulting from the intentional or negligent acts of Tenant.

18. Landlord agrees to return said security deposit to Tenant within ten days of the Tenant's vacating the leased premises subject to the terms and conditions set forth herein.

19. Tenant shall, at reasonable times, give access to Landlord or his agents for any reasonable and lawful purpose. Except in situations of compelling emergency, Landlord or his agents shall give the Tenant at least 24 hours' notice of intention to seek

access, the date and time at which access will be sought, and the reason therefore.

20. In the event of default by Tenant, Tenant shall remain liable for all rent due or to become due during the term of this lease. Landlord or his agents shall have the obligation to relet the premises in the Landlord's name for the balance of the term, or longer, and will apply proceeds of such reletting toward the reduction of Tenant's obligations enumerated herein.

21. Tenant shall permit Landlord or his agents to show the premises at reasonable hours, to persons desiring to rent or purchase same, _____ days prior to the expiration of this lease, and will permit the notice "To Let" or "For Sale" to be placed on said premises and remain thereon without hindrance or molestation after said date.

22. In the event of any breach by the Tenant of any of Tenant's covenants or agreements herein, Landlord or his agents may give Tenant five days' notice to cure said breach, setting forth in writing which covenants or agreements have been breached. If any breach is not cured within said five-day period, or reasonable steps to effectuate said cure are not commenced and diligently pursued within said five-day period and thereafter until said breach has been cured, Landlord or his agents may terminate this lease upon five days' additional notice to the Tenant, with said notice being in lieu of a Notice to Quit, which Tenant hereby waives. Said termination shall be ineffective if Tenant cures said breach or commences and diligently pursues reasonable steps to effectuate such cure at any time prior to the expiration of said five-day termination. Upon terminating this lease as provided herein, Landlord or his agent may commence proceedings against Tenant for his removal as provided for by law.

23. In the event of any breach by Landlord of any of Landlord's covenants or agreements herein, Tenant may give Landlord ten days' notice to cure said breach, setting forth in writing the manner in which said covenants and agreements have been breached. If said breach is not cured within said ten-day period, or reasonable steps to effectuate said cure are not commenced and diligently pursued within said ten-day period and thereafter until said breach has been cured, rent hereunder shall be fully abated from the time at which said ten days' notice expired until such time as Landlord has fully cured the breach set forth in the notice provided for in this paragraph.

24. In no case shall any abatement of rent hereunder be effected where the condition set forth in the notice provided for herein was created by the intentional or negligent act of the Tenant, but Landlord shall have the burden of proving that rent abatement may not be effected for the foregoing reason.

25. Landlord agrees to deliver possession of the leased premises at the beginning of the term provided for herein. In the event of Landlord's failure to deliver possession at the beginning of said term, Tenant shall have the right to rescind this lease and recover any consideration paid under terms of this Agreement.

26. Tenant agrees that this lease shall be subject to and subordinate to any mortgage or mortgages now on said premises or which any owner of said premises may hereafter at any time elect to place on said premises.

27. Unless otherwise provided for elsewhere in this lease, any notice required or authorized herein shall be given in writing, one copy of said notice mailed via U.S. certified mail, return receipt requested, and one copy of said notice mailed via U.S. first-class mail. Notice to Tenant shall be mailed to him at the leased premises. Notice to Landlord shall be mailed to him, or to the managing agent, at their respective addresses as set forth herein, or at such new address as to which the Tenant has been duly notified.

28. This lease constitutes the entire agreement between the parties hereto. No changes shall be made herein except by writing, signed by each party and dated. The failure to enforce any right or remedy hereunder, and the payment and acceptance of rent hereunder, shall not be deemed a waiver by either party of such right or remedy in the absence of a writing as provided for herein.

29. In the event legal action is required to enforce any provision of this Agreement, the prevailing party shall be entitled to recover reasonable attorney's fees and costs.

30. Landlord and Tenant agree that this lease, when filled out and signed, is a binding legal obligation.

IN WITNESS WHEREOF, the parties hereto have executed this Agreement on the date first above written.

By: _____ _____

By: _____ _____

If you chose #6 and 23, you were correct!

TENANCIES RECOGNIZED BY LAW

- Sole ownership
- Joint tenants with right of survivorship
- Tenancy in common
- Tenancy by the entirety

HOW ARE PROPERTY INTERESTS HELD?   L05

How property interest is held addresses how many people own a property together, and what legal rights arise from the type of ownership they possess (see Take Away 7-2, "Tenancies Recognized by Law").

Sole Owner

If title to the property is held by only one person, then ownership rests solely with that single owner. The single owner owns the property and does not have to consult with anyone to determine how the property can be used. The sole owner is the only one responsible for paying for the property, repairs, taxes, and harm that occurs to another from use of the property.

Tenants in Common

It is possible for more than one person to hold title to a piece of property at the same time. Each of the owners has an undivided proportionate share of the whole. What share each has depends on what portion they have agreed to hold, but in the absence of an agreement to the contrary, each holds an undivided share proportionate to the total number of owners. If there are five owners, each would own an undivided one-fifth interest in the property. If there are two, each would own an undivided half, and so on. Each owns his or her share and can do with it as he or she pleases, including willing it to a nonowner upon his or her death.

EXAMPLE

However, the interest each tenant in common has is an undivided one and is subject to the ownership of the other owners. That means that each of the owners owns each inch of the land. The practical result is that none of the owners can do anything with the land unless the others agree. If three siblings own a piece of land and one wishes to build a store on his portion, he cannot do so without the agreement of the others since they all own an undivided interest in each part of the property.

If the tenant in common owners wish to deal with their interests separately, they can request from the court a **partition** of the property into their respective interests. If a partition is granted by the court, each of the parties would own his or her interest separately and would not need the permission of the others to use the property as he or she wished.

Joint Tenants with Right of Survivorship

EXAMPLE

Joint tenancy is much like a tenancy in common except that when one of the owners dies, his or her share automatically goes to the other owners and is divided up proportionately. If the three siblings owned their property as joint tenants and one died, the interest of that tenant could not be willed away to someone else. Instead, the two remaining siblings would now each own title to half of the property instead of one-third each. The decedent cannot pass his or her interest by will to anyone other than the other joint tenants.

Tenants by the Entirety

Tenants by the entirety is a form of holding property that is specific to married couples. In most states, when the purchasers of property are married, they must hold title to the property as tenants by the entirety. This is usually the same as a joint tenancy with right of survivorship, except that the owners are married. Some states have done away with this form of ownership. In the *Capital Bank* case (Case 7.1) the court had to determine if a husband's sole name on certain business documents was sufficient to rebut the presumption of a married couple holding property as tenants by the entirety.

CASE 7.1   The Capital Bank v. Barnes

277 SW3d 781; 2009 Mo. App. LEXIS 256 (Ct. App. Mo. 2009)

Facts: Husband and wife operated an Italian restaurant together for 43 years, owning the property on which their business stood for the past 20. When the business failed and the bank received a judgment against the husband, the bank sought to execute the judgment against the assets of the restaurant. The husband argued that he and his wife held the property jointly as tenants by the entirety and thus, the bank could not take the wife's property, only the husband's. The bank argued that because the husband's was the only name to appear on certain business documents such as the business liquor license, it was sufficient to rebut the presumption of holding the property as tenants by the entirety, and therefore the bank should able to execute the judgment against the assets.

Issue: Whether the presumption of a married couple holding property as tenants by the entirety is rebutted by the fact that only the husband's name appears on certain business documents.

Decision: No

Reasoning: Nancy Steffen Rahmeyer, J.: The law requires a presumption that jointly owned property is held as a tenancy by the entirety, which can be rebutted by a showing of severance by consent, agreement, or acquiescence. Despite Appellant's evidence, the trial judge found credible the testimony that Respondent and his wife both contributed to the operation of Rocky's, and they consulted on "major decisions." Furthermore, Respondent and his wife owned the real estate on which Rocky's sits for approximately 20 years, and all the proceeds from Rocky's were deposited into a joint bank account. On review we are required to accept the trial judge's credibility determination and view the evidence in the light most favorable to the judgment. Under that standard, substantial evidence supported the trial court's obvious doubt that Respondent's wife had acquiesced in the sole ownership by Respondent and we, therefore, find no error in the court's judgment finding that Appellant failed to rebut the presumption that the property was held in a tenancy by the entirety. The judgment for the bank is AFFIRMED.

CASE QUESTIONS

1. Does the court's decision make sense to you? Explain.
2. Do you believe it is possible for only the husband's name to have appeared on documents because they truly intended for him to be the sole owner?
3. Is there a way the husband and wife could have held their property so that the tenancy by the entirety was not presumed?

HOW IS TITLE TO REAL PROPERTY TRANSFERRED?

L02

The owner of property may at some point wish to no longer own it. Transferring title to the property can occur in several different ways. The owner can give the property away as a gift, will the property to another upon his or her death, or sell the property to another. No matter how the property is transferred it is imperative that the title to the property and the documents transferring title have a specific legal description of the real property being conveyed. If it does not, the transfer is not effective. We previously spoke of our law considering land as unique in our legal system. This is one of the ways in which it is manifested. When someone sells a house or building, it is not enough to simply include the street address of the property in the deed. The full legal description must be given or the transfer will not convey the property to the transferee. The full legal description will generally include the plat number and lot number of the land, which is generally found in the county office of land records (such as the registry of deeds) for the county in which the land is located.

It is also important to register the land transaction with the proper land authorities in the county in which the land is located so that the public will be put on notice of the transfer and lessen the possibility that the same property will be sold again without the purchaser knowing it belongs to someone else. Purchasers generally have a title search conducted and acquire title insurance to protect them against such a contingency. It is a wise investment. Can you imagine spending thousands of dollars to purchase a piece of property, only to discover that there is a problem with your having sole title to the property? That is why before purchasing property, a title search should be conducted and even when it is, title insurance should be acquired, just in case.

What Is Personal Property and How Is It Different from Real Property?

L01

EXAMPLE

Now that we have discussed land or real property, we will turn to personal property. The two are not considered the same in our legal system and the law deals with them in quite different ways. For instance, you can own a refrigerator or a sweater without necessarily having a document to represent ownership and if you give this property away or sell it, you can do so without having to convey documents that represent them. Not so with land. So, let us take a look at some of the attributes of personal property and see how it might be different from real property.

WHAT CONSTITUTES PERSONAL PROPERTY?

EXAMPLE

Personal property is anything other than land. It can be anything from a desk to cows; from a car to a couch; from accounts receivable to book royalties to patents. Anything other than land or something permanently attached to land is considered to be personal property. Sometimes the two can be fairly close. For instance, an agreement to sell to buyer trees cut from your property is an agreement for personal property. However, an agreement to allow the buyer to come in and cut down trees from your property is an agreement for an interest in land. The two can have different consequences if anything goes wrong with the agreement, as they are covered by different laws that impose different requirements for pursuing rights under the agreement. You will recall from our contracts chapter that land contracts are governed by the common law or Restatement while the sale of goods, a type of personal property, is governed by the Uniform Commercial Code.

L02

HOW IS TITLE TO PERSONAL PROPERTY ACQUIRED?

As with land, an owner of personal property may wish to relieve herself of the property at some point. Indeed, the owner may instead accidentally lose his or her personal property also. This gives rise to various ways that personal property can be transferred (see Take Away 7-3, "Acquiring Title to Personal Property").

TAKE AWAY 7-3

ACQUIRING TITLE TO PERSONAL PROPERTY

Transfer of personal property may be by:

- Claiming abandoned property
- Claiming lost property
- Claiming mislaid property
- Stealing (possession, no title)
- Will
- Purchase
- Rent/lease
- Gift

Abandoned Property

Personal property to which an owner has relinquished all right and title has been abandoned. The first to claim abandoned personal property acquires title to the personal property and becomes the owner of the property.

Lost Property

Lost property is personal property that the owner has accidentally allowed to leave his or her possession and control. The finder has superior claim to the property against all except the true owner. Most states have statutes dictating how much time must pass and how the owner must be searched for before the finder can claim the property. If you have ever turned in a lost item at Disney World you now understand why they tell you to check back after a certain period and if the property has not been claimed, you can claim it.

EXAMPLE

Mislaid Property

Mislaid property is personal property that has been placed somewhere by the owner or rightful possessor and he or she has forgotten where the property is located. The owner of the premises where the property is found is entitled to claim the mislaid property if the true owner is not found.

As you can imagine, it can often be difficult to determine if a particular item of personal property is abandoned, lost, or mislaid. Courts generally look at the totality of the circumstances to make a determination. In our chapter opening scenario, since Clarice found expensive electronic items that would rarely be thrown away in the manner in which she found them, it is a pretty good indicator that the property was either lost or mislaid rather than abandoned. Once we determine that it is not abandoned, but either lost or mislaid, we must see if there are clues that might point us in one direction or the other.

EXAMPLE

The fact that the property was expensive electronic equipment in a protective bag, in a protected place that it would not otherwise have been kept indicates that the property was probably mislaid. That is, someone intentionally put the bag by the stump intending to pick it up, and probably forgot where he or she put it. The fact that it has apparently been there for quite some time may indicate that the owner either forgot where he or she put it, or has not been able to retrieve it. Since the property is most likely mislaid, the owner of the premises where it was found has the right to claim it until the true owner is found. Since the land belonged to Clarice's company, the company would have the right to keep the property for the true owner and if the true owner is not found within a certain time, usually determined by the state, the company can claim it.

Gift

Property may be acquired as a gift. For a gift to be created the donor must (1) have a present intention to give the property to another with no intent to receive consideration in return; (2) deliver possession of the property or something that represents the property (such as keys and title to a car); and (3) the donee must accept the property. The one giving the gift is the donor and the one to whom the gift is given is the donee. A valid completed gift cannot be taken back by the donor, and the donee can now do whatever he or she wishes with the gift. In the *Ware* case (Case 7.2) the court was faced with

CASE 7.2 Ware v. Ware

161 P.3d 1188; 2007 Alas. LEXIS 63 (Alaska 2007)

Facts: A mother is being sued by her daughter. The mother had previously made a will leaving her homestead, including five houses and other buildings, as well as acreage, to her four children equally. The mother changed her mind and instead gave all the property to one son as a gift. The mother referred to the transaction as a sale and the son gave the mother $10 for the property. The mother's daughter, sister of the son, sued to have the gift from her mother to her brother rescinded.

Issue: Whether there will be a presumption of a gift even if the donee gives the donor a minimal consideration in exchange.

Decision: Yes

Reasoning: Carpeneti, J.: We adopt this majority view that transfers of property, including real property, money, and cash advances, from parent to child are presumptively gifts. In the present case, Margaret gave Brandie the land in exchange for ten dollars. The first issue we must resolve, then, is whether Margaret intended to gift the land to Brandie, or to sell it. To determine whether an individual has gratuitous intent we ask whether the parties had a close relationship; whether the plaintiff failed to request compensation; and whether the services performed were the sort one would expect to receive as a mere gratuity. Margaret and Brandie share a close mother-son relationship. She testified at her deposition that she decided, on her own, to transfer the homestead to Brandie, and that she wanted him to keep it. She stated that even if Brandie were willing to sign back the deed to her, she would decline. These facts indicate that Margaret's behavior meets the tests for gratuitous intent.

The only contrary indication is that Brandie paid Margaret ten dollars for the property and Margaret referred to having sold the property to Brandie. While the purpose of this payment is not clear, the amount is so nominal that it should not invalidate the gratuitous nature of Margaret's act.

Based on this analysis, the transfer from Margaret to Brandie is presumptively a gift. Superior Court judgment granting summary judgment for the son Brandie is AFFIRMED.

CASE QUESTIONS

1. Do you understand why the sister brought the case challenging the gift? Explain.

2. Do you agree with the court that the $10 was not enough to destroy the gratuitous intent necessary for the mother's act to be considered a gift?

3. Would it have been ethical for the court to determine that the mother should not leave her three other children out of her estate, and thereby declare the gift to the single son invalid?

REALITY CHECK 7-3

WHO GETS THE ENGAGEMENT RING?

Did you ever wonder what happens to the engagement ring when an engaged couple breaks up? When you think about the different ways we said property could be transferred, the ring is a gift. The question becomes, does the donor get to take it back or does the donee get to keep it? The law varies from state to state and there have been many different theories for the different approaches, from the ring being a symbolic gift that signifies transfer of ownership of a woman from her father to her husband and the donee would be able to keep the ring even if the engagement was broken, to determining who was at fault to decide rights in the ring.

States still vary, but the majority of courts now hold that engagement rings are conditional gifts conditioned on getting married and as such if the marriage does not take place, the condition is not met, therefore there is no gift and the donor can take back the ring. Most states, either by case law or statute, still leave room for exercising discretion so that if something unusual happens the court can address it appropriately. For instance, a New York court held that even though New York had a statute entitling the donor to return of the ring if the engagement was broken, because the donor was already married at the time he became engaged to someone else and gave his new fiancée an engagement ring, the engagement ring was a gift and the fiancée could keep it. The ring was not a gift conditioned on marriage because he was already married to someone else.

Source: Marshall v. Cassano, 2001 N.Y. Slip Op. 40320U.

EXAMPLE

whether a son giving his mother $10 in exchange for an entire homestead was enough to negate the mother's intent to give the son the homestead as a gift.

Not all gifts arise the same way. What most of us think of as a gift (such as for a birthday) is actually an **inter vivos gift,** that is, a gift made during the donor's lifetime, as opposed to through a will that takes effect upon the donor's death. Again, if the three requirements for a gift inter vivos are present, the gift is complete and cannot be taken back by the donor. The law also recognizes **gifts causa mortis,** a conditional gift (see Reality Check 7-3, "Who Gets the Engagement Ring?") where the donor gives a gift to the donee because the donor is contemplating the possibility of death, (for instance, the donor is going on a dangerous trip to climb Mt. Everest) or is gravely ill at the time of giving the gift and expects to die. If the donor does not die as contemplated, there is no gift to the donee. Since the gift is a present gift but is conditioned upon the donor dying and the donor does not die, the condition is not met, and the gift is not realized. The promise to make a future gift is ineffective.

EXAMPLE

Will

A **will** is a legal document providing for the disposition of the property of the one making a will, called a **testator** (if female, **testatrix**) after the death of the testator. The owner of property can provide for his or her personal property to be given to another after his or her death through a validly executed will. If the will is executed correctly under the state's law regarding wills, title passes to the one to whom the personal property is **bequeathed.** A will is not effective until the testator dies, and can be changed any time until the death. No one given anything in a will has any rights in the property until the testator dies and before the testator's death, the will can be revoked or property dispositions changed as often as the testator wishes.

Purchase

Like real property, personal property can be acquired through giving something of value to the owner in exchange for the property. Of course, you recognize this as a sale. What is given need not be money. It can be whatever the parties agree upon as consideration for the exchange. It is important to note that a seller can only convey to the buyer the title that the seller has. This will be discussed in more detail under stolen property below.

Rent

As with real property, if the owner of personal property wishes to retain title to the property, but allow another to possess the property for a period, this can be done through rental or lease. Again, the renter/lessee does not have title or ownership of the property, but only legal possession. As such, the renter must act in accordance with the rental agreement. Renting a car for spring break does not give the renter the right to sell the car while on vacation. Neither does leasing a car rather than buying it.

EXAMPLE

Stolen Property

Which brings us to the matter of acquiring personal property through receiving stolen personal property or goods or through unlawfully dispossessing another of his ownership or possession in the goods.

One who steals personal property does not acquire title to the property and thus, cannot convey title to a buyer by selling the property to the buyer. The true owner retains the right to the goods, even though he or she is not in possession of them, and that right is good against all others.

Generally speaking, if someone steals property from the owner, then sells the property to a third party, even to an innocent purchaser who has no notice that the property is stolen, the true owner can still reclaim the property. The duped buyer's cause of action is against the one who sold him or her the property, and the buyer would have no basis for keeping the property from the true owner.

What Intentional Torts against Property Does the Law Recognize?

None of this interest in ownership of property would be worthwhile if the law did not recognize an owner's right to be able to exclude others from his or her property or its use. In light of this, there are several actions available to property owners that address this right to exclude. (See Take Away 7-4, "Intentional Torts against Property.")

INTENTIONAL TORTS AGAINST PROPERTY

- Trespass to real property
- Trespass to personal property
- Conversion

TRESPASS TO REAL PROPERTY

L07

Trespass to real property is intentionally coming onto the real property of another.

Intentionally—Coming onto the property must be intentional rather than accidental. Choosing to climb a property owner's fence and come onto their property is not legally the same as having a car accident which causes you to run into the fence and onto the property. The former is a trespass, the latter is not, though the latter may constitute negligence.

EXAMPLE

Coming onto the land—The tort must involve real property, not personal property.

Of another—The land does not belong to the trespasser or the trespasser otherwise does not have permission to be on the property. The action can be brought by either the

EXAMPLE

owner of the property or someone in legitimate possession of the property. For instance, as the renter of an apartment, you can sue someone who breaks into your apartment for trespass even though you do not actually own the premises. Since your lease gives you the right to possession of the premises to the exclusion of others, you have a right to bring a trespass action against an intruder (aside from any criminal action that may be brought).

Without his or her permission—In the absence of permission we don't have the right to be on property that does not belong to us. If the owner or possessor of the real property has given permission to the trespasser to be on the property, then there is no trespass.

If the trespasser intended to come onto the property (rather than accidentally doing so) it does not matter whether or not it was done innocently. The tort is for the protection of the integrity of an individual's ownership or possession of land, and why a trespasser enters is not important to establishing the tort, beyond intent versus accidentally coming on. No harm need be proved to establish the tort of trespass to real property. Instead, the amount of damages is related to the harm done, and the less harm done to the property, the less damages will be awarded by the court.

EXAMPLE

Keep in mind that a possessor can also bring an action for trespass. For instance, the landlord of one of our students frequently came into her apartment with his own key, unannounced, for no reason, just as she or one of her female roommates was stepping out of the shower. She was only renting the property, but doing so gives her the right to exclusive possession and control over the premises for the period of her lease, even against the owner of the property. Although the landlord owned the property, he has contracted away his possession of the property to the renter. The rental agreement gives exclusive possession and control to the tenant and that can form the basis of a trespass to real property action, though the lease can give the landlord permission to come on for emergency purposes or general upkeep such as periodic pest control. Even then, as you saw in Reality Check 7-2 (the lease), paragraph 19, leases generally require that the landlord provide adequate notice to the tenant.

TRESPASS TO PERSONAL PROPERTY

Trespass to personal property actually involves two different torts: trespass to personal property and conversion. Both have the same basic requirements, but it is as if the two are on a continuum and trespass to personal property is the less severe trespass, while conversion is a more substantial interruption of the owner or possessor's right to own or possess personal property.

Trespass to personal property involves intentionally interfering with the possession and control of another's personal property.

Intentionally—As with trespass to real property, the interference with the plaintiff's property must be intentional, not accidental.

Interfering with possession and control—This is taking the owner or possessor's personal property so that he or she no longer has possession of it. The tortfeasor does not have to actually do anything with the property once taken or to harm it in any way. Simply taking it out of the owner or possessor's control is enough for the tort to be committed. For instance, if one roommate borrows the sweater of another roommate without permission and wears it out on a date for a couple of hours, it is trespass to personal property even though the sweater was not harmed. The sweater owner has the right to exclusive possession and control over her property and this was interfered with by the borrower.

EXAMPLE

Of someone else's—As with trespass to real property, the trespass must be against the true owner of the property or someone in legitimate possession of the property.

Personal property—This tort applies only to personal property, not real property.

If all requirements of the tort are met, then the owner or possessor of the property can recover for trespass to personal property and receives damages for being deprived of the property and any harm to it.

Conversion is intentionally exercising dominion and control over the personal property of another and is a more serious interference with the owner or possessor's personal property. This might include taking it for a longer period of time, doing something to it that is not consistent with not being the owner of the property with ultimate control over the property (dyeing the borrowed sweater a different color or selling it on eBay), or substantially harming the property (setting the sweater on fire).

EXAMPLE

Intentionally—Again, as an intentional tort, the taking must not be an accident on the part of the tortfeasor.

Exercising dominion and control—This is more than a mere interference with the owner or possessor's right to the property. It is virtually excluding the owner from the property and treating the property as if it belongs to the converter. For instance, you loan your roommate your car to go home for the weekend, 30 miles away, and instead your roommate paints your car and takes it on a three-week, 2000-mile road trip.

EXAMPLE

Over personal property—Again, it involves personal property, not real property.

Of another—Again, the property can be that of the true owner or someone in legitimate possession of the property, i.e., if you loan your roommate your car, your roommate is in legitimate possession of your property. As a practical matter, conversion cases are generally brought by the owner of the property because he or she has more of an interest that would lead to such an action.

EXAMPLE

Do the two personal property torts sound similar? They are. The line is not always clear when the tort is one or the other. Just know that the more serious the interference with the rights of the property's owner or possessor, the more likely the action will be deemed conversion rather than trespass. The real difference between trespass to personal property and conversion lies in the remedy. The remedy for trespass to personal property is to give the property back to its owner and have the trespasser pay damages for any harm to the property or the owner or possessor's loss of use while it was no longer in his or her possession.

Conversion is a more serious intrusion into the possessory rights of the owner, and the remedy is a forced sale. The converter pays the owner the value of the personal property and the converter keeps the property rather than give the property back to the owner. The interference with control can come from a taking of the property from the owner, or a possession that starts out lawfully but becomes unlawful because of not being returned in a timely fashion.

When you open a bank account, your agreement with the bank is that you will deposit money into your account and the bank will disperse the money only upon your

SPAM AS AN ETHICAL ISSUE IN PROPERTY?

Spam, or spamming, refers to the use of mailing lists to blanket listservs or private e-mail boxes with indiscriminate advertising messages. The first bulk e-mail spam message was from an attempt by a DEC marketing representative to send an e-mail to every networked computer address on the west coast announcing a demonstration of DEC computers at several California locations.[1] It is amusing to note that the source of the term *spam* for this form of e-mail is generally accepted as the Monty Python song, "Spam spam spam spam, spam spam spam spam, lovely spam, wonderful spam." Like the song, spam is an endless repetition of worthless text. Others believe that the term came from the computer group lab at the University of Southern California, which applied the name because it has many of the same characteristics as the lunchmeat Spam:

- Nobody wants it or ever asks for it.
- No one ever eats it; it is the first item to be pushed to the side when eating the entree.
- Sometimes it is actually tasty, like 1 percent of junk mail that is really useful to some people.

Some believe that spamming should be protected as the simple exercise of the First Amendment right to free speech while others view it as an invasion of privacy or even theft of resources or trespass to property, as Intel argued when a disgruntled ex-employee spammed more than 35,000 Intel employees with his complaints. In that case, the court agreed, considering his e-mail spamming equivalent to trespassing on Intel's property and recognizing that Intel was forced to spend considerable time and resources to delete the e-mail messages from its system.

The Controlling the Assault of Non-Solicited Pornography and Marketing (CAN-SPAM) Act of 2003 requires unsolicited commercial e-mail messages to be labeled as commercial (rather than a deceptive subject line or false header) and also to contain instructions for opting out. It also requires that the sender include an actual return address. Unfortunately, as anyone with an e-mail address knows, the act lives up to the nickname offered by anti-spam activists, the "Yes, you CAN spam Act," since the Act actually does permit mass marketing messages, as long as the above parameters are met. Consider the arguments that spammers might make in favor of the ethics of their actions, since some of those who engage in these activities may justify the behavior on ethical grounds when, in fact, sending spam takes your time and resources without your permission. You will probably see this even more clearly when you think about unsolicited text messages and calls on your cell phone for which you must pay!

Source: Templeton, Brad, "Reaction to the DEC Spam of 1978," http://www.templetons.com/brad/spamreact.html#msg (accessed August 2, 2007).

---

signature. When someone forges your signature on a check and the bank cashes the check for the forger, the bank has converted your funds. They have not paid out the money on your signature, but that of another, and they are liable for the money taken from your account (see Diversity in the Law 7-3, "Legal Government Conversion," for an extreme example).

An interesting ethical question arises as to whether computer spamming can be considered a taking of someone's property (Reality Check 7-4, "Spam as an Ethical Issue in Property?").

In addition to owning personal property, it is also possible to have only legitimate possession of the property, though not own it. This can occur through leasing, such as a car lease, an equipment lease, or even a textbook lease, or it may occur through a bailment. In both cases, the owner of the property does not give up title to the property, but instead allows someone else to take possession for a limited time and/or purpose. It is expected that the possessor, either lessee or bailee, return the property in substantially the same condition it was in when he or she took possession. Of course, in the case of bailments, if the bailment is for the purpose of allowing the possessor to perform a service on the personal property, such as repair a car or clean an outfit, the property will be changed in the agreed way.

LEGAL GOVERNMENT CONVERSION

During World War II, after Japan attacked the U.S. by bombing the Pacific fleet at Pearl Harbor in Hawaii on December 7, 1941, President Franklin D. Roosevelt ordered at least 110,000 inhabitants of Japanese descent living on the west coast to be moved to internment camps. Sixty-two percent of those moved to internment camps were American citizens. They were given little time to gather their belongings and without knowing where they were going, did not even have appropriate clothing. They lost their homes, jobs, and businesses. Three years later in January 1945, internees were allowed to leave the camps after receiving $25 and a ticket home. Many returned to ruined or nonexistent businesses and homes. Property put in storage was often ruined. Many had quickly sold their homes for a pittance before they left for the camps and buyers made a fortune. Three years later in 1948, the American Japanese Claims Act was passed allowing detainees to file claims for their losses, but having left in such a hurry for the camps, few had proper documentation and IRS tax files had mostly been destroyed by then. Only $37 million was disbursed of the $148 million claimed. The final claim was not paid out until 1965.

In signing into law The Civil Liberties Act of 1988, President Reagan apologized for the removal and internment of the Japanese, saying that government actions were based on "race prejudice, war hysteria, and a failure of political leadership." The apology included reparations of $20,000 for those removed to the camps, totaling $1.4 billion. In 1992, $48 million more was provided to make sure all detainees received their due and President George W. Bush once again apologized. The last payment was made in 1999. In all, 82,210 internees or their families were given reparations.

Do you believe the payments were enough to compensate detainees for their personal and real property? If not, why do you think the apology and reparations were provided? Would this situation have been as drastic if property had not been involved? Do you see a difference between reparations and apologies for the Japanese because of their three-year internment and African Americans for their 246-year enslavement plus the additional 100 years of Jim Crow? Discuss the property issues involved in each situation, as well as the apologies and their timing (43 years vs. 144 years). What ethical considerations are there in the situations that may dictate the responses to each? What ethical considerations for apologizing? Should time play a factor in determining what to do ("i.e., it's been so long, why don't we just forget about it")? Can you see how being able to have control over property, its acquisition, and so on would have made a difference in the lives of the two groups?

Sources: Executive Order 9066, February 19, 1942, Internment Archives.com, http://www.internmentarchives.com/showdoc.php?docid=00055&search_id=19269&pagenum=4; Oracle ThinkQuest Educational Foundation, http://library.thinkquest.org/TQ0312008/; The Japanese American Legacy Project, http://www.Densho.org.

Summary

Land and personal property is a very big deal in our legal system and has been from the very beginning of our foray into what would later become the United States of America. Property ownership is the basis of power and wealth, and its ownership can have many legal implications. How property is held, who owns it together, how it is acquired, how it is transferred, and what can be done with it relative to the interest possessed are all important legal considerations for business. In order to best protect its assets, it is important for a business to understand not only what property it has, but what limitations there may be on its use and conveyance.

Review Questions

1. Tina was walking to her car in the mall parking lot when she saw a man standing by an open car trunk. In the trunk were several items that Tina had been searching for in the mall but either could not find, or they were too expensive. Tina asked the man about the items and he told her they were for sale. The price he offered was well within what Tina could pay and the goods were still in their original packaging. Tina purchased several items. One she gave to her sister for a

birthday gift, and one she sold to her aunt who had also been searching for the item. Later Tina sees a news story about the guy who sold her the goods being involved with a big theft ring that sold stolen goods. The description of the goods included the items Tina purchased. What title does Tina have to the goods? What title does Tina's sister have to the good Tina gave her? What title does Tina's aunt have to the item she bought from Tina? LO2, 7

2. Peters and Lane enter into an oral agreement to create a military museum using military memorabilia that Peters and Lane have gathered over the years. Before this can take place, Peters dies. Peters' son sues Lane for trespass to personal property and conversion, alleging that Lane came into Peters' house and took Peters' memorabilia and commingled his own military memorabilia with that of Peters so that it is extremely difficult to separate out Peters' property. If proven, will Peters' son be more likely to push for conversion or trespass to personal property? (*Peters v. Lane*, 2005 Cal. App. Unpub. LEXIS 4052 [Ct. App. Cal., 4th App. Dist., Div. 3 2005]) LO7

3. Three parties, including a partnership, own real property as tenants in common. The parties are involved in a dispute about what should be done with the property and they cannot reach an agreement. What can they do? (*Owens v. M.E. Schepp. P'ship*, 218 Ariz. 222; 2008 Ariz. LEXIS 74 [2009]) LO5

4. If personal property is found to be mislaid, then superior right to the property lies with _____. If personal property is found to be lost, then superior right to the property lies with _____. LO6

5. Tammy executed a deed granting a house to Esmerelda, and after Esmerelda's life ended, to Tammy's grandchildren. What interests has Tammy conveyed? LO3, 4

6. Jay's parents granted Jay title to their home. In return, Jay entered into an agreement with his parents stating that the coveyancing agreement was created "to protect and preserve an interest in the premises for the parents to insure that the parents may reside in the premises for so long as they shall live." Additionally, the conveyancing agreement provides that the parents have the right "to reside in the premises for so long as they choose and for the rest of their lives." Finally, the conveyancing agreement states that Jay "agrees to provide living accommodations for his parents, either on the premises or at some other premises in which Jay resides." Has Jay granted his parents a life estate in the property? (*Altomari v. Altomari*, 2008 Conn. Super. LEXIS 2142 [Super. Ct. Conn. 2008]) LO3, 4, 5

7. Gerald's mother shared with him that in her will she was leaving him half of her substantial estate. Several months later, Mother discovers that Gerald has been taking drugs and stealing to support his habit. Mother takes Gerald out of her will and gives the portion she was going to give to Gerald to a cat shelter instead. Gerald sues his mother for return of his interest. Does Gerald win? LO2

8. By the time Blythe realized that she no longer wanted to marry Danner, he had given her a $10,000 engagement ring and a beautiful diamond bracelet as an engagement gift. When Blythe tells Danner she no longer wishes to marry him, he asks for the return of his engagement gift and engagement ring. Use the information you were given in the chapter to analyze whether Blythe must return the jewelry. LO2

9. Using what you know from the chapter about the importance of property, including our own right to the fruits of our labor, make an argument for giving reparations to African Americans for the taking of the right to their property in themselves and their work from 1619 to 1865. Once you create that argument, make an argument against reparations. In crafting your argument, try to do it without addressing the issues of how to determine who is to receive the reparations and where the money will come from to pay for it. Once you have developed your position, think about those issues also. LO8

10. Four sisters plan to purchase a piece of real estate together. If they wish to each be able to will their share to their significant others and children, the best way to hold the property would be as: LO3, 4, 5

    a. Tenants in common.

    b. Joint tenants

    c. Tenants by the entirety

    d. Sole owners

Ethics Issue

When Myra's boyfriend, Byron, unexpectedly lost his roommate and could no longer afford to live in his apartment, he moved in with Myra. Myra's lease did not allow anyone who was not on the lease to occupy the premises. The landlord was not on the premises, so Myra was not worried about it being discovered. Myra's neighbor on the left, Tyra, is really incensed about Byron moving in with Myra. Tyra's best friend is Myra's neighbor on the right, Preston. When the same thing happened to Preston's girlfriend, Preston did not let her live with him because of the lease prohibition. Tyra is thinking seriously about whether to tell the landlord that Myra has an unauthorized person living with her. Discuss the ethics of Myra's actions and whether Tyra should tell. "It's none of her business" is not an option. Discuss Myra's situation as an ethical issue. Who are the stakeholders? Think hard. What do they stand to lose by Myra's situation? What do they stand to gain? Is it a form of stealing? Is there a public policy at play? Does it have monetary implications? For whom? Think broadly.

Group Exercise

Make a list of 25 pieces of real or personal property which you or someone you know owns or possesses. By each piece of property indicate what type of property it is, what interest is held in the property, and how the property was acquired. In addition, note whether there has ever been a trespass to the property. Try to include as many pieces of property as possible, including property owned by others such as parents or other relatives, and friends. For instance, you may have as one of the items your car that was rented and stolen, and so on. Once you have made the list, think about whether you fully understood the property rights involved before reading the chapter and making the list.

Key Terms

abandoned property 166
adverse possession 159
bequeath 169
conversion 171
deed 159
eminent domain 159
estate for years 160
estates (interests) 159
fee simple 159
gift 167
gift causa mortis 168
grantee 159
grantor 159
implied warranty of habitability 161

inter vivos gift 168
joint tenant with right of survivorship 164
landlord 161
life estate 159
life tenant 159
lost property 166
mislaid property 167
partition 164
purchase 169
remainder 161
rent 169
reversion 161

sole owner 164
stolen property 169
sublease 161
sublessee 161
tenant 161
tenants by the entirety 164
tenants in common 164
testator 168
testatrix 168
title 159
trespass to personal property 170
trespass to real property 170
will 168

Business Crimes

Learning Objectives

After reading this chapter, you should be able to:

LO1 Define white collar crime

LO2 Discuss the initiation of a criminal case

LO3 Identify the constitutional protections offered a criminal defendant

LO4 Define the constitutional protections offered to companies and corporations

LO5 Identify the types of white collar crimes most associated with business

LO6 Discuss sentencing guidelines as they relate to white collar criminals

LO7 Discuss the Sarbanes-Oxley Act's impact on investor confidence

LO8 Determine appropriate ethical considerations regarding business crimes

Opening Scenario

A. H. Robins Company produced the Dalkon Shield, an intrauterine device (IUD) used for birth control. From the time the Shield was first marketed, issues arose concerning its design and the research that its developers had conducted. The Shield was being blamed for causing bacteria to be stored in the uterus of its users, causing illness and injury to thousands of women. In spite of the warning signs, Robins aggressively marketed the Shield worldwide. Between 1971, when the Shield was first sold, to 1974, when it was pulled from the market, 4 to 5 million Shields were distributed globally. Is the company potentially criminally liable for harm to users? Can company personnel be held criminally liable and imprisoned and/or fined for the company's acts?[1] Should the developers who knew about the defects before marketing the Shield have put those warning labels on the Shield? What if they decided not to? Do they owe the women who used them a duty to reveal what they knew?

Introduction and Background

It would be impossible to list and explain all of the crimes that may be committed by and against businesses. If you listen to the news and read about current events you know that the list is long. Because many of the crimes are committed in the business context,

---

we refer to most business crimes as **white collar crimes.** White collar crimes are defined by the federal government as "illegal acts that use deceit and concealment—rather than the threat of physical force or violence—to obtain money, property or service or to avoid the payment or loss of money. . . . [W]hite collar criminals occupy a position of responsibility and trust in government, the professions, industry, and civic organizations."[2] Many white collar crimes are not violent and do not target specific victims; hence society has treated these crimes differently from other, so-called blue collar or violent crimes committed by those not identified as white collar criminals.

Today the distinction has become less meaningful as we realize just how dangerous and cruel white collar crime can be. For example, we now recognize that a business that chooses to dump toxic waste into a city's storm drains can cause illness, brain damage, and even death to great numbers of people, animals, flora, and fish. Or, as the opening scenario illustrates, people can be maimed in pursuit of profits above all else.

Think about what you know about the traditional characterization of white collar crimes: they tend to be thought of as less dangerous, less violent, and somehow even more respectable, and we may not really classify the perpetrators as criminal. But think about it. Should a perpetrator who sneaks into someone's house and steals a TV and computer or mugs them on the street for their money be thought of as "more criminal" than a CEO who causes thousands of people to lose their savings, homes, and children's college funds? Which type of criminal causes the most damage? Why do you think we perceive them so differently? What is the value of doing so? Do you think our perception of who it is that commits each of these types of crimes has anything to do with how we perceive the crimes? Finally, do we treat white collar criminals differently than we do burglars or robbers? Is such different treatment justified? Is it ethical for us to treat violations of the law differently?

In this chapter we will discuss crimes that occur in the business context, how businesses are treated when they engage in criminal activity, what protections are afforded to businesses under the Constitution, and, where appropriate, how any of this can be impacted by diversity factors.

We should note here that an important aspect of business crimes is how our legal system views business entities that may engage in criminal activity. Although we cannot imprison a corporation, we can send corporate officers and managers to prison if they participate in a crime or should have known that a crime was committed. The theory behind holding corporate officers and managers liable is similar to respondeat superior. We hold the corporate executives and managers liable for crimes committed by corporate employees over whom they exercise control or could have exercised control. If we did not hold a CEO and other high-level officers and managers liable for the acts of their employees, then those executives could delegate their duties to subordinates and possibly avoid liability. The developers of the Shield could have prevented the wide dissemination until the Shield was proven safe. The *Freed* case (Case 8.1) describes liability for management actions.

Case 8.1 raises important questions to answer. If, in response to question 2 in Case 8.1, you think the punishment should not include jail or prison time for the executive who ordered the violation, does it seem fair to allow a corporation to avoid its responsibilities this way? If you think the employee who knows should be held accountable, does this ignore the fact that employees work for corporations and do what they are told to do or suffer the repercussions? Do you think that ultimately it is top management that must be held accountable?

---

[2]Annual Rept. Att. Gen. of the U.S. 39 (1983).

CASE 8.1 U.S. v. Freed

189 Fed. Appx. 888 (11th Cir. 2006)

Facts: Freed owned Enota Mission Trust, which owned a campground called Enota in the Chattahoochee National Forest. In 1999, a Forest Service ranger discovered blaze marks on vegetation, reparation of an old dam, and a bridge constructed on the Enota property. Freed was ordered to remove all improvements made by his staff. Two years later another ranger returned to the park and discovered the improvements to the land were still in place. A year after that, two more undercover Forest Service officers visited the park. They discovered repairs to the dam, two log bridges, and several paths that had been maintained. Additionally, the officers found damage to the vegetation for better viewing of the local waterfall. The two officers spoke with Freed and issued citations for the violations. In 2004, the undercover agents again returned to find all the improvements still in place and issued yet another citation to Freed. Freed challenged the citations being issued to him as owner of the Trust.

Issue: Whether the owner of a trust that owned a campground in a national forest can be held responsible for the acts of trust employees who repeatedly ignored federal forest personnel's orders to stop causing damage to vegetation and to remove changes the employees made to the forest to benefit the campground.

Decision: Yes

Reasoning: It is settled law that the only way in which a corporation can act is through the individuals who act on its behalf. This makes the person in position of responsibility or decision making liable for acts of the corporation or company. Here, Freed was the person who was in a position of responsibility in the company. Even though he personally did not build or maintain any of the improvements he was the person in charge and was the individual that allowed the corporation to act.

CASE QUESTIONS

1. What is the similarity between the court's position and the theory of respondeat superior?
2. Owners and executives are held accountable for the actions of their employees that they direct. Should this accountability include prison or jail time? Why or why not?
3. If the employee also knew it was a violation of the law to do the conduct they were directed to do by their employer, should they be held accountable also?

Reality Check 8-1, "Tracking White Collar Crime," lists some of the categories of crime that are routinely tracked by the U.S. government. Notice that within each category there are a number of different crimes. Of course, these categories can easily overlap. For example, you can commit fraud against the government that involves a health care institution, and maybe even a financial institution, all at once. For specifics about how each of these is categorized, see http://memphis.fbi.gov/mewcc.htm.

REALITY CHECK 8-2

WHY ARE FEDERAL GRAND JURIES SECRET?

A juror placed on a grand jury is sworn to secrecy. Why? The model rules published by the United States Courts give the reasons for requiring secrecy. The model rules instruct the jurors that the proceedings are secret and must remain secret permanently. The rules prohibit a juror from relating to family, to news or television reporters, or to anyone what happened in the grand jury room. The reasons are that a "premature disclosure . . . may . . . giv[e] an opportunity to the person being investigated to escape . . . or to destroy evidence. Also . . . , the witness may be subject to intimidation, retaliation, bodily injury, or other tampering before testifying at trial. [T]he requirement of secrecy protects an innocent person who . . . has been cleared by the actions of the Grand Jury. . . . [I]nvestigation by a Grand Jury alone carries with it a suggestion of guilt. Thus great injury can be done to a person's good name even though the person is not indicted. And . . . the secrecy requirement helps to protect the members of the Grand Jury themselves from improper contacts by those under investigation. . . . [T]herefore, the secrecy requirement is of the utmost importance and must be regarded . . . as an absolute duty. If you violate your oath of secrecy, you may be subject to punishment."

Source: Model Grand Jury Charge, Charge 33, United States Courts, http://www.uscourts.gov/FederalCourts/JuryService/ModelGrandJuryCharge.aspx.

L02 How Are Criminal Cases Initiated against the Individual?

The steps taken by law enforcement to initiate a criminal case are essentially the same for white collar criminals as for any other. Once a crime has been reported or sufficiently investigated to establish that the person has committed the crime, the person is taken into custody by the police either on the scene of the crime, or through the use of an **arrest warrant.** If the police have **probable cause** to suspect that you have committed a crime, you can be taken into **custody.** In some cases, the prosecutor will convene a **grand jury** to hear the facts of the case as they know them so far. If the evidence is believed to be strong enough to establish you as a suspect in the crime, the grand jury will return an **indictment,** which gives the police the right to take you into custody (see Reality Check 8-2, "Why Are Federal Grand Juries Secret?").

Once arrested, suspects are in the custody of either the state or the federal government. While in custody suspects are protected by the U.S. Constitution and by state constitutions. That means that the police and other state officials must provide suspects with the constitutional protections to which they are entitled. These protections are set forth in the following sections. Take Away 8-1 lists a few of the main incidents that trigger a suspect's constitutional rights.

L03 FOURTH AMENDMENT PROTECTION

The **Fourth Amendment** protects a person against unreasonable searches and seizures by the police or other government official. Warrantless searches are generally not allowed unless the police have a reason recognized by law to conduct a warrantless search. For example, if the police stop a person on the street because they suspect he or she is carrying an illegal substance, they are permitted to conduct a pat-down search for their own protection to make sure the person is not carrying a weapon that can be used against them. The police do not need to have a warrant to conduct such a search because of the circumstances. On the other hand, if the police want to search a home for evidence of contraband, they would have to obtain a **search warrant** in order to enter the home to conduct a search. If the

TAKE AWAY 8-1

CRIMINAL PROCEDURE FOR DEFENDANTS

Probable Cause—a reasonable, particularized basis for believing an arrest is necessary

Arrest Warrant—issued by a judge calling for the arrest of the individual

Custody—under physical restraint by law enforcement

Grand Jury—the group of individuals selected to be on the panel to hear evidence presented by the prosecution in order to determine whether there is sufficient evidence to return an indictment

police cannot convince an impartial judge that a suspect is likely to have the evidence of a crime in the home, the search warrant will be denied by the judge and no search can be conducted. If the suspect gives the police permission to search either the home or person, they do not need to obtain a warrant. Questions arise when there is more than one occupant of the home. For instance, what if the one giving the consent is only visiting? Does this give him or her right to consent to a search? What if the person providing consent is underage? What if two people live together but only one is on the lease and the one giving consent is not the one on the lease? What if more than one person lawfully occupies the premises with authority to consent, but one agrees to the search and the other does not? The latter is illustrated by the *Georgia v. Randolph* case (Case 8.2) that follows.

CASE 8.2 Georgia v. Randolph

547 U.S. 103 (2006)

Facts: Scott and Janet Randolph separated in 2001 when Mrs. Randolph left the residence for Canada. She returned a few months later with her child. Later that month, the police responded to a domestic dispute at the home during which Mrs. Randolph pointed out to the police that her husband was a habitual cocaine user. Mr. Randolph rebutted his wife's allegations and said she was the one with the cocaine and alcohol problem. Mrs. Randolph volunteered evidence within the house. The officers were taken upstairs and discovered a drinking straw with powdery residue that was taken to the police station. Mr. Randolph was later indicted for possession of cocaine. He moved to suppress the evidence as product of a warrantless search. The trial court suppressed the evidence, but the Georgia Court of Appeals reversed the trial court's decision. The Georgia Supreme Court granted certiorari.

Issue: Whether a police search that results in evidence of unlawful activity by a tenant of the premises violates the 4th Amendment prohibition against unreasonable search and seizure if permission for the search was refused by the tenant, but given by another co-tenant of the premises.

Decision: Yes

Reasoning: Since the co-tenant wishing to open the door to a third party has no recognized authority in law or social practice to prevail over a present and objecting co-tenant, his disputed invitation, without more, gives a police officer no better claim to reasonableness in entering than the officer would have in the absence of any consent at all. Accordingly, in the balancing of competing individual and governmental interests entailed by the bar to unreasonable searches, the cooperative occupant's invitation adds nothing to the government's side to counter the force of an objecting individual's claim to security against the government's intrusion into his dwelling place. Disputed permission is thus no match for this central value of the Fourth Amendment, and the State's other countervailing claims do not add up to outweigh it. Yes, we recognize the consenting tenant's interest as a citizen in bringing criminal activity to light. And we understand a co-tenant's legitimate self-interest in siding with the police to deflect suspicion raised by sharing quarters with a criminal This case invites a straightforward application of the rule that a physically present inhabitant's express refusal of consent to a police search is dispositive as to him, regardless of the consent of a fellow occupant. Scott Randolph's refusal is clear, and nothing in the record justifies the search on grounds independent of Janet Randolph's consent.

CASE QUESTIONS

1. Do you think it was a determining factor that Mrs. Randolph had recently returned from Canada and that her and Mr. Randolph's reconciliation was unclear?

2. In fact, Mrs. Randolph's complaint about her husband was allegedly made because she was afraid for her child, who had been removed by her husband from the house. If the child was still present, would that have been enough of an exigent circumstance to allow the police to search without a warrant? Why or why not?

3. What police conduct is being encouraged or discouraged by the court's decision?

FIFTH AMENDMENT

The **Fifth Amendment** provides constitutional protection against self-incrimination. This means that you cannot be compelled to testify against yourself as to criminal matters and can refuse to talk to the police about any crime that you might have committed. The reason for this is that if the government thinks that you have committed a crime it is up to them to prove it. This they must do on their own, not with your forced help. This is, in part, the basis for the Miranda warnings, with which you are likely familiar from TV programs, books, and movies. The Miranda warnings, outlined in the *Miranda v. Arizona*[3] case, are

`EXAMPLE`

the following: "You have the right to remain silent. Anything you say can and will be used against you in a court of law. You have the right to speak to an attorney, and to have an attorney present during any questioning. If you cannot afford a lawyer, one will be provided for you at government expense."

In Reality Check 8-3, "Juveniles Cannot Be Forced to Incriminate Themselves to Stay Out of Adult Prison," the issue was whether a court could require a juvenile to admit to his guilt in order to get certain benefits. As you can see, the Nevada Supreme Court viewed those admissions as a violation of a juvenile's constitutional right.

Do you think this decision by the Nevada Supreme Court binds the hands of the judge who wants to help a drug-addicted teen by offering him help or a mentally incompetent teen who might benefit from treatment rather than incarceration? What might be a middle ground that serves the purpose of both parties? Does society have an ethical duty to juveniles different from that to adults? If so, what? Why? Who are the various stakeholders and what are their interests to be served?

SIXTH AMENDMENT

The **Sixth Amendment** establishes our constitutional right to an attorney through the important phases of the criminal process. It also provides the defendant the right to a speedy trial, the right to subpoena witnesses to speak on his or her behalf, the right to confront witnesses, and the right to a jury of his or her peers.

One of the ways that diversity impacts the criminal justice system is in African American defendants arguing that they do not receive a jury of their peers when their jury is overwhelmingly white. Do you think it could make a difference? If you think that the criminal justice system and society are beyond such considerations, in Diversity in the Law 8-1, "Entitled to a Lawyer? Yes; Entitled to an Unbiased Lawyer? No," look at what happens when it is not the jury that presents the problem, but the attorney. The consequences of such actions can be quite serious. Here, the defendant was essentially executed without a defense being mounted because of the racial prejudice held by his attorney.

In the criminal justice system, finality is one of the hallmarks. Clearly, no one wants jury decisions to be overturned without a compelling reason. Was there such a reason in

---

[3]384 U.S. 436 (1966). See also http://www.usconstitution.net/miranda.html.

ENTITLED TO A LAWYER? YES; ENTITLED TO AN UNBIASED LAWYER? NO

Just because you are entitled to a lawyer does not mean you are entitled to a good one. That is what Curtis Osborne found out when he was appointed an attorney to represent him in a case for which he was sentenced to death. Osborne argued that his attorney, Johnny Mostiler, was a racist, and never lifted a finger to help defend him. The irony of his claim is that the former Chief Justice of the Georgia Supreme Court, Norman S. Fletcher, agreed with him. Although Justice Fletcher voted to affirm Osborne's conviction, he later agreed that perhaps he had made a mistake in doing so. To his credit, Justice Fletcher did not find out until after he heard the case that Osborne's attorney was a known racist and had been overheard many times to refer to black clients as "n******" and supposedly admitted that Osborne deserved the death penalty, and for that reason he was not going to lift a finger to try to get him acquitted of the murders for which he was on trial. A second attorney who was appointed to represent Osborne along with Mostiler confirmed Osborne's and others' allegations that Mostiler did not attempt to mount a defense on Osborne's behalf. Osborne, facing the death penalty, continued to appeal his case. Before his execution on June 3, 2008, by lethal injection, Osborne's appeal was heard and rejected by the U.S. Supreme Court.

Source: Alan Berlow, "Lose That Lawyer; Do Defendants in Georgia Have Any Right at All to Competent Representation?" Slate.com, June 3, 2008, http://www.slate.com/id/2192831/pagenum/all/.

the Osborne case? Was Osborne essentially on trial without the benefit of an attorney in violation of the Sixth Amendment? Whose obligation was it to ensure Osborne had a defense? What about the second attorney who was appointed along with Mostiler who quit the case because she didn't want to work with him? Did she have an ethical obligation not to "throw Osborne to the wolf"?

As we can see, our constitutional right to an attorney can actually operate as only a bare minimum. A right to an attorney, yes, but not necessarily a right to the best attorney or even a good attorney. In the final analysis it can make a big difference. Osborne would certainly agree.

EIGHTH AMENDMENT

The **Eighth Amendment** protects us against the imposition of cruel and unusual punishment by the government. It also ensures our right to **bail.** However, this right to bail can be compromised if the crime for which defendant is charged is serious enough. For example, most people charged with a capital offense, that is, one for which the death penalty can be imposed, are denied bail. Bail can also be denied if defendant presents a flight risk pending the case. While defendants have a right to bail, that right is not absolute. As noted in the *Madoff* case (Case 8.3), flight is not the only reason for denying bail.

`EXAMPLE`

CASE 8.3 U.S. v. Madoff

586 F.Supp.2d 240 (S.D.N.Y. 2009)

Facts: In December of 2008, the government charged Bernie Madoff with masterminding the largest Ponzi scheme in history. At his initial hearing Madoff and the prosecution reached a bail agreement that included a $10 million bond secured by Madoff's Manhattan apartment, surrender of his passport, travel restrictions, home detention, electronic monitoring, and a 24-hour guard service. The bail agreement also forbade Madoff from transferring any assets belonging to him or his company. Within a week after the agreement was reached Madoff and his wife mailed several packages, which he classified as "gifts of sentimental value," to his family and friends. The Government learned of the transfers and sought a hearing to revoke the conditions of his bail and detain Madoff

until trial. The Government further contended there are no bail conditions that can be set to address the flight risk of Madoff or his potential harm to the community, thus, he must be held without bail.

Issue: Whether a defendant can be held without bail if it is difficult to impose conditions that will assure his appearance in court and protect the community.

Decision: No

Reasoning: Generally, a court must release a defendant on bail on the least restrictive condition that will lead to the defendant's appearance and the safety of the community.

The legal issue before the Court is whether the Government has carried its burden of demonstrating that no condition or combination of conditions can be set that will reasonably assure Madoff's appearance and protect the community from danger. First, the court must determine whether the Government has established by a preponderance of the evidence that [Madoff] . . . presents a risk of flight or obstruction of justice. If the Government carries this initial burden, the Court must determine whether there are reasonable conditions of release that can be set or whether detention is appropriate. To support detention based on danger, the Government's proof must be clear and convincing, while detention based on risk of flight must be proven by a preponderance of the evidence. Furthermore, in making this determination, the Court must consider a set of four factors established by Congress. These include the nature of the offense, the weight of the evidence against the suspect, the history and character of the person charged, and the nature and seriousness of the risk to the community. The Government's burden regarding risk of flight is made more difficult because the record reflects that conditions have already been put in place to address this concern and, until this motion was filed, the Parties had agreed that the measures in place were adequate. The Government contends, nevertheless, that circumstances have changed markedly since the defendant's bail was set and that detention is now warranted [because] . . . Madoff has assets that cannot be effectively restrained . . . and . . . Madoff's recent act of distributing valuable personal property to third parties. Aside from the bare assertion that there remains some risk of flight, the Government has failed to articulate any flaw in the current conditions of release. The question of whether Madoff's distribution of assets, whether characterized as sentimental effects or $1 million worth of valuable property, constitutes a serious risk of obstruction of justice . . . in the future[, t]he statute, by its nature, is always looking forward. To be sure, the Court should consider past behavior in assessing the likelihood of prohibited behavior in the future, but the Government needs to show that there is a serious risk that these potential harms exist going forward. The Government has failed to demonstrate that no conditions can be set to reasonably protect the community from this form of obstruction. The Court also finds that the Government has failed to carry its burden of showing that no condition or combination of conditions of pretrial release will reasonably assure the safety of the community. [As an additional condition of bail, the court ordered an inventory of the personal items in the Madoff home and that the inventory be checked every two weeks by the security company. The court also ordered that all outgoing mail be checked for valuables.]

CASE QUESTIONS

1. What was the government's basis for filing the motion to revoke Madoff's bail?
2. What potential harm to the community was being alleged here? Can the court consider financial harm to individuals as harm to the community?
3. Are the additional conditions likely to address the government's concern about Madoff's ability to transfer his assets? Does it include liquid assets or assets not within his home?

If your rights are violated by law enforcement, the law provides a remedy in the form of exclusion of the evidence that was discovered in violation of your rights. For example, suppose the police knock on your door and ask if they can search your home without a warrant. If you do not give your consent, but they search anyway, and find marijuana and bring drug charges against you, they will be prohibited from entering any evidence against you that was found during that warrantless search including the drugs. Without being able to introduce the drugs found, it is difficult, if not impossible, to prosecute a drug possession case. This deters law enforcement from violating the constitutional rights of citizens. If the police know they will not be able to use the evidence against defendant unless they comply with the law, they are more likely to comply. Keep in mind that these constitutional rights are limitations on the government, not on the private sector.

The Corporate Criminal

A corporation can be held criminally liable for acts performed by its officers, directors and employees. The employees who perform those acts can also be held criminally liable for the acts. In the Dalkon Shield case, the corporate executives who pushed through the manufacture of that product might have been held liable had it been proven that they knew of its harmful effects.

DO BUSINESSES HAVE CONSTITUTIONAL RIGHTS?

A corporation has most of the rights that individuals have under the constitution. Although a corporation cannot be taken into custody, the individuals who represent the corporation can. If the criminal charge is against the corporation itself, however, then the government can ask that the corporation be prohibited from continuing the criminal behavior until the charges are proven. If the court agrees that there is enough evidence for the government to prove its case, the court will issue a **restraining order** prohibiting the charged behavior. A corporation can also have its assets frozen by the court, which will essentially shut down operation of the business.

Under the constitution, businesses are protected from illegal searches and seizures by the Fourth Amendment much like individuals are. There are exceptions to the warrant requirement for businesses. For example, if the business is highly regulated (such as nuclear plants) government agencies like the Occupational Safety and Health Administration (OSHA) can enter the premises without a warrant or any notice to the business.

Corporations have no Fifth Amendment rights against self-incrimination. The Fifth Amendment states "No person . . . " and has been interpreted to apply only to natural persons, not entities such as businesses. A business can incriminate itself through the introduction into evidence of its business records. If there is evidence of criminal activity in those records, a business cannot claim a Fifth Amendment right against self-incrimination to keep those records out.

The Sixth Amendment gives the corporation the right to counsel through its officers or agents. This right ensures that the corporate officers of agents cannot be **interrogated** without the presence of counsel should they invoke that right. Just like individuals, the Sixth Amendment right to counsel can be waived by the corporate officers and they can speak to the police without counsel being present if they decide to do so.

The Eighth Amendment's prohibition against cruel and unusual punishment has no application to corporate punishment. The Eighth Amendment prohibits physical or mental cruelty which cannot very well be inflicted upon a corporation. See Take Away 8-2, "Corporate vs. Individual Constitutional Rights" for a comparison of personal and corporate constitutional protections.

 TAKE AWAY 8-2

CORPORATE VS. INDIVIDUAL CONSTITUTIONAL RIGHTS

Amendment	Protection Offered Against	Corporation/Individual
4th	Warrantless search and seizure	Yes/Yes
5th	Self-incrimination	No/Yes
6th	Right to an attorney and to confront witnesses	Yes/Yes
8th	Cruel and unusual punishment; right to bail	No/Yes

Types of White Collar Crimes

EXAMPLE

It would be impossible to list every type of crime a corporation could commit, but there are categories of criminal activity that are associated with business. Generally, if a corporation commits a crime it is for the specific purpose of gaining an advantage in the market. For example, the Dalkon Shield was a product that a corporation wanted to be the first to fill a need in the market with—birth control that was not an oral contraceptive—and the company may have cut corners to obtain this advantage. That is, a kind of greedy groupthink may have prevailed generally. If individual corporate officers and managers commit white collar crimes, however, it is generally done for their own personal gain, but their presence in the corporate setting allows the crime to be committed. Diversity in the Law 8-2, "The Whiter the Collar the Whiter the Criminal," discusses the racial disparity between blacks and whites as they progress up the white collar crime ladder. It also raises the interesting issue of a similar characteristic between both groups, however.

DIVERSITY IN THE LAW 8-2

THE WHITER THE COLLAR THE WHITER THE CRIMINAL

According to a recent book by Michael L. Benson and Sally S. Simpson, race is a characteristic that is highly correlated with the type of offense committed. Studies show that generally, compared to whites, racial minorities have a higher rate of crime. However, when you examine participants among the middle to upper white collar offenses, especially securities fraud and antitrust violations, nonwhites are nonexistent.

What accounts for this disparity? Surely, the paucity of minorities as CEOs, presidents, and other top managers is one answer. But opportunity, or lack thereof, does not account for it completely, according to these authors. Human nature under different circumstances seems to prevail as the two groups share a peculiar overlap of criminal mindset.

Studies suggest that the mindsets of low-level criminals and high-level criminals are similar in that they both possess a shared characteristic—lack of fear when it comes to committing a crime. On the one hand, elite whites believe that their chance of getting caught is very low. An underclass black[4] believes prison is a [housing] "project that feeds you."[5] In other words, neither has much to lose in committing the crime, one because they won't get caught so their lives won't change; the other because they will get caught and their lives won't change.

Source: Michael L. Benson and Sally S. Simpson, *White-Collar Crime: An Opportunity Perspective* (Routledge, 2009).

The following paragraphs (see Take Away 8-3, "Business Liability") address a few of the white collar crimes involving corporations, but the discussion is not intended to be exhaustive.

SECURITIES FRAUD

Securities are regulated by the Securities Exchange Act of 1934. The primary purpose of the statute is to protect investors from fraudulent activity involving the purchase or sale of securities on the stock market. This act criminalizes certain activity that comes under the broad heading of securities fraud. The act covers acts by the managers, officers and employees of the corporation as well as any other person who commits a fraud against the market by buying or selling stocks in violation of the rules. Security violations are prosecuted by the Department of Justice if the charges are criminal. The Securities and Exchange Commission can also impose civil penalties against a corporation or person who violates the Securities Exchange Act.

TAKE AWAY 8-3

BUSINESS LIABILITY

- Securities Fraud
- Insider Trading
- Mail Fraud
- Misappropriation
- Conspiracy
- Bid Rigging
- Antitrust Crimes
- Price Fixing
- Obstruction of Justice

---

[4]These attributes are not this author's, but the attributes given by Benson and Simpson.

[5]Michael L. Benson and Sally S. Simpson, *White-Collar Crime: An Opportunity Perspective* (Routledge, 2009), p. 175.

CHINA EXECUTES TWO FOR MULTIMILLION DOLLAR FRAUDULENT SCHEME

Two business people were executed in China for defrauding hundreds of investors out of approximately $127 million. China's highest court found that the scheme to defraud had seriously damaged the country's financial regulatory order and social stability, a requirement for having the death penalty imposed for this type of crime. Nonviolent offences which threaten social order or which involve large sums of money are eligible for the death penalty.

One defendant was a beauty shop owner who promised her investors monthly returns of up to 10 percent and had received more than $102.5 million in investment. She allegedly spent the money on a lavish lifestyle, including investments in beauty parlors, real estate, and mining businesses. The other woman who was executed collected $24 million from 300 people by telling them they could receive up to 108 percent interest.

China executes more people than any other country, including people accused of financial crimes.

Source: AP, "China Executes Two for Defrauding Investors," August 6, 2009, http://www.law.com/jsp/law/international/LawArticleIntl.jsp?id=1202432826454&src=EMC-Email&et=editorial&bu=Law.com&pt=LAWCOM%20Newswire%20Update&cn=LAWCOM_NewswireUpdate_20090806&kw=China%20Executes%20Two%20for%20Defrauding%20Investors.

Keep in mind that the main intent of securities laws is to make sure investors are aware of all they need to know to make prudent business decisions. Many of the violations of securities laws arise from failure to report information required by law. Securities laws are often called "blue sky" laws precisely because if you want to invest in blue skies, you are free to do so, as long as you are fully informed of what you are getting into. The law is not made to protect people from bad investment decisions, but rather, to make sure they are made aware of all they need to know before investing.

The United States is not the only country that punishes those who defraud investors out of their money. However, as yet, we have not levied capital punishment for such wholesale theft. Look at Reality Check 8-4, "China Executes Two for Multimillion Dollar Fraudulent Scheme." Perhaps if capital punishment were considered in the U.S., those who are in the position to commit this type of fraud would think twice. Given our system of law, is this a possibility? What are the ethical and jurisprudential theories involved in such an approach? If we really want this crime to stop, would this be appropriate if it accomplished its end? Why or why not? What ethical considerations do we include in making this determination?

INSIDER TRADING

The most prominent criminal activity involving fraud on the market is insider trading. Insider trading also allows you to see why having pertinent information provided to all investors is so important to investors. **Insider trading** occurs when someone, usually a corporate insider, buys or sells a security while in possession of inside information. Inside information is any material information about the stock that is unknown to the public. The purpose of engaging in insider trading is to get a jump on the market. In other words, if you are in possession of information that indicates a big merger between two corporations is about to occur, you might purchase shares of the corporation's stock so that when the merger is announced and the stock value increases, you will have received the benefit of that increase to the detriment of the public who did not know that information. The same thing occurs in the reverse if you learn information about the stock that indicates the value is about to fall. If you can sell stock that you own before the public learns of the decrease in value, then you do not lose the amount of money you would have lost had you not acted on that information before the public learned of the bad news. Under either scenario, one using such information has committed a fraud on the market and is guilty of insider trading.

Lastly, insider trading can occur if a person is not a member of the corporation but works for the corporation in an outside capacity and, as a result of the position, learns of and acts upon nonpublic information. For example, if you are hired as an accountant for the corporation and, in that capacity you learn of inside information and act on it, you have committed a form of insider trading known as **misappropriation.** In other words, you have taken information that you were privy to as a result of your position with the corporation and acted on it for your benefit while the information was not public. You have also committed the crime of insider trading through misappropriation of information. Misappropriation also occurs if you learn of the information and pass it on to others, such as friends, a spouse, or other relatives and they act on the information to their benefit. In the *Rocklage* case (Case 8.4), this is exactly what occurred.

CASE 8.4 S.E.C. v. Rocklage

470 F.3d 1 (1st Cir. 2006)

Facts: Mr. Rocklage joined Cubist Pharmaceuticals in 1994 as CEO of the company. He routinely communicated nonpublic information to his wife thinking she kept it confidential. While attending a meeting in 2001 Mr. Rocklage learned that one of the company's key drugs had failed its clinical trials. Under the impression that his wife would keep the information confidential, as usual, he phoned her and told her the bad news. He again reminded her to keep the information private and as usual she agreed.

Unknown to him, his wife had a prior understanding with her brother that she would inform him if she learned significant negative news about the company. After learning that the news would negatively impact the company Mrs. Rocklage told her husband that she planned to signal her brother to sell the stock and Mr. Rocklage objected. Nevertheless, Mrs. Rocklage gave her brother information regarding Cubist. Three days later her brother dumped 5,500 shares of the stock. Her brother also tipped off a friend who sold all of his 7,500 shares of stock. By selling the stock before the announcements the friend and brother avoided losses of over $200,000.

The S.E.C alleged all the defendants violated insider trading. Mrs. Rocklage was found guilty of insider trading which she appeals.

Issue: Whether the wife of an insider, who divulges insider information told to her by her insider husband, can be found guilty of insider trading for disclosing the information which is then acted upon to the advantage of the one to whom the wife told the information.

Decision: Yes

Reasoning: We think that Mrs. Rocklage's actions fit within a natural reading of the "in connection with" requirement. Mrs. Rocklage's preexisting arrangement with her brother can easily be understood as a scheme or practice or course of business whose goal was to enable her brother to trade in Cubist securities at a substantially reduced level of risk. Her deception of her husband was a natural and integral part of this scheme; she induced her husband to reveal material negative information to her about Cubist, knowing full well that in obtaining that information she would enable her brother to execute a securities transaction. She then actively facilitated a securities transaction by tipping her brother, and securities were in fact sold based on her information. These events show that her deceptive acquisition of material inside information was "in connection with" a securities transaction. We find that the complaint states a claim under the misappropriation theory.

CASE QUESTIONS

1. A person in Mrs. Rocklage's position is called a tippee. Tippees are guilty of insider trading when they pass material nonpublic information on to others that they received from a tipper, Mr. Rocklage, in this case. Mrs. Rocklage gave information obtained from her husband in confidence to her brother, who used it to save himself money. Why would receiving information, unsolicited, be a criminal act, if her brother did not ask her for it?

2. If the friend of the brother were prosecuted, would it matter if he did not know that the information was not public? Would he still be guilty of insider trading?

3. What is the definition of material? If Mr. Rocklage told his wife that the CEO of Cubist was going to quit, and that information was shared with her brother, would that constitute insider trading? Does the information have to affect the market in order to make it material? Should it?

CONSPIRACY, OBSTRUCTION OF JUSTICE, MAIL FRAUD, AND PERJURY

These criminal charges are often a part of the government's prosecution for white collar crimes. These charges are added on, sometimes for leverage, and are different and separate from the underlying crime charged.

EXAMPLE

Conspiracy is an agreement between two or more persons to commit a crime or to conspire to commit an act that is not unlawful by unlawful means. For example, in the crime of insider trading involving a tipper and tippee, there is almost always the crime of conspiracy as well, because both parties would likely have made an agreement to buy or sell the stock in question while the information was unknown to the public. Adding a charge of conspiracy (thus increasing the potential penalty) often acts as an incentive for the guilty party to plead to the underlying charge in exchange for dropping the ancillary charge of conspiracy. This negotiation is called **plea bargaining** and is very common. While it may seem to you unfair for someone alleged to have committed a crime to be able to plead to a lesser offense or have other offenses dropped in exchange for the plea bargain, the truth is, not every case should or can be tried in a court of law. It is expensive, time consuming, and risky. If a prosecutor can plead out a case and still punish the perpetrator, it saves time, money, and court resources and clears up the courts and prosecutors for the truly important cases. Plea bargaining has been called by some a necessary evil, and given our shrinking resources and overburdened court system, this is probably a pretty accurate description.

EXAMPLE

Perjury is the willful and corrupt false swearing or affirming, under oath, as to a material matter in question. Perjury is another ancillary charge that often gets added on to the more serious charge by the prosecutor because of the frequency with which it occurs in conjunction with the underlying crime. For example, in the case involving Martha Stewart it was alleged that she and her broker lied under oath when they gave a statement saying they had agreed ahead of time to sell Stewart's Imclone stock when it fell below a certain value. That was not true, and her broker was charged with perjuring himself because the statement was made under oath to federal authorities.

EXAMPLE

Mail fraud is using the mail to obtain money or property in a scheme to defraud. **Wire fraud** is the same, but requires use of a telecommunications device of any kind if the communication crosses state lines. Under either, if the intent of the scheme is to defraud, the mail or wire fraud charge can be added. This is true even if the underlying crime is not charged. Using Martha Stewart as an example again, she and her broker could have been charged with wire fraud once they made the phone call to plan how they were going to sell the Imclone stock while in possession of inside information.

EXAMPLE

The crime of **obstruction of justice** can be used to address conduct that overlaps with other categories of crime, for example, perjury. It is generally defined as any corrupt attempt to influence, interfere with, or impede an investigation conducted by any officer of the court or of the law by threats, intimidation, or corrupt persuasion. It also covers the destruction or altering of documents and witness tampering. Obstruction of justice was the crime that Martha Stewart was ultimately convicted of based on her corrupt persuasion of her broker to change the documents involved in the Imclone sale to look as if there was a standing order to sell the shares when they fell below a certain value.

ANTITRUST CRIMES

America is a capitalist country. Capitalism is grounded in the idea of a free market and competition. That is, sellers can sell at whatever price the market will bear and competition hopefully results in the best product, service or support having the larger share of the market. Anything that significantly interferes with this scheme is therefore prohibited.

Antitrust crimes involve unfair marketing techniques and conduct designed to eliminate competition through unfair means. Antitrust statutes that regulate trade practices in this country are numerous. The primary statutes, the Sherman Act,[6] the Clayton Act,[7] the Robinson-Patman Act,[8] and the Federal Trade Commission Act,[9] all have as their purpose keeping competition in check. All of these statutes are intended to protect competition, not individual competitors. What follows is a brief description of a few types of violations.

Price discrimination is an antitrust violation under the Robinson-Patman Act. Price discrimination occurs when different purchasers of the same product are charged differently for an item that costs the same to produce if the purpose is to decrease competition or create a monopoly. For example, let's suppose it costs $1 to produce an item and there are 2 producers of that item. In order to be competitive, Producer 1 sells the items for $2 to all his purchasers, regardless of where they are located, which gives him a profit of $1 on each item. Producer 2, on the other hand, sells his items for $2 if they are located in an area that competes with Producer 2, but $1.50 if they are located in an area that doesn't compete with Producer 2. Thus, Producer 2 will make $1 on some items and $.50 on others. If this tactic is used to keep Producer 1 out of the market that's currently not served by him, it's a violation of the Robinson-Patman Act. While this example is an oversimplification, it illustrates the effect of price discrimination. The *Li Xi v. Apple, Inc.* case (Case 8.5) illustrates that not all differently priced items are discriminatory.

The Sherman Antitrust Act makes it a crime to enter into a contract or engage in a conspiracy that restrains trade. The Sherman Act's purpose is to ensure free enterprise and open competition in the market. For a Sherman Act violation, the government must prove that there was a conspiracy between two or more persons that unreasonably restrained interstate trade with the intent to violate the law. Enforcement of the Sherman Act is by the Department of Justice, although violations of the act can be investigated by the Federal Trade Commission.

Price fixing is an antitrust violation under the Sherman Act. Price fixing occurs when two or more competitors conspire to sell a product for the same price. As you can see, the idea of competition, upon which capitalism is found, goes out the window. The reason price fixing occurs is to make the cost of the product so high that it puts the buyers at a disadvantage. For example, let's suppose two competitors provide all of one product in a geographical market. In order for each of them to make money, they agree that they will raise the price of their goods to a certain amount, and that neither of them will decrease the price of that product. Eventually, they could collude to raise the price even higher giving the buyers no choice but to purchase one of their products. This could continue until the price is at the maximum that the buyers are willing to pay. Price fixing can occur with products, services, advertising prices, or credit terms. If two or more firms engage in a conspiracy to fix prices, they have formed a **cartel.** Entering into the agreement to perform an illegal act is called **collusion.** Collusion and the forming of a cartel are easier when the market has only a few competitors, because the operation of the cartel depends on secret, collusive agreements being enforced. The smaller the number of competitors, the easier it is to keep the secret.

Bid rigging is another form of illegal antitrust activity prohibited by the Sherman Act. Bid rigging involves interference with the competitive bidding for the awarding of a contract. The essence of bid rigging is when the bidders agree ahead of time who will

---

[6]15 U.S.C. §1.

[7]15 U.S.C. §12.

[8]15 U.S.C. §13(a).

[9]15 U.S.C. §41.

CASE 8.5 Li Xi v. Apple, Inc.

603 F.Supp.2d 464 (E.D.N.Y. 2009)

Facts: In 2007, Apple announced it would no longer produce the 4GB iPhone and was cutting the price for the 8 gigabyte (8GB) from $599 to $399. Apple's price protection policy allowed customers who purchased the iPhone within 14 days of the price cut to be eligible for a refund of the difference in price. A class action suit was commenced against Apple by people who purchased the phone within a month of the price cut. Each class member purchased the phone to resell it and Apple's decision to lower the price of the iPhone hurt these purchasers because now they could not resell their phones and earn the profit they anticipated. Plaintiffs asserted a violation of the Robinson-Patman Act. Apple moved to dismiss the claim.

Issue: Whether Apple committed price discrimination in violation of the Robinson-Patman Act when it reduced the price of the 8GB iPhone and discontinued producing the 4GB iPhone.

Decision: No.

Reasoning: To establish a claim under §2(a), a plaintiff has the burden of establishing four facts: (1) that seller's sales were made in interstate commerce; (2) that the seller discriminated in price as between the two purchasers; (3) that the product or commodity sold to the competing purchasers was of the same grade and quality; and (4) that the price discrimination had a prohibited effect on competition. Section 2(a) "addresses price discrimination in cases involving competition between different purchasers for resale of the purchased product." Absent actual competition between a disfavored purchaser and a favored purchaser, a plaintiff cannot establish the requisite injury. To have standing under §2(a), a private plaintiff must make some showing of actual injury attributable to something the antitrust laws were designed to prevent. To establish an antitrust injury, a plaintiff must show (1) an injury in fact; (2) that has been caused by the violation; and (3) that is the type of injury contemplated by the statute. Plaintiffs assert that they were injured because they could not resell their iPhones for as high a profit as later purchasers. However, plaintiffs do not allege that they are competitors engaged in the business

of reselling iPhones, that they are in actual competition with a favored purchaser, or that they even resold or attempted to resell their iPhones. Moreover, the Amended Complaint incorporates by reference the sales agreement between Apple and plaintiffs, in which plaintiffs expressly acknowledged and agreed that they were "end user customers," and that Apple's retail customers "may not purchase for resale." Thus, plaintiffs fail to allege actual competition with a favored purchaser or antitrust injury. Moreover, plaintiffs allege that the purchasers of an iPhone prior to September 5, 2007, paid identical prices and received identical terms of sale. Apple subsequently reduced the price to all purchasers, so that all later purchasers paid the identical price and received identical terms of sale. Plaintiffs' allegations do not describe any price discrimination, only a reduction in the price of the iPhone after their purchase. Indeed, a seller is free to change its prices as much and as often as it wants, provided it charges the same price to all competing customers at the same time. Each plaintiff bought an iPhone before September 5 for exactly the same price and under exactly the same terms as every other contemporaneous purchaser of the iPhone; each plaintiff could have purchased an iPhone after September 5 at exactly the same price and terms as every other contemporaneous purchaser. Plaintiffs have not alleged any price discrimination, only that Apple lowered the price of the iPhone for *all* customers—action that is legally permissible under §2(a).

CASE QUESTIONS

1. What would a plaintiff have to prove to bring a valid discrimination claim?
2. The court held that a seller is free to change its prices as much and as often as it would like as long as it does so for everyone at the same time. Does this control the wholesale or retail price? Can a retailer sell below what the manufacturer sets as the price?
3. How does price discrimination negatively impact the market? How does it help to create a monopoly?

win the award. The bids they submit then reflect who they have appointed as the winner through the use of the lowest bid. It undermines the bidding process by not allowing the true cost of the bid to be reflected and, again, it interferes with a free and competitive market. For example, if four companies are in the same market for a bid, the normal process is for all four companies to submit bids independently of one another using figures they have obtained from the resources necessary to complete the job. If the four companies are engaged in bid rigging, they agree ahead of time that the lowest bidder will be one of them, but the bid that is submitted will be higher than it should be. The others then will bid higher than the winning bid, assuring that the appointed winner receives the bid. They do this in turn with other bids, assuring themselves work when it is their turn to win the bid. This type of conduct is illegal under the Sherman Act.

EXAMPLE

ENVIRONMENTAL CRIMES

Crimes against the environment encompass many different crimes ranging from air pollution to illegal dumping of toxic wastes on land and in water. There are several statutes that have been enacted to criminalize this behavior. Under the overall umbrella of the Environmental Protection Act, these statutes are used to prevent harm to the environment. Businesses engaged in manufacturing that have by-products that are polluting substances are generally violators of the EPA in specific ways, discussed below.

The Clean Air Act regulates the amount and type of particles that can be dispelled into the environment from such things as manufacturing and chemical plants. The law recognizes that some material must be sent into the environment in order to produce materials needed to produce goods, but there is a limit to how much harmful material can be contained in that waste product. Emissions standards are strictly regulated and a false report can create liability for the violator.

The Clean Water Act is designed to control and regulate the amount of pollution that can be sent into the waterways of this country. Emissions are strictly regulated and a false report will result in a violation of the act.

The disposal and storage of hazardous waste in this country is regulated under the Resource Conservation and Recovery Act (RCRA). RCRA establishes standards, in conjunction with state regulations, for proper disposal and storage of these toxic wastes. The minimum civil and criminal penalties are set by the state in compliance with guidelines set by RCRA. Corporations are largely responsible for violations of RCRA because pollutants are usually emitted at the point of production which is usually a manufacturing or chemical plant controlled by a corporation. How far these environmental restrictions go is the question in Reality Check 8-5, "Environmental Protection for Global Dumping."

REALITY CHECK 8-5

ENVIRONMENTAL PROTECTION FOR GLOBAL DUMPING

With a lawsuit that started in New York in 1993, the small town of Lago Agrio, Ecuador, is anxiously awaiting their court's ruling on whether Chevron is liable for environmental damage to its small village. There's no question that the rain forests contain streams topped with shimmering layers of oil and their pastures contain diesel-smelling sludge. Also without question is that local natives are experiencing illnesses that they blame on the contamination of their lands by Texaco, now owned by Chevron. In April 2008, an Ecuadorian geological engineer recommended to the court that Chevron pay between $8 and $16 billion for environmental damage if they are found to be guilty of causing the damage. Texaco has admitted it dumped more than 18 billion gallons of toxic waste water into Ecuador's Amazon waterways when it was the exclusive operator of an oil consortium from 1964 to 1990. The waste included carcinogens such as benzene, and five indigenous groups assert their traditional lifestyles have been decimated by the contamination. No timetable has been given for the decision. Many other third world countries are anticipating the outcome of this case, and intend to file their own suits if they get a favorable ruling. Chevron is challenging the finding by the Ecuadorian engineer and will be certain to appeal any adverse ruling by the court.

Source: Kelly Hearn, *CSMonitor.com,* "$16 Billion Lawsuit Tests Chevron," April 9, 2008, http://www.csmonitor.com/2008/0409/p06s01-woam.html?page=2.

WORKPLACE CRIMES

Workers are protected in the workspace by the Occupational Safety and Health Act.[10] This act tries to set minimum standards for a safe work environment by imposing training, equipment guidelines, and reporting requirements on employers. Even with this effort, thousands of workers are killed each year and many more injured due to workplace accidents. Violations of the OSHA can result in civil and criminal penalties imposed by the Department of Justice, the enforcement arm of OSHA. For example, OSHA requires chemical manufacturers and importers to obtain or develop a material safety data sheet (MSDS) for each hazardous chemical they produce or import. It further requires that employers provide information to employees about the chemicals to which they are exposed.[11]

EXAMPLE

RACKETEER INFLUENCED AND CORRUPT ORGANIZATIONS ACT (RICO)

RICO was originally aimed at organized crime prosecutions, but has become a useful tool in prosecuting white collar crimes. RICO requires a pattern of predicate acts in furtherance of an illegal activity. These predicate acts can be any number of illegal acts, including fraud, extortion, bribery, and obstruction of justice. If two or more of the predicate acts occur within a 10-year period, RICO can be charged. For example, suppose a broker engaged in a pattern of activity involving the illegal sale of stocks (fraud) over a 5-year period of time. In addition to being charged with the underlying crimes, a RICO charge will increase the potential penalty.

CORRUPTION

Although **corruption** may conjure up thoughts of politicians, the politicians engaged in corrupt activity are often enticed into doing so by corporate officials. Political corruption occurs when the acts of public servants deviate from their appointed duties for the politicians' personal enrichment. The corporate officials engaged with those politicians also face criminal charges. For example, judges are forbidden from accepting any form of remuneration (payment) for a favorable disposition of a case. Suppose the corporation whose case is before the judge offers a bribe (money or something of value) for disposing of the case in favor of the corporation. That is corruption, and both the judge who accepts the bribe and the corporation who offered or paid it will be guilty of a crime. Reality Check 8-6, "A Horrendous Breach of Trust Lands Judges in Jail," illustrates this crime.

EXAMPLE

---

[10]29 U.S.S. §651 et seq.

[11]Hazardous Communication Standards, 29 CCFR 1910.1200.

EMBEZZLEMENT

Embezzlement is a breach of trust done for private gain by an employee or agent of the corporation. For embezzlement to occur there has to be a breach of trust and the relationship allowed the employee or agent to obtain money or property. For example, a bank teller who takes funds from the cash drawer has embezzled. Likewise, an accountant who falsifies the books of a company to reflect improper transactions and who steals the money from the company has embezzled.

EXAMPLE

Computer Crimes

Computer crime refers to the intentional use of a computer to commit fraud or for other illegal purposes. The difference between computer crimes and crimes committed on the computer is difficult to distinguish. If a crime can be committed without the use of a computer, for example, extortion,[12] but the communication is by computer (the letter demanding payment for the act), it is not a computer crime, but just a crime committed via use of the computer. On the other hand, a crime that can only be committed via use of the computer is what "computer crime" refers to. Cyberterrorism and Internet fraud are distinctly computer crimes (see Take Away 8-4). The area of computer crime is obviously vast and evolving as fast as the technology. Since 9/11, cyberterrorism is a major and growing concern. A thorough discussion is beyond the scope of this chapter, but the other categories are briefly discussed in the following sections.

INTERNET FRAUD

The Controlling the Assault of Non-Solicited Pornography and Marketing Act (CAN-SPAM) is used to target unsolicited e-mails that are often used to commit **Internet fraud.** This fraud requires the multijurisdictional approach to try to seek out and stop the vehicle of the fraud, this spam or e-mail. Generally the e-mail may originate in a foreign jurisdiction, require the victim's payment to be sent to a second jurisdiction, and then the funds are wired to a third jurisdiction. Although it is difficult to apprehend these fraudulent transfers, an effort has been made to work globally to do so.

Many of the Internet fraud cases implicate legitimate corporations. For example, one common scheme replicates a national bank's letterhead and asks the receiver of the e-mail to verify their bank information because there has been a break-in at the bank and the system has been compromised. Unsuspecting consumers who think this is a legitimate attempt to verify their account will confirm their bank information in response to this e-mail only to later discover that the thief has emptied out their account. Corporations have to spend money either responding to these e-mails or protecting the accounts of their customers from these illegal attempts to fraudulently obtain the funds.

EXAMPLE

IDENTITY THEFT

Identity theft could happen anytime and might be difficult to avoid. Have you ever left your magnetic hotel entry card in your room at the end of your stay, thinking you didn't need it anymore, so it could be thrown away?

TAKE AWAY 8-4

COMPUTER CRIMES

- Internet Fraud
- Cyberterrorism
- Identity Theft
- Hacking

---

[12]The use of position or power to obtain money or favors illegally.

THE COST OF COMPUTER CRIME

In 2008, of 552 responses by computer security practitioners in U.S. corporations, government agencies, medical institutions, and universities, the average reported loss per incident was about $300,000. For those companies that experienced financial fraud, the loss averaged $500,000. The majority of the types of incidents reported were viruses (49%) followed by insider abuse of networks (44%) and theft of laptop computers (42%). Only 1% of the respondents did not have a formal security policy in place or in development within their companies.

Source: Robert Richardson, *2008 CSI Computer Crime & Security Survey,* http://i.cmpnet.com/v2.gocsi.com/pdf/CSIsurvey2008.pdf.

Did you know it contains all sorts of information about you and your credit card? Did you ever use your social security number as a school ID number? Did you ever throw away unsolicited credit card applications sent to you? All of this could have led to theft of your identity causing you untold heartache, not to mention the time, energy, effort, and money to deal with it. **Identity theft** has become a fast-growing industry in the U.S., and the Internet makes this crime especially pernicious. Corporations are implicated in this crime because often it is from the corporation's database that the identities of its customers are pilfered, usually through **hacking** methods. For example, several retailers have been victimized when hackers have stolen names, credit card information, dates of birth, social security numbers, and other proprietary information from their databases. This information is stored because the customer has requested a retail credit card or has conducted business with the retailer. The government has also been the victim of stolen identity crime. A briefcase containing a computer which held approximately 26.5 million names and sensitive information of veterans was stolen from a Veterans Administration data analyst's home.[13] The assumption is that false identities will be created using the stolen information. Reality Check 8-7, "The Cost of Computer Crime," indicates the money companies are investing to prevent this crime.

Businesses pay for identity theft in numerous ways. Most obvious is the need to compensate victims of stolen identity. Most corporations who have been victimized have offered to pay for credit monitoring of each victim for several years to allow the potential victim to be sure his or her credit is not being used illegally. Another cost is in the replacement of stolen credit card information. Each credit card takes $5.00 to $6.00 to replace.[14] If 8 million credit card numbers are stolen via hacking,[15] it costs $40 to 48 million to replace them. This cost is passed on to the consumer. In addition, the cost of increased security methods to prevent the hacking is added to the already high cost of security for major corporations.

Defenses

A defense is a legal position taken by someone accused of a crime to defeat the charges made against him or her. Corporations have the same right to defend themselves as do individuals. Corporations can make use of constitutional defenses such as search and seizure laws, as well as substantive defenses such as defendant alleging and proving he

---

[13]The briefcase was later recovered and it was determined that the information had not been accessed in this case. Nonetheless, the VA agreed to a $20 million settlement to be used to pay for anyone whose information was stored on the computer who suffered damages as a result of this theft (http://www.vetsfirst.org/are-you-entitled-to-a-share-of-the-20-million-va-identity-theft-lawsuit-settlement/).

[14]Timothy C. Barmann, "Banks Cancel Debit Cards after BJ's Wholesale Club Warns of Theft," *Providence Journal,* March 16, 2004, available at 2004 WL 59429202.

[15]It is alleged that 8 million debit and credit cards accounts were compromised by the Data Processors International security breach. "Hacker Breach Dents Confidence in Card Security," *ATM & Debit News,* February 27, 2003.

or she did not do the act alleged. Immunity, self-defense, and criminal insanity are some substantive defenses. For example, if a corporation cooperates with the government in exchange for **immunity** from prosecution, the government cannot later decide to prosecute the corporation for crimes for which they were granted immunity. Personal defenses, such as insanity and self-defense, are not available for corporate crimes, although they are available for use by the corporate officers and managers who might be charged with crimes.

L06 Sentencing Guidelines

The **Sentencing Guidelines** are designed to create uniformity in sentencing. Although the structure of the guidelines is too extensive to go into here, the guidelines use a gridlike approach to allocate points that then get translated into time measurements. For example, one aspect of the Guidelines calculates the offense level. The offense level is determined by the severity of the crime and is allocated points based on the severity level designation. Added to that is the specific offense characteristics. This category allows points to be added or deducted based on the specific factors of the crime committed. This goes on until a number is reached which then corresponds to a number of months.

Sentencing Guidelines are used for calculating white collar and corporate sentencing as well as individual sentencing. In 2002 the recommended punishment in the Sentencing Guidelines for corporate crimes was increased as a part of the response to the Enron and other corporate scandals. This exponentially increased individual penalties for white collar crime. For example, the penalty for mail fraud pre-2002 was a maximum of five years in prison. That penalty was increased by the 2002 amendments to a maximum of 20 years. In addition, an individual engaged in criminal activity that caused more than $1 million in losses now faces up to 10 years in prison. Reality Check 8-8, "Are Victims Really Victims if They Have Been Repaid?" illustrates one of the issues that are currently being debated about the Sentencing Guidelines.

L07 The Sarbanes-Oxley Act

After the Enron scandal of 2002 and others that followed on the heels of Enron, Congress enacted the **Sarbanes-Oxley Act** (SOX) of 2002. This act attempted to reform corporate culture and to give the SEC more oversight and control over corporations and

THE COST OF SOX COMPLIANCE

One company that has charted the cost of SOX compliance since its passage reported that costs for compliance for section 404 reached an average of $1.7 million for a company averaging $75 million in market capitalization. That figure represented a slight decrease in cost over the 2006 figures, and the cost has decreased in each of the four years since SOX was passed. Section 404 requires management to produce an internal control report as part of each Exchange Act report. The report must also contain an assessment of the effectiveness of the internal controls for financial reporting.

Source: FEI Survey: "Average 2007 SOX Compliance Costs $1.7 Million," http:// fei.mediaroom.com/index.php?s=43&item=204.

to impose more ethics and accountability rules on corporations. The purpose was to avoid a continuation of Enron-type scandals.

The Act also increased the criminal penalties imposed for violations covered under the Act. Used more as a deterrence factor than a reality, this fear factor has nonetheless had some effect on the corporate culture.

One of the most important sections of the Sarbanes-Oxley Act is Section 906 which requires corporate officers to certify the financial reports of the corporation. Penalties of up to $5,000,000 and 10 years in prison can be imposed on a Chief Executive or Chief Financial Officer for willfully certifying that the records comply with the reporting requirements imposed by the SEC if it is known that they do not. The Act also created the private, nonprofit **Public Company Accounting Oversight Board,** or **PCAOB.** PCAOB is designed to oversee the auditors of public companies. By overseeing the auditors, PCAOB protects investors and maintains the public confidence in corporations. Congress thought it wise to do this since Enron showed what an integral part CPAs played in Enron's doomed scheme that, among other things, nearly brought Houston to its knees when the bottom fell out of the company. See Reality Check 8-9, "The Cost of SOX Compliance," for some figures which might surprise you concerning the cost to businesses to comply with the new Act.

PCAOB also investigates and disciplines auditing firms and those who work for and with them. Violations of the Sarbanes-Oxley Act or specific PCAOB rules may result in sanctions being levied against the violators. Such sanctions can include monetary penalties, remedial measures, or for more serious violations, revoking a firm's registration or barring a person from participating in the audit of public corporations.

EXAMPLE

For example, the PCAOB revoked the registration of one firm and suspended its CPA for a period of one year for making misleading statements in connection with a PCAOB inspection and violating auditing standards regarding auditing documentation. It was alleged that the CPA changed reports he submitted to the PCAOB to appear more favorable to its inspection team concerning the firm's quality control procedures. Citing the need to protect the public, the PCAOB ordered the firm's license to audit revoked and suspended the auditing practice of the CPA for one year.[16]

LO8

The PCAOB was created to police what had not been policed before—the moral compass of corporate culture. While corporations were left to do well or not, they were never intended to be left to do harm, but that is what the culture had given birth to. Corporations turned their backs on ethical behavior at the expense of the corporate shareholders and the investing public. What Sarbanes-Oxley and PCAOB do is create an accountability system that is so exact that any breach other than the most innocent is penalized. Corporate America brought that on itself.

---

[16]PCAOB Release No. 105-2009-002, June 16, 2009, http://www.pcaobus.org/Enforcement/Disciplinary_Proceedings/2009/06-16-DellaDonna.pdf.

Summary

There is no doubt that most businesses conduct their business on the right side of the law, but there is also no doubt that there are many ways businesses can get into trouble or be the victim of crimes. Because businesses are associated with the suit-and-tie style of management, their misconduct is called white collar crime. Businesses are subject to the constitutional protections offered to individuals with a few exceptions. To the extent that businesses have rights, they have the right to be protected to the fullest extent of the law.

Corporate crimes are called so because it is the proximity to the business that gives employees, managers, and officers of the corporation opportunity to commit crimes. Many crimes are breaches of fiduciary relationships: embezzlement, bribery, and corruption are a few examples. Securities fraud also often involves a breach of trust by corporate employees. Businesses can engage in crimes designed to manipulate the market for their profit to the detriment of commerce. When this happens, antitrust laws are used to level the competitive playing field.

Environmental crimes harm everyone and have come under increasing scrutiny with the green movement. Global awareness of past practices, illegal or not, is requiring former corporate players in nonindustrial countries to clean up where they have caused harm. Indigenous people are beginning to discover the harm to the environment many of these companies have caused, and are seeking money damages to help in cleaning up their localities.

Computer crimes are the fastest rising crimes and are a plague on businesses. Money is spent protecting the computer systems that businesses rely upon from hackers and other potential security breaches. Information stored by the business for legitimate reasons also has to be protected so information about clients and customers can remain private.

Sentencing Guidelines have begun to reflect the seriousness with which this country regards corporate crimes that stem from avarice and greed. Corporate officers and directors who position themselves within the corporation only to pilfer money from the legitimate shareholders are being harshly sentenced under the Guidelines. This is a difference from years past when white collar criminals were not placed into the justice system for committing financial crimes.

Review Questions

1. A building inspector asks a restaurant owner for a bribe. Without the bribe, the inspector will issue a summons to close the restaurant for safety violations. The owner directs you to make the payment. What should you do? LO2

2. Alvaro was stopped by the police on his way home from the gym. After asking him for identification, which he gave them, the police asked Alvaro if they could search the gym bag he was carrying. When he asked why they wanted to search his bag, they said they thought he might have been part of a robbery that had taken place on the same street he was on about one hour before. He refused, but the police took the bag and searched it anyway, saying his refusal gave them the right to be suspicious. Alvaro's best argument to suppress the search would be that: LO3

   a. It violated his Fourth Amendment right.

   b. It violated his Fifth Amendment right.

   c. It violated his Sixth Amendment right.

   d. It violated his Eighth Amendment right.

3. Jamile was the Chief Financial Officer of Dayglo Corporation. During the course of her three years as CFO, she created several secret accounts to which she diverted funds that she used for her personal finances. An audit finally caught on to what she was doing and Jamile was arrested. What crime(s) has she committed? LO5

4. What are some of the characteristics that might be evidence of bid rigging? LO5

5. Frantz, a waste engineer for a company that manufactured particle board, managed the company's pollution control system. He ordered his subordinates to discharge pollutants from his plant into a municipal sewer causing the mineral content to greatly exceed federal standards and then falsified the records at the plant to cover up what he had done. What environmental law would he likely be guilty of violating? Can you think of any other laws that he might be charged with violating? LO6

6. You arrive for your new job in a photo processing plant. While being given a tour of the facilities, you notice that many of the employees you are meeting do not speak English and you suspect they cannot read the warning signs posted around the workplace machinery. The machinery consists of very dangerous chemicals used to process photos. You also see that some of the chemicals appear to be used improperly. For example, one worker seems to be inhaling the toxic fumes of the chemicals without wearing the mask that is required. When you ask your tour guide about it, she answers that "these workers all seem to have their own way of doing things" and that "as long as they get the job done, there's no problem." You, however, are sure this is a problem. Whom would you complain to and which agency do you think would investigate the workplace conditions at this plant? LO5

7. You are a maintenance worker at a brokerage firm. One night while emptying the trash, you notice a sheet of paper which appears to be a note describing a big merger that is about to happen between two companies. You are not experienced at all in the stock market, but you use your life savings to buy stock in the company that was listed as the takeover company. As it turns out, you are right about the merger, and your stock increases more than you can imagine once the merger occurs. What crime are you guilty of committing? LO5

8. HP Suppliers was in the habit of bidding on county projects involving road construction. Chery Contractors also bid on the same type of contracts with the county. One day, the presidents of the two companies met for lunch to talk over business. During the course of their conversation, it was suggested that it would be nice if they could alternate low bids between them, so they could both stay in business. Both agreed that that would be a good idea. Although nothing else was said, the fact is that for three years

after that, their bids seemed to be awarded alternatively between them. When one bid came in, the other was always placed higher than the first. Would this be evidence of a pattern necessary to charge them both with bid rigging? LO5

9. Diane appeared before the grand jury to testify about an incident she had witnessed several months before. When she appeared at the courthouse she saw the defendant and became afraid to testify truthfully, so while on the stand she denied ever seeing anything on the night in question. What crime has Diane committed? LO5

10. Corporations are the major polluters of the earth; yet, the EPA rarely imposes the kind of fines and punishment that deter pollution. If you were able to change this situation, what would you do to ensure that corporations would not use the earth as a dumping ground for hazardous waste and other toxic pollution? What kinds of punishment do you think would be necessary to deter corporations from harming the earth through pollution? How would you measure these solutions with the Eighth Amendment's "Excessive Fines Clause"? LO8

11. Using his bank's Web page, Israel created an authentic-looking fake e-mail to send to everyone he knew asking them to give him their personal information concerning their bank account. He intended to use that information to hack into the bank's Web page and steal the money from anyone who answered his e-mail. What crime has Israel committed? LO5

12. A large manufacturer of food products anticipated a rise in the cost of sugar, one of its important raw materials for food processing. It bought large amounts of this commodity and stockpiled it pending the increases. Other companies did not purchase bulk supplies. Shortly, the cost of sugar tripled. Competitors were now forced to buy their supplies at the higher market price. This made the cost of their finished products higher for consumers. The company that prepurchased sugar was not faced with the same cost increases as its competitors. Nevertheless, it increased its prices on products made from sugar to meet the competitors' prices. Is this an ethical decision? Is there a legitimate reason why this company would choose to act this way? Would it matter if the public knew about the increased profits the company was earning because of its foresight? LO8

Ethics Issue

You are the Head of Security for your multimillion-dollar corporation. Recently, you have been restoring your computer system because of a serious breach that occurred over a period of several weeks before it was detected by your computer analysts. You estimate that the financial loss associated with this attack is $27,148,000. This cost is based on tangible losses such as lost productivity, network downtime, and the expense of getting rid of the virus that infected the network. You've been called into a meeting with the Board of Directors and the CEO to determine whether the company should go public with the breach. The discussion centers on how this information will be used by customers and competitors, i.e., the intangible costs. What will the media do with this information? What will be the impact on your reputation? Will your customers lose confidence in your ability to protect their private information? Will this result in a negative impact on your bottom line?

Consider all the stakeholders in this scenario. What is the primary consideration here? Other than what is being considered at the board meeting, are there other things that should be considered? What is the ethically right thing to do?

Group Exercise

Take a look at newspapers, the Internet, or magazines and find a story about a business crime committed recently (make sure it is not one mentioned in the chapter). Determine the details of the crime or alleged crime and which of the laws we discussed have been violated. Discuss both the legal as well as the ethical issues involved.

Key Terms

www.mhhe.com/bennett-alexander1E1e

Secured Transactions and Bankruptcy

Learning Objectives

After reading this chapter, you should be able to:

L01 Describe a secured transaction

L02 Discuss the formation of a security interest

L03 Identify the different types of collateral

L04 Describe how a security interest is perfected

L05 Discuss the characteristics of a surety

L06 Explain the bankruptcy process

L07 Discuss the types of bankruptcy

L08 Describe the bankruptcy exemptions

 ## Opening Scenario

Olympia was a writer who had been able to support herself on the advance she received for a book deal she entered into with a small publishing company. It had been five years since her advance, however, and she was no closer to finishing her book than she had been this time last year. She used the last of her advance about two years earlier, and had been forced to take a low-paying job to support herself and still have time to write. Before she knew it, creditors began to call and her credit cards were maxed out. Olympia had borrowed $7,500 from her uncle who made her sign a promissory note giving him all of her art work as collateral. He had not filed to perfect his interest, however, since she was family. She had purchased a new set of appliances some time ago because everything seemed to have stopped working at once. She was paying those off in installments. Her car was in its fourth year of a six-year financing deal.

Olympia had procrastinated for so long on her book that the publisher backed out when several books with her theme hit the market. When Olympia stopped to take a look at her financial situation, she was $53,000 in debt, not counting what she owed her uncle. She had credit card payments of about $1000 per month, and was only able to make interest payments on them. She was mortified that she had let her situation get this bad. She immediately made an appointment to see an attorney. Was bankruptcy a possibility? Olympia had heard bad stories of people who filed bankruptcy, but she really had no choice. What will Olympia hear from her attorney?

Introduction and Background

Imagine the world you grew up in without the availability of credit. Chances are, if you are like most, you would not have been able to live in a house, because most homes are purchased through loans called mortgages. There would likely have been no family car, because most cars are bought through giving a small down payment with the remainder to be paid with a loan, rather than total cash payment for the car. Your parents likely used credit cards for purchases of school clothes, vacations, and other things. In fact, since most students do not pay their full tuition, fees, room and board up front in cash, chances are, without credit you would not even be in college. Unlike days of yesteryear when credit was thought of as almost shameful and a luxury in which few consumers indulged, credit has today become an almost vital part of life as we have come to know it.

As you can then imagine, making sure the credit relationship is protected and kept secure is of grave importance to our economy. If those making loans cannot be assured that the loan will be repaid, they are less likely to make the loans. If the loans are not made, fewer goods will be purchased. If fewer goods are purchased, there will be less manufacturing. If there is less manufacturing, there will be less need for taxpaying workers to make the goods, and so on.

This is where secured transactions come in. Secured transactions involve a debt to pay money that is made stronger by the debtor giving an interest in his or her property as a means of securing the promise of repayment. When all else fails and loans cannot be repaid, there is bankruptcy. **Bankruptcy** involves a debtor who cannot afford to repay his or her debts having those debts legally discharged by the court. Given this, you can see why we would discuss secured transactions and bankruptcy in the same chapter, as you can see how closely they can be linked.

Most of the credit you may be aware of is based on a simple contract with a debtor's promise to pay a debt owed to the creditor such as that involved in a credit card transaction. A **debtor** is one who owes a debt to a creditor. A **creditor** is the one who has given something of value to the debtor in exchange for a promise that the debtor will repay the creditor. However, sometimes those who extend credit wish to have something more than a mere promise to secure their interest in having the debt repaid. A promise may be fine, but some creditors want more assurance that the loan they have made to the debtor will be repaid.

This further assurance generally comes in the form of the creditor asking the debtor for **collateral** to secure repayment of the debt. Collateral is the debtor's property in which the debtor gives the creditor an interest, which ensures that if the debt is not repaid, the creditor will be able to take the property. This interest in the debtor's property must be given by the debtor to the creditor if the creditor is to be able to cash in on the property if the debtor **defaults** on the loan since without the debtor giving the creditor such an interest the creditor has no right to the debtor's property.

Notice that we said it gives the creditor an interest in the property. That is because most property used by debtors as collateral remains in the possession of the debtor. Not only do most creditors not have the space or wish to possess such property, but there may well be no need, since the creditor only needs the interest in the property if the debt is not repaid. Although we may have been going through tough financial times as a country lately, the reality is that most debtors repay their debts as agreed.

However, debts are often secured by collateral owned by the debtor. If a creditor has collateral, then if the debtor does not repay the loan, the creditor has some other means of receiving payment, usually by taking the collateral into his or her possession and selling it.

Yet the creditor receiving an interest in the debtor's collateral is not enough to fully protect the creditor. In order for a creditor to be able to secure her debt with that collateral, she must file a **financing statement** with the clerk of the local court giving notice to the public that the creditor has a security interest in the debtor's property so that if anything should happen and the debtor cannot pay, the creditor has put the public on notice that she has an interest in the collateral. This is called **perfecting** a security interest, and is discussed in more detail below. A creditor with a perfected security interest is called a **secured creditor.** Being a secured creditor gives creditors the most protection they can have in our system to ensure repayment of what is owed them.

If a business fails or an individual cannot pay her debts and has to file for bankruptcy protection, the creditors get in line for repayment of the business's or individual's debts. Secured creditors are paid before unsecured creditors. In other words, they are at the front of the line to get whatever collateral they have secured. An **unsecured creditor** is a creditor without a security interest in a debtor's property, such as a credit card company that has extended credit to the consumer. Unsecured creditors are paid after the secured creditors. Often, especially with consumer debtors, unsecured creditors will receive nothing in bankruptcy because nothing is left after the secured creditors take their collateral.

The link between debtors, secured creditors and bankruptcy will be further explored in this chapter.

Secured Transactions

L01

A **secured transaction** involves a debtor/creditor relationship and includes two elements: (1) a debt to pay money, and (2) an interest of the creditor in specific property that secures performance of the obligation. An obligation needs no security to exist; many debts are unsecured. For example, in the opening scenario, all of Olympia's credit card debts were unsecured. In many situations, however, an individual or business cannot obtain credit without giving security. It is totally up to the creditor and what terms the creditor is willing to use to extend credit to the debtor. This section covers those credit transactions in which the obligation is secured by personal property owned by the debtor and secured by the creditor.

Financing secured transactions is covered by Article 9 of the UCC. Article 9, which covers secured transactions in personal property only, is designed to provide a simple structure within which secured transactions can be accomplished with relative ease and certainty. Article 9 excludes security interests that arise as a matter of law, such as mechanic's liens (see below) and landlord's liens.[1]

L02

CREATING THE SECURITY INTEREST

In every consensual secured transaction there is a debtor, a secured party/creditor, collateral, a security agreement, and a security interest. A debtor is a person who owes payment or performance of an obligation. A **secured party** is the creditor/lender, seller, or other person who owns a security interest in the collateral. Collateral is the debtor's property subject to the security interest. **Security agreement** is the agreement that creates or provides for a **security interest** in debtor's property, which is generally defined as an interest in personal property that secures payment or performance of an obligation. Keep in mind that ownership of property is a cornerstone of our system of law. When one owns property, either personal or real property, part of the rights that go with it is that the property ownership is exclusive and no one has a right to the property except the owner. Even if a creditor is owed a debt, a creditor has no right to exercise

---

[1]A landlord's lien allows a landlord to sell abandoned personal property left on rented or leased premises by a former tenant to cover unpaid rent or damages to the property.

TAKE AWAY 9-1

SECURED TRANSACTION NECESSITIES

Debtor	Person who promises to pay a debt owed to the creditor
Creditor	Person or company that has given something of value in exchange for a promise that the debtor will repay the creditor
Collateral	Debtor's property in which the debtor gives an interest to the creditor as security for its debt
Secured Party	Creditor who owns a security interest in the collateral
Security Interest	Interest in the debtor's property placed as collateral for the debt that is enforceable against the debtor if he or she defaults on the debt
Security Agreement	The agreement that creates or provides for a security interest in the debtor's property

dominion and control over the debtor's property without the debtor's permission to do so. The security agreement is the debtor's consent to allow his or her exclusive possession of his or her property to be subjugated to the right of the creditor who has agreed to extend credit to the debtor using the property as collateral. For example, in the opening scenario, Olympia is the debtor, the finance company that financed her car is the creditor and the secured party, the car she is purchasing is also the collateral for the loan, and the financing agreement she signed which obligated her to pay for six years is the security agreement. The car is Olympia's, but the security agreement she signed gives the creditor the right to return of the car (repossession) if Olympia does not repay the car loan as agreed. A security interest in property cannot exist apart from the debt that it secures, and upon discharge of the debt in any manner, the security interest in the property is terminated. See Take Away 9-1, "Secured Transaction Necessities."

CLASSIFICATION OF COLLATERAL

L03

Not all property is the same under Article 9, and different types of property are handled in different ways to provide security interests in them and to perfect those security interests. Collateral that is covered under Article 9 can be classified as (1) goods, (2) collateral involving indispensable paper, and (3) intangibles.

Goods

Goods are tangible personal property that is movable at the time the security interest in them becomes enforceable. Goods are further divided into (1) consumer goods, (2) equipment, (3) farm products, (4) inventory, and (5) fixtures. At times, these definitions can overlap depending on how the property is being used. For example, the refrigerator purchased by a physician to store medicines in her office is classified as equipment, while a refrigerator used in the home of a consumer for household purposes is classified as a consumer good. If you look around your home, most of the furniture you see would be classified as goods; if you look around your classroom, most of the furniture you see is equipment. In the opening scenario, Olympia's appliances are household items that are considered goods.

Indispensable Paper

In business many transactions are evidenced only by the paper that describes or represents the transaction. Some of these transactions create paper that can be used in other transactions by the person holding that paper as collateral. This paper is generally labeled indispensable paper. **Indispensable paper** can be categorized as (1) chattel paper, (2) instruments, and (3) documents. **Chattel paper** is a writing or writings which evidence both a monetary obligation and a security interest in, or a lease of, specific goods when a creditor sells the security agreement of his debtor along with his interest in the collateral to a third party. If he does, the secured party's collateral is described as chattel paper.

For example, if Olympia's car dealer assigns his contract and financing agreement with Olympia to the bank to receive a line of credit to purchase new inventory, as between the bank and the car dealer the agreement would then be chattel paper. Or, suppose a farm equipment dealer sells a tractor to a farmer via a security agreement using the tractor as collateral. The dealer then uses this security agreement as collateral in a bank loan that he arranges for himself. The security agreement between the dealer and the farmer now becomes chattel paper. In this transaction between the dealer and the bank, the bank becomes the secured party and the dealer is the debtor. The dealer's debts owed to him, secured by the items purchased, are, in and of themselves, valuable interests that the dealer can use as collateral for a loan of his own.

The term **instrument** includes negotiable instruments, stocks, bonds, and other investment securities. It is any paper that evidences a right to payment of money that is not itself a security agreement. Negotiable instruments can be used as collateral. For example, suppose Olympia owned stock in a company. When her uncle loaned her money, he could have taken her stock as collateral for the loan. A **document** includes documents that are negotiable or nonnegotiable. For example, suppose a buyer has a receipt for goods that are being stored in a warehouse. He can use that receipt as collateral in another transaction.

Intangibles

Transactions that are not represented by a writing or other paper cannot be possessed; thus, the only way to use them as collateral is to file a security interest. The UCC recognizes two types of intangible collateral: (1) accounts and (2) general intangibles. The term **accounts** or **accounts receivable** refers to the right to payment for goods sold or leased or for services rendered which are not evidenced by chattel paper or an instrument. For instance, in our example above with the tractor dealer, if the dealer had not taken a security interest in the tractor he sold the farmer, the debt would simply be an account receivable. Since the dealer secured the credit sale to the farmer with a security interest in the tractor, the documents representing the transaction became chattel paper.

The term **general intangibles** applies to any personal property other than goods, accounts, chattel paper, documents, instruments, and money. This is used as a catch-all phase for interests not otherwise covered unless they are specifically excluded. It includes literary rights, rights to performance of a contract, patents, trademarks, and copyrights and gives flexibility to the UCC to allow for new kinds of collateral. For instance, if Britney Spears wrote a book and had the copyright to it, and was to receive royalties from sale of the book, both the royalties and the copyright are a type of property that she can use as security. For a real life version of how the intangible property can be used as collateral, see Reality Check 9-1, "Annie Leibowitz's Life in Pictures."

ATTACHMENT

A security interest is said to **attach** (1) once the secured party has given something of value, (2) the debtor has rights in the collateral, and (3) either the collateral is in the possession of the secured party or the security agreement is in a writing which contains a description of the collateral and is signed by the debtor. Notice the requirements are conjunctive and all three are necessary for the security interest to attach. For example, when the uncle took Olympia's art work in exchange for the $7,500 loan, his security interest in the art work attached because he gave Olympia the money, Olympia had a right to her art work, and she gave the art work to her uncle. Since the uncle was in possession of the art work, he did not need to have an agreement signed by Olympia describing the art work. Once a security interest attaches, it can be enforced against the debtor. Attachment is a prerequisite for a security interest to be perfected.

Perfection provides notice to the public of a security interest and therefore makes a security interest enforceable against third parties, including a bankruptcy trustee, other creditors, and transferees of the debtor. Thus, the difference between attachment and perfection lies in whom the interest can be enforced against. For attachment, the creditor can enforce the security interest against the debtor; for perfection, the creditor can enforce the security interest against third parties. This becomes very important if the debtor wants to, or does, enter into more than one security interest in a particular property. Keep in mind that the creditor wants to have as much protection as possible if the debt is not repaid. If the debtor does not repay the loan to the creditor and the creditor attempts to exercise her security interest in the collateral, only to find that the debtor has used the property as collateral for a loan from another creditor, the first creditor's position is threatened and she may now have to engage in litigation to determine who has superior rights (called priority, and discussed later) in the collateral.

REALITY CHECK 9-1

ANNIE LEIBOWITZ'S LIFE IN PICTURES

In early 2009 the world was shocked to learn that the most famous photographer of the 21st century was forced to sign away the copyrights, negatives, and contracts to all her work done in the past and in the future in exchange for $15.5 million in an attempt to stave off bankruptcy. Photographer to the stars, as well as to most of the notable politicians since the 1960s, Leibowitz was about to lose it all before making a deal in which she used her life's work as collateral for a $15.5 million loan. She has to continue working to pay off the $15.5 million in order to regain her property rights in her photographs. Perhaps best known for her 1981 *Rolling Stone* cover of a naked John Lennon wrapped around Yoko Ono, which she shot on the last day of John Lennon's life, Leibowitz is also known for her more recent covers on *Vanity Fair* magazine. She made headlines with her *Vanity Fair* cover showing a very pregnant and naked Demi Moore in 1991, Tom Cruise and Katie Holmes with their son Sun Cruise in 2006, and Tina Fey sporting the American flag in 2009. She also made news when her provocative pictures of then 15-year-old Miley Cyrus, a Disney pop star and actress and idol to many young girls, appeared in the same magazine in 2008. In the most controversial pose, Miley was photographed wrapped only in a sheet.

Source: Jason Cochran, "Photographer Annie Leibowitz, Overexposed, Is Forced to Sell Her Life's Work," February 25, 2009, http://www.walletpop.com/blog/2009/02/25/photographer-annie-leibovitz-overexposed-is-forced-to-sell-her/.

PERFECTING A SECURITY INTEREST

Why perfect a security interest? Perfection assures priority over other third parties. That is its biggest impact. **Perfection** means that the security interest will generally be valid for the creditor in the event of a debtor's bankruptcy. A security interest is perfected when it has attached and when all the applicable steps required for perfection have been taken. A security interest may be perfected:

1. By filing a financing statement signed by the debtor,
2. By the secured party's taking or retaining possession of the collateral, or
3. Automatically upon the attachment of the security interest.

In order to receive as much protection as the law allows, creditors not only must perfect their interest but must first search for interests which others have perfected in

EXAMPLE

the collateral before they commit their own funds to a debtor. For example, Remi approaches First National Bank seeking a loan and offering as collateral an interest she has in a piece of real estate she owns. First National Bank would investigate Remi's credit history and the proper records to see if Remi has used the real estate to secure any other loans she may have received earlier. Creditors are often assisted in perfecting and searching by companies with specialized knowledge of state or local filing requirements that can uncover earlier perfections on collateral.

FILING A FINANCING STATEMENT

EXAMPLE

In order to properly file a financing statement to perfect a security interest, the UCC in the state in which the property lies must be consulted. Rather than have one rule that governs nationwide, the UCC provides alternative methods for filing a **financing statement** depending on the type of collateral filed against. For example, in some states, if the collateral is minerals, timber, or fixtures, the proper place to file is usually with the county in which the property is located. In other states, local filing is required for fixtures, farm products, consumer goods, timber, minerals, and farming equipment. Other states require a creditor to file locally and with the Secretary of State. Consultation with the state rules is required to make sure the creditor has perfected his or her financing statement in accord with the applicable laws so that there is maximum protection of the creditor's interest.

FAILURE TO PERFECT A SECURITY INTEREST

The test for a security interest under Article 9 is whether it can withstand an attack by a third party, especially a bankruptcy trustee. A lender who fails to perfect his or her security interest faces certain defeat by the **avoidance powers** of the bankruptcy trustee. Avoidance powers are an arsenal of ways bankruptcy trustees have to avoid recognizing financing agreements that the trustee must recognize and pay out of the bankrupt's estate; they use them whenever possible. It is critical to understand how avoidance powers work, what is necessary to perfect a security interest, and how these two areas intersect. Only by understanding the relationship can secured creditors be fully protected.

If a creditor has failed to file the financing statement properly the filing is ineffective, unless the mistake was made in good faith or the person against whom the statement is filed has knowledge that the collateral is covered by the financing statement.

Have a look now at Reality Check 9-2. In thinking about Reality Check 9-2, "What's in a Name?" you can see how important it is to perfect correctly.

Given what you know now, from having read Reality Check 9-2, what would be the purpose of filing a financing statement under a name different from a legal name? Should the rule under the revised Article 9 allow for any variation? See one answer to this question in the *Kinderknecht* case (Case 9.1).

While filing is the usual way a security interest is perfected, in some situations a security

REALITY CHECK 9-2

WHAT'S IN A NAME?

The debtor's name has always been the most crucial item on the financing statement because under the UCC statements are indexed by the debtor's name and third parties search with reference to potential debtors' names. What happens if a financing statement was filed under an incorrect name and the searcher did not find the statement? Under an earlier version of Article 9, most courts held that the filing was ineffective if the searcher should have found it under the wrong name. Under the revised Article 9 rules, and as computerized filing becomes more prevalent, secured parties must work harder to file the financing statement under the correct name if they wish to perfect their security interest.

For a corporate debtor, the name shown on the Articles of Incorporation will be the correct name. Thus, for corporations if there is any discrepancy between the name as shown in the organizational records and the name as shown on the financing statement, and a search does not produce the filing, then the financing statement is ineffective and the security interest is not perfected.

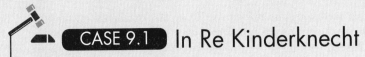

CASE 9.1 In Re Kinderknecht

308 BR 71 (10th Cir. BAP 2004)

Facts: Terry Kinderknecht ran a Kansas farming operation as a sole proprietorship. His legal name was Terrance Joseph Kinderknecht, but he was informally known as Terry. When he borrowed money from John Deere Credit Services to buy two new pieces of farm equipment, Deere filed its financing statement using the name Terry J. Kinderknecht in designating the debtor. When Kinderknecht filed Chapter 7 bankruptcy, the trustee brought an adversary proceeding to avoid Deere's security interest on the ground that the debtor's name used by Deere in the financing statement was seriously misleading and thus invalid. Deere countered that the use of a nickname was proper under Article 9 as long as it was an individual. The bankruptcy court concluded that Deere's financing statement was sufficient to perfect its interests. The trustee appealed.

Issue: Whether the bankruptcy court was correct in finding that the secured creditor's interest in the debtor's property was perfected under Kansas law even though the name on the filing was the debtor's nickname rather than his legal name?

Decision: No. The bankruptcy court was incorrect in finding that the financing statement was perfected. Under Kansas law, the secured creditor must list an individual debtor by his or her legal name, not a nickname.

Reasoning: Section 84-9-502(a) of the Kansas Statutes Annotated states that "a financing statement is sufficient only if it: (1) Provides the name of the debtor[.]" This requirement is to facilitate "a system of notice filing" under which multiple security interest documents need not be filed, but rather only a single document notifying parties in interest that a creditor may have an interest in certain property owned by the named debtor. Because notice of a secured interest in property is accomplished by searching the debtor's name, "[t]he requirement that a financing statement provide the debtor's name is particularly important." Accordingly, pursuant to §84-9-506(b), if a financing statement "fails sufficiently to provide the name of the debtor" it is "seriously misleading."

Although §84-9-503 specifically sets parameters for listing a debtor's name in a financing statement when the debtor is an entity, it does not provide any detail as to the name that must be provided for an individual debtor—it simply states that the "name of the debtor" should be used. This could be construed, as it was by

the bankruptcy court, as allowing a debtor to be listed in a financing statement by his or her commonly used nickname. But, we do not agree with that interpretation because the purpose of §84-9-503, as well as a reading of that section as a whole, leads us to conclude that an individual debtor's legal name must be used in the financing statement to make it sufficient under §84-9-502(a)(1).

Our conclusion that a legal name is necessary to sufficiently provide the name of an individual debtor within the meaning of §84-9-503(a) is also supported by four practical considerations. First, mandating the debtor's legal name sets a clear test so as to simplify the drafting of financing statements. Second, setting a clear test simplifies the parameters of UCC searches. Persons searching UCC filings will know that they need the debtor's legal name to conduct a search; they will not be penalized if they do not know that a debtor has a nickname, and they will not have to guess any number of nicknames that could exist to conduct a search. Third, requiring the debtor's legal name will avoid litigation as to the commonality or appropriateness of a debtor's nickname, and as to whether a reasonable searcher would have or should have known to use the name. Finally, obtaining a debtor's legal name is not difficult or burdensome for the creditor taking a secured interest in a debtor's property. Indeed, knowing the individual's legal name will assure the accuracy of any search that creditor conducts prior to taking its secured interest in property.

CASE QUESTIONS

1. The court clearly opted in favor of a bright line rule. How was this policy articulated by the court?

2. Does this decision seem fair? Ethical? What burden does this place on the creditor that was not there before? What about those whose ethics are not what they should be? Would the lower court's decision give them a way to avoid being found by allowing any name they wished to provide?

3. The federal law has requirements similar to the old Article 9 requirements. Would it be better if states were to unify their filing requirements to meet the federal standard? Does it create less certainty to have different filing rules for each location?

interest is automatically perfected upon attachment. Recall that attachment occurs when the creditor gives value to the debtor, the debtor has rights in the collateral, and the collateral is either in the creditor's possession or the creditor has a security agreement signed by the debtor. This is important to know because the filing requirement is then not an issue if the security interest is automatically perfected. This also means that since perfection notifies third parties, third parties may be put at a disadvantage if no filing is required in order to perfect. The two most important situations in which **automatic perfection** applies are (1) purchase money security interests (PMSI) in consumer goods and (2) temporary perfection with respect to instruments, documents, and proceeds.

PURCHASE MONEY SECURITY INTEREST

A seller of goods who provides the purchase price to the buyer retains a security interest in the goods by a security agreement and has a perfected interest without doing anything more such as filing a security agreement. No filing or other step is required to perfect a **purchase money security interest (PMSI)** in consumer goods. A consumer good is defined as goods that are used or bought for use primarily for personal, family, or household purposes. For example, in the chapter's opening scenario, Olympia's purchase of her appliances, and probably her automobile, were consumer goods. If the store where she purchased the goods loaned her the money to make the purchase, then the store's security interest attaches and is automatically perfected. The rationale for this exception is to allow a creditor who extended the money to purchase the collateral to keep an interest in the collateral and disallow other creditors from gaining a priority interest in it greater than that of the creditor whose money bought the collateral.

Although PMSI perfection is automatic, ancillary filings, for example, a motor vehicle that must be filed with the state to obtain a title, can also be challenged by the bankruptcy trustee. Attention should be paid to the requirements for these ancillary filings, lest the bankruptcy trustee try to avoid the PMSI's automatic perfection ensuring that the creditor has priority in the goods, and instead try to avoid the creditor's interest and include the collateral in the bankrupt's estate for potential liquidation to pay creditors as in the case of *Laursen*. Contrast the court's decision in the *Laursen* case (Case 9.2) with the decision in *Kinderknecht* (Case 9.1) and answer the questions below.

A security interest in negotiable instruments is automatically perfected upon attachment for 21 days without filing or taking possession. However, if the instruments are

---

CASE 9.2 In Re Laursen

391 BR 47 (Bankr. D. Ida. 2008)

Facts: Whitney Laursen purchased an automobile from a General Motors dealer. Laursen financed the purchase by signing a six-year retail instrument with the dealer, who then assigned the contract to GMAC. Under the contract, Laursen granted the dealer a purchase money security interest in the automobile. Shortly thereafter, the dealer applied for a certificate of title from Idaho's Department of Transportation (IDOT). In the application, the dealer made a one-character typo in Laursen's first name—Whitnet instead of Whitney. When the IDOT issued the certificate, it carried through the typo. When Laursen subsequently filed for Chapter 7 bankruptcy, the trustee challenged GMAC's security interest based on an analogy to Article 9 rules and a recent Idaho case that found a one-character typo to invalidate a security interest under Article 9—Andrew Fuel rather than Andrew Fuell. That decision was based on a finding by the court that the Idaho search logic for searching names had failed to produce Andrew Fuell's name when it was entered Andrew Fuel. The trustee in Laursen's case argued that the Article 9 rules should be applied by analogy because the trustee conducted a search under the name Whitnet Laursen and came up empty; therefore, the security interest should not apply and the car should be included in the estate rather than go to the creditor because it did not appear to be a perfected security interest since it did not appear to be filed.

Issue: Whether the Article 9 standard for perfecting a security interest should be used for perfecting a purchase money security interest in an automobile when the automobile's ancillary Department of Transportation filing is by the vehicle's VIN number rather than name?

Decision: No.

Reasoning: Under Idaho law, security interests in vehicles may be perfected only by complying with the state's certificate of title laws. Section 49-504, in turn, requires persons applying for a certificate of title to complete the form furnished by IDOT, and to supply "a full description of the vehicle" including the make, identification numbers and odometer reading, as well as "a statement of the applicant's title and of any liens or encumbrances upon the vehicle, and the name and address of the person to whom the certificate of title shall be delivered[.]" Upon receiving a completed application, IDOT's first duty is to check the vehicle's identification number (its "VIN") against the VIN index the department is required to maintain. Then, if satisfied that the application is in proper form, IDOT must issue a certificate of title "in the name of the owner of the vehicle[.]"

The Trustee, however, contends that authorities regarding Uniform Commercial Code (UCC) financing statements are applicable by analogy. Recently, several courts have held that errors in UCC financing statements—even seemingly minor ones—can be fatal. For example, creditors who listed a debtor's first name as Roger instead of Rodger (or Mike instead of Michael or Terry instead of Terrance) in the financing statement failed to properly perfect their security interests.

Recently this Court held that a creditor failed to properly perfect its security interest because it used the name Andrew Fuel, rather than the correct name, Andrew Fuell, in a financing statement. The harsh results in these cases were justified, however, because third parties searching for existing security interests in goods look in the appropriate secretary of state's database for UCC-1 financing statements. Further, these databases must be indexed by the debtor's name. Thus, in order to accurately and reliably notify third parties of existing security interests in goods, it is crucial the debtor's name is correctly and exactly listed on the financing statement. In fact, the form financing statement supplied in Idaho's UCC instructs the preparer to provide the "DEBTOR'S EXACT FULL LEGAL NAME." There is no equivalent instruction in IDOT's application for a certificate of title. Idaho's certificate of title laws requires IDOT to index motor vehicles by VIN—not by name.

The UCC's filing system is fundamentally different from IDOT's: accuracy of names is paramount in the UCC filing system, while accuracy of numbers (the VIN) is critical in Idaho's motor-vehicle filing system. Thus, under Idaho's motor vehicle code, third parties who want to buy a car or take a security interest in one will either examine the certificate of title in the owner's possession, and see any existing liens, or search IDOT's records. The fact that IDOT's records can be searched by name does not alter the fact that its *required* indexing protocol is by VIN. For example, assume a creditor wished to obtain a lien in a debtor's vehicle. Performing an IDOT name search (as the Trustee did in this case) and finding no vehicles listed under the debtor's name would not allow this third party creditor to believe it could safely obtain a first priority position in the debtor's vehicle, as it would if performing the same search under the UCC. Instead, it would alert the creditor that the debtor may not have an ownership interest in the vehicle. Upon further investigation, searching by the VIN, the creditor could substantiate ownership or lack thereof.

CASE QUESTIONS

1. It was the state's different filing system that allowed the court to reach a conclusion in this case that was different from the decision reached in *Kinderknecht*. Does the court's conclusion make sense in this case?

2. The court could have required a stricter standard for PMSI filings analogous to the Article 9 standards. What was the court's primary reason for rejecting that standard here?

3. Would a one-character error in the VIN number but a correct filing of the name have rendered the same result? Does it seem ethical for a creditor to lose his or her secured status because of such a minor difference in spelling? What are the pros and cons? Who are the stakeholders and what do they have to gain or lose? Does it matter that they can lose their secured status through no fault of their own, but instead a clerical error over which they had no control? What about the sheer numbers of potential errors when a business like GMAC, which finances millions of cars, has the potential for such losses? What about the impact of our country becoming more diverse with many new names from other countries with spellings that are so easily entered incorrectly?

negotiated to a holder in due course during that period, the holder in due course will take priority over the original secured party.

Priorities

The whole purpose of a security interest is to make sure the creditor has the most protection possible if the debtor does not repay the loan the creditor extended. As we have seen this is accomplished by the creditor taking a security interest in collateral owned by the debtor. Further, this security interest, in order to be protected, must be perfected by filing or possession.

However, perfection of a security interest may not be the end of the secured creditor's concerns about the property. What if the debtor has given other creditors a security interest in the same collateral? What if the second creditor perfected before the first? Perfection itself does not provide the secured party with a priority over other third parties with an interest in the same collateral. When more than one party has an interest in the same collateral, Article 9 establishes a set of rules that determines the relative priorities among these parties. A creditor with a perfected security interest has greater rights in the collateral than a creditor with an unperfected security interest, but when there is more than one creditor with a perfected security interest, Article 9's priority provisions come into play.

In order for credit to be extended to a debtor using a security interest in collateral, the creditor wants to be sure that if the debtor becomes bankrupt the creditor will be able to shield the collateral from the reach of the debtor's other creditors or from disposal by the debtor. That is what **priority** is all about; a creditor seeks to be first in line to reclaim her collateral when the debtor defaults on a security agreement.

There is a set of general rules that can be applied. Generally, where there is more than one secured creditor, victory goes to the first creditor to file or otherwise perfect (keep in mind that perfection can also be accomplished by the creditor taking possession of the collateral). In a sense, this rule creates a race to the proper filing office.

However, the reality is that there are so many exceptions to this general rule that the rule is practically swallowed up by the exceptions, and the exceptions are too numerous and complicated to include here. To be certain, Article 9 should be consulted for the rules and exceptions concerning how priorities are established and enforced in your jurisdiction. For our general purposes however, the first secured party to file or otherwise perfect has priority. For instance, Jose extends a loan to Giancarlo, taking an interest in Giancarlo's coin collection as collateral. Unknown to Jose, Giancarlo then receives a loan from Xavier using the same coin collection as collateral. Xavier files immediately, but Jose files later than Xavier. When Giancarlo defaults on both loans, Xavier will have priority in the collateral because he was the first to file to perfect his interest. If Jose had taken the coin collection into his possession when extending the loan, or had filed his security interest before Xavier, the loan would have been perfected and Jose would not only have been the first to receive a security interest in the coin collection, but also would have been the first to perfect and would therefore have priority over Xavier.

EXAMPLE

Miscellaneous Liens

A lien is created by state statute for the purpose of securing priority of payment of the price or value of work performed and materials furnished in enhancing the value of property. There are many liens that can be secured for many reasons. For example, a **mechanic's lien** (sometimes referred to as an **artisan's lien**) is the right given to a skilled person to retain possession of an item, produced with his or her labor and materials, until paid. The lien gives the repairer the right to continue to hold on to the goods

EXAMPLE

that were worked on or materials that were supplied until the customer pays them. If the customer does not pay for the work, the repairer can sell the property to fulfill payment of the debt. Prior to the sale, the repairer must give the debtor notice and an opportunity to pay for the item. When you take your clothes to the cleaners or your car to a mechanic or your computer to the computer technician for repair, you are, by virtue of the transaction, giving them a mechanic's lien on your property. Fail to pay and they can sell the item and thereby obtain the amount you owe them for repairing your property.

A lien can be created by the state for almost any service or performance. For example, there are liens for labor for raising crops, labor on vessels, labor on logs or timber, furnishing material for vessels, professional services for veterinarians, and liens for towing and storing vehicles. Such liens cover suppliers of material, tradespeople, suppliers, laborers, and others who furnish services or labor or materials on construction or improvement of property.

The important thing to remember about a lien is that the lien holder has priority over all other creditors. That means that if you had given a creditor a security interest in your computer, and you later took your computer to a computer technician for repairs and did not pay your computer repair bill, and also did not pay the creditor for the computer, the repairer's lien on your computer would have priority over the creditor's security interest in the computer as collateral.

Surety

As you may well know if you tried to buy a car or rent an apartment on your own as a young adult, it is common in many business transactions involving the extension of credit for the creditor to require that someone in addition to the debtor promise to fulfill the obligation. This promisor generally is known as a **surety.**[2] For example, Charlie Brown wanted to borrow $10,000 from Peanuts National Bank, but the bank would not loan Charlie any money unless his note was backed by four responsible people. Charlie then asked Lucy, Schroeder, Pig Pen, and Peppermint Patty to agree to be his sureties, which they all did. The bank loaned Charlie the money. When the money becomes due, if Charlie cannot pay, the bank will look to his sureties to pay his debt. You usually know the person who signs for another as a co-signor. You may have been required to have your parents' signature before you were able to purchase your car, rent your apartment, or obtain a credit card.

Sureties are also frequently utilized by employers to protect against losses caused by **defalcations** (breaches of trust, such as embezzlement) by employees, as well as in construction contracts for commercial buildings to bond the performance of the contract. Similarly, it is common practice to require contracts for work to be done for government entities to have the added protection of a surety.

NATURE AND FORMATION

A surety promises to answer for the payment of a debt or the performance of a duty owed to the creditor by the debtor upon the failure of the debtor to make payment or otherwise perform the obligation.

The creditor's rights against the debtor are determined by the contract between them. The creditor may seize any collateral securing the debtor's performance that the debtor or the surety holds. In addition, the creditor may proceed against the surety if the debtor defaults. If the surety is an **absolute surety,** then the creditor may hold the surety liable

---

[2]Technically, under the common law there is a difference between a surety and a guarantor. A surety is bound on the same instrument as the principal debtor, whereas a guarantor is bound by a separate or collateral writing. However, for convenience, we will apply surety to mean both. Under the UCC, Article 3, a guarantor is a surety who adds words of guaranty to his or her signature, but these words add nothing to the suretyship obligation.

as soon as the debtor defaults. The creditor need not first proceed against the debtor. However, if the surety is a **surety for collection** only, then before the creditor can collect from the surety, the creditor must exhaust all other legal remedies to collect from the debtor. Thus, a surety for collection is only liable if the creditor first obtains a judgment against the debtor and is unable to collect under the judgment.

Now you can see why anyone who is asked to co-sign for someone should think about it hard and long. The surety gets nothing out of the process and has total responsibility for the debtor's liability. Even with the best of intentions, something may go wrong and the surety winds up being responsible for paying a debt the surety never thought he or she would have to pay. Can you imagine how frustrating that would be? Paying for a car that does not belong to you? Can you imagine all the broken friendships that have occurred over the years as co-signers who just lent their signature to be a good friend, but never thought they would have to pay on a debt, have been required to do so because their friend or family member fell on hard times, lost their job, was downsized, or otherwise was adversely impacted by the floundering economy? Now, you can see why your parents did not jump at the chance to co-sign for you but instead probably had to be convinced—big time. When someone asks you to co-sign a loan for them, it is not just a signature. Think about whether you want to retain the friendship or your money, because many times you will not be able to do both.

Upon the debtor's default, the surety has a number of rights against the debtor, third parties, and co-sureties. These rights include (1) exoneration, (2) reimbursement, (3) subrogation, and (4) contribution.

EXONERATION

It is expected that the debtor will perform the obligation and the surety will not be required to perform. The right of **exoneration** allows the surety to obtain a court decree ordering the debtor to pay the creditor. The surety's remedy of exoneration is against the debtor and in no way affects the creditor's right to proceed against the surety. For example, in the Charlie Brown hypothetical above, once the note becomes due, all or any of the sureties can seek an order from the court ordering Charlie to pay. Doing so, however, does not release them from their surety responsibility to the creditor.

REIMBURSEMENT

When a surety pays the creditor upon the default of the debtor, the surety has the right of **reimbursement** against the debtor. The surety, however, has no right to reimbursement until he actually pays the creditor and then only to the extent of the payment made.

Thus, a surety who makes an advantageous negotiation of a defaulted obligation with the creditor and settles the debt at a compromise figure less than the original amount owed by the debtor may not recover from the debtor any more than the surety actually paid. In the hypothetical involving Charlie Brown, if Charlie fails to pay his loan and Peppermint Patty pays the full amount, she may sue Charlie Brown to reimburse her for the full amount she paid. If she succeeds, Charlie will have to pay Peppermint Patty the amount she paid the bank. If, however, Peppermint Patty is able to negotiate with the bank to pay less in full satisfaction of the debt, Peppermint Patty would be able to collect from Charlie Brown only the amount she paid the bank, not the full amount of the debt she co-signed.

SUBROGATION

If the surety is forced to pay off the creditor, the surety is subrogated to whatever rights the creditor had. Put another way, the surety steps into the shoes of the creditor. This becomes important if the creditor is holding collateral of the debtor, because now that collateral will go to the surety once the surety pays the debtor's obligation. This is called **subrogation** and confers upon the surety all the rights the creditor has against the debtor. In the Charlie Brown example, if the bank had required Charlie to place the title to Charlie's car with the bank as collateral to secure the loan, the title to the car would transfer to Peppermint Patty once she paid off the debt to the bank, because the creditor's right to that title would be subrogated to Patty.

EXAMPLE

CONTRIBUTION

When there is more than one surety, the co-sureties are jointly and severally liable for the debtor's default, up to the amount of each surety's undertaking. The creditor may proceed against any or all of the co-sureties and collect the entire amount the surety has agreed to guarantee. Joint and several liability means that each of the sureties is responsible for the entire amount or for their share of the amount. The creditor can go against any or all of the sureties, but only collect a total of the entire amount, not the entire amount from each surety. As a result, it is possible that one co-surety may pay the creditor the entire amount of the principal debtor's obligation.

When a surety pays a debtor's obligation, the surety is entitled to have the co-sureties pay to the surety their proportionate share of the obligation the surety paid to the creditor. This right of **contribution** arises when a surety has paid more than her share of the debt. For example, if Charlie had defaulted on his loan, and the bank sued Peppermint Patty for the full amount, which the bank is entitled to do since the sureties are jointly and severally liable, and Peppermint Patty paid off the entire loan, Peppermint Patty would have the right to seek a proportionate share of the loan from her co-sureties, Schroeder, Lucy, and Pig Pen. Under the theory of contribution, they would have to pay her $2,500 each ($10,000 divided by the 4 sureties).

EXAMPLE

For a review of our discussion of surety so far, see Take Away 9-2, "Suretyships."

TAKE AWAY 9-2

SURETYSHIPS

Surety	Person or company other than debtor that agrees to assume liability on the debt in case the debtor defaults
Exoneration	Court decree that orders the debtor to pay the creditor, thereby releasing the surety of its obligation to pay
Reimbursement	Right given to a surety that pays the debt for the debtor allowing the surety to collect from the debtor
Subrogation	Rights given to surety which enables the surety to step into the shoes of the creditor to collect against the debtor
Contribution	Rights given to surety who pays creditor to collect pro rata share from other sureties on the debt

DEFENSES OF THE DEBTOR AND SURETY

If a debtor lacks capacity to contract, then he may disaffirm the contract. However, if the consideration is not returned by the debtor, the debtor's infancy may not be used by the surety as a defense—the surety will still owe the creditor. Likewise, if the debtor declares bankruptcy, it does not discharge the surety's liability to the creditor.

The surety may use her own defense of incapacity to disaffirm her suretyship. As with any other contract, the surety may use the defense of a violation of the Statute of Frauds, duress, or fraud as discussed in the contracts chapters. If a co-signer is intended and has agreed to be a surety but does not sign the contract, the suretyship agreement cannot be enforced against the surety.

If the creditor who is holding collateral as security impairs the value of the collateral, the surety is discharged to the extent of the decrease in value. Lastly, if the debtor performs, both the debtor and surety are discharged from the obligation.

All in all, secured transactions are an important part of making sure that creditors who extend credit to debtors have some means of obtaining repayment if the creditor defaults. Whether that means is through the debtor giving the creditor an interest in property used as collateral, or through the debtor having someone co-sign his or her loan, if done correctly, these vehicles extend the most protection our system provides to creditors for loan reimbursement.

DISTINCTION BETWEEN SURETY AND GUARANTOR

Although a surety and a guarantor are both parties who make an agreement to bind themselves for the act of another, a surety makes a promise on the original agreement, becoming a party to that agreement. Therefore, a surety is obligated to pay the debt as soon as it becomes due and the debtor does not pay. Nothing further need occur to obligate the surety.

A **guarantor,** on the other hand, usually does not become a part of the original agreement. A guarantor usually enters into a separate contract which binds him to the first contract, and which requires a separate consideration to be given to the guarantor in exchange for his agreement to be bound. Thus, a guarantor does not become obligated unless the debtor does not pay, but the creditor must first try to collect from the debtor before the guarantor becomes obligated on the debt.

EXAMPLE

For example, Ishaq is a businessman who seeks capital to purchase goods from Sam Seller, and needs a loan to do so. He cannot obtain a loan on his own because he does not have a sufficient credit history, so the bank tells Ishaq that he will need a co-signer, or surety, if he is to obtain a loan. Ishaq convinces Joaquin to co-sign the note, making Joaquin a surety on the note. Both Ishaq and Joaquin are liable on the note simultaneously.

But suppose Ishaq would like to obtain those goods from Sam Seller, but Joaquin does not wish to become liable on a note with Ishaq to the bank? Joaquin could also enter into a contract with Sam Seller in which he guarantees that if Ishaq does not pay for the goods, Joaquin will pay for them. In most states, Sam Seller will have to sue Ishaq, or show that a suit would not be fruitful, before Sam can collect from Joaquin.

EXAMPLE

There are different kinds of guaranties. The most common are an **absolute guaranty** and a **guaranty for collection** only. An absolute guaranty puts the guarantor in the same position as a surety, i.e., he is guaranteeing payment, and the creditor can look to the guarantor immediately as if he was a surety. A guaranty for collection only requires the creditor to take extra steps before he can collect from the guarantor. The guaranty described between Ishaq and Joaquin above is a guaranty for collection only, meaning that the creditor would have to perform due diligence before he can collect from Joaquin, including but not limited to suing Ishaq.

Guaranty and surety create essentially the same relationships, that is, the obligation of one person to answer for the debts of another. Neither relationship should be entered into without a full understanding of those obligations.

Bankruptcy

Financial ruin is a reality in today's market. Despite good intentions and maximum effort by business owners, not all businesses are successful. When a business fails or individuals become mired in debt, businesses and individuals have the choice to take advantage of the bankruptcy codes that give them the opportunity to either have their debts completely discharged, or allow them an opportunity to be protected from creditors while they reorganize their debts so that the business can be maintained and creditors can be paid off over time.

Providing this opportunity for relief was so important that the Founding Fathers not only included bankruptcy in the U.S. Constitution, but did so in its first article, authorizing Congress to legislate in this area (Article 1, Section 8, Clause 4). In 1934,[3] the U.S. Supreme Court recognized that a fundamental goal of the federal bankruptcy laws enacted by Congress is to give debtors a financial "fresh start" from burdensome debts. This goal is accomplished through the bankruptcy **discharge,** which releases individual and business debtors from personal liability from specific debts and prohibits creditors from ever taking any action against the debtor to collect those debts. When you realize what a difference 40 days in bankruptcy made for General Motors from June 1 to July 10, 2009,[4] you realize how important such a **fresh start** can be. Take Away 9-3, "Bankruptcy Roots," gives you an interesting, comical flavor for how far we have come in handling businesses that cannot pay their debts.

THE BANKRUPTCY PROCESS

L06

Article I, Section 8, of the U.S. Constitution authorizes Congress to enact uniform laws on the subject of bankruptcies. Congress enacted the present-day **Bankruptcy Code** in 1978 (the Code) and has amended it several times, the latest major amendment occurring in 2005. While states may have their own bankruptcy provisions, it is the uniform federal law that governs all bankruptcy cases.

Accompanying the Code are the Federal Rules of Bankruptcy Procedure (the Rules), which, much like the civil and criminal rules we discussed in the court chapter, are the rules that must be followed to successfully proceed through a bankruptcy in federal court. In addition, there are local rules that courts within each district follow in bankruptcy cases. Used together, the Code, the Rules, and local rules govern filing a petition for bankruptcy for individuals and businesses. The Code has recently undergone major changes and in the financial situation the United States has found itself in in the last few years, more have been contemplated (see Reality Check 9-3, "What Is a 'Cramdown' and How Can It Hurt You?").

TAKE AWAY 9-3

BANKRUPTCY ROOTS

The term *bankruptcy* is derived from the Italian term "banca roota," or broken table, which referred to a medieval practice of breaking the money table of a tradesman who failed to pay his debts.

Source: Stephanie Wickouski, *Bankruptcy Crimes,* 3rd ed. (Beard Books, 2007), p. 5.

---

[3]*Local Loan Co. v. Hunt,* 292 U.S. 234, 244 (1934).

[4]John D. Stoll and Sharon Terlep, "GM Takes New Direction: Car maker Leaves Bankruptcy, Will Slim Down, Court Consumers," *The Wall Street Journal,* July 11, 2009. http://online.wsj.com/article/SB124722154897622577.html.

WHAT IS A "CRAMDOWN" AND HOW CAN IT HURT YOU?

A "cramdown" is where the value of a home has fallen below the mortgage's outstanding balance. The cramdown occurs when a bankruptcy judge would be allowed to reduce the principal of the loan. The idea is, in effect, to bail out those homeowners who paid a small deposit on a huge mortgage only to have their property foreclosed upon at the worst possible time. That was when the housing market as a whole collapsed because there were so many subprime mortgages created thus putting so many people into bankruptcy.

And just how can it hurt others? The answer is in who ultimately pays for it—taxpayers. Taxpayers would pay by helping to subsidize the loans initially. They would pay again when they needed a mortgage and had to pay higher interest rates because of the increased risk that they would ultimately go bankrupt. Next, they would have to pay a third time when they were asked to bail out banks who had too many of their loans crammed down.

Does this sound like a fair system? It does for some members of Congress. However, their constituents have made their opposition heard and the bill that would allow cramdowns has failed to get the Senate vote necessary to pass.

Source: Megan McArdle, "Sink and Swim," *The Atlantic*, June 2009, pp. 30–32.

Each judicial district in the U.S. has a **bankruptcy court.** Some states have more than one, totaling 90 throughout the country. Presiding over each bankruptcy is the **bankruptcy judge,** who is a judicial officer of the court. The judge decides all matters of the case, including whether an individual or business qualifies to use bankruptcy to discharge their debts. Accompanying the judge is the **trustee** in bankruptcy. The trustee is actually the person most likely to be involved with the individual who files for bankruptcy (see Reality Check 9-4, "Whom Does the Bankruptcy Trustee Represent?"). Unless there is a dispute, many cases are resolved without an appearance in court before the judge.

A debtor usually meets with his or her creditors in a "341" meeting, so named because of the section of the bankruptcy code which requires such a meeting. The debtor must attend this meeting run by the bankruptcy trustee, and the creditors may question debtor about property owned which may be used to satisfy the debts. If the debts are not resolved at the **"341" meeting,** the trustee will have the case set before the bankruptcy judge for litigation.

WHOM DOES THE BANKRUPTCY TRUSTEE REPRESENT?

A trustee in a bankruptcy proceeding represents the property of the bankruptcy estate. A bankruptcy estate consists of all property owned by debtors on the filing date of the petition and all property acquired by debtors within one year of filing bankruptcy. The trustee's job is to preside at the "341" meeting of the creditors and the debtor.

Most trustees that preside over Chapter 7 and 13 proceedings are private individuals, not federal employees. They are supervised by **U.S. Trustees** who are appointed by the U.S. Trustee Program, a component of the U.S. Department of Justice. The Program "monitors the conduct of bankruptcy trustees, oversees related administrative functions, and acts to ensure compliance with applicable laws and procedures."

Generally, a bankruptcy trustee goes unnoticed. However, that has not been the case for the trustee appointed to handle the Bernie Madoff estate liquidation. He has drawn the ire of Madoff's victims by valuing the amount of their loss based on the amount they actually invested. The victims want the value of their loss to be determined by what the Madoff firm showed they made on their investment. In addition, the trustee has charged $37 million in 2009 for handling the bankruptcy. That, too, has upset the victims.

That could be just the tip of the iceberg for some of Madoff's investors. The bankruptcy trustee filed a "clawback" suit against one investor. A clawback suit seeks the return of money an investor may have withdrawn from his investment account within a certain time frame. Vizcaya Partners withdrew $150 million of its $327 million investment just six weeks before Madoff confessed to his Ponzi scheme. The U.S. bankruptcy code allows the trustee to sue investors for any fictional profits plus the investment that they withdrew anytime in the past six years. There may be more angry investors before the bankruptcy trustee is finished.

Sources: U.S. Trustee Program, http://www.usdoj.gov/ust/eo/ust_org/about_ustp. htm; Alison Gendar, "Victims of Ponzi Schemer Bernard Madoff Outraged over Bankruptcy Trustee Irving Pickard's Pay," December 18, 2009, http://www. nydailynews.com/money/2009/12/18/2009-12-18_madoff_vics_rage_at_trustees_ pay.html; Lita Epstein, "Madoff Trustee Files First Clawback Suit to Recover from Investors," *Daily Financial*, April 10, 2009, http://www.dailyfinance.com/story/ madoff/madoff-trustee-files-first-clawback-suit-to-recover-funds-from-i/1513640/.

TYPES OF BANKRUPTCY

When you hear the term *bankruptcy,* you tend to have one thing in mind: someone gets rid of their debts in court and the slate is wiped clean. But there is not simply one type of bankruptcy. There are actually several different kinds and they do not all operate the same way or do the same thing.

Bankruptcy is a very serious matter. In a society like ours an individual can barely exist without credit. Even if a person is rich and uses only cash for everything, having a bad credit score can make life pretty miserable. Many businesses take only credit cards rather than cash, and a credit card is used almost as universally for identification as a driver's license. A credit score can determine everything from whether you can obtain a mortgage to purchase a home, to what your interest rate will be if you do; from whether you can obtain car insurance, to how much you will pay for it.

In this sense, even though we may think of bankruptcy as a way to wipe the slate clean, having a bankruptcy on your credit record can create major stumbling blocks to achieving the life you may want. It is for that reason that it makes a big difference what type of bankruptcy a debtor chooses. Needing time to get your self together financially through a reorganization is not the same as having the slate wiped clean. As we saw in July 2009, GM, which had filed for bankruptcy protection from its creditors just 40 days before, made front page news when it was able to clean up its act and get out from under bankruptcy just 40 days later. You can imagine how much differently it would have been perceived by the buying and investing public if GM had filed for complete bankruptcy. In this section we will discuss the various types of bankruptcy and what they require and accomplish.

EXAMPLE

INVOLUNTARY BANKRUPTCY

L07

Most bankruptcy cases are voluntarily filed by the debtor. However, in certain cases, creditors can file a Chapter 7 or Chapter 13 involuntary **bankruptcy petition.** A debtor is eligible for involuntary bankruptcy if either (1) it is generally not paying its debts, or (2) a custodian has been appointed during the last 120 days to take charge of substantially all of the debtor's property. Once proof of either of these is made, the court must place the debtor under either Chapter 7 or Chapter 13 bankruptcy. In order to file the petition, creditors must have total outstanding **unsecured debt** of at least $10,000. If you are wondering how your creditors would know your financial situation or who your other creditors are, we have two words for you: credit report. If there are more than 12 creditors, three must participate in the involuntary petition. Where there are fewer than 12 creditors, a single creditor may file. In addition, the debts must not be contingent nor subject to any bona fide disputes. For the court to find in favor of the creditors, it must find that the debtor is not generally paying its debts as they become due and that the creditor's petition was filed in good faith.

An involuntary petition should be filed if:

- The debtor is squandering assets or is grossly incompetent;
- The debtor is transferring unsecured assets to a third party for less than value;
- The debtor is paying one creditor to satisfy the debt to it but not paying the other creditors;
- The debtor is transferring assets to a successive company;
- The debtor is paying debts only to company insiders; or
- A bankruptcy is imminent but it is in a state that makes it cost-prohibitive for an unsecured creditor to participate.

The benefit to the unsecured creditor of filing involuntarily against its debtor is the ability to recover transfers of assets from the debtor that should not have been made.

Those transfers include a transfer of assets to an insider within two years of the filing; fraudulent transfers made within one year prior to filing; and noninsider transfers made within 90 days of filing. Another benefit is that the court will appoint a trustee immediately for a Chapter 7 bankruptcy, or if the court believes one is necessary, for a Chapter 13 bankruptcy. Lastly, the creditors who file can get an award for expenses for filing, including attorney's and accountant's fees.

So what is the downside to using this remedy? The courts will look closely at the motivation of the creditors in filing. The fact that a few creditors are not being paid is not enough. In order to satisfy the requirement that the debtor is not paying debts as they become due, the creditors have to show that the debtor is missing a significant number of payments. If the debtor can dispute the debts, the court can disqualify the claim. If the creditor files just to protect her claims rather than the group of creditors, the court will impute that to mean bad faith and dismiss the filing.

Just as in a voluntary filing, the filing triggers an **automatic stay** of the debts owed. Thus, until the court issues an order, creditors are precluded from taking any other course of action to collect from the debtor, even though they filed the petition for involuntary bankruptcy.

VOLUNTARY BANKRUPTCY

There are six types of bankruptcy that can be filed under the code. They are referred to according to the Chapters that create them. The most often used and those we will focus on are Chapters 7, 11, and 13. The others are Chapter 12, entitled Adjustment of Debts of a Family Farmer or Fisherman with Regular Annual Income; Chapter 9, entitled Adjustment of Debts of a Municipality; and Chapter 15, entitled Ancillary and Other Cross-Border Cases. In addition to the basic types of bankruptcy, Congress has provided the Servicemembers' Civil Relief Act, which provides protection to members of the military against the entry of default judgments and gives the court the ability to stay proceedings, including bankruptcy proceedings, against debtors who are in the military.

WHAT IS A DISCHARGE IN BANKRUPTCY?

A bankruptcy discharge releases the debtor from personal liability for certain specified types of debts. After being discharged in bankruptcy the debtor is no longer legally required to pay any debts that are discharged. The discharge is a permanent order prohibiting the creditors of the debtor from collecting discharged debts, including legal action and communications with the debtor, such as phone calls, letters, and personal contacts.

EXAMPLE For example, in the opening scenario, Olympia would be entitled to a discharge of her debts if she qualifies for bankruptcy. Afterward, her creditors would not be able to call or otherwise communicate with her about the debts because the debts no longer legally exist. As we mentioned in discussing liens in the context of secured transactions, a discharge in bankruptcy does not discharge a valid lien filed against property upon which there is a valid lien. If, after bankruptcy, the lien has not been avoided, it will still be enforceable against the property owner/debtor. (See the earlier section of this chapter, "Miscellaneous Liens.")

While recent changes in the bankruptcy code have made filing for bankruptcy more difficult (see Take Away 9-4, "End of an Era"), in Take Away 9-5, "Bankruptcies Return at Record Pace," the discharge still occurs automatically, unless there is litigation involved. All creditors are notified by the clerk of the court. This notice informs the creditors that they are not to continue to collect from the debtor and that continued collection efforts could result in a contempt order being issued against them for failing to follow the court order of discharge.

TAKE AWAY 9-4

END OF AN ERA

In 2005, the Bankruptcy Code was amended to make it more difficult for consumer debtors to file Chapter 7 bankruptcy. Below is the difference between personal and business filings for the year 2005 and the three years following.

Year	Totals Filings	Business Filings	Nonbusiness Filings	Consumer Filings as a Percentage of Total Filings
2005	2,078,415	39,201	2,039,214	98.11%
2006	617,660	19,695	597,965	96.81%
2007	850,912	28,322	822,590	96.67%
2008	1,117,771	43,546	1,074,225	96.10%

Source: Annual Business and Non-Business Filings by Year, http://www.abiworld.org/AM/AMTemplate.cfm?Section=Home&CONTENTID=57826&TEMPLATE=/CM/ContentDisplay.cfm.

WHICH DEBTS ARE DISCHARGED?

Not all debts are **dischargeable** in bankruptcy. Each chapter has its own exemptions that preclude some debts from being discharged. If the debt is exempted, the debtor must still pay those debts. Generally, debts are exempted for public policy reasons. For example, if a debt was incurred as a result of a drunk driving conviction, it is not discharged by the Code. Other exemptions include tax claims, debts omitted by the debtor from the list of debts, child support or alimony, debts for willful injuries to property or others, educational loan debt, housing fees, and tax-advantaged retirement plans. Both individuals and businesses have been quite creative in trying to circumvent the bankruptcy laws (see Take Away 9-6, "Bankruptcy Crimes").

EXAMPLE

Chapter 7 Bankruptcy

Chapter 7 bankruptcy is most likely the type of bankruptcy you generally think of when you think of bankruptcy. In a Chapter 7 bankruptcy, in exchange for a discharge in bankruptcy, a debtor is required to turn over all nonexempt property to the trustee so that it may be sold and the proceeds distributed among the unsecured creditors. There are two policies that are being furthered:

TAKE AWAY 9-5

BANKRUPTCIES RETURN AT RECORD PACE

In 2005, the new bankruptcy law went into effect. Aimed at curbing the high number of bankruptcy filings by consumers, the Bankruptcy Abuse Prevention and Consumer Protection Act of 2005 seemed to do just that. Bankruptcies fell from an average of 6,339 per day in 2004 to 2,372 per day in 2006. However, bankruptcies are being filed at an average of 5,593 per day in 2009.

Because of the increased difficulty of filing personal, or Chapter 7, bankruptcy, experts are blaming the economy for the increase. Debtors are willing to pay the higher fees, suffer through the increased means test, go through **credit counseling,** and pay the cost of an attorney to qualify. It is predicted that by the end of 2009, about 1.45 million bankruptcy petitions will be filed.

Source: Martin Merzer, "Bankruptcy Filings Return to Pre-reform-law Pace," http://www.creditcards.com/credit-card-news/bankruptcy-filings-back-to-pre-reform-levels-1282.php.

TAKE AWAY 9-6

BANKRUPTCY CRIMES

Four of the most common fraudulent schemes used in bankruptcy are:

Bustout This scheme involves a protracted plan to con a creditor into thinking it is dealing with an upstanding debtor. The debtor makes payments on time and lulls the creditor into shipping more and more goods. The debtor then begins missing payments and tells the creditor it is having cash flow problems. The truth is the debtor has sold the creditor's merchandise and made off with the money.

Bleedout Bleedout occurs when the owners of the company bleed the company dry over a period of time, depleting assets by making themselves "loans," engaging in complicated corporate transactions, using pension funds and trust fund taxes. By the time the creditors realize what is happening, it is too late.

Looting Looting occurs when a failing company moves its assets to a new business which is thriving after convincing the creditors that they should accept what the new buyer is offering for its debts. After the creditors accept pennies on the dollar for the sold company, they learn that the "new" company was a straw company set up by the principal of the failed business.

Skimming This occurs when the debtor does not make the mortgage payments on property that is generating income. The debtor takes the money and uses it for himself and lets the real estate go into bankruptcy. This is often seen in the commercial real estate market.

Source: Stephanie Wickouski, *Bankruptcy Crimes*, 3rd ed. (Beard, 2007), pp. 11–12.

a fresh start for the debtor and equity among competing creditors. Chapter 7 bankruptcy involves total liquidation of the debtor's assets. The trustee gathers and sells the debtor's assets and uses the proceeds of such assets to pay creditors (see Reality Check 9-5, "Bankruptcy Trustees: Who Are They? What Do They Do? How Do They Get Paid?"). Exempt property is items that cannot be liquidated, including the debtor's current residence, pension, clothing, and present household items such as furniture. Any property that is not exempt will be used to satisfy the creditor's claims. Items that are not exempt may include extra vehicles, second houses, and family heirlooms.

If the debtor has no assets, the trustee will file a "no asset" report with the court, and there will be no distribution to the creditors. Most Chapter 7 cases are no asset cases. Generally, the debt that is discharged is unsecured credit card debt. This is very likely the type of bankruptcy that Olympia will qualify for if she chooses to pursue bankruptcy in the chapter's opening scenario.

EXAMPLE

While a discharge in Chapter 7 bankruptcy may appear to give the debtor a clean slate, the slate is not exactly totally clean. A discharge in bankruptcy will negatively affect the debtor's credit rating for 10 years. Given the number of ways in which we indicated credit scores matter in our society, even outside the actual credit sphere, that is a heavy price to pay and should only be very carefully chosen and only as a last resort.

Most Chapter 7 bankruptcies are filed by individuals, but debtors qualify for Chapter 7 bankruptcy if they are an individual, a partnership, or a corporation or other business entity. After the 2005 amendments to the Bankruptcy Act, individuals must undergo a **means test** to determine if they qualify for Chapter 7 bankruptcy. Under the means test, if the debtor earns less than the median income for a family of its size in the state, debtor can automatically file for Chapter 7 bankruptcy. But if debtor's income from the last six months is greater than the median income of debtor's state income and debtor can pay at least $6,000 over five years or $100 per month toward his or her debt, debtor cannot file for Chapter 7 protection, but must instead file under Chapter 13. Chapter 13

BANKRUPTCY TRUSTEES: WHO ARE THEY? WHAT DO THEY DO? HOW DO THEY GET PAID?

There are approximately 1,100 bankruptcy trustees in the United States; they handle mostly Chapter 7 bankruptcies. In FY 2007 there were approximately 500,000 Chapter 7 bankruptcies filed.[5] Many trustees handle 500 to 1,000 cases per year. Most Chapter 7 debtors never appear before a judge; rather, their cases are resolved by the trustee. The trustees are private individuals whose duties are under the purview of the Office of the U.S. Trustee, which is a part of the Department of Justice. In FY 2007, the Office of the U.S. Trustee made 1,163 criminal referrals, most resulting from Chapter 7 trustees. Chapter 7 trustees distributed $2.86 billion to creditors. If the trustee's efforts do not result in a dividend to creditors, they receive only the $60 (see below).

A **no-asset** case is a Chapter 7 bankruptcy case in which there are no assets available to satisfy any portion of the unsecured claims of the creditors, or a case in which all of the individual debtor's property is exempt. Approximately 95% of the Chapter 7 cases are no asset cases. For handling these cases, the trustee currently receives $60 per case. The trustee still must perform all of the duties listed in §704 of the Code, such as preparing 341 meetings, verifying information sought by the U.S. Trustee, ensuring that tax returns are filed, and examining documents filed by the debtor. Additional duties are imposed by the 2005 amendments to the Bankruptcy Code such as verifying the means test, Form 22A documentation, confirming credit counseling, and monitoring misconduct issues concerning attorneys, petition preparers, and debt relief agencies.

In an asset case, the trustee receives 25% of the first $5,000, plus 10% of any amount over $5,000, but less than $50,000, plus 5% of any amount over $50,000 and under $1,000,000, and 3% of any amount above $1,000,000.

Source: Senate Hearing on Bankruptcy Compensation, Subcommittee on Commercial and Administrative Law, September 16, 2008, http://judiciary.house.gov/hearings/hear_090916_1.html.

---

will require debtor to repay a portion of his or her debts over three to five years (see Take Away 9-7, "Florida Means Test").

A debtor does not have an absolute right to have debts discharged after filing for bankruptcy (see Take Away 9-8, "What Must Be Filed with a Petition to Begin a Chapter 7 Bankruptcy Proceeding?"). Under the Code, a creditor may object to the discharge by

TAKE AWAY 9-7

FLORIDA MEANS TEST

There is a formula to use to determine whether a debtor qualifies for bankruptcy under Chapter 7. First, look at the government website that publishes your state's median income. Determine what your income is for the past six months. If your income is less than that, you qualify under Chapter 7; if it's more than that, you must continue to determine your eligibility by answering questions posed on the form you must submit along with your petition. If you do not qualify, you cannot file a Chapter 7 petition. Rather, you must file under Chapter 13.

If Less than Median Income	Median Income for 1 person household in Ft. Lauderdale, FL	If More than Median Income
You Pass: Chapter 7 is an option for you.	Average monthly income is $3,539.	You must complete means test to determine eligibility for Chapter 7.

Source: U.S. Trustee Program, Department of Justice, 11 U.S.C. §707(b)(7) exclusion, Official Form 22A, Line 15.

---

[5]In FY 2008, that number reached over 714,000; http://www.uscourts.gov/bnkrpctystats/statistics.htm.

WHAT MUST BE FILED WITH A PETITION TO BEGIN A CHAPTER 7 BANKRUPTCY PROCEEDING?

1. Schedules of assets and liabilities;
2. A schedule of current income and expenditures;
3. A statement of financial affairs; and
4. A schedule of executor contracts and unexpired leases.

If it is an individual debtor, he or she must file

1. A copy of debtor's tax returns;
2. A certificate of credit counseling and a copy of a debt repayment plan developed through the counseling service;
3. Evidence of employment from employers;
4. A statement of monthly net income and any anticipated increase in income or expenses after filing;
5. Any record of any interest the debtor has in federal or state qualified education or tuition accounts;
6. A list of all the creditors and the amount and nature of their claims;
7. The source, amount, and frequency of the debtor's income;
8. A list of all the debtor's property; and
9. A detailed list of the debtor's monthly living expenses, i.e., food, clothing, shelter, utilities, taxes, transportation, medicine, etc.

Source: Fed. Rules Bankr. P. 1007(b).

filing an objection in the time allowed for doing so. The filing of the complaint begins an adversary proceeding ending in litigation. The court or trustee in bankruptcy may also deny a discharge for other reasons. For example, the court may deny discharge because the debtor failed to file the proper tax documents, or failed to complete a course in personal financial management, or transferred or concealed property with the intent to defraud creditors. The grounds for denying an individual debtor a discharge in a Chapter 7 case are narrow. The burden is on the creditor to prove the debtor is not entitled to discharge once he or she files for bankruptcy under Chapter 7. Even with this virtual default to granting discharge in bankruptcy, as Diversity in the Law 9-1, "Why Are Blacks' Debts Discharged Less than Whites?" demonstrates, there are still racial disparities in bankruptcy discharges.

A debtor can have his or her discharge revoked if the court or trustee determines that the discharge was obtained fraudulently, the debtor failed to reveal all property that would satisfy the debts, or there are other failures to comply that would revoke the discharge. A debtor cannot receive a second discharge if he or she received a discharge within eight years of filing for the second discharge.

A debtor can voluntarily repay a debt even after it has been discharged and will choose to do so if, for example, the reputation of the debtor is important, or the debt is owed to a family member, even though it can no longer be legally enforced. This is called **reaffirming a debt.** For example, even if Olympia's debt to her uncle is discharged by Olympia's bankruptcy, Olympia might want to repay her uncle since he is a family member and because she may wish to maintain him as a resource. If a debt is to be reaffirmed, it must be done before the discharge is entered.

EXEMPTIONS

For most consumer debtors, no section of the Code is more important than §522 which governs the debtor's rights to exempt property. The Code contains no definition of "exempt," but this designation is given to prevent the trustee from liquidating these assets and the debtor is entitled to keep them under Chapter 7 **liquidation.** The rules require a debtor to list all exempt property at the outset of the case.

Exempt property includes homestead, motor vehicle, household goods, clothing, jewelry, and a general exemption that can be applied to any property. It is important to note that this exemption does not mean that these items will not be liquidated by the trustee to pay the creditors. The exemption means that the debtor will be given a certain interest in these items up to a dollar amount. Any value in the items above that exempted dollar amount belongs to the trustee (see Take Away 9-9, "Federal Exemptions under §522"). In Olympia's case, she would list all her household items, jewelry, and other items covered by §522.

EXAMPLE

DIVERSITY IN THE LAW 9-1

WHY ARE BLACKS' DEBTS DISCHARGED LESS THAN WHITES?

When Congress amended the Bankruptcy Code in 2005 it meant that more debtors would have to take advantage of Chapter 13's payment plan than Chapter 7's immediate relief from discharge through liquidation. Why, then, are whites who enter bankruptcy less likely than blacks to use Chapter 13? Black debtors are three times more likely to use Chapter 13 than Chapter 7. Because the overall relief rate for Chapter 13 was only 23%, blacks are getting less relief than whites based on the Chapter they choose. Once selected the chance that blacks and Hispanics will have their debts discharged is 40% less than that of whites under Chapter 13.

This is unfortunate since it has already been shown that blacks and Hispanics are already far more likely to enter bankruptcy than whites. Scholars have shown that this is in part because low income blacks and Hispanics are far more likely to have subprime mortgages than residents in low income white neighborhoods. In addition, whites disproportionately have the kind of assets that bankruptcy protects, and blacks disproportionately have the types of debts that bankruptcy does not relieve.

Source: Rory Van Loo, "A Tale of Two Debtors: Bankruptcy Disparities by Race," *Albany Law Review* 72 (2009), p. 231.

TAKE AWAY 9-9

FEDERAL EXEMPTIONS UNDER §522[6]

Exemption	Amount Exempted	Doubled for Married Couple?
Homestead	$20,200	Yes
Motor Vehicle	$3,225	No
Household Goods	$10,775 aggregate	No
Jewelry	$1,350	Yes
Any Property (Wild Card Exemption)	$1,075	Yes

Source: 11 U.S.C. §522 (2008).

---

[6]These dollar values are adjusted for inflation every 3 years. 11 U.S.C. §104.

For example, suppose a married couple jointly owns a home valued at $60,000 with a $30,000 mortgage. Under current law, each party will be able to exempt $20,200. For a married couple, that amount is doubled, so a married couple can exempt $40,400. Because their exemption comes to less than that allowable ($60,000 − $30,000 = $30,000 ÷ 2 = $15,000) the debtor's interest would be fully exempt.

Pensions are exempt from bankruptcy. We are seeing an intersection with the bankruptcy laws of factors as diverse as an aging population with the Baby Boomers coming of age, Congress trying to do its part to encourage us to save (if for no other reason than to ensure that the elderly are not left with public relief as their only alternative), Congress creating new means of investing and stimulating the economy, and the persistent (at least perceived) threat of Social Security running out of money. One of the issues that has arisen in bankruptcy cases is how to treat assets such as alternative retirement income. Congress passed legislation creating IRAs (individual retirement accounts) as an effective, and, at times, tax-friendly way for people to save for retirement.

Yet, as *Rousey v. Jacoway* (Case 9.3) shows, even though pensions and IRAs are both designed for retirement, they may not necessarily be considered to be the same. It took a U.S. Supreme Court case to make a determination as to whether to treat IRAs like pensions for bankruptcy purposes.

CASE 9.3 Rousey v. Jacoway

544 U.S. 320 (2005)

Facts: Several years after the petitioners deposited distributions from their pension plans into IRAs, they filed a petition for Chapter 7 bankruptcy. They sought to shield their IRAs from their creditors by claiming the IRAs were exempt from the bankruptcy estate under 11 U.S.C. §522(d)(10)(e), which provides that a debtor may withdraw from the estate his right to receive a payment under a stock bonus, pension, profit-sharing, annuity, or similar plan on account of age. The bankruptcy trustee objected and asked the court to force the Rouseys to turn over the IRAs. The bankruptcy judge agreed with the trustee and ordered the IRAs to be moved into the estate. The 8th Circuit court, on appeal, agreed with the bankruptcy court. The Rouseys appealed to the U.S. Supreme Court.

Issue: Whether IRAs are similar to the type of retirement assets listed in the bankruptcy code as exempt from belonging to the estate in bankruptcy, such that they, too, are exempt?

Holding: Yes

Reasoning: Assets in IRA accounts are protected under the bankruptcy code because, like the assets in §522, they provide a payment on account of age. Just because the money in the IRAs is payable on demand does not change the fact that there is a penalty of 10% if withdrawn before age 59. If the 10% is levied, it prevents access to the entire balance in their IRAs and limits their right to payment of the balance. Because this condition is removed when the accountholder turns 59, the Rouseys' right to their balance is a right to payment on account of age. The Rouseys' IRAs are similar plans to the stock bonus, pension, or profit-sharing or annuity plans listed in §522. To be similar, the IRA must be like, but not identical to, the listed plan. Because the Bankruptcy Code does not define the listed plans, looking to their ordinary meaning shows their common feature is that they provide income that substitutes for wages earned as salary or hourly compensation. In that respect, they are unlike savings accounts, which are not exempt, even though the IRAs are capable of withdrawal like a savings account. The fact that there is a penalty makes it more like an exempt asset.

CASE QUESTIONS

1. What do you think the policy is for allowing pension plans and other retirement-type income to be exempt?
2. The difference between an IRA and other exemptions is discussed by the court. Do you accept the argument that an IRA should be like a pension? Explain.
3. Since the court announced this ruling, do you think it will act as an incentive for people to put their money in an IRA rather than other types of savings vehicles to protect it from the possible reach of a bankruptcy trustee? Should it? Do you perceive any potential ethical issues involved in the Court's position? Explain.

Chapter 11 Bankruptcy

Chapter 11 is frequently referred to as the reorganization bankruptcy. A Chapter 11 case begins with the filing of a petition with the court. A petition may be a voluntary petition filed by the debtor, or it may be an involuntary petition, which is filed by creditors meeting certain requirements.

Chapter 11 is usually used to reorganize a business—a corporation, partnership, or proprietorship. The distinguishing feature is that a sole proprietorship does not have assets separate from the business's assets, and thus, a bankruptcy case involving such an entity includes both personal and business assets. On the other hand, partnerships and corporations exist separate from their owners (see Reality Check 9-6, "What Happens When a Corporation Files for Bankruptcy?"). In a partnership bankruptcy, the partners' personal assets may be used to pay the creditors.

A debtor that files under Chapter 11 can remain "in possession of the assets" while undergoing reorganization under Chapter 11, without the appointment of a trustee. A debtor will remain in possession until the debtor's plan of reorganization is confirmed, the debtor's case is dismissed, or a Chapter 11 trustee is appointed. The latter occurs in only a handful of situations. The debtor in possession performs many of the functions that a trustee would perform.

Generally, a **disclosure statement** must be filed with the court that contains information concerning the assets, liabilities, and business affairs of the debtor; this is used to enable a creditor to make an informed judgment about the debtor's plan of reorganization. This information varies with the size of the business and is more elaborate for a large business than for a small business, which may be excused altogether if information can be determined by the plan itself. The important thing is to discuss how each creditor will be treated under the plan.

A debtor in possession is placed in a fiduciary relationship with the powers and rights of a trustee. The Code includes the rules for the debtor in possession and requires him or her to account for the property, examine and object to claims, and file informational reports as required by the court.

In a Chapter 11 case, the court may appoint a trustee. See Reality Check 9-7, "GM Files for Bankruptcy." In the case of a large reorganization, there will often be a trustee appointed. A trustee plays a major role in monitoring the progress of a Chapter 11 case. The trustee oversees the disbursements of the business and regulates banking, employee compensation, and the hiring of professionals to work with the business. Most important is the creditor's committee. This committee is appointed by the trustee and usually consists of the

REALITY CHECK 9-6

WHAT HAPPENS WHEN A CORPORATION FILES FOR BANKRUPTCY?

Several major corporations file for bankruptcy protection each year. In 2009, several major auto companies were forced to file for bankruptcy because of extreme losses suffered as a result of the downturn in the economy. But what happens to the investors/shareholders when the company files for Chapter 11 bankruptcy protection?

If a corporation files under Chapter 11, the company continues to be managed by the existing managers, but every significant decision has to be approved by the bankruptcy court. A company's securities may continue to trade, but very often trade is halted because of the stock exchange rules. Even if the company is delisted, however, the stocks can still be bought or sold. However, very often the creditors of the company will emerge out of reorganization as the new owners of the company, and the equity (shares) will be canceled, leaving common shareholders with the loss. There is a designation used on the market for shares that have been involved in a bankruptcy. The new shares that exist will be designated differently.

In addition, during the bankruptcy proceeding, shareholders will stop receiving dividends and can be asked to surrender their old shares for reissued new ones which may be fewer in number and worth less. The reorganization plan will spell out their rights as investors and what they can expect to receive, if anything, from the company. The trustee may decide that shareholders do not receive anything because the company has no assets.

If the company files a Chapter 7 bankruptcy petition, usually the stocks are worthless and shareholders have lost their investment. If you hold a bond that represents a loan to the company, you may get a fraction of its face value, depending on the amount of assets the company has.

The SEC has no part in the plan of reorganization, but will take a stand on investor issues, should they arise.

Source: U.S. Securities and Exchange Commission, http://www.sec.gov/investor/pubs/bankrupt.htm.

GM FILES FOR BANKRUPTCY

In a stunning move, General Motors filed for Chapter 11 bankruptcy protection on June 1, 2009. It became the fourth largest bankruptcy in U.S. history. When it filed, GM had $172.81 billion in debt and $82.29 billion in assets. The company intended to reorganize with an infusion of $30 billion from the Treasury Department and $9.5 billion from Canada. Their intention was to form a smaller, leaner GM that is profitable again. They discontinued GM brands Hummer, Saab, Saturn, and Pontiac. With the bankruptcy court being required to approve all expenditures under GM's reorganization plan, the country was pretty shocked when GM emerged from reorganization only 40 days later. As promised, it said it was smaller, leaner, and more attuned to consumers.

Source: "Humbled GM Files for Bankruptcy Protection," June 1, 2009, http://www.msnbc.msn.com/id/31030038/; John D. Stoll and Sharon Terlep, "GM Takes New Direction: Carmaker Leaves Bankruptcy, Will Slim Down, Court Consumers," *The Wall Street Journal*, http://online.wsj.com/article/SB124722154897622577.html. July 11, 2009

seven largest unsecured creditors of the business. The committee investigates the debtor's conduct and operation of the business, consults with the debtor, and formulates a plan. The intent of the Chapter 11 reorganization is for the debtor to emerge from the reorganization not totally debt free, but after having been given a hiatus in which to regroup and come up with a viable plan, much more in control of his or her finances.

Chapter 13 Bankruptcy

A Chapter 13 bankruptcy is also called a "wage earner's plan." It enables individuals with regular income to develop a plan to repay all or part of their debts and provides protection from creditors while they do so. Under this Chapter, debtors propose a repayment plan to make installments to creditors over 3 to 5 years (see Take Away 9-10, "What Must Be Filed to Begin a Chapter 13 Bankruptcy"). A corporation or partnership may not be a Chapter 13 debtor.

The advantage of choosing Chapter 13 over Chapter 7 is the opportunity Chapter 13 gives the debtor to save his or her home from foreclosure. By filing Chapter 13, individuals can stop foreclosure proceedings and may cure delinquent mortgage payments

TAKE AWAY 9-10

WHAT MUST BE FILED TO BEGIN A CHAPTER 13 BANKRUPTCY

1. A petition;
2. Schedules of assets and liabilities;
3. A schedule of current income and expenditures;
4. A schedule of executor contracts and unexpired leases;
5. A statement of financial affairs;
6. A copy of tax returns;
7. A certificate of credit counseling and a copy of a debt repayment plan developed through the counseling service;
8. Evidence of employment from employers;
9. A statement of monthly net income and any anticipated increase in income or expenses after filing;
10. Any record of any interest the debtor has in federal or state qualified education or tuition accounts;
11. A list of all the creditors and the amount and nature of their claims;
12. The source, amount, and frequency of the debtor's income;
13. A list of all the debtor's property; and
14. A detailed list of the debtor's monthly living expenses, i.e., food, clothing, shelter, utilities, taxes, transportation, medicine, etc.

Source: Fed. Rules Bankr. P. 1007(b).

over time. They must still make all payments during the duration of their plan. But the automatic stay that attaches with the filing of the petition will stop the foreclosure proceeding.[7] Another advantage is that it allows individuals to reschedule **secured debts** and extend them over the life of the plan. Lastly, Chapter 13 acts like a consolidation loan, in that all payments are made to the trustee, who then makes the payments to the creditors. In the chapter opening scenario, if Olympia does not have a wage, she would not be a candidate for Chapter 13.

Within 20–50 days after the petition is filed, the trustee will hold a creditor's meeting. Unsecured creditors who wish to participate in the distribution of payments must file their claims within 90 days after the date set for the meeting.

The debtor must file a repayment plan within 14 days after the petition is filed. The plan must be submitted for court approval and must provide for payments of fixed amounts to the trustee on a regular basis. The trustee then distributes the funds to creditors according to the terms of the plan. Creditors may get less than full payment on their claims under the plan. Once the plan is confirmed, it binds both the creditor and the debtor. Interestingly, research indicates that most people on repayment plans under Chapter 13 bankruptcy fail, sending debtors into Chapter 7 liquidation.[8]

There are three types of claims the plan must provide for under Chapter 13: priority, secured, and unsecured. Priority claims are those granted special status by the bankruptcy law, such as most taxes and the cost of the bankruptcy proceeding. Secured claims are those for which the creditor has the right to take back certain property (collateral) if the debtor does not pay the underlying debt. Unsecured claims are generally those for which the creditor has no special rights to collect against particular property owned by the debtor.

The plan must pay the priority claims in full. If the debtor wants to keep the collateral securing a particular claim, the plan must include a provision that gives the creditor the value of the security.

A debtor under Chapter 13 is usually entitled to a discharge upon completion of all payments under the plan. As in Chapter 7, however, discharge may not be automatic. If the debtor received a prior discharge in another case within certain time frames, he or she cannot seek a second discharge. However, creditors do not have the right to object to a Chapter 13 discharge. They can object to the repayment plan, but once the repayment plan is complete, creditors cannot object to the discharge. A discharge can be revoked if the discharge is obtained through fraud.

As a general rule, the discharge releases the debtor from all debts provided in the plan or disallowed, with the exception of certain debts. Debts such as long-term obligations like a home mortgage, debts for alimony or child support, educational loans, personal injury–caused debts, or debts for restitution or a criminal fine are not discharged. See Take Away 9-11, "Bankruptcy."

Servicemembers' Civil Relief Act

It probably comes as no surprise to you that members of the military do not make a great deal of money. In fact, some give up better salaries in order to join the military and fight for our country. Joining the military does not suspend financial obligations of service members. The combination of the stress of leaving family, job, and familiarity, especially to go to war, as well as minimal pay and trying to support family while fulfilling

---

[7]The homeowner may still lose her home if the mortgage company completes the foreclosure before the debtor files the Chapter 13 petition.

[8]Megan McArdle, "Sink and Swim," *The Atlantic*, June 2009, pp. 30-32. Quoting McArdle, "[P]eople who weren't previously good at living on a budget don't magically get better at it with a court order. Moreover, job losses or other unexpected events can derail the highly structured payment plans. And the costs of administering an ongoing plan are much higher than for a simple discharge and write-off."

BANKRUPTCY

Chapter 7	Requires debtor to turn over all nonexempt property to trustee for liquidation to satisfy the debtor's creditors
Chapter 11	Used to reorganize debts so that business may remain operating and present a plan to the creditors for paying its debts
Chapter 13	Enables individuals to develop a plan to repay all or part of their debts and provides protection from creditors while they do
Voluntary	Any one of six types of bankruptcy that can be filed by the debtor for protection against creditors
Involuntary	Filed by creditors when a debtor is not paying its debts or a custodian has been appointed to take charge of the debtor's property

military obligations leaves many members of the military stretched and stressed. Congress took this into account and passed the Servicemembers' Civil Relief Act (SCRA).[9] The purpose of the Servicemembers' Civil Relief Act is to strengthen and expedite national defense by giving service members certain protections in civil actions. By temporarily suspending judicial and administrative proceedings and transactions that may adversely affect service members, the SCRA allows service members to focus their energy on defense issues.

The SCRA applies to all active duty military and to citizens serving in the military. It allows forbearance and reduced interest on certain obligations incurred prior to military service, and restricts default judgments against service members and rental evictions of service members and their dependents.

There are three primary areas of coverage under the SCRA: (1) protection against the entry of default judgments; (2) stay of proceedings where the service member has notice of the proceeding; and (3) stay or vacation of execution of judgments, attachments, and garnishments. The SCRA also applies to any bankruptcy proceedings before a bankruptcy court. The provisions end when the service member is discharged (but can be extended by the court to 90 days after discharge if necessary for pending matters), or when the service member dies.

Summary

The relationship between secured transactions and bankruptcy has to do with the relationship between debtors and creditors. Creditors take the risk when extending credit that the debtor will not be able to repay the debt. One way to decrease that risk is to use debtor's property as collateral to secure the transaction so that if debtor is unable to repay the debt the creditor can recoup some if not all the money by selling the collateral.

---

[9]50 U.S.C. 501-596 (2003).

Debtors, on the other hand, need at least some protection against the unexpected event of bankruptcy. The rules of bankruptcy that allow debtors to wipe out their debt and get a fresh start come with costs. Not only do debtors have to qualify for liquidation, but their credit is ruined for a period of time. That means they may not receive credit and if they do receive it, it will cost more for a long time to come. Additionally, debtors who wish to liquidate their assets to become debt free can only do so under the amended bankruptcy law if they qualify to do so. If not, they must enter into a repayment plan to pay their creditors at least part of what they owe. They do not have the benefit of having their debts wiped out, even if they would choose to do so.

Reorganization allows a business that gets into financial trouble to devise a plan to get out of trouble. For some businesses, like GM, this proves to be a lifeline. Society benefits from businesses being able to thrive, create jobs, and produce goods and services. Perhaps more frugal management or better management is what is needed to allow the business to reorganize and prosper. Chapter 11 gives a business that chance.

Overall, the bankruptcy laws serve as an effective safety net for those whose finances get the better of them. Absent fraud and overreaching, it an important tool for those in need.

Review Questions

1. McClendon's Appliances sold to Rodney a refrigerator for his personal use. Rodney signed an installment contract promising to pay in installments of $50 per month for 24 months. Rodney is adjudicated bankrupt 5 months after purchasing the refrigerator. The bankruptcy trustee has included the refrigerator in Rodney's assets. Who will object to the inclusion of the refrigerator as an asset, and what will the objection be? LO4

2. When Butch borrowed $10,000 from Olympia Bank, the bank not only made him get a surety, but also demanded that the inventory of Butch's feed store stand as collateral. Butch talked his brother Arnold into signing the promissory note as surety and signed the necessary papers for the bank to get an Article 9 security interest in the inventory. Unfortunately, the bank failed to file the Article 9 financing statement in the correct place, so when Butch had financial difficulties, other creditors prevailed over the bank's attempt to claim the inventory. The inventory was worth $6,000. What is the effect of the bank's Article 9 difficulties on Arnold, Butch's surety? LO5

3. In problem 2, suppose the bank had filed the Article 9 security interest properly. When Butch's note was due, he was not in a position to pay the money back to the bank, so Arnold paid the bank the $10,000. What is Arnold's recourse against Butch? What can he do under his subrogation rights? LO5

4. Will and Grace are husband and wife and are filing a Chapter 7 bankruptcy petition jointly. They own a home worth $120,000 with a mortgage of $100,000 remaining. What is their homestead exemption under §522? LO8

5. Silver Dollar LLC was organized under Tennessee law and properly filed with the Secretary of State as an LLC. When they began to do business, they opened their store under the assumed name of Silver Dollar Stores. In 2007 they borrowed money from Community Bank and signed a security agreement which the bank filed under the name Silver Dollar Stores. Shortly after they filed for Chapter 7 bankruptcy. The trustee sought to avoid the security agreement based on it having been filed under the assumed name. What is the likely outcome of the challenge by the bank? LO6

6. House of Design is an interior decorating store. Until the economy began to tighten, it had a thriving business. However, lately, House of Design has been spotty in paying its creditors, choosing to pay regularly only the two main suppliers of its inventory. Many of the other creditors have become concerned that House of Design will be forced to close its doors. What options do they have before that happens? LO7

7. Alicia, a 17-year-old student, purchased a car using her own money as a down payment and signed an installment contract for the remaining

$7000. Her father co-signed on the contract with her. Alicia, unhappy with her choice of car, gave the car away to her boyfriend, stopped making payments, and disaffirmed the sale with the car dealer. Her father was notified by the dealer immediately for the remainder owed. Does her father have any defense he can assert against the car dealer that will prevent him from having to pay the remaining debt? LO4

8. Bellamy took his farm equipment into Genoa's Repair Shop to have it repaired. Harvest season was approaching, and Bellamy really needed the equipment so he did not lose his crops. When Genoa's presented him with the bill for the repair, Bellamy could not pay it. Genoa refused to allow Bellamy to take his equipment unless his bill was paid. What legal ground did Genoa's have to keep Bellamy's farm equipment? LO5

9. Martha borrowed $20,000 from the Mt. Vernon Finance Company. To secure the note, the finance company took a mortgage on Martha's vineyard. Martha failed to pay her taxes on the vineyard, and the state placed a tax lien against it. When Martha defaulted on the note with the finance company, they attempted to take the vineyard in satisfaction of her debt. What is the outcome of the dispute that arose between the state and the finance company over Martha's vineyard? LO2

10. Jon and Kate had always paid their bills, but their daughter's unexpected illness had eaten up all their savings and they were forced to file for Chapter 7 bankruptcy. They had a home, furnishings, one car, and their wedding rings. They had already sold their other jewelry to pay the bills, except for a diamond ring valued at $30,000 that was an heirloom given to Jon by his grandfather. The ring had belonged to his grandmother and Jon vowed to his grandfather to keep it forever in the family. What is likely to be the trustee's position on whether Jon and Kate can keep their heirloom? LO8

Ethics Issue

One ethical dilemma facing lawyers is the concept of "asset planning" or "bankruptcy planning." These terms are often buzzwords for hiding assets from creditors. For example, suppose a client sought advice from his attorney because he was about to be sued and he realized that his assets might be at risk. What would be his lawyer's obligation? Should she convert his nonexempt assets to exempt assets? Create a spendthrift or other protective trust for his spouse or family member that is exempt? Transfer real estate that he owns into property he shares with his spouse in a tenancy by the entirety? Place his assets in a foreign account? Or just advise him to go on a spending spree?[10]

Authorities agree that conversion of nonexempt property into exempt property is not fraudulent per se,[11] but that begs the question. Should an attorney advise a client to hide or remove assets from his creditors?

Group Exercise

In order to determine whether an individual is eligible for a Chapter 7 bankruptcy, the individual has to first pass the "means test." Go online and determine what income is acceptable for a family of four to be able to file for bankruptcy protection under Chapter 7 in your state. Then go online and determine how many individuals have filed for bankruptcy in your state last year. Given your state's financial situation, and that of the U.S. in general, why do you think the number is what it is?

---

[10]All of these devices would be exempt from the bankruptcy estate or would use assets that some would argue belong to the creditor.

[11]*In re Moreno*, 892 F.2d 417 (5th Cir. 1990).

Key Terms

www.mhhe.com/bennettalexanderLE1e

10

Agency and Business Organizations

Learning Objectives

After reading this chapter, you should be able to:

LO1   Describe the types of authority an agent has to bind the principal

LO2   Describe the duties between agents and principals

LO3   Discuss how authority is terminated

LO4   Distinguish between various types of business organizations

LO5   Describe the factors for determining the appropriate businesses organization to use

LO6   Explain the corporation and its attributes

LO7   Determine when courts can step outside corporate protection and why

LO8   Explain the government regulations that impact corporations

 ## Opening Scenario

Aunt Ruth, an elderly widow, asked her nephew to act on her behalf because she felt she was getting too old to handle her affairs and did not want to be taken advantage of by other family members or her associates. Duke, her nephew, was a lawyer and agreed that this was a good idea. He prepared a power of attorney that gave him authority to "handle her business affairs, banking affairs, and legal affairs." He also prepared a separate power of attorney that listed Duke as her proxy should she suffer any accident or illness that would leave her incompetent or unable to make end-of-life decisions.

Over the course of the next few years, Duke paid Aunt Ruth's bills, prepared her will, closed her accounts at the brokerage firm where she had her investments, and generally prepared Aunt Ruth's finances for her remaining years. Duke also used Aunt Ruth's money to pay his own outstanding debts and create a trust fund to pay for his daughter's college education.

After Aunt Ruth became slightly demented in her thinking, Duke had Aunt Ruth's home transferred into his name. Duke then "sold" her home to his corporation, of which he was the sole shareholder, and began to borrow money using Aunt Ruth's house as collateral to finance legitimate, but shaky, investments. He soon ran into financial trouble and his corporation was forced to file bankruptcy. Aunt Ruth's home was to be sold to pay for his debts. All of Duke's use of Aunt Ruth's money and home for his own purposes was done without Aunt Ruth's knowledge or permission.

Was Duke acting within the scope of his agency in handling Aunt Ruth's property? What rights does Aunt Ruth have to undo any of Duke's actions? Do you think there should be a third party to keep this from happening? How often do you think elderly relatives are taken advantage of in this way? Are family situations especially susceptible to abuses such as this one? Who, other than an attorney, might help keep this from happening? When should the courts step in? Can Aunt Ruth's home be saved from being taken from her by Duke's corporate creditors?

Introduction

People begin doing business together and with each other in all kinds of ways. Some business relationships, like that of Aunt Ruth and Duke, are very informal and grow out of their family or personal relationships. Others are more formal and develop because of necessity. Still others are very formal and are created only by the state in which they will operate, and do not exist legally until the state issues them a charter to begin operations. When Duke formed his corporation, it could not operate until the state issued it a corporate charter.

All of these forms of business have rules and regulations that govern them. Business owners, as well as those who interact with business, should be mindful of these rules so that their conduct can comply and their interests remain protected. These relationships, formal and informal, and the liability that they create, are the subject of this chapter.

Principals and Agents in the Commercial Context

Many relationships in business involve **agency.** Most of the world's work is performed by **agents,** the one performing for another, on behalf of **principals,** the one for whom the work is performed. The purpose of the agency relationship is to accomplish acts by utilizing the services of others. Agency enables a person to broaden his or her activities by having someone else render services on his or her behalf, and then receive the benefit of those services. An agency can be created for any legal purpose. Consideration is not required for an agency to be formed between a principal and an agent. As in our chapter's opening scenario involving Aunt Ruth and her nephew Duke, no money was paid in exchange for Duke's services, but an agency relationship was established without it. In this chapter we will focus primarily on the commercial or business aspects of agency relationships.

AGENT DEFINED

An agent is a person who by agreement with the principal acts on behalf of and subject to the control of the principal. A principal must have capacity to contract, but anyone can be an agent, even a minor or an incompetent person. An agency relationship is always created by the words or actions (or lack of action) of the principal. The fact that a person acts on behalf of another does not make him an agent without the appointment by the principal. The assent to act is what creates the agency relationship.

An agency results in a fiduciary relationship between an agent and a principal. A **fiduciary** is one who acts primarily for the benefit of another. An agent's obligation is to act only in the interest of the principal. He may not act contrary to or without the principal's consent nor may he act secretly in the same transaction for his own account. In the opening scenario, Aunt Ruth is the principal, Duke is her agent, and he owes Aunt Ruth a fiduciary duty to act only on her behalf within the agency relationship. When Duke began taking Aunt Ruth's property and using it for his benefit, he violated the fiduciary relationship owed to her as part of his status as her agent.

The principal source of agency law today is the **Restatement of Agency 3d** (Rest. 3d),[1] and its earlier edition, the Restatement of Agency 2d. The Restatement puts the common law of agency into a volume of rules that outline, to the extent possible, the

---

[1]Restatement of the Law of Agency 3d, American Law Institute, 2006. The Restatement 2d was published in 1958 and remains influential in some states.

TAKE AWAY 10-1

RESTATEMENT OF THE LAW OF AGENCY 3D: §1.01 AGENCY DEFINED

Agency is the fiduciary relationship that arises when one person (a "principal") manifests assent to another person (an "agent") that the agent shall act on the principal's behalf and subject to the principal's control, and the agent manifests assent or otherwise consents so to act.

Source: Rest. 3d of Agency, §1.01.

relationships involved in agency (i.e., the relationship between the three parties contemplated in an agency relationship): the principal, the agent, and the third party. The Restatement is useful because it provides a comprehensive set of definitions and examples for studying the subject. As with the Restatement of Contracts or the Restatement of Torts discussed in earlier chapters, although the Restatements are not law, in the area of agency many jurisdictions have adopted and follow the Restatement. Important sections of the Restatement will be given in the chapter to illustrate the law that governs this area, beginning with Take Away 10-1 ("Restatement of the Law of Agency 3d: §1.01 Agency Defined"). Reality Check 10-1 ("When Does an Agency Exist?") illustrates a case in which whether an agency had been created had to be established by the court.

Agents are classified as general agents and special agents. A **general agent** is one who has authority to transact all of the business of the principal, of a particular kind, or in a particular case. A **special agent** is an agent who is authorized to conduct only a single transaction, or only a series of transactions not involving continuity of service. In the opening scenario, Duke was a general agent for Aunt Ruth because he was transacting all of Aunt Ruth's business for her.

EXAMPLE

REALITY CHECK 10-1

WHEN DOES AN AGENCY EXIST?

M.D. Associates rented space to Sears for one of its stores. During the lease, Sears was notified to make its rent payable to Paul Hogg, c/o McLane Investment Company at a post office box. Shortly before the lease was to be renewed, Hogg notified Sears that McLane Investment Co. was purchasing the building and the rent checks were to be sent to a different address. When it came time to renew the lease, Sears sent the lease renewal notice to the post office box, return receipt requested. The return receipt was signed by Paula Fraley, who worked at McLane with Hogg.

McLane Investment alleges the lease renewal was invalid because it was mailed to the post office box, and not the most recent address; therefore it did not receive notice of the renewal. However, evidence indicated that Fraley, who worked with Hogg and who signed the return receipt, had picked up Hogg's mail for him from his post office box for months and delivered it to him. Hogg denied that Fraley was his agent; that she worked "with" him and not "for" him, thus, notice to her could not serve as notice to McLane's. However, the court found that even if she did not have express authority to act as his agent, because it was the regular procedure to deliver mail to him, he consented to her agency by acquiescence. The court indicated that by circumstances, words, acts, and conduct, an agency relationship can be found. Thus, notice to Fraley was notice to Hogg.

Source: M.D. Associates v. Sears, Roebuck & Co., 749 S.W.2d 454 (Ct. App. Mo. 1988).

PRINCIPAL DEFINED

L01

A principal is a person on whose behalf an agent acts. Of course, since they have an agency relationship, the agent knows who the principal is, However, that is not always the case when the agent is interacting with third parties outside the agency relationship. Keep in mind that an agent, by nature, acts on behalf of a principal when dealing with third parties. Sometimes issues arise with those third parties regarding their knowledge of the principal. For that reason, principals are divided into three classes: disclosed, unidentified (partially disclosed), and undisclosed. A principal is **disclosed** if the third party with whom the agent interacts knows the agent is acting on behalf of a principal, and he or she knows who the principal is. A principal is **partially disclosed** if, when an agent and a third party interact, the third party has notice that the agent is acting for a principal but it does not know the principal's identity. A principal is **undisclosed** if, when an agent and a third party interact, the third party has no notice that the agent is acting for a principal. The primary difference is in the how the agent is legally viewed in the contract that he or she enters into with the third party. For example, Duke can act on behalf of

EXAMPLE

Aunt Ruth in any of these capacities, depending on what type of transaction he is engaging in on her behalf. This relationship is further discussed below.

DISTINGUISHING AGENCY FROM OTHER RELATIONSHIPS

Disputes between the principal and agent over agency relationships usually focus around two issues: the principal's right to control the agent or the fiduciary nature of the relationship. Both of these characteristics must be present in order to have an agency relationship. There are many other relationships that could exist that at first glance resemble an agency. Some have a fiduciary relationship, but lack control, such as a trustee to a beneficiary. Others are subject to control, but are not fiduciaries, such as the distributor to a supplier. Some relationships lack both control and a fiduciary relationship, such as an independent contractor. Of these, the independent contractor most typically gets confused with an agent.

An **independent contractor** is a person who contracts with another to do something but who is not controlled by the other with respect to his physical conduct in the performance of the undertaking. She does a job for a price, but the manner and control of doing the job are entirely up to her. For example, if a business hires a painter, the painter is normally an independent contractor, because although the color of the paint and other details might be discussed, the business owner does not control how the painter does her job of painting, and there is no fiduciary relationship between them that arises from the painter being hired to do the job. Take Away 10-2, "Electronic Agents," poses the interesting question of whether electronic "agents" are created by the software systems you use every day.

`EXAMPLE`

`L02`

THE CREATION OF AUTHORITY

One of the important attributes of an agent is the power to bind the principal to third parties and to bind third parties to the principal. This power is described as the ability to

TAKE AWAY 10-2

ELECTRONIC AGENTS

The UCC §2-103(g) defines an electronic agent as a computer program, or an electronic or other automated means, used independently to initiate action or respond to electronic records or performances in whole or in part, without review or action by an individual. Just as people turn to agents to handle many routine tasks of daily life, today there is another option—employing software operating over the Internet to take care of these chores. Software "agents" will interact on your behalf with all the websites demanding your attention. These software agents are called "bots," short for robots.

Can you enter a contract with a robot? Do the common law agency and contract principles apply to software agents?

The first question has been answered by the enactment of several federal and state statutes, like the UCC, which have created statutory law for electronic agents governing the use of bots in electronic contracting. The second question is answered in the common law of agency, contracts, and torts that have applied existing principles to bots and other forms of electronic agents. As more business and personal lives are conducted over the Internet, there will be increasing reliance on bots and electronic agents to automate access and enter contracts and other agreements. For instance, one national loan company runs radio ads saying that the entire home mortgage loan process can be transacted online, including signatures, taking the place of loan officers that used to meet face to face with customers. The law is just beginning to address the existence of bots and formulate legal principles to govern their use and misuse. Over the next few years, litigation will test the limits of those laws, new and old, to this new agent.

If you think the idea of bots is strange, imagine life if you had to stop and speak with a live agent by phone or in person each time you were doing something online that required you to agree. Right now, all you have to do is click the "I agree" button that is a part of the software. But it would be quite different if you had to actually speak with a live agent each time.

Source: S. Middlebrook and J. Muller, "Thoughts on Bots: The Emerging Law of Electronic Agents," *Business Law* 56 (November 2000), p. 341.

produce a change in a given legal relationship between the principal and third parties by doing or not doing a given act.[2] This power gives the agent the authority to act on behalf of and bind the principal. When Duke acted for Aunt Ruth by, for example, hiring her nurses or contracting for medical services to provide for her, Aunt Ruth was legally obligated to pay for these services even though Duke was the agent who contracted for them. An agent has **actual authority** to act in a given way on a principal's behalf if the principal's words or conduct would lead a reasonable person in the agent's position to believe that the principal wishes the agent to act. The authority is actual if the principal notified the agent that he had such authority. Actual authority may be express or implied.

Express Authority

Express authority is communicated to the agent in writing or orally. For example, Dante was hired as the purchasing agent for Goodyear. He was told that he was responsible for purchasing the supplies needed to run the Goodyear plant. Dante has express authority to make the purchases and Goodyear is legally bound to pay for supplies ordered by Dante. If the agent has express authority and acts within the scope of that authority, the principal is bound. Duke was given express authority to be an agent for Aunt Ruth when she asked him to take over her finances and pay her expenses for her.

Implied Authority

Actual authority may also be **implied.** In general, an agent has the power to do those acts that are usual and incidental to the authorized acts and those which are reasonably necessary to accomplish the principal's purpose. Implied authority may come from several sources.

1. A principal may *consent* to the agent's acts:
   A clerk in a retail store may not have been expressly told to sell the items from the store, but where the clerk has been told to report for work at a certain hour and be trained by the senior clerk, it is implied that the clerk will sell the items from the store.

2. The agent may be acting within the *custom and usage* of the principal's trade or business:
   If the sale of real estate requires that a warranty accompany the deed, and the agent extends the warranty along with the deed, he had implied authority to do so because of the custom and usage of that business.
3. The agent may act on an *ambiguity* created by the principal's instructions:
   Where a principal instructs an agent to buy "the best boat he can for the money," the principal implies that he will accept the boat that the agent buys.
4. The agent may be acting in an *emergency:*
   If an agent is a store manager, he may do certain acts outside the normal course of his authority if there is an emergency that would cause the principal loss if the agent did not act to protect the principal's property. For example, during severe flooding, a store manager may remove goods from a store to a dry warehouse and the principal would be legally bound to pay the warehouse expenses even though the principal did not tell the agent to incur the expenses, since it was an emergency.

5. The agent may act based on the *conduct* of the parties:
   If an agent has always done a certain act that was not expressly authorized by the principal, but the principal has acquiesced in the conduct, the principal assents to the conduct. For example, if an agent always includes a tip in paying for services given to his principal, the principal implies that the agent has the authority to include a tip in paying for the services.

---

[2]Rest. Agency 2d §6.

In any of these cases, the agent may be acting on implied authority to do the act. In each case, the principal will be liable for the acts of the agent. Here, implied authority simply means an absence of express authority, but authority nonetheless. In both express and implied authority, the authority is derived from some instruction from the principal to the agent. If the principal can show that the agent did not have the implied authority to do an act, the principal will not be responsible for the agent's act. In such a case, the agent will be responsible. Since an agent agrees to act on behalf of a principal and not be personally liable for the acts the agent is doing for the principal, no agent wants to end up having to take responsibility for something the agent did not think he had responsibility for. That is why it is important for an agent to make sure that he or she understands exactly what the principal wants done and does only that.

Apparent Authority

L02

In order for there to be **apparent authority,** the principal must act in such a way as to clothe the agent with the authority. An agent has apparent authority to act if actions of the principal to the third party would lead a reasonable person in the third person's position to believe that the principal has authorized the agent to act. Another way apparent authority has been described is as *inherent* authority. However, as Take Away 10-3, "Death of a Power—Inherent Agency Power," illustrates, that term is being phased out.

If an agent has apparent authority and acts within the scope of that authority, the principal is bound. Apparent authority may arise in a number of ways. It arises usually when the principal allows a situation to exist causing the third party to be misled. It may arise because of what the principal has said or because of some document, such as a power of attorney, that the principal has given the agent and which the agent has shown to the third party. It may also arise because the agent has been placed in such a position that a person of ordinary business prudence would be justified in believing that the agent was authorized. **EXAMPLE** If you walk into a store and there is a person at the cash register ringing up customer purchases, you expect that this person has the authority to do so. In addition it may come into existence where the agent has acquired a reputation for having authority because of the fact that he has acted in the past for the principal with the principal's knowledge and without any indication of the principal's dissent. **EXAMPLE** For example, Duke had authority to act for Aunt Ruth in managing her financial affairs, even though that authority did not extend to creating a college fund for his daughter. However, because of the extent of his authority, a banker who routinely dealt with Duke concerning Aunt Ruth's affairs may not have questioned Duke when he opened a trust account for his daughter, assuming that Aunt Ruth had given her permission for such an account to be opened. This would be true especially if Aunt Ruth had never objected to anything Duke had done in the past, and the banker knew of the relationship between Duke and Aunt Ruth. In this case, the banker might be justified in believing that Duke was authorized to open a trust account for his daughter because of Aunt Ruth's prior acquiescence to Duke's actions in the past.

TAKE AWAY 10-3

DEATH OF A POWER—INHERENT AGENCY POWER

Inherent agency power was a term used to indicate the power of an agent that is not derived from authority, apparent authority, or estoppel, but solely from the agency relation and exists for the protection of persons harmed by or dealing with a servant or other agent. For example, Peter, owner of a manufacturing plant, tells Anson, his sales agent, to purchase widgets from Trader Company. Anson, finding Trader's widgets to be inferior, instead places an order for widgets with Jackson's, using Peter's stationery to place the order. Jackson's supplies Peter with the widgets, but Peter refuses to pay for them because he did not authorize Anson to buy them from Jackson's. Peter would be liable to Jackson's for payment because Anson had the inherent power to place the order. If this sounds like apparent authority to you, then you are like most others who would view this situation. For this reason, inherent authority has been discontinued as a theory in agency law, and has been replaced in the Restatement 3d by apparent authority or estoppel doctrines. The use of inherent authority, however, is still popular in some jurisdictions and will be found in older cases. Because of its similarity to apparent authority, however, it should be discontinued.

DUTIES OF AGENTS AND PRINCIPALS TO EACH OTHER AND THIRD PARTIES

When an agency is created, not only is there a relationship in which the agent must act for the principal, but there are rights and duties created on both sides of the equation. In this section we will address those.

Duty of Agent to Principal

Agency is a fiduciary relationship that requires an agent's complete loyalty to the principal—the principal's objectives and wishes are dominant. There are several specific duties the agent has that are designed to protect the principal's interest.

Duty of Good Conduct

An agent must act with reasonable skill and care in the performance of the work for which he is employed. He must also exercise any special skill that he may have. The level of care that is imposed on an agent depends on whether the agent is or claims to be an expert in the area to which his fiduciary relates. If an agent does not exercise the required care and skill he is liable to the principal for any resulting loss. For example, Foley hired Jermaine to manage his rental property because of Jermaine's accounting background. Jermaine engages in sloppy bookkeeping and causes Foley's checking account to be overdrawn. Jermaine would be liable for any overdrawn charges because his services as Foley's agent fell below the standard of care for an accountant.

Duty to Obey

When an agent acts on behalf of the principal, the agent must follow all lawful instructions of the principal. This duty to obey exists apart from the express provision in the contract. Exceptions include emergencies and instances in which instructions are not clearly stated. For example, Ricky Williams, the Heisman Trophy–winning running back from the University of Texas, was represented by an agent when he was negotiating with the New Orleans Saints of the NFL in 1999. His agent was assailed for allegedly making a bad deal for Ricky by negotiating a contract laden with incentives rather than accepting an offer which would have given Ricky a guaranteed signing bonus of $26 million. Instead, Ricky's contract guaranteed him $8.8 million, but required him to meet performance objectives. If he did not meet the objectives, he would receive the league minimum of $175,000–$400,000 per year for seven years. In response to criticism of his agent, Ricky Williams stated, "I don't work for my agent. My agent works for me. This was my decision and my decision alone. . . . He told me I shouldn't do it." This is an example of an agent's duty to obey.[3] Ricky's agent did exactly as the law requires: he obeyed his principal regardless of what the agent may think of the principal's decision. After all, keep in mind that the principal hired the agent to act on the principal's behalf, not the agent's own.

Duty to Account

Where the agent has received money and/or property from her principal for the principal's benefit, the agent is under a duty to account for those things received if the principal reasonably requests such **accounting.** The agent also has a duty to account for any profits that arise out of the agency. For example, if the principal authorizes the agent to sell an item for $1000 and the agent sells it for $1500, the agent may not secretly keep the extra $500.

Duty of Care

When an agent places his own interests above those of the principal there is a breach of fiduciary duty to the principal. An agent must use reasonable efforts to give the principal information that is relevant to the affairs entrusted to her and which, as the agent knows or

---

[3]Bryan Burwell, "Think Williams Got a Bad Deal? Don't Try to Tell Him That," *Sports Business Journal,* October 11, 1999, http://www.sportsbusinessjournal.com/article/15761.

should know, the principal would desire to have and which the agent has been given. A breach of the duty of care would occur when an agent fails to convey to his principal a message from a business partner that a deal had been called off, causing the principal to expend money in anticipation of the deal. The agent would be in breach of his duty of care for failing to convey that information and would be liable to the principal for the money spent by the principal unnecessarily.

EXAMPLE

Duty of Loyalty

An agent is said to owe a duty of undivided loyalty. The duty of an agent to his principal is a fiduciary one. It arises out of a relationship of trust and confidence. It is a duty imposed by law and is one of utmost loyalty and good faith. For example, if an agent is entrusted with confidential information concerning construction projects of his employer, the agent breaches his duty of loyalty by going to work for the business's competitor at the same time. Diversity in the Law 10-1 ("Redlining, Then and Now") and

EXAMPLE

DIVERSITY IN THE LAW 10-1

REDLINING, THEN AND NOW

In the 1950s, Albert and Sallie Bolton purchased a home on the south side of Chicago. The Boltons had to purchase their home on an installment plan, because in the 1950s, the federal government did not insure mortgage loans for buyers in racially integrated areas—just one way the government was implicated in creating ghettos that still exist today. The Boltons' real estate agent, Jay Goran, was a typical agent of the times. Blacks looking for homes would only be steered to certain areas—those in which blacks already lived or in which real estate owners wanted them to live. Goran bought the white home owner's house for a song—merely $4,300—and sold it a week later to the Boltons for $13,900. The installment contract required the Boltons to make every payment on time or they would suffer immediate eviction, which Goran could obtain for a $5.00 fee paid to the courthouse. After entering into the contract, Goran began to add fees on to the Boltons' monthly payment. When the Boltons complained, he refused to speak to them. They then started receiving repeated visits from the housing inspectors, first requiring new shutters, then a new front porch, then a new back porch. The inevitable ultimately happened, and the Boltons fell behind in their payments. They were evicted. The same pattern occurred over and over again to Goran's black clients. Some black families began dividing the property and taking on more roomers to generate income to make the inflated payments. Overcrowding created other social problems: for example, the school system increased 286 percent in 14 years.

The process that allowed such atrocities to happen is known as **redlining.** Appraisers would rate properties using a color scheme: green for all white areas, blue and yellow for areas with some foreigners or Jews, and red for areas with blacks; hence the term *redlining*. It was the government's Fair Housing Administration's pre-1965 policies and private banks who were in collusion with them that excluded blacks from obtaining mortgage loans, as the FHA would not approve any red loans. The presence of a single black family would cause the redlining of an entire neighborhood. Whites as well as blacks were unable to obtain a loan in that neighborhood. White homeowners were frightened by agents like Goran who would scare them off with the threat of their neighborhood becoming all black. Blacks, who could not obtain a mortgage at all, had no choice but to deal with agents like Goran. As the Boltons' real estate agent, Goran was supposed to be protecting the Boltons' interests, but instead, he created a completely untenable situation that resulted in the loss of their home. Note that here Goran started out as the real estate agent, but when he purchased the house and then sold it to the Boltons, he became a seller, which, of course, created an inevitable conflict of interest for his duties as an agent. Add to that his unscrupulous business dealings, and it was a recipe for disaster. No one minds making an honest profit. That is what capitalism is all about. But does what Goran did seem ethical to you?

Think it's over? Unfortunately, it is not. Today this practice continues in Chicago and other cities. In 2004, the Department of Justice announced it had settled with Chicago's First American Bank that it had charged with redlining. Noting that not one of First American's 34 branches was located in a minority area, the DOJ ordered First American to stop discriminating on the basis of race, to open four new full-service branch offices in areas affected by its discriminatory practices, and take other steps to correct its practices.

How ethical is this practice? Certainly it raises ethical issues for agents who steer black and Hispanic clients into areas where their loans cost more money, loans are generally subprime, and homes decrease in value because of foreclosures, abandonment, and other related issues set up by the agents themselves. Agents count on the fact that these families are poor, largely uneducated, may be unsophisticated real estate purchasers, have little voice in making policy, and not only do not know how to fight back, but are so busy trying to work to live, that they have little time to do so.

Sources: Beryl Satter, *Family Properties: Race, Real Estate, and the Exploitation of Black Urban America* (Metropolitan, 2009); DOJ Release, "Chicago Bank Charged with Discriminatory Redlining Lending," July 13, 2004, http://www.usdoj.gov/opa/pr/2004/July/04_crt_478.htm.

REVERSE REDLINING: PREDATORY LENDING PRACTICES

Here's another hair-raising example of a borrower taken advantage of by those who are generally more sophisticated and do not apply ethical concepts to their business dealings: Florence McKnight, an 84-year-old widow, signed a $50,000 loan from her hospital bed to put new windows in her home—a $10,000 job. The loan called for her to pay a total of $72,000 in payments over 15 years, at the end of which time she would still owe a $40,000 balloon payment. Needless to say, her home went into foreclosure.

Racial minorities and low-income families in poor communities have often been victimized by such predatory lending practices. Often seen as *reverse redlining,* predatory lending practices are practiced in these vulnerable communities because of the withdrawal of conventional financial services in these neighborhoods. Predatory practices include subprime mortgages, balloon payments which require borrowers to make a huge payment at the end of making small payments over time, single-premium life insurance payments which call for a single yearly payment to be paid up front, high prepayment penalties that trap the lender into the loan, fees for nonexistent services, loan flipping causing homeowners to refinance loans with subprime lenders, and other practices. The Joint Center for Housing Studies at Harvard University reported that subprime loans increased between 1993 and 2000 from 1 to 13 percent and that they are most frequently found in neighborhoods with high unemployment rates and declining housing values. The study also found that 20 percent of refinanced loans were to borrowers earning less than 60 percent of the median income and were made by subprime lenders. In response to this and other reports, the FTC took enforcement action against 19 lenders and brokers for predatory practices and negotiated a settlement with Citigroup for $215 million to resolve charges against a subsidiary it owned for various deceptive practices.

Redlining and predatory practices take advantage of a population that has no alternative but to deal with these agents. The government has stepped in to regulate and eliminate some of these practices, and private agencies have started educational campaigns to try to educate these communities to forestall some of these practices, but they continue almost unabated.

Think about what these practices do to entire groups of people, to neighborhoods, schools, small businesses, recreation areas, home values, neighborhood aesthetics, and in the way of increasing crime. We saw a great deal of this recently when so many homes were foreclosed creating blighted neighborhoods with empty houses, devaluing remaining properties. Crime increased as people broke into empty homes. The look of neighborhoods took a beating as houses lay empty, with lawns overgrown and unattended. In Diversity in the Law 10-1, an inevitable consequence of the demands the real estate agent Goran made was that people took in roomers to help make more money, so single family homes suddenly became rooming houses with moveable populations rather than stable families. With the prevalence of such unscrupulous practices, schools become overcrowded, and in overcrowded living situations, the social environment often suffers and degrades. All of this greatly impacts local businesses too. This is a prime example of how diversity, law, and business have intersected in our country in a tragic way. The issues are very difficult to untangle. If people know the possibilities going into making decisions it can greatly impact the outcome, but of course people like the Boltons or Florence McKnight rarely have the leeway to acquire such knowledge. Such situations are not isolated business decisions. Their impact is far greater. Mr. Goran's wish to make money at the expense of others had a far-reaching impact on the neighborhood he chose to decimate.

Source: Gregory D. Squires, "Predatory Lending; Redlining in Reverse," NHI, *Shelterforce Online,* Issue 139, January/February 2005, http://www.nhi.org/online/issues/139/redlining.html. accessed 8/8/09.

Diversity in the Law 10-2 ("Reverse Redlining: Predatory Lending Practices") illustrate abuses of the duty of loyalty that resulted in long-term harm to the African American community and the continued harm to that community made possible by disloyal agents. Take Away 10-4 ("Duties of Agents to Principals") summarizes the duties agents have to their principals.

L03 Duty of Principal to Agent

Although the principal-agent relationship does not require a contract to arise, the general rules of contract apply to any agreement between the parties. Thus, the principal has a duty to perform any contract of employment that he has made with the agent and he may be held liable for breach of contract if he fails to do so.

DUTIES OF AGENTS TO PRINCIPALS

Duty	Description of Duty
Good Conduct	To act with reasonable skill and care
Obey	To follow all lawful instructions
Account	To account for those things received and profits that arise
Care	To use reasonable efforts to give relevant information
Loyalty	To maintain a relationship of trust and confidence

Duty to Indemnify

An agent may incur expenses or make payments on behalf of the principal. If so, the principal has a duty to **indemnify** the agent for such payments made or expenses incurred within the scope of the agency. For example, Construction Company is in the construction business and is erecting a building. Construction Company hires Acme Insurance company as its insurance agent for the construction. Acme signed an indemnity clause with Construction Company that required Acme to indemnify Construction Company for any harm caused to a third party unless Construction Company was 100 percent liable. An employee was injured and sued Construction Company for damages. Construction Company was found to be 99 percent liable for harm, and the employee was found to be 1 percent liable. The employee was awarded $425,000 in damages against Construction Company for injuries suffered. Under the indemnity provision, Acme has agreed to indemnify the Construction Company for the $425,000 Construction Company had to pay the employee because Acme promised to indemnify Construction Company unless Construction Company was found to be 100 percent liable.

Duty to Compensate

A principal is under a duty to perform his part of the contract according to its terms. The most important duty of the principal toward his agent is to compensate him according to the terms of the contract. If the contract does not specify the terms of compensation, the principal is under a duty to pay the reasonable value of the authorized services.

Where an agent is to be paid according to the results he accomplishes, the principal has a duty to provide a means by which the agent can earn his compensation. The principal has a further duty not to interfere with the work of the agent.

Duty to Reimburse

A principal is under a duty to reimburse his agent for authorized payments made by the agent on behalf of the principal and for authorized expenses incurred by the agent. For example, an agent who reasonably and properly pays insurance for the protection of her principal's property is entitled to reimbursement for the payment. In the opening scenario, if Duke had incurred expenses, for example, in closing out Aunt Ruth's investment accounts, Aunt Ruth would have been responsible for reimbursing Duke for those expenses.

Duty of Principal to Third Party under Contract

General rules of contract govern the liability of a disclosed or partially disclosed principal on an authorized contract. In those cases, the agent, principal, and third party are known to exist. Some of the rules applied to disclosed or partially disclosed principals are not applicable to transactions conducted by an undisclosed principal.

EXAMPLE

Agent for Disclosed Principal Where the principal is fully disclosed, the agent is not a party to the contract. That is because the third party knows the agent is acting on the principal's behalf and understands that though she is dealing with the agent, it is only in a representative capacity, and she is actually dealing with the principal only. For example, Roberto is an acquisitions manager for a large corporation. The corporation has decided to purchase a warehouse to use for storage of its product. Roberto, on behalf of his corporation, contacts the warehouse owner and begins to negotiate for its purchase. Roberto makes it known that he is making an offer on behalf of his corporation, and not for himself. In this scenario, Roberto is an agent acting for a disclosed principal, his corporation. Even if Roberto's signature appears on the contract of sale, it will appear as an agent for the corporation only and Roberto is not liable for the expense of the warehouse.

EXAMPLE

Agent for Partially Disclosed Principal Where the principal is partially disclosed (known to exist but unidentified), it is implied that the agent is a party to the contract. Because he or she is known to be acting as an agent, however, it is inferred that the third party also wants the principal to be a party to the contract, and that is the normal inference given. However, the agent remains liable on the contract because it is unreasonable for the third party to bind himself to an unknown party. But, why, you ask, would a principal want to be unknown? Let us suppose someone like Oprah Winfrey wishes to purchase a vacation home. Rather than disclose her interest in the property (which will likely cause a significant increase in the asking price), she sends her agent to negotiate on her behalf. The seller of the home is told that the agent is not purchasing the home for herself, but her client (the principal) does not wish to disclose her identity. In this case, the agent is working for a partially disclosed principal. Because the third party seller knows that a principal is involved, the third party would expect that principal to be a party to the contract, and release the agent once the third party and principal enter into the contract.

EXAMPLE

Agent for Undisclosed Principal When an agent purports to be acting in his or her own behalf but is, in fact, acting for a principal, the agent alone is party to the contract. The undisclosed principal is also liable on the contract to the third party if the agent was acting within the scope of his actual authority, because of the basic agency concept that the authorized act of an agent binds his principal.

The use of undisclosed agency agreements in the commercial world is common. For example, if you enter into a contract to lease a truck from Lease America, Inc., you would ordinarily assume that you have contracted with that company. However, you may in truth, have contracted with another company which, as principal, gave Lease America, Inc., the authority to act as its agent and contract on its behalf. In

TAKE AWAY 10-5

AGENTS AND LIABILITY

Type of Agent	Definition	Liability
Disclosed	Third party knows identity of principal	Principal
Partially Disclosed	Third party knows of principal but does not know identity	Agent then Principal
Undisclosed	Third party does not know of existence of principal	Agent and Principal

this example, both the agent and the undisclosed principal may sue and be sued on the contract, unless the terms of the contract expressly or impliedly confine the right to sue or be sued to the named parties. For example, an agent purchases a car for an undisclosed principle. The car dealer does not know that the true owner of the car is the principal. In a contract dispute that arises later because the payments are not made, the car dealer sues the agent. When the agent informs the car dealer that he is only the agent and that the true owner is the principal, the car dealer has three options: he can maintain his suit against the agent, he can sue the principal, or he can sue both (but only collect what he is owed from one).

Normally, the principal intends that transactions be conducted in her or his individual or corporate name. Very often, the other party to the transaction is relying on the reputation and credit standing of that principal. In that case, the identity of the agent is not important. However, there are times when it is the agent's reputation that is important. For example, in the purchase and sale of stock, the identities of the buyer and seller are usually of no consequence; it is the broker-agent who they are dealing with that is important. Stockbrokers, in most cases, transact securities transactions on behalf of clients, but do so in a manner which makes them appear as principals. Take Away 10-5 ("Agents and Liability") summarizes the liability of agents depending on the type of principal in dealing with third parties.

RATIFICATION

Ratification is the **affirmation** by a person of a prior act which did not bind him but which was done on his account. A principal's ratification confirms or validates an agent's right to have acted as the agent did. If an agent assumes to act for a principal without authority, and the principal later affirms the agent's act, it is ratification. The principal is then bound to the same extent as if previous authority had been granted. For example, suppose Aunt Ruth subsequently learned that Duke opened the unauthorized trust account for his daughter. Intending to open an account for her anyway, Aunt Ruth allowed the trust account that he had created to continue. Aunt Ruth would be said to have ratified Duke's prior unauthorized creation of the trust account.

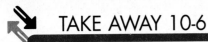

TAKE AWAY 10-6

RESPONDEAT SUPERIOR

An employer is subject to liability for torts committed by employees while acting within the scope of their employment.

Source: Rest. 3d Agency §2.04.

RESPONDEAT SUPERIOR

The liability of a principal for the tort of an agent is referred to as **respondeat superior.** A principal is responsible for the unauthorized torts of his agent if committed while the agent is acting within the scope of his employment. The agent's tortious conduct is said to be imputed to the principal. See Take Away 10-6 ("Respondeat Superior") for the Rest. 3d's liability statement.

An agent acts within the **scope of employment** when performing work assigned by the principal or engaging in a course of conduct subject to the principal's control. An agent's act is not within the scope of employment when it occurs within an independent course of conduct not intended by the agent to serve any purpose of the principal. The fact that a principal has specifically forbidden the agent from doing the acts will not prevent the acts from being within the scope of his employment, if they are connected with the act the agent is authorized to perform. The *O'Connor v. Davis* case (Case 10.1) explores the limitation of scope of employment.

CASE 10.1 O'Connor v. Davis

126 F.3d 112 (C.A. NY 1997)

Facts: Bridget O'Connor majored in social work at Marymount College, in Tarrytown, New York. As part of her curriculum she was required to perform 200 hours of field work at a hospital in New York. Dr. James Davis worked as a psychiatrist at the same hospital at which O'Connor was interning. After she had interned for two days, Dr. Davis referred to O'Connor as "Miss Sexual Harassment"—a term which he later explained was a compliment because O'Connor was attractive and was likely to be the target of sexual harassment. O'Connor complained about the comments and was instructed by the hospital's supervisor to "ignore him." After the complaint, Dr. Davis continued with the comments. He told O'Connor one morning she looked tired and that she and her boyfriend must have had "a good time last night." On another day, Dr. Davis suggested that he and O'Connor should participate in an orgy. Finally, on a separate occasion, Dr. Davis told her to take her clothes off during a meeting and explained to her that you always take your clothes off when you go to the doctor's office. O'Connor complained to the school and was allowed to leave the hospital to complete her internship requirement at another hospital. Later O'Connor brought suit against the hospital alleging sexual harassment by Dr. Davis.

Issue: Whether, as a college intern, O'Connor is able to bring suit for workplace sexual harassment of an employee?

Decision: No.

Reasoning: To recover under Title VII [of the Civil Rights Act of 1964 which prohibits gender discrimination including sexual harassment] sexual harassment, one must be an employee of the organization one is attempting to hold liable under the Act. When Congress uses the term "employee" without defining it with precision, courts should presume that Congress had in mind "the conventional master-servant relationship as understood by the common-law agency doctrine." A prerequisite to considering whether an individual is one or the other under common-law agency principles is that the individual have been hired in the first instance. That is, only where a "hire" has occurred should the common-law agency analysis be undertaken. Where no financial benefit is obtained by the purported employee from the employer, no "plausible" employment relationship of any sort can be said to exist because although "compensation by the putative employer to the putative employee in exchange for his services is not a sufficient condition, . . . it is an essential condition to the existence of an employer-employee relationship." It is uncontested that O'Connor received from Rockland no salary or other wages, and no employee benefits such as health insurance, vacation, or sick pay, nor was she promised any such compensation. Because the absence of either direct or indirect economic remuneration or the promise thereof is undisputed in this case, we agree with the district court that O'Connor was not a Rockland employee within the meaning of Title VII and thus that her discrimination claim under that statute must fail. We conclude by saying that we are not unsympathetic for O'Connor's situation. We recognize that her success was dependant on completing her internship; however, it is for Congress not the court to provide a remedy.

CASE QUESTIONS

1. Earlier, it was explained that a gratuitous agent is an agent nonetheless. Why do you think the court was unwilling to expand the definition of employee here?

2. If Ms. O'Connor had complained to her university and nothing had been done, would that have provided her with an alternative form of relief? In other words, would a university that received such a complaint have a duty to act?

3. Should Congress include people like Ms. O'Connor within the definition of employee? If they don't, what avenue will she have to recover? Does this send the wrong message to people like Dr. Davis? Does this decision make students sent to hospitals for internships vulnerable to people like Dr. Davis who may take advantage of the fact that they cannot be sued for violation of Title VII?

Whether the agent is within the scope of his employment is the main issue to be decided when attaching liability to the principal. For example, suppose an agent was sent on an errand, and while performing, decided to go 10 blocks out of the way to fill out an application for another job. On this side trip, he causes injury to a third party. Is the principal liable for the third party's injuries caused by the agent? Reality Check 10-2 ("Frolic and Detour") raises this question of what happens if an agent goes off course and injures someone.

 EXAMPLE

An employer will not be liable for the torts of an independent contractor, even if the independent contractor is acting for the benefit of the employer. The crucial factor in all cases is whether the employer has retained the right to control the physical movements of the one employed. Where the one employed has a particular skill or occupation of his own and is paid by the job or commission, he is more likely than not an independent contractor. For example, plaintiff was knocked unconscious and injured when an 8 X 10 panel of wood blew over onto her while she was walking on a public sidewalk. The property was owned by Olympic Savings and Loan who had hired Drury Construction Company to erect the fence. The court ruled that Drury was an independent contractor and that Olympic was not liable for plaintiff's injuries.[4]

EXAMPLE

Liability has been deemed not to apply where the harm to a third party arises from a personal dispute rather than the principal's business, where the act is the result of personal compulsion, or where the acts did not occur as an outgrowth of employment.

REALITY CHECK 10-2

FROLIC AND DETOUR

When an employee is on a "frolic," he is outside the scope of employment. A "detour," however, is a deviation within the scope of employment. Test yourself with this scenario: Freddie sent a truckload of its merchandise from Manhattan to Staten Island, instructing Ishaq, the driver, to return to the garage on the west side of Manhattan. After making the delivery, Ishaq instead drove to Hamilton Street on the east side of Manhattan to visit his mother, where a neighborhood carnival was in progress. He took a group of boys on a tour of the district, stopping at a café on Catherine Street to say a word to his friends. As he drove off with some of the boys still on the truck, an 11-year-old boy trying to join them was injured. Ishaq stated that he was on his way back to the garage. Assuming this was true, what would your conclusion be? Frolic or detour?

The Restatement of Agency §228 states "(1) Conduct of a servant is within the scope of employment if, but only if: (a) it is the kind he was employed to perform; (b) it occurs substantially within the authorized time and space limits; (c) it is actuated, at least in part, by a purpose to serve the master, ..." Additionally, §229 states "(1) To be within the scope of employment, conduct must be of the same general nature as that authorized, or incidental to the conduct authorized." Frolic or detour?

---

[4]*Blodgett v. Olympic Savings & Loan Asso.,* 646 P.2d 139 (Ct. App. Wash. 1982).

TERMINATION OF AUTHORITY

TERMINATION OF ACTUAL AUTHORITY—IN GENERAL

An agent's actual authority may be terminated by:

1. the agent's death, cessation of existence, or suspension of powers . . . ; or
2. the principal's death, cessation of existence, or suspension of powers . . . ; or
3. the principal's loss of capacity . . . ; or
4. an agreement between the agent and the principal or the occurrence of circumstances on the basis of which the agent should reasonably conclude that the principal no longer would assent to the agent's taking action on the principal's behalf, . . . ; or
5. a manifestation of revocation by the principal to the agent, or of renunciation by the agent to the principal . . . ; or
6. the occurrence of circumstances specified by statute.

Source: Rest. 3d Agency §3.06.

Authority may be terminated by the act of the parties or by operation of law. As a general rule, a principal has the power to terminate an agent's authority at any time, even if doing so violates a contract between the principal and agent, and even if it had been agreed that the agent's authority was irrevocable. The agent's authority terminates once he has received notice of the revocation. This does not mean that the principal may escape liability if it in fact breaches the contract giving the agent authority.

An agent has the power to **renounce,** which terminates the principal-agency relationship. As in the case with the principal, if there are issues of liability, this renunciation does not terminate them.

The occurrence of certain events will terminate the agency relationship as a matter of law. Where this occurs, no notice is necessary. For the most part, these are events that make it impossible for the agent to perform or those that would make it unlikely that the principal would wish him to act. See Take Away 10-7 ("Termination of Actual Authority—In General") for the Rest. 3d of Agency's summary. Termination occurs by operation of law upon:

1. An outbreak of war between the principal's country and the agent's country which makes it impossible or illegal for the agent to act;
2. The death of the principal even though the agent has no notice of it;
3. The permanent loss of capacity by insanity or otherwise of the principal; however, brief periods of insanity will not terminate the agent's authority;
4. The death of the agent, but not the loss of capacity of the agent by insanity, whether temporary or permanent, since an agent does not need capacity to possess authority;
5. Termination by a change in circumstances which makes the agent realize that the principal would no longer desire him to act (such as changes in the value of the property or subject matter, bankruptcy or insolvency of the principal, failure to obtain or acquire a necessary license, or the act becomes unlawful).

Forms of Business

Business is a broad term describing all kinds of profit-making and nonprofit activity. It covers activities ranging from the street vendor to the billion-dollar Walmart Corporation. It covers nonprofit organizations like the Girl Scouts as well as mega-foundations like the Bill and Melinda Gates Foundation. Duke's corporation, although he was the sole shareholder, was a form of doing business.

Businesses may be looked at in different ways. They are conducted either by a single individual or a collection of individuals. The street vendor is an example of a sole proprietorship—an unincorporated business owned by a single person. Microsoft is an example of a huge corporation with thousands of shareholders. We'll examine other forms of business, namely the general partnership, limited partnership, limited liability company, and professional corporation. There are still other forms of business that are less used or used only for a particular purpose such as joint ventures and franchises. While these forms of business are important, they are beyond our focus in this chapter.

Businesses may be classified as corporations, either privately or publicly owned, or as unincorporated business entities. An unincorporated business entity is every form of business but a corporation. Reality Check 10-3 ("Business Courts") describes the attention businesses are getting in the court system with the formation of courts that specialize in business disputes.

CHOOSING A BUSINESS FORM

L06

When choosing a business form, many things should be considered. What is the purpose of the business? What liability does the owner want to assume? What are the tax implications for one business choice over another? Is the business going to be owned by one person or a group of people? Are those people related or are they strangers to one another? Does the owner want the business to function in perpetuity or end when he or she retires or dies? Do the owners want to be able to pass the business on to others? Do the owners intend for the business to ultimately become publicly owned? These and other questions should determine what type of business enterprise is chosen.

SOLE PROPRIETORSHIPS

One unincorporated business owned by a single individual is called a **sole proprietorship.** The sole proprietor is personally liable on all business obligations since there is no legal separation between the owner and the business. The more successful the business becomes, the more successful the business owner becomes, but the risks to the owner's personal assets also increase. If the owner wishes to minimize her personal risk, she may have to switch to a different type of business that will allow her to protect her personal assets. For example, Roger started his business as a young boy who cut his neighbor's lawns on the weekends while in high school. After graduation, Roger wanted to expand his business so that he could save money for college. He purchased lawn equipment and solicited for business outside of his neighborhood, eventually building up a clientele that kept him busy all week. Roger eventually bought a home, car, and a truck that he used to haul his equipment. Roger, as a sole proprietor of his lawn business, now risks his assets (his home, car, truck and equipment) if he should become personally liable for damage to the property he services or harm to someone while performing his services. He should begin to think about protecting his assets by using another form of business.

EXAMPLE

REALITY CHECK 10-3

BUSINESS COURTS

Business courts are cropping up all over the U.S. They are designed to hear cases involving business-on-business disputes and complex commercial litigation. In some states they are designed to reduce the backlog of cases in regular courts, and in other states the approach is that they can more easily attract business to their states by the creation of these specialized courts.

The Delaware Court of Chancery was the first business court. It hears about 500 cases per year, but it is limited to cases in which equitable relief, rather than money damages, is sought.

New York uses a different type of business court model in which the business court hears cases within a defined monetary amount, or within a business subject area, including antitrust, corporate governance, and contract disputes.

North Carolina has a third model in which the only cases heard are those with complex disputes that have the potential to impact business.

Whatever the model, the trend seems to be for states to develop business courts to try to create a specialty among its judiciary for handling complex business litigation.

Source: Gary W. Jackson, "Do Business Courts Really Mean Business?" June 1, 2006, http://www.thefreelibrary.com/Do+business+courts+really+mean+business%3f+Many+nonbusiness+cases+are+...-a0147568319.

CHARACTERISTICS OF SOLE PROPRIETORSHIPS IN THE U.S.

According to the latest available U.S. Census statistics (2002), self-employed individuals who have no paid employees operate three-fourths of U.S. businesses. Forty-nine percent of the nation's businesses are operated from home and 77% of those business owners used their own money to start the business. Ethnically, home-based businesses made up 56% of American Indian or Alaska Native–owned firms, 56% of women-owned firms, 53% of black-owned firms, 53% of Hawaiian and Pacific Islander–owned firms, and 45% of Hispanic-owned firms. In contrast, of the Asian-owned firms, 66% reported that they operate their firms from nonresidential locations.

What types of businesses are run from home? The majority were accommodation and food services (79%), manufacturing (78%), wholesale trade (74%), and retail trade (72%). Twenty-eight percent of businesses started with no capital at all, and one in ten started with just capital generated by personal or business credit cards.

Almost two-thirds of all business owners had more than a high school diploma: 23% had a bachelor's degree and 17% had a graduate degree. One in four business owners had a high school education or less.

Thirty-one percent of business owners were over 55 years old, 29% were between 45 and 54, 24% were between 35 and 44, and 2% were less than 25 years of age.

Source: U.S. Census Bureau, press release, September 27, 2006, http://www.census.gov/newsroom/releases/archives/business_ownership/cb06-148.html.

For a summary of some of the characteristics of business in the U.S., see Reality Check 10-4 ("Characteristics of Sole Proprietorships in the U.S.").

GENERAL PARTNERSHIPS

A **partnership** is an association of two or more persons to carry on a business for profit. Partnerships do not need to be expressly created, that is, no special words need be spoken between the parties or documents signed or filed to make a partnership.

Some partnerships are governed by a partnership agreement. This can be either a written agreement or an oral agreement. Like the formation of a partnership itself, some of these agreements are elaborate and lengthy, and others are simply understood between the partners. An oral agreement to share profits may be enough to create a general partnership even though the financial contributions are unequal. If two or more parties enter an agreement to perform together and split the profits, a general partnership is formed. Even if the parties did not intend to be partners, the law will treat them as such regarding the affairs of that business. For example, Duke, a lawyer, may have partners in a law firm with whom he shares profits and losses.

Of course, many general partnerships are carefully planned. But even without such a plan, a partnership may exist. If a business has the essential characteristics of a partnership, it is a partnership. For an illustration of this principle, see *Wiggs v. Peedin* (Case 10.2).

Notice that the sharing of losses is not a key characteristic of a partnership. Loss sharing may be a consequence of being a partner, but is not a condition of partnership.

CASE 10.2 Wiggs v. Peedin

669 S.E.2d 844 (N.C. App. 2008)

Facts: In 1995 the Wiggs and Peedin's husband entered into an oral partnership to operate a commercial hog farm. The partnership was later reduced to writing. Peedin and her husband owned the property on which the hog farm was to operate, and used this property as collateral to get a loan to start the farm. The terms of the partnership agreement stated that if the loan was repaid within 10 years, each plaintiff would get a 10% interest in the profits and assets of the partnership, and Peedin and her husband would own the remaining 60%. After Peedin's husband died, she became the sole owner of the property. The Wiggs alleged that the partnership did not end with the death of the husband pursuant to the partnership agreement.

Issue: Was there a partnership agreement between the Wiggs and Peedin to carry on the partnership after Peedin's husband's death?

Decision: Yes.

Reasoning: As a general rule partnerships dissolve upon the death of any partner, unless expressed otherwise in the partnership agreement. Here, Peedin proposed that his and defendant's partnership interest be passed to their surviving children if both of them died prior to March 2005. Although *both* Peedin and defendant did not die before March 2005, this provision shows an intent for the business relationship with plaintiffs to continue in the event of Peedin's death. This intent is also evidenced by the provision in the document which states their children "will not be allowed to break this agreement." Presumably, upon Peedin's death, the benefits and burdens of his interest in the partnership passed to defendant.

Here, a partnership may have resulted from either: (1) defendant's spoken words or (2) plaintiff's and defendant's continued conduct after Peedin's death. Although defendant denies that she had knowledge of the exact terms of the agreement between Peedin and plaintiffs, Defendant specifically testified that from [1999] through 2004, . . . the arrangement did not change in terms of [plaintiffs'] and [defendant's] involvement in the farm. Defendant also reaped the benefits of this continued arrangement for the five years after Peedin's death. The record shows that from 2001 to 2004, the hog farm operation was generating a net cash flow between $150,000.00 and $200,000.00 per year. This indicates that she was fully aware there was some sort of arrangement for plaintiffs to work for the hog farm operation.

CASE QUESTIONS

1. The Defendant argued that she was not bound by the partnership agreement between the Wiggs and her deceased husband. On what grounds did the court find that she was bound?

2. What was the most convincing evidence that compelled the court to find that she was a part of the partnership agreement entered into by her husband?

3. How could she have ensured that upon the death of her husband, the partnership would terminate?

The Uniform Partnership Act

Beginning in 1914, it was recognized that in order to conduct business nationally, partnerships needed to function with consistent rules and regulations. Thus, the Uniform Partnership Act of 1914 (UPA) was promulgated. These rules were quickly adopted by 49 states (Louisiana was the lone holdout), and have been amended in subsequent years. Now, all 50 states and the District of Columbia, Guam, and the Virgin Islands have adopted some version of the UPA or the Revised Uniform Partnership Act (RUPA). These rules allow partnerships, wherever formed and operating, to have predictability in functioning and in interacting with other businesses.

As with the Restatements and the Uniform Commerical Code, each state, through its legislature, decides which UPA or RUPA rules to adopt for the state. The rules are to be used only if the partnership agreement does not determine how the partnership wishes to handle its affairs. These are known as **default** rules—they are there to be used if the partnership agreement, either written or oral, is silent. We will speak of partnership rules generally without referring to any UPA or RUPA rule specifically.

DUTIES OF PARTNERS TO EACH OTHER

Generally, partners share equally in the profits and losses of the partnership, unless otherwise agreed. Partnerships are somewhat risky in that one partner's actions can bind the rest of the partners and the partners' personal assets may be used to cover partnership liability if the partnership assets are insufficient. Partners owe each other a fiduciary duty of loyalty. In general a partner may not profit at the expense—either direct or indirect—of the partnership. In particular, without the consent of the other partners, a partner may not compete with the partnership, take business opportunities from which the partnership might have benefited or that the partnership might have needed, use partnership property for personal gain, or engage in a transaction that presents a conflict of interest. These restrictions begin with the partnership formation and end with the termination of the partnership or the partner's withdrawal from the partnership.

EXAMPLE

Occasionally, partners deal on opposite sides of a transaction. When this occurs, a partner is obliged to provide full disclosure to the partnership, and engage in fair dealing with the partnership concerning the transaction. For example, full disclosure would mean that if a partner is selling his or her partnership interest to another partner, he or she has an affirmative duty to disclose any **material information** that relates to the value of the partnership interest itself that cannot be learned by examining the partnership books. The partner who possesses the information must volunteer it and cannot use

EXAMPLE

the "you did not ask" excuse that would be permitted if they were not partners and were dealing at arm's length. An example of fair dealing would mean that as a matter of process, partners are required to deal with each other in a candid, noncoercive manner. In addition, partners are required to provide a fair price in partner-to-partner transactions.

LIMITED PARTNERSHIPS

A **limited partnership** consists of one or more general partners and one or more limited partners. Both the right to manage and the right to bind the limited partnership are reserved to the general partners. Limited partners are essentially passive investors in the partnership who do not make management decisions. Generally, limited partners share profits and losses in proportion to their investment. The general partners of a limited partnership are personally liable for the partnership's debts. Thus, limited partners are protected from lia-

EXAMPLE

bility beyond their investment in the limited partnership. Suppose, for example, that a partnership needed capital to continue growing its business. It could borrow the money to expand, but that would require it to pay the money back. Another option available is to have a limited partner who would invest in the partnership and take money out of the partnership much like a partner would do. The limited partner would provide the cash needed, but the liability would remain with the general partners. The limited partner would only be at risk for the amount of money that he or she invested. For an example of a very successful limited partnership, see Reality Check 10-5 ("Bloomberg Finance, L.P.").

In order to form a limited partnership, the owners must file a certificate of limited partnership with the state and operate under the state's statute. The certificate is a public document that can be referred to by outsiders looking to do business with the limited partnership. Most limited partnerships are governed by a partnership agreement and it is the partnership agreement, not the certificate of limited partnership filed with the state, that details and determines the rights, responsibilities, and relationships of the partners. The limited partnership agreement is not a public document. Like general partnerships, in a limited partnership, no partner may substitute another person for itself as a partner without the consent of all the other partners.

Only general partners manage the business and only the general partners have the power to bind the partnership. Because of their management role, general partners owe fiduciary duties of loyalty and care to the partnership. Limited partners have the right to information about the partnership business, but they do not have any say in the ordinary operations of the partnership. This role can be enlarged under the partnership agreement. For example, some partnership agreements give limited partners the right to remove the general partners.

LIMITED LIABILITY COMPANIES

The **limited liability company** (LLC) is a hybrid form of business that combines the liability shield of a corporation with the federal tax classification of a partnership. (See Corporations below.) LLCs have been in existence only since 1988. The benefit of doing business in this form is that the owners of the business (called "members") can operate the business like a partnership, but without the risk of unlimited liability. Another benefit is that the LLCs enjoy partnershiplike tax status. Today, all 50 states and the District of Columbia have LLC statutes, and LLCs are a fast-growing choice for doing business in the United States. Take Away 10-8 ("Advantages and Disadvantages of Limited Liability Companies") lists some things to consider when thinking about forming an LLC.

LLCs are organized under state statutes that allow the LLC to exist and provide rules for operating the LLC. Generally, an LLC is formed by filing **articles of organization** with the secretary of state in the state where it is formed. Once this is accomplished, the LLC, much like a corporation, exists as a legal entity separate from its owners. This existence allows

TAKE AWAY 10-8

ADVANTAGES AND DISADVANTAGES OF LIMITED LIABILITY COMPANIES

Advantages	Disadvantages
• No double taxation—profits taxed at member level	• Earnings of members subject to self employment tax
• Limited liability of members	• If partnershiplike status chosen, LLC terminated if more than 50% of capital sold within 12-month period
• Can be set up with one person which can be an entity	• If partnership treatment elected, cannot issue stock, stock options, or tax-free reorganizations
• No required annual meeting for members (unless required by state law)	• Lack of uniformity among LLC statutes leading to inconsistent treatment if operated in more than one state
• No loss of power to board of directors	• Some states tax LLCs but not partnerships
• Perpetual business entity	
• Less record keeping and paperwork	
• LLC may have foreign investors	

the owners to have a liability shield against the debts of the LLC. Unless the statutory filing requirements are complied with, however, the courts are not likely to recognize the LLC. For the danger that that can pose, see *In the Matter of Hausman* (Case 10.3).

Unlike a partnership, an LLC can be formed by one person, and can operate like a sole proprietorship and is called a Single Member LLC (SMLLC). The SMLLC, although managed by a single owner, is still legally operative as long as the filing is complete. It maintains the liability shield and the partnership tax status as well.

Flexible management rules allow LLCs to function like a corporation, if they choose, or to function like a partnership. LLCs are governed by an **operating agreement** similar

CASE 10.3 In the Matter of Hausman

858 N.Y.S.2d 330 ((NY App. Div. 2008)

Facts: On October 16, 2000, the decedent executed a will dividing her residuary (whatever is left after bills are paid and will items are disbursed) estate between her son George, her daughter Susan, and seven of her grandchildren. At the time she executed her will, the decedent was the owner of real property located at 1373 56th Street in Brooklyn. Almost one year later, on October 4, 2001, George executed articles of organization to form 1373 Realty Co. LLC (hereinafter the LLC) for the purpose of owning, operating, and managing the real property. On the same day, George and Susan also signed an operating agreement, which provided that they were to be the sole members of the LLC. On November 2, 2001, the decedent executed a deed transferring ownership of the real property to the LLC. However, the LLC's articles of organization were not filed with the Department of State until two weeks later on November 16, 2001. It is undisputed that the property was purportedly transferred to the LLC before the LLC came into legal existence.

Following the decedent's death, a dispute arose among George, Susan, and the seven grandchildren over whether the deed transferring the real property to the LLC prior to its legal formation was valid and belonged to the LLC, or invalid and belonged to the decedent's estate to be divided among the 9 beneficiaries under the will. George, in his capacity as executor of the decedent's estate, filed a petition asking the Surrogate's Court to make a legal determination as to the validity of the deed and its transfer. The Surrogate Court concluded that the deed was valid because the LLC was a de facto entity on the date the conveyance was made. This is an appeal from that decision.

Issue: Was the LLC the owner of the property?

Decision: No.

Reasoning: As a general rule, a purported entity which is not yet in legal existence cannot take title to real property. However, New York has recognized that an unincorporated entity can take title or acquire rights by contract if it is a *de facto* (defectively filed) corporation and we agree with the Surrogate's finding that the *de facto* corporation doctrine is equally applicable to limited liability companies. However, to establish that an entity is a *de facto* corporation or limited liability company, there must be a showing that a colorable attempt was made to comply with the statutes governing incorporation or organization prior to the purported acceptance of the deed. Here, while it is undisputed that George executed the LLC's articles of organization on October 4, 2001, there is no evidence that an attempt to file the articles of organization was made prior to the execution of the deed on November 2, 2001. In the absence of a colorable attempt to comply with the statute governing the organization of limited liability companies by filing, we cannot find that the LLC was a *de facto* entity capable of taking title on the date the deed was executed. Accordingly, the decedent's purported conveyance of the real property was void.

CASE QUESTIONS

1. In order for the court to be able to find that the LLC was able to take title, it would have to find that the Hausmans attempted to file under the state's filing rules. Why would the court make that requirement?

2. Why was it necessary for the court to find that the laws governing corporations also governed LLCs regarding *de facto* filing?

3. What is the danger in allowing entities that are not recognized by the state to take title or be otherwise recognized? Why wouldn't the same danger be present with a *de facto* LLC?

to a partnership agreement or corporate bylaws. This is a nonpublic internal document that represents the agreement the owners have as to how they will operate the LLC and their relationship. If the owners of the LLC decide to function more like a partnership, then they elect to be **member-managed,** which means that the owners themselves will manage the day-to-day operation of the LLC. If the owners decide to function more like a corporation, then they elect to be **manager-managed,** which means that the owners will elect officers to run the LLC. Governance in a member-managed LLC is like a general partnership. Governance in a manager-managed LLC is like a corporation. The election is stated in the articles of organization. If the LLC is managed by its members, the power to bind the LLC attaches to its members. If the LLC is managed by managers, the power to bind the LLC attaches to the managers and not to all of its members. In the earlier example involving Roger's lawn business, he could elect to become an SMLLC rather than remain a sole proprietor. The benefit he would receive is that his personal assets would be protected from exposure to personal liability.

EXAMPLE

LLC statutes can differ substantially in how they address the fiduciary duties of members. Generally, those who manage an LLC owe a duty of loyalty and care to the entity. It is not as clear that there is a duty of loyalty or care owed to the members themselves. It depends on the statute under which the LLC was formed and the operating agreement under which it operates. Many statutes allow the duty of care to be eliminated but typically prohibit eliminating the duty of loyalty or self-dealing.

TERMINATION OF A PARTNERSHIP

Termination of a partnership is governed by the law of the state in which the partnership operates. In order to terminate a partnership, the partnership must first dissolve itself. There are two rules that govern partnership **dissolution** used by states. Under the UPA, dissolution *must* occur whenever a partner withdraws from the partnership. Under the RUPA, dissolution *may* occur when a partner withdraws, but does not necessarily do so. Withdrawal of a partner under the RUPA is called **dissociation.** Under both the UPA and RUPA, dissolution of the partnership can be brought about by three ways: (1) an act of the partners; (2) operation of law; or (3) court order.

A partnership is rightfully dissolved by an act of the partners if one partner expresses a will to withdraw from the partnership (this creates mandatory dissolution under UPA-governed states but not RUPA-governed states), all partners expressly agree to dissolve the partnership, when the partnership agreement expires in accordance with the time provided in the agreement, or by the expulsion of a partner done in accordance with the terms of the partnership agreement. Under the UPA, a partner always has the *power* to dissolve the partnership by withdrawing as partner, but whether he or she has the *right* to do so is determined by the partnership agreement.

Under the UPA, a partner who withdraws in violation of the partnership agreement is liable to the remaining partners for damages resulting from the wrongful dissolution. For example, if the partnership agreement is for a specific term and a partner withdraws before the expiration of that term, that would be considered a wrongful termination of the partnership even though he has the power to withdraw (remember that partners cannot be forced to be in or stay in a partnership). The partner who withdrew, then, would have liability to the other partners for whatever damage was caused by his withdrawal because under the partnership agreement, he had no right to withdraw.

EXAMPLE

A partnership is dissolved by **operation of law** upon (1) the death of a partner; (2) the bankruptcy of a partner or of the partnership, or (3) the subsequent illegality of the partnership. For example, a partnership formed to manufacture alcohol would be dissolved as a matter of law by a law prohibiting the production or sale of alcoholic beverages, such as during Prohibition.

EXAMPLE

TAKE AWAY 10-9

TERMINATING A PARTNERSHIP

Dissolution	**Act of Partners** Withdrawal of partner (UPA); partnership agreement; partnership expires; expulsion of partner
	Operation of Law Disability of partner; bankruptcy of partner or partnership; subsequent illegality of partnership
	Court Ordered Incompetence or incapacity of partner; conduct of partner prejudicial to partnership; financial irresponsibility of partnership; equity required
Winding Up	Completing unfinished business, collecting debts, reducing assets to cash, taking inventory, auditing partnership books, distributing remaining partnership assets

A **court-ordered dissolution** will occur if court finds that (1) a partner is incompetent or suffers some other incapacity preventing him from functioning as a partner; (2) a partner is guilty of conduct prejudicial to the business or has willfully or persistently breached the partnership agreement; (3) the business can only be carried on at a loss; or (4) other circumstances render a dissolution equitable. See Take Away 10-9 ("Terminating a Partnership") for a summary of partnership termination.

Dissolution brings about restrictions on the authority of the partners to act for the partnership. Once the partnership is dissolved, the partnership continues until the **winding up** of the partnership affairs is completed. The process of winding up involves completing unfinished business, collecting debts, reducing assets to cash, taking inventory, and auditing the partnership books. After all the partnership assets have been collected and reduced to cash, they are then distributed to the creditors and partners. Partners are not permitted to bring any new business into a partnership that is winding up its affairs.

TERMINATION OF A LIMITED PARTNERSHIP

A general partner in a limited partnership has the power to withdraw at any time but that withdrawal does not necessarily cause dissolution of the partnership if the partnership has at least one general partner left, the partnership agreement allows the remaining general partners to continue without the withdrawing partner, or, within 90 days after the withdrawal, all the remaining partners (limited and general) agree in writing to continue the partnership. If a general partner's withdrawal does result in dissolution, the consequences are the same as for a general partnership.

Limited partners in a limited partnership for a specified term have no power to withdraw unless the partnership agreement gives them that power. If no term is given, a limited partner can withdraw by giving six months notice or under the terms of the partnership agreement. The withdrawal of a limited partner does not cause dissolution of the partnership.

TERMINATION OF THE LIMITED LIABILITY COMPANY

In the early LLC statutes, dissolution occurred on the death or withdrawal of a member. Today, most statutes have been amended to make dissolution at the option of the members and to provide that the entity will continue automatically unless a certain percentage of the

CHARACTERISTICS OF UNINCORPORATED ENTITIES

Entity	Formation	Liability	Management	Termination
Sole Proprietorship	No filing	Personal	Sole management	By sole proprietor
General Partnership	No filing	Unlimited liability	Each partner has equal voice	Dissolved by withdrawal, operation of law, court order, or voluntary
Limited Partnership	Filing Req'd	Unlimited liability of general partners; ltd partners not liable for debts of partnership	Each general partner has equal voice; ltd partners silent	Dissolved by withdrawal of all general partners, operation of law, court order, or voluntary; not dissolved by withdrawal of ltd partners
Limited Liability Company	Filing Req'd	Members not liable	Members have control unless manager managed	Perpetual duration unless agreed to terminate

members (the default rule is a majority) vote to dissolve. See Take Away 10-10 ("Characteristics of Unincorporated Entities") for summary of above.

Corporations

L07

The unincorporated business entities discussed so far have placed ownership and management of the business in the same hands (with the exception of a manager-managed LLC). The corporate form of business is different in that the ownership of the corporation and the management of the corporation are in separate hands. Corporations are also different because unlike sole proprietorships and general partnerships that are limited to the money they can gather from themselves, friends, family, or from borrowing from banks or other lending institutions, without participation in the enterprise in return, corporations sell shares of stock to investors. Those investors, in turn, become owners of the corporation and get to have a say in its management on an indirect basis by voting for board members. So, if you want to have the full run of the business, a sole proprietorship or SMLLC is for you. If you don't mind sharing the reins a bit, partnership may suit you. But if you need lots of money and you don't mind sharing control, and you want protection of personal assets, a corporation may be your best avenue.

Corporations are legal fictions. They exist only as allowed by law. Unlike a sole proprietorship that is created as soon as the proprietor operates the business, or a partnership that is created as soon as two or more people engage in a business for profit, corporations do not exist unless there is a statute permitting them. All corporations, regardless of their type, are created by statute, either federal or state, and each statute determines the corporation's powers. Duke's investment business was operated by a corporation.

EXAMPLE

CORPORATE FORMATION

Forming a corporation under modern state corporation statutes is quick and easy. You have probably heard advertisements that talk about businesses that will incorporate you in no time, and do so right over the Internet. Make sure the company is reliable and fully protects your interests. The process of incorporating creates a public record of incorporation and binds the corporation to the state corporate laws that govern all corporations in the state. This is important to do because as a legal fiction, a corporation is not like a human being you can go to when something goes wrong with your interaction. So, incorporating is an important step to create the legal fiction that allows the state to keep track of the corporate entity and gives the public a means of being able to know who it is dealing with. Once the decision to incorporate is made, the next logical step is to file the incorporation papers with the proper state agency, usually the Secretary of State, to get the corporation recognized.

CREATING THE CORPORATION

Corporate existence begins when the articles of incorporation are filed, or, in some states, when they are issued. Under modern statutes, state law requires the articles of incorporation to include the name of the corporation, its registered agent and the location of its office, the name of at least one incorporator, and the number of shares of stock the corporation is authorized to issue. The articles may also include the purpose of the corporation, the size and composition of the board of directors, voting provisions for approval of corporate actions, management provisions, and indemnification provisions, but these latter items are optional. State law either recognizes the corporate existence when the articles are filed, or when the filing office issues the corporate certificate.

PROMOTER LIABILITY

Before the business is incorporated, someone is working behind the scenes to ensure that the corporation, once formed, has the capital and means to begin operation. This person is called the **promoter.** A promoter, in addition to working on behalf of the corporation, has a fiduciary duty not to engage in unfair activities with the corporation, such as self-dealing, and to provide future shareholders with full disclosure during the capital-raising process.

Promoters, in addition to raising the capital necessary to begin a business, may enter into contracts with employees, lessors, and customers, or they may secure loans or lines of credit for the business. At some point, it is anticipated that the promoter will turn over all its activity to the corporation. The question is when does this happen, and what is the promoter's liability until it does?

If the contract or other obligation arises before the corporation comes into existence, the promoter remains liable on the contract or obligation. That is because under the law of agency and contract, a party cannot be part of a contract until it exists. Thus, a promoter is personally liable on a pre-incorporation contract. For example, in a case where the promoter for a to-be-formed corporation entered into an architectural contract that authorized the architect to begin work before the corporation was formed, the court held that the promoter was personally liable for the contract, because no corporation had been formed at the time of the contract.[5]

An exception to this rule exists when the party with whom the promoter contracts agrees to look only to the corporation for payment. For example, in a case where the salesman for a supplier of nursery stock insisted on closing a supply contract before the buyers incorporated their business, the court held the promoters not liable because the seller, by its agent's actions, had agreed to look only to the corporation for payment.[6]

---

[5]*Stanley Howe & Asso. v. Boss,* 222 F. Supp. 936 (S.D. Iowa 1963).

[6]*Quaker Hill, Inc. v. Parr,* 364 P.2d 1056 (Colo. 1961).

Promoters may also escape liability for pre-incorporation contracts if the corporation adopts the contracts after incorporating. This adoption can be explicit, through a formal corporate resolution, or implicit, through acquiescence in the contract by making payments under the contract or accepting its benefits.

CORPORATE STRUCTURE

Corporations operate through three mechanisms: the board of directors, the officers, and the shareholders. Each has its own rights and duties to the corporation.

The **shareholders** are the true owners of the corporation. They elect the board of directors, vote on fundamental corporate transactions, and may initiate bylaw changes. **Bylaws** are the corporation's rules and regulations, and govern such things as how many directors a corporation may have, how many votes it takes to pass a resolution, and how many officers a corporation may have. Although they are owners of the corporation, shareholders do not participate in managing the corporation's business or affairs. The shareholders, even a majority, cannot act on behalf of the corporation.

The **board of directors** is the center of management authority for the corporation, and all corporate power flows from the board. The board is not an agent for the shareholders; it has independent status. The directors have fiduciary duties to the corporation and the shareholders.

The **officers** are delegated the day-to-day management of the corporation and are answerable to the board. All authority to act for and to bind the corporation originates in the board of directors.

CORPORATE ATTRIBUTES

Limited Liability

A major attribute of corporate ownership is the limited liability of its owners, the shareholders. Shareholders invest in corporations by purchasing their shares. Their liability is limited to the amount they invest. Even though a corporation's debt may exceed its assets causing the corporation to go into bankruptcy, unlike sole proprietorships or partnerships, creditors can look only to the corporation to satisfy their debts. A shareholder will never be liable for the corporate debts. This is always true for publicly owned corporations. For closely held corporations, this shield of liability can be pierced. (See Piercing the Corporate Veil, later in the chapter.)

Taxation

Under the current federal income tax laws, a corporation is taxed as a separate entity, meaning that the corporation itself pays taxes on its earnings. In addition, when the shareholders receive their share of the corporate earnings through the distribution of dividends, the individual shareholders are taxed. This is known as double taxation.

If the corporation qualifies, the effects of double taxation can be avoided by choosing to be taxed as a Subchapter S corporation. Named after the section of the IRS Code that allows it, a Subchapter S corporation is taxed much like a partnership: taxes are paid by the shareholders and no tax is paid by the corporation. There are restrictions to becoming a Subchapter S corporation. Currently, any corporation with over 100 shareholders cannot qualify for Subchapter S treatment. Corporations with corporate or nonresident (non-U.S. citizen or those without resident status) shareholders or more than one class of shares are prohibited from electing Subchapter S status. See Take Away 10-11 ("Form 2553: Election of Subchapter S") for the IRS form that allows a corporation to elect to be taxed as a partnership.

FORM 2553: ELECTION OF SUBCHAPTER S

Form **2553** (Rev. December 2007) Department of the Treasury Internal Revenue Service	**Election by a Small Business Corporation** (Under section 1362 of the Internal Revenue Code) ▶ See Parts II and III on page 3 and the separate instructions. ▶ The corporation can fax this form to the IRS (see separate instructions).	OMB No. 1545-0146

Note. This election to be an S corporation can be accepted only if all the tests are met under **Who May Elect** on page 1 of the instructions; all shareholders have signed the consent statement; an officer has signed below; and the exact name and address of the corporation and other required form information are provided.

Part I	**Election Information**		
Type or Print	Name (see instructions)	**A** Employer identification number	
	Number, street, and room or suite no. (If a P.O. box, see instructions.)	**B** Date incorporated	
	City or town, state, and ZIP code	**C** State of incorporation	

D Check the applicable box(es) if the corporation, after applying for the EIN shown in **A** above, changed its ☐ name or ☐ address

E Election is to be effective for tax year beginning (month, day, year) (see instructions) . . . . . ▶ ___/___/___

   Caution. A corporation (entity) making the election for its first tax year in existence will usually enter the beginning date of a short tax year that begins on a date other than January 1.

F Selected tax year:

   (1) ☐ Calendar year

   (2) ☐ Fiscal year ending (month and day) ▶ _____

   (3) ☐ 52-53-week year ending with reference to the month of December

   (4) ☐ 52-53-week year ending with reference to the month of ▶ _____

   If box (2) or (4) is checked, complete Part II

G If more than 100 shareholders are listed for item J (see page 2), check this box if treating members of a family as one shareholder results in no more than 100 shareholders (see test 2 under **Who May Elect** in the instructions) ▶ ☐

H Name and title of officer or legal representative who the IRS may call for more information   **I** Telephone number of officer or legal representative ( )

If this S corporation election is being filed with Form 1120S, I declare that I had reasonable cause for not filing Form 2553 timely, and if this election is made by an entity eligible to elect to be treated as a corporation, I declare that I also had reasonable cause for not filing an entity classification election timely. See below for my explanation of the reasons the election or elections were not made on time (see instructions).

Sign Here ▶ Under penalties of perjury, I declare that I have examined this election, including accompanying schedules and statements, and to the best of my knowledge and belief, it is true, correct, and complete.

Signature of officer	Title	Date

For Paperwork Reduction Act Notice, see separate instructions.   Cat. No. 18629R   Form **2553** (Rev. 12-2007)

Notice the limitations for who can file for Subchapter S according to the IRS Form 2553.

Source: www.IRS.gov/pub/IRS-pdf/f2553.pdf.

Constitutional Rights

A corporation has constitutional rights for some purposes, but not for all purposes. The U.S. Supreme Court has determined that corporations cannot be deprived of their property under the Due Process Clauses of the Fifth and Fourteenth Amendments.[7] Corporations are entitled to equal protection under the Fourteenth Amendment [8] and have limited First Amendment rights to advertise their products.[9]

Corporations do not have rights under the Privileges and Immunities Clause. The court ruled that a corporation was not a "person" in this context.[10] Nor can a corporation claim a Fifth Amendment right against self-incrimination.[11] In addition, a corporation has a lesser expectation of privacy for search and seizure under the Fourth Amendment. The court has limited it on the basis that business privacy is less compelling than personal privacy.[12]

Types of Corporations

Corporations may be classified as government, private or public, closely held, for profit or not for profit, domestic or foreign, or as a professional corporation. These labels are not mutually exclusive. For example, a corporation can be public, not for profit, and domestic at the same time.

EXAMPLE

GOVERNMENT-OWNED CORPORATIONS

A **government corporation** is one that is created to administer a unit of local civil government, such as a county, city, town, village, school district, or one created by the U.S. government to conduct pubic business. Two well-known government corporations are the Tennessee Valley Authority and the Federal Deposit Insurance Corporation. Government corporations are also known as municipal corporations. As Reality Check 10-6 ("Government Corporations") shows, government corporations have been used for a variety of reasons in this country.

PUBLIC CORPORATIONS

A **public corporation** is one created to conduct a publicly owned business enterprise for profit or not for profit. One of the characteristics of a publicly

REALITY CHECK 10-6

GOVERNMENT CORPORATIONS

Why does the U.S. government need corporations? A look at the variety of corporations chartered by the government suggests they are needed to carry on some of the government's most important business. The U.S. Postal Service, one of the largest government corporations, and UNICOR, the Federal Prison Industries run by the Department of Justice, are but two of many important corporations run by the government.

Each government corporation is chartered by an act of Congress. The Government Corporation Control Act of 1945 regulates budget, auditing, debt management, and depository practices for those corporations listed in the act. Many government corporations are established to exist in perpetuity, and others are chartered for specific purposes and then de-listed while others are used as transition corporations. For example, the U.S. Enrichment Corporation was used to transition enriched uranium into a private corporation; the U.S. Postal Service is intended to act in perpetuity; and a bill introduced into the 109th Congress to create a Louisiana Reconstruction Corporation designed to engage in commercial-like activity, purchasing and selling real estate in areas affected by Hurricane Katrina is intended to be a transition government corporation. The purpose of a transitional government corporation is to demonstrate marketability and asset value for eventual sale to the private sector. New corporations are added occasionally.

One of the biggest criticisms of government corporations is the lack of oversight. Corporations are assigned to committees by subject matter. The General Accounting Office has recommended that Congress reconsider its corporate controls. Although government corporations have been around for as long as the government has been in existence, there still needs to be better oversight and accountability over them.

Source: Kevin R. Kosar, "CRS Report for Congress, Federal Government Corporations: An Overview," updated January 28, 2008, http://assets.opencrs.com/rpts/RL30365_20080131.pdf.

---

[7]*Oklahoma Press Publ. v. Walling,* 327 U.S. 186 (1946).

[8]*Santa Clara County v. Southern Pac.* Ry, 118 U.S. 394 (1886).

[9]*Va. State Board of Pharmacy v. Va. Citizens Consumer Council,* 425 U.S. 748 (1976).

[10]*Paul v. Va.,* 75 U.S. (8 Wall.) 168 (1868).

[11]*Bellis v. U.S.,* 417 U.S. 85 (1974).

[12]*G.M. Leasing v. U.S.,* 429 U.S. 338 (1977).

HOW TO READ A STOCK MARKET QUOTE: THE CRASH OF BRITISH PETROLEUM STOCK AFTER THE GULF OIL SPILL

Did you ever look at the financial pages of a newspaper and wonder how to read the stock market quotes that are listed? To the untrained eye, those tiny numbers can seem unintelligible. However, the information reveals a lot about a company's fortunes. Take the international corporation, British Petroleum. This company is being blamed for the worst oil spill in U.S. history, which occurred on April 23, 2010. Since that time, BP's market shares have plummeted. Looking at the reading of its stock quote reported on July 5, 2010, reveals a considerable amount about how its fortunes have fallen. Below is reproduced the stock quotes for that day. And below that is the explanation for the columns, which have been numbered for convenience.

1	2	3	4	5	6	7	8	9	0	11	12
52 week hi	52 week low	Stock	Ticker	Div	Yield %	P/E	Vol 00s	High	Low	Close	Net Chg
62.38	26.75	British Petroleum	BP	3.36	11.45	5.59	31.48	29.91	28.99	29.39	−0.14

1. This represents the highest price that BP was traded at within the past year.
2. This is the lowest price that BP was traded at within the past year. Notice that BP was trading over $35 higher one year before this date.
3. This is the name of the corporation.
4. This is the ticker name, i.e., the name given to it by the stock exchange for trading.
5. This is the dividend per share; if this is blank no dividend was given.
6. This is the dividend yield, i.e., the percentage of return on the dividend.
7. This is the price/earnings ratio, calculated by dividing the current stock price by the earnings per share for the last four quarters.
8. This is the trading volume, the total number of shares traded per day, by hundreds.
9. This is the market high that was paid that day (July 5, 2010).
10. This is the market low that was paid that day (July 5, 2010).
11. This is the last trading price recorded when the market closed.
12. This is the net change, i.e., the dollar value change in the stock price for the previous day's closing price. If a stock is "up," the number is positive. Notice that BP's trading is "down," i.e., a negative number.

Source: http://moneycentral.msn.com/detail/stock_quote?Symbol=US:BP.

owned corporation is the trading of its shares on a stock exchange. See Reality Check 10-7 ("How to Read a Stock Market Quote: The Crash of British Petroleum Stock after the Gulf Oil Spill") for information on the public record of stock market trading.

CLOSELY HELD CORPORATIONS

A corporation is described as **closely held** when its outstanding shares of stock are held by a small number of persons, frequently family relatives or friends. In most closely held corporations, the shareholders are active in the management and control of the business. Accordingly, the shareholders are concerned with who their fellow shareholders are and they typically enter into a buy-sell arrangement at the time of incorporation in order to prevent the stock from getting into the hands of persons outside the original group of shareholders. Closely held corporations comprise the majority of corporations in the U.S., but account for only a small fraction of corporate revenues and assets.

PIERCING THE CORPORATE VEIL

The separate legal status of a corporation as a business organization acts as a corporate veil, a shield that prevents creditors from reaching the personal assets of stockholders. This is a very powerful legal relationship of protection. In order to enjoy the protection of the corporate veil, efforts must be made to keep the corporation separate from the individuals who own it. This means that the shareholders should make an effort to keep their personal assets separate from those of the corporation by using separate bank accounts, bookkeeping and so on. Assuming that this is done, when the corporation fails or owes money, its creditors can normally look only to corporate assets for satisfaction of their claims.

In closely held corporations, the joint and active management by all the shareholders frequently results in a tendency to forgo adherence to all the formalities that are expected of corporations, such as holding meetings of the board of directors and shareholders, recording minutes, voting regularly, and keeping corporate assets separate from personal assets. When the closely held corporation gets into financial trouble, its creditors will often ask the court to **pierce the corporate veil** and impose personal liability on the shareholders to satisfy corporate debts. Courts are likely to pierce the corporate veil where the shareholders have not conducted the business like a corporation, have not provided adequate funding for the corporation's debts, or when the corporation is used to commit wrongdoing or fraud or circumvent the law. When the court pierces the corporate veil of a corporation, the shareholders are held personally liable for the debts of the corporation. In the chapter's opening scenario, Duke's use of his Aunt Ruth's personal property to fund his business might be questioned. However, creditors may still be able to take Aunt Ruth's home to extinguish the debt of Duke's corporation unless the court finds that Duke's wrongdoing should somehow exempt her home from collection. This is unlikely, and Aunt Ruth may very well lose her home. Reality Check 10–8 ("Piercing the Corporate Veil—in Reverse") may give Aunt Ruth some hope for stopping the sale.

EXAMPLE

PROFIT AND NOT FOR PROFIT CORPORATIONS

A profit corporation is one that is founded for the purpose of operating a business for profit from which payments are made to shareholders in the form of dividends.

A **not for profit corporation** can earn a profit, but the profit may not be distributed to its members, officers or directors but must be used exclusively for the charitable, educational, or scientific purpose for which the corporation was organized. Libraries, hospitals, private schools, fraternities

REALITY CHECK 10-8

PIERCING THE CORPORATE VEIL—IN REVERSE

What happens if you form a corporation to obtain one benefit, but it costs you an even more valuable benefit that was not intended? One possible but rare equitable remedy is the concept of a reverse pierce. A reverse pierce of the corporate veil occurs when a corporate owner, who formed the corporation in order to protect personal assets, asks the court to disregard the corporate form. It is called reverse pierce because ordinarily the creditors are trying to get through the corporate veil to gain access to personal assets. In the reverse case, the corporate owner is trying to get through the corporate veil to dissolve the corporation. For example, a farmer formed a corporation to run her farm and sold her home to the corporation so it could act as collateral for a loan. Unknown to her at the time, this meant that she was not qualified to claim her home under homestead exemption, which protects a person's home from personal creditors. Her corporation became financially insolvent, and she stood to lose her home to the corporation's creditors. She asked the court to reverse pierce—let her out of the corporation—so that she would not lose her home, a consequence she would not have invited had she known what incorporating would do. The court allowed her to dissolve the corporation, file homestead exemption, and save her home. The court did require her to sell the remaining acreage of the farm to pay the creditors.

What's the harm in reverse piercing? One argument against such a policy is that it acts as a fraud on creditors who might extend credit based on property the corporation owns. Had the farmer in the above scenario not had her farm to place as collateral, it's very possible that she would not have been able to receive credit at all. Once the home was removed, the creditors were left with nothing except the remaining property.

Source: Cargill v. Hedge, 375 N.W.2d 477, 479 (Minn.1985).

CASE 10.4 Airlie Foundation v. IRS

283 F. Supp. 2d 58 (D.D.C. 2003)

Facts: Airlie had at one time operated as a tax-exempt charitable organization, but had its tax-exempt status revoked by the IRS after IRS found that the earnings went to the founder, Murdoch Head, and that the center was run for nonexempt commercial purposes. After 10 years, the foundation applied for reinstatement of its tax-exempt status and was denied by the IRS, again on the basis that plaintiff operated its conference center for a commercial purpose. Plaintiff appeals the IRS ruling.

Issue: May a tax-exempt corporation engage in commercial activity and still retain its tax-exempt status?

Decision: No.

Reasoning: Pursuant to Section 501(c)(3), an organization is entitled to federal corporate income tax exemption if the following requirements are met: (1) the organization is organized and operated exclusively for exempt purposes (i.e., religious, charitable, educational purposes); and (2) no part of the organization's net earnings benefits any private shareholder or individual; and (3) no substantial part of the organization's activities consists of carrying on propaganda, or otherwise attempting to influence legislation; and (4) the organization must not participate in any political campaigns.

Only the operational test is at issue in this case. According to the booking report for 1999, the year in which plaintiff applied to the IRS for tax-exempt status, in fact, approximately 30–40 percent of plaintiff's patrons were of a private or corporate nature. The fact that plaintiff's conference center derives substantial income from weddings and special events and competes with a number of commercial, as well as noncommercial, entities constitutes strong evidence of a commercial nature and purpose. Furthermore, it maintains a commercial website and has paid significant advertising and promotional expenses. While plaintiff was organized for an exempt purpose, the Court cannot find, under the totality of the circumstances, that it is operated similarly. Having considered the facts before it, the Court is not persuaded that plaintiff has met its burden of demonstrating that an incorrect determination was made by the Internal Revenue Service.

CASE QUESTIONS

1. Clearly a nonprofit can earn profit from some of its activities without losing its exemption. What is the test the court used for making that determination?
2. Of the factors listed by the court, which do you think was most persuasive in allowing the court to deny tax-exempt status to Airlie?
3. What's the best way to make sure an organization does not cross the line between commercial and noncommercial. Could this be a potential problem for nonprofits?

and sororities are examples of not for profit corporations. The dangers of losing the tax exempt status are illustrated in the case of *Airlie Foundation v. IRS* (Case 10.4).

PROFESSIONAL ASSOCIATION

All states have a **professional association** act that permits the practice of professions by duly licensed individuals under the corporate form. The purpose of the statute is to permit licensed professionals to obtain tax benefits not allowable to individuals or partnerships.

DOMESTIC OR FOREIGN CORPORATIONS

A corporation is **domestic** in the state in which it is incorporated. It is **foreign** in every other jurisdiction. A corporation may not do business in a state other than the state of its incorporation without the permission of the other state. Every state, however, provides for the issuance to foreign corporations a certificate to do business in the state and for the taxation of such foreign businesses. Obtaining a certificate usually involves filing certain information with the Secretary of State, the payment of fees, and the designation of a resident agent.

Corporate Governance

Certain positions in the corporation carry with them a fiduciary duty. This duty is generally placed on those who manage the corporation or who have the requisite control of votes necessary to control the outcome of shareholder decisions. This section will detail the duties of each of the relevant governing bodies within a corporation.

DUTIES OF THE BOARD OF DIRECTORS AND OFFICERS

Board members and officers have two primary duties: the duty of care and the duty of loyalty. The duty of care requires directors and officers to perform their duties with the diligence of a reasonable person in similar circumstances. Directors and officers can be liable for acts they commit that are grossly negligent, and for not acting when they have a duty to act.

However, decisions made by directors and officers are protected by the **business judgment rule.** Under this rule, the decision made by the directors and officers is given a presumption of correctness that can only be overcome by a showing of gross negligence in making the decision. The purpose of the rule is to allow directors and officers to act in the best interest of the corporation, even if the decision results in loss to the corporation. The business judgment rule requires the court to look at the process the directors and officers undertook in making the decision, focusing on whether the directors and officers informed themselves of all relevant information, relied on expert evidence where needed, and deliberated the pros and cons of the decision. If the process was correct, the court does not look at the substance of the decision; the decision is protected by the business judgment rule. For example, a corporation's board was asked to approve of a risky undertaking. If the undertaking had worked out, the corporation would have earned significant profits from it. However, the undertaking did not go well, causing huge losses to the corporation and, consequently, its shareholders. The shareholders sued to challenge the board's decision in voting for the undertaking. If the board engaged in a proper process to make its determination, the decision would be protected and the suit would be dismissed. The board is not required to be right in all its decisions; it is simply required to be deliberative and circumspect and consider all the issues properly before making them.

The duty of loyalty requires the directors and officers to act in the best interest of the corporation and in good faith. A lack of good faith can involve any intent to harm the corporation or in an intentional disregard for one's responsibilities. The duty of loyalty also focuses on conflicts of interest where the director's or officer's personal interests are advanced over the corporation's interests. Generally, the standard for determining whether the director or officer has breached his or her duty of loyalty is whether the transaction was fair to the corporation. Thus, the duty of loyalty breach will involve more judicial scrutiny than a duty of care violation.

DUTIES OF CONTROLLING SHAREHOLDERS

Generally, a shareholder has no fiduciary duties to other shareholders or to the corporation. The exception arises when the shareholder is a controlling shareholder. A **controlling shareholder** is any shareholder with sufficient voting shares to determine the outcome of a shareholder vote. Directors are usually elected by shareholder vote, and any shareholder who has a voting majority has control of the board. With the power to select the board and approve fundamental changes, a controlling shareholder can act to the detriment of minority shareholders. For this reason, courts impose a fiduciary duty that generally parallels those of directors. In a public corporation, this majority might be

EXAMPLE

as little as 20 percent ownership. In a closely held corporation, it is usually closer to 50 percent ownership.

GOVERNMENT REGULATION OF CORPORATIONS

There is no federal corporate law statute, but federal regulation adds a significant layer of corporate regulation to corporations. Probably the most significant part of this extra layer for corporations is federal securities regulation. You probably know this best as the regulation of selling corporate stock or other securities. The primary purpose of federal securities regulation is to prevent fraudulent practices in the sale of securities and to maintain public confidence in the securities market. Federal securities law consists primarily of two statutes. The Securities Act of 1933 regulates disclosure when corporations raise capital in public markets. The Securities Exchange Act of 1934 imposes periodic reporting requirements and proxy disclosure rules on corporations whose stock is publicly traded. In addition, the Exchange Act regulates the trading of securities in public and private markets, including insider trading. Both acts are administered by the Securities Exchange Commission (SEC). The SEC is empowered to bring civil actions against violations of the Acts and to recommend to the Department of Justice that they bring criminal actions against violators.

The Securities Act of 1933

The Securities Act of 1933 (the '33 Act) has two basic purposes: to provide investors with material information concerning securities offered for sale to the public and to prohibit misrepresentations, deceit, and other fraudulent acts in the sales of securities generally. For the purpose of securities laws, a security is an investment of money, property, or other valuable consideration made in expectation of receiving a financial return solely from the efforts of others.

The Securities Exchange Act of 1934

The Securities Exchange Act of 1934 (the '34 Act) extends protection to investors trading in securities that are already issued. The '34 Act also imposes disclosure requirements on publicly held corporations. The '34 Act requires companies to register their securities and subjects them to the Act's periodic reporting requirements.

Blue Sky Laws

In addition to federal laws, the states have their own laws regulating such sales within the state called **blue sky laws.** These statutes all have provisions prohibiting fraud in the sale of securities. In addition, a number of states regulate brokers and dealers of securities.

Any person selling securities must comply with the federal securities laws and the state laws regulating the sale of securities.

Insider Trading

Rule 10b of the 1934 Act and SEC Rule 10b-5 make it unlawful for any person by use of the mails or facilities of interstate commerce in connection with the sale of a security to defraud or make material untrue or misleading facts or omit to state a material fact to any person. Rule 10b-5 applies to any purchase or sale of a security whether it is registered or not, whether it is publicly traded or closely held, whether it is listed on an exchange or sold over the counter, or whether it is part of an initial issuance or a secondary distribution. There are no exempted securities under Rule 10b-5. Rule 10b-5 applies to misconduct by buyers or sellers and allows either defrauded buyers or sellers to recover damages.

Rule 10b-5 applies to sales or purchases made by an insider who possesses material inside information. Information is said to be material if a reasonable person would attach importance to the information in making a decision. **Inside information** is information known by a corporate officer or board member (and in some cases others who have a relationship with the corporation) that is not known to the public. Such persons are called **insiders.** An insider will be liable under Rule 10b-5 if he fails to disclose the material nonpublic information before trading on the information unless he waits until the information becomes public. Insiders include directors, officers, employees and agents of the issuer as well as those with whom the issuer has entrusted information solely for corporate purposes, such as underwriters, accountants, lawyers, and consultants. In some instances, persons who receive material nonpublic information from insiders—**tippees**—are also precluded from trading on that information. A tippee is under a duty not to trade on inside information when the insider has breached his fiduciary duty to the shareholders by disclosing the information to the tippee who knows or should have known that there has been such a breach.

Sarbanes-Oxley Act

Major corporate scandals have influenced the development of regulation to try to limit the ability of managers or controlling shareholders to harm public shareholders. The first major scandal was the fall of the company called Enron, which you have no doubt heard of, but it was quickly followed by other major scandals. The entire corporate governance structure was called into question, and Congress was quick to act to restore investor confidence in the market. The Sarbanes-Oxley Act of 2002 was enacted in response to these scandals.

The Sarbanes-Oxley Act (SOX) deals with accounting, corporate governance issues, increased disclosure, and conflicts of interest in the securities business. In terms of accounting, a new Public Company Accounting Oversight Board (PCAOB) was established to set auditing, quality control, and ethics standards for public accounting firms. In the past, many of these functions were done with self-policing by private bodies. This new board consists of full-time members that have the authority to investigate and impose sanctions.

SOX also deals with accounting issues. Many accounting firms had supplied the corporations they audit with other services that were often more lucrative to the accountants. The variety of roles accountants played raised issues of whether the auditing function was compromised. SOX limits the activities of the accountants while they are auditing the company.

SOX tries also to increase the monitoring of the business and its managers. The law seeks to review auditing and makes the accountant responsible to the directors, not to the managers. The chief executive officer and chief financial officer must now sign off on the auditor's reports, and incur personal liability should the reports be falsified. SOX mandates internal procedures to ensure the compliance with its rules.

Foreign Corrupt Practices Act

In response to revelations in the 1970s that U.S. companies were doctoring their books and setting up slush funds to bribe foreign government officials, Congress passed the Foreign Corrupt Practices Act of 1978. The purpose of the FCPA was to crack down on publicly held corporations that had lax internal controls that allowed these payments to be made and remain undetected by auditors of the corporation. The FCPA requires reporting companies to maintain financial records in reasonable detail to reflect company transactions accurately and to put into place internal accountability and proper accounting. These requirements became part of the SEC's reporting requirement. The FCPA also prohibits reporting companies from making payments to foreign government officials to influence their official actions or decisions. Compliance is ensured by requiring

HOW TO ENSURE COMPLIANCE WITH THE FCPA

When the SEC learned of the slush funds and secret payments corporations were engaged in in the 1970s, something had to be done to ensure that corporations complied with the FCPA and that looking at corporate books would reveal such payments if they had to occur. To make corporations compliant, the FCPA requires publicly held U.S. companies to keep books, records, and accounts which detail the transactions involving the assets of the company. They are also required to have a system of internal controls in place so that each transaction is authorized and recorded, and that there is periodic review of these transactions to prevent illegal payments.

How is this enforced? Any person that knowingly implements or fails to implement an internal accounting system, or any person that knowingly falsifies books or records of the corporation, is subject to criminal liability. Even if no illegal payment is made, falsifying the books or records of the corporation subjects the person to this criminal liability.

Source: Michael Crites and Greg Mathews, "What You Need to Know About the Foreign Corrupt Practices Act," May 20, 2009, Inhouselcounsel.com, http://www.law.com/jsp/ihc/PubArticleIHC.jsp?id=1202430820195.

reporting to the SEC and constant audits, as Reality Check 10-9 ("How to Ensure Compliance with the FCPA") illustrates.

Corporate Dissolution

Although a corporation may have perpetual existence, its life may be terminated in a number of ways. Incorporation statutes usually provide both for dissolution without judicial proceedings and for dissolution with judicial proceedings. Dissolution does not terminate the corporation's existence but does require that the corporation wind up its affairs and liquidate its assets.

Nonjudicial dissolution can be brought about by an act of the legislature of the state of incorporation, expiration of the period of time provided for in the articles of incorporation, voluntary action by all the shareholders, or voluntary action by the board of directors which is approved by a majority of shareholders entitled to vote at a meeting called for this purpose.

Involuntary dissolution by judicial proceeding may be instituted by the state, the shareholders, or the creditors. Judicial dissolution can occur by court action taken at the instance of the attorney general of the state of incorporation when the corporation has failed to comply with the filing requirements of the state, by court action brought by the shareholders when it is established that the directors are deadlocked in the management of the corporate affairs and the shareholders are unable to break the deadlock, or by court action instituted by the creditors of the corporation upon a showing that the corporation has become unable to pay its debts and obligations as they become due, if the creditor can show that it has a judgment that cannot be executed against the corporation.

Upon dissolution the assets of the corporation are liquidated and used to pay the expenses of creditors. Any remainder is distributed to shareholders. When the liquidation is voluntary, it is carried out by the board of directors. When it is involuntary, it is carried out by a court-appointed receiver.

Summary

Business is the backbone of American enterprise. Whether the business is large or small, it contributes to the economic success of the capitalist society. Without the entrepreneurial spirit of business men and women, this country would not have had the success it has had nor would it be a leader in the global economy.

In order for business to thrive, it must have an environment conducive to doing so. Our country has walked a thin line between trying to give business the environment it needs to thrive, while protecting the public from harm that can be caused in the process. As you have seen, capitalism is not for the faint of heart. There are times when the public must be protected, but we do not want it to be at the expense of a thriving engine of commerce.

Business takes all forms. Sole proprietorships take the most risk because their business is run by one person whose personal assets are at stake. While they have the most control, answering only to themselves, their assets are exposed each time they go to work. Partnerships spread the risk among at least two people and allow each person to contribute what they have in either money or skill to the enterprise. Limited liability companies have become the business entity of choice for many because of the flexibility the form offers small and large companies alike. Corporations, of course, have the capability of operating readily in the global market and are a recognized way of organizing business ownership with little risk.

Regardless of what type of business model is chosen, government regulation helps to keep businesses and their customers operating within the law. Some might argue that there is too much government regulation of business. Others argue there is not enough. The point is that it is there to protect the end product and to keep the system running smoothly and productively.

Review Questions

1. Bernadette rented a house from Franz for one year. Six months later, a saleswoman for Exteriors Company stopped by and seeing Bernadette in the yard, offered a contract to paint the house for $1500. Bernadette said, "Okay, but I'm renting the place from Franz. I'll enter it on his behalf." The contract was entered into. Subsequently, Franz refused to allow Exterior to do any painting. Exterior sues for breach of contract. Is Franz liable to Exterior? LO2

2. Nathaniel, an Italian who speaks no English, employed Dan, an interpreter, to make an offer to Sherman that Nathaniel will buy certain described goods from Sherman. Dan misunderstands Nathaniel and makes an offer for different goods also sold by Sherman, which Sherman in good faith accepts. Is Nathaniel bound to Sherman? LO2

3. Bob and Edna are husband and wife. Edna runs an interior decorating business. Bob is a high school administrator. Recently, Edna bid on a redecorating job for Rustic Inn, owned by an acquaintance of Bob and Edna. The owner decides to accept the bid. She sees Bob at a local cross-country race and says to him "Tell Edna I've decided to accept her bid on Rustic Inn." Bob agrees to do this, but forgets to tell Edna. Is there an acceptance of the bid? LO1

4. Donna suffered food poisoning at Skewers Restaurant, located inside Northside Mall. Northside exercised considerable control over all the tenants in the mall by regulating the hours of operation, restricting the kinds of advertising its tenants may publish, and the scope of the goods sold, reserving the right to inspect the premises, and requiring all tenants to belong to a tenant's association formed to promote the mall. Donna claimed that these facts created an agency relationship. Do you agree? Why? LO2

5. Suppose Camille, an agent, negotiates a transaction her principal wants and takes a little "gratuity" that the third party has offered her in order to hurry the deal through. The principal, satisfied with the transaction, pays Camille and then learns about the gratuity. Has Camille violated her fiduciary duty to her principal? LO2

6. Joon-Sik, who makes deliveries for the Nye Drug Company, while on route negligently flips her cigarette out of the car window on to dry grass, causing a fire. Is Nye Drug liable? Would your answer change if instead Joon-Sik, while driving en route, had taken both hands off the wheel in order to light the cigarette and had caused an accident? LO2

7. The board of directors of a corporation makes a decision that is not popular with the shareholders because it results in a bad investment which loses the corporation money. What judicial rule will protect the board members from liability for their decision? LO7

8. Glennis and Brad were partners in a bakery. Brad wanted to expand the bakery and took out a loan in the bakery's name without consulting Glennis. If the partnership defaults on the note, is Glennis liable for repayment of the note as well as Brad? LO5

9. Sylvester worked as a broker in a securities firm. One day, he called his friend and told him about a merger that was about to happen that had not been made public. What rule did Sylvester violate? LO8

10. Regina was involved in putting a corporation together for her and her brothers to operate a beauty salon. They agreed that Regina would buy the equipment, lease the beauty salon space, and hire the employees, which she did. Her brothers then got into a huge argument with each other and refused to pursue the business as planned. What role did Regina play and what is her liability in regard to each of the things that she did for the nonexistent corporation? LO6

Ethics Issue

The corporation for which you are on the board of directors operates globally. One of their subsidiaries is a banana growing farm in Colombia, South America. You have learned that the company has been paying bribes to a terrorist organization in Colombia in order to protect the people who work for your company, and that the only way to keep them safe is to pay the terrorists. You know that it's wrong, but other American companies in Colombia have complained of workers disappearing, being murdered, plants being vandalized, and other really awful things happening if they refused to support the terrorist organization there. You know also that it's illegal to pay bribes to government officials, but you wonder if the terrorists are considered to be a government. In any event, you do not want the blood of any murdered civilians on your hands. What do you do?

Group Exercise

Read a business magazine, newspaper, or website—anything with a number of articles included in it. Identify all the agency relationships you can and identify the duties each has in their respective capacity. Are their duties prescribed by the common law, statutes, administrative rules, or specifics of the agency position?

Key Terms

accounting 238
actual authority 236
affirmation 243
agency 233
agent 233
apparent authority 237
articles of organization 251
blue sky laws 264
board of directors 257
business judgment rule 263
bylaws 257
closely held corporation 260
controlling shareholder 263
court-ordered dissolution 254
default 249
disclosed principal 242
dissociation 253
dissolution 253
domestic corporation 262

express authority 236
fiduciary 233
foreign corporation 262
general agent 234
government corporation 269
implied authority 236
indemnify 241
independent contractor 235
inside information 265
Insider 265
limited liability company 251
limited partnership 250
material information 250
manager-managed 253
member-managed 253
not for profit corporation 261
officers 257
operating agreement 252
operation of law 253

partially disclosed principal 242
partnership 248
piercing the corporate veil 261
principal 233
professional association 262
promoter 256
public corporation 259
ratification 243
redlining 239
renounce 246
respondeat superior 244
Restatement of Agency 3d 233
scope of employment 244
shareholders 257
sole proprietor 247
special agent 234
tippee 265
undisclosed principal 242
winding up 254

The Employment Relationship and Equal Employment Opportunity

Learning Objectives

After reading this chapter, you should be able to:

L01   Explain why there is a need for employment discrimination laws

L02   Give the requirements of Title VII of the Civil Rights Act of 1964

L03   Compare and explain the two theories of recovery under Title VII

L04   List the five protected categories of Title VII

L05   Set forth the provisions of the Age Discrimination in Employment Act

L06   Explain the provisions of the Americans with Disabilities Act

L07   Distinguish the employer defenses of BFOQ, business necessity, and legitimate nondiscriminatory reason

L08   Discuss what affirmative action is and is not

 ## Opening Scenario

Amy is a real estate agent for a large national firm. Each year the firm has a festive gathering of its agents from all over the country. The event has gained quite a reputation over the years as a free-for-all, over-the-top event that no one wants to miss. Each year the male agents ask their favorite female agents to act as servers for the party. Servers are expected to look glamorous, bring the agents drinks, light their cigars, and anything else the male agents want them to do. Female agents vie for invitations to be a server because it is the best way they know of to be accepted by the male agents and get the leads and other information they need to do their jobs effectively. This year, Amy has been invited to be a server, but she is not feeling comfortable about either going to the event or being a server there. Amy doesn't feel like the event is in the firm's best interest, but she is afraid she will be targeted and harassed as a killjoy if she does not go along. Does Amy have reason to be concerned for her employer or her employment?

Introduction

Of all the chapters in this text, this is probably the one in which you would most likely expect to see diversity issues. They are here. But what we have come to realize over the time workplace protective laws have been in existence is that these issues do not just show up in the workplace. They show up in virtually every aspect of our lives. Because of that, the information cannot, in good conscience, be limited to just this one chapter if we are to teach you what you need to know to legally and ethically conduct business in a diverse society. Instead, this chapter is in some ways the fountainhead of the other information throughout the text. In this chapter you are given much of the underlying basis for why diversity would be such an issue in our society. It is done within the context of the workplace, since that is probably the single most active area of our laws about these issues.

There is probably no one reading this text who has not heard a news story about some type of workplace discrimination. Whether it was Bill Clinton being sued by Paula Jones for sexual harassment while he was sitting as president of the United States, musician Santana being sued by his employees for religious discrimination because Santana wanted to impose his religious views upon them, or popular clothing store Abercrombie and Fitch paying out a $54 million settlement for race and national origin discrimination after its store managers were told to terminate perfectly fine Asian, black, and other minority employees because they "did not fit with the A&F image," the workplace discrimination issue has come onto our radar screen in ways that we could never have imagined.

After hearing such stories, you may well have thought to yourself that it all seems like such nonsense; people seem to be so touchy nowadays; you can't seem to even *look* at someone in the workplace without their being ready to sue you for discrimination. And affirmative action! Don't even start on that one! Hopefully in this chapter you will come to understand the reason for such laws and the awesome job our country has done in trying to live up to the Constitutional promise of equality and justice for all. We are the world's greatest social experiment in this area, and we are not finished yet. We have done most of the heavy work, and it has led the way and fired the imaginations of people all around the world to yearn for the freedom and equality that we strive for here in the U.S., but we are still a work in progress.

Since most of you were born well after the struggle that put these laws on the books and you live in a world in which electing a black president did not seem to be too difficult a task for a society to do, it can be pretty hard to imagine what all the fuss is about when it comes to workplace discrimination. After all, you've seen women and minorities sit next to you in class, get elected to office, and run major corporations. However, we are not nearly where we should be with women's and minorities' representation in these areas and, unfortunately, a lot of that has to do with workplace discrimination and denial of equal employment opportunity.

In this chapter we will explore the different laws employers must consider in making workplace decisions consistent with fair employment practices and equal employment opportunity as required by law. Our ultimate goal is to ensure that you will learn not to make employment decisions that may later serve as the basis for costly, time-consuming, embarrassing, discrimination litigation. We will do so by making sure that we tell you what the law requires and how to avoid common pitfalls in this area.

These laws exist to ensure equal employment opportunity to all qualified applicants or employees, regardless of immutable characteristics such as race or gender. The intent of the law is to provide equal employment *opportunity* for all, *not* equal *employment*, as many take the law to mean. Employers do not have to hire someone simply because she is female, African American, Hispanic, etc., if she is not qualified for the job. Rather, they must ensure that if she is qualified, she be allowed an equal opportunity to be employed. They may not keep her out based on her gender, race, ethnicity, and so on. Since fair employment laws vary from state to state, and the federal laws apply the same across the country, it is the federal law that will be primarily addressed in this chapter, though most of the considerations are the same.

As you can imagine, ethical lapses abound in this area: employers who do not wish to hire those of a certain group, employers who have "unwritten rules" about hiring certain groups and not others or treating them differently or paying them differently while imposing rules against discussing wages, or employers allowing certain kinds of harassing activity to go on despite the discomfort it causes the employees who are the object of such harassment. On the other hand, many people think of the whole area of equal employment opportunity as an ethical issue that employers should be able to decide for themselves, rather than have to follow laws that the government imposes. But keep in mind that corporations exist only as legal fictions permitted by law. In exchange for the existence and protection they receive, there are certain laws to which businesses must adhere. Equal employment opportunity laws are only one such set of laws, but they are as important as those dealing with incorporating, securities regulation, labor unions, or paying taxes. Congress has made the determination that having equal employment opportunity in the workplace is a worthwhile goal and has passed legislation to achieve it. While EEO laws may seem like ethical judgments an employer should be able to make privately, they have been determined by Congress to be the law and must be obeyed or an employer will take the consequences. Congress made this determination after 99 years of letting employers handle it on their own. Discrimination was still the ironclad law and custom virtually everywhere, so Congress stepped in.

Since most of you have lived only in a time when employment discrimination is illegal, some may wonder why antidiscrimination laws are needed—particularly since the laws regularly receive such a lambasting around the issue of affirmative action. The reason is as complex as it is simple. We need such laws because people do discriminate. While this may be one's choice in one's personal life, it is quite another matter when it comes to the workplace and denying someone who is qualified a job simply because of their gender, race, ethnicity, or religion.

To address essentially the after-effects of slavery and Jim Crow in our country, The Civil Rights Act of 1964 was passed by Congress. The law contained several titles addressing discrimination in various areas such as public accommodations, education, and the receipt of federal funds. But one of the most important was Title VII which addressed employment discrimination. Title VII was the first significant employment discrimination law enacted in this country, was needed to address the reality that 100 years after the 13th Amendment to the U.S. Constitution abolished slavery, Jim Crow was still alive and well and African Americans were nowhere near parity with whites in virtually any facet of society because of discrimination. This reality, by the way, may be also seen in the history of the law itself, in the way discrimination has been enshrined in the law until recently.

Before passage of the Civil Rights Act, several states had legalized discrimination and segregation in housing, education, employment, and public accommodations. Even though it had been nearly 100 years since slavery ended, it was perfectly legal to refuse to hire based purely on race. Newspaper classified ads were divided into help wanted ads for "colored" and "white," as well as for males and females.

Since the U.S. Supreme Court's decision in *Brown v. Topeka Board of Education*,[1] desegregating public schools, the civil rights struggle to end legalized discrimination

---

[1]347 U.S. 483 (1954).

had been fought in earnest. In 1963, on the 100th anniversary of the Emancipation Proclamation, the famous March on Washington took place, at which Rev. Dr. Martin Luther King, Jr., gave his "I Have a Dream" speech. It was past time to start breaking down the barriers to full participation of all Americans in the American dream of equality for all. A year later, Title VII was passed. It became effective a year later, in 1965 100 years after the Civil War ended. Title VII and the later workplace discrimination laws were some of the tools used to dismantle Jim Crow and the barriers of discrimination. States and municipalities have comparable employment laws. They may be called human rights laws, equal employment opportunity laws, or fair employment practice laws. State and municipal laws generally track the federal law, but many expand coverage to include other categories in their prohibitions such as marital status, affinity orientation (sexual orientation), receipt of public assistance benefits, physical appearance, and so on.

Before we conclude this introduction to the chapter, we want you to be aware that the refusal to hire, unfairly disciplining an employee, sexually harassing employees, or other violations of the equal employment opportunity laws may also serve as the basis for tort or even criminal claims. For instance, sexual harassment is a violation of Title VII, but if the harasser inappropriately touches or attempts to have forced sex with the harassee, it may constitute civil and criminal assault or battery, or both. Preventing an employee from getting a deserved promotion may be an interference with contractual relations in addition to employment discrimination based on race, and so on.

Finally, if the employer is the federal, state, or local government, employment discrimination may also be redressed by the state or federal constitution. For instance, if a federal agency refused to hire females as engineers, it is a denial of equal protection of the laws and a deprivation of due process, in violation of the 5th and 14th Amendments to the U.S. Constitution.

What is Title VII of The Civil Rights Act of 1964?

L02

The single most important piece of legislation that impacts the workplace in the area of discrimination is the Civil Rights Act of 1964. This federal law prohibits discrimination in any way in employment, including hiring, firing, promotion, compensation, benefits, training, discipline and other workplace decisions. (See Take Away 11-1, "Title VII in a Nutshell.")

To whom does Title VII apply? Title VII applies to employers with 15 or more employees, as well as to labor organizations and other organizations that perform hiring or job referral functions. If the law applies to an employer, the employer must make all workplace decisions in accordance with appropriate federal civil rights laws. Equivalent state fair employment practice laws may set the minimum number of employees limit even lower, say at 4 rather than 15 employees. Under such laws, for

TAKE AWAY 11-1

TITLE VII IN A NUTSHELL

Title VII applies to:

- All employers with 15 or more employees, public, private or nonprofit
- All unions
- All job referral businesses

Title VII prohibits discrimination on the basis of:

- Race
- Color
- Religion
- Gender
- National origin

Title VII prohibits discrimination in all workplace decisions including, but not limited to:

- Hiring
- Raises
- Termination
- Pay
- Discipline
- Retaliation
- Training
- Workplace assignments
- Promotions
- Transfers

instance, employers will not be able to refuse to hire qualified males as secretaries because they think it inappropriate for males to hold that position.

L04

Who is protected under Title VII? Title VII protects employees on the basis of race, color, gender, religion or national origin. Gender discrimination also includes discrimination on the basis of pregnancy, as well as sexual harassment. Title VII does NOT prohibit discrimination on the basis of sexual orientation.

Are there exceptions to Title VII? Yes, there are exceptions to Title VII. Keep in mind that the federal law does not even apply to employers with fewer than 15 employees. Religious organi-

EXAMPLE

zations are also allowed to act consistently with their religious faith in employment. For example, a Catholic church would not be liable for not hiring a Jewish rabbi to lead its parish. The law also permits employers to discriminate in favor of Native Americans working on or near reservations, and to discriminate against communists (the reason for the latter has to do with the "Red scare" the country was coming out of as the law was passed). See Take Away 11-2, "Exceptions to Title VII."

What remedies are available under Title VII? With the passage of the Civil Rights Act of 1991 which amended Title VII, Title VII now permits jury trials as well as the recovery of compensatory and, where appropriate, punitive damages, although the latter may not be assessed against the federal government. Title VII originally limited damages to make-whole relief including backpay, reinstatement, injunctions, and retroactive seniority and benefits. (See Take Away 11-3, "The Civil Rights Act of 1991.")

TAKE AWAY 11-2

EXCEPTIONS TO TITLE VII

Title VII does not apply to employers:

- Who wish to discriminate on the basis of the employee being a communist
- Who wish to favor Native Americans living near an Indian reservation
- Who are religious organizations making workplace decisions on the basis of their religious beliefs

TAKE AWAY 11-3

THE CIVIL RIGHTS ACT OF 1991

The 1991 Civil Rights Act was a major overhaul for Title VII. The law's long history was closely scrutinized and Congress chose to strengthen the law in many ways rather than weaken it. Among other things the new amendments to Title VII permitted:

- Jury trials where compensatory or punitive damages are sought
- Compensatory damages in religious, sex and disability cases (such damages were already allowed for race and national origin under related legislation)
- Punitive damages for the same
- Unlimited medical expenses

The new Title VII law also

- Limited the extent to which "reverse discrimination" suits could be brought
- Authorized expert witness fees to successful plaintiffs
- Codified the disparate impact theory

- Broadened protections against private race discrimination in 42USC section 1981 cases (see later discussion)
- Expanded the right to bring actions challenging discriminatory seniority systems
- Extended extraterritorial coverage of Title VII to U.S. citizens working for U.S. companies outside the U.S., except where it would violate the laws of the country
- Extended coverage to and established procedures for Senate employees
- Established the Glass Ceiling Commission
- Established the National Award for Diversity and Excellence in American Executive Management (known as the Frances Perkins–Elizabeth Hanford Dole National Award for Diversity and Excellence in American Executive Management) for businesses which "have made substantial efforts to promote the opportunities and development experiences of women and minorities and foster advancement to management and decision making positions within the business"

What Are the Discrimination Theories Under Title VII?

Employees who believe they have been the object of discrimination may file a claim with the Equal Employment Opportunity Commission (EEOC), the federal agency charged with enforcing Title VII and other equal employment opportunity laws. The EEOC is required to accept and address virtually all complaints filed with them, free of charge. EEOC may have an agreement with a state's fair employment practice office for the office to serve as a complaint-handling agency for EEOC (called 706 agencies for the part of Title VII that permits the arrangement).

It is important to realize that it is easy and economical for employees to assert their rights under Title VII—at least initially. Since it is so easy for employees to file claims, it makes it even more important for employers to have careful policies that are consistently applied. If the claimant is not satisfied with EEOC's disposition of the claim the claimant may bring suit in federal court after exhausting administrative remedies at EEOC and receiving a **right to sue letter.** You may recall from the administrative law chapter that this means the claimant going through all the agency procedures to reach a final agency decision. At this point, the employee would have to bear the cost of litigation. The cost would also be on the employee if the employee brought a civil suit or a suit on constitutional grounds rather than on the basis of Title VII.

Bringing a discrimination claim involves much more than filing a claim with EEOC. Those who feel they have been discriminated against in employment must be able to prove it in one of two ways: **disparate treatment** or **disparate impact.** Disparate treatment is used when an employee alleges treatment different from others similarly situated. Disparate impact is used when a seemingly neutral employment policy adversely affects an entire group of employees protected by the law. An example of disparate impact would be a workplace requirement that applicants be at least 5 feet 2 inches and weigh at least 120 pounds, which is neutral on its face and appears to apply the same to everyone, but in reality screens out women and certain shorter and slighter ethnic minorities at a higher rate.[2]

EXAMPLE

DISPARATE TREATMENT

In disparate treatment the employee alleges that he or she was treated differently from other similarly situated employees regarding some aspect of employment based on one of the prohibited reasons, that is, based on race, gender, and so on. The allegation is that but for the employee's race, color, gender, religion, or national origin, the employee would not have been treated differently. Disparate treatment is an individual concept of discrimination. That is, the employee alleges that he or she as an individual was treated differently from others of a different group because of a prohibited basis. For instance, claimant could show disparate treatment if he was terminated for engaging in a workplace "stall-in" deemed to be "disruptive or illegal activity," then not rehired, if whites terminated after engaging in "disruptive or illegal" activity were, in fact, rehired.[3]

EXAMPLE

Intent to discriminate must be shown, in a disparate treatment case, but it can be shown directly or indirectly. For instance, for direct proof, the employee may allege that the employer said "I do not hire women." Or, the employer's discrimination may be

---

[2]*Dothard v. Rawlinson,* 433 U.S. 321 (1977).

[3]*McDonnell Douglas Corp. v. Green,* 411 U.S. 792 (1973).

shown indirectly by the employee establishing that (1) the applicant is a member of a group protected by Title VII, (2) the employer had a job available for which the applicant was qualified and applied, (3) though the applicant was qualified, the employer did not hire her, and (4) upon rejecting her, the job remained open and the employer continued to search for applicants with her qualifications. (See Take Away 11-4, "Disparate Impact Requirements.") The latter, indirect approach, demonstrates discrimination by ruling out all of the usual reasons that a person would not be hired (i.e., no job is available, lack of the necessary qualifications, and so on) so that all that is left is the applicant's membership in a protected class. Employer must therefore be sure that his treatment of all employees is consistent and fair, so that the basis for a disparate treatment claim does not exist. As we will discuss, the employer is then free to rebut this presumption of discrimination if the facts so warrant.

DISPARATE IMPACT

Disparate impact is not quite so simple. With disparate impact the employee must show that an employment policy that is neutral on its face has a harsher impact on a group protected by the law. It is a group concept of discrimination rather than an individual one. No intent to discriminate need be shown. It is the result which is important.

For instance, in our example above, an employer had a policy requiring that anyone who works in a security capacity be 5 feet 2 inches and weigh at least 120 pounds. The policy applied across the board to anyone applying for the job. Statistically, women as a group are not as likely as men to meet this requirement because most are shorter and lighter. Therefore the policy would have the effect of screening out women from security jobs at a higher rate than men, thus creating a disparate impact upon women. It would also create a disparate impact upon certain ethnic groups that tend to be shorter and slighter in stature, such as Asians and some Hispanics.

The employer's policy appears on its face to be neutral, but courts have found it has a disparate impact upon women and other minority groups and therefore violates Title VII. In order to continue to use the policy the employer would be required to show that the policy is necessary for the job, that is, that in order to perform necessary security functions, employees must be 5 feet 2 inches and a minimum of 120 pounds. This would be difficult to do since people who do not fit these requirements routinely perform quite well as security personnel. Keep in mind that the employer may well have legitimate job requirements; however, the appropriate basis for who meets them must be demonstrated.

Disparate impact is generally defined as the employer using a **screening device** to choose employees where a minority group does not perform at least 80 percent as well as the majority group under a given policy. This is known as the **80% or 4/5 Rule.** But courts have not held this theory to strictly numerical terms. Because of the many ways in which policies may have disparate impacts upon different groups, it may be difficult for an employer to discern that a given policy has a disparate impact. Listening to concerns of employees can greatly aid in this, as the *Bradley* case (Case 11.1) somewhat startlingly demonstrates. See Take Away 11-5, "Disparate Impact Requirements," for an overview of disparate impact.

TAKE AWAY 11-4

DISPARATE TREATMENT REQUIREMENTS

In order to prove a prima facie case of indirect disparate treatment under Title VII, claimant must show:

1. That he or she is a member of a class protected under Title VII;
2. That the claimant applied for an available job for which he or she was qualified;*
3. The employee was rejected for the job despite being qualified; and
4. The job remained open and the employer continued to search for applicants with claimant's qualifications.

Once this is shown, the employer can rebut claimant's case by demonstrating that there was a legitimate, nondiscriminatory reason for the action taken against claimant.

Once the employer demonstrates this, the claimant has the opportunity to rebut the employer's reason by showing that it is mere pretext for discrimination.

*the facts can be changed as appropriate, for other workplace actions other than hiring such as discriminatory termination, discipline, raises, and so on.

EXAMPLE

939 F.2d 610 (8th Cir. 1991)

Facts: Domino's Pizza, the employer, had a policy requiring all male employees to be clean shaven. An African American employee who did not want to shave because it exacerbated a common African American male skin condition was terminated for failure to comply with the policy.

Issue: Whether a policy that is neutral on its face but has a disparate impact upon a group protected under Title VII can stand if there is no business necessity for the policy.

Decision: No

Reasoning: Fagg, J.: Domino's grooming policy prohibits employees from wearing beards. Pizzaco, a Domino's franchisee, hired Bradley to deliver pizzas, but fired him within two weeks because he would not remove his beard. Bradley is a black man who suffers from pseudofolliculitis barbae (PFB), a skin disorder affecting almost half of all black males. The symptoms of PFB—skin irritation and scarring—are brought on by shaving, and in severe cases PFB sufferers must abstain from shaving altogether. Domino's policy, however, provides for no exceptions. As Pizzaco's owner explained, "You must be clean-shaven to work for Domino's."

This case, then, is about a seemingly neutral employment policy that discriminates against black males when applied. Title VII forbids employment policies with a disparate impact unless the policy is justified by legitimate employment goals. Through expert medical testimony and studies, the EEOC demonstrated Domino's policy necessarily excludes black males from the company's work force at a substantially higher rate than white males. In so doing, the EEOC has shown Domino's facially neutral grooming requirement operates as a "built-in headwind" for black males. *Griggs v. Duke Power Co.*, 401 U.S. at 432.

The record shows PFB almost exclusively affects black males and white males rarely suffer from PFB or comparable skin disorders that may prevent a man from appearing clean-shaven. Dermatologists for both sides testified that as many as forty-five percent of black males have PFB. The EEOC's dermatologist offered his opinion that approximately twenty-five percent of all black males cannot shave because of PFB.

PFB prevents a sizable segment of the black male population from appearing clean-shaven, but does not similarly affect white males. Domino's policy—which makes no exceptions for black males who medically are unable to shave because of a skin disorder peculiar to their face—effectively operates to exclude these black males from employment with Domino's. Decision against the driver REVERSED in part, AFFIRMED in part, and REMANDED.

CASE QUESTIONS

1. Why do you think there was a no-beard policy? Does it make sense to you? Should it, when you think of an applicant being hired to deliver pizza? Is it enough reason to keep a qualified pizza deliverer from a job he is otherwise qualified for? Is not having a beard a marketing scheme or an actual qualification to be able to drive the truck to deliver pizzas? Should it matter? How much weight should be given to marketing schemes and why? Is it ethical to keep someone from a job for which they are otherwise qualified because of a marketing scheme? Explain.

2. Do you agree with the court's decision? Why or why not?

3. Can you think of a better legal approach to this situation? If so, what? If not, why not?

Note that we are discussing beards here in the procedural context of disparate impact, rather than the substantive issue of the wearing of beards. The issue of wearing beards also arises in the context of religion and of safety. That is can someone be allowed to wear a beard if it is for religious reasons, or can they be required to shave it off for safety reasons, such as so that a required safety mask fits as it should? As we will see when we discuss religion, an employer has the duty to reasonably accommodate the religious conflict unless to do so would cause an undue hardship. As for safety, if the mask is required for safety and there is no way the mask can be worn over a beard worn for religious reasons, then the employer can change the job of the employee so that safety is not an issue.

L04 Is There More about Protected Categories Under Title VII?

Title VII protects everyone from employment discrimination, but the discrimination prohibited falls into certain categories. Those categories are race, color, gender, religion and national origin. The sections below outline the requirements for each of these.

RACE AND COLOR

Because of the particular history of the United States, with nearly 250 years of slavery and its inevitable Jim Crow vestiges in the ninety-nine-year aftermath, racial discrimination is an ongoing concern in the workplace. You saw as much in Congress's 2008 apology for slavery in the property chapter. While Title VII was enacted to address the 100-year post–slavery segregation and Jim Crow legal and custom-based discrimination against blacks, Title VII applies to *everyone* equally. Whites are protected, just as are blacks are. While the category of race has been undergoing a metamorphosis as our country has grown more and more ethnically diverse, those from other countries or whose heritage is of nonwhite or nonblack origins generally bring their discrimination claims on the basis of national origin rather than race. We will discuss national origin discrimination shortly. Employers must ensure that all employees are treated equally or comparably, regardless of their race or ethnicity.

Discrimination on the basis of race may be overt or covert, disparate impact or disparate treatment, but it should not be tolerated in any of its manifestations. The *Bradley* case (Case 11.1) was a good example of the subtle ways in which race can enter into the workplace without an employer even realizing it. At times, it is totally unintentional, but nonetheless has a devastating impact on the group discriminated against. For instance, in *Bradley*, a qualified pizza deliverer, was terminated for what amounted to racial reasons. Do not only look for discrimination in its more obvious manifestations. Look for the subtle as well, and have zero tolerance for it. Not only does it waste precious resources, but it lowers productivity, sends the wrong message to other employees, and is simply not good business. Notice that it is not ill will or intent that matters in these situations. The law looks at the discriminatory act done, not its motivation. This leads to an entirely different way of looking at discrimination than you may be used to.

Closely related to the issue of race is that of color. While Title VII always included color as one of its categories, the first case was not brought until the 1990s. Since then, the number of claims has increased. If you have never been particularly attuned to racial issues, as a manager or supervisor you could well miss color discrimination. The claim is generally that an employee is being treated less favorably because his or her skin color is darker than a similarly situated employee. Of course, it is no secret that many cultures favor fairer skin over darker skin, but in our country, if it is the basis for treating an employee differently, then it is illegal.

Keep in mind that color is not the same as race. While race addresses the racial group one belongs to, color has to do solely with skin color within that group. For instance, in the first color discrimination case brought, a fair complexioned African American

TAKE AWAY 11-5

DISPARATE IMPACT REQUIREMENTS

If a claimant is using disparate impact as her or his theory of discrimination against the employer, in order to prove a prima facie case, the claimant must show that:

1. The employer used a screening device to determine which applicants or candidates would receive some workplace benefit such as hire or promotion;
2. The complaining group did not perform at least 80% as well as the group that received the benefit (traditionally it has been that women have not done as well as men, or that blacks and Hispanics have not done as well as whites).

Once this is shown, the employer's policy has a disparate impact under Title VII and may be prohibited unless the employer can prove there is a business necessity for the screening device used.

If the employer shows a business necessity for the screening device, claimant may then demonstrate that while this may be true, there is a way to address the business necessity with less of a disparate impact than the screening device used by the employer. If this is shown to the court's satisfaction, the less harmful means must be used by the employer.

EXAMPLE

EXAMPLE

employee charged that her darker African American supervisor treated her poorly and made statements indicating the supervisor thought the lighter employee believed she was better than the darker supervisor because of her lighter skin color.[4]

GENDER

Gender is another of those areas where the discriminatory treatment and policies had been generally accepted for a long period of time, and Title VII attempted, much as with race, to change ingrained notions. Delightful, 80-year-old Lorena Weeks of Wadley, GA, remembers at 18 going to work for Southern Bell Telephone Company to support her orphaned sister and brother. Working at Southern Bell and also working as a waitress for tips and a free meal for her brother, she knew the impact of hard work, having seen her widowed mother die at 38 from working three jobs to support her children. So, when the higher paid switchmen's job became available, Lorena applied. She was quickly told she could not have the job because it was for men only. Asked her reaction, Lorena said "Well, I had seen this new law posted on the board and I knew I was going to get that job some kind of way." Lorena sued and eventually became the first employee to win a gender suit under the then-new Title VII legislation. (Weeks v. Southern Bell, 467 F.2d 95 (5th Cir. 1972) interestingly enough, gender was placed in the Title VII bill the day before its passage by Judge Howard Smith, a southern legislator and civil rights foe but also a longtime supporter of women's rights who was searching for a way to stop passage of legislation that would outlaw segregation. It did not work, and research shows that women have been the biggest beneficiaries of the law. Employers must guard against such ingrained notions finding their way into employment policies that discriminate on the basis of gender. Again, because of the particulars of our history, while most of the discrimination in the workplace has been against females rather than males, the law equally protects men from gender discrimination.

Gender discrimination has many different manifestations of which employers must be aware. The problem does not lie in not knowing that one cannot discriminate on the basis of gender, but as can be seen in Diversity in the Law 11-1, "The Many Faces of Gender Discrimination," it lies in recognizing when it occurs.

The list in Diversity in the Law 11-1 could go on. The important thing to note is that employers must ensure that their workplace policies do not adopt notions of what is "appropriate" work or activity for one gender or another, but instead, limit consideration to qualifications for the job. As *Price Waterhouse v. Hopkins*

DIVERSITY IN THE LAW 11-1

THE MANY FACES OF GENDER DISCRIMINATION

Gender discrimination has been found by courts to exist in such diverse situations as:

- Refusal to hire males as airline flight attendants.
- Refusal to hire females as bartenders.
- Hiring men, but not women, who are the parents of pre-school-aged children.
- Hiring unmarried men, but not women, who have children.
- Refusing to hire anyone not at least 5 feet 2 inches and 120 pounds.
- Having only "filthy" toilets on the worksite premises and refusing to allow the female employee access to an off-limits cleaner restroom.
- Refusal to hire males as servers for a restaurant.
- Refusal to hire males at an all-women's health spa.
- Prohibiting women of childbearing age from working in jobs with exposure to lead, and not prohibiting men of childbearing age from doing so, when both were at reproductive risk.
- Requiring men to wear "business attire," but requiring similarly situated women to wear uniforms.
- Requiring that in order to be acceptable as a partner the female (who had outperformed her male competition) dress more femininely, have her hair styled, wear jewelry, not use curse words and be less aggressive.
- Requiring that female flight attendants be unmarried, but male flight attendants had no such restriction.

---

[4]*Walker v. Secretary of the Treasury, IRS,* 742 F. Supp. 670 (N.D. Ga., Atlanta, Div. 1990).

CASE 11.2 Price Waterhouse v. Hopkins

490 U.S. 228 (1989)

Facts: A female associate who was refused admission as a partner in an accounting firm brought a gender discrimination action against the firm. The U.S. Supreme Court held that the gender stereotyping which took place was impermissible under Title VII.

Issue: Whether making a workplace decision based on stereotyped notions of gender is permitted under Title VII's prohibition on gender discrimination.

Decision: No

Reasoning: Brennan, J.: In a jointly prepared statement supporting her candidacy, the partners in Hopkins' office showcased her successful two-year effort to secure a $25 million contract with the Department of State, labeling it "an outstanding performance" and one that Hopkins carried out "virtually at the partner level." None of the other partnership candidates had a comparable record in terms of successfully securing major contracts for the partnership.

The partners in Hopkins' office praised her character and her accomplishments, describing her as "an outstanding professional" who had a "deft touch," a "strong character, independence and integrity." Clients appeared to have agreed with these assessments.

Virtually all of the partners' negative comments about Hopkins—even those of partners supporting her—had to do with her "interpersonal skills." Both supporters and opponents of her candidacy indicate she was sometimes "overly aggressive, unduly harsh, difficult to work with and impatient with staff."

There were clear signs, though, that some of the partners reacted negatively to Hopkins' personality because she was a woman. One partner described her as "macho"; another suggested that she "overcompensated for being a woman"; a third advised her to take "a course at charm school." Several partners criticized her use of profanity; in response, one partner suggested that those partners objected to her swearing only "because it['s] a lady using foul language." Another supporter explained that Hopkins "ha[d] matured from a tough-talking somewhat masculine hard-nosed manager to an authoritative, formidable, but much more appealing lady partner candidate." But it was the man who bore responsibility for explaining to Hopkins the reasons for the Policy Board's decision to place her candidacy on hold who delivered the coup de grace; in order to improve her chances for partnership, Thomas Beyer advised Hopkins should "walk more femininely, talk more femininely, dress more femininely, wear makeup, have her hair styled, and wear jewelry."

As for the legal relevance of gender stereotyping, we are beyond the day when an employer could evaluate employees by assuming or insisting that they matched the stereotype associated with their group, for "[i]n forbidding employers to discriminate against individuals because of their gender, Congress intended to strike at the entire spectrum of disparate treatment of men and women resulting from sex stereotypes." An employer who objects to aggressiveness in women but whose positions require this trait places women in the intolerable and impermissible Catch-22: out of a job if they behave aggressively and out of a job if they don't. Title VII lifts women out of this bind. Decision against Hopkins REVERSED and REMANDED.

CASE QUESTIONS

1. What was Price Waterhouse's fatal flaw?
2. Does Hopkins' treatment here make good business sense?
3. How would you avoid the problem in this case?

(Case 11.2) demonstrates, liability can ensue when this advice is not followed and employees are instead stereotyped based on gender. (See Diversity in the Law 11-2, "Upcoming Bases for Discrimination?")

SEXUAL HARASSMENT

Sexual harassment is also a form of gender discrimination. It is discriminatory to have employees of one gender and not the other subject to workplace requirements or oppressive and offensive behavior that interfere with the employee's ability to do his or her job. Although in excess of 80 percent of sexual harassment claims are brought by females both males and females are protected and the number of males filing complaints with EEOC has steadily increased to a 2009 high of 16 percent. Contrary to popular

UPCOMING BASES FOR DISCRIMINATION?

One of the bases of discrimination that we are frequently asked about is discrimination on the basis of appearance, including obesity. It is well documented that there are differences in perception based on appearances. Very attractive men and women earn at least 5 percent more per hour than people with average looks. Plain women earn an average of 5 percent less than women with average looks, most employers pay overweight women 20 percent less per hour than women of average weight, and overweight men earn 26 percent more than their underweight counterparts (men are "supposed to be sturdier"), and so on.

These differences have increasingly become the bases of lawsuits by employees who believe it is unfair to have their jobs or pay be put in jeopardy because of their appearance. As mentioned in an earlier chapter, in June 2010, the media played up the story of a New York female employee who alleged she was terminated because her male bosses told her that her body and shape were too distracting for male employees to concentrate. In the spring of 2010, a 132 pound, 5 foot 6 inch waitress was told she had to lose weight because she no longer looked good enough in her Hooter's Restaurant outfit.

As more employees receive coverage under Title VII and related laws for issues that form the basis of what these employees perceive as non-qualification-based judgments that cost them their jobs, they are getting more assertive at trying to obtain relief. Presently, there is little or nothing that can be done unless the issues can be fitted into one of the protected categories (for instance, the female whose body was too distracting might allege gender discrimination). Michigan is the only state that includes obesity in its workplace discrimination laws so far. Keep an eye out. As appearances and weight become more of an issue, state or federal regulators may well decide to include these categories in the law.

Sources: Cameron Tuttle, *The Paranoid's Pocket Guide* (Chronicle Books, 1997); Jeff Biddle and Daniel Hamermesh, "Beauty and the Labor Market," *American Economic Review* 83, no. 1174 (December 1994); John Cawley, *Body Weight and Women's Labor Market Outcomes,* Joint Center for Poverty Research, 2000; Elizabeth Dwoskin, "Is This Woman Too Hot to Be a Banker?" *The Village Voice,* June 10, 2010, http://www.villagevoice.com/2010-06-01/news/is-this-woman-too-hot-to-work-in-a-bank/1; and Steven Greenhouse, "Obese People Are Taking Their Claims to Court," *New York Times,* August 4, 2003, http://www.globalpolicy.org/component/content/article/217-hunger/46082.html.

thought, sexual harassment need not necessarily involve sex. Courts have found sexual harassment where the activity was not necessarily sexual in nature, but instead exhibited **anti-female animus** toward the harassee so that because of her gender she is made to endure a negative work environment. Take Away 11-6, "EEOC Sexual Harassment Guidelines," provides the specific language that defines sexual harassment.

There are two types of sexual harassment: **quid pro quo sexual harassment** and **hostile environment sexual harassment.** Quid pro quo sexual harassment involves the employee directly or indirectly being threatened with not receiving workplace benefits or entitlements such as hire, promotions, raises, training, and so on, unless the employee engages in sexual activity with the harasser.

Hostile environment sexual harassment is quite different and not always as clear-cut. Under the EEOC sexual harassment guidelines virtually any unwanted activity directed to one gender but not the other which creates for an employee a hostile or offensive

TAKE AWAY 11-6

EEOC SEXUAL HARASSMENT GUIDELINES

Unwelcome sexual advances, requests for sexual favors, and other verbal or physical conduct of a sexual nature constitute sexual harassment when (1) submission to such conduct is made either explicitly or implicitly a term or condition of an individual's employment, (2) submission to or rejection of such conduct by an individual is used as the basis for employment decisions affecting such individual, or (3) such conduct has the purpose or effect of unreasonably interfering with an individual's work performance or creating an intimidating, hostile, or offensive working environment. 29 C.F.R. Section 1604.11 (a)

environment and unreasonably interferes with the employee's ability to perform can be the subject of a sexual harassment claim. This includes such activities as:

- Physical contact
- Sexual jokes
- Negative or stereotyped gender-based jokes
- Teasing
- Gestures
- Display of nude or sexually explicit photos, drawings, plaques, calendars, magazines, cartoons or the like in the workplace
- Repeated requests for dates or sexual activity

After reading the information about sexual harassment and gender discrimination just presented, you should be able to surmise that in our opening scenario, real estate agent Amy has a reason to be concerned about the event that her firm gives each year. Asking the women who work at the firm as equals to get dressed up and serve liquor and cigars to the other agents is not only offensive and demeaning, it will most likely be deemed illegal. It clearly evidences that the females at the firm who are on par with the males in terms of the jobs they hold are not considered in the same professional light. Even though some women want to engage in the activity, it is pretty clear that they view doing so as a way to be on par with the men. Consensual activity is not a violation of sexual harassment laws; however, it must be clear that the activity is truly consensual. In this scenario based on an actual real estate firm, even though the female agents participated, a court would likely find that they felt they had no choice under the circumstances if they wanted to continue to work at the firm.

Though there has been a great deal of attention to the issue of sexual harassment over the past few years, many people, even business people and employers, do not understand sexual harassment. Many think that an allegation of sexual harassment is tantamount to proving it. That is not so. In order to be actionable the activity must meet certain requirements which ensure that the activity alleged to be sexual harassment is not a mere isolated incident which simply annoys an employee or hurts his or her feelings or even offends him or her. (See Take Away 11-7 "Sexual Harassment Requirements.")

The requirements make clear that simply asking someone for a date or telling them they look nice in an appropriate way (for instance not staring at their breasts or licking your lips as your eyes slowly travel up and down their body) is not the sort of activity which will serve as a basis for liability. Even at that, there can be differing opinions as to what is merely inappropriate behavior and what constitutes sexual harassment.

Supervisory or managerial employees who sexually harass employees may cause the employer to be held liable whether or not the employer knew of the harassing activity. Such employees are agents of the employer and act on the employer's behalf. Employers must be vigilant in choosing supervisory employees and ensure that they are not likely to engage in such costly, unnecessary behavior. If the harassment is perpetrated by a co-worker (rather than a supervisory employee) employers are liable if they knew or should have known of the harassment. They should know of it if they are notified by the harassee, they witness it, or the matter is so pervasive and obvious until a prudent employer would be aware of it.

Employers are also responsible for harassment perpetrated by outsiders who deal with the company and harass

TAKE AWAY 11-7

SEXUAL HARASSMENT REQUIREMENTS

In order to sustain a finding of hostile environment sexual harassment, it is generally required that:

- The harassment is unwelcome by plaintiff.
- The harassment is based on gender.
- The harassment is sufficiently severe or pervasive to create an abusive working environment.
- The harassment affected a term, condition or privilege of employment.
- The employer had actual or constructive knowledge of the hostile environment and took no prompt adequate remedial action

EXAMPLE

CREATING A NON-HOSTILE WORK ENVIRONMENT

Suggestions for creating an atmosphere in which sexual harassment is minimized include:

- Making sure, from the top down, that all employees understand that sexual harassment in the workplace simply will not be tolerated.
- Adopting an anti-sexual harassment policy discouraging such activity. This should not be part of a general anti-discrimination policy, but should instead be separate
- Creating and disseminating information about an effective reporting mechanism for those with sexual harassment complaints including alternatives when the supervisor is the harasser.
- Providing employees with training or information which apprises them of what sexual harassment is and what specific activities are appropriate and inappropriate to engage in.
- Ensuring that reported incidents of sexual harassment are taken seriously by supervisors.
- Ensuring that there is immediate appropriate corrective action taken against employees engaging in sexual harassment.

its employees. For instance, a computer repairer who comes in to service the office's computers on a regular basis and harasses employees while there may be the basis for a sexual harassment complaint.

It is important for employers to provide immediate corrective action to address sexual harassment once they discover it has occurred. The best approach an employer can take in avoiding liability for sexual harassment is to create an atmosphere in which it is not permitted to exist. (See Reality Check 11-1, "Creating a Non-Hostile Work Environment.")

If the steps in Reality Check 11-1 are taken, they will go a long way toward helping employers avoid the unnecessary liability of sexual harassment claims. Courts address whether given activity constitutes sexual harassment on a case by case basis, and considering all relevant factors in context. What may be appropriate in one circumstance or setting may not be in another. Employers should ensure that employees are aware of what types of activities are more likely to result in liability for sexual harassment, and strive to avoid them.

PREGNANCY

While many have notions regarding the "frailty" of pregnant employees, the law takes the position that it is gender discrimination on the basis of pregnancy to treat pregnancy differently from any other short-term disability that any other employee has. Pregnant employees cannot be made to leave work early and take maternity leave at a certain arbitrarily set date, as was once the case with teachers and others. They also cannot have their job duties taken away unless there is some basis for doing so, such as inability to perform. Otherwise, pregnancy is to be treated just as an employer would treat any other short-term disability.

EQUAL PAY AND COMPARABLE WORTH

While Title VII prohibits discrimination in any aspect of employment, the matter of gender discrimination in wages was addressed even before Title VII was passed. The Equal Pay Act was passed in 1963, the year before Title VII. The Act prohibits discrimination in pay on the basis of gender, except in certain circumscribed situations such as where the difference in pay is based upon the amount produced, quality of production, and so forth. Employers may not circumvent the law to justify wage differentials by simply calling the same job by different titles when it is performed by males and females (i.e., a male "orderly," but a female "nurse's aide," though both perform the same tasks).

Since Title VII came into being so soon after the Equal Pay Act and also addressed the matter of gender-based wage discrimination, the Equal Pay Act has not been used as much as it might have otherwise. However, its biggest contribution may well be that it also gave rise to the concept of **comparable worth.**

Comparable worth permits jobs that are not the same, but are of comparable worth to the employer, to be examined for wage disparities. For instance, it can be used to argue that secretaries are paid less because it is a female dominated profession, while construction workers are paid more because it is male dominated, yet both are of comparable value to the employer. It thus gets around the EPA limitation on comparing jobs that are essentially the same. It permits arguments for those situations where pay within a profession may not be discriminatory among males and females, but the profession itself, being female dominated, may have lower wages for reasons more related to gender than anything else.

Comparable worth has not been fully accepted by the courts, and legislation does not require it. However, employers should ensure that the wages paid to their employees are free of possible claims in this area. This is even more important now that the Lilly Ledbetter Fair Pay Act of 2009, the first piece of legislation signed into law by President Barack Obama, renews the statute of limitations each time an employee receives a paycheck that is based on discrimination. A study by the U.S. Government Accountability Office on gender and wages between 200 and 2007 released September 28, 2010, indicated that female managers, on average, made 81 cents for every dollar a male manager made. This is up from 79 cents in 2000.[5]

AFFINITY ORIENTATION

Employers should recognize that the gender classification of Title VII has been deemed *not* to include discrimination on the basis of **affinity orientation.** This category includes gays, lesbians, bisexuals, transgenders, and others on the basis of gender identity. Discrimination on the basis of affinity orientation and gender identity is not covered under Title VII, but many state and municipal governments have laws providing protection from job discrimination on this basis, and the list changes almost daily. In addition, thousands of employers have such policies and amending Title VII to include such protection will no doubt occur at some point. (See Reality Check 11-2, "Societal Changes.").

To date, laws extending employment protection and benefits on the basis of affinity orientation have been enacted in Washington, Nevada, California, Illinois, New Mexico,

---

REALITY CHECK 11-2

SOCIETAL CHANGES

As we have previously stated, law does not occur in a vacuum. It is often a reflection of what is going on in society and this fact contributes to the organic nature of our law. We are presently experiencing changes in the area of the treatment of the Lesbian Gay Bisexual and Transgender (LGBT) community. In addition to state and local workplace protections, many other rules and regulations in the area reflect a growing move toward inclusion. For instance, the first half of 2010 saw President Obama issue a federal executive order requiring nondiscrimination in visitation rights in hospitals receiving federal funds (aimed at gays and lesbians being excluded from visiting their hospitalized partners). This was followed in June 2010 by the Joint Commission, the largest organization accrediting hospitals nationwide, requiring all American hospitals to have an antidiscrimination policy for LGBTs. The Department of State announced in June 2010 that it was issuing new guidelines on its gender marker policy, changing its policies with regard to transgenders to reflect that they need not have had surgery in order to have their passports reissued with their new gender, with appropriate documentation from a doctor saying they are undergoing transition. Though the 2010 Gallup Poll's Annual Values and Beliefs Survey marked a milestone as being the first time in the history of the survey that the acceptance rate for gay relationships was over 50 percent (52 percent), these changes will not be made easily. Such is life in a democracy.

What are the ethical considerations in making determinations about who should be protected from discrimination and who should not; who should be accepted and who should not? Should it be a matter of polls? Is there an inherent right or wrong in judging others this way? How is this issue similar to or different from that of blacks being accepted via the Civil Rights Act of 1964? The Irish being accepted more after John F. Kennedy was elected president of the U.S. and did not, as was feared in some quarters, "take his marching orders from the Pope"? Are we facing the same issue of acceptance of other groups such as Hispanics and Muslims? What groups do not seem to have these issues of societal acceptance? Can you determine why? Is there any ethical difference?

---

[5]"Women Managers Paid Less Than Male Counterparts," Reuters, http://www.reuters.com/article/idUSTRE68R1O020100928

MUNICIPALITIES WITH ANTI-DISCRIMINATION LAWS BANNING DISCRIMINATION AGAINST GAYS AND LESBIANS

- At least 14 states have executive orders.
- At least 71 cities and counties have civil rights ordinances.
- At least 41 cities or counties have council or mayoral proclamations banning discrimination in public employment.

Jurisdictions include:

Laguna Beach, CA	Marshall, MN
Berkeley, CA	St. Paul, MN
Sacramento, CA	Essex Co, NJ
Davis, CA	St. Louis, MO
San Diego, CA	Albany, NY
Oakland, CA	Alfred, NY
San Francisco, CA	New York, NY
Los Angeles, CA	Ithaca, NY
Santa Monica, CA	Watertown, NY
Key West, FL	Tompkins County, NY
West Hollywood, CA	Columbus, OH
Miami Beach, FL	Harrisburg, PA
Washington, DC	Yellow Springs, OH
Champaign, IL	Lancaster, PA
Ames, IA	Philadelphia, PA
Chicago, IL	Pittsburgh, PA
Rockville, MD	Austin, TX
Iowa City, IA	Alexandria, VA
Howard County, MD	Seattle, WA
New Orlean, LA	Madison, WI
Detroit, MI	Portland, OR
Gaithersberg, MD	
Minneapolis, MN	*Source:* hrc.org.

New York, Wisconsin, California, Massachusetts, Hawaii, Connecticut, Rhode Island, New Jersey, Maine, Maryland, Minnesota and Vermont, plus the District of Columbia. Over 200 municipalities also have such enactments. Even more jurisdictions have provisions protecting state, city and county government employees and over 400 of the Fortune 500 companies have such policies as well. (See Reality Check 11-3, "Municipalities with Anti-Discrimination Laws Banning Discrimination against Gays and Lesbians.") You should also be aware that the Fifth and Fourteenth Amendments to the U.S. constitution may also protect government employees as a denial of equal protection unless it is justified by a legitimate state interest.

Under the circumstances, the better approach for employers is to choose their employees based on relevant, job-related criteria which address the ability to do the job rather than a judgment about their non-job-related personal lives. If there are specific problems that are presented by the gay or lesbian employee, these should be addressed as would any infringement of workplace rules, rather than as if their orientation is the deciding factor.

For instance, many heterosexual employees **EXAMPLE** and employers have the perception that if gays are permitted to be open about their orientation, they will have explicit sexual discussions in the workplace and make others uncomfortable. Of course, this is a myth, but even if such inappropriate conversation did occur, it should be addressed as it would if it were any other employee discussing inappropriate matters in the workplace. It need not be thought of as a "gay or lesbian issue," as gays are no more likely to discuss their sex life at work than other employees.

An emerging issue in this area is gender stereotyping as it relates to gays and lesbians. As you saw in the *Hopkins* case, gender stereotyping is a form of illegal gender discrimination under Title VII. Some courts have used the case to protect males who have been stereotyped in the workplace as being too feminine and thus not meeting the standard of a "stereotypical" male. This has permitted recovery in cases that might otherwise have been dismissed since Title VII does not cover affinity orientation. However, in this line of reasoning, the claim is not that the employee is being discriminated against on the basis of affinity orientation, but rather, on the basis of gender stereotyping. While the two can be essentially the same, the form of the claim makes all the difference since one is not permitted under Title VII and the other is. For instance, claimant **EXAMPLE** was teased as being effeminate and not the "usual oil field worker."[6]

---

[6]*Sisco v. Fabrication Technologies, Inc.*, 350 F. Supp. 2d 932 (D. Wyo. 2004). See also, *Theno v. Tonganoxie Unified School District No. 464*, 2005 U.S. Dist. LEXIS 12537 (D. Kan. 2005); *Nichols v. Azteca Rest. Enters*, 256 F.3d 864 (9th Cir. 2001).

RELIGION

Discrimination on the basis of religion is also prohibited by Title VII. Not only should employers refrain from asking applicants or employees their religious affiliation, they should also refrain from treating employees differently based upon religion unless the law so permits. Unlike the prohibitions on race or gender, the prohibition on discriminating on the basis of religion is limited in that employers cannot discriminate unless to do so would present an undue hardship. What constitutes an undue hardship is determined on a case by case basis by the courts. (See Take Away 11-8, "Factors in Undue Hardship").

The religion need not be one which the employer recognizes in order for Title VII to apply. As long as the employee's belief is sincerely held and takes the place of religion in his or her life, the employer cannot dismiss it as not being a "legitimate" religion (i.e., a recent situation involved The Church of Body Modification.[7] In trying to reach an accommodation, the employee must cooperate with the employer rather than put the full responsibility on employer to find an accommodation. If it can be shown that the employer attempted an accommodation and the employee refused to cooperate, there is no liability for the employer. Religious conflicts can arise in any number of ways, including an employee not being able to work certain days or hours because of his or her Sabbath, not being able to engage in certain activity because it is against his or her religion (Muslim grocery store cashiers who cannot handle pork or alcoholic products), desiring the wearing of certain clothing, or inability to wear workplace required clothing, and so on.

Many of the issues arising around religion have involved Muslims in the years since 9/11. Not only has there been a significant increase in religious harassment directed toward Muslims or those perceived to be Muslims, but there is also much litigation about employers not accommodating the religious needs of this group's requirement that they pray five times per day and perform ablutions before doing so. For instance, a Muslim employee was terminated for using an empty patient bathroom to perform her required ablutions of washing her hands, feet and forehead before praying. The court held that the employer failed to reasonably accommodate the religious conflict.[8] Again, an employer must accommodate on the basis of religion unless it would present an undue hardship to do so. Two interesting cases have arisen recently involving the wearing of the hijab, or scarf by Disney employees who are required to dress in Disney-dictated costume for their position. It will be interesting to see the outcome. Who do you think should prevail? Why?

NATIONAL ORIGIN

Discrimination on the basis of national origin addresses the reality that in our country of a multitude of ethnicities, many employees will not be of the dominant culture. This can present problems when this becomes a basis for treating them differently. National origin discrimination addresses this and deals with discrimination against employees because their ethnic origins.

TAKE AWAY 11-8

FACTORS IN UNDUE HARDSHIP

EEOC has provided employers with guidelines as to what factors it will consider in answering the question of whether the employer's accommodation would cause undue hardship. Such factors include:

- The nature of the employer's workplace
- The type of job needing accommodation
- The cost of the accommodation
- The willingness of other employees to assist in the accommodation
- The possibility of transfer of the employee and its effects
- What is done by similarly situated employers
- The number of employees available for accommodation
- The burden of accommodation upon the union

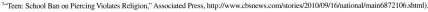

[7]"Teen: School Ban on Piercing Violates Religion," Associated Press, http://www.cbsnews.com/stories/2010/09/16/national/main6872106.shtml).

[8]*Tyson v. Clarian Health Partners, Inc.,* 2004 U.S. Dist LEXIS 13973 (S.D. Ind. 2004).

National origin discrimination can take a number of forms. It can be an employer refusing to hire or firing those of a particular nationality, such as Asians or Iranians; having policies not permitting those with a native language other than English to speak their native language in the workplace even when it does not interfere with their jobs; not permitting those with accents to hold certain jobs; and so on. None of this is permissible under Title VII.

EXAMPLE

"English only" rules may be permissible if the speaking of English is actually a job requirement. However, if the employer imposes such a rule on employees when they take their lunch or other breaks, or when they otherwise do not need to speak English, it is discriminatory. Likewise, with accents. For instance, having an accent was insufficient basis for an employer not to promote an employee who had previously held the position of laboratory director on an intermittent basis in the absence of the director, when it could not be shown that the accent interfered with his ability to do the job.

The more subtle, but nonetheless devastating issue with national origin as we see more and more different nationalities and ethnicities coming into the workplace is how to avoid the subtle ways in which such employees are given the message that they do not belong. A situation involving one of our Hispanic students is a good example. Pablo was born in Puerto Rico but had been in the U.S. most of his life. Pablo had a great college experience and the grades to show for it and upon graduation took a job with a prestigious corporation and was quite excited to do so. It did not take long for him to notice the subtle, but definite differences in the way he was treated in the workplace. Unlike other employees who were hired with him and had comparable education and grades, his work was constantly closely monitored and checked, as if it was expected that he would not perform as well. There were constant "joking" references to his ethnicity. These subtle messages of "difference" and "otherness" made him feel like an outsider. He was stunned by them. It had never occurred to him he would experience such a thing in a professional setting. All he wanted was to be taken seriously as a professional, as had happened with the whites who had been hired with him. One of the things that also annoyed Pablo was that each day when he returned from lunch with his office mates, the only person security ever checked was him. It went on for weeks. The guards knew everyone except Pablo, even though Pablo always went to lunch with the same people every day. Pablo tried discussing these issues with higher ups, but to no avail. They could not understand why he was upset. Finally, after struggling with the issue for several months, Pablo left his prestigious job. Not only did he not have another job lined up, he could not find one for a year.

Pablo was deeply disappointed that the job did not work out, but he felt he could not take the humiliation for even one more day. The company continues to think it values diversity and Pablo is left with this sad experience with corporate America. What a waste for both. They lost a good and productive employee, and subjected themselves to unnecessary potential liability. As you become managers, supervisors and business owners, make sure to check for the subtle ways in which messages are given to employees that they are unwelcome and discriminated against.

LO5

The Age Discrimination in Employment Act of 1967

We live in a society that seems obsessed with youth. Some cultures revere their older members. Our culture, particularly in the work arena, seems to cast them away despite research showing older workers to be more reliable, harder working, more committed and absent less than other employees. To counter the effect of devaluing older workers, Congress passed protective legislation for employees 40 and over. If an employee is age 40 or over, the employee cannot be discriminated against in any aspect of employment on the basis of age.

Often employers will attempt to cut costs by terminating older, often higher-paid employees. During the country's economic crisis beginning in 2008, EEOC's age discrimination claims rose significantly. Or perhaps the employer wishes to bring a more youthful look to a retail establishment and terminates older employees or transfers them to lower paying jobs. Such targeting on the basis of age is a violation of the Age Discrimination in Employment Act, or ADEA.

The Employee Retirement Income Security Act (ERISA) also prevents employees from being excluded from a pension plan because of age. In addition, it has vesting requirements protecting the older employee from being terminated before vesting of his or her pension plan.

While age, as religion, can be a **bona fide occupational qualification (BFOQ)** reasonably necessary for the operation of the employer's particular business, it is not to be used merely to justify not hiring older employees. If it can be shown that there is a connection between age and performance of the job the employee is hired to do, the BFOQ may be allowed. For instance, airlines and bus companies in the business of safely transporting passengers from one place to another have been able to successfully argue, based on expert medical testimony, that after a certain age, deterioration starts to set in and affect features critical to the pilot's or driver's ability to safely transport passengers. It is also required to show that the older workers' attributes being challenged are such that they occur so frequently within the targeted population that it would be unwieldy to test each applicant for the problem, so the rule is permitted to be applied to all. Under these circumstances, making decisions based upon age and imposing a maximum age for employment have been upheld. However, the BFOQ cannot be based solely upon the employer's perception that the older worker is simply too old. It must be supported by credible information.

EXAMPLE

Of course, the ADEA is also not a "full employment law for older workers." The law does not mean that they are guaranteed a job regardless of age or level of performance. If the employee can no longer perform the job, then there is a nondiscriminatory, job-related basis for termination, that is, inability to perform the job the employee was hired to do. The trouble comes in assuming that age is the reason for the deteriorating performance and using it as the basis for termination when there is no credible information upon which to base the decision. The reality is, the employer should not be as concerned with age as with performance. No matter what age, the employee must be able to perform or termination or training is appropriate.

Initially the ADEA was the only workplace protective legislation which permitted a jury trial. Because of the Civil Rights Act of 1991, this is no longer true. However, willful violations of the ADEA may result in treble damages or three times the damages the claimant would ordinarily have received. Imposing such stiff damages is intended to act as a deterrent for willful violators. The employee win-rate for ADEA cases is high. Sympathetic jurors tend to put themselves in the place of the employee and while everyone may not be a female, or a minority, or of a different religion, everyone thinks of growing old and fears being cast away without resources. The thought of an employee being "dumped" by an employer just because he or she grows older, does not sit well with juries.

Employers should be careful not to allow preconceived notions about age and its relation to ability to enter into their employment decisions and cause potential liability. This is particularly true since treble damages are permitted under the law.

The Americans with Disabilities Act of 1990

L06

The passage of the Americans with Disabilities Act (ADA) in 1990 provided Title VII-type relief to those who are disabled. The Act was hailed as the "Declaration of Independence" or "Emancipation Proclamation" for the disabled and the most

TAKE AWAY 11-9

far-reaching civil rights law since the Civil Rights Act of 1964. The disability discrimination law is similar to the religious discrimination law in that it prohibits employers with 15 or more employees from discriminating against qualified applicants who are disabled unless to do so would present an undue hardship. As you can imagine, if the law was sweeping enough to receive the types of nicknames it did, it has a far-reaching impact on employers.

The law addresses three types of barriers to those who are disabled: (1) intentional discrimination due to social bias; (2) neutral standards with a disparate impact upon those who are disabled; and (3) barriers to job performance that can be addressed by accommodation.

Under the ADA a disability is a physical or mental impairment that substantially limits one or more of a person's major life activities. Employers, however, were offered little guidance about this since neither the ADA nor the Section 504 of the Rehabilitation Act, the forerunner to the ADA, defined with any certainty the terms "physical or mental impairment or "major life activities." Take Away 11-9, "ADA Definitions," provides the definitions given by the EEOC's ADA implementing regulations.

Under the law a person is disabled if he or she:

- is actually disabled
- is perceived as disabled, or
- has a record of being disabled

While the law covers both mental as well as physical disabilities, it does not include a definitive list of what is and is not a disability. Rather, courts must address the issue on a case by case basis. For instance, it has been held that breathing is impaired if an employee has emphysema; learning is impaired when a person is dyslexic; functioning and procreation is impaired if the employee is HIV+. Employees are entitled to equal employment opportunity if, aside from the disability and any appropriate accommodation, they are otherwise qualified for the job and do not present a risk of harm to themselves or others.

"Qualified for the job" can include reasonable accommodation of the disability or not, as necessary. The most difficult issue for employers is learning when and what it is they must do to accommodate a disabled employee. This will take a substantial effort on the part of those who think of the disabled only as those in wheelchairs or with white canes. This is not what the law contemplates, and in fact, it is illegal to act on such presumptions by classifying employees in ways which restrict their status, opportunities, or what they can do unless it can be shown to be job-related and consistent with business necessity. As with the Title VII categories, employers may not discriminate against qualified disabled applicants or employees in recruitment, hiring, promotion, training, discipline, layoffs, pay, terminations, assignments, leave policies, benefits or any other matter in employment.

Unlike Title VII, under the ADA, employers must take a proactive approach rather than waiting until a problem occurs. Not only must they not discriminate against qualified disabled applicants or employees in any aspect of employment, they must also make the workplace accessible to disabled workers. For instance, if necessary and appropriate, employers must restructure their workplace and job descriptions to allow the disabled access.

EXAMPLE

Not only does the law force us to change our perception of who a disabled person is, but also what they are capable of—both of which may go against our ingrained notions. We must learn to think of employees as being able to perform in a multitude of ways and with abilities which may be different from those we generally think of. If we do, we are less likely to be held liable for violating the ADA by failing to accommodate disabled employees.

For instance, a blind teacher applied for a position as a physical education instructor. The teacher was denied employment because of his blindness and no attempt was made to accommodate the disability. The teacher was able to show the possibility that his disability could be accommodated by having someone act as his eyes to tell him, for instance, if a ball went in the basket or if everyone was performing as directed. The school system had to at least attempt an accommodation.

EXAMPLE

As with the other protective legislation, the ADA does not guarantee a job to any disabled person regardless of qualifications. It merely requires that we consider what qualifications are actually necessary for the job and alternative ways of performing the job. We may have always thought of typists as having fingers, but if someone has no arms and can type just as well with their toes, having fingers may not actually be a job requirement after all.

EXAMPLE

In the *Arline* case (Case 11.3), widely perceived to have direct implications for AIDS cases, the U.S. Supreme Court was called upon to determine if Arline's contagious

CASE 11.3 School Board of Nassau County v. Arline

480 U.S. 273 (1987)

Facts: Employee Arline, a teacher with tuberculosis, was terminated from her job. The employer argued that the termination was not because of Arline's disease, but instead because of the threat that her relapses posed to the health of others since tuberculosis is contagious. The Court held for Arline.

Issue: Whether an employer violates The ADA by terminating a teacher from her job because she has a contagious disease.

Decision: Yes

Reasoning: Brennan, J.: We must consider whether Arline can be considered a handicapped individual. This impairment was serious enough to require hospitalization, a fact more than sufficient to establish that one or more of her major life activities were substantially limited by her impairment. Thus, Arline's hospitalization for tuberculosis in 1957 suffices to establish that she has a "record of

impairment" within the meaning of the regulations and is therefore a handicapped individual.

The Board maintains that Arline's record of impairment is irrelevant in this case, since the School Board dismissed her not because of her diminished capabilities, but because of the threat that her relapses of tuberculosis posed to the health of others.

We do not agree that, in defining a handicapped individual, the contagious effects of a disease can be meaningfully distinguished from the disease's physical effects on a claimant in a case such as this. Arline's contagiousness and her physical impairment each resulted from the same underlying condition, tuberculosis. It would be unfair to allow an employer to seize upon the distinction between the effects of a disease on others and the effects of a disease on a patient and use that distinction to justify discriminatory treatment.

The fact that *some* persons who have contagious diseases may pose a serious health threat to others under certain circumstances does not justify excluding from the coverage of the Act *all* persons with actual or perceived contagious diseases. It would mean those accused of being contagious would never have the opportunity to have their condition evaluated in light of medical evidence and a determination made as to whether they were "otherwise qualified." The fact that a person with a record of a physical impairment is also contagious does not suffice to remove that person from coverage under the law.

The remaining question is whether Arline is otherwise qualified for the job of elementary schoolteacher. The basic factors to be considered should include: findings of facts, based on reasonable medical judgment given the state of medical knowledge, about (a) the nature of the risk (how the disease is transmitted), (b) the duration of the risk (how long is the carrier infectious), (c) the severity of the risk (what is the potential to harm third parties), and (d) the probabilities the disease will be transmitted and will cause varying degrees of harm. The next step in the "otherwise qualified" inquiry is for the court to evaluate whether the employer could reasonably accommodate the employee under the established standards for that inquiry.

Because there were few factual findings by the district court, we are unable at this stage to resolve whether Arline is otherwise qualified for her job. We remand the case to the district court to determine whether Arline is otherwise qualified for her position. REMANDED.

CASE QUESTIONS

1. Do you agree with the Court's decision? Why or why not? Would your answer change if the contagious disease was AIDS or HIV? Explain.
2. If it is shown that Arline could perform some other function in the school system besides teaching, and contact with others was not as prevalent as in the classroom, would you allow her to stay on? Discuss.
3. Do you think there is adequate protection of both the employee and the public in this case? What should the courts do to diminish discrimination against the disabled built upon myth and misconceptions?

disease substantially limited her major life activities and whether she could be terminated simply because of its contagiousness.

The ADA takes equal employment opportunity for the disabled very seriously; therefore, employers must do so also. According to the preamble to the legislation, Congress's intent in enacting the law was to open opportunities for a fuller life to the nation's 43 million disabled citizens. Employers should be aware that in order to comply with the law, it will take thinking about disabilities and the disabled in a different way. The thought should not be "how can they perform if they are disabled?" but instead, "how can we accommodate this otherwise qualified disabled employee in a way which enables him or her to do the job?" As more differently abled employees enter the workforce, employers must be flexible in trying to accommodate their needs to the extent it does not present an undue hardship. That may not always be easy. Marc Elliot, a handsome, engaging, lively, gracious 25-year-old Washington University graduate with Tourette's Syndrome which causes uncontrollable tics including exaggerated facial expressions and random sounds and outbursts (http://www.whatmakesyoutic.com/WhatMakesYouTic/Homepage.html) tells of being ordered off a Greyhound bus because his disease caused him to blurt out the "n-word", highly offending the patrons on the bus. Though the bus driver had made an announcement over the public address system when Marc notified her of his disease upon boarding the bus, and the riders were gracious, when his disease caused him to yell out the "n-word," their view changed. They were willing to accommodate his malady only to the extent it did not cause them discomfort. Had this been the workplace, how would you have handled accommodating Marc's disease while not stepping on the toes of other employees who are also protected under the law? Questions like this are bound to increase as more employees exert their rights under the law.

Are There Defenses to Employment Discrimination Cases?

L07

Employers sued for discrimination have several defenses available to prevent liability from attaching. Not all defenses may be used for every case, but they provide protection if the employer meets the requirements for their usage. For instance, it is a defense to a discrimination action if an employer is using a bona fide seniority plan, even though it may have an adverse impact on a group protected by Title VII. Generally, having a bona fide plan means the plan was not enacted for the purpose of discrimination.

EXAMPLE

BFOQ

Title VII (and as we saw, the ADEA) permits employers to use a defense of the discriminatory characteristic being a bona fide occupational qualification which is reasonably necessary for the employer's particular business. Since the BFOQ defense is actually legalized discrimination, as you can imagine, it is very narrowly interpreted. The BFOQ defense is used in situations where, for instance, authenticity is necessary, such as being female as a BFOQ for modeling women's clothes, or playing the female part in a theater production—even though we know that there are excellent impersonators. It can also be used where safety may be at stake, for instance using males to guard male prisoners in a maximum security facility. As we saw, courts have upheld a maximum age as a BFOQ in such situations as airline pilots and bus drivers, both of whose business is to safely transport passengers from one point to another. Employers were able to demonstrate through expert testimony their necessity for putting a age cap on job applicants by showing that after a certain age, attributes important to the transportation task began to deteriorate.

EXAMPLE

A BFOQ cannot be used simply as part of a marketing scheme, such as an airline having a BFOQ of being female for the position of flight attendant in order to be consistent with its "love" theme.[9] Race and color cannot be the subject of a BFOQ. While employers can use BFOQ if the requirements are met, they should do so sparingly. Courts are not fond of permitting legalized discrimination under a law intended to prevent discrimination.

BUSINESS NECESSITY

Employers can also use the defense of **business necessity** to defend against discrimination claims. If the employee establishes a prima facie case of discrimination using the disparate impact theory, employers can counter by demonstrating that the offending policy is necessary for performance of the employee's job.

EXAMPLE

For instance, if the employer has an employment policy which required all employees to be able to lift at least 50 pounds, if the requirement was legitimate, it would be allowed even if it screened out women at a higher rate. If the employee would only rarely have to lift 50 pounds, the requirement would not be allowed. Lorena Weeks, who we mentioned in the gender discrimination chapter, was told she could not have the better paying job at Bell South because she was a female and the job required that she be able to lift at least thirty pounds. Not only was it presumed that she would not be able to do this because she was a female, but they failed to realize that in the job she held, she routinely was required to carry around a 35-pound typewriter!

However, even when business necessity is demonstrated by the employer, the employee would still be able to show that while this may be true, there is a way for the employer to get what the employer needs with less of a disparate impact upon women than his present policy involves.

---

[9]*Wilson v. Southwest Airlines Company,* 517 (F. Supp. 292 (N.D. Tex. Dallas Div. 1981).

Business necessity permits the employer whose workplace policies are necessary for performance, but which have an adverse impact, to still use them if the requirements are legitimate. In this way, the employer is more likely to have policies with a disparate impact only where they are necessary to performing the employer's business.

Students often wonder if BFOQ and business necessity are the same. While they may seem the same, they are not. While a BFOQ is an employer's assertion that a particular requirement is necessary for the job, which in lay terms seems to be a business necessity, legally the two arise quite differently.

A BFOQ is discriminatory on its face in that the job requirements state the BFOQ and applicants not meeting the qualifications need not apply. For instance, bus companies having a maximum age of 30 for applying for a job as a bus driver. Business necessity, on the other hand, arises when the employer's policy is neutral on its face, but once challenged by an applicant or employee, the employer may use business necessity as a defense. Business necessity is also subject to the claimant's assertion that though the employer's requirement may be a business necessity, there is a less discriminatory way to accomplish what the employer requires.

With BFOQs, the employer must be able to demonstrate that the qualification required is so unavailable in the group being excluded that virtually everyone in the group cannot meet the qualification and it would be too burdensome to require an employer to handle cases on an individual basis. There is no such requirement with business necessity. So, when you think of business necessity, think of it as a specialized legal concept rather than in its lay terms of simply something needed for the job.

Legitimate Nondiscriminatory Reason

In disparate treatment cases where the claim is for individual discrimination against an employee, the employer may defend against the claim by proffering a legitimate nondiscriminatory reason for treating the employee differently that had nothing to do with illegal discrimination.

Affirmative Action and "Reverse" Discrimination

LO8

Before we leave the area of employment discrimination, we will address one other issue of major importance. Executive Order 11246 prohibits those who contract to provide the federal government with goods or services worth $10,000 or more from discriminating in the workplace on the same bases as Title VII. If the contract is for $50,000 or more, in addition to not discriminating, the employer must conduct an audit of the workplace to determine if there is an underrepresentation of women or minorities in job categories traditionally closed to them. The government originally took this step during World War II to make sure that human resources necessary for winning the war were not excluded from the war effort because of race discrimination. The government understood that race discrimination that had been in place since the country began excluded African Americans from jobs based on race. The Executive Order has been in place ever since, and has been amended to add other categories such as gender. The Executive Order is enforced by the Office of Federal Contract Compliance Programs which can **debar** a federal contractor from further participation in government contracts if the contractor does not comply with the Executive Order.

If there is an underrepresentation, the employer/contractor must also develop a remedy. The employer must establish a goal of the number of employees which will make the workforce more representative of the population from which the employees are drawn and timetables within which to accomplish the goal. This is called an **affirmative action plan** in the context of a scheme of **affirmative action.** Affirmative action is merely making a plan to include in the workplace those who have traditionally been excluded from the workplace due to generations of discrimination which otherwise would favor only whites and males, who have been the ones in the workplace longest due to intentionally excluding women and minorities.

In addition to federal contracting, affirmative action plans may arise as remedies imposed by a court after discrimination is found, or they may be voluntarily adopted by an employer to redress underrepresentation. The latter must be done in strict conformity with certain requirements ensuring that the rights of other employees are not unnecessarily trammeled, the plan is made to attain, not maintain, a workforce that more accurately reflects the area the employees are drawn from, and the plan unsettles no legitimate expectations of majority employees. (See Take Away 11-10, "Affirmative Action Requirements.")

When an affirmative action plan is instituted, often other employees who belong to the group not discriminated against will feel they are being discriminated **EXAMPLE** against by implementation of the plan. For instance, an employer may have been found by a court to have a long history of discrimination against women in hiring and promotions. The court may order the employer to promote one woman for every man promoted until the percentage of women in the managerial ranks reflects their availability for such positions in the workforce drawn from. The men who would have been in line for promotion feel that they are being discriminated against because they must now wait longer to be promoted. They may bring a suit alleging **reverse discrimination.** If the plan is drawn up as required by law, then when employees who feel harmed by the plan sue, they will lose. The requirements for creating the plan recognize that there is an urgent need to break the cycle of discrimination, yet a need to harm as few people as possible in the process. If the requirements are met, this is accomplished by the plan.

Actually, there is only one type of discrimination under the law. Everyone is protected equally. Suits alleging "reverse" discrimination will only be successful if the employer or court did not establish the goals with a sufficient basis to do so, or did not do so in the least harmful way.

TAKE AWAY 11-10

AFFIRMATIVE ACTION REQUIREMENTS

In order for an affirmative action plan to withstand judicial scrutiny when challenged by employees who feel they have been adversely impacted by application of the plan, the court requires that the plan meet certain criteria that will limit its negative impact.[10]

- The plan is made to attain, not maintain, a balanced workforce reflective of the area from which employees are drawn.
- The plan does not unnecessarily trammel the rights of majority employees or create an absolute bar to their advancement.
- The plan sets aside no specific number of positions for minorities or women, but only authorizes consideration of race or gender as a factor when evaluating qualified candidates for jobs in which members of such groups are traditionally poorly represented.
- The plan does not upset any legitimate settled expectations of the majority employees.

Summary

Title VII and other antidiscrimination laws ensure that employers afford all qualified employees an equal opportunity for employment. Rather than be viewed as a nuisance which interferes with the employer's right to hire and fire however the employer wishes, the law should be viewed as a necessary part of doing business. It forces the employer to use all available resources rather than screen out, for arbitrary reasons, certain groups which may be productive members of the workplace. Discrimination on the basis of race, color, gender, religion, national origin, age and disabilities will not be tolerated in the workplace under the law.

---

[10]*Johnson v. Transportation Agency, Santa Clara County, California,* 480 U.S. 616 (1987).

Review Questions

1. Betty and Laura, two females, apply for a position at Walter Construction Co. as flag holders at construction sites. Walter has a policy of not hiring females. If Betty and Laura sue Walter Construction Co. for gender discrimination, it will likely be under the theory of: LO3

   a. disparate impact

   b. hostile environment

   c. quid pro quo

   d. disparate treatment

2. An African American firefighter is transferred to a different engine company. The fire captain at the engine company the firefighter is being transferred from tells him to take his bed with him. The captain says the other firefighters, who are white, will not want to sleep on his bed. Would the firefighter have a cause of action under Title VII? Explain. LO4

3. List the states which have enacted state legislation protecting employees from discrimination on the basis of affinity orientation. LO4

4. Richard retires from the Post Office after a 35-year career. After being at home and dealing with his wife for a few days, he's sorry he retired. Richard then applies for a position with the local recreation center as an after-school recreation coordinator. The superintendent does not hire Richard because he says Richard would not be able to keep up with the children in the recreation program because he is too old. Does Richard have a cause of action? Explain. LO5

5. Pablo Velasquez, owner of Velasquez Cruise Lines, wishes to make his workplace more reflective of the community in which it is located. Pablo tells Suardana, his personnel director, not to hire any more African Americans or Hispanics until 20 new whites have been hired. Has Pablo violated Title VII? Discuss. LO8

6. If Suardana, Pablo's personnel director, refuses to hire Christians because employees are required to work on Sunday and Suardana has had a problem with Christians refusing to work on Sunday because it is their Sabbath, has Suardana violated Title VII? Why or why not? LO4

7. Jayce's Transportsit, Inc., is in the business of moving office furniture. Jayce does not hire women because he says women shouldn't be doing this kind of work, and anyway, they aren't strong enough to do what he needs done. Debbie, a bodybuilder who can bench-press 350 pounds, applies for a position with Jayce's and is not even given an application. What can Debbie do? LO4

8. Laurabeth comes into work dressed up in a business suit because she is going on an interview. Roger, one of the security personnel, approaches her and says to her, "Is it okay if I tell you that you look very nice today?" Karen, one of Laurabeth's co-workers, overhearing the comment, tells Laurabeth that Laurabeth ought to report Roger to his supervisor for sexual harassment. Should she? LO4

9. An airline hires only female flight attendants, saying it is a marketing tool they use as part of their "Love Airlines" logo. If a male sues for gender discrimination and the airline uses BFOQ as a defense, the airline will win since it is protected as part of a marketing plan. True or false? LO4

10. Affirmative action is a legal way of taking jobs from qualified white males and giving them to unqualified women and minorities. True or false? LO8

Ethics Issue

Raymond is truly upset. He works for Priscilla's business. Priscilla intentionally keeps her staff at 14 employees so that she will not have to comply with federal equal employment opportunity laws. The problem is that her business has been growing by leaps and bounds. At first it was okay with Raymond, because the extra work was not too much to handle. But as the business has grown more and more, it has really become a problem. All the employees are frazzled from working too hard. They enjoy the better pay and benefits, but they cannot really enjoy them because they are working all the time. Several of the employees have spoken with Priscilla about the increased work load and the need for more employees to help, but Priscilla refuses to budge. She says that this is her business that she built from the ground up and she refuses to have the government tell her who she can and can't hire. She says the government is in her business enough without having EEO laws to deal with too. Discuss the ethical implications of Priscilla's decision, including all the relevant stakeholders, what Priscilla gains by taking her position, what she loses, and what you think she should do.

Group Exercise

Divide the class into groups based on the areas provided protection by law, e.g., a group for age, gender, disability, race, etc. For a week, have the groups collect news articles, magazine stories, TV or movie stories, and personal stories about the kind of discrimination their group is responsible for. Report back to the class on what you find.

Key Terms

80% or 4/5 Rule 275

affinity orientation 282

affirmative action 291

affirmative action plan 291

anti-female animus 279

bona fide occupational qualification 286

business necessity 290

comparable worth 282

debar 291

disparate treatment 274

disparate impact 274

hostile environment sexual harassment 279

quid pro quo sexual harassment 279

reverse discrimination 292

right to sue letter 274

screening device 275

sexual harassment 278

12

Labor and Management Relations

Learning Objectives

After reading this chapter, you should be able to:

LO1 Explain the need for labor laws and how the laws came to be

LO2 Give the names of the major labor laws and tell what they do

LO3 Distinguish between unfair labor practices and unfair management practices

LO4 Recite several collective bargaining agreement clauses

LO5 Explain the need to have curbs put on union power

LO6 Understand the diversity and ethics issues involved in labor-management relations

 ## Opening Scenario

Cynthia Laverle, owner and CEO of Laverle Carbide, is worried. For the 15 years Laverle Carbide has been in business they have always gotten along with their employees. Cynthia thought the employees were satisfied. Apparently not. Jefferson Myuki, the production manager for the company, has come to Laverle and told her that he has been hearing rumblings on the plant floor lately that the workers want to bring in a union. Laverle Carbide has never had a union, and Cynthia never saw the need for one. She tries to treat her employees well so that there would be no need for a union. In brainstorming about how to respond, Cynthia thinks a straightforward attack on the union idea is best. Cynthia believes that if management takes a strong stand now, it will nip this union idea in the bud, and the workers will see the value of being nonunion. She believes a hard-line campaign of threatening the leaders proposing the idea and firing anyone who is caught discussing the union will quickly quell the union talk. Jefferson thinks that if they throw a little bonus into the mix, say on the employees' next paycheck, that might help things out too. Does this approach seem like a good idea?

 LO1

Introduction and Background

Imagine doing the hard work of building the business of your dreams. You come up with the idea; you manage to find funding sources, a place to conduct business, employees to do what needs to be done; and you spend untold nights and weekends doing whatever it takes to make it work. Finally, the business that you put so much of yourself into is a success. You have made every decision necessary to make that happen. They were not always the best decisions; you made some mistakes along the way. But it all worked out and the business is now a stable, growing concern. You couldn't be more proud.

Then your employees come to you and tell you they want a union. You know that if there is union, no longer will you be able to call the shots. You know that while the law gives business owners entrepreneurial discretion under the labor laws, you will no longer be able to make unilateral decisions you think are in the best interest of the business you worked so hard to create and build. Now, instead, you will have to negotiate about wages, hours, and other terms and conditions of employment. You are really, really angry. This is *your* business that you built up with *your* blood, sweat and tears, and *no one* should have the right to interfere with your decisions. Why in the world should you have to consult with anyone?! *You* took the risk. It was *your* money, ideas, and hard work. And now someone wants to come in and tell you how to run the business? The next thing you know they will be trying to tell you what you should produce and what markets to move into. You're not even going to let this conversation get started. No way!

Now, let us look at it from one of the employees' point of view.

You've been with your employer since the beginning when this business was hardly more than a dream. You worked your hardest to help him build it up. Whatever he asked you to do, you did. As it grew and he took on more and more employees and the business managed to grow, it was as if things got further out of hand. It was as if once he could see the possibility of success, he got harder and harder to deal with. He pushed the employees harder, requiring overtime if they wanted to keep their jobs. He imposed absence policies that treated employees as if they had no life outside of work. He imposed unreasonably short break times, wouldn't allow employees to even listen to music in the break room, refused to pay employees more as business picked up, and work got tougher and they worked harder for him. He even wanted to ship parts of the production overseas because he said costs would be cheaper! The workers constantly grumble to you because you have been with the company the longest. You've tried talking to the employer about the workers' concerns, but he refuses. He says it is his business and he built it up from nothing and no one is going to tell him how to run it. If they don't like it, he says, they can leave and there will be others waiting in line to take their jobs.

After trying over many months to talk to him about their concerns, the workers finally decide that if he won't talk to them, they will have to form a union. They are not sure of all the details, but they know the law says they can form a union and their employer can't refuse to deal with the union.

What a difference one's point of view makes! Both sides have very legitimate concerns. The law, however, sides with the employees. The law allows employees to form and join unions and the employer cannot interfere with their legal ability to do so.

The above scenario may help you see the arguments on both sides of the equation for why an employer would not want to have a union and why the employees would want to do so. Given how diametrically opposed those two positions can be at times, it is a wonder labor relations goes as smoothly as it does. Feelings may run high. But the law is a powerful tool.

Union membership that we take for granted today was not always a part of our workplace landscape. At one point in U.S. history, it was actually illegal for employees to work together in concert to gain workplace benefits. You can imagine how repressive this was in light of the advantage many employers took over employees virtually at their mercy who could not band together to request redress from the employer. It caused great distress. In 1932 in recognition of the toll that increasing labor unrest was taking on interstate commerce, Congress enacted legislation that led the way to organized labor in the United States. In 1953, the percentage of unionized employees was at an all-time high of just under 27 percent. That percentage has steadily decreased since 1970. According to the latest U.S. Department of Labor's Bureau of Labor Statistics released in 2010, in 2009 about 12.3 percent of the

COLORED NATIONAL LABOR UNION

Established in 1869, four years after the Civil War ended, the Colored National Labor Union (CNLU) was started by Isaac Myers, a ship caulker who had been free all his life and 214 other African Americans. Most white unions had refused to allow blacks into their ranks, particularly for industrial or skilled labor jobs, and Myers believed that collective action was the only way that blacks would be able to move ahead in the aftermath of the post-Civil War production boom. Myers had organized his fellow-workers into a cooperative whose employees had been fired and eventually bought a shipyard of their own. The organization accepted males and females, skilled and unskilled workers as well as industrial as well as agricultural workers. In 1872, noted abolitionist, Frederick Douglass headed the organization. Eventually, the organization succumbed to economic pressures of the Depression of 1873.

Source: U.S. History Encyclopedia, http://www.answers.com/topic/colored-national-labor-union. www.associatedcontent.com/article/388414/the_colored_national_labor_union_one.html?cat=37 mdoe:org/myersisaac.html

workforce was unionized.[1] However, the economic woes of 2008–2009 had caused the number to increase from 12.1 percent the year before. The percentage went up to 12.4 in 2008, but dropped in 2009 primarily due to the number of employees losing their jobs in the economic downturn.

The steadily declining union membership rates can be attributed in part to factors such as reduction in the labor force of traditionally heavily unionized industries like steel and other manufacturing, international competition, aggressive nonunion campaigns by employers, union concessions during downturns in the economy, and loss of jobs to other countries with cheaper labor. Union membership may have declined drastically but labor-management relations are still an important consideration in the workplace landscape.

Like everything and everyone else in a country in which race and gender discrimination has played such an important role in history, labor unions have had their problems in the areas of diversity and ethics too. When it came to protecting work for only those who were considered "worthy" of their efforts, unions led the way. Discrimination by the unions against certain groups was the order of the day. This merely reflected the greater society, but also at play was the notion that if women, blacks, and Hispanics, among others, were excluded from unions and workplaces, that left more jobs for whites and males. Thus, there were unions that did not permit women or minorities to become members at all. In others, women and minorities were only grudgingly given membership. They had to fight to get into unions and had to fight to be represented equally once there. As in the baseball leagues, and other institutions in society, at one time blacks created their own labor unions since they could not join white unions. (See Diversity in the Law 12-1, "Colored National Labor Union.")

Ethical issues have always been at the heart of labor-management relations. Most employers would prefer not to have to deal with a union. Employers would prefer to be able to make unilateral decisions without any employee input. They have over the years either vigorously opposed unions altogether, or once unions were established, cooperated with them to the minimum that avoided violating the law. Certain parts of the country, particularly the South, have had a long history of escaping being successfully unionized.

Once totally without the power that comes from being able to band together in concert to effect change, perhaps it was predictable that once workers were able to do so, they took full advantage of the power derived from being unionized. So much so that Congress finally had to pass legislation prohibiting unions from engaging in certain nefarious activities that had taken hold, including strong-arming members, using union funds as the union leaders' own personal piggy banks, rigging union elections, selective representation of union members, and so on.

There are four main federal laws that form the statutory basis for labor law and unionization. The legislation initiating a move toward collective bargaining in the

---

[1]http://www.bls.gov/news.release/union2.nr0.htm.

United States began with restricting court response to union activity (courts usually enjoined such activity) and establishing the right of employees to form labor organizations and be protected against unfair labor practices. Legislation also provided union members with a bill of rights to protect them from union abuses. We will discuss each of these laws and their impact on the workplace. First, however, we will provide an overview of the labor relations landscape.

What Is a Union For and How Does It Work?

The purpose of a union is to represent the interests of employees to management. The law recognizes that the company may be owned by the owner and managed by management, but Congress has determined that when an employer is to make decisions about wages, hours, or other terms and conditions of employment, the decisions cannot be unilaterally decided and imposed by the employer. If there is a union representing employees, then proposed changes must be negotiated with the union.

The relationship between the union and management is governed by a **collective bargaining agreement** or union contract entered into between management and labor. The collective bargaining agreement contains all relevant issues that may arise in the workplace and will provide a means of resolving conflicts. If the employee has a problem in the workplace with areas covered by the agreement, the employee goes to his or her union representative or **shop steward,** who, in turn, speaks with management to seek a resolution.

By having a union representative to represent the employees' interests with management, management has an efficient way to handle labor conflicts. Rather than dealing with hundreds or thousands of different employees, management simply deals with the union representative and tries to resolve the conflict. If it cannot be resolved between the two, the employees can choose to arbitrate the matter. Most collective bargaining agreements have an arbitration clause requiring disputes to be resolved through arbitration. The obvious benefit for management is not having to run to court for every dispute an employee may have. For employees, it is less costly and more timely for resolving disputes.

Every so often, depending on the terms of the contract, management and labor will have to meet and hammer out a new collective bargaining agreement. Each will bring proposals to the table and negotiate them, hopefully, to resolution. If no resolution is reached, the parties may have the matter arbitrated or, in the worst case scenario, the employees may strike. What provisions are in the collective bargaining agreement are up to the parties. We will discuss some of the more common ones shortly.

The labor-management relationship is governed by a collective bargaining agreement, but things do not necessarily always go as planned. Either management or labor can engage in activities that breach the agreement or labor laws. When this occurs the parties can file an **unfair labor practice** or an **unfair management practice** with the NLRB to have the matter resolved. Now that you have an overview, let us take a look at the laws governing labor-management relations.

THE NORRIS-LAGUARDIA ACT OF 1935

L02

The Norris-LaGuardia Act was the first major U.S. labor law statute. When it was illegal for employees to engage in concerted activities like strikes against the employer, courts routinely issued injunctions against employees prohibiting them from continuing this concerted activity. The Norris-LaGuardia Act restricted the right of courts to issue such injunctions.

The Act also outlawed **yellow dog contracts** that many employers required pledging that the employee did not belong to a union and would not join one while working for

INSTITUTIONALIZING DISCRIMINATION IN LAW

With the U.S. now having an African American president and in your lifetime having seen women and minorities participating in all aspects of society, it can be difficult to imagine a time when race, ethnic, and gender discrimination were simply the way things were. One of the ways this was manifested was in legislation enacted that created the middle class as we now know it except that those benefits were to be given to whites only. Central to this were three pieces of legislation: the National Labor Relations Act allowing employees the right to collectively bargain, the Fair Labor Standards Act requiring minimum wages and overtime pay, and the GI Bill. The latter was passed by Congress as a way to show its appreciation to those who served their country in the military in World War II by providing several very important benefits to veterans, including loans for housing and businesses, as well as educational stipends. As a result of these three pieces of legislation, the fruits of the expanding economy were spread to more people and the country was able to experience a boom in building, new businesses and industries, and home buying and economic stability unlike anything previously seen. New homes meant expansion of cities, which resulted in the suburbs many of you may have grown up in. Suburbs meant homes, schools, office buildings, malls, and yet new expansions of business and transportation. Where once home ownership or having a college degree was reserved for the elite few, it was now accessible to the masses who took advantage of it and grew into the broad middle class we now know. Just before World War II, 160,000 people graduated from college each year, but by the end of the 1940s, this had tripled.

But not everyone benefited from the laws. At the time this legislation was passed African Americans were still suffering under the Jim Crow laws of segregation. Jim Crow was a system of segregation that existed virtually everywhere in the U.S., either by law or custom, from the end of Reconstruction after the Civil War, until well after passage of the Civil Rights Act of 1964. Blacks and whites were separated in every way you can imagine, from birth till death, from the midwives who abounded in the black community because many doctors and hospitals did not service blacks, to the strictly segregated undertakers who handled them after death. Blacks were barred from or only allowed access on an extremely restricted basis to schools, parks, stores, theaters, libraries, and any other venue you can think of. Some towns had a specific day of the week blacks could shop and many towns were "sundowner towns" which did not permit blacks to be in the town after sundown.

The southern states wanted to keep it that way. While southerners, like any other politicians, held a variety of views and positions, they were all united on one: segregation. This made them a powerful force as a voting bloc in Congress. Any legislator who wanted any piece of legislation passed, no matter how important, no matter how civic minded, no matter how much good it did for the populace, had to get past the southern voting bloc.

When it came to these new pieces of legislation (National Labor Relations Act, the GI Bill and the Fair Labor Standards Act), which would have the power to drastically change life in the U.S. for the better, the southern bloc was a force to be reckoned with. Blacks making the same wages as whites? No. Blacks getting equal access to money to build homes, start businesses, and obtain an education? Not gonna happen. Blacks being able to collectively bargain as farmers and domestics? No way. The bloc did not mind the legislation itself—as long as it was reserved for whites. They simply

the employer. When the Norris-LaGuardia Act removed these two important obstacles to employees engaging in concerted activity, the way was paved for the National Labor Relations Act.

L02

THE NATIONAL LABOR RELATIONS ACT (WAGNER ACT) OF 1935

This law established the right of employees to form unions, to bargain collectively, and to strike. It also prohibited unfair labor practices and created the National Labor Relations Board (NLRB). NLRB is the independent federal agency that enforces the labor laws. Among other things, the NLRB conducts elections to determine which union is to represent employees once they have decided to bring a union in, decertifies unions that employees no longer wish to represent them, issues labor regulations, hears unfair labor practice complaints at the agency level, and otherwise administers the NLRA.

Employees may unionize by signing a sufficient number of authorization cards, by voting in a union during a representation election, or in some cases by NLRB ordering an employer to bargain with a union. Unions are composed of nonsupervisory or nonmanagerial employees, including part-time workers. Specifically excluded from the law are agricultural and domestic workers, independent contractors,

were not about to have blacks have even the possibility of being put on par with whites. As Representative Martin Dies, Jr., of Texas said, "What is prescribed for one race must be prescribed for the others, and you cannot prescribe the same wages for the black man as for the white man."

The vast majority of blacks lived in the South at the time, and because they had not been able to break out into other avenues of employment because of outright discrimination, which was not illegal, blacks held mostly jobs in agriculture and as domestics who cared for the children and homes of whites. In the South, 75 percent of blacks and nationwide 60 percent held these jobs. That such people would be able to earn as much as anyone else would not only take money out of the pockets of the southern legislators who employed them who would now have to pay their domestics a minimum wage, but far worse this would also potentially begin to put blacks on a social and legal par with whites. That could not be.

So, the southern legislators built into the Fair Labor Standards Act the condition that agricultural and domestic workers were excluded from minimum wage and overtime provisions. In the National Labor Relations Act the southern legislators insisted upon the exclusion of agricultural workers and domestics from the right to collectively bargain. The impact was to exclude the vast majority of blacks from a means of increasing their low wages or bettering their working conditions as was now to be provided for whites.

Florida legislator James Wilcox said at the time:

> There has always been a difference in the wage scale of white and colored labor. So long as Florida people are permitted to handle the matter, the delicate and perplexing problem can be adjusted; but the Federal Government knows no color line and of necessity it cannot make any distinctions between the races. We may rest assured, therefore, that when we turn over to a federal bureau or board the power to fix wages, it will prescribe the same wage for the Negro that it prescribes for the white man. Now, such a plan might work in some sections of the United States but those of us who know the true situation know that it just will not work in the South. You cannot put the Negro and the white man on the same basis and get away with it.

Edward Cox of Georgia said that "organized Negro groups of the country are supporting [the Fair Labor Standards Act] because it will . . . render easier the elimination and disappearance of racial and social distinctions, and . . . throw into the political field the determination of the standards and the customs which shall determine the relationship of our various people of the South."

With the GI Bill, the southern bloc insisted that administration of the proposed legislation be taken from the federal government and put in the hands of locals for the same reasons Rep. Wilcox said. By requiring local control, the legislators knew that when black veterans went to a bank in their home town to obtain a mortgage or a business loan under the GI Bill, they would be told, as was usually the case, that the bank did not lend to blacks. When they went to apply for admission to a college or university, they would be told the institution did not admit blacks. In this way, the GI Bill effectively shut out the vast majority of black veterans from the benefits extended to whites, and thus out of the breathtaking increase and uplift of the middle class.

Sources: Ira Katznelson, *When Affirmative Action Was White: The Untold History of Racial Inequality in Twentieth Century America* (Norton, 2005); and James W. Loewen, *Sundown Towns: A Hidden Dimension of American Racism* (Touchstone/ Simon & Schuster, 2005).

and those employed by a spouse or parent. Do you wonder why domestic and agricultural workers were excluded from this law (as well as the Fair Labor Standards Act requiring minimum wages for American workers)? Therein lies an incredible tale of institutionalized racism. (See Diversity in the Law 12-2, "Institutionalizing Discrimination in Law.") Since 75 percent of blacks in the south, and 60 percent nationwide held such jobs at the time the law was being considered, in excluding domestics and agricultural workers from the NLRA, as the southern legislators insisted, the law effectively excluded the vast majority of blacks from its benefits. Given this Jim Crow racial landscape at the time, it should come as no surprise that African Americans had a hard time becoming a part of unions and enjoying the benefits of their membership.

Nowadays, however, unions are not only open on a nondiscriminatory basis because of Title VII of the Civil Rights Act of 1964, but the law also requires unions to fully and fairly represent all employees. But what if the union refuses to represent a group of employees even though the law requires them to? That is precisely what happened to African American and Hispanic sheet metal workers in New York, and the case went all the way to the U.S. Supreme Court, as explained in Case 12.1.

CASE 12.1 — Local 28, Sheet Metal Workers v. EEOC —

478 U.S. 421 (1986)

Facts: The union and its apprenticeship committee were found to have discriminated against Hispanics and blacks in not allowing them to join the union through the union's mandatory apprenticeship program. The court ordered them to be admitted and the union refused and delayed for twenty years. The court finally imposed as part of a contempt order that the union, among other things, admit a certain percentage of nonwhites by a certain date, and set up counseling and tutorial programs for them, as had traditionally been done for whites. The union challenged the court's requirements as unlawful.

Issue: Whether a union found to discriminate on the basis of race or ethnicity in its membership can be ordered by a court to engage in race-conscious relief to unidentified victims of discrimination under Title VII of the Civil Rights Act of 1964.

Decision: Yes

Reasoning: Brennan, J.: In most cases, the court need only order the employer or union to cease engaging in discriminatory practices, and award make-whole relief to the individuals victimized by those practices. In some instances however, it may be necessary to require the employer or union to take affirmative steps to end discrimination effec-

tively to enforce Title VII. Where an employer or union has engaged in particularly longstanding or egregious discrimination, an injunction simply reiterating Title VII's prohibition against discrimination will often prove useless and will only result in endless enforcement litigation. In such cases requiring a recalcitrant employer or unions to hire and admit qualified minorities roughly in proportion to the number of qualified minorities in the workforce may be the only effective way to ensure the full enjoyment of the rights protected by Title VII. Here, the membership goal and fund were necessary to remedy the union and apprenticeship program's pervasive and egregious discrimination and its lingering effects. AFFIRMED.

Note: Would you believe that twenty-four years later the union is still fighting this case? Yep.

CASE QUESTIONS

1. Do you agree with the court's decision? Explain. Do you think there is some other way to address what the union did that might work better?
2. Why do you think the union refused to have black and Hispanic members? How should employers educate employees to avoid these attitudes that result in liability?
3. Are you surprised that this is a 1986 case? Explain.

How Does a Workplace Become Unionized?

In order to begin the process of bringing a union into a workplace, employees with a **community of interests** come together as a **bargaining unit** that the union will represent. The community of interests, that is, similar workplace concerns and conditions, is based on factors such as similarity of the jobs the employees perform and similar training or skills required. A bargaining unit is the employees with a community of interests that the union will represent. Employees of the bargaining unit conduct a **card check,** indicating that they wish to have a union represent them.

Congress is currently considering the highly contentious Employee Free Choice Act.[2] If passed, it would have a direct impact on the way union representation decisions are made by amending the NLRA to make it easier to form, join, or assist labor organizations. For a long while union members have been complaining that union busting and intimidation by management is out of control (see Reality Check 12-1, "Union Busting").

[2]H.R. 1409, S560.

One of the areas of contention is the **union representation election** process itself. As it presently stands, once management has been presented with cards signed by least 30 percent of the members in the bargaining unit indicating that they want a union to represent them (known as card check), employers can object and require a separate secret ballot election to determine if a majority of the bargaining unit wants union representation. Unions believe that this intimidates employees and makes it more difficult for unions to organize employees.

Under the proposed law, The Employee Free Choice Act, once management has been presented with cards signed by a majority of the bargaining unit indicating they wish to have a union, management cannot hold a secret ballot election and matters may proceed to choosing a union.

The legislation was introduced into both houses of Congress on March 10, 2009. It only missed passage by nine votes when it was voted on the year before, so there has been speculation that the proposed legislation may have more of a chance of passing under the Obama administration.

Generally, there must be at least two employees in a bargaining unit, but an employer may agree to a one-person unit if necessary—for instance, an on-site carpenter who belongs to a carpenter's union being employed at a worksite as the only carpenter.

Unions may be **industrial unions** or **craft unions.** Industrial unions are composed of the employees of a workplace who perform like jobs. They may be part of a larger union network of the same type of employees at other workplaces. The **business agent** of the craft union (e.g., carpenters) represents the union craft workers' interest at a given job site. Employers often contact a craft union when they need the type of employees represented by that union.

Once it is decided that the bargaining unit will be represented by a union, a union representation election must be conducted by the NLRB. NLRB conducts the election under federal regulations and certifies the results. Once a union has been elected, union and management must negotiate a collective bargaining agreement. In order to reach such an agreement, many factors are at play, some of which will be discussed below.

GOOD FAITH BARGAINING

To prevent management from unilaterally implementing workplace policies that closely affect employees, the NLRA requires employers to bargain in good in good faith with union representatives over **mandatory subjects of bargaining.** This includes wages, hours, and other terms and conditions of employment. Examples would be an employer wanting to impose mandatory overtime, termination policies for absenteeism, subcontracting out work, pay raises, break times, and so on. If they wish to, employers may also bargain over **permissive subjects of bargaining,** but only a refusal to bargain

CÉSAR CHAVEZ: NEGOTIATING OUTSIDE THE LAW

If you do not know who Cesar Chavez is, you should. Chavez is probably the most important Latino civil rights figure in U.S. history. Along with Dolores Huerta, Chavez organized farm workers to fight for better pay and conditions, even though agricultural workers are not covered by the NLRA. The National Farm Workers Association (NFWA), later called the United Farm Workers (UFW), had over 50,000 members at the height of its power. Using many of the tactics of one of his heroes, Dr. Martin Luther King, Jr., during the 1960s and 70s, Chavez organized marches, strikes, boycotts, and other nonviolent means of getting his message out about the conditions that workers suffered to get food onto the American dinner table.

Chavez's March 31 birthday is celebrated as a state holiday to promote service in California and other states, and a bill has been introduced in Congress to make it a national holiday. On his birthday in 2010, President Obama signed a presidential proclamation praising Chavez for his contributions to American society. Posthumously presented with the Presidential Medal of Freedom by President Bill Clinton, Chavez's work is an example of the power of collective bargaining, even when there is no legal framework for doing so.

Source: United Farm Workers, http://www.ufw.org/_page.php?inc=history/07.html&menu=research; http://www.chavezfoundation.org/_cms.php?mode=view&b_code=003007000000000&b_no=1698&page=&field=&key=&n=.

about mandatory subjects of bargaining will form the basis of an unfair labor practice. Permissive subjects of bargaining are any matters that do not fall into the category of mandatory subjects of bargaining.

Bargaining in good faith means that the parties act in a responsible, businesslike manner regarding the bargaining process. They must provide necessary information to support their bargaining proposals, must attend meetings, and must conduct themselves as if they are engaged in the serious business of bargaining. Bargaining in good faith does not mean that one party must agree to the other party's proposal, but only that the parties must seriously negotiate and do so in good faith. It would not be bargaining in good faith if a party continually missed negotiation meetings or refused a proposal without seriously considering it or offering any alternatives. If the parties do not reach an agreement, the union may exercise pressure tactics like strikes to try to get management to change its mind. In Reality Check 12-2 you get to see how effective these tactics can be even if the organization engaged in them is not protected by law in doing so.

DUTY OF FAIR REPRESENTATION

The NLRA imposes on unions the duty of fair representation. The duty of fair representation is not defined in the NLRA and is often used as a catchall category for grievances against the union by union members who are unsatisfied with how an issue turned out. Given the history of unions discriminating against minorities and women, you can easily see the need for such a provision.

As the employees' bargaining representative, the union must fairly represent all members of the bargaining unit, whether the employee belongs to the union or not. Those employees who do not believe their interests have been fairly represented by the union can pursue the matter through an unfair labor practice against the union alleging failure of the union in its duty of fair representation.

Despite the thrust of the law, Diversity in the Law 12-3 suggests that minorities and women still may feel that the duty of fair representation is not carried out by unions as consistently as it should be.

If there is a statutorily imposed duty of fair representation required of unions, why do you think the CLUW found it necessary to have a union for women to deal with their interests? If the unions did not adequately address issues of importance to women, aside from the legalities, think about the ethics of not doing so. Who are the stakeholders involved? What are their interests? Why would the unions risk and unfair labor practice? How would discrimination benefit them?

COLLECTIVE BARGAINING AGREEMENTS

If negotiations go well, the end product of the negotiations between management and labor will be a **collective bargaining agreement** for a specified period. There is no set form that such an agreement must take, and it may be any length and contain any provisions agreed upon by the parties. Job and union security constitute the main issue for employees; freedom from labor strife such as strikes, slowdowns, and work stoppages is paramount for employers. The agreement also contains provisions regarding strikes, arbitration of labor disputes, seniority, benefits, employment classifications, and so on. (See Take Away 12-1, "Selected Collective Bargaining Agreement Clauses").

UNFAIR LABOR PRACTICES

Activities that would tend to attempt to control or influence the union or interfere with its affairs or that discriminate against employees who join or assist unions may also be **unfair labor practices.** Actual interference by an employer need not be proved in order for it to be considered an unfair labor practice. Rather, the question is whether the activity tends to interfere with, restrain, or coerce employees who are exercising rights protected under the law. Management may not promise or give benefits, or, in the alternative, reduce benefits,

in an effort to discourage unionizing efforts. To do so is an unfair labor practice.

So, in our chapter opening scenario, the proposed responses to the possibility of Cynthia's company unionizing would constitute an unfair labor practice. The threats to, and termination of, employees, and giving them a bonus, all in the effort to thwart efforts at unionizing, would constitute an unfair labor practice since they interfere with the employees being able to form, join or assist a labor union.

The NLRB and the courts take seriously any interference with the right of employees to organize and bargain collectively without the interference or pressure of management. (See Take Away 12-2, "Management Unfair Labor Practices.") Given this, it probably will surprise you to know that it is not an unfair labor practice for an employer to totally go out of business even if the reason is anti-union animus. Although an employer can go totally out of business, the employer cannot close only part of its business (for instance, it closes one plant and has two others it leaves open) if the reason is to discourage unions and the employer has reason to know that would be the effect.[3] If employers with at least 100 employees (not including those working for less than six months) decide to go out of business or have a massive layoff, they are required by law to give the employees at least 60 days notice under the Worker Adjustment Retraining and Notification (WARN) Act of 1988.

Case 12.2 (*Electromation*) demonstrates just how seriously unfair labor practice is taken by the courts. In this case the court found an unfair labor practice in a nonunion employer's setting up and administering committees to look into various workplace issues.

---

[3]*Textile Workers v. Darlington,* 380 U.S. 263 (1965), *NLRB v. Dorsey Trailers, Inc.,* http://laws.findlaw.com/4th/991390p.html.

TAKE AWAY 12-1

SELECTED COLLECTIVE BARGAINING AGREEMENT CLAUSES

Wages—including cost-of-living increases, production increases, learners and apprentice differentials, and overtime

Benefits—including vacation leave, sick pay, holidays off, and insurance

Hours—including overtime and determinations as to assignment

Seniority—setting forth how employee seniority is determined and used

Management security—management may make their own decisions as to how to run the business as long as the decisions are not contrary to the collective bargaining agreement or the law

Union security—the union's legal right to exist and to represent the employees involved

Job security—how management will maintain employment, including procedures for layoffs, downsizing, worksharing, and so on

Dues checkoff—right of a union to have management deduct union dues directly from employees' wages and turn them over to the union rather than have the union try to collect them from members after they receive their paychecks

Union shop—all employees are required to join the union within a certain amount of time after coming into the bargaining unit

Modified union shop—requires that new employees join the union after an agreement becomes effective, as must any employees who were already union members, but those already working who were not union members and do not wish to join, need not do so

Maintenance of membership—employees who voluntarily join a union may leave only during a short window period prior to agreement expiration

Agency shop—requires that employees of the bargaining unit pay union dues whether they are union members or not

Grievances—sets forth the basis for grievances regarding conflicts over the meaning of the collective bargaining agreement and procedures for addressing them

Exclusive representation—the union representative will be the only party who can negotiate with management over matters affecting bargaining unit employees

Arbitration—matters that cannot be otherwise resolved will be submitted to arbitration to be resolved by a neutral third part whose decision will usually be binding

Midterm negotiations—permits agreed-upon topics to be reopened to negotiation prior to the contract's expiration

No strike, no lockout—employees either will not strike or will do so only under limited circumstances and management will not engage in locking employees out of the workplace; instead the grievance procedure will be used to handle labor disputes

TAKE AWAY 12-2

MANAGEMENT UNFAIR LABOR PRACTICES

It is a violation of the law for management to engage in the following activities:

- Trying to control the union or interfering with union affairs such as trying to help a certain candidate get elected to union office
- Discriminating against employees who join a union or are in favor of bringing a union in or who exercise their rights under the law (e.g., terminating, demoting, or giving unfavorable working schedule to such employees)
- Interfering with, coercing or restraining employees exercising their rights under labor law legislation (e.g., telling employees that they cannot have a union and they will be terminated if a union is organized)
- Refusal to bargain or to bargain in good faith

CASE 12.2 Electromation, Inc. v. NLRB

35 F3d 1148 (7th Cir. 1994)

Facts: In response to employee workplace complaints in a non-union setting, Electromation management set up five action committees that were to meet and try to come up with solutions in various areas of concern. Electromation administered the committees, set up meetings, and determined the issues and committee composition without employee input. An unfair labor practice charge was filed claiming that the committees violated the NLRA's prohibition on domination or interference with employees' right to form a labor organization. The NLRB agreed.

Issue: Whether it is the unfair labor practice of dominating a labor organization for an employer to set up committees of employees to discuss areas of workplace concern.

Decision: Yes

Reasoning: Will, J.: We find substantial evidence supports the Board's factual finding that the action committees were labor organizations within the meaning of the NLRA and that the employer dominated the labor organization. Section 2(5) of the Act defines labor organization as "any organization of any kind, or any agency or employee representation committee or plan, in which employees participate and which exist for the purpose, in whole or in part, of dealing with employers concerning grievances, labor disputes, wages, rates of pay, hours of employment, or conditions of work.

This is not to suggest that management was antiunion or had devious intentions in proposing the creation of the committees. But even assuming [the committees] acted from good intentions, their procedure in establishing the committees without employee input, their control of the subject matter to be considered or excluded (chosen without employee input), their membership and participation on the committees, and their financial support of the committees by providing paid time for meetings, meeting places, pencils, paper, phones and so forth, all combine to make the committees labor organizations dominated by the employer in violation of the Act. Accordingly, we AFFIRM the Board's findings.

CASE QUESTIONS

1. Do you agree with the court's decision? Explain.
2. What impact do you think the *Electromation* decision had on employers wanting or permitting work concern groups to operate in the workplace?
3. What do you think the employer here could have done differently to avoid being found to have committed this unfair labor practice? What do you think the result would have been in workplaces had the Court not decided the way it did?

Legitimate strikes may be called by the union either for economic reasons or because of unfair labor practices. If employees strike for legally recognized reasons, their actions are protected under the NLRA and they retain their status as employees. Strikes that are not authorized by the union are called **wildcat strikes** and are illegal and subject to unfair labor practice charges if they force the employer to deal with the employees rather than the union or impose the will of the minority rather than the majority. Unauthorized strikes have been found not to be unlawful if they are merely to make a statement of some sort. Many collective bargaining agreements contain **no-strike, no-lockout clauses** which either prohibit or limit the availability of such action and instead agree to use the grievance procedure to handle issues.

The Taft-Hartley Act of 1947

At one time in this country employees had no right to engage in concerted activity, but after considerable struggles they won the right to be able to have unions. As it is perhaps in the nature of things, some unions eventually abused their newfound power and went overboard with it and committed abuses themselves. The Taft-Hartley Act

UNION UNFAIR LABOR PRACTICES

- Refusal to bargain or bargaining in bad faith (e.g., not attending bargaining sessions).
- Coercing or restraining employees in exercising their rights to join (or not join) a union. If the union and employer have a provision in their collective bargaining agreement that states that a nonunion member coming into the bargaining unit must join the unit within a certain amount of time, then union members performing that activity does not present a problem.
- Charging discriminatory or very high dues or entrance fees for admittance into the union.
- Threatening, encouraging, or influencing employees to strike in a effort to pressure management to join a management organization or to get management to recognize an uncertified union, or to stop doing business with an employer because management is not doing this.
- Influencing management to discriminate against, or otherwise treat differently, employees who do not belong to the union, or are denied union membership for some reason other than nonpayment of union dues or fees.

of 1947 was a response to this and was an attempt to curb union abuses and excesses. Under the Act, unions could now be subject to unfair labor practices for engaging in activity that overstepped their role as employee representatives.

The Taft-Hartley Act was enacted as an amendment to the NLRA to curb excesses by unions. Unfair labor practices by unions include such activities as the union refusing to bargain or refusing to do so in good faith, coercing employees to join unions (or not join, as the case may be), and charging members discriminatory dues and entrance fees. (See Take Away 12-3, "Union Unfair Labor Practices.")

An important concept in relation to the Taft-Hartley Act is **right to work laws.** Before the Act was passed, employers and employees often had a **closed shop** provision in their collective bargaining agreement. Under this provision, labor and management agreed that union membership was a condition of employment for anyone coming into a unionized workplace. He or she could even be terminated for failure to pay dues or some other violation of the union's rules, even though they may not have done anything wrong regarding their work for the employer. The Taft-Hartley Act outlawed closed shops.

The law, however, did not outlaw **union shops** provisions. In union shops an employee must become a member of a union within a certain time of being hired and can only be terminated (regarding union membership) for failing to pay dues. This provision in a collective bargaining agreement is called a **union security clause.** An **agency shop** is one in which the employee need not join the union, but must still pay the equivalent of union dues, often called **fees.** An **open shop** is one in which the employee can be a member of the union or not and need not pay dues or their equivalent.

RIGHT TO WORK STATES

The following states, by law or state constitution, are right to work states. Guam is also a right to work jurisdiction.

Alabama	Nevada
Arizona	North Carolina
Arkansas	North Dakota
Florida	Oklahoma
Georgia	South Carolina
Idaho	South Dakota
Iowa	Tennessee
Kansas	Texas
Louisiana	Utah
Mississippi	Virginia
Nebraska	Wyoming

The Act gave states the right to outlaw union and agency shops if they wished to do so. The 22 states that did so are called "right to work states." (See Reality Check 12-3, "Right to Work States.") In right to work states, collective bargaining agreements cannot contain union security clauses. Employees are free to join unions or not and do not have to pay union dues or their equivalent.

As you can imagine, there are powerful arguments on both sides. Unions do not want to have **free riders** who get the benefits of the union's work without having to be a part of the union or pay the equivalent of union dues. On the other side, employees believe that they should have the right to decide whether or not they wish to join a union and should not be forced to if they do not wish to do so. Can you think of an alternative that would satisfy both sides?

L02 # The Landrum-Griffin Act of 1959

The Landrum-Griffin Act, also called the Labor Management Reporting and Disclosure Act, was enacted to establish basic rules of union operation that would ensure a democratic process, provide union members with a minimum bill of rights attached to union membership, and regulate the activities of union officials and the use of union funds. The bill of rights was enacted in response to union abuses found during a two-year Congressional investigation. The act set forth procedures unions must adhere to in union elections, including voting for officers by secret ballot, elections at least every three years (other frequencies for various levels of the union such as international officers), candidates' being allowed to see lists of eligible voters, and provisions for members having an election. (See Take Away 12-4, "Union Member Bill of Rights.")

TAKE AWAY 12-4

UNION MEMBER BILL OF RIGHTS

Among other things, the Landrum-Griffin Act provides that:

- Union members have the right to attend union meetings, vote on union business, and nominate candidates for union elections.
- Members may bring an agency or court action for violations against the union after exhausting union procedures.
- Certain procedures must be followed before any dues or initiation fees increase.
- Except for the failure to pay union dues, members must have a full and fair hearing when being disciplined by the union.

Labor Relations in the Public Sector

Much of what has been discussed relates to the private sector. Of more recent vintage is the matter of collective bargaining in the public sector. The NLRA applies only to the private sector. Federal, state, and local government employees (e.g., public employees such as government workers, police officers, and so on) are governed by other laws. Federal employees are covered by the Civil Service Reform Act of 1978 which established the Federal Labor Relations Authority to administer federal sector labor laws. State and local employees are covered by their state's public employee relations statute, usually administered by a state public employee relations commission.

The most significant difference between public and private collective bargaining is that government employees are generally not permitted to strike or to bargain over wages, hours, and benefits. The former prohibition against striking is grounded in the need to protect public health and safety. For instance, if police officers or firefighters went on strike, crime would rise and buildings would burn. It is also due to the sovereignty doctrine that deems striking against a government employer as inconsistent with the federal government being the highest authority.

EXAMPLE

Summary

Management must be mindful that employees have a legal right to form, join, or assist unions in the workplace. Collective bargaining does not apply to every workplace, as the employees must determine whether they wish to have a union represent their interests, but where such is the case, management must be careful to obey the laws that address unions. Attempting to interfere with union business, trying to coerce union members or otherwise acting not in accordance with the labor laws will result in unfair labor practice charges before the NLRB. Unions, too, must be vigilant about their responsibilities to their union members and to management as they collectively bargain, as failure to do so can result in unfair labor practice charges against unions also.

Review Questions

1. When Pearson signed on to work for Fancy Nancy's Famous Ironworks, one of the documents he was required to sign was a statement saying he did not belong to a union and would not join one while working for Fancy Nancy's Famous Ironworks. Pearson does not remember ever having to sign such a document before and is not sure he should have done so. If Pearson decides to join the union, can his employer use the document against Pearson? LO3

2. Bennina Industries is nonunion, and wants to stay that way. In an effort to do so, it wants to be proactive about employee concerns. Bennina tells some of the more popular employees it thinks they should meet after work for dinner, for which Bennina will pay, and hash out some of their issues and present them to management. Does this violate the law? LO3

3. In an effort to stay in office, Chino Guttieriez, president of Local 576 Iron Workers, persuades the union members to put off holding elections for the next two years (he has been in office for three years) because the union and management are engaged in delicate negotiations that will be seriously disrupted by holding elections as scheduled. The union members are aware of the negotiations, they realize the value of continuity and of Chino's good relationship with management, and they think their chances of getting what they want are better if they do as Chino requests. Can they grant his request? LO3

4. Haley is the president of a small local union with only 10 members. The union is holding elections, and when it is time for voting, Haley reads out the names of the candidates for office, has them give a brief speech, then asks members to hold up their hands if they want to vote for the candidate. Patrick is uncomfortable with this. Is there anything he can do? LO2, 3

5. Management unfair labor practices were introduced by LO2
   a. The Taft-Hartley Act
   b. The Wagner Act
   c. The Norris-LaGuardia Act
   d. The Landrum-Griffin Act

6. When Tibia Swanson told her union representative that she wanted to have action take against Chuck Bassin, a co-worker, for sexual harassment, the union rep told Tibia that not only was Chuck one of his friends and he was sure Chuck was just kidding but also that it would look bad for union contract negotiations next time around if Tibia pushed this. Does Tibia have a right to relief? LO 3

7. If in the previous question the union representative told Tibia what he did because she was not a member of the union, though she was a part of the bargaining unit, would it change things? LO3

8. The labor laws do not apply to part-time workers. True or false? LO2

9. Union and management are locked in contract negotiations. The union is requesting a 7.5% across the board raise for the bargaining unit. Management is only willing to give a 3.8% raise to the top 15% of the best performing employees. Management refuses to provide the union with any documentation explaining why it can only provide the raises the union proposed. When the union continues to insist on some sort of documentation, management stops meeting with the union, saying it is not getting anywhere. Is this okay for management to do? LO3

10. The union president loaned his friends money from the union strike fund at favorable interest rates. This is permissible as long as interest is charged for the loans and they were promptly repaid. True or false? LO2

Ethics Issue

Discuss the ethics of "union busting," wherein employers who do not wish to have unions hire specialized firms to resist such efforts, up to and including using physical force to intimidate employees who are so afraid of losing their jobs that they comply. Without addressing the actual legalities of such efforts, discuss the ethical implications. Who are the stakeholders? What are the real issues involved in such efforts by the employer? What do the stakeholders stand to lose or gain? Think broadly and don't forget to include issues like consumers, higher prices, competition, managerial power, depressed wages, and so on. In the end, does it make sense to you for an employer to engage in such activity?

Group Exercise

Have the class divide up into management and labor, with more labor than management. Have labor select a few union leaders. Have union leaders hold a meeting with employees to decide what they wish to approach management about in negotiating their collective bargaining agreement. Then have labor and management meet and negotiate the items. Draw up the collective bargaining agreement, then have the union take it back to the membership for ratification. How much of what the union wanted did it get? How much did management get? Which terms seemed the most important? Were there any terms that were not permissible subjects of negotiation? Which were permissible? Was there a difference in negotiating the two? How did the negotiating process go? Did you get a feel for what it might be like to be a business fighting to control your investment or a worker fighting for economic well-being or security?

Key Terms

agency shop 308

bargaining unit 302

business agent 303

card check 302

closed shop 308

collective bargaining agreement 299

community of interests 302

craft union 303

fees 308

free riders 308

industrial union 303

mandatory subjects of bargaining 303

no-strike, no-lockout clause 307

open shop 308

permissive subjects of bargaining 303

right to work laws 308

shop steward 299

unfair labor practice 299

unfair management practice 299

union representation election 303

union security clause 308

union shop 308

wildcat strike 307

yellow dog contracts 299

Chapter 3

Securities Regulation and Compliance

Learning Objectives

After reading this chapter, you should be able to:

L01 Discuss the purpose for regulation of the security industry

L02 Define a security

L03 Explain the purpose of securities regulation in the U.S.

L04 Explain how a company becomes a commodity on the market

L05 Describe insider trading and the effects of fraud on the market

L06 Discuss the Sarbanes-Oxley Act of 2002

L07 Describe the blue sky laws

L08 Analyze some of the ethical issues involved in the securities area

Opening Scenario

Maher Fayez Kara, a former director in Citigroup's Global Market's investment banking division in New York, had learned information too good not to pass on. Maher told his brother Michael some of the information he found out and Michael began making trades in companies involved with Citibank's clients. Michael told his friend Emile Youssef Jilwan and other family and friends about the information and they also made trades. They made the trades just in time too, because in one instance, the family members traded stocks and options of one company less than three days before the acquisition was announced. Now, thanks to Maher's info, they arre $6 million richer. Will they be allowed to keep the money?[1]

Introduction: The Need for Regulation

The estimated value of the world's **stock market** in 2008 was $36.6 trillion.[2] That is a lot of money and power being entrusted to others. (See Reality Check 13-1, "Exchanges of the World.") It should then come as no surprise that in the United States, the securities industry is one of the most highly regulated industries we have. You can imagine why. People who want to gain the potential benefits of a return, called *investors*, give

---

[1]Sarah N. Lynch, "Ex-Citigroup Banker Indicted in Insider Trading Scheme," *WSJ.com,* April 30, 2009, http://online.wsj.com/article/BT-CO-20090430-722756.html.

[2]http://seekingalpha.com/article/99256-world-equity-market-declines-25-9-trillion.

EXCHANGES OF THE WORLD

Although the focus of this chapter is on the stock markets of the U.S., there are stock markets worldwide. Three are African exchanges, 23 Asian exchanges, 34 European exchanges, 5 Middle Eastern exchanges, 17 North American exchanges, and 15 South American exchanges. In the U.S., there are three exchanges located in New York, three in Chicago, and one each in Arizona, Kansas City, and Minneapolis. Ten major world exchanges include:

U.S.	New York Stock Exchange	China	Shanghai Stock Exchange
Japan	Tokyo Stock Exchange	Hong Kong	Hong Kong Stock Exchange
U.S.	NASDAQ	Canada	Toronto Stock Exchange
Europe	Euronext	Spain	BME Spanish Exchanges
United Kingdom	London Stock Exchange	India	Bombay Stock Exchange

Source: http://www.tdd.lt/slnews/Stock_Exchanges/Stock.Exchanges.htm.
Retrieved 7/19/2009.

their money over to perfect strangers in hopes that the broker investing the money and/or company in which it is invested will act wisely, prudently, and honestly and make the money grow. This is a lot of power that investors give to someone along with their money. Investors, who are the backbone of the industry, need protection from swindlers who would take their money and give little or nothing in return. If investors cannot trust that their money is safe from misuse, they will not invest. If they do not invest, companies cannot even begin to make the kinds of research and innovation strides that we have come to expect.

So, what begins as a personal issue for one person investing his or her money quickly becomes a huge business issue when multiplied by millions of investors, and sometimes a disaster if not handled well. Since the investor is usually not right there with the broker making decisions, you can imagine the ethical issues that are presented. With so much money and seeming anonymity involved, there is a good deal of temptation to do the wrong thing. Thus, strict regulation is a must. In the opening scenario the behavior of the Kara brothers is called *insider trading* and is illegal and one type of behavior the laws are intended to prevent.

EXAMPLE

Because investors are so important to the capitalist system that our country as a whole enjoys, the U.S. Congress has created a complicated regulatory system to protect these investors. The **Securities Exchange Commission** (SEC) oversees all the U.S. stock exchanges and any organization connected with the selling of securities. Its anti-fraud provisions provide strong protections for individual investors and the markets as a whole. Each state also has its own regulatory authority to protect investors and the securities that are sold within the state. In the opening scenario, the Kara brothers were charged with a federal offense by the SEC.

EXAMPLE

Does all of this regulation guarantee that you will not get swindled? Obviously not. We have all heard and seen the failures of regulation lately. Since the late 1990s, the stock market has been hit with several large-scale failings. The collapse of the dot-com companies followed by the collapse of the telecommunication industry started to erode investor confidence in the market. The collapse of Enron, Arthur Andersen, WorldCom,

EXAMPLE

WHAT IS A PONZI SCHEME?

Ponzi schemes are a type of illegal pyramid scheme named for Charles Ponzi, who duped thousands of New England residents into investing in a postage stamp speculation scheme back in the 1920s. Ponzi thought he could take advantage of differences between U.S. and foreign currency used to buy and sell international mail coupons. Ponzi told investors that he could provide a 40% return in just 90 days compared with 5% for bank savings accounts. Though early investors were paid off to make the scheme appear legitimate, an investigation found that Ponzi had only purchased about $30 worth of international mail coupons. In a Ponzi scheme, the money early investors receive generally comes from the money the schemer is given by later investors rather than from profits from the thing invested in, thus insuring that at some point, the funds will run out and there will be investors who are not paid.

Source: http://www.sec.gov/answers/proxydelivery.htm.

Adelphia, Quest, Global Crossing, and Tyco, all between 2001 and 2002, and the convictions of their executives who benefited from their misconduct further eroded public confidence in the ability of the regulatory system to protect investments.

In 2007, the market essentially collapsed from the mortgage and credit crises. In addition to structural failures, the market was stricken with news of **Ponzi** schemes and financial fraud perpetrated by greedy individuals. (See Reality Check 13-2, "What Is a Ponzi Scheme?") Bernard Madoff was sentenced to serve 150 years for being the mastermind of a Ponzi scheme that bilked investors out of $65 billion. His clients, some of whom were wealthy individuals and others who were very well known charitable institutions and universities, saw their fortunes evaporate. (See Reality Check 13-3, "Madoff Gets Maximum Sentence.")

Listed by Forbes as one of the richest men in the world, R. Allen Stanford of Stanford Financial Group, along with his executives, was charged with running financial schemes involving a $7 billion fraud. They ran a scheme that stole money from customers who paid for certificates of deposit they bought for investments, destroying the lives of their customers while enriching their own portfolios. In spite of the breadth and scope of regulation in the security industry, people will find ways to steal other people's money if determined enough to do so. An example of this is our opening scenario. Maher Kara, a former director in Citigroup's Global Market's investment banking division, was accused of trying to enrich his family to the detriment of the public.

`EXAMPLE`

MADOFF GETS MAXIMUM SENTENCE

At age 71, Bernard Madoff is almost guaranteed to die in prison. That's what his 150 year prison sentence earned him for his "extraordinarily evil . . . financial crime." While his victims cried and displayed anger at him, the judge wanted the sentence to fit the "bloodless" crime that took a "staggering human toll."

One investor recounted how she and her husband invested their life savings with Madoff. Two weeks later, her husband died suddenly. Madoff put his arms around her and told her that her investment was safe with him and that she had nothing to worry about. When Madoff was arrested, this widow lost everything. Justice Chin, who sentenced Madoff, pointed to this letter as an example of what made Madoff worthy of the 150 year sentence he imposed.

Madoff was one of the world's most sought-after investors. Actors such as Steven Speilberg and Kevin Bacon, and Hall of Fame baseball pitcher Sandy Koufax, among many other notables, were his clients. The investigation found that he used money from new investors to pay old investors, and that he took money to support his lavish lifestyle. He and his wife were stripped of $171 billion worth of personal property, including real estate investments and his wife's $80 million she claimed were her assets. She was left with $2.5 million. Madoff claims to have acted alone, although his sons were also in his business. Beside Madoff, one other person has been charged so far.

Source: "Madoff Sentenced to 150 Years in Prison," http://www.msnbc.msn.com/id/31604191/ns/business-us_business/.

What Is a Security?

L02

A **security** is defined as a **negotiable instrument** that represents financial value. What is meant by negotiable is that the instrument may be bought, sold, or pledged freely on the market. A security is an umbrella name for a variety of different negotiable instruments. **Stock**, also known as **shares,** is one type of security. Stock represents investors buying ownership in a company and becoming stockholders or shareholders. However, sometimes, it is not clear whether an instrument meets the definition of a security. That is the issue in *Howey,* Case 13.1.

There are two primary types of securities: debt and equity securities. **Debt securities** are represented by bank notes, for example. **Equity securities** are represented by stocks and other instruments that qualify as assets. The primary difference between debt and equity is that debt represents money owed while equity represents an asset owned. While stocks represent buying ownership in a company, bonds are loans to companies which companies promise to repay with interest.

For example, the AB Corporation is a profitable manufacturer that wishes to expand its operations. In order to expand, it has to raise money. It has basically two ways it can raise money. It can take out a loan, which of course requires the corporation to repay the loan, with interest, over time. This is a debt to the corporation. Or it can raise money by selling stock. If it does this, it takes on new additional owners, and gets money to

CASE 13.1 Securities and Exchange Commission v. W. J. Howey Co.

328 U.S. 293 (1946)

Facts: W. J. Howey, Inc., and Howey-in-the-Hills Services, Inc., were corporations owned by W. J. Howey. Howey owned large tracts of land on which he grew citrus. He sold real estate contracts to investors and then sold the investors service contracts which gave Howey-in-the-Hills Services the right to tend, harvest, pool, and market the produce for a fee. Most investors were out of state investors who had no knowledge of how to farm or market crops. Howey had not registered the sale of the land or service contracts with the SEC. The SEC filed suit to enjoin Howey from selling the service contracts, claiming that these were investment contracts and had to be registered before they could be sold.

Issue: Whether the service contracts met the definition of an investment contract.

Decision: Yes, the investment contracts sold by Howey were securities under the SEC regulations.

Reasoning: The Court developed a 3-part test to determine whether a contract represents an investment. The test is whether the scheme involves (1) an investment of money; (2) in a common enterprise; (3) with profits to

come solely from the efforts of others. The Court found that all 3 prongs of the test were met, thus, W. J. Howey was required to register these investments under §5 of the Securities Act of 1933.

CASE QUESTIONS

1. This 3-part test is known as the Howey test and is still used to define an investment today. A key element in Howey's defense was that he was not the sole provider of these service contracts; in fact, the lessor of the land could choose anyone to service it. Why was this defense not successful?

2. What evil was inherent in what Howey was doing? What was the SEC trying to do in requiring registration of this investment contract?

3. In a recent case, *Davis v. Chase*, 453 F. Supp. 2d 1205 (C.D. Ca. 2006), the court ruled that a credit card was not a security, even though the plaintiff argued that it was an interest that has financial value. What part of the Howey test does a credit card fail to meet?

operate that it does not have to repay. This becomes equity—an asset of the corporation. Of course, there are many, many things to consider before making this decision, but this illustrates the difference between acquiring debt to raise money and selling stock to raise money.

Each stock that is sold represents an ownership interest in the corporation that sells it. Bringing buyers and sellers of these stocks together is a primary function of the stock market. Stock may be represented by a **stock certificate,** but most often is represented only in electronic form known as a **noncertificated stock.** Stock can be **nonregistered,** meaning it can be negotiated by whoever possesses the stock, or it can be **registered,** meaning that the only person who has a right to negotiate it is the person whose name is registered on the books of the corporation as the owner.

Securities get distributed by issuers. **Issuers** can be corporations, government agencies, local authorities, or international organizations.

The Securities Act of 1933

L03

The Securities Act of 1933 was the federal government's first involvement in the sale of stocks and other securities. Up to this point, stocks and securities had been regulated solely by state law. The Act was part of the New Deal legislation enacted by Congress in response to the Great Depression. Congress believed that the stock market crash of 1929 precipitated the depression, and that the primary reason for the collapse of the market was the fraudulent transactions which created a false financial bubble. Once the bubble burst, the market crashed. Congress viewed this as having an impact on the national economy, not just private investors; thus, legislation to address this was enacted.

Congress assumed that the best way to protect investors from future fraud was to require complete and accurate disclosure. This was the antithesis of state law regulation, which regulated the sale of securities by refusing to approve the sale unless the agency thought it was a good one. Congress's position was that if the investor had all the information about the investment, he or she could protect himself or herself. Thus, full disclosure became the lynchpin of the legislation.

The **Securities Act of 1933** is directed primarily at the original distribution of securities into the market. The Act has two basic objectives: (1) to require that investors receive financial and other significant information concerning securities being offered for public sale, and (2) to prohibit deceit, misrepresentation, and other fraud in the sale of securities.[3] The Act generally requires the registration of all securities being placed in the hands of the public for the first time. As discussed in the "Business Crimes" chapter, Congress opted to require full disclosure of all material information in the registration process. The theory behind full disclosure is that the public is adequately protected if all aspects of the securities being marketed are fully and fairly disclosed. The scope of the Act is limited: it reaches only distributions of securities, and its investor protection reach extends only to purchasers of securities. Investors who purchase securities and suffer a loss as a result of false or misleading registration information have legal remedies to recover their losses. Losses based on the vagaries of the market cannot be recovered. Again, the primary goal is to make sure investors have all the information they need in order to make a prudent decision as to investing. Investing is inherently risky, and since anything can happen in business, there are no guarantees of return. Investors invest at their own risk, and as long as they have been provided with all the legally required relevant facts regarding the investment, there is no liability on the part of the company or broker if the investment does not make money.

---

[3]http://www.sec.gov/about/laws.shtml.

LO4 Initial Public Offering

EXAMPLE

Not every business is a public one. Walmart, for instance, was a family-owned business for years. However, there may come a time when the business decides that it wishes to expand or otherwise have an infusion of capital by allowing the public to own shares in the business. This is a big decision, because rules for public corporations are quite different from those of private corporations. As you can imagine, having the government now able to regulate you through the SEC, as well as 10,000 people who now have a say in how you run your business, is not quite the same as running it by yourself or with your family. But the financial rewards tend to be great.

If and when a corporation decides to "go public" it offers its shares for sale through an **initial public offering (IPO).** (See Reality Check 13-4, "IPO for Skype to Be Offered in 2010.") Going public requires a company to be evaluated from top to bottom by a team consisting of an **underwriter,** lawyers, accountants, and auditors.

As you have no doubt heard in the news, the infusion of cash from an IPO for a company with a great product can be staggering. (See Reality Check 13-5, "Google's IPO.") However, fees for staging the IPO can be prohibitively costly. Attorney's fees modestly range from $150,000 to $450,000. In addition, accounting fees can add another $100,000 to $250,000; printing expenses may add another $75,000 to $175,000 and the SEC's filing fee of 1/33 of 1% of the maximum aggregate offering price of the securities will be incurred.[4]

FILING A REGISTRATION

When going public, full compliance with the Securities Act of 1933 involves the filing of a **registration statement** with the SEC. A registration statement consists of two parts: (1) a **prospectus,** a document that is to be distributed to potential and actual investors (remember we mentioned printing costs above?); and (2) additional information that must be submitted to the SEC and is publicly available but need not be included in the prospectus. While the SEC requires the information to be accurate, it does not guarantee its accuracy. Since 1996, the SEC has required electronic filing of most reports. (See Take Away 13-1, "Electronic Data Gathering, Analysis, and Retrieval (EDGAR) Online.")

REALITY CHECK 13-4

IPO FOR SKYPE TO BE OFFERED IN 2010

EBay announced that it would spin off its Skype Internet telephone company in the first half of 2010. EBay had purchased Skype from its founders for $2.6 billion in 2005. The reason for its sale is so Skype can compete more effectively with other telecommunications companies. Skype currently appears on over 6 percent of all iPhones and iPods.

Source: Mark Heffinger, "EBay Announces IPO for Skype in First Half of 2010," *DMW Media.com,* April 14, 2009, http://www.dmwmedia.com/news/2009/04/14/ebay-announces-ipo-skype-first-half-2010.

REALITY CHECK 13-5

GOOGLE'S IPO

On April 30, 2004, Google, the world's No. 1 search engine, filed for its initial public offering. When their stock finally sold on August 19, 2004, it opened at $100.01, $15.01 higher than Google's asking price of $85 per share, which reflects what the purchasers were willing to pay over the asking price because of what they saw as the potential value of the shares. Google sold over 20 million shares at this price, raking in an estimated $27 billion.

On its five-year anniversary, August 19, 2009, Google was still profitable beyond all projections. Citing a high per share of over $600 in 2007, on its anniversary, Google was trading at $445.28. The estimated value of the company rose to approximately $140 billion.

Scott Reeves, "Google's Flub, Flop and Bomb," *Forbes.com,* http://www.forbes.com/2004/09/17/cx_sr_0917ipooutlook.html; and "Google's IPO, Five Years Later," *New York Times,* http://dealbook.blogs.nytimes.com/2009/08/19/googles-ipo-5-years-later/.

---

[4]Robert Hamilton and Jonathan Macey, *Corporations,* 9th ed. (West, 2005), p. 350.

ELECTRONIC DATA GATHERING, ANALYSIS, AND RETRIEVAL (EDGAR) ONLINE

The Electronic Data Gathering, Analysis, and Retrieval (EDGAR) system performs automated collection, validation, indexing, acceptance, and forwarding of submissions by companies and others who are required by law to file forms with the SEC. Since 1996, the SEC has required all public domestic companies to file all forms, including registration forms, through the computerized system. As of 2002, the SEC requires all foreign companies to file via EDGAR. Filings with the SEC can also be retrieved from EDGAR if they are public documents.

Source: http://www.sec.gov/edgar/aboutedgar.htm.

The registration form must include:

a. A description of the company's property and business;
b. A description of the security to be offered for sale;
c. Information about the management of the company; and
d. Financial statements certified by independent accountants.[5]

The financial statements must be certified for the past three years. Much more information is gathered by other parts of the registration forms that must be submitted to the SEC.

Prior to the final prospectus being filed with the SEC, the company must issue a **red herring prospectus,** named for the red writing that usually appears across the front of the document that identifies it as a preliminary prospectus. The purpose of the red herring prospectus is to give potential investors as much information as possible before the sale is actually consummated. The red herring prospectus will include such things as the purpose of the offer, the offering price range, the promotion expenses, earnings statements for the previous three years, and the underwriting costs.

Once complete, the SEC reviews the registration statement and issues a comment to the corporation that usually contains areas in which the registration needs clarification. No securities can be sold until the registration becomes effective; however, **tombstone ads** may be published to announce the anticipated offering. (See Take Away 13-2, "Tombstone Ad.") A registration becomes effective 20 days after the final change has been submitted to the SEC. The securities may then be sold. A prospectus must then be delivered to every person who purchased the security.

EXEMPT SECURITIES

Not all public offerings of securities must be registered with the SEC. Some offerings, like those filed under a "Regulation D" exemption, are **exempt** because the offering is being made to a select group of individuals, called **accredited investors.** An accredited investor is one who qualifies under the SEC's definition of sophisticated investor. The idea is that these investors do not need the SEC's disclosure requirements to make sound investments. They are not the type of investor the SEC is concerned with protecting. Offerings of a limited size or that are being sold strictly intrastate and securities of municipal, state, or federal governments are also exempt from registration. Because of the cost of registration, registration is to be avoided if at all possible, and offering exempt securities is one way to accomplish this.

Corporations wishing to take advantage of Regulation D exemptions must first file a Form D, which notifies the SEC of their intent to sell securities under Regulation D. Those investors wishing to take advantage of an exempt sale should first check to make sure the proper filing has been made to obtain the exemption, and that they qualify as accredited investors.

---

[5]http://www.sec.gov/about/laws.shtml.

⬈ TAKE AWAY 13-2

TOMBSTONE AD

A tombstone ad is an announcement by the issuer of the sale of the stock and the parties involved in the IPO. It is not an offer for the sale; it is just an announcement of the upcoming sale to generate interest. This is an example of what a tombstone ad looks like:

This announcement is neither an offer to sell nor a solicitation of an offer to buy any of these Securities. The offer is made only by the Prospectus.

May 26, 1999

5,750,000 SHARES

WORLDGATE™

WORLDGATE COMMUNICATIONS, INC.

COMMON STOCK

Price $21.00 Per Share

Copies of the Prospectus may be obtained in any State from only such of the undersigned as may legally offer these Securities in compliance with the securities laws of such State.

GERARD KLAUER MATTISON & CO., INC.

JEFFERIES & COMPANY, INC.

JANNEY MONTGOMERY SCOTT INC.

BANCBOSTON ROBERTSON STEPHENS	CIBC WORLD MARKETS	DONALDSON, LUFKIN & JENRETTE
HAMBRECHT & QUIST	ING BARING FURMAN SELZ LLC	LEHMAN BROTHERS MERRILL LYNCH & CO.
SALOMON SMITH BARNEY	SG COWEN	WASSERSTEIN PERELLA SECURITIES, INC.
AUERBACH, POLLAK & RICHARDSON, INC.		DAIN RAUSCHER WESSELS
		A DIVISION OF DAIN RAUSCHER INCORPORATED
FRIEDMAN, BILLINGS, RAMSEY & CO., INC.		HOAK BREEDLOVE WESNESKI & CO.
PACIFIC CREST SECURITIES INC.		PREFERRED CAPITAL MARKETS, INC.
RAYMOND JAMES & ASSOCIATES, INC.		THE ROBINSON-HUMPHREY COMPANY
SOUNDVIEW TECHNOLOGY GROUP	STEPHENS INC.	C.E. UNTERBERG, TOWBIN

Source: http://www.asklux.com/tomb2.htm.

VIOLATION OF THE SECURITIES ACT OF 1933

Investors who are injured by purchasing shares from corporations whose registrations contain false or misleading information have remedies available under the law. The most important of these is Section 11 of the Act that allows investors to bring a suit for losses incurred if the prospectus contains misleading statements of material facts unknown to the purchaser when making the purchase. Section 11 is a strict liability statute; the issuer is liable if the false or misleading statement appears in the prospectus. The officers, directors, underwriters, and other persons named in the registration statement may be liable unless they can prove that they relied on experts and made a reasonable investigation into the truthfulness of the statements.

Investors may also bring a lawsuit under Section 12(1) of the Act. Section 12(1) allows any purchaser of securities that should have been registered but were not to rescind the purchase without regard to fault or misstatement. Section 12(2) imposes liability on any seller for material misstatements or omissions in connection with the sale of securities. The only defense permitted under this section is that the seller did not know or should not have known that the statement was false or omitted. Purchasers also have the right to bring suit if there are incomplete or inaccurate disclosures of material facts in the prospectus, without regard to intent or negligence.

Purchasers have one year from the date of the discovery of the false or misleading statement to bring an action under Sections 11 or 12. Purchasers cannot bring an action if more than three years have passed since the purchase of the security.

L03

The Securities Act of 1934: Formation of the Securities and Exchange Commission

With the Securities Exchange Act of 1934, Congress enacted a more expansive act and created the Securities and Exchange Commission to oversee and enforce the law. The Act empowers the SEC with broad authority over all aspects of the securities industry. This includes the power to register, regulate, and oversee brokerage firms, transfer agents, and clearing agencies as well as the nation's securities **self-regulatory organizations (SROs).** (See Take Away 13-3, "Securities Exchange Acts of 1933 and 1934.")

EXAMPLE

SROs are important to the regulation of the security industry. The SEC alone cannot enforce all aspects of the market. Congress empowers SROs as enforcement agencies. An example of an SRO is the **Financial Industry Regulatory Authority (FINRA)** (formerly National Association of Securities Dealers—NASD). FINRA is responsible for regulatory oversight of all securities firms that do business with the public. Another SRO related to securities is the **Municipal Securities Rulemaking Board (MSRB).** Congress created the MSRB to adopt investor protection rules governing broker-dealers, banks that underwrite, trade, or sell tax-exempt bonds, college savings plans, and other types of municipal securities. Enforcement occurs regularly through the use of the agencies appointed to regulate this activity. (See Reality Check 13-6, "Firms Fined for Excessive Commissions on IPOs.")

 TAKE AWAY 13-3

SECURITIES EXCHANGE ACTS OF 1933 AND 1934

Securities Exchange Act of 1933	Securities Exchange Act of 1934
Requires *original* issuers to publicly disclose significant information about themselves and the terms of the sale	Regulates *secondary* trades of securities between persons having no relationship to the original issuer

Liability under Rule 10b-5

L05

The foundational rule against fraudulent activities is SEC Rule 10b-5. **Rule 10b-5** is the most famous rule in securities law. (See Take Away 13-4, "Rule 10b-5.")

A cause of action exists under Rule 10b-5 for every person who buys or sells securities as a result of fraud or misrepresentation. Rule 10b-5 is applicable to both closely held (privately owned) corporations and those corporations whose shares are traded on the stock market because it is triggered by the use of interstate commerce. Thus, Rule 10b-5 is applicable to virtually every securities transaction. See the *Gann* case (Case 13.2).

EXAMPLE For example, if a telephone call is used to sell shares from one broker to another located in the same building, Rule 10b-5 applies if the sale is made based on false or misleading information because of the use of interstate commerce—the telephone. Or if a buyer of all the shares of a private corporation made the purchase based on false or misleading information, Rule 10b-5 applies because the shares of a closely held corporation are securities within the meaning of the rule.

It is important to note that any suit alleging a Rule 10b-5 violation arises in federal court. States do not have jurisdiction to hear a Rule 10b-5 case.

Rule 10b-5 not only applies to false and misleading statements, but also applies if the seller fails to disclose or makes only half-true statements if those statements are misleading and material.

MATERIALITY UNDER RULE 10b-5

What is material? A statement is **material** if a reasonable person would attach importance to the information in determining a course of action. In other words, if the information would affect the value of the securities, then it should be considered material and it should be disclosed. If the statement is made in a public manner, e.g., it is made by a public corporation via a public press release, then any person who purchases or sells shares based on that public information can recover without establishing specific knowledge of the statement. The theory is that a misrepresentation made in a public manner misleads all investors. Rule 10b-5 requires intent to deceive.

INSIDER TRADING LIABILITY UNDER RULE 10b-5

Rule 10b-5 is also a rule that prohibits trading on the basis of inside information. Information is said to be "inside" when it is known to certain individuals inside the

TAKE AWAY 13-4

RULE 10b-5

It shall be unlawful for any person, directly or indirectly, by the use of any means or instrumentality of interstate commerce, or of the mails or of any facility of any national securities exchange,

   a. to employ any device, scheme, or artifice to defraud;

   b. to make any untrue statement of a material fact or to omit to state a material fact necessary in order to make the statements made, in the light of the circumstances under which they were made, not misleading; or

   c. to engage in any act, practice, or course of business which operates or would operate as a fraud or deceit upon any person, in connection with the purchase or sale of any security.

CASE 13.2 S.E.C. v. Gann

565 F.3d 932 (5th Cir. 2009)

Facts: In 2002, Gann and a co-worker traded funds under the company name of Southwest Securities for a customer named Haidar Capital Management. Southwest agreed to trade the funds by using "market timing." Market timing is a legal practice in which traders buy and sell shares quickly to take advantage of short-term differentials to turn a profit. Many mutual funds prohibit trading of their shares by market timers. Gann opened up 21 accounts for his customers and engaged in market timing by fraudulently creating different account numbers to make detection by the mutual funds nearly impossible. Over seven months Gann conducted about 2,500 trades in the amount of $650 million and turned a profit of nearly $60,000. The SEC asserted a civil enforcement action under Rule 10b-5 after learning of the activity and won at trial. Gann appealed.

Issue: Whether the SEC had the power to issue an injunction against Gann.

Decision: Yes.

Reasoning: The SEC is the enforcement body of the government relating to the sale and trade of securities. In this instance they are enforcing corporate regulations on behalf of mutual funds. Even though timing itself is not illegal, it is illegal for one like Gann to intend to defraud companies by creating various accounts to fly under the radar of their regulations. This type of behavior is harmful to all investors and the SEC was well within its powers to step in.

CASE QUESTIONS

1. This case demonstrates how using a legal process illegally can be a violation of the stock market rules. It also demonstrates how much deference is given to the SEC enforcement by the courts. Is this wise?
2. Should the SEC have to prove that Gann caused harm by using his process on mutual fund purchases and sales?
3. How exactly was Gann defrauding the companies by buying and selling quickly? Why did he need to create 21 companies to accomplish this?

corporation, but that information has not been disseminated to the general public. Of course, if an **insider** knows what is about to happen in the market with certain stocks, buying or selling on the basis of that information can be extremely beneficial to either avoid loss or create gain to the buyer or seller. For that reason, it is forbidden by Rule 10b-5. In the chapter's opening scenario, Maher Kara was an insider possessed with nonpublic information that he passed on to his brother.

EXAMPLE

In our scenario, the Kara brothers were able to gain nearly $6 million by trading their shares before the public knew what was going to happen. If they learned that a company whose shares they owned was going to announce adverse information which would negatively impact the value of their shares, the brothers sold their shares before the announcement, thereby avoiding the loss. If, on the other hand, a positive statement about the company was going to be announced so that immediately after the company's shares would skyrocket, the brothers bought the shares while they were priced low, and gained the benefit of the increased value of the shares once the announcement was made public. Buying and selling on this basis is unfair to the public. Any trade made on the basis of inside information is unlawful.

EXAMPLE

Because the rule speaks of "any person," it has been interpreted to apply to insiders and any person with whom the insider shares the information—a tippee. A **tippee** is a person who gets an inside tip, that is, learns of the nonpublic information from the insider. In the opening scenario, Michael Kara was a tippee; he learned of the information from an insider. In addition, as we discussed in the "Business Crimes" chapter, those who receive insider information from the issuer in connection with other duties such as accountants or lawyers are said to have **misappropriated** information and are considered insiders under Rule 10b-5. Thus, they are subject to the same rules as corporate officers, directors, or employees. For example, a lawyer at a law firm was handling a merger for her client, Corporation X. She knew that once the merger was announced, Corporation X's shares would triple in value. If she purchased shares of Corporation X before the merger was announced, she would be guilty of misappropriating that information.

Insider Trading Liability under Section 16

Section 16 is designed to prevent certain persons from unfairly profiting from inside information by engaging in transactions that may have a temporary effect, and to prevent in-and-out transactions that might be used to manipulate securities. These transactions are called **short swing profits** and are prohibited. Persons are covered by Section 16 if they are officers, directors, or 10 percent shareholders of the issuer, including spouse, relatives, or nominees. If they are covered, they cannot buy stock then sell it within six months of the purchase (or vice versa). For example, if there is a purchase of stock on January 1, Section 16 would prohibit a sale of that stock any time from six months before to six months after the purchase. Unlike Rule 10b-5, Section 16 imposes automatic liability once the purchase or sale is proven. For example, a sale of securities for entirely justifiable reasons, like to raise money to cover unexpected medical expenses, triggers Section 16 liabilities if there has been an offsetting purchase within the previous six months.

Even though both Rule 10b-5 and Section 16 apply to insiders, there are substantial differences:

- First, Section 16 only applies to transactions involving registered equity securities, while Rule 10b-5 applies to all securities, registered or nonregistered, debt or equity.
- Second, the term *insider* is much broader under Rule 10b-5, whereas Section 16 is limited to those persons covered by the section.
- Third, Section 16 does not require that the insider possess material nonpublic information; Rule 10b-5 only applies if that information is not disclosed.
- Fourth, Section 16 only applies to transactions within six months of each other. Rule 10b-5 has no such limitation.
- Fifth, under Rule 10b-5, injured investors may recover damages on their own behalf, while under Section 16, although shareholders may bring suit, recovery is on behalf of the corporation.

The SEC monitors for Section 16 transactions by requiring all persons covered by the section to file periodic reports with the SEC. The first report must describe the person's initial ownership of the shares, and subsequent reports must be filed showing the acquisitions and dispositions of securities. (See Take Away 13-5, "Differences between Rule 10b-5 and Rule 16.")

Communication between Shareholders and the Corporation

How does a corporation communicate with its shareholders? How does a corporation conduct its business? For a small, closely held corporation, it simply calls a meeting and the shareholders gather to meet and vote. But what if the corporation has thousands of shareholders scattered all over the world? How is its business conducted? How are its

DIFFERENCES BETWEEN RULE 10b-5 AND RULE 16

Rule 10b-5	Rule 16
Applies to all securities	Applies to equity securities only
Applies to all insiders	Applies only to persons covered by rule
Requires action on nondisclosed inside information	Does not require action to be on inside information
Does not matter when transactions occurred	Requires transactions to have occurred within 6 months of each other
Damages recoverable by shareholder	Damages recoverable by corporation

elections held? Rule 14 regulates the information and circumstances under which the corporation or its members can give information to the shareholders.

PROXY STATEMENTS

Virtually every public corporation has an obligation to disclose information to shareholders and to members of the general public.[6] This is done via a proxy statement. A **proxy statement** is a statement required of a U.S. corporation when soliciting shareholders' votes. Remember that shareholders are owners of the corporation, and, as such, get to participate in its governance. Much like we, as citizens, participate indirectly in government through voting for representatives we hope will vote the way we want on issues, shareholders participate indirectly in corporate governance through electing directors of the corporation who then make corporate policy and conduct corporate business. A proxy statement includes the voting procedures, background information about the company's nominated directors, director compensation, the compensation of its executives, and information about auditor fees.

Corporations are generally required to have at least an annual meeting of the shareholders. A proxy statement must be filed with the SEC in advance of the annual meeting.

PROXY SOLICITATIONS

Because shareholders very seldom attend annual meetings, most shareholders are solicited via a proxy solicitation. Proxy solicitations are communications with potential absentee voters. A **proxy solicitation** is a writing signed by a shareholder of a corporation authorizing a named person to vote his or her shares of stock at a specified meeting of the shareholders. Solicitations, whether by management or shareholders, must disclose all important facts about the issues on which shareholders are asked to vote. The goal of federal proxy regulation was to improve those communications and enable proxy voters

---

[6]There are some exceptions to this requirement based on the number of shareholders and value of assets.

to control the corporation as effectively as they might have by attending a shareholder meeting. See Reality Check 13-7, "Electronic Delivery of Proxy Statements Allowed by SEC," for information about electronic proxy statements.

ANNUAL REPORTS

If a corporation is holding an annual meeting for the purpose of voting on a board of directors, Rule 14 requires that the proxy be accompanied by an **annual report** containing financial information on the corporation. The annual report to shareholders is the principal document used by most public companies to disclose corporate information to their shareholders. It is usually a comprehensive report containing market information, new products, research and development and other detailed information about the corporation. In addition to the annual report, corporations must file a report with the SEC that contains more detailed information about the corporation that is available to the investing public.

Annual reports generally contain easy to read information that informs the shareholders about the company. Even though the shareholder is a company owner and needs an accurate and realistic picture of the company she owns, the reality is that most annual reports are advertising pieces for the companies designed to keep investors upbeat about their investment in the company so they will continue to invest.

MANAGEMENT'S DISCUSSION AND ANALYSIS

Management's Discussion and Analysis (MD&A) is often the most important disclosure item in the annual report. It consists of a discussion of the company's financial condition, changes in financial condition, and results of operations, specifically with respect to liquidity and resources. It must also contain any other information the corporation believes to be necessary to an understanding of its financial condition. The object is to give the investor a look at the company through the eyes of management. It is required to have a short-term and long-term view of the company.

The SEC's rules governing MD&A allow disclosure about trends, events, or uncertainties known to management that would have a material impact on reported financial information. The purpose of the MD&A is to provide investors with information that the company's management believes to be necessary to an understanding of its financial condition, changes in condition, and results of operations. While it is intended to help investors see the company through the eyes of management, it is also intended to provide context for the financial statements and information about the company's earnings and cash flow.

The SEC allows management to include **forward looking statements** in the MD&A. Forward looking statements do not include historical factual information; rather, they contain projections for future performance. You can imagine that any company wishing to retain its investors would want to paint a glowing picture of the future of the company in this section. However, projections do not always work out as planned. To prevent individuals who read the projections from holding the company liable if the projections are not met, the SEC adopted the **safe harbor** rule. The safe harbor rule provides that such statements are not false or misleading as long as they are made in good faith or

CASE 13.3 In re Humana, Inc. Securities Litigation

2009 WL 1767193 (W.D. Ky. 2009)

Facts: This is a class action suit initiated by investors who traded common stock of Humana, Inc. Plaintiffs alleged that Humana violated Rule 10(b) and 20(a) of the Securities Exchange Act of 1934.

In February 2008, Humana issued a press release divulging its fourth quarter and annual earnings for 2007. Using language like "we anticipate," "we do not foresee," and "we remain confident of our ability to . . . ," Humana issued statements projecting that its earnings per share (EPS) would increase in 2008 approximately 9–13%. Humana also attributed this increase in earnings to a lower tax rate for 2008. This information was disseminated via a press release.

On March 12, 2008, Humana announced via another press release revised financial projections downward $360 million or 47% from the number it released just five weeks prior. Plaintiffs alleged that their original projection was false and misleading on the part of Humana's CEO, CFO, and COO, who issued the releases. Plaintiffs alleged that Humana's internal control system used to verify and make these projections was so faulty that they had no way of determining what their projections should be. They also alleged that Humana knew of these problems and that Humana made the faulty projections to induce people to invest with Humana through deception.

Issue: Whether Humana's statements were forward looking statements and protected by the "safe harbor" provision?

Decision: Yes.

Reasoning: Under certain circumstances the defendants' statements are protected under the safe harbor provision. Forward looking statements are allowed to include future financial conditions based on predictions. The court held that "If a forward-looking statement is accompanied with cautionary language, the issuer is immune from liability and state of mind is irrelevant." Here, the court agreed with Humana that the statements were, in fact, forward looking statements and contained the necessary cautionary language; therefore, they were immune from liability.

CASE QUESTIONS

1. The plaintiffs were convinced that the short time period between the press release and the restatement indicated wrongdoing on the part of Humana. Can you imagine a scenario where the facts would have come to light in such a short period of time?

2. The amount of the revision is also what the plaintiffs used to bring their complaint. How do words like "projected," "estimated," or "possible" allow an investor to be cautious of what follows those words?

3. Does the safe harbor rule give management an opportunity to cover up its wrongdoing, or should there be a way to be able to estimate and be wrong?

made with a reasonable basis. You can see how this rule works in the *Humana* case (Case 13.3).

 ## Mandatory Reporting under the Sarbanes-Oxley Act

The **Sarbanes-Oxley Act of 2002 (SOX)** is a federal law enacted in reaction to a number of major corporation and accounting scandals. The Act established new standards for all U.S. company boards of directors, management, and accounting firms. (See Take Away 13-6, "The Sarbanes-Oxley Act of 2002.") It entrusted the SEC to enact rules and regulations mandating corporate compliance. It was enacted to restore public confidence in the financial markets, which had been shaken by corporate scandals that resulted in millions of dollars of investment lost by corporate mismanagement and mal-management.

The Sarbanes-Oxley Act created a new agency, the **Public Company Accounting Oversight Board,** or **PCAOB.** PCAOB is charged with overseeing, regulating, and disciplining accounting firms when they act as auditors of public corporations. (See Reality Check 13-8, "Is the PCAOB Constitutional?")

SOX covers auditor independence, corporate governance, internal control assessment, and financial disclosures. Notice that we have been discussing public companies, but see Reality Check 13-9 ("Agent for Public Company Held for Violation of Sarbanes-Oxley Whistleblower Provision") about a decision that found SOX to extend to private companies.

ACCOUNTANT ACTIVITIES

In dealing with corporations and their responsibilities to provide investors with relevant information, auditing plays a vital role. Not only are there legal requirements regarding proper auditing of corporate assets and financial position for information purposes, but the information auditors provide is crucial to the making of effective decisions. As we saw with the Arthur Andersen firm in the Enron case, when the auditors who are supposed to provide an accurate picture of the company's financial situation begin to allow their relationship with the company to compromise the accuracy of their jobs, trouble ensues and investors are usually on the losing end. Prior to Sarbanes-Oxley, auditing firms were self-regulated. They also performed significant consultant work for the companies they audited. Many times, the consultant work was more lucrative than the auditing functions. Thus, auditing firms often had conflicts of interest in the performance of their dual duties. Such conflicts can run afoul of PCAOB rules.

TAKE AWAY 13-6

THE SARBANES-OXLEY ACT OF 2002

There are eleven sections of the act. They are:

1. Public Company Accounting Oversight Board
2. Auditor Independence
3. Corporate Responsibility
4. Enhanced Financial Disclosures
5. Analyst Conflicts of Interest
6. Commission Resources and Authority
7. Studies and Reports
8. Corporate and Criminal Fraud Accountability
9. White Collar Crime Penalty Enhancement
10. Corporate Tax Returns
11. Corporate Fraud Accountability

Source: sec.gov.

REALITY CHECK 13-8

IS THE PCAOB CONSTITUTIONAL?

Some are questioning the constitutionality of PCAOB on the grounds that Congress exceeded its authority in enacting it. Specifically being challenged is the fact that the five members who run the PCAOB are appointed by the five commissioners of the SEC, not the President. According to its critics, the power exerted by PCAOB requires that the President not the SEC commissioners should appoint—and have the power to remove—members of the PCAOB.

In support of their argument, they point out that the President has the power to appoint heads of every Cabinet-level department, and to remove them for cause or at will, and this should be no different. They state that the PCAOB decides which accounting firms to inspect and how to conduct investigations, as well as interpret the Sarbanes-Oxley Act.

Arguing that the constitutional flaws are not merely matters of "etiquette or protocol," Judge Cavanaugh of the Second D.C. Circuit, who dissented in the opinion which held the PCAOB's authority to be constitutional, stated that the restriction over the board divorces the Presidential control in a way not contemplated by the Constitution.

The critics sought an appeal of the D.C. Circuit decision to the U.S. Supreme Court. Oral arguments were heard in the U.S. Supreme Court on December 7, 2009. On June 28, 2010, the Court held the PCAOB's authority to be unconstitutional. It held that the President, and not the SEC, has power to appoint and remove members of PCAOB.

Source: Kenneth W. Starr and Viet Dinh, "The PCAOB: An Obstacle to Obama's Success," *The Wall Street Journal,* May 13, 2009, http://online.wsj.com/article/SB124216925017912671.html. Free Enterprise Fund v. PCAOB, 561 U.S. ___ (2010)

AGENT FOR PUBLIC COMPANY HELD LIABLE FOR VIOLATION OF SARBANES-OXLEY WHISTLEBLOWER PROVISION

In a decision that should give notice to privately held companies, the Department of Labor ruled that private companies that perform work for public companies will be held accountable under the Sarbanes-Oxley Act if they act as an agent for the publicly held company.

An attorney who worked for a public company, DVI Financial Services, Inc., "reported up" to her Board of Directors that her company had sent misleading information to the SEC. The Board hired an outside private company, AP Services, LLC, to help reorganize the company. When the attorney followed up on her report to the DVI Board she was fired by Mark Toney, an employee of AP Services who had been given authority to terminate DVI's employees.

The attorney sued DVI and AP Services for violating the whistleblower provisions of Sarbanes-Oxley. The administrative law judge who heard the case agreed with her, and that ruling was affirmed by the Department of Labor's Administrative Review Board (ARB).

The ARB judge found that although Toney worked for AP Services and not DVI, AP Services was an agent of DVI. Sarbanes-Oxley imposes liability on "any officer, employee, contractor, sub-contractor, or agent" of a publicly held company for retaliation because of the employee's whistleblowing activity. AP Services, a privately held company, as an agent of DVI, was able to affect the employment of the attorney, therefore was subject to the whistleblower provision. The ARB further found that the whistleblowing complaint was a motivating factor in Toney's decision to fire her. Thus, the ARB held both DVI and AP Services liable under §806 of the Sarbanes-Oxley Act. She was awarded back pay, damages for pain, suffering, and mental anguish, and reimbursement costs, including attorney's fees.

Source: Kalkunte v. DVI Financial Services, Inc. & AP Services, LLC, USDOL/OALB Reporter, ARB Case Nos. 05-139 and 05-140, February 27, 2009, http://www.oalj.dol. gov/PUBLIC/ARB/DECISIONS/ARB_DECISIONS/SOX/05_139.SOXP.PDF.

(See Reality Check 13-10, "Deloitte Slammed with $1 Million Penalty for Violation of PCAOB Standards.")

BOARD OF DIRECTORS ACTIVITIES

Boards of directors, especially those directors that sit on the **audit committee,** are charged with establishing oversight mechanisms for financial reporting. In several of the major scandals that occurred in 2001–2002, many board members were identified that did not exercise their responsibilities. In many cases, audit committee members were not independent of management and that created a conflict of interest.

Section 202 of the Sarbanes-Oxley Act imposes significant new responsibilities on audit committees. All audit services must be preapproved by corporate management and the company's audit committee. Section 201 makes it unlawful for accounting firms that audit public companies simultaneously to provide the company with a variety of nonaudit services: bookkeeping, information systems design and implementation, fairness opinions, management or human resource functions, legal services, and expert services unrelated to the audit.

Section 301 provides that the audit committee shall be directly responsible for the appointment, compensation, and oversight of

DELOITTE SLAMMED WITH $1 MILLION PENALTY FOR VIOLATION OF PCAOB STANDARDS

Deloitte was fined $1 million for allowing an auditor whose competency was questioned to continue leading the auditing team of a pharmaceutical company for a four-year period. Involved was an auditing standard which Deloitte's executives noticed was irregular. The PCAOB found fault with the auditing procedure during the previous years' review but Deloitte issued a clean report indicating that the company's accounting had conformed to the GAAP standards. However, in mid-2005, the pharmaceutical company announced that it had to restate nearly three years' worth of financials, estimating downward $59 million less than it had previously reported. Deloitte admitted it kept the auditor on too long but attributed it to poor communication. It has since corrected the problem.

Source : Sarah Johnson, "PCAOB Fines Deloitte $1 Million," *CFO.com,* December 10, 2007, http://www.cfo.com/article.cfm/10277538?f=related.

the work of any accounting firm employed by the issuer. The auditors must report to the audit committee all critical accounting policies and practices, all alternative treatments of financial information within GAAP, the ramifications of such alternative procedures, and all significant conversations between management and the accounting firm.

Perhaps the best known and most controversial provisions of Sarbanes-Oxley are the new rules that require the CEO and CFO of each public company to certify that he or she has reviewed each quarterly or annual report filed with the SEC and that to his or her knowledge the report does not contain any material false statements or omissions and fairly represents, in all material respects, the financial condition and results of the operations of the company for the period being reported. Knowingly false certifications may be punishable by fines up to $1 million and imprisonment not exceeding 10 years.

THE ROLE OF ATTORNEYS UNDER THE SARBANES-OXLEY ACT

Attorneys appearing and practicing before the SEC in the representation of issuers are covered by the reporting requirements of Sarbanes-Oxley. Any company registering securities with the SEC and any company required to file reports or a registration statement by the SEC is an issuer. An attorney who practices before the SEC includes any attorney transacting business or corresponding with the SEC, representing issuers, providing advice on securities law or SEC rules and regulations regarding documents to be filed with the SEC, and any attorney advising issuers as to whether any document must be filed with the SEC.

The attorney's duty to report is triggered whenever there is credible evidence that a material violation has occurred, is ongoing, or is about to occur. Any material violation of federal or state securities law, breaches of fiduciary duty arising under federal or state law, or similar violations of any U.S. federal or state law triggers an attorney's duty to report.

An attorney has the duty to "report up" any evidence of material violation by an issuer, its officer, director, employee or agent. To **report up** means the report has to be made to a chief legal officer or qualified legal compliance committee.

Many states permit withdrawal by an attorney when the highest authority of the corporation insists on a criminal action that will substantially injure the corporation. This is called **reporting out.**

OTHER KEY PROVISIONS OF SARBANES-OXLEY

There are other provisions of Sarbanes-Oxley—both criminal and civil. Section 302 of the Act mandates a set of internal procedures to ensure accurate financial disclosure. First, Section 302 mandates **signing officers** to certify that they have established and maintain internal controls to ensure that material information relating to the company is made known to the signing officers. Second, **external auditors** are required to state whether effective internal control over financial reporting was maintained in all material respects by management.

The most contentious aspect of SOX is Section 404. This section requires management and the external auditor to report on the adequacy of the company's internal control over financial reporting. Documenting and testing important financial manual and automated controls requires tremendous effort and expense for the company to ensure. Section 404 requires management to produce an internal control report as part of each SEC report that their internal controls are working. Of course, expensive or not, investors would think it only makes sense that, given the extensive corporate financial fiascoes of late, such a provision would be a given.

On the criminal side, Section 802 makes it a crime to alter, falsify, or destroy any record with an attempt to impede an investigation. Section 1107 makes it a criminal

SARBANES-OXLEY REQUIRES PLANNING BEFORE DOCUMENTS ARE DESTROYED

Both private and public companies must comply with Sarbanes-Oxley's requirements for destroying documents. Otherwise, companies run the risk of prosecution and criminal penalties for destruction of evidence or obstruction of justice regarding any actual or contemplated federal investigation.

The law requires that every company, public or private, have "litigation holds" so that routine purges of information are suspended when litigation is contemplated. The problem is a company does not always know when the government is contemplating an investigation. Pre–Sarbanes-Oxley, companies were not as aware of the triggers for litigation holds. Sections 802 and 1102 were enacted partly in response to the Enron/Arthur Andersen collapse and since their enactment companies have some, but not enough, guidance as to when routine purges become document destruction in violation of the Act. Both statutes require "intent to impair, impede, instruct, or influence" a matter, but there has been little case law to determine what that means. For heavily regulated industries, such as the securities industry, Sections 802 and 1102 "holds" can be perilous waters to navigate.

Source : Robert D. Brownstone, "Ignore Sarbanes-Oxley at Your Peril," *The National Law Journal,* March 20, 2008, http://www.law.com/jsp/legaltechnology/pubArticleLT.jsp?id=1205923895814.

offense to retaliate against any person who provides any truthful information relating to any crime committed under the Act. (See Reality Check 13-11, "Sarbanes-Oxley Requires Planning before Documents Are Destroyed.")

CRITICISM OF THE SARBANES-OXLEY ACT

L08

Some critics of the Act state it places an unnecessary burden on U.S. companies to comply with the Act and this burden places U.S. companies at a competitive disadvantage with foreign companies. As proof, they point to the de-listing of companies with the New York Stock Exchange within the first year of enforcement of SOX according to a study conducted by the Wharton Business School.

Others criticize the cost of compliance. According to one survey, Sarbanes-Oxley cost Fortune 500 companies an average of $5.1 million in compliance expenses in 2004, while another survey found that the Act increased costs of a publicly held company by 130 percent.[7]

Other criticism states that international business is listing on foreign exchanges instead of the NYSE[8] and that IPOs have dried up because of the cost issues of complying with SOX.[9]

In spite of the criticism, SOX seems here to stay. Although the SEC has fine-tuned it somewhat, especially regarding adjusting the filing requirements for small companies, most critics have stopped calling for its repeal.

L07

State Securities Laws

In addition to the federal laws regulating the sale of securities, the states have their own laws regulating such sales within the state. They are known as **blue sky laws**.[10] These statutes all have provisions prohibiting fraud in the sale of securities. A number of states also require the registration of securities, while some states regulate brokers and dealers.

Each state has a regulatory agency that administers the law, generally known as the state Securities Commissioner. Even though antifraud provisions are most often brought by the SEC and various SROs, states also have the power to bring actions

---

[7]Ron Paul, "Repeal Sarbanes-Oxley!" before the House of Representatives, April 14, 2005, http://www.house.gov/paul/congrec/congrec2005/cr041405.htm.

[8]Joseph D. Piotroski and Suraj Srinivasan, "Regulation and Bonding: The Sarbanes-Oxley Act and the Flow of International Listings," SSRN, January 2008, http://ssrn.com/abstract=956987.

[9]Newt Gingrich and David Kralik, "Repeal Sarbanes-Oxley," November 5, 2008, http:// www.sfgate.com/cgi-bin/article.cgi?f=/c/a/2008/11/05/ED2813T8O9.DTL.

[10]The phrase was coined by U.S. Supreme Court Justice McKenna in *Hall v. Geiger-Jones,* 242 U.S. 539 (1917), in which he referred to evil "speculative schemes which have no more basis than so many feet of blue sky."

against securities violators pursuant to state law. Each state has its own security act, or blue sky law, which regulates the offer and sale of securities, registration and reporting requirements for broker-dealers and individual stock brokers doing business in the state, and investment advisors seeking to offer their investment advice and services in the state. Federal law preempts many state laws; however, there are notice and filing requirements in each state with which companies must comply before selling securities in the state.

Accountability for Actions: Ethical Responsibility

One of the most controversial parts of the Sarbanes-Oxley Act was Section 404 which requires the attorney to "report up" if he or she suspects the company is violating federal or state laws. When it was first proposed, attorneys viewed it to be in direct conflict with the attorney's oath to maintain a client's confidence. If an attorney had to report suspected activity to the SEC, which was the first proposal, what about a lawyer's duty to his client? The compromise was to report "up" or "out" if the client would not cease the activity or do something about it. But a lawyer who undertakes a withdrawal signals that there is something amiss that might give authorities reason to begin an investigation, even if there was not one already under way. Do you see this as a conflict of a lawyer's obligation to his client? Do you think that either reporting up or out violates a lawyer's oath of confidence? What do you think the impact would be on the relationship between companies and their attorneys?

Summary

Investing someone's hard-earned money is serious business, both for the company that needs the money as well as the investor who is trying to make a profit. There is no question that the securities industry has benefited from regulation. Although there have been fluctuations in the stock market since the 1929 crash, including the financial instability of the markets that occurred in 2008–2009, none have been as bad as that notorious episode in American financial history. The regulatory system that Congress has crafted and continues to fine-tune seems to have responded to the investor's need for security.

However, many of the financial crises of the 21st century seem to be born from greed, not predictable financial fluctuations. Or maybe it is the inventive financier who saw a big payday in the hedge fund and mortgage bundling markets. Either way, some have posited that the law's ability to regulate the market has come to an end, or close to it.

Securities, whether the old-fashioned kind or new ones, still have to be regulated. The Securities Exchange Commission, while not able to stop every swindler, has done a laudable job in managing to keep the American economy bright. Legislating morality is not within its scope.

Both the Securities Act of 1933 and the Securities Exchange Act of 1934 have used full disclosure as their foundation. Knowledge of the market should be the best regulator of who invests and who does not and what they invest in. Whether an investor is willing to invest in a little or a lot, the best gauge is information about the company. To that end, the rules and regulations, whether they be filing requirements, reporting requirements, or enforcement provisions, all attempt to provide the investor with what he or she needs to know to invest wisely, or not at all. Additional laws that Congress may enact should be designed to shine a brighter light on the market.

Review Questions

1. Francesca is a director and vice president of AB Software, Inc., whose common stock is listed on the NY Stock Exchange. Francesca engaged in the following transactions involving her company stock: on Jan. 1st she sold 500 shares of stock; on Jan. 15th she bought 300 shares of stock; on Feb. 1st she sold 200 shares of stock; on March 1st she bought 100 shares of stock. The SEC alleges that Francesca is guilty of violating the SEC Act of 1934. What specifically would she be guilty of doing? LO5

2. Inventco, Inc., had applied for a patent for one of its inventions and learned that it was going to be issued. Inventco suspected that its stock would increase once the patent was announced. Elaine, the president's secretary, overheard his conversation with the company attorney and called her husband telling him about the impending stock increase. Her husband, hearing of an opportunity to make some money, purchased as much of the company's stock as possible. As anticipated, the stock increased and Elaine and her husband made a considerable sum on their purchase. What violation occurred and how would they be prosecuted for it? LO5

3. Assume the same facts as above, only rather than Elaine's husband acting on the information, it was the lawyer who worked on the patent. Under what theory would she be prosecuted? LO5

4. Nova, Inc., sought to issue new stock but included false and misleading information in its registration statement and the prospectus. Coleman purchased shares when they were issued at $6.00 per share. When the false and misleading information became public, the shares fell to $1.00 per share. What violations occurred here? LO5

5. The accounting firm of Cane and Co. was hired to perform an audit on Prestige Foods. During the course of its audit Cane and Co. discovered that the inventory of the company was overvalued. When Cane and Co. approached Prestige Foods' president about the improper valuation, he became enraged and told Cane and Co. that if they did not accept the valuation, they would not be paid. Cane and Co. are thinking about not reporting the problem on their audit report. Discuss the implications of not reporting what Cane has learned about Prestige Foods.

6. Assume the same facts as above. Cane and Co. completed their audit using Prestige Foods' overvalued inventory numbers. Leslie, Prestige Foods' attorney, learned of this and has reported up to the Board of Directors who, led by the president, have refused to do anything. What is Leslie's option? LO6

7. Gant Enterprises has filed its annual report with its shareholders. One of its major subsidiaries is located in Bolivia. In its annual report, Gant states that if the political climate in Bolivia stabilizes, it expects that its profits will exceed the previous year by at least 20 percent. The truth is, Gant knows the political climate is about to destabilize, and it is making arrangements to sell its subsidiary to a local producer. Is Gant's statement protected under the forward looking statement safe harbor rule? Why or why not? LO4

8. Ethics Question: In *Virginia Bankshares v. Sandberg,*[11] the corporation, in contemplation of a merger that had already been approved by a majority of its shareholders, solicited for proxies (votes) from the minority shareholders. Clearly, the minority votes were not needed to approve the merger. The proxy solicitation contained false and misleading statements and the minority shareholders brought suit, alleging proxy violations. The Supreme Court held that since the minority shareholders could not affect the vote, there was no "causal necessity" between the statements and the actions of the minority shareholders. In other words, the minority voters could not have had an effect on the outcome of the vote, because there were already enough votes to approve of it. What, then, was the purpose of the proxy solicitation? The purpose was to get them to buy into the merger and forego their right to formally protest it. A merger that occurs without protest by its shareholders is favored over a merger that has shareholders who are protesting the merger.

   The rule makes clear that false and misleading statements are actionable. Do you think corporations who mislead their shareholders, even if their votes are not needed, should have their conduct condoned? LO8

---

[11]501 U.S. 1083 (1991).

Ethics Issue

Prior to Sarbanes-Oxley, auditing companies had engaged in nonauditing functions with the corporations they audited. Although this had been cause for concern by the SEC, rules were not promulgated until mandated by Sarbanes-Oxley. Now, auditing companies are forbidden to perform nonauditing services simultaneously with auditing services. Auditing companies must now contract with the audit committee of the corporation they propose to audit, rather than with the management of the corporation, as had been the practice before. The Act also made the audit committee directly responsible for the appointment, compensation, and oversight of any work done by the auditors. Do you think this will change the nature of how an audit is done? Do you think it will prevent the auditors from engaging in practices that could undermine the intent of Sarbanes-Oxley? Do you think the added layer of requiring the CEO and CFO to certify the work of the auditing committee helps to bring back the balance that was lost by commingling accounting practices and auditing practices?

Group Exercise

Choose your favorite clothing, music, car, food, or other company and see what public information you can find from SEC filings. Any surprises? Did you find anything that makes you uncomfortable? Anything missing that you would want to know?

Key Terms

accredited investors 318

annual report 325

audit committee 328

board of directors 328

blue sky laws 330

debt securities 315

equity security 315

exempt securities 318

external auditors 329

Financial Industry Regulatory Authority (FINRA) 320

forward looking statements 325

initial public offering (IPO) 317

insider 322

issuer 316

Management's Discussion and Analysis (MD&A) 325

material statement 321

misappropriation 322

Municipal Securities Rulemaking Board (MSRB) 320

negotiable instrument 315

noncertificated stock 316

nonregistered 316

ponzi scheme 314

prospectus 317

proxy solicitation 324

proxy statement 324

Public Company Accounting Oversight Board (PCAOB) 327

red herring prospectus 318

registered stock 316

registration statement 317

reporting out 329

report up 329

Rule 10b-5 321

safe harbor rule 325

Sarbanes-Oxley Act of 2002 326

security 315

Securities Act of 1933 316

Securities Exchange Commission 313

self-regulatory organizations (SRO) 320

shares 315

short swing profits 323

signing officers 329

stock 315

stock certificate 316

stock market 312

tippee 322

tombstone ad 318

underwriter 317

Antitrust and Trade Regulation

Learning Objectives

After reading this chapter, you should be able to:

LO1   Describe the federal regulation of antitrust law

LO2   Discuss the importance of the Sherman Antitrust Act

LO3   Explain the state antitrust enforcement system

LO4   Describe the difference between per se and rule of reason approaches

LO5   Discuss the different antitrust violations

LO6   Describe the special problems with antitrust enforcement of groups

LO7   Describe monopolistic behavior

LO8   Discuss mergers and acquisition antitrust laws

LO9   Explain the impact on the U.S. of international antitrust laws

 ## Opening Scenario

Apple Inc. has one of the largest computer operations in the world. It designs and manufactures consumer electronics and computer software products, including the MacIntosh (Mac) computer, and the i-products, including the iPhone, iTouch, and iPod. Its software includes the Mac OS X operating system, the iTunes media browser, the iLife multimedia suite, the iWork software, Final Cut Studio, a suite of professional audio and film industry software products, and Logic Studio, a suite of audio tools.[1]

In October 2001, Apple introduced the iPod, a digital music player. Other versions of the iPod followed, giving users a wide range of choices. The iPod is the largest selling media player.

During the Macworld Expo in January 2007, Steve Jobs announced the iPhone. In July 2008, Apple launched the App Store to sell applications for the iPhone and iTouch. Within a month, the App Store sold 60 million applications and brought in $1 million per day. On April 24, 2009, the App Store surpassed 1 billion downloads.[2]

Although Apple's market share has grown, it still lags far behind its competitor Microsoft, with only about 8 percent of desktops and laptops in the U.S.[3] It wants to change that, and is coming up with ideas as to how to capture a greater percentage of the market. Some ideas are to slash the prices of its computers below manufacturing costs to entice buyers from

---

[1]See www.apple.com.

[2]http://www.apple.com/pr/library/2009/04/24appstore.html.

[3]http://www.nytimes.com/2009/08/30/business/media/30ad.html?em.

Microsoft, match Microsoft's prices for personal computers, seek an agreement with Apple retailers on a maximum price for the computers, get Microsoft to agree not to sell in certain areas in exchange for giving over other territory to Microsoft exclusively, offer incentives to suppliers of both Microsoft and Apple not to deal with Microsoft, and the best idea of all, require purchasers of iPhones to purchase a Mac computer in order to have a complete product. That will surely boost the sales of the Mac computers. Finally, the suggestion is to merge with Microsoft, so that the competition would be eliminated but the value of Apple and Microsoft combined would allow innovation and development of new models.

The CEO of Apple asks the legal department for their advice on these suggestions. You are the antitrust guru for the firm. What do you tell her about her ideas? (Note: While the facts stated herein are true (see footnotes), this scenario is fiction and used only as a pedagogical tool for this chapter.)

Introduction

When you endeavor to place your goods or services into the stream of commerce, law demands that you be held liable for them. This chapter focuses on one type of liability which can potentially affect your business: liability for trade practices, otherwise known as **antitrust.**

Business cannot start up and operate in a vacuum. When a business enters into a market, there are generally others there with similar goods or services. Chances are the business entered the market with the idea or intent of doing a better job in the market than those already there. In firms' trying to gain a competitive advantage, our capitalist system is based on the idea that the market will determine the winner. Those with better goods or services will beat out others and rise to the top. However, in gaining that competitive advantage, goods or services must not unfairly compete with other like goods or services, or a business will run afoul of the antitrust laws. Failure to comply with these antitrust laws and regulations can result in liability for the business and decreased competition for consumers, leading to higher prices and less quality. That, Congress does not want. That is why we have laws to insure that competition remains free, fair and open.

The heart of the American system of economics is its **capitalist** approach to business. The basic guiding principal is that the market of goods and services should remain free and open to all who care to enter. Under this theory, those who deliver shoddy goods or services will fall by the wayside, and the market will thus regulate itself. This, in turn, inures to the benefit of the consumer because as long as they have a choice and can use personal preference, quality, price and service to determine their buying decisions, those who must compete for their business will have no choice but to keep up with their competitors or fall by the wayside. To that end, our system regulates the production and marketing of goods so that those markets stay open and free to whoever wishes to compete. Antitrust is the area of law which keeps the market open by regulating business activities. In this chapter, we look at laws that regulate competition between U.S. businesses. These are the laws that the legal department of the Apple Corp. will have to consult to evaluate the suggested measures to gain a larger market share of the computer industry.

Earlier in this text you were introduced to white collar crimes and some of the statutory law making certain business practices illegal. Many of the white collar crimes involve marketing practices. Marketing involves many factors such as the pricing, packaging, promotion, and placement (distribution) of goods and services. Each of these factors is regulated by common law, statutory law, or administrative rules and regulations. The thrust of the laws is to make sure businesses do not act in ways which will suppress competition, inhibit free trade, and ultimately harm the consumer. These are some of the considerations to be held in mind in evaluating the suggestions for Apple in our opening scenario.

Suppression of free trade could include, for instance, a business buying or merging with all of its competition so that consumers no longer have a choice. Lack of choice means the business would be able to charge whatever it wants or provide shoddy services. A merger of Microsoft and Apple, while producing innovative products, might also allow the merged company to raise prices because the competition between them is eliminated. Harmful also to free markets could be competing businesses getting together to agree on what prices they will charge so that they are no longer really competing with each other. There are other prohibited practices. Knowledge of the antitrust laws ensures that your business stays within the law as you market your product and the consumer benefits as you do so.

Federal Regulation of Antitrust

As you examine the federal antitrust acts, keep in mind that this area of the law is constantly evolving. Just as the economy is not static, neither is business. New forms of business may emerge, and new relationships may offer different ways of doing business. Whether these new ideas are threatening to the market, and how threatening they are, are often not agreed upon by the economists, the government, or the courts. Also, as economists and the government learn about how markets function and what restrains competition in the marketplace, different measures are used to determine the competitive outcomes. Thus, a practice that was once viewed as inherently anticompetitive may now be viewed as not so much so, or only so when accompanied by other behavior. This tension should be kept in mind when judging the effects of competitive behavior in the U.S. marketplace. Reality Check 14-1, "The Antitrust Modernization Commission," discusses the periodic updating of the antitrust laws that Congress authorizes to ensure that the laws don't become antiquated or lose their purpose to protect competition.

REALITY CHECK 14-1

THE ANTITRUST MODERNIZATION COMMISSION

In 2002 Congress authorized the Antitrust Modernization Commission whose purpose was to undertake a comprehensive review of the U.S. antitrust laws to determine whether they should be modified. In April 2007, the Commission rendered its finding in the Antitrust Modernization Commission Report and Recommendations.

The Commission recommended that the Sherman and Clayton Acts remain intact. They did, however, make several recommendations that would improve mergers, focusing on efficiency and enforcement studies. The Commission also recommended that in cases where there is dual jurisdiction between the FTC and DOJ, that Congress authorize some mechanism for them to work together.

Not surprisingly, the Commission recommended the repeal of the Robinson-Patman Act as an arcane remnant of the depression-era mentality. This was not new. Three earlier commission reports had recommended the same thing.

It remains to be seen whether and to what extent Congress will move to implement the recommended changes. Some of the recommendations have been implemented, and some were done in anticipation of the report. The Commission pointed out, however, that the overall structure of antitrust law in this country was based on sound principles that are still applicable today.

Source: The Antitrust Modernization Commission Report and Recommendations, April 2007, http://govinfo.library.unt.edu/amc/report_recommendation/letter_to_president.pdf.

The Sherman Antitrust Act

LO2

Antitrust law began to develop in 1890 with the passage of the Sherman Antitrust Act. The Act was passed after a growth period in our economy which led to cutthroat competition and the formation of holding companies, trusts, and monopolies which restrained free competition. A monopoly would be the danger in the merged computer companies mentioned in the opening scenario. The provisions of the Sherman Antitrust Act are enforced by the Antitrust Division of the Department of Justice. Take Away 14-1, "The Sherman Antitrust Act," gives the pertinent parts of the Act. It also allows you to focus on the difference between §1 and §2.

Section 1 of the Act prohibits contracts, combinations, or conspiracies in **restraint of trade** or commerce and focuses on agreements made to restrain trade. This language clearly requires at least two participants. Section 2 of the Act prohibits monopolizing or the attempt to monopolize. This section can be applied to a lone participant and focuses on the creation or misuse of monopoly power through wrongful exclusionary means. These prohibitions might be implicated in Apple's evaluating some of the suggestions made in the opening scenario.

As the federal statute is written, every "restraint of trade" is illegal. In the early court interpretation of §1 courts used a literal interpretation of this section. It soon became clear to the courts that a literal interpretation would hinder commerce, in that every agreement has the potential to restrain trade in some form, even those that were legal under the common law such as partnerships or the formation of corporations. In the landmark case involving the *Standard Oil Company*[4] the U.S. Supreme Court announced that §1 of the Sherman Act did not prohibit all trade restraints, but only outlawed **unreasonable restraints of trade.** That is, restraints of trade are not in and of themselves illegal, but will only be deemed so if they meet certain requirements. This **rule of reason,** as it is known, requires a two-step analysis. First, there must be proof of a contract, combination, or conspiracy, and secondly, the combination must be found to be unreasonable under the circumstances, and therefore illegal. *Standard Oil* has stood the test of time and the rule of reason articulated by the court in its 1911 decision has become one of antitrust's basic measurement tools. It would have to be determined by Apple's legal department whether any of the ideas for improving market share suggested in the opening scenario would be subject to this approach.

In contrast to the rule of reason approach, courts can use a *per se approach* to antitrust analysis. Both approaches are examined later in this chapter.

The Sherman Act provides powerful remedies. It punishes trade restraints and monopolization as crimes, with responsibility imposed on natural persons and corporate persons. The Act makes equity's broad powers available to enjoin specific behavior, to dismantle monopoly positions acquired or sustained lawfully, and otherwise to service antitrust policy. Private parties who are successful are entitled to **treble damages,** making the legal risks

TAKE AWAY 14-1

THE SHERMAN ANTITRUST ACT

Section 1. Trusts, etc., in restraint of trade illegal; penalty

Every contract, combination in the form of trust or otherwise, or conspiracy, in restraint of trade or commerce among the several States, or with foreign nations, is declared to be illegal. [Violators] . . . shall be deemed guilty of a felony, [punishable by fine and/or imprisonment].

Section 2. Monopolizing trade a felony; penalty

Every person who shall monopolize, or attempt to monopolize, or combine or conspire with any other person or persons, to monopolize any part of the trade or commerce among the several States, or with foreign nations, shall be deemed guilty of a felony, . . . [punishable by fine and/or imprisonment].

Source: 15 U.S.C. §§1–2.

---

[4]*Standard Oil Company v. U.S.,* 221 U.S. 1 (1911).

TAKE AWAY 14-2

THE CLAYTON ACT

No person engaged in commerce or in any activity affecting commerce shall acquire, directly or indirectly, the whole or any part of the stock . . . , [if] the effect of such acquisition may be substantially to lessen competition, or to tend to create a monopoly.

Source: 15 U.S.C. §18.

very significant. This provision alone would give any legal department pause in implementing any conduct that could potentially create §1 or §2 liability.

The Clayton Act

After the *Standard Oil* decision, opponents of the rule of reason approach lobbied for more precise guidelines that business could use to determine when the business was violating the antitrust laws. Congress enacted the Clayton Act in 1914[5] to address the problems left open by the Sherman Act. The Clayton Act declared four practices unlawful but not criminal: (1) price discrimination—selling a product at different prices to similarly situated buyers; (2) exclusive dealing contracts including tie-ins—sales on condition that the buyer stop dealing with the seller's competitors; (3) corporate mergers—acquisitions of competing companies; and (4) interlocking directorates—common board members among competing companies. See Take Away 14-2, "The Clayton Act," for the text of this statute. Along with the Department of Justice, the Federal Trade Commission shares enforcement of the Clayton Act. It sounds like an unlawful tie-in might characterize one of the suggestions in the opening scenario about improving market share for Apple. We'll look more closely at that when we examine the requirements for tying.

The courts' interpretation of the reach of the Clayton Act limited the Congressional intent of the act. For example, courts initially ruled that §2 of the Act did not reach competition between rival buyers.[6] By the time the Court decided it did reach competition between buyers in 1929,[7] chain stores, Congress's biggest worry at the time, had taken over and begun running small businesses out of the market because of their ability to mass purchase at cheaper prices. Congress decided to act once again.

TAKE AWAY 14-3

THE ROBINSON-PATMAN ACT

§13. Discrimination in price, services, or facilities

a. Price; selection of customers

It shall be unlawful for any person engaged in commerce, . . . either directly or indirectly, to discriminate in price between different purchasers of commodities of like grade and quality, . . . where the effect of such discrimination may be substantially to lessen competition or tend to create a monopoly in any line of commerce, or to injure, destroy, or prevent competition with any person . . .

Source: 15 U.S.C. 13(a).

The Robinson-Patman Act

The Robinson-Patman Act was enacted in 1936 to amend §2 of the Clayton Act. See Take Away 14-3, "The Robinson-Patman Act," for text of the act. It applies only to sales of commodities of like grade and quality in commerce. Congress's concern was the small Mom-and-Pop stores who were being run out of business by the buying power of the chain stores and the inability of the Clayton Act to effectively abate this practice. The Act barred price discrimination unless it was supported by cost savings or was proved necessary to meet a competitor's price offer. Section 2 of the Act was enforceable against unjustified discounts offered to buyers for the sole purpose of running other suppliers out of the market.

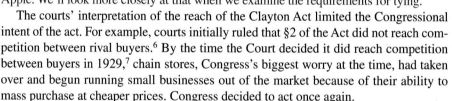

---

[5]15 U.S.C.A. §§12–27.

[6]*National Biscuit Co. v. FTC,* 299 F. 733 (2d Cir. 1924).

[7]*George Van Camp & Sons v. American Can Co.,* 278 U.S. 245 (1929).

ANTITRUST STATUTES

Statute	Conduct Prohibited	Enforcement Agency
Sherman Act §1	Unreasonable restraints of trade	DOJ
Sherman Act §2	Monopolization or attempts to monopolize	DOJ
Clayton Act	Price discrimination, exclusive dealing contracts, corporate mergers, interlocking directorates	DOJ and FTC
Robinson-Patman Act	Discrimination in price, services, or facilities	DOJ and FTC
Federal Trade Commission	Unfair or deceptive practices	FTC

The Federal Trade Commission Act

Section 5 of the Federal Trade Commission Act (FTC) of 1914 (amended in 1938 and 1975) provides that "unfair methods of competition in or affecting commerce and unfair or deceptive acts or practices in or affecting commerce are hereby declared unlawful."[8] The Act provides no criminal penalties and limits the FTC to equitable remedies. Section 5 is a catch-all provision which has been construed to include all the prohibitions of the other antitrust laws and is used to fill loopholes in the more explicit statutes. This means that in our opening scenario about the challenge confronting Apple even conduct that doesn't specifically violate one of the federal acts might be challenged by the FTC as being anticompetitive.

EXAMPLE

Congress also created the Federal Trade Commission to enforce antitrust violations and to improve and develop antitrust policy. To help with establishing this policy, the FTC was staffed with personnel from a variety of disciplines, including accounting, economics, and law. As with other agencies, the FTC has broad investigative powers and uses the agency's administrative adjudication process, subject to court review, to resolve conflicts. It has no criminal jurisdiction; rather, it is subject to civil jurisdiction and to issuing equitable decrees only. See Take Away 14-4, "Antitrust Statutes."

State Antitrust Efforts

L03

Before the enactment of the federal Sherman Act, at least 26 states had laws governing competition within the state.[9] Although the laws that were enacted were inconsistent with each other they all served the same purpose, and that was to preserve the balance of power between the citizens of the state.

---

[8]15 U.S.C.A. §45.

[9]David Millon, "The First Antitrust Statutes," *Washburn Law Journal* 29 (1990), p. 141.

In the period since the enactment of federal legislation, state laws have continued to have an effect on antitrust activity within the states. States continue to permit indirect suits on behalf of aggrieved citizens who are impacted by antitrust violations. These actions are generally orchestrated by the National Association of Attorneys General (NAAG), an organization formed in 1907. In 1983, NAAG formed the Multistate Antitrust Task Force. This task force has engaged in activity to bring about a uniform approach to antitrust law in the states and to pursue federal cases in which there is a strong state interest. NAAG has published guidelines designed to assist states in developing uniform laws and procedures by which antitrust laws can be enforced nationwide, but through state activity. Even if the federal government does not object to one of the activities contemplated in our opening scenario, the state attorneys general may bring an action if they think the measures taken by Apple are anticompetitive.

State attorneys general are also free to litigate on behalf of their state citizens individually. For example, in conjunction with the federal monopoly case filed against Microsoft, 20 state attorneys general filed the same action on behalf of their states. In the consolidated action, the states that participated in the settlement agreement reached in the Microsoft case are part of the monitoring of Microsoft's compliance with its obligations under the settlement.

Antitrust Violations: Per Se or Rule of Reason Approach?

When conduct is alleged to be anticompetitive, a court has two ways in which it can measure the anticompetitive effects of that conduct: the per se approach and the rule of reason approach. The rule of reason approach requires courts to look at the specific activity that is alleged to be anticompetitive and determine whether it unreasonably restrains trade or whether the behavior is monopolistic. The court does not presume that the behavior is or is not unreasonable; rather, it makes that determination only after examining the effects of the behavior on the particular market.

Not all restrictive conduct is inherently anticompetitive. Conduct that the court has not previously categorized as per se illegal, or conduct that the court has not had much experience in evaluating, is generally treated on a case-by-case basis. The court will scrutinize the conduct, its purpose, and its effect on the market before determining whether it is unreasonable.

There are a few activities, however, that if proven, are held by courts to be *inherently* unreasonable. These are known as **per se violations.** Per se means "in and of itself." Thus, if an act is a per se violation, it is inherently unreasonable and proof of the prohibited activity is proof of the guilt. Per se treatment of activities is appropriate because courts in the past have determined that if the business engages in the behavior, it will unreasonably restrain trade. In other words, there is nothing that is beneficial to the market that this conduct has to offer. No further inquiry is needed to determine the reasonableness of the restraint or its competitive effect. The per se analysis is a conclusive presumption of illegality.

An example is illustrative. Suppose two competitors engage in price fixing. A court reviewing that conduct will hold the price fixing agreement to be a per se violation of the antitrust laws. Price fixing agreements always have the effect of restricting competition in a harmful way. On the other hand, suppose a cement company wishes to expand its production capacity by purchasing its supplier of sand. If the cement company purchases the sand supplier, it might negatively affect the other cement companies who can no longer purchase sand from the purchased company. But does this per se violate

GOOGLE—SO BIG IT HAS NO PLACE TO HIDE

Google started out wanting to be the world's information index—a place where everyone could go to get all their questions answered. It achieved major success with its search engine, and has branched out into other avenues, but not without drawing attention to itself. It seems that everything Google does now brings scrutiny from the government. In 2007, Google canceled its plans to enter into a long-term contract with Yahoo when the DOJ raised concerns about it. Rather than continue under the government's scrutiny, it chose to forgo the deal.

Now Google has again drawn attention to itself with its plans to put all out-of-print books on its website and enter the retail market for these books. To accomplish this, Google has made a deal with publishers and other rights holders to allow the books to be scanned and made available.

Because of the small profit margin available for this type of endeavor, all other competitors have dropped out of this market, leaving Google and its resources to capitalize on the opportunity.

But not so fast. This activity has captured the attention, once again, of the DOJ, which is now looking into the settlement Google reached with the publishers and rights holders. Even librarians, who are parties to the settlement, are raising questions about Google's possible monopoly power and suggesting perhaps the DOJ put Google under a long-term monitoring plan to make sure that doesn't happen.

Clearly, Google would like to fly under the government radar, but at this point it's like the 8000-pound elephant in the room. How do you do anything without drawing attention to yourself?

Source: John Timmer, "Google's Diversity Causing It Antitrust Trouble," *ars technica,* May 11, 2008, http://arstechnica.com/business/news/2009/05/googles-diversity-causing-it-antitrust-trouble.ars.

---

anticompetition laws? Probably not, but only by looking at the specific market in which these two companies operate will a court be able to tell. This kind of conduct, then, would be decided by using the rule of reason approach. There's nothing per se wrong with one company purchasing a supplier, if that purchase will allow the company to expand. However, in a particular market, it might damage the competition too much, or the company's motives might be to monopolize competition in cement, and thus be unreasonable.

After reviewing the specific antitrust violations discussed next, you should be able to determine whether there are any activities contemplated by Apple to increase its competitiveness in the market that may be evaluated under the per se approach. Reality Check 14-2, "Google—So Big It Has No Place to Hide," discusses the constant scrutiny mega-corporations like Google receive whenever they venture into businesses that increase their market power.

Courts determine whether an antitrust violation has occurred by looking at whether it involves a per se offense or one which requires the court to evaluate the offense under the rule of reason. Further, the courts look at whether the companies involved are horizontal to each other, meaning in competition with each other, or vertical to each other, meaning in a relationship of a supplier and its customer. For example, two grocery stores in the same market are horizontal competitors. A shoe manufacturer and a company that supplies leather to the shoe manufacturer are vertical competitors.

In determining whether an antitrust violation has occurred, then, courts look at whether the relationship is horizontal or vertical, and whether the behavior requires a per se or rule of reason analysis. **Horizontal per se violations** generally are looked at more stringently than vertical ones, and include price fixing, allocation of territory or customers, cartels, and group boycotts. **Vertical per se violations** include price fixing, tie-ins, and boycotts. There are a host of other behaviors for which the rule of reason is applied, including exclusive selling agreements, vertical territorial and customer allocations, and exclusive dealing contracts.

Antitrust Violations

Antitrust violations are not limited to any particular industry, nor are they limited to a particular behavior. New relationships are challenged all the time. There are a few categories of activity, however, that remain fairly constant among those that are challenged. The specific violations below name just a few of them, identify them as involving horizontal or vertical relationships, and further identifying them as being subject to per se or rule of reason approach by the courts.

Antitrust violations are measured by looking at the power a company has in a particular market. Markets are measured by two concepts: product market and geographic market. A **product market** is determined by looking at like products in a particular market—like products meaning those products that can be substituted for one another. An example of this would be food wrap—foil and plastic might be the same or like products if they are shown to be used interchangeably and thus be in the same product market. Another market is the **geographic market.** Some producers have nationwide markets, i.e., their products are sold everywhere in the U.S. Manufacturers such as Pillsbury, Kraft, and others with household names might qualify as having a nationwide geographic market. Other manufacturers might have a global geographic market, thus are seen to be in competition with manufacturers all over the world. Companies such as Microsoft, Sony, and Kodak might qualify as having a global geographic market. But most companies are smaller than those and operate in a much smaller geographic area. Think of your local movie theater, regional grocery chain, or other local company. Whether national, global, regional, or local, the ability to affect the market is measured within their geographic area.

HORIZONTAL PRICE FIXING

The most serious horizontal per se violation is **price fixing.** Price fixing is an agreement between two or more competitors to set prices. It is illegal for competitors to set prices whether the price set is high, low, fair, or reasonable to the consumer. It is simply illegal. The law applies to buyers and sellers alike, in large or small companies in all industries. Even if the agreement to fix prices is made to be able to meet the price of the large competitor in the market, price fixing is illegal per se.

One way to attain price fixing is to form a **cartel.** Cartels are prohibited under §1 of the Sherman Act. Cartels are most successful when there are just a few members in the cartel, the cartel can raise prices without affecting the consumer's buying habits, and the members of the cartel have no reason to stray outside of the agreement. The purpose of a cartel is to try to control prices through control of the output. For example, if a few manufacturers produce a product and compete with each other for sales, they are competing in the same market. However, if they form a cartel and agree to produce only so many of the products causing the product to be scarce, they can raise the price of the product and maximize the overall return. A tightly organized cartel, whatever the size, can have the same effect on prices as a monopoly.

Price fixing covers more than just naked agreements to fix prices. It also covers agreements that affect prices, even if it is not an agreement to set the price. For example, competitors cannot agree on a price range within which they will set their price, they cannot agree on a common list or book price that limits their ability to set the price, nor can they set the terms and conditions of sale which indirectly affects the price. Competitors cannot agree to limit the supply of a product to a market because that would affect the price as well. If one of the suggestions in the opening scenario implied that Apple and Microsoft would agree on the price of their computers, it would violate this section for sure. Apple should be careful in how it tries to secure the market share it desires.

The agreement need not be in writing and signed by the parties. In fact, there need not be a contract at all. What is required to be proved is that the agreement was made, directly or indirectly, to set prices or affect them. Whenever competitors conduct themselves in a way that would not otherwise be done by competitors, it might give rise to an inference that there is an agreement. If there are contacts between the competitors, there is an inference that can be drawn that an agreement was made.

The idea of finding the inference of an agreement by looking at parallel conduct was used successfully by plaintiffs in several lower courts and unsuccessfully in others. In 2007, the Supreme Court was asked to determine when inferring an agreement from parallel action between competitors, or **conscious parallelism,** was sufficient to infer an agreement between competitors.[10] The court held that "[a] statement of parallel conduct, even conduct consciously undertaken, needs some setting suggesting the agreement necessary to make out a §1 claim; without that further circumstance pointing toward a meeting of the minds, an account of defendant's commercial activity stays in neutral territory."[11] Since 2007, plaintiffs have been less successful when alleging only parallel conduct without evidence of the agreement. For example, in one case, the plaintiffs alleged only that Mastercard and Visa conspired with participating banks to fix transaction fees for retail transactions, but did not show any evidence of the conspiracy. The court dismissed the case.[12] In another example, the case was dismissed when the plaintiff could only allege parallel conduct in trying to prove a conspiracy to boycott him without evidence of an agreement to do so.[13] The court concluded that vague allegations, without more, could not be used to establish an agreement. In our continuing example, similar parallel pricing between Microsoft and Apple, absent more, would not violate the antitrust laws.

VERTICAL PRICE FIXING

Vertical price fixing agreements are those between a supplier and customer with respect to the price at which the customer will resell the products. As with horizontal price fixing agreements, it does not matter how reasonable the agreed-upon price may be or how good the reasons are for the agreement, such agreements are per se illegal.

To fall within the per se rule, there must be an agreement between the buyer (customer) and seller (supplier) that the buyer will resell at a specified price or price level. Unlike horizontal agreements, the per se rule does not apply to vertical agreements which merely affect prices. The crucial question is whether an agreement exists. A seller may properly *suggest* a resale price to its vendor; the fact that the suggested price is followed is not enough to show the presence of conspiracy. It is thus advisable for a manufacturer or other supplier, in mentioning resale price, to use the word "suggested" in order to make the intention clear. Now you know why the items you purchase have this notation on them! In our continuing example, depending on how the suggestion is worded between Apple and its distributors, there could be a violation here.

HORIZONTAL MARKET RESTRAINTS

An agreement among competitors to divide markets by territory is analyzed under the per se approach. This type of agreement may be to divide an area geographically or to divide among customers or products. The competitors usually argue that they can achieve efficient production by this allocation, but if the division were truly efficient then the economy would achieve the division naturally. This type of agreement has a greater effect than even price fixing, since the remaining competitor is free of competition in the given territory.

---

[10]*Bell Atlantic Corp. v. Twombly,* 127 S. Ct. 1955 (2007).

[11]*Id.* at 1966.

[12]518 F.3d 1042 (9th Cir. 2008).

[13]2008 U.S. App. LEXIS 25810 (6th Cir. 2008).

The *Toledo Mack Sales & Service v. Mack Trucks* case (Case 14.1) illustrates the territorial restrictions discussed in this section and the dangers they pose to competition and thus to consumers.

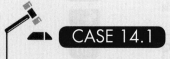

CASE 14.1 Toledo Mack Sales & Service, Inc. v. Mack Trucks, Inc.

530 F.3d 204 (3d Cir. 2008)

Facts: Mack manufactures heavy duty trucks and Toledo was one of its dealers. Mack has a nationwide network of authorized dealers, each of which is assigned an area. A dealer's area is not exclusive; Mack's policy is that dealers are free to sell anywhere. When a customer contacts a dealer to purchase a truck, the dealer can shop around for the lowest price from Mack, and that will determine the price he offers the customer. Dealers are permitted to bid against each other inside or outside their area.

Toledo produced evidence that although this was the stated policy of Mack, there was actually a series of agreements to the contrary. For example, to support allegation of a horizontal conspiracy between the managers at Mack, Toledo produced evidence of an agreement among Mack dealers not to compete outside of the assigned areas, producing notes which referenced a "gentlemen's agreement," conversations between two Mack salesmen about how things worked in New Jersey, and testimony from a former manager that there were unwritten agreements contrary to official policy. Toledo also introduced evidence in support of vertical conspiracy allegations that sales assistance would be withheld on out-of-area sales, recordings and notes of conversations referring to an informal policy, and proof that the unwritten policy was followed up to the time of trial. Toledo argued that this practice artificially inflated the price of the truck because although theoretically a dealer could seek the best price by going out of area, the agreement not to assist out-of-area sales prevented the best price from being obtained. Toledo argued this constituted a horizontal and vertical conspiracy in violation of §1 of the Sherman Act.

Issue: Whether Toledo produced sufficient evidence of a conspiracy to take the case to the jury.

Decision: Yes.

Reasoning: Section 1 of the Sherman Act prohibits "a conspiracy . . . in restraint of trade or commerce among the several States. . . ." Toledo's burden was to present evidence sufficient to allow a rational jury to conclude that Mack and its dealers committed overt acts in furtherance of an illegal conspiracy or conspiracies. . . . To avoid punishing lawful conduct, the Supreme Court has placed certain limits on the inferences that may be drawn from

the evidence in antitrust cases. The Court has explained that certain evidentiary restrictions are necessary in antitrust cases since "mistaken inferences . . . are especially costly because they chill the very conduct the antitrust laws are designed to protect." Therefore, "antitrust law limits the range of permissible inferences from ambiguous evidence in a §1 case. . . . [C]onduct as consistent with permissible competition as with illegal conspiracy does not, standing alone, support an inference of antitrust conspiracy." In addition, "if the factual context renders the plaintiff's claim implausible—if the claim is one that simply makes no economic sense—a plaintiff must come forward with more persuasive evidence to support its claim than would otherwise be necessary." Finally, "in evaluating whether a genuine issue for trial exists, the antitrust defendants' economic motive is highly relevant. If the defendants had no rational economic motive to conspire, and if their conduct is consistent with other, equally plausible explanations, the conduct does not give rise to an inference of conspiracy. Nevertheless, we have held that those limits on inferences do not apply to a plaintiff's direct evidence of an unlawful agreement under §1. In the present case, Toledo presented several pieces of direct evidence for the existence of one or more agreements among Mack dealers not to compete with each other. Because we conclude that Toledo's direct evidence is sufficient to allow a jury to conclude that a conspiracy not to compete existed among Mack dealers, we need not apply the rules restricting inferences drawn from circumstantial evidence.

CASE QUESTIONS

1. The court cited the rules of interpretation for inferring conspiracy through indirect evidence. The court ruled, however, that there was direct evidence here and thus the evidence was sufficient to go to trial. Why did the court discuss the inference limitations?

2. Why does the court require the plaintiff to have extra proof against actions that are ambiguous?

3. The court discussed horizontal and vertical conspiracy. Who was involved in the horizontal conspiracy, and who was involved in the vertical conspiracy?

EXAMPLE Proof of the agreement is required here also. However, indirect proof is permitted. In a case involving direct proof, in 2008, Dick's Sporting Goods Store was enjoined by the FTC from enforcing a territorial agreement with a Canadian sporting goods store in which they agreed that the Canadian store **EXAMPLE** would not enter the U.S. market.[14] Territorial restraints are especially scrutinized and draw the attention of the DOJ or FTC, so in our continuing example concerning Apple, they would need to be concerned with this, too.

VERTICAL MARKET RESTRAINTS

Marketing plans have often had arrangements whereby dealers agree to resell the product only within specified territories and to solicit business only from specified classes of customers. Such restraints are subject to the rule of reason; as long as the agreements are purely vertical and economically justified, they will not be found to be anticompetitive.

But what if the seller refuses to allow sales in a certain territory for other reasons? See Diversity in the Law 14-1, "How About Restricting Territory for Image Reasons?" to learn how Bally stopped allowing sales to stores in predominantly black and Asian territories because of image issues linked to race and ethnicity. Diversity in the Law 14-2, "Women Assisted by Organization in Antitrust Law," addresses the dearth of women in the antitrust legal field.

While most vertical customer and **territorial restrictions** have been sustained, if the seller has a significant market share, the practice can still be risky, and less restrictive methods of marketing should be considered.

HORIZONTAL BOYCOTTS

A **boycott,** or concerted refusal to deal, is an agreement between two or more competitors not to sell to or buy from an individual or company or group. Competitors boycott individuals or companies for a variety of reasons including to punish the individual or company or to advance their own interests. Regardless of the reason, the boycott restrains trade and impedes competition and is per se illegal. Apple suggesting this to the suppliers of Microsoft in our continuing example would certainly violate the antitrust laws.

For example, credit card holders alleged that the credit card companies conspired to insert mandatory arbitration clauses in credit card member agreements and engaged in a **group boycott** of customers who refused to sign the agreements. They alleged that beginning in 1998 or 1999, the companies held meetings and formed an Arbitration Coalition to recruit other credit card issuers into using arbitration clauses and over the next four years the Coalition shared plans for the adoption of arbitration clauses, which

---

DIVERSITY IN THE LAW 14-1

HOW ABOUT RESTRICTING TERRITORY FOR IMAGE REASONS?

We see that it is anticompetitive to conspire to split up territories to limit competition. But what if a supplier refuses to service certain territories based on race or ethnicity? Does that violate the antitrust law?

Swiss shoe manufacturer, Bally, in 1996, ordered its sales personnel to stop servicing stores in predominantly Asian and African American territories. During an age discrimination lawsuit by several of the sales personnel, it came to light that Bally did, indeed, tell the sales personnel to stop servicing such areas. Seems they had a shoe that, even at $175, was flying off the shelves in these areas. "Bally did not want to see its shoes on black or Asian feet," said Jim Tuohy, a former Midwest salesman. It ordered the sales people to stop servicing scores of stores in black and Asian areas across the country. In depositions, interviews and written documents, Bally did not deny this. Bally CEO Richard Wycherley said that Bally wasn't racist, just snobby. "We control the actual image of the brand," said Wycherley. "The function is to keep the brand clean. So we don't have distribution in unsatisfactory kinds of vendors. You don't see Ferragamo discounting their brands all over the place and selling them in locations in Harlem."

Bally's refusal to allow its products in certain territories is not illegal. It has the right to control its brand and only selling in certain territories is one way to accomplish this.

Source: Jim Dwyer, "Bally's Mean Feet No Shoes in Black Areas," *The Daily News*, November 17, 1996, http://www.nydailynews.com/archives/news/1996/11/17/1996-11-17_bally_s_mean_feet__no_shoes_.html.

---

[14]2008 FTC LEXIS 141 (FTC 2008).

WOMEN ASSISTED BY ORGANIZATION IN ANTITRUST LAW

More than one person has noticed that there is a shortage of women practicing in the antitrust area. What's the reason? Some suggest it has to do with the scarcity of women in the economics field, which is a large part of antitrust law. Others suggest it has to do with the "old boys' network" that is still at play in the antitrust field. Looking at the government employment side of it, while there are women at the FTC and DOJ in the antitrust divisions, at the top echelon women remain underrepresented.

Women themselves have begun to fight back. In New York, Washington D.C., and other major cities, women's groups are emerging to help themselves. Formed basically to get to know each other, they are branching out to include help with developing a client base, as well as introducing younger women in the profession to the area. Noting that 49 percent of the law school population is female, women remain hopeful that this area of the law will be broken into by women.

On the international front the same types of networks are springing up. For example, in September 2009 the Women's Competition Network in Brussels was started by two practitioners in Europe.

What are their issues and how are they different from those faced by men? Everything from what to wear at the office, to how to juggle child care with the long hours that are required in the field. Not that these issues aren't being faced by men, but with men, the issues are somehow novel, whereas with women, these issues apparently should have been decided when they chose antitrust as their field.

Many signs are evident that the networking has paid off. For example, for the first time ever women head both the DOJ's Antitrust Division and the European Competition Commission. Christine Varney was confirmed as the new assistant attorney general at the DOJ, and across the Atlantic, Neelie Kroes heads up the ECC where she was appointed in 2004.

Source: Lauren S. Albert, "Antitrust Law—Women Seek Power in Numbers," *Women's Lawyers Journal,* 2003, p. 11; and "Women in Antitrust 2009," *Global Competition Review* 12, Issue 5, May 2009, http://www.lw.com/upload/pubContent/_pdf/pub2637_1.pdf.

resulted in the companies forcing the cardholders into accepting arbitration for credit card disputes on a "take-it-or-leave-it" basis. The cardholders argue that this collusion violated the antitrust laws and that failure to issue cards to individuals who did not agree to arbitration was a group boycott.[15]

VERTICAL BOYCOTTS

Vertical boycott agreements occur when a seller agrees with some of its customers that it will not sell to another. If such an agreement is shown, the refusal to deal is per se illegal.

EXAMPLE

That does not mean that a seller is limited in choosing his customers. A seller has always been afforded the right to choose as long as the decision is independently made. For example, a seller may announce that he will not deal with anyone who does not comply with certain suggestions (such as resale prices), but if such a seller agrees with others to carry out this policy, it is not an independent action and an unlawful agreement may be found.

All of the above per se violations have the anticompetitive effect of prohibiting suppliers from finding buyers for their goods and prohibiting consumers from having a variety of suppliers from which to choose. It is primarily for this reason that these violations are viewed as unreasonable in all circumstances.

TYING ARRANGEMENTS

Sellers with more than one product may seek to tie the sales of one (which the consumer desires) with the sales of another (which the consumer does not want). Such **tying arrangements** are prohibited by Section 3 of the Clayton Act and are per se illegal if the seller coerces the buyer into taking the tied product as a condition to obtaining the desired product. This is the most blatant of the ideas suggested by Apple in our chapter opening scenario. If the iPhone is the desired product and the Mac is the tied product, requiring the purchase of one in order to get the other would violate the Clayton Act.

EXAMPLE

---

[15]*Ross v. Bank of America,* 524 F.3d 217 (2d Cir. 2008).

One of the problems with tying arrangements is in defining when the products are tied. Certainly, a shoe store can require that you purchase the right shoe with the left. The question is whether the products have two discrete functions so that a consumer will ordinarily purchase them separately.

In order to establish a per se violation alleging tying, a number of steps are required. First, there must be two products, one of which is the tying product and one of which is the tied product. Second, there must be power in the tying product market. Third, there must be a "not insubstantial" amount of commerce affected in the tied product market. Fourth, the power in the tying product must be used to prevent competition between products in the tied market. Fifth, the tying firm must have an economic interest in the sales of the tied firm.

This tying analysis was used in the *U.S. v. Microsoft Corp.*[16] case in which the appellate court found several of the Microsoft practices were not illegal per se tying arrangements. These practices included requiring licensees of Windows 95 and 98 also to license Internet Explorer (IE), refusing to allow equipment manufacturers to uninstall from the desktop, designing Windows 98 so that IE could not be removed by use of the add/remove program, and designing Windows 98 to override users' efforts to choose a default web browser. In refusing to apply the per se analysis, the court ruled that it was not wise to separate the operating system from the browser as two separate products. According to the court, to allow these products to be considered two products might mean that even integration of the spell check function in word processing programs could potentially violate the tying prohibitions. The court ruled that it was not confident that bundling in computer software was not more efficient, thus not per se anticompetitive.[17]

For example, looking at the relationship between Apple's iPod products and iTunes raises the question of which product is the tying product and which is the tied product. Throw in the launch of the iPhone, and the question becomes more complicated. Is the iPhone the most desired product? Is the AT&T service, which is the only service with which the iPhone will work, the tied product? Are the applications that are available for use on the iPhone tied to the iPhone or to the Apple? Questions like these are difficult to answer and are necessary for a tying charge to be raised. Reality Check 14-3, "Loyalty Rebates—Are They Tying Arrangements in Disguise?" raises the tying arrangement in another context.

REALITY CHECK 14-3

LOYALTY REBATES—ARE THEY TYING ARRANGEMENTS IN DISGUISE?

What if you are a seller and wish to offer "rebates" to your loyal customers? Is this a violation of Section 2 of the Sherman Act? That's exactly what the court was asked to address in the case of *Southeast Missouri Hospital v. C. R. Bard, Inc.* In this case, the hospital complained because it was being required to purchase a certain amount of urological catheters from Bard in order to receive discounts, rebates, and lower prices on all of its catheter purchases. This left only about 10 percent of the needs of the hospital unfilled, which meant it could only purchase that much from Bard's competitors if it wanted to maximize the incentives. The hospital was complaining because it said it was prohibited from purchasing an innovative product from a competing vendor. The court agreed with the hospital in this case and ruled that the practice was a form of exclusive dealing and anticompetitive.

A recent DOJ report indicated that it was likely to apply predatory pricing to loyalty rebates, but cautioned that it would look to real world examples before imposing such an approach in all cases.

Source: Southeast Missouri Hospital v. C. R. Bard, Inc., 2008 U.S. Dist. LEXIS 4480 (E.D. Mo. 2008).

---

[16]253 F.3d 34 (D.C. Cir. 2001).

[17]Although these tying arrangements were found not to violate Section 3 of the Clayton Act, they formed the basis of the monopolization charges against Microsoft which were successful.

EXCLUSIVE SELLING AGREEMENTS

Sellers may grant an **exclusive selling agreement** to a particular dealer in a specified territory by agreeing to sell only to that dealer within its area of responsibility. Such restraints, which are limitations upon the seller's freedom, are governed by the rule of reason and are, in most instances, valid. Even if the seller is induced to grant such an "exclusive" by the dealer, the courts have not found an illegal agreement.

EXCLUSIVE DEALING AGREEMENTS

Exclusive dealing agreements, pursuant to which the buyer undertakes to purchase all its requirements for the product from the seller, are governed by Section 3 of the Clayton Act; this prohibits such contracts if they are likely to substantially lessen competition. The principal vice of exclusives is that, if they tie up a significant portion of the market, the seller's competitors will be foreclosed from market access and competitively disadvantaged.

The development of the law in this area has been muddled. The application of the rule of reason to exclusive dealings does not mean that all such arrangements are lawful. Particularly for a seller with a large market share, the careful course is to avoid any widespread use of exclusive dealing arrangements or any single agreement or group of agreements which would tie up a large number of outlets. Antitrust risk can be minimized by requiring dealers to purchase absolute minimum quantities instead, or by utilizing similar undertakings to assure adequate inventories.

EXAMPLE

For example, a Michigan retailer of medical devices sued the administrators of an insurance plan that required its insurance enrollees to obtain their medical devices from a network of suppliers, of which the plaintiff was not one,[18] claiming that this exclusive deal left him and other medical device suppliers who were not part of the network of suppliers out of a major source of customers. The court rejected his claim finding that the arrangement accounted for only 6.5 percent of the medical device sales revenue in the state and only 12.5 percent of the revenue in the Detroit area. The court found this to be an insignificant restriction of commerce.

PRICE DISCRIMINATION

Price discrimination is charging different prices to buyers of the same product in essentially the same time period. Section 2 of the Robinson-Patman Act makes it illegal for any person to discriminate in price. A seller discriminates when the difference in price charged to different customers does not reflect the difference in the cost of selling to those customers.

The Act allows two defenses to price discrimination: the **cost justification defense** and the **meeting competition defense.** Under the cost justification defense, §2 states that there shall be no liability where the discount to the buyer reflects the lower cost to the seller of selling to the favored customer. Under the meeting competition defense, §2 states that there shall be no liability where the seller granted the discount in order to meet a competing seller's price. In addition to the statutory defenses, the FTC recognizes the **practical availability** defense. The FTC will find an absence of competitive injury where discounts are generally and practically available to competitors of the favored customer. Apple might be tempted to use the meeting competition defense, but unless they can show that they were meeting the price of Microsoft's computers, it will be in violation of the Robinson-Patman Act.

EXAMPLE

For purposes of the Robinson-Patman Act, the price includes all promotional materials, discounts or gifts given in connection with the sale of a product. All buyers

---

[18]*B&H Medical v. ABP Administration, Inc.,* 526 F.3d 257 (6th Cir. 2008).

must be treated the same and thus must be given a proportionate amount of these "freebies." While a company may meet its competitor's price in a specific market in order to remain competitive, as soon as the threat is gone, the seller must raise the prices again so that all of her buyers are receiving the same price in all areas of the country.

Price discrimination (charging different prices to different buyers) and **predatory pricing** (selling below cost for the purpose of eliminating competition) have similar effects. These aspects of the Robinson-Patman Act remain controversial. It was thought that small businesses were being hurt by the large-scale buying power of retail chains and corporate giants who entered the retail field. While that may be true, the result is generally lower prices for consumers overall. Antitrust law is designed to protect competition, not competitors. Thus, unless the corporate giants and large retail chains are engaged in predatory pricing or other forms of price discrimination, it is unlikely that their mere presence in the market is harmful to competition. This has been the primary reason why every Antitrust Commission that has studied the effects of the Robinson-Patman Act has called for its repeal. (See again Reality Check 14-1.)

There are two sides to this argument. It is argued that consumers will benefit in the short run by low prices from the big discounters but if retail giants can put small operations out of business, they may then raise its prices, thus hurting consumers in the long run. However, what has happened is that there has developed competition between the giant retailers. For example, in most markets there is competition between Walmart and Target or K-Mart, Sam's Club v. Costco, etc. Thus, the market remains competitive and consumers are well served in both the short and long run. The inefficient small businesses will leave the market and scarce resources will be better allocated, so the theory goes.

Walmart has been challenged a number of times for predatory pricing. For example, in 2001, Wisconsin became the first state to challenge Walmart's pricing policies. It alleged that, for example, Walmart was charging its customers $5.00 for detergent that cost it $6.51, a move Wisconsin claimed was designed to put its competitors out of business. As usual, Walmart settled the case rather than litigate it. In its settlement agreement, Walmart agreed to pay double or treble damages for future violations.[19] See Take Away 14-5, "Antitrust Violations."

EXAMPLE

Special Problems in Antitrust

LO6

Some industries have presented special problems to courts that have been asked to review the exclusive nature of the business. Two such industries that warrant a closer examination are trade associations and sports franchises.

TRADE ASSOCIATIONS

Trade associations require agreements to deal with each other and for that reason may violate antitrust laws. The question is whether the trade association is engaged in activity that is anticompetitive. Behavior such as closed business meetings, closed membership, and decisions to exclude buyers or sellers that do not support the trade association may be viewed as anticompetitive; thus, their behavior may violate the antitrust law. One act that trade associations often engage in is price sharing, which can be a lawful activity and beneficial to the industry. Because of the many benefits to the trade association that price sharing brings, courts apply a rule of reason approach to this activity. For example, courts determined price sharing to be anticompetitive where the trade

EXAMPLE

---

[19]"Wal-Mart Settles Predatory Pricing Charge," http://www.newrules.org/retail/news/walmart-settles-predatory-pricing-charge.

ANTITRUST VIOLATIONS

Violation	Conduct Prohibited	Standard Applied
Horizontal Price Fixing	Agreement between 2 or more parties to set prices	Per Se
Vertical Price Fixing	Agreement between supplier and customer to set prices	Per Se
Horizontal Market Restraint	Geographic division of territory served or division by customer or product	Per Se
Vertical Market Restraint	Agreement to resell products within certain territories or solicit business from certain customers	Rule of Reason
Horizontal Boycott	Agreement not to buy or sell from an individual, company, or group	Per Se
Vertical Boycott	Agreement between seller and customer that it will not sell to another	Per Se
Tying Arrangements	Tying the sale of a product to the sale of a different product	Per Se
Exclusive Selling Arrangements	Agreement to sell only to a one dealer within his or her area of responsibility	Rule of Reason
Exclusive Dealing Arrangement	Agreement whereby buyer purchases all it needs from seller	Rule of Reason
Price Discrimination	Charging different prices to buyers of the same product	Rule of reason

association also required its member to make daily reports, subjected them to audits on sales, purchases, and production, and required members to notify them immediately of any price changes.[20] However, the Court upheld a plan where the sharing only included the exchange of statistical data which included only past prices and not identification of individual customers.[21]

In order to prevent an appearance of antitrust activity, trade associations should be open to all qualified firms, especially where membership confers a significant competitive benefit over nonmembers. Reality Check 14-4, "NAR Cited for Anticompetitive Policies,"

---

[20]*American Column Lumber Co. v. U.S.,* 257 U.S. 377 (1921).

[21]*Maple Flooring Manufacturing Asso. v. U.S.,* 268 U.S. 563 (1925).

illustrates how policies adopted by associations, here, the National Association of Realtors (NAR), can be challenged as anticompetitive.

SPORTS LEAGUES

Generally, competing sports teams are capable of forming a conspiracy, but this rule is subject to statutory and court-directed exceptions. In *NCAA v. Board of Regents*, the Supreme Court considered an allegation that the NCAA had unreasonably restricted trade in the televising of college football games. The Court's holding, that the NCAA's price and output restrictions were unlawful restraints of trade, implicitly recognized that an association of sports league teams is capable of satisfying §1 of the Sherman Act.

This holding in *NCAA* was challenged in *Chicago Professional Sports v. NBA*. Here, plaintiffs challenged the NBA's ability to cap at 30 the number of games televised on Chicago television station WGN. In considering the claim, the Court of Appeals held that the NBA bore greater resemblance to a single firm than an independent group of firms. This is true even though the teams are not subsidiaries of the national organization; they all have separate ownership. The Court accepted the position offered by the NBA that it functions as a single entity, creating a single product that competes with other basketball leagues, other sports, and other entertainments. Here, it was protected from §1 liability.

Baseball, however, has a different status in antitrust law. Two Supreme Court cases have exempted baseball from antitrust laws: *Federal Baseball Club of Baltimore, Inc. v. National League of Professional Baseball Clubs*[22] is the first, and *Flood v. Kuhn*[23] is the second. In *Federal Baseball,* the court found that interstate commerce was not present in baseball; thus, it cannot be reached by the Sherman Act. In the *Flood* case, the Court refused to repeal the professional baseball exemption to antitrust law. Professional sports other than baseball are not exempt from antitrust laws.[24]

In a more recent application, the court considered a challenge to Major League Baseball Properties' (MLBP) collective licensing of team logos and other intellectual property owned by MLB's member teams. A manufacturer that had been denied a license brought a §1 claim alleging that MLBP was a cartel engaged in horizontal price fixing and output restraints. The court concluded that the manufacturer failed to rebut the MLBP's evidence of procompetitive efficiencies. Rejecting the plaintiff's request to analyze the case using the per se approach, the court found that the case was similar to other cases which had been analyzed under the rule of reason approach. The Court found the plaintiff also did not rebut MLBP's assertion that it actually increased output by increasing the number of licenses issued. Reality Check 14-5, "*American Needle v. NFL*—Poised to Change the Face of Sports," discusses the latest case challenging the antitrust status of sports leagues. Experts predict that a favorable ruling for American Needle will change the face of sports.

REALITY CHECK 14-4

NAR CITED FOR ANTICOMPETITIVE POLICIES

Real estate brokers share listings of homes through the Multiple Listing Service (MLS), which lists all the homes for sale in a local market. Some real estate agents are taking advantage of technology by listing their homes through a password-protected website on which all the homes are listed. The MLS system works only if all the homes are listed on the system. The National Association of Realtors (NAR) adopted a policy which allowed its members to withhold listing their clients' homes on the website. The DOJ charged that this would enable NAR brokers (those who are not listing on the website) to block their competitors' customers from having full access to the homes for sale in the area, preventing web-based brokers from providing all MLS listings, effectively inhibiting the new technology. This, the DOJ charged, altered the rules that govern MLS listings by denying consumers access to information in a new way. The court found this to be anticompetitive.

Source: Department of Justice, "Justice Department Sues National Association of Realtors for Limiting Competition Among Real Estate Brokers," press release, September 8, 2008, http://www.usdoj.gov/atr/public/press_releases/2005/211008.htm.

---

[22]259 U.S. 200 (1922).

[23]407 U.S. 258 (1972).

[24]See, for example, *Brown v. Pro Football, Inc.,* 518 U.S. 231 (1996).

AMERICAN NEEDLE V. NFL—POISED TO CHANGE THE FACE OF SPORTS

In *American Needle v. NFL,* a unanimous Supreme Court held that the member teams of the NFL are subject to antitrust scrutiny for licensing activities carried out through a joint venture—the National Football League Properties (NFPL). The case began when American Needle filed an antitrust action against the NFL alleging that the league was using its monopoly power illegally to deprive the company of its share of the market for caps and hats bearing the logos of NFL teams. American Needle had made knit caps and baseball hats bearing NFL logos for decades under a nonexclusive contract until the NFL ended the relationship in 2000, awarding an exclusive contract to Reebok. Both the district court and the court of appeals dismissed the claim filed by American Needle.

In an unusual move, the NFL announced that it was in agreement with American Needle's request for a hearing and a Supreme Court decision even though the party winning a case usually argues against Supreme Court review. The reason for the NFL's agreement? It thought it had the opportunity to challenge more than the issue placed before it by American Needle; it wanted to convince the court to grant the NFL total immunity from antitrust laws and to extend that immunity to the NFL, NBA, and NHL, as the Court had done for baseball.

The NFL tried to convince the court that, just as it found for baseball, the NFL is not 32 separate entities, but one single entity and should be treated as such for antitrust purposes, making it immune from Section 1 claims. (If they are one separate entity, they cannot compete against themselves.) But the Court took a different analysis. It looked not at whether the teams are separate entities, but whether they have a unity of interest. The heart of the argument is whether the teams compete against each other in the football market. As for that question, the court held that they do. The fact that the NFL forms a joint venture (NFLP) to produce a product or services does not make it immune from antitrust scrutiny. Subjecting it to the rule of reason approach, the Court did not decide whether the NFLP had in fact violated Section 1, but that its granting of a 10-year, exclusive license to Reebok to produce its trademarked caps for all 32 teams *could* violate Section 1. The issue of whether it does will be decided upon remand. If the court on remand sides with American Needle in finding that the exclusive licensing agreement violates Section 1, it will completely change the face of sports, affecting players unions, free agency, and other concerted activities by the NFL.

Why do you think baseball is treated differently than the NFL?

Source: American Needle v. NFL, 130 S. Ct. 2201 (2010).

L07

Monopolies

The problems that we have examined so far have focused on *behavior* that violates the antitrust law. Antitrust law is also concerned with the overall market structure and how competition operates within it. **Market structure** looks at certain things that might lessen competition. Antitrust law in this country is based on the assumption that the more competitors you have the better competition is overall. To this end, antitrust law also looks at how to keep markets from becoming too concentrated in one or a few sellers. When there are only a few sellers in a market, they are said to have a large **market share.** Large market shares lead to **market power.** A concentration of market power is to be avoided. Market power leads to **monopolies.** Thinking again of our continuing scenario, Apple might be able to establish that Microsoft has a monopoly over the market since they own 82 percent of it, but unless Microsoft reached their monopoly power by exhibiting monopolistic behavior, they will not be deemed to be in violation of the law.

Section 2 of the Sherman Antitrust Act makes it unlawful to monopolize, attempt to monopolize, or conspire to monopolize a line of commerce. The Supreme Court has defined monopoly power as the power to control prices or exclude competition. Market power is measured by the monopolist's share of the relevant market. The offense of monopolization has two elements: (1) possession of monopoly power in the relevant market, and (2) willful acquisition or maintenance of power.

Absolute monopoly, i.e., 100 percent of the market, doesn't happen. The question is how much of a share of the relevant market does a business have to have to monopolize the market? A report from the DOJ suggests that for firms with less than 50 percent

CASE 14.2 LiveUniverse, Inc. v. MySpace, Inc.

304 Fed. Appx. 554 (9th Cir. 2008)

Facts: LiveUniverse alleges monopolization and attempted monopolization against MySpace, a social networking website. The allegation specifically is that MySpace has refused to deal with LiveUniverse whereas before it allowed LiveUniversae customers to link to LiveUniverse from the MySpace page.

Issue: Has MySpace violated §2 of the Sherman Act by monopolizing or attempting to monopolize the social networking websites?

Decision: No.

Reasoning: LiveUniverse's exclusionary conduct claim is predicated on MySpace's "refusal to deal" with LiveUniverse. As a general matter, the Sherman Act does not restrict the long recognized right of a trader or manufacturer, engaged in an entirely private business, freely to exercise his own independent discretion as to parties with whom he will deal. Even a firm with monopoly power has no general duty to engage in a joint marketing program with a competitor. This right, however, is not unqualified, and under certain circumstances, a refusal to cooperate with rivals can constitute anticompetitive conduct and violate §2. This court has since recognized the narrow scope of the refusal to deal exception, which requires, *inter alia,* the unilateral termination of a voluntary and profitable course of dealing. LiveUniverse's only allegation is that, before MySpace redesigned its platform, individual users were able to link to content on vidiLife.com. Though this may indicate a prior course of dealing *between MySpace and its users,* nothing in the complaint suggests an agreement, or even an implicit understanding, *between MySpace and LiveUniverse* regarding the functionality of embedded links. Even if we were to assume a voluntary course of dealing, LiveUniverse has failed to allege that it was profitable to MySpace, such that MySpace's conduct was contrary to its short-term business interests. LiveUniverse's failure to allege causal antitrust injury,

which is an element of all antitrust suits, serves as an independent basis for dismissal. Antitrust injury is injury of the type the antitrust laws were intended to prevent, which means harm to the process of competition and consumer welfare, not harm to individual competitors.

LiveUniverse's allegation that MySpace's conduct in disabling links on MySpace.com to other social networking websites reduces consumers' choices in the relevant market, thereby diminishing "the quality of consumers' social networking experience," falls short. LiveUniverse does not explain how MySpace's actions *on its own website* can reduce consumers' choice or diminish the quality of their experience on *other* social networking websites, which is the relevant market. There is no allegation that MySpace has prevented consumers from accessing vidiLife.com (or any other social networking website). Indeed, it would be impossible for MySpace to do so: any consumer desiring such access need only type "vidiLife.com" into the address bar of his or her web browser, or into a search engine such as Google. All MySpace has done is prevent consumers from accessing vidiLife.com *through MySpace.com.* Consumers remain free to choose which online social networks to join, and on which websites they upload text, graphics, and other content. LiveUniverse's failure to allege antitrust injury serves as an independent ground on which we affirm the decision of the district court.

CASE QUESTIONS

1. The court ruled that businesses were free to do business with whomever they wanted, but that right was not unqualified. What limits are placed on that right, according to this court?
2. What was the exclusionary conduct LiveUniverse alleged in this case?
3. How did the exclusionary conduct lead to an attempted monopoly charge by LiveUniverse?

---

market share there be a rebuttable presumption that market power is lacking, and when a firm has maintained a market share exceeding two-thirds for a significant period of time with no likelihood of erosion, that market power be presumed.[25] Under the DOJ guidelines, Microsoft would certainly qualify as a monopoly with 82 percent of the market in personal computers. *LiveUniverse, Inc. v. MySpace, Inc.,* Case 14.2, shows what must be proved if allegations of monopolizing behavior are to be substantiated.

---

[25]Department of Justice Report, "Competition and Monopoly: Single-Firm Conduct Under Section 2 of the Sherman Act," September 24, 2008, http://www.usdoj.gov/atr/public/reports/236681.pdf.

Once a monopoly is found to exist, the question is how was it obtained or maintained? Monopolies can exist lawfully—they are not in and of themselves unlawful. However, monopolies that are created through the use of monopolistic behavior are unlawful. The statute does not require that there needs to be an evil intent to eliminate competitors. Conscious acts designed to further or maintain a monopoly market position will be enough to find willful acquisition. Acts such as acquisition of competitors, exclusive dealing contracts, or charging unreasonably low or below cost for products could be evidence of monopolistic behavior.

For example, Fair Isaacs is a corporation that takes the combined scores of the three national credit bureaus and, using an algorithm, generates a bundled score used by lending institutions. The three credit bureaus, which combined own 100 percent of the national market, created their own bundled score using the same algorithm that Fair Issacs uses, and called it VantageScore. They then began to sell their services so that the lenders could purchase their bundle of the three scores plus the VantageScore bundle, or the lenders could purchase the bundle sold by Fair Isaacs. The problem was that if the lender purchased the bundles containing VantageScore, the product cost considerably less than if the lender ordered the Fair Issacs bundle. In addition, in order to obtain the scores from the three credit score companies, Fair Issacs was required to pay significantly more than other resellers of credit scores. Even though Fair Isaac's algorithm dominated the market at the time, the court ruled that the behavior of the credit score companies created a dangerous probability that they would successfully monopolize the credit scoring market, and denied their motion to dismiss.[26]

Another indication of market power is the **product market**. The product market is all of those products that are available to a buyer of the business's product. This includes all products that are similar in price, use, and quality. The price test looks to see if the buyer would reasonably interchange between the products even though the cost is different. The use test looks to see if the use of the product is the same. One example is whether IBM computer equipment has the same use as non-IBM computer equipment. In that case, the non-IBM computer equipment could be easily modified to do the same tasks as the IBM computer equipment. The quality test is whether there are any physical attributes of the product that consumers desire over other products. These tests help determine the product market from which the market power analysis can begin.

Monopsony Power

The concept of monopoly refers to the power of *sellers* of a good or service. In some instances, the power is on the buying side, called **monopsony** power. A buyer having price and quantity power is said to have a monopsony on the buying or demand side of the market. Monopsony power falls within §2 of the Sherman Act and has been examined in courts much like monopoly power. Microsoft might have monopsony power over supplies it uses in its computer manufacturing because of the size of the market it owns. If, for example, Microsoft was the largest user of chips, it might be able to demand a discount for itself, or require that they be offered the lowest price, causing an increase price for other users of the same product.

For example, in *U.S. v. Griffith*,[27] the defendants operated movie theaters; in some towns they were the only theater, in others there was competition. As purchasers of film from distributors in towns where they were the only theaters, they possessed monopsony power. By linking the distribution of the films in the towns where they were the only theater with those theaters in towns where there was competition, they were able to

---

[26]*Fair Issacs Corp. v. Equifax, Inc.*, 2008 U.S. Dist. LEXIS 16664 (D. Minn. 2008).
[27]334 U.S. 100 (1948).

negotiate first showings in both towns. The effect on the market was that they were able to increase the market power of the theaters in the towns where they were competitive. The Supreme Court ruled that to be a violation of §2, condemning the buying power of the entire circuit of theaters.

Oligopoly

Section 2 of the Sherman Act is designed to prevent anticompetitive behavior by a single firm. Section 1 of the Sherman Act concerns the behavior of one or more firms acting in agreement with each other. The result is that there is a gap in coverage in industries where there are a few competitors who own the entire market. This type of market is called an **oligopoly,** or, more recently, a shared monopoly.

To be an oligopolistic market, the market has to have a limited number of competitors who are interdependent on each other. For example, if there were three airlines serving the Atlanta to Houston route, one would be able to gain a greater market share by lowering the fare on that route. However, they would have to contend with the others' lowering their fares as well to keep the market shares relatively equal. If one raises fares, it may find its market share will decrease. This interdependence keeps the three fares relatively stable and equal. This parallel behavior is not monopolistic, so it does not fit within §2 of the Sherman Act, nor is it the result of collusive agreement, thereby escaping §1 liability as well. Apple and Microsoft would not qualify as an oligopoly because they are not equals in the market, and thus, would not be likely to exhibit parallel conduct or interdependence.

Although appearing anticompetitive, the courts have made clear that unless the Sherman Act is violated, this behavior does not violate the law. For example, the court in *E.I. DuPont v. FTC*[28] held "in the absence of proof of a violation of the antitrust laws or evidence of collusive, predatory, or exclusionary conduct, business practices are not unfair in violation of §5 unless those practices have an anticompetitive effect or cannot be supported by independent legitimate reason."[29] In that case, the FTC challenged practices by DuPont and the Ethel Corporation, both dominant in the antiknock gasoline additive industry. Earlier, the FTC had received an adverse ruling in *In re Kellogg Co.*[30]

In that case, the four cereal manufacturers were attacked by the FTC, alleging violations of the Sherman Act. The cereal manufacturers possessed a combined 90 percent of the market share and were charged with excluding entry by engaging in brand proliferation, misleading advertising, controlling retail shelf space, and acquisition of competitors. They were not charged with being a monopoly; however, they were charged with being a shared monopoly (oligopoly). The case was dismissed. The Commission ruled that without proof of shared profits via a monopoly, there was no Sherman Act or §5 violation.

Thus far, oligopolies are free to interact independently outside the reach of the Sherman Act and the FTC §5. For an overview of our discussion, see Take Away 14-6, "Market Structure Violations."

TAKE AWAY 14-6

MARKET STRUCTURE VIOLATIONS

Violation	Characterization
Monopoly	Power of seller to dominate market
Monopsony	Power of buyer to dominate market
Oligopoly	Few competitors in a market

---

[28]729 F.2d 128 (2d Cir. 1984).
[29]*Id.* at 140.
[30]99 F.T.C. 8 (1982).

Mergers and Acquisitions

A **merger** is the joining together of two companies that were previously separate. In order to expand business, reduce costs, or increase market power, firms often seek to merge with or acquire other firms. Mergers are covered by the Sherman Act §1 if they anticompetitively restrain trade because every merger involves an agreement. Mergers are also covered by §5 of the FTC Act, and a merger that would create a firm with monopoly power would also violate §2 of the Sherman Act. Mergers are also covered under the Clayton Act. The *FTC v. Whole Foods Market, Inc.* case (Case 14.3) demonstrates how the decision of which market you compete in can determine the outcome of whether the merger will be approved or not.

CASE 14.3 FTC v. Whole Foods Market, Inc.

548 F.3d 1028 (D.C. Cir. 2008)

Facts: Whole Foods and Wild Oats operate, collectively, over 300 stores in the U.S. In 2007, Whole Foods announced that it would acquire Wild Oats and notified the FTC pursuant to the Hart-Scott-Rodino Act required for the $565 million merger. The FTC opposed the merger on the grounds that the merger would create monopolies in 18 cities because Whole Foods and Wild Oats were the only premium, natural, organic supermarkets (PNOS). The expert testimony for Whole Foods showed that there was no way that the merger could produce a monopoly because raising prices (the danger for a monopoly) would drive people to other supermarkets. The expert witness for the FTC argued that the merger would chill entry of other PNOS supermarkets into the area and would drive up prices in the PNOS market. If the court accepted the FTC's witness's testimony, it would mean that Whole Foods and Wild Oats were a distinct market unto themselves and a monopoly would be formed. If the Whole Foods expert was to be believed, the PNOS market was one within the larger supermarket market and competition would not be adversely affected.

Issue: Whether the PNOS market is a discrete market or one that operates within a larger market of supermarkets.

Decision: PNOS is a discrete market.

Reasoning: The district court concluded "the relevant product market in this case is not premium natural and organic supermarkets . . . as argued by the FTC but . . . at least all supermarkets." Thus, considering the defendants' evidence as well as the FTC's, as it was obligated to do, the court was in no doubt that this merger would not substantially lessen competition, because it found the evidence proved Whole Foods and Wild Oats compete among supermarkets generally. However, the court's conclusion was in error.

A market must include all products reasonably interchangeable by consumers for the same purposes. The FTC's evidence delineated a PNOS submarket catering to a core group of customers who "have decided that natural and organic is important, lifestyle of health and ecological sustainability is important." It was undisputed that Whole Foods and Wild Oats provide higher levels of customer service than conventional supermarkets, a "unique environment," and a particular focus on the "core values" these customers espoused. The FTC connected these intangible properties with concrete aspects of the PNOS model, such as a much larger selection of natural and organic products, and a much greater concentration of perishables than conventional supermarkets.

Further, the FTC documented exactly the kind of price discrimination that enables a firm to profit from core customers for whom it is the sole supplier. [Their expert] compared the margins of Whole Foods stores in cities where they competed with Wild Oats. He found the presence of a Wild Oats depressed Whole Foods' margins significantly. Notably, while there was no effect on Whole Foods' margins in the product category of groceries where Whole Foods and Wild Oats compete on the margins with conventional supermarkets, the effect on margins for perishables was substantial. Confirming this price discrimination, Whole Foods' documents indicated that when it price-checked conventional supermarkets, the focus was overwhelmingly on "dry grocery," rather than on the perishables that were 70 percent of Whole Foods' business. Thus, in the high-quality perishables on which both Whole Foods and Wild Oats made most of their money, they competed directly with each other, and they competed with supermarkets only on the dry grocery items that were the fringes of their business.

Additionally, the FTC provided direct evidence that PNOS competition had a greater effect than conventional supermarkets on PNOS prices. [Their expert] showed the opening of a new Whole Foods in the vicinity of a Wild Oats caused Wild Oats' prices to drop, while entry by non-PNOS stores had no such effect. Similarly, the opening of

Earth Fare stores (another PNOS) near Whole Foods stores caused Whole Foods' prices to drop immediately. The price effect continued, while decreasing, until the Earth Fare stores were forced to close.

CASE QUESTIONS

1. This was a motion for a preliminary injunction that was on appeal. Why was it important to identify which market the PNOS competed in?

2. The court made it a point to mention that when Whole Foods did their comparison they used dry goods, but their distinction was in produce. What point was the court making in pointing this out? What did it say about their expert?

3. Determining the market in which you compete largely determines whether your merger will be contested by the FTC. For this purpose, is it better to be in a large market or a small one?

Generally mergers occur through either a stock or asset purchase of one firm by another. Mergers may present threats to competition, depending on the type of merger and the size and strength of the companies involved. The merger regulations attempt to prohibit the merging of firms that will create a monopoly under the theory that it is better to prevent than to untangle a merger. The Hart-Scott-Rodino Act of 1976 was enacted to allow the DOJ to review these mergers before they were completed. For this reason, notice of intent to merge between companies of a certain size must first be given to the DOJ. This gives the DOJ the opportunity to assess the effects the merger will have on the market, and to make recommendations as to whether the merger should go forward. See Reality Check 14-6, "The Threshold Limits for Filing Merger Notification with the DOJ." Failure to notify the proper agency can result in the merger being challenged by either the FTC or DOJ, whichever has jurisdiction of the merger. In our continuing scenario regarding Apple, merging would offer advantages. Rather than working in two research and development departments, there would be one effort to produce the best personal computer, perhaps combining the finest features of both existing computers. Another advantage would be the price that may be charged for the computer. Without competition, the price could drop if it becomes cheaper to produce. On the other hand, lack of competition can also be a danger, in that the prices can be set higher because of the demand.

EXAMPLE

NUMBERS 2 AND 3 TRY HARDER TO COMPETE WITH NUMBER 1

In what is building up to be an epic battle, Microsoft and Yahoo are trying to combine their muscle to take on the number one search engine, Google. Experts admit, however, that it's going to be a difficult task to get the merger approved by the FTC, which rarely grants approval to the second and third players in an industry, fearing that the merger of three companies into two will create a market that's too concentrated and more likely to become anticompetitive. In 2000, the FTC quashed a move by number two Beech-Nut to merge with number three Heinz in the baby food industry, which were anxious to team up to take on the number one Gerber, which controlled 65 percent of the baby food market. Here, the numbers are similar—Google owns 65 percent of the market, while together, Yahoo and Microsoft control about 28 percent of the search engine market.

Source: Spencer E. Ante, "Microsoft-Yahoo: Antitrust Hurdles Loom," *BusinessWeek*, July 29, 2009, http://www.businessweek.com/technology/content/jul2009/tc20090729_672770_page_2.htm.

The entire structure of an industry can be altered by a merger. See Reality Check 14-7, "Numbers 2 and 3 Try Harder to Compete with Number 1," in which the dangers of having too concentrated a market are feared. There are three types of mergers that can threaten competition: horizontal, vertical, and conglomerate mergers.

HORIZONTAL MERGERS

Horizontal mergers involve firms selling the same or similar products in the same geographical markets. These firms compete directly. By merging, firms often eliminate competition between themselves. Because of direct impact within a given market, horizontal mergers are given the most scrutiny.

It is not that they are all bad. Horizontal mergers can result in greater efficiency. Price reductions to consumers may follow. Courts that are asked to review a horizontal merger must balance the market size and power with the consequences of the merger. The antitrust concern is whether the resulting firm will result in market power so great that the merged firms act monopolistic, or whether it is likely to cause the remaining firms to collude to survive.

EXAMPLE Even where there are only two firms competing in a market, the merger may still not violate the antitrust rules. An example of that is the merger between XM Satellite Radio Holdings Inc. and Sirius Satellite Radio Inc. which was approved by the DOJ in 2008. Although XM and Sirius were the only two providers of satellite radio service, the DOJ decided not to oppose the merger, stating that the merger did not exclude various alternative sources of audio entertainment. The DOJ also pointed out that in the future, consumers would likely have new technologies that will enter the market that would offer new and improved alternatives to satellite radio, such as streaming Internet radio to mobile devices.

VERTICAL MERGERS

Vertical mergers occur when one firm purchases either a customer or a supplier, with the result that the resulting firm expands into a new market. When a computer producer purchases a microchip business it then operates in two markets—computer and microchip production. Mergers may be upstream or downstream. **Upstream mergers** occur when a consumer acquires a supplier—the computer company purchases the microchip company. A **downstream merger** occurs when the supplier acquires the purchaser—the microchip company acquires the computer firm. In either an upstream or downstream merger, the same number of competitors remains in the market. What has changed is the *ownership* of those competitors.

The anticompetitive effects this could create stems from the ready source of supply and demand of the vertically merged firms. To produce computers, the computer company has the supply of microchips that it needs. If a shortage of microchips should exist, the merged firm will have a competitive advantage over other computer firms. This might have the effect of forcing the other firms to merge to stay competitive.

358   Part Three ■ Business and Employment Regulation and Financing

What if the acquired firm, here the microchip company, has been supplying other computer companies in the market and there are no competing microchip companies in the area? This creates **foreclosure,** meaning other firms can no longer deal with the acquired firm. This would also create an anticompetitive effect.

Vertical mergers can also be created by acquiring a license rather than a firm. For example, if a company purchased an exclusive license to provide a drug needed in treatment and the company also was the largest treatment provider, it might have an anticompetitive effect. In the example of Fresenius that's exactly what happened. Fresenius, a drug manufacturing company and the largest provider of dialysis in the U.S., purchased the exclusive right to manufacture, distribute, and sell the intravenous drug Venofer to dialysis clinics in the U.S.[31] In reviewing the sale of the license, the FTC was concerned that Fresenius would have the ability to increase the cost of the drug and treatment to Medicare, the sole insurer of dialysis treatment in the U.S. The FTC required Fresenius to enter into a consent decree to cap the price Fresenius can report for Venofer, which is linked to the current market price.

CONGLOMERATE MERGERS

Conglomerate mergers are those in which the merging firms had no prior relationship. The firms may have been potential competitors but they were not customers or suppliers of each other. True conglomerate mergers have no overt effect upon competition or market shares; they merely change the ownership of firms in the markets. There are, however, anticompetitive effects of forming a conglomerate.

Conglomerate mergers occur when the producer of one product extends its production into another product line that is closely related—detergent and bleach, for example. Conglomerate mergers also occur when a company located in one geographic market decides to open a same firm in another geographic market—a bank from one location opening in another location, for example.

Two anticompetitive effects can occur from conglomerates: reciprocity and entrenchment. **Reciprocity** occurs when one firm agrees to purchase items from another firm that agrees to purchase products from it. For example, a silicon chip manufacturer may agree to purchase computers from a computer firm that buys its silicon chips from the first firm. Neither may buy from outside competitors, thereby closing off the markets of the two firms.

If a firm acquires another firm that is already near monopoly size, the acquisition may allow the larger firm to solidify its share of the market, thereby decreasing competition. This is called **entrenchment** because of the possibility that the large firm will become further entrenched in the market. This happens especially when the acquiring firm and the acquired firm are near monopoly. The merger of these two firms may discourage competitors from remaining in or entering the market. Because of the vast resources of the two companies, cost savings may be passed on to the consumer, but not without harm to the market.

International Antitrust Enforcement

As cross-border transactions become more common, parties are faced with complex international trade regulations. While a detailed and exhaustive review is beyond this chapter, some information about existing and emerging issues will help any student to appreciate the global market and need for cooperation and respect for laws outside the U.S. As the sales of computers and the i-products produced by Apple are worldwide,

---

[31]Fresenius Med. Care File No. 081-0146 (FTC, September 15, 2008), http://www.ftc.gov/os/caselist/0810146/080915freseniusanal.pdf.

UNITED KINGDOM NATIONALS PLEAD GUILTY IN U.S.—DO THEIR TIME IN THE U.K.

An unusual plea agreement between three United Kingdom nationals and the DOJ prosecutors will require the U.K. residents to enter a plea in a U.S. court and then be escorted back to the U.K. to serve their time. The three U.K. citizens have agreed to serve 30, 24, and 20 months in prison, respectively. The three were charged with participating in a price-fixing and bid-rigging cartel which conspired to inflate the price of marine hose used to transfer oil between tankers and storage facilities. It is alleged that during the cartel's operations, hundreds of millions of dollars worth of marine hose was affected. The case was investigated by the U.S. authorities in cooperation with the U.K.'s Office of Fair Trading, which is investigating them for violations of the Enterprise Act of 2002.

Source: "Three United Kingdom Nationals Plead Guilty to Participating in Bid-Rigging Conspiracy in the Marine Hose Industry," DOJ Release, December 12, 2007, http://www.usdoj.gov/atr/public/press_releases/2007/228561.htm.

for example, care needs to be taken to make sure the international rules of trade are not violated.

THE EUROPEAN UNION APPROACH TO TRADE REGULATION

In the European Union (EU), almost all the antitrust enforcement is done by the European Commission (EC), which is roughly analogous to the FTC. EC competition law does not provide for criminal sanctions, although some of the member states' laws do provide for criminal penalties. The EC has only injunctive powers and has no private causes of action permitted.

However, member states, i.e., each country with membership in the EC, have the authority to bring an action against violators, and can impose criminal as well as civil and injunctive relief. Whether a member state brings the action depends on the size of the action and its relative importance to all the other member states.

The EC Treaty, under which the EC gains its authority, contains provisions very similar to those found in the U.S. For example, Article 81 and 82 mirror the Sherman Act's §§ 1 and 2. Other provisions contain rules which prevent anticompetitive measures between the member states. Most important are the merger rules established in 1989, and revised in 1994 and 2004. These guidelines, much like the Hart-Scott-Rodino Act in the U.S., set thresholds for notification of the EC, and the EC is the exclusive jurisdiction for mergers in the EU. Reality Check 14-8, "United Kingdom Nationals Plead Guilty in U.S.—Do Their Time in the U.K.," shows the interconnectedness of antitrust in the global economy. There really is a global financial effect in some markets, illustrated by this global cartel.

THE NEW CHINESE ANTI-MONOPOLY LAW

Antitrust laws are not new to Asia. Japan and Korea have long had antitrust regimes, and India, Indonesia, Singapore, and Taiwan now have laws in place that multinational corporations must acknowledge when doing business in these countries.

But the most significant antitrust development in Asia was the enactment of the new Chinese antimonopoly law in August 2007. Integration of such a law into a communist country leaves some puzzling about how this will work.

The law's purpose is stated to prohibit monopolistic conduct, protect fair market competition, promote efficiency, safeguard the interests of consumers and the public, and promote the healthy development of the socialist market economy.[32]

The law specifically prohibits monopoly agreements and abuse of dominant market positions, regulates the concentration of undertakings (mergers), and prohibits agencies and state organizations from preventing the free flow of goods throughout China. Fines, civil liability, and the loss of the right to do business are remedies which may be imposed for violations of the statute.

---

[32]Nathan Bush, "The PRC Antimonopoly Law: Unanswered Questions and Challenges Ahead," *The Antitrust Source,* www.antitrustsource.com.

Already criticized for its lack of transparency, the Ministry of Commerce, the Chinese agency responsible for enforcement of its antitrust laws, rejected a bid by Coca-Cola to buy its Huiyuan Juice Group Ltd. for $2.3 billion.[33] The Ministry made no attempt to explain its reasoning.

Summary

A business has liability for several different aspects of its operations. Ensuring that it complies with the applicable laws regarding its liability can greatly lessen the likelihood that it will incur the unnecessary expense of litigation and judgments. In addition, complying with the laws will increase the likelihood of a business prospering because it will build customer loyalty and support for engaging in conduct consistent with the laws.

Antitrust law is important because of the free enterprise system in this country. The system works because it assumes that the market will allow all competitors to have an equal opportunity to secure their share of the market and that market forces will determine who has the best product and whose business ultimately succeeds. The antitrust laws attempt to ensure that smaller enterprises have an opportunity to present their goods on the market and are not forced out by the presence of larger, more established businesses. This, in the long run, best serves both the free market system and the consumers.

Review Questions

1. Clarina and Moses, the owners of a small family-owned pharmacy, complain to their supplier, the Liles Pharmaceutical Supply Company, that the prices Liles charges them for their pharmaceuticals are higher than those they charge Belvinco, a national drug store chain which also purchases from Liles. Since this makes Clarina and Moses have to charge more for their prescriptions than the larger chain, they allege that it is anticompetitive and illegal. Is it? LO5

2. Clarina and Moses find out that Belvinco lowered its prices on some items which Clarina and Moses sold to consumers for cheaper than Belvinco. Moses and Clarina think this is unfair, since they know this means Belvinco is not even charging the cost of the items to the consumers and their small operation cannot afford to cut costs any further. Is it illegal for Belvinco to lower its prices to below cost? LO7

3. Several pizza parlors are located near a university. Since there are so many of the parlors, owned by different people, none of them is particularly successful. In an effort to become more so, one of the parlors begins to lower prices. The other parlors, seeing the increase in business, do

the same. The first parlor continues to lower prices to meet competition. Eventually, though volume has increased, prices are so low for the parlors, that none of the owners is really making any money. The owners get together after a local chamber of commerce meeting and decide that they will divide up the area around the school and only service customers within their area. In this way, they can go back to charging higher prices and not all lose out because of undercutting each other to meet competition. They don't feel customers would be harmed because they will be able to still come to the parlor closest to their area and will only have to pay the prices they paid before for pizza. Can they take care of the problem this way? LO5

4. Fujido made photocopiers and sold service agreements as part of its sales for the photocopiers. The parts that were used in the photocopiers were not interchangeable with other parts, and thus, if you bought a Fujido copier you had to buy its repair service agreement because they did not make their parts available to any other dealers. Sumy was a copier repair shop that could not repair Fujido copiers because Fujido did not sell

[33]Dune Lawrence, "China, Coca-Cola Deal Blocked under Chinese Monopoly Law," *The Huffington Post*, March 18, 2009, http://www.huffingtonpost.com/2009/03/18/china-cocacola-deal-block_n_176271.html.

its supplies outside of its market. Sumy claims this is unlawful tying. What do you think? LO5

5. Stoney was a supplier of crushed stone to the building industry. He had one competitor, which he purchased. Stoney then refused to supply crushed stone to HiRise Co. because of a disagreement that he had with the owner personally. Because HiRise could not get any crushed rock from Stoney, it caused HiRise to abandon his contracts and he eventually filed bankruptcy. HiRise now alleges an antitrust injury because of Stoney's boycott. Is he able to recover from Stoney for his injury? LO5

6. Several business people attended a trade show. In an elevator ride in which all the owners of tool companies were present, one suggested that they could all make money if they would simply increase prices 10 percent above last year's price of his product. Nothing else was said. The prices of all the tools were increased 10 percent over last year's individual price. Are they guilty of violation of the Sherman Act? LO2

7. Briscoe was a regional seller of machine parts. One part of his region was remote and it cost him twice as much to deliver machine parts to that part of his region. To make up the cost, he charged his customers in that region more for machine parts that they purchased than he charged his customers in the other part of his regions. Is charging two different prices for the same product in the same region a violation of the antitrust laws? LO5

8. Barnaby's and Books for Less were the two big retail chains for books in the U.S. When Barnaby's would have a sale on its books, Books for Less would offer the same sale for the same length of time. When the book prices were raised, they were raised by both sellers. What is this called, and is this behavior a violation of the antitrust laws. LO7

9. Milestone, a clothing manufacturer, entered into an exclusive dealing contract with Macy's in which Macy's was the sole distributer of Milestone's line of clothes. Dillard's, a competitor, wanted to be able to stock Milestone's line as well, but Milestone refused to authorize Dillard's to sell their line. Is this an antitrust violation? LO5

10. Diamond Rocks wanted to purchase all the diamonds one major South African exporter could produce. In order to convince the exporter to sell to only Diamond Rocks, it promised to buy only from the exporter. Diamond Rocks had only one other competitor who also bought diamonds from the exporter. The exclusive deal with Diamond Rocks precluded the competitor from being able to obtain enough diamonds to keep him in business. Could he bring an antitrust action against Diamond Rocks and the exporter? LO8

Ethics Issue

Dell Corporation, a computer manufacturer, was a member of VESA, a voluntary standard-setting association to which almost all members of the computer industry belonged. For several years, VESA sought to implement a process by which a certain platform would transfer video between a computer's CPU and its peripherals. Several times it asked its members if anyone had any patents which would prevent VESA from utilizing its discovery but no one replied that they had a patent on the process. VESA then announced its new platform and was immediately sued by Dell for patent infringement. It turns out that Dell had a patent on the process all along but did not reveal that to VESA.

In an action by the FTC based on unfair practices, the FTC charged Dell with acting unfairly toward VESA in not revealing its patent. It alleged that Dell caused an industry delay and that uncertainty about acceptance raised the cost of implementation. Dell was required to relinquish its rights to enforce its patent against any computer manufacturer using the new design in its products and prohibited from engaging in comparable behavior in future standard-setting activities.

What would have motivated Dell's management to lie to VESA, an organization of which it is a member? What benefit would be gained by putting its reputation as an upstanding organization at risk? If the organization makes a request to reveal, is there a duty to cooperate, to disclose intellectual property? If such a patent is legitimately missed by management, is it the duty of Dell to forgo the royalties' fee requirements that could be charged against users of the new product?

Group Exercise

Look at the two largest retailers (or manufacturers, or grocery stores) in your area. What would be the likely result if they merged? What would be the response of the FTC to the proposed merger? What impact would it have on your community? Who would be the likely losers in the deal? Who would be the winners? What jobs would it cost? Who would likely complain? Who would be the proponents of the merger? What interest would all the parties have?

Key Terms

www.mhhe.com/bennettalexanderLE1e

chapter

15

Intellectual Property

Learning Objectives

After reading this chapter, you should be able to:

L01 Distinguish the different types of intellectual property

L02 Discuss the laws that regulate copyright protection

L03 Describe how the copyright protects works of original artistic creativity

L04 Explain the fair use doctrine

L05 Describe the patent law process

L06 Explain the types of patents available

L07 Describe trademark protection law

L08 Discuss domain names

Opening Scenario

YouTube has approximately 160,000 free videos that have been viewed at least 1.5 billion times. Comedy Central's mock news show, the Colbert Report, is one of the more popular videos that are viewed. Viacom, the parent company of Comedy Central, has asked the court to make YouTube stop posting videos that are unauthorized. Viacom seeks $1 billion in damages and asks the court to make YouTube stop the practice.[1]

Two questions have to be answered by the lawsuit. The first is whether owners of the content can sue the host site for putting the content on its site. In other words, can the owner block all content? The second question is whether a consumer of the content, say, a viewer of the Colbert Report, can capture the show or portions of it and share it through YouTube distribution. In other words, is this fair use?

Before we learn what the law is regarding this area, what are your thoughts about this case? Should the owner of a show's content have some right to control its distribution? Should the viewer be able to share with others? Is the problem similar to the *Sony* case in which the Supreme Court held that time-shifting, i.e., videotaping a television show for later viewing by the consumer, is fair use? Or is this more like the *Napster* case in which the court held that peer-to-peer sharing of music is a copyright infringement because it is meant to avoid paying for the recording thereby cheating the artists of earned royalties? Does it make any difference if the content that is distributed on YouTube comes from a cable show in which the viewer only has access if they pay the cable company versus a network show that can be viewed by anyone? Is that a valid distinction? Viacom is arguing that what they lose is the advertising dollars

---

[1]Complaint, *Viacom Int'l Inc. v. YouTube, Inc.,* and Google, Inc., C.V. No. 02103 (S.D.N.Y., filed March 13, 2007).

that they charge when a show is on television. Is this a reason for prohibiting content on the Web, or is the remedy for that loss charging YouTube each time someone views the particular video? The real question is whether the law will ever keep up with technology.

Introduction

L01

Have you ever copied music to give to a friend? Scribbled a poem on a napkin while waiting for your meal to be served? Been in a school play of a theatrical production you've seen on TV or in the movies? Played popular CDs at an event people paid to attend? Used a favorite cartoon character on a T-shirt logo? Photocopied chapters from a friend's textbook because you couldn't afford to buy your own? Played a popular song on your guitar? Uploaded a TV clip you liked to YouTube? Made copies of your professionally taken photos because it was too expensive to order copies from the photographer? Well, then you need to know the law regarding intellectual property.

Intellectual property consists of concepts, information, symbols, or creative expression and therefore has no physical boundaries. Such activity becomes property once it is protected by patents, copyright, or trademark. Issues may involve patenting of some novel invention, deciding to protect a business name by trademark, or copyrighting written information, or some combination thereof. As you can see from the opening scenario, technology plays a hand in these determinations.

EXAMPLE

The Founding Fathers considered the protection of one's creative work to be extremely important to the forging of a new nation. They believed that the country would need all the innovation and creativity it could muster to make this new experiment in democracy all that it could be. They also understood that people would be less likely to put the necessary time, money, and energy into that creative process unless the fruits of their labor were provided protection from others treating those fruits as their own. While this new government was to be one in which free enterprise predominated, they understood this must be balanced with the creator's right to the fruits of his or her labor. One way to accomplish this was by providing at least limited protection for fruits of the creative process. The Founding Fathers considered this concept so important that they accomplished it by providing for copyright and patent protection in the U.S. Constitution itself.

The Copyright-Patent Clause of the U.S. Constitution, Article I, section 8, gives Congress the power "to promote the progress of science and useful arts, by securing for limited times to authors and inventors the exclusive right to their respective writings and discoveries." This provision authorizes the federal government to protect authors and inventors from unauthorized use of their writings and discoveries, but only for limited times. The clause is concerned with the right of the authors and inventors to control the use and reproduction of their original work. This constitutional clause balances the tension between encouraging intellectual, artistic, and technological progress on the one hand, and allowing the dissemination and use of these developments for the enjoyment and betterment of society on the other. This is an important issue for artists and authors who are trying to hold on to exclusive use of their artistic creations in spite of the ease with which these items can now be copied due to technological advances.

EXAMPLE

There are three types of federally protected intellectual property: copyrights, patents, and trademarks. **Copyright** protects authors, illustrators, photographers, musical composers, and lyricists, among others. **Patents** protect inventors and their inventions. **Trademarks** protect goods and services. All three are protected by federal acts. Copyrights and patents, unlike trademarks, are designed to promote the progress of science and useful arts; the constitutional source of Congress's power is the Copyright and Patent Clause. The purpose of trademark law is to prevent confusion in the marketplace and ensure accurate information and the maintenance of quality of goods and services. The constitutional source of Congress's power is the Commerce Clause. Other types of business information such as **trade secrets** are protected by state statutes or unfair competition laws.

The Copyright Office lies within the Library of Congress and is an arm of the legislative branch. Administratively, the Copyright Office and the Registrar handle the bulk of the work on copyright registration and recording. The Office handles applications for copyright, issues regulations about copyrights, sets and distributes fees, and handles the mechanics of registration. The Registrar of the Copyright Office is appointed by the Librarian of Congress.

Copyright Laws

While copyright protection has been around since the country was founded, laws have changed a good deal over the years. Keep in mind that when the Constitution was written, books were not something that most people had and there was no recording of music. As society has changed, technology has changed and even societal mores have changed, so too, have copyright laws. The basic copyright law that now governs is the Copyright Reform Act of 1976.

THE COPYRIGHT REFORM ACT OF 1976

The Copyright Reform Act of 1976 (the Act) grants to copyright holders the exclusive right to use and authorize use of their work with certain exceptions. A copyright protects original works of authorship that are fixed in any medium of expression, now known or later developed, from which they can be perceived, reproduced, or otherwise communicated, either directly or with the aid of a machine or device, whether published or unpublished. A copyright does not protect an idea itself, but protects the manifestation of the idea. For example, in the opening scenario, the content of the programs played on YouTube is the expression of an idea. That is the protectable product. Works of authorship include literary works; musical works, including words; dramatic works, including music; pantomimes and choreographic works; pictorial, graphic, and sculptural works; motion pictures and other audiovisual works; sound recordings; and architectural works. The Act states that the list is not meant to be exclusive.

For works created or published on or after January 1, 1978 (the effective date of the Act), copyright protection lasts for the life of the creator plus 90 years.[2] In the case of joint authorship, the last surviving author plus 50 years is the term of protection. Thus, all of an author's works enter the public domain at the same time.

Works that are in the **public domain,** i.e., works whose copyright has expired or was never requested, are not eligible for copyright protection. Such works are freely useable; there is no restriction whatsoever on the use of the work. This raises the question—if someone replays a movie made before 1923 on YouTube, is it infringement?

SECTION 1101 OF THE COPYRIGHT ACT

With the growth of technology came greater and greater opportunities for copyright infringement. Whether it was omnipresent tape machines that allowed dubbing of music cassette tapes or recording of music from the radio, or photo copiers that

---

[2]An amendment to the Act in 1998 added 20 years onto the original grant of 70 years for works published after January 1, 1978. Works created but not published or registered before January 1, 1978, are protected for 95 years after publication Works created and published or registered before January 1, 1978 are protected for 95 years..

allowed for professional-looking copies of graphics, scanners that allowed the printed word to be digitized and manipulated, smaller and smaller video cameras that allowed for surreptitious recording of live shows or movies, Betamax and VHS technology that ushered in VCRs, music sharing technology over the Internet, or social networking sites that made sharing so easy, copyright infringement grew exponentially with each new technology.

In response, Congress passed several laws that tried to keep up with the explosion of assaults on intellectual property. In 1994 Congress enacted section 1101 of the Copyright Act. This section was enacted to implement the treaty known as the Agreement on Trade Related Aspects of Intellectual Property (TRIPs). The purpose of section 1101 is to prevent unauthorized fixing or broadcasting of live musical performances, also known as **bootleg** copying. Unauthorized recording or public performance of a bootleg copy played for the public is a violation of this federal statute. For example, if you attend a live play and videotape it, it's a violation of federal law to replay it for the public. A videotape of the singer/dancer/actress Beyonce falling down the steps as she entered the stage for one of her concerts was removed from YouTube after the sponsors of the show complained that the concert was copyrighted. This was an example of an unauthorized showing of copyrighted material.

EXAMPLE

THE NO ELECTRONIC THEFT ACT

The No Electronic Theft Act (NET Act) was passed in 1997 largely in response to the *U.S. v. LaMacchia*[3] case. In that case the district court dismissed the case against LaMacchia, a college student at Massachusetts Institute of Technology (MIT) who infringed as a hobby, because there was no commercial intent in the infringement. Without commercial motive there could be no criminal prosecution.

Congress quickly responded to this case by enacting the NET Act, which makes it a crime to engage in copyright infringement even when there is no commercial motive, i.e., there is no money earned or benefit gained. Maximum penalties are five years in prison and a $250,000 fine.

THE DIGITAL MILLENNIUM COPYRIGHT ACT

The Digital Millennium Copyright Act (DMCA)[4] was enacted in 1998 specifically for the purpose of recognizing two treaties that had been adopted by the international community through the World Intellectual Property Organization (WIPO). Title I of the DMCA criminalizes production and dissemination of technology, devices, or services intended to circumvent measures that control access to copyrighted works even where there is no infringement and increases the penalty for infringement on the Internet. In other words, if there is an **encryption** device placed on copyrighted material, Title I makes it a federal violation to decode that device. Thus, the court had no problem in finding infringers guilty of violating Title I when they decoded a scrambling system placed on copyrighted works by several major motion picture studios and placed the decoding software on their website for others to download and decode the DVDs on which they were placed.[5] In a more recent case, a federal judge issued a preliminary injunction prohibiting the sale of RealDVD, a DVD copying software that allows users

EXAMPLE

---

[3]871 F. Supp. 535 (U.S. Dist. Mass. 1994).

[4]17 U.S.C. §512 et seq. The DMCA contains five Titles, but only Titles I and II are pertinent to this discussion. Title III is entitled the Computer Maintenance Competition Assurance Act and addresses infringement that might occur during computer repair; Title IV, entitled Miscellaneous Provisions, addresses topics such as education, statutory licenses, libraries, and movie rights; and Title V entitled Vessel Hull Design Protection Act adds protection for boat hull designs previously not covered by copyright law.

[5]*Universal City Studios v. Corley,* 273 F.3d 429 (2d Cir. 2001).

to copy DVDs on up to five computers. Seven movie companies had argued that the copying software violates the DMCA, and that the argument offered by RealDVD that it constituted fair use was invalid for software that allows five copies of copyrighted material to be made. The federal judge agreed with the studios, and held that RealDVD promoted piracy and violated the DMCA.[6]

Title II of the DMCA limits the liability of online service providers for copyright infringement by their users, providing a safe harbor for those providers who adhere to the safe harbor guidelines. Reality Check 15-1 ("And the Winner Is . . . ?") looks at what happens when the winners of a contest to see who could decipher an encrypted code wished to publish his findings.

Copyright Requirements

Not everything is subject to copyright protection. Even if it is, there are requirements that must be met in order to receive the maximum protection the law allows. Following are the requirements for copyright.

L03

THE MEANING OF "FIXED" IMAGE

The Copyright Act protects a work fixed in either a copy or phonorecord as defined in section 101 of the Act. Examples of a phonorecord are a vinyl disk, an audiotape, a CD, or a computer hard-drive or, more generally, anything that can be heard. A copy is defined as a material object other than a phonorecord in which a work is fixed and from which it can be communicated or, more generally, anything that can be seen. In order to bring a work under the federal act, then, it must be **fixed** in one of these tangible objects.

EXAMPLE

New technology has challenged the definition of "fixed." For example, cases once raised the question of whether a video game has fixed images. Before this issue was decided, users argued that the screen images were unfixed and subject to human manipulation, thus subject to being freely copied. The courts consistently rejected that argument.[7] The issue was finally resolved when the courts held that computer programs, whether operating systems or application programs, were literary works (works expressed in words, numbers, or other verbal or numerical symbols), that, once fixed in computer hardware, are eligible for copyright protection.[8]

IDEAS VERSUS EXPRESSIONS

Section 102(b) of the Act specifically states that copyright does not "extend to any idea, procedure, process, system, method of operation, concept, principle, or discovery, regardless of the form in which it is described, explained, illustrated, or embodied in such work."

---

[6]Drew Combs, "Real Networks Loses Another Round in DVD Copying Case," *The American Lawyer,* August 12, 2009, http://www.americanlawyer.com.

[7]See, e.g., *Williams Elecs, Inc. v. Artic Int'l, Inc.,* 685 F.2d 870 (3d Cir. 1982).

[8]See, e.g., *Apple Computer Inc, v. Franklin Computer Corp.,* 714 F.2d 1240 (3d Cir. 1983).

EXAMPLE The line between idea and expression is not always clear, especially in certain areas. For example, in the area of literature, an author's work is copyrightable, but general themes, story ideas, or character prototypes are not copyrightable. Facts or groups of facts are not copyrightable—the court takes the position that facts are merely discovered, and discoveries are not copyrightable under the Act. Likewise, blank forms, graph paper, account books, address books and the like are not copyrightable, because they are designed for recording information and not for conveying information.

Another area that presents some confusion is in the area of pictorial, graphic and sculptural works. Familiar symbols or designs are not copyrightable, but things such as colorized black and white movies,[9] and Barbie's nose, lips, and eyes **EXAMPLE** [10] are copyrightable. There is no question that the content contained in the television and movies being contested by Viacom are copyrightable images. Reality Check 15–2 ("What About Movie Characters?") discusses another medium in which the line between ideas and expressions can be blurred.

REALITY CHECK 15-2

WHAT ABOUT MOVIE CHARACTERS?

Could you make a movie in which a young blond woman is captured by a giant menacing gorilla, taken to the top of the Empire State Building, gets shot by aircraft and dies on the streets of NYC? What if you called the gorilla King Kong? Even if this scene is not familiar to you, it is the final scene of the movie *King Kong,* originally made in 1933 by RKO and remade by Universal Pictures in 2005. And the answer is No. You cannot make a film with these specific characters, at least according to one court. In one case, where the infringer made an automobile commercial in which a handsome man in a tuxedo and his female partner were cast driving recklessly to escape a high tech villain, the court held that that was too close to a James Bond movie not to infringe. The more a character is identifiable, the more it is expressed and the less it is just an idea, and thus the more copyrightable it is. Here, the characters had been expressed and defined beyond just the idea.

Source: MGM Inc. v. American Honda Motor Co., 900 F. Supp. 1287 (C.D. Cal. 1995).

OWNERSHIP OF COPYRIGHT

The Copyright Act is straightforward on ownership; ownership is in the author. If the work is a joint work, the authors are co-owners. If, for example, a song is written by a lyricist and a composer, they are both co-owners and either one may license the performance or recording of the song. If, however, the music was written by the composer and published that way, and lyrics were added later, the work is not jointly owned. In that case, the composer would own the music only and the lyricist would own the words only. Consent to record or use the song must be obtained from both. Diversity in the Law 15-1 ("Another Reason Blacks Have the Blues") examines the history of the copyright laws pertaining to black recording artists in the U.S., many of whom experienced copyright infringements without realizing it. As illustrated by the opening scenario, films and television are not owned by the actors who portray the parts, but by the owners of the material or those who own a license to it.

EXAMPLE

NOTICE AND REGISTRATION

Registration of the copyrighted work with the Copyright Office is not a prerequisite for a valid copyright. For copies and photographs distributed to the public between January 1, 1978, and February 28, 1989, the Copyright Act requires the presence of three elements for a published work to be protected. First, the symbol © or the word *copyright* or the abbreviation *copr.* must appear on the document. Second, the year of first publication of the document or, if the document is unpublished, the year completed must appear. Third, the name of the owner of the copyright should appear. All information should be obvious, not hidden or inconspicuous, on the document. On

---

[9]52 Fed. Reg. 23,442 (1987).

[10]*Mattel, Inc. v. Goldberger Doll Mfg. Co.,* 365 F.3d 133 (2d Cir. 2004).

ANOTHER REASON BLACKS HAVE THE BLUES

American music has a strange history in this country. Reflecting the culture of the times, during the 1920s and 30s, the sale of "coon" or "nigger" sheet music was the most profitable segment of the music business. Black-faced minstrelsy, another popular form of entertainment during that time and the most degrading form of entertainment in America for decades, exacerbated the stereotypes of blacks in this country. In this mode of entertainment whites performed on stage with their faces blackened by burnt cork, all over except the lip and eye area, meant to portray the caricature of blacks having huge lips and eyes that bugged out.

The music industry was no exception to the institutionalized racism and discrimination practiced against black Americans. Before the 1950s, black Americans could not perform with any opera company and, in fact, were excluded from the music industry except through playing the "Chitlin' Circuit"—a group of theaters around the country known to cater only to black audiences. Many performers today are products of the "Chitlin' Circuit." Record companies relegated black recording artists to "race record" divisions of record companies. Major black recording artists such as Bessie Smith were subjected to unconscionable contracts that deprived black artists of royalties they were entitled to under the law. Not only did they deny them compensation, they also never gave them credit for their contributions.

Music scholars have credibly refuted the notion that whites invented rock and roll, although there are still histories that insist it was invented solely by Elvis Presley. Other black contributions have been attributed to white artists as well. Blacks sang the blues long before the all-white Original Dixieland Blues Band sang them. Negro spirituals, long the songs of slavery and freedom, are said to have been copied from white Christian songs. Black contributions have been devalued throughout the history of music in this country.

Copyright laws themselves have contributed to the lack of credit given to blacks. Copyright law requires the work to be in a fixed medium. Many forms of black music are not based on a written format. In fact, many of the original blues singers were illiterate and had no formal way of notating their music. In addition, copyright requires original works. Many blues and other forms of black music have as their trademark "borrowing" one song to the next, forming the cultural context of the music. As a result, these forms of music may not lend themselves to copyright. Lastly, at least before 1976, there were a series of formal requirements for registering work that was forbidding even to schooled musicians and promoters. Failure to maneuver through the rules often thrust the work into the public domain where anyone could record it without attribution.

The exclusion continues into the 21st century, where rap artists are prevented from copyrighting their originality because of the idea vs. expression cultural divide. Early black rappers are said to have exhibited "style" and not originality, thus their style is not protectable under the law. What this means is that when their "style" is captured and repeated by others—Vanilla Ice comes to mind—the originators receive no credit or compensation from their contribution.

There is an irony here. Fast-forward to the criticism of musicians and artists today who decry the piracy of their music—wholesale theft by file-sharing digital thieves. Looked at through a different lens, it could be argued that this is a mere repeat of the theft perpetrated by the music industry upon equally helpless artists and musicians at the turn of the century, legally disenfranchised by societal norms rather than technology. Perhaps what the anti-copyright youth of today understand and rebel against is that the copyright laws tend to make the music companies richer, while keeping the creative artists and musicians in relative poverty. Perhaps not for artists who are conglomerates, but for those who are the creative innovators, the music industry has taken a step back.

Source: K. J. Greene, "What the Treatment of African American Artists Can Teach About Copyright Law," in Peter K. Yu, ed., *Intellectual Property and Information Wealth: Issues and Practices in the Digital Age,* Volume 1 (Greenwood, 2006).

EXAMPLE

March 1, 1989, to comply with international rules regarding copyright, Congress eliminated the mandatory notice provisions in the law. Thus, the words "shall be placed" in the Copyright Act were replaced with the words "may be placed." The fact is, most commercial endeavors—movies, television, and the like—are registered.

For works that were created before the notice provisions were eliminated, failure to comply is fatal to protecting the works; thus, if they did not comply they are in the public domain. For works after the March 1, 1989 change, an omission is of no consequence, other than to deter infringers. Reality Check 15-3 ("Statute of Limitations Bars Suit for Infringement") illustrates the other limitations for filing an infringement action.

Prior to the enactment of the Copyright Act of 1976, whether a work was published was very important and determined which jurisdiction could hear the case—federal or state, whether there was compliance with the formalities, and whether a 28-year or 56-year term of protection applied. Because the term *publication* was not defined in the previous act, courts were left to define the term. The courts generally agreed that only a general publication would divest a work of copyright protection, while a limited publication would not. Thus, in 1991 the courts held that the dissemination between 1929 and 1941 of 159 Oscar statuettes by the Academy of Motion Picture Arts and Sciences without notices of copyright was not a general publication because it was awarded to only a select group of people. [11] In 1999, the same question arose surrounding the publication of Dr. King's "I Have a Dream" speech. Diversity in the Law 15-2 ("Who Owns the Dream?") details the fight over ownership of his most famous speech. What do you think the motive was for CBS to argue it was published to them?

Although registration with the Copyright Office is not necessary (copyright attaches at the moment of creation), it is required before seeking certain legal remedies, and it is best for legal protection. If a work is filed within five years of creation, the work has the presumption of authenticity; if filed after that, authenticity may

---

[11] *Academy of Motion Picture Arts & Sciences v. Creative House Promotions, Inc.*, 944 F.2d 1446 (9th Cir. 1991).

have to be proven. Registration requires an application, a fee, and two copies of the work, excluding movies.

INFRINGEMENT

To **infringe** upon a copyright means that the exclusive rights of the copyright owner have been violated. This can be accomplished by reproducing the copyrighted material; using the copyrighted material in a derivative work, such as a collection, without permission; or distributing, performing, or displaying copyrighted work. If an infringement claim is successful, the copyright owner could elect to enjoin the continued use of the work or could receive either actual damages—including profits made by the infringer—or statutory damages of up to $50,000.

In order to infringe, the owner must prove that the work was copied and that what was copied was substantial in degree. For example, if an infringer copied only isolated or minor elements that did not create an appearance of similarity, then the copying would be **de minimis** and not infringing. This will present an interesting issue for the *Viacom* lawsuit. The programs displayed are generally played in their entirety. In addition, if the words copied are not copyrightable, it is not infringement. For example, where a list of facts is compiled in a copyrightable pattern, the pattern may be infringed upon, but the facts in the list are not protected and may be copied and used. Reality Check 15-4 ("Section 115 of the Copyright Act: A Look under the 'Covers'") answers the question of why so many recording artists can record one song without infringing on the copyright owner's interest. The reality is the artist can't stop it.

FAIR-USE DOCTRINE

 L04

An exception to the unauthorized use of copyrighted material is the **fair-use doctrine.** This judicially created exception to the protection normally afforded copyrighted material recognizes that in certain instances, public policy dictates that use of the material is fair and that its use would not conflict with the constitutional mandate to protect such work for the purposes of promoting intellectual growth and development. Going back to our opening scenario, it is anticipated that YouTube and Google will attempt to use the fair-use doctrine to defend their position in the Viacom lawsuit. Can you see how it would be used?

The Act lists four criteria to be used in a determination of whether use of material is fair. First, the purpose and character of the use are measured; this considers both how the material is used and the intent for which use was made. Second, the nature of the copyrighted work is measured; this examines both the expectations of the author and whether the work is scholarly or for commercial use. Third, the amount and substantiality of the portion used in relation to the copyrighted work as a whole are measured; this examines both the qualitative and quantitative use of the work. Last, the effect of the use upon the potential market is measured; this examines the value of the copyrighted portions on the potential purchasing market. Reality Check 15-5 ("What Happened to Napster?") discusses the demise of Napster, the peer-to-peer file sharing computer program created by a college student to share music with his friends that began the whole music downloading phenomenon, which was enjoined after trial.

The Act gives six examples of purposes to which the fair-use doctrine normally applies. Those examples are criticism, comment, news reporting, teaching, scholarship, and research. Not listed, but almost always protected by fair use, is the use of copyrighted material in parody and satire. Are any of these exceptions available to YouTube?

Technology has impacted this area of the copyright law also. In January 2009, Gatehouse Media, a publisher of 125 newspapers in the Boston area, sued the *New York Times* and the Boston.com website alleging copyright infringement. [12] In this suit, Gatehouse is asking the court to rule on whether Internet news providers will be able to continue the practice of posting headlines and lead sentences from stories they link on to other sites. A ruling in Gatehouse's favor will have far-reaching implications for other Internet news providers, including bloggers, Internet researchers, and companies that aggregate news online. Such organizations and individuals are watching the case closely. Case 15.1 also illustrates how significant an adverse ruling can be for a company seen to infringe on the copyright.

EXAMPLE

EXAMPLE

Fair Use and Photocopying

To the specific issue of photocopying (including by audiovisual or computer), three tests apply: brevity, spontaneity, and cumulative effect. Generally considered fair are uses that constitute less than 10 percent of a total body of work (brevity), are created so quickly that there is not time to request permission for use (spontaneity), and that the use is limited to one time or such a small number that there is no aggregate use that could harm the potential market (cumulative effect).

Thus, two different courts have rejected the fair-use doctrine in two important cases with similar facts where teaching materials that comprised substantial portions of copyrighted books were copied without seeking permission of the copyright owners. [13] In another case, the court rejected the fair-use doctrine where a single copy was made to assist researchers. In that case, researchers for an oil company received the table of contents of scientific journals. Once they circled the titles of articles they wished to possess, copies of the articles were made for them. The court held that use of the copies was a substitute for purchasing additional subscriptions or licensing fees. [14]

 EXAMPLE

---

[12]Susie Madrak, "Lawsuit to Determine Fair Use for Blogs, Links, Headlines," January 23, 2009, http://crooksandliars.com/susie-madrak/lawsuit-determine-fair-use-blog-links.

[13]See *Basic Books, Inc. v. Kinko's Graphics Corp.*, 758 F. Supp. 1522 (S.D.N.Y. 1991); and *Princeton University Press v. Michigan Document Services, Inc.*, 99 F.3d 1381 (6th Cir. 1996 en banc).

[14]*American Geophysical Union v. Texaco Inc.*, 60 F.3d 913 (2d Cir. 1994).

CASE 15.1 Bourne v. Twentieth Century Fox

602 F. Supp.2d 499 (S.D.N.Y. 2009)

Facts: Bourne owns the copyright to the unpublished version of the song "When You Wish Upon a Star" originally written for *Pinocchio*. The song has been used by over 100 artists in movies, ads, and television shows. Fox's show, *Family Guy*, is an animated TV show that regularly contains irreverent, pop-cultural plotlines. One episode was entitled "When You Wish Upon a Weinstein." The comedy was centered on the show's character Peter and his inability to manage the company's finances. After learning how others have used people with Jewish names to achieve success Peter decides he needs a "Jew" to help him. In the episode Peter sings a song entitled "I Need a Jew" with the same rhyme scheme, beat, and music of "When You Wish Upon a Star." Plaintiff refused to license the song for use and the show used the song anyway. Bourne filed suit for copyright infringement.

Issue: Whether the show's use of the song constituted copyright infringement or fell within the fair use exception.

Decision: Fair use existed.

Reasoning: According to the Supreme Court, the fair-use doctrine permits and requires courts to avoid rigid application of the copyright statute when, on occasion, it would stifle the very creativity which that law is designed to foster. Further, the task is not to be simplified with bright-line rules, for the statute, like the doctrine it recognizes, calls for case-by-case analysis. Because the four factors in Section 107 are applied differently to parodies and satires, the starting point of the Court's analysis is determining whether the Defendants' use of "When You Wish Upon a Star" is properly considered satire, parody, or neither, as those terms have come to be defined by fair-use case law. The distinction between parody and satire turns on the object of the "comment" made by the allegedly infringing work.

The Defendants in this case have sought to justify their use of Plaintiff's copyrighted material as parody in two ways: (1) as a comment on the "saccharine sweet," "innocent" and "wholesome" worldview presented in and represented by "When You Wish Upon a Star" and (2) by evoking "the song most associated with Walt Disney and his company" commenting "on the song while simultaneously making a sharp point about Walt Disney's reputed anti-Semitism." Defendants argue that their song works to "lampoon the 'purity' and 'wholesome' values expressed in 'Wish Upon a Star' "; the song "turns the sweetness of this idyllic message on its head by having Peter ignorantly sing about stereotypes of Jewish people, while at the same time earnestly, and innocently, wishing for a Jew, as if they were some kind of mystical beings who, naturally, could help him solve his financial problems." Plaintiff argues that Defendants' song "I Need a Jew" does not criticize, ridicule, or in any way comment upon its song but rather "ridicules anti-Semitism and Jewish stereotypes." It argues there is absolutely nothing about "I Need a Jew" that overtly comments on or criticizes the subject matter, quality or style of "When You Wish Upon a Star."

The creators of the Episode were clearly attempting to comment in some way on the wishful, hopeful scene in *Pinocchio* with which the song is associated. Consequently, "I Need a Jew" is properly understood as a parody of "When You Wish Upon a Star."

CASE QUESTIONS

1. The court focused on the nature of the song and what it was trying to communicate. Why is this necessary? Why is the court interested in protecting parody as in this case?

2. What benefit does society get from the protection of parody and satire?

3. The court went on to find that the four factors listed in 107—(1) the purpose and character of the use, (2) the nature of the copyrighted work, (3) the amount and substantiality of the portion used in relation to the work as a whole, and (4) the effect on the market—all weighed in favor of the parody, and thus constitutes fair use. Once a court finds the infringing work to be a parody, under what circumstances would it be likely to find infringement that was not fair use? Wouldn't a parody always be so?

WORK FOR HIRE

The **work-for-hire doctrine** states that an employer automatically owns copyright in employees' works that are prepared within the scope of employment. The doctrine covers such things as writings, art, photography, music, and computer programs.

The critical inquiry to be made is whether a person has created the material while within the scope of employment. Generally, absent a written agreement to the contrary, an employer owns any material created while an employee is working at a task directed by the employer, whether that task is performed at home or on the job. Conversely, an employer is not entitled to ownership of material simply because the employer's assets, time, and place of business were used during the creation of the material.

A second inquiry revolves around the definition of who is an employee. An employer can more easily claim copyright privileges on material created by an employee than it can on material created by an independent contractor. In fact, some courts suggest that if a person is not a bona fide employee (i.e., an employee for tax and benefit purposes), then the employer is not entitled to any ownership of property created by the independent contractor. The Supreme Court had the opportunity to clarify the difference between an employee and an independent contractor in the case of *Community for Non-Violence v. Reid.*[15] In that case, the court made clear that under the Copyright Act of 1976, an employee is defined under typical agency rules that are applied in tort cases. The Court held that for a person to be an employee, factors must be considered, such as

> control by the employer, the skill required by the worker, the source of instrumentalities and tools, the location of the work, the duration of the relationship between the parties, whether the hiring party has the right to assign additional duties, the extent of the hiring party's discretion over when and how long to work, the method of payment, the hired party's role in hiring and paying assistants, whether the work is part of the regular business of the hiring party, whether the hiring party is in business, the provision of employee benefits, and the tax treatment of the hired party.[16]

For clarity's sake, the better practice is to have employees enter into contracts that give an employer the ownership of property created by an individual that is generally enforceable. Alternatives to consider might be a license to the employer to use the product created by an independent contractor or an assignment of the copyright by the creator of the property to the person who commissioned the work.

TRANSFER OF COPYRIGHT OWNERSHIP

Ownership of copyrights is freely transferable. This means the copyright can be assigned or licensed, bequeathed by will, or given away. The Copyright Office registers initial ownership and records transfers of ownership and acts much like the recording of real property.

Transfer of ownership has been subject to uncertainty in the face of new technology. Questions now arise with the advent of e-books and digital books. In most cases, the contract that transferred ownership or licensed use was entered into long before these newer technologies were invented. Who can say whether an author of a book written in 1980 who granted a publisher the right to publish the book intended to give the author the right to digitalize the book and/or publish it in e-book format—technologies that were not available then? In a 2001 case in which a publishing company challenged the right of several authors to transfer rights to publish in e-book form to a digital publisher, the court sided with the authors in finding that they acted lawfully when conveying e-book rights to digital publishers, even though they had a prior print contract with the publishing company.[17]

EXAMPLE

REMEDIES FOR COPYRIGHT INFRINGEMENT

Once the plaintiff has proven infringement, injury is presumed and either an injunction will be issued or damages assessed. The court can also impound the infringing copies and order them destroyed.

---

[15]400 U.S. 730 (1989).

[16]*Id.* at 751-52.

[17]*Random House, Inc. v. Rosetta Books, L.L.C.,* 150 F. Supp. 2d 613 (S.D.N.Y. 2001).

Section 504 of the Act provides for the award of statutory damages consisting of actual damages and additional profits. Actual damages can be measured by the cost of a license or the loss of profits by the unlawful distribution of the copyrighted work. The statute also allows, in the court's discretion, the award of attorney's fees and costs to the prevailing party. In our opening scenario, what do you think the appropriate remedy should/will be if Viacom is successful in its lawsuit against YouTube?

EXAMPLE

L05

Patents

The U.S. Constitution, Article I, Section 8, gives Congress the power to enact laws relating to patents. The Patent Act of 1952 (the Act) and the American Inventors Protection Act of 1999 provide the laws regulating patents. The Act establishes the U.S. Patent and Trademark Office (USPTO) as the agency to administer the laws relating to the granting of patents. Its role is to grant patents to protect inventions and to register trademarks.

A **patent** for an invention is the grant of a property right to the inventor to preclude others from using the patent without the patent holder's permission. Patents provide the strongest protection of any type of intellectual property. During the term of a patent, its protection is virtually absolute; in exchange, at the end of the term, full disclosure of the patented invention to the public is required. A patent does not give the inventor the right to make, use, or sell the invention; rather, it gives the inventor the right to *exclude others* from making, using, offering for sale, or selling, the invention or design for a 20-year-period from the date of the application, which cannot be renewed. Patent grants are effective only within the U.S., U.S. territories, and U.S. possessions. Once issued, the patentee must enforce the patent; the USPTO does not assist in enforcing its patents.

Beginning in 1995, the USPTO provided for the provisional application for a patent designed for two purposes. First, it provides for a lower cost, first-patent filing in the U.S. Second, it gives U.S. applicants parity with foreign applicants. Once a provisional application is filed, the term "Patent Pending" is permitted to be used with the invention. The words "Patent Pending" on an article gives no protection at all during the period prior to the actual grant of the patent. Rather, it puts the public on notice that the item is subject to potential patent rights. A provisional application expires by operation of law 12 months after the application is filed, and this 12-month period is not included in the 20 year patent grant. Provisional applications may not be filed for design inventions. Diversity in the Law 15-3 ("Women's Contributions Seen through Patent Grants") shows the contributions made by minority women in the area of inventions throughout history and Diversity in the Law 15-4 ("Henry Baker, Patent Examiner and Historian") discusses the contribution made by Henry Baker regarding minority inventors throughout history.

L06

TYPES OF PATENTS

There are three types of patents in the United States: utility, design, and plant patents.

A **utility patent** is available for "any new and useful process, machine, manufacture, or composition of matter, or any new and useful improvement thereof."[18] These are the most common types of patents.

A **design patent** covers any new original and ornamental design for an article of manufacture. Design patents differ from utility patents in that (1) they do not cover utilitarian function; (2) the drawing of the design is the focus of the protection; (3) the standards for infringement are different; and (4) the measures of damages are different for infringement. Reality Check 15-6 ("How Do I Know if My Invention Is Already Patented?") tells how to do an initial search of the patent office to see if your invention is original.

---

[18]Title 35 U.S.C. 101 (2010)

WOMEN'S CONTRIBUTIONS SEEN THROUGH PATENT GRANTS

Women and minorities have contributed to the advancement of this country through their inventions. Here are a few of the contributions made by women.

In addition to these few inventors, *Buttons to Biotech, U.S. Patenting by Women, 1977 to 1996,* a USPTO report published in February 1999, listed the following statistics for patents granted between 1977 and 1996:

- 5.7% of the 985,319 patents granted were to women inventors

- Patents to women inventors rose from 2.6% to 9.2% during that time
- 82.6% of patents granted were for utility patents (inventions); 16.4% for design patents; and 0.5% for plant patents
- 49.5% of utility patents pertained to chemical technologies; 36.2% pertained to mechanical technologies; and 14.3% pertained to electrical technologies

Source: U.S. Patent and Trademark Office, press release, March 1, 2002, http://www.uspto.gov/web/offices/com/speeches/02-16.htm.

Year	Name of Inventor	Invention and Use
1809	Mary Dixon Kies	Weaving straw with silk or thread; used in making hats
1884	Judy W. Reed: First African American woman to receive a patent; she signed her patent application with an "X"	Dough kneader and roller; baking product
1885	Sarah E. Goode	Folding bed that could be formed into a desk when not in use
1903	Mary Anderson	Windshield wipers; used to clean windshield on automobiles
1971	Patsy O. Sherman (along with co-inventor Samuel Smith)	Scotchguard; stain repellent and soil removal product

HENRY BAKER, PATENT EXAMINER AND HISTORIAN

Henry Baker was an assistant patent examiner who is credited with chronicling the history of black inventors in the U.S. He was dedicated to uncovering and publicizing the black contributions of black inventors. His work began when the Patent Office sent letters to patent attorneys, company presidents, and others soliciting information about black inventors. This information was to be used to create an exhibit for the Cotton Centennial in New Orleans, the World's Fair in Chicago, and the Southern Exposition in Atlanta, all of which occurred around the early 1900s. Baker was responsible for cataloguing the letters that were received. By the time of his death, he had compiled four volumes detailing the contributions of black inventors.

Baker uncovered what was believed to be the first patent issued to a black inventor. Thomas Jennings, born in 1791, received a patent in 1821 for a dry cleaning process. At the time, slaves could not receive a patent, but Jennings was a free black who had a dry cleaning business in New York City. The second black man, Henry Blair, received his patent in 1834 for a seed planter, and in 1836 for a cotton planter. He was identified in the patent records as a "colored" man.

One of the more interesting persons uncovered was Lewis Latimer. Born in 1848, Latimer studied drafting and invented a method of making filaments for electric lamps. He ultimately became the draftsman for Thomas Edison and became a star witness in many infringement trials involving Edison's inventions.

Perhaps the most famous black inventor is George Washington Carver, who, from his laboratory at Tuskegee Institute, developed 325 different uses for peanuts and 118 products from the sweet potato. Carver received only three patents; he believed that God gave him the ideas and it was wrong to sell them. He was inducted into the National Inventors Hall of Fame in 1990.

Source: Mary Bellis, "Colors of Innovation," http://inventors.about.com/od/blackinventors/a/Early_History_3.htm.

HOW DO I KNOW IF MY INVENTION IS ALREADY PATENTED?

What if you have invented something and want to know if there is already a patent protecting it? The Patent Search Room located in Alexandria, Virginia, is where the public may search and examine patents that have been granted since 1790. The facility contains state of the art searching workstations. The Patent Search Room of the USPTO also provides facilities where the public can search for patents, and many public libraries have been designated as Patent and Trademark Depository Libraries (PTDLs). You can look through prior patents to determine whether one similar to your invention has been granted a patent and when. For complicated inventions, inventors often hire patent attorneys to do the search. Even these searches won't be as thorough and exhaustive as the search conducted by the patent examiner once the application is submitted. Often, a patent examiner will reject a claim in a patent application on the basis of patents not found in the preliminary search. The USPTO and PTDLs also contain forms and classification information for those wishing to patent their inventions.

Source: U.S. Patent and Trademark Office, http://www.uspto.gov/go/pac/doc/general/#functions.

Sometimes a design patent and a utility patent can overlap or be confusing. The easiest way to distinguish one from the other is to remember that a utility patent protects the way an article works, whereas a design patent protects the way an article looks. Think about a simple chair. While at one time a patent could have been obtained for whoever invented the chair, it would be a hard sell to the patent office to re-invent a simple chair. However, in 1905, Harry Bunnell applied for and received patent no. 794,777 for the Adirondack chair, then called the Westport chair. The design that was patented was a rounded back and contoured seat chair, a look that was specific to his chair and whose design was recognized as unique and patentable.

EXAMPLE

The **plant patent** covers "distinct and new" varieties of plants that are produced asexually. This excludes seed plants and most commercially valuable crops. Plant patents differ from utility patents in two ways. First, the plant has to be distinct rather than have any utility, thus a plant may be (and often is) merely an ornamental plant asexually produced. Second, there is a relaxation of disclosure requirements for plants, as their varieties are deemed incapable of accurate description. The description must simply be as complete as possible.

OBJECTS NOT SUBJECT TO PATENT

Certain things have been judicially deemed unsuitable for patent. Those things are laws of nature, physical phenomena, and abstract ideas. They are not patentable. Examples include fundamental scientific principles, mathematical formulas and algorithms, and abstract business ideas. The rationale for excluding such things is that they are discovered, not invented, and therefore patent laws do not protect them.

EXAMPLE

One continuous discussion within the patent community concerns cutting edge medical testing, especially concerning metabolic processes that occur in the body. For example, one debate currently is whether genetic testing for certain cancers involves a naturally occurring process which cannot be patented, or whether the tests themselves which measure this occurrence are within the patentable range. The ACLU and the Public Patent Foundation have challenged Myriad Genetics, the company that has patented all genetic testing for breast and ovarian cancer and thus controls all genetic testing for those diseases.[19] The way the issue has been framed—Do intellectual property rights trump life and death information?—means that the court will clearly have to resolve the ethical issue raised by the question. If the court rules that this is a phenomenon that cannot be patentable, then other labs that wish to work on curing or preventing these diseases will have the means to do so. If the process is patentable, then any work that is done will have to be done by Myriad Labs or the other labs will have to pay them to use the test they developed. Either way this case is decided, the issues are more than the patent court should have to decide.

[19]Alison Frankel, "Patent Litigation Weekly: Medical Testing and IP Rights Clash Again," *The American Lawyer,* July 20, 2009, http://www.americanlawyer.com.

REQUIREMENTS FOR PATENT PROTECTION

An invention must meet three criteria to qualify for patent protection: **novelty, utility,** and **nonobviousness.** Those three criteria, and the strictness with which they are applied, are the reasons why patent protection is the most difficult and expensive to obtain. The difficulty and expense are well worth it, because once patented, the owner has exclusive use of it for 20 years. Each of these criteria is governed by the Patent Act and consists of a strict and complicated set of rules that guide the issuance or nonissuance of a patent. Diversity in the Law 15-5 ("Michael Jackson's Shoes") describes an unusual contribution to dance and recording history of the late singer, which exemplifies the patent requirements of novelty and utility.

Case 15.2, *Procter & Gamble Co. v. Teva,* involves the patent requirement of nonobviousness.

DIVERSITY IN THE LAW 15-5

MICHAEL JACKSON'S SHOES

The National Inventors Hall of Fame presented a special display featuring some of Michael Jackson's inventions after his death in June 2009. Prominently displayed was his invention of a pair of shoes described as "a system for allowing a shoe wearer to lean forward beyond his center of gravity by virtue of wearing a specially designed pair of shoes which will engage with a hitch member movably projectable through a stage surface." The move can be seen in his video for Smooth Criminal, in which he is wearing what appears to be a pair of shoes with spats. Included in the display are Michael Joseph Jackson's signature on his patent application and his trademarks for his recordings.

Source: http://www.invent.org/hall_of_fame/1_5_0_museum.asp.

CASE 15.2 Procter & Gamble Co. v. Teva Pharmaceuticals, USA Inc.

566 F.3d 989 (C.A. Fed.) (Del.) 2009

Facts: Procter & Gamble (P & G) patented risedronate, the active ingredient in an osteoporosis drug. In 2004, P & G sued Teva when Teva tried to market a generic version of their drug. In its defense Teva argued the patent was invalid due to double-type patenting and obviousness. The trial court held for P & G and Teva appealed.

Issue: Whether the subject matter of the patent is obvious?

Holding: No

Reasoning: A party seeking to invalidate a patent based on obviousness must demonstrate "by clear and convincing evidence that a skilled artisan would have been motivated to combine the teachings of the prior art references to achieve the claimed invention, and that the skilled artisan would have had a reasonable expectation of success in doing so." Teva argues that the patent identifies 2-pyr EHDP as the most promising molecule for the inhibition of bone resorption. The trial court disagreed and concluded from the evidence that a person of ordinary skill in the art would not have identified 2-pyr EHDP as a lead compound for the treatment of osteoporosis. We need not

reach this question because we conclude that even if 2-pyr EHDP was a lead compound, the evidence does not establish that it would have been obvious to a person of ordinary skill at the time of the invention to modify 2-pyr EHDP to create risedronate.

Additionally, there was an insufficient showing that a person of ordinary skill in the art would have had a "reasonable expectation of success" in synthesizing and testing risedronate. The Supreme Court stated that when an obvious modification "leads to the anticipated success," the invention is likely the product of ordinary skill and is obvious. "[O]bviousness cannot be avoided simply by a showing of some degree of unpredictability in the art so long as there was a reasonable probability of success. Here, the district court's findings indicate that there was no reasonable expectation in 1985 that risedronate would be a successful compound. In this case, there is no credible evidence that the structural modification was routine. The district court found that the appellee's expert was evasive on this topic, stating that the witness "did not directly respond to most questions posed to him about whether it would be common for a chemist who develops a pyridine compound to conceive of and make [2-pyr

EHDP, 3-pyr EHDP, and 4-pyr EHDP] isomers." But evidence of evasion is not necessarily evidence that the testimony would otherwise have been favorable. The only direct evidence that the structural modification was routine was presented by an expert witness that the district court judge discredited.

CASE QUESTIONS

1. One way to avoid patent infringement is for the defendant to argue that the patent you are trying to enforce against them is invalid. What was Teva's invalidity argument here?

2. The court held that in 1985, Teva would not have been able to duplicate the results of Procter & Gamble's process because the ingredient would not have been predictably able to anticipate the results that were obtained. Why was this an important part of the decision?

3. The court ruled that the chemist/expert for Teva was evasive in answering the questions about whether Teva would have been able to create a successful compound. In noting that the lower court discredited the expert's testimony, what was the court saying about Teva's claims?

PATENT INFRINGEMENT

Anyone who without permission, makes, uses, or sells a patented invention infringes upon the right of the owner. The remedies for infringement are provided by the Patent Act. Those remedies are (1) an injunction, (2) damages, (3) attorney's fees, and (4) costs. It can be very expensive to litigate patent infringement cases. Reality Check 15-7 ("Abbott Labs to Pay Johnson & Johnson $1.67 Billion for Infringing") shows how expensive it can be to lose a patent infringement case.

L07

Trademarks

Think of a refreshing cola drink. What comes to mind? Chances are that you didn't think of an off-brand, but rather a popular brand of cola. Even the fact that we can call some colas an "off-brand" says a lot. It presumes there is a standard brand, then all others. The company's trademark has done its job. It has identified in the minds of consumers its product rather than any other, the standard by which others are to be judged. That is what trademarks are designed to do. A **trademark** is "any word, name, symbol, or device, or any combination thereof . . . used by a person . . . to identify and distinguish his or her goods . . . from those manufactured or sold by others."[20] Depending on the nature of the business, it can be extremely important for the business to establish customer loyalty by using a trademark for product identification. It is also important for the business not to infringe on the trademarks of other businesses.

TRADEMARK LAW

Trademarks are protected under a federal statute known as the Trademark Act of 1946, commonly referred to as the Lanham Act.

REALITY CHECK 15-7

ABBOTT LABS TO PAY JOHNSON & JOHNSON $1.67 BILLION FOR INFRINGING

A federal judge has ordered Abbott Labs to pay Johnson & Johnson $1.67 billion for infringing on its patent involving a rheumatoid arthritis drug. At issue was whether Johnson & Johnson's product, Remicade, was the same product as Abbott's Humira. Abbott claimed that Remicade is partially made from mouse DNA and that Abbott's Humira was the first fully human rheumatoid arthritis drug. The jury did not believe the distinction, and ruled that Abbott owes Johnson & Johnson for infringement.

Source: Jennifer Malloy Zonnas, "Abbott Ordered to Pay 1.67B in Patent Case," *TheStreet.com*, June 30, 2009, http://www.thestreet.com/story/10530739/2/abbott-ordered-to-pay-167b-in-patent-case.html.

[20]USPTO, http://www.uspto.gov/web/offices/pac/doc/general/whatis.htm.

This statute allows owners of trademarks to register them with the Patent and Trademark Office. Divided into four Subchapters, Subchapter III is the primary subchapter that includes Section 43(a). This section sets the "likelihood of confusion" standard for infringement of an unregistered trademark or trade dress. In our opening scenario, could trademark infringement be an action that Viacom pursues as well? What would be the complaint?

In 1999, Congress enacted the Trademark Cyberpiracy Prevention Act. This act was intended to create liability for any person who tries to make a bad faith attempt to profit by registering or using a domain name that belongs to a trademark. For example, shortly after Apple launched its iMac computer, Abdul Traya, a 16-year-old Calgary student, registered the domain name appleimac.com for the purpose of requiring Apple to purchase the domain name from him. This was a clear violation of the Act and Apple was able to recover damages under the Act.[21] More recently, Hells Angels has sued a woman alleging she registered domain names related to the group and placed them on eBay for sale. The group claims trademark infringement and cyberpiracy. They are asking the court to transfer the domain names to them and any profits she makes as a result of the sale to be given to them. They are also asking for $100,000 in damages for each domain name found to belong to the club.[22] Reality Check 15-8 ("Quick Extinction of a Cyberpirate") demonstrates how effective this law is in stopping this type of piracy.

Although words are probably the principal form of trademarks, names (once they become known), symbols, and devices can also serve as trademarks. Names such as McDonald's and Pillsbury are trademarks, as is John Hancock and Sam and Libby's. Symbols such as AT&T, 7-Eleven, and V-8 also form trademarks. Devices such as the shape of a Coca-Cola bottle have been ruled trademarks. The act covers a wide variety of things such as the color pink for insulation (Owens Corning fiberglass insulation), loop stitching and cloth tabs on pants (Levi Strauss), shapes of bottles (Mogen David wine), and slogans (Don't Leave Home Without It—American Express).

Unlike the other intellectual properties we have discussed, trademark protection has no limited term, but rather is protected for as long as it is used in commerce. That protection, however, is not absolute. It operates only to avoid confusion resulting from conflicting use of similar words or symbols in the same geographic area, and trademark principles do not protect words or symbols in the abstract, but only as they are used in commerce. Because of the commercial value of trademarks, however, trademark licensing has become enormously profitable business.

QUICK EXTINCTION OF A CYBERPIRATE

Shortly after passage of the Trademark Cyberpiracy Prevention Act, Stanley Steemer International obtained a judgment against George Donaldson, a Florida man who registered the name on the Internet under the name stanleysteemer.cc and then contacted the company via e-mail and offered to sell the name to the company. Advised that he was violating federal law, Donaldson refused to relinquish the name, bringing on the lawsuit. A federal judge quickly ruled that he had violated the Act. The law makes it much easier to pursue cybersquatters, as the domain name thieves are known. Formerly, a trademark owner had to pursue his claims under the original trademark statutes, which usually involved a long, expensive process. This law makes it easy to prove infringement, especially where the bad faith intent is so easy to prove.

Source: Robert Ruth, "Stanley Steemer Wins Cyberpiracy Suit," *The Columbus Dispatch,* August 9, 2000, http://www.ustrademarklawyer.com/steamer2.htm.

EXAMPLE

---

[21]Reuters, Dispute Settled, New Strait Times, April 29, 1999. http://news.google.com/newspapers?id=COcVAAAAIBAJ&sjid=3BQEAAAAIBAJ&pg=5474,6098014&dq=abdul-traya&hl=en

[22]Complaint for Cyberpiracy; Trademark Infringement; False Designation of Origin; Dilution; and Unfair Competition, Civil Case No. 1:09-cv-261-AWI-SMS, filed in the U.S. District Court, E.D. California, *Hells Angels Motorcycle Corp. v. Fawn Myers, GoDaddy.com, et seq.,* filed February 20, 2009, http://www.slideshare.net/LegalDocs/hells-angels-cyberpiracy-trademark-infringement-lawsuit.

eBAY SUED FOR SELLING COUNTERFEIT JEWELRY ON THEIR SITE

In a case currently on appeal in the second circuit, Tiffany's and eBay are fighting it out. At issue is whether eBay has done enough to stop the sale of counterfeit "Tiffany" jewelry on their popular website. In the district court, the first round went to eBay when the judge ruled that eBay was not liable to Tiffany's for the sale of fake jewelry when all the information they had was unspecified knowledge that trademark infringement might be happening. Tiffany's argued, and continues to argue, that eBay can hold back listing suspicious goods until they can be verified. eBay counters that it already spends $18 million per year to trace and remove fake items, and that they are fulfilling their obligation. All eyes are watching this important case as it could have a ripple effect on the online retail sales vendors who market name brand products on their websites.

Source: Susan Beck, "All Eyes on eBay-Tiffany Fight," *The American Lawyer,* July 17, 2009, http://www.american lawyer.com.

TRADEMARK REGISTRATION

Trademarks are not required to be registered; you can, in fact, establish rights in a mark without registering it with the USPTO. If you choose to register your trademark, you can do so using the Trademark Electronic Application System (TEAS), the electronic application system of the USPTO, or you may apply by sending in a printed form. Owning a registered trademark has the advantage of providing notice to the public of your claim to the mark, provides a presumption of ownership of the mark, allows for federal enforcement of the mark through access to the federal courts, offers a basis for obtaining trademark protection in foreign countries, and offers the ability to bring an infringement action for importing infringing goods. Reality Check 15-9 ("eBay Sued for Selling Counterfeit Jewelry on Their Site") shows the difficulty the owner of a mark encounters in trying to keep control of a trademark.

Any time you claim a right to a trademark, you may use the "TM" designation to alert the public to your ownership. However, you may use the federal registration symbol ® only after the USPTO actually registers a mark, and not while an application is pending.

Encompassed within the law of trademark are related forms of intellectual property, including service marks, titles and character names, trade names, trade dress, certification marks, and collective marks. Related to trademarks, but regulated under state law, are trade secrets.

SERVICE MARKS

Section 3 of the Lanham Act provides for registration of **service marks.** It defines the term service mark as a mark used in the sale or advertising of services that identifies and distinguishes the services of one person, including a unique service, from the services of others. A service mark differs from a trademark in that a service mark identifies the source of a service, whereas a trademark is used to indicate goods.

EXAMPLE

If the service of the company deals with communications, the service mark can be a sound. For example, AT&T uses a tone sound followed by a woman's voice speaking the company's name to identify its long distance service. MGM uses the sound of a lion's roar for its motion pictures. The Harlem Globetrotters have marked their whistled theme song "Sweet Georgia Brown." Other companies have successfully marked their sounds,[23] but not all have been successful. Harley Davidson for years unsuccessfully tried to mark the sound of its motorcycle engine. After several challenges from other motorcycle manufacturers, Harley Davidson withdrew its application.

Service marks have been given broad meaning, and a service mark differs from a trademark only in that it identifies services rather than goods. Service marks may not be registered for services that are expected, routine, or legally required upon the purchase of goods, such as a warranty. Rather, service marks used for such services as motel and hotel services, restaurants, and insurance services are permitted.

---

[23]Sound marks can be heard by logging on to http://www.uspto.gov/go/kids/kidsound.html.

TITLE AND CHARACTER NAMES

Creative property, such as the titles of and the characters in creative works, are commercially important, and trademark principles also protect them. Titles of films, comic book characters, and characters created for commercials or merchandising promotions may be protected. Such well-known characters as Batman, Conan the Barbarian, and the peanut in the Planter's peanut logo have been afforded trademark protection under this theory.

TRADE NAMES

A **trade name** is the name of a firm or business and differs from a trademark in that it identifies the producer rather than the products or services produced. Because trade names are not trademarks, they cannot be registered under the Lanham Act, but they are instead protected under nearly identical principles housed in the common law. Some states have enacted statutes that provide for registration of trade names. Those states that do not provide for registration generally operate on the theory that the first to use the name in a particular line of activity within a geographic region have the common law right to the name.

REALITY CHECK 15-10

HOOTERS CONFUSES ORANGE WITH BLACK

In another attempt by Hooters to protect the trade dress of its waitresses, they sued Winghouse, alleging that customers of Winghouse might get the black shorts and shirt–wearing waitresses confused with Hooters' waitresses, who wear orange shorts and white shirts. The judge who ruled in the case thought it was an attempt by Hooters to prevent any other wing-selling establishment from selling wings with a scantily clad waitress staff. The judge found that no reasonable person would confuse Winghouse girls with Hooters girls and threw out Hooters' suit. In addition, Hooters was slapped with a $1.2 million breach of contract award of damages because it had agreed to settle such suits with Winghouse in 1997.

Source: Source: Ted Frank, "Update: Hooters Trade Dress Suit," December 7, 2004, http://overlawyered.com/2004/12/update-hooters-trade-dress-suit/.

TRADE DRESS

The term **trade dress** refers to the total image of a product, including the size, shape, color, texture, graphics, or particular sales technique employed. Almost any feature may be protected under this term if it is distinctive and performs an identifying function. Trade dress is protected by section 43 of the Lanham Act, which refers to unregistered trademarks. This section has been universally applied to trade dress and applies to such items as Rubik's Cube, Ls Sportsac luggage, Harlequin romance novels, Hallmark cards, and "adoption" of Cabbage patch dolls. As Reality Check 15-10 ("Hooters Confuses Orange with Black)" demonstrates, the trade dress has to be specific to the product.

EXAMPLE

TRADEMARK INFRINGEMENT

Recall that the underlying purpose for trademarks is to distinguish the trademark holder's products, services, and so on, from those of others. It is not then difficult to understand that the single standard for **trademark infringement** is likelihood of confusion, whether that infringement action takes federal, statutory, or common law grounds and whether that action is against registered or unregistered trademarks. Basically, under this standard, infringement exists if the two marks, under all the circumstances of the marketplace, make confusion on the part of the consumer likely. The confusion created must be confusion as to the source of origin of a service or product. As Reality Check 15-11 ("'Walocaust' Items OK over Walmart Objection") demonstrates, there must be a real possibility of confusion between the marks, and parody is protected in this area.

How many times have you asked someone if you could "xerox" a document? What you actually wanted to do was photocopy it. The word "xerox" has come to mean the same thing. In order to protect a right to a trademark, efforts must be made to prevent the trademark from falling into general use as a generic term for a product.

EXAMPLE

"WALOCAUST" ITEMS OK OVER WALMART OBJECTION

Georgia resident Charles Smith does not like Walmart's business practices and decided to do something to alert the public. He reserved the domain name walocaust.com, designed T-shirts, hats, bumper stickers, and other items with the words Walocaust and a star and smiley face on them, and put them for sale on Cafepress.com, a website that sells novelty items. Then he heard from Walmart.

Walmart sent him a letter demanding that he immediately stop selling the items. They claimed that they owned trademarks in the name Walmart, the star, and the smiley face associated with it. They also threatened Cafepress.com, which immediately stopped selling Smith's items.

When Smith refused to back down, Walmart sued alleging trademark infringement. Smith admitted to all the facts, but countered that the designs themselves are noncommercial speech which is protected by the First Amendment. Smith also stated that there is no chance of confusion between his products and Walmart's designs.

The court agreed, stating that the Walmart name is a strong and recognizable mark and it is unlikely that a parody, especially one that parallels to the killing of millions of people and that aligns itself with a terrorist organization, would confuse the minds of the people into believing that that represented the real Walmart. To date, Smith has sold only 62 T-shirts, 15 of them to Walmart's law firms.

Source: "Wal-Mart Critic Has First Amendment Right to Sell 'Walocaust' Items, Maintain Web Site Critical of Retail Giant, Public Citizen Tells Court," http://www.nebraskatrademark.com/news.cfm/Article/60976/Wal-Mart-Critic-Has-First-Amendment.html; and "Wal-Mart Critic Wins Judgment in 'Walocaust' Lawsuit," AP, March 26, 2008.

This often happens with popular products, as when the trademark name of the product becomes so associated with the product that the two have become one and the same in the minds of consumers. For instance, many people simply ask for a Kleenex, rather than a facial tissue, yet Kleenex is a brand name. The same can be said for Jell-o brand gelatin, Band-aid brand adhesive strips, Pop Tarts brand toaster pastries, and Kool-Aid brand powdered drink mix. **EXAMPLE**

If a business does not take steps to protect its trademark from general use, it can lose the right to bring suit for trademark infringement. From time to time you may see a magazine advertisement by Xerox that simply says Xerox is a trade name of the Xerox Corporation and the ad is to serve as a reminder that all photocopies are not Xeroxes. That ad can then be used by Xerox to show it has taken steps to prevent general use of its name and can maintain an action for trademark infringement. **EXAMPLE**

Section 2(a) of the Lanham Act prohibits the use of a trademark for disparaging, scandalous, and immoral marks. The examiner of the requested mark makes a determination, along with a supervisor, whether the mark requested falls within this definition. If so, the mark will be refused. This section applies to all types of marks, including service marks, certification marks, and collective marks.

For example, the USPTO has refused Bullshit as a mark.[24] However, they allowed the use of the word Badass for a musical instrument. Challenged have been words such as O.J. Simpson by Christian men who equate the words with wife-beater and wife-murderer; the N-word, the F-word, and Dykes on Bikes, as examples. **EXAMPLE**

CERTIFICATION MARKS

The Lanham Act also provides for **certification marks.** A certification mark is used to indicate that certain goods or services originated in a particular region, or that they are of a particular nature, quality, or characteristic, or that they were produced by a member of a particular organization. The owner of a certification mark must maintain control over its use, but may not engage in actual production or marketing of the goods.

 EXAMPLE

For example, the mark Good Housekeeping Seal of Approval indicates that particular products meet standards imposed by owners of that certification mark. Good Housekeeping magazine, however, as the owner of the mark, must not allow itself to use the certification mark and must design the mark so that it is distinguishable from the magazine itself. Because trademarks indicate origin and certification marks indicate a guarantee of a certain characteristic, a common owner must ensure that the marks are distinguishable.

---

[24]*In re Tinseltown,* 212 U.S.P.Q. (BNA) 863 (T.T.B.A 1981).

The importance of this to an industry is shown in Reality Check 15-12 ("Chemical Company Liable for Improper Use of Certification Mark").

Another difference between certification marks and trademarks is that use of a certification mark cannot be denied to anyone who maintains the characteristics that the mark certifies. Exclusive ownership, therefore, is contrary to the purpose of certification marks.

COLLECTIVE MARKS

A **collective mark** indicates that goods or services are produced by members of a collective group or simply indicates membership in a particular group. Ownership of the collective mark is vested in a group, of which each producer or provider is a member. Most of us have seen collective marks in clothing, which often carries a tag stating it was made by the ILGWU or International Ladies' Garment Workers Union. Those who wish to support unions may assure themselves of it by purchasing only items that contain a union collective mark. See Take Away 15-1, "Intellectual Property Comparison," for a comparison chart.

TAKE AWAY 15-1

INTELLECTUAL PROPERTY COMPARISON

	Copyright	Trade/Service Mark	Patent	Trade Secret
Interest protected	Original works of authorship fixed in tangible form	Word, name, symbols or device used in trade of goods or services	Utility, design, or plant invention	Information of value not generally known to the public or outside of company
Governing law	Copyright Act of 1976	Patent and Trademark Act	Patent and Trademark Act	Uniform Trade Secrets Act if adopted by state
Right obtained	Exclusive right to reproduce, distribute, or perform	Prevention of others from using confusingly similar mark	Exclusive right to make, use, or sell, or right not to do such for 20 years from date of filing application	Right to keep valuable information from public

continued

Limitations	Covers form of expressions, not subject matter of works; 20 year period them goes in public domain	Cannot prevent others from making same product under different mark	None once patent is obtained; cannot obtain patent unless novel, utile, and nonobvious	None, as long as information is not divulged; once divulged, trade secret is lost
Registration required	Yes, Copyright Office of the Library of Congress	Yes, Trademarks Office of the Patent and Trademark Office	Yes, Patent and Trademark Office	No
Insignia of registration	©	™ or ℠ (nonregistered) or ® once registered	"Patent" and number of patent (example: Patent 1234567) on article	None
Examples	*Gone with the Wind,* Beatles recordings, video games	Roar of MGM lion, pink of Owens-Corning insulation, shape of Coca-Cola bottle	Fiber optics, computer hardware, medications (utility); look of athletic shoe, bicycle helmet, Star Wars characters (design); silver queen corn, Better Boy Tomatoes, hybrid tea roses (plant)	

Trade Secrets

If there is a secret formula or important ingredient, recipe, or client list that is important to the business and not an item of general knowledge, they may wish to protect it as a trade secret. A **trade secret** may be any formula, pattern, device, or compilation of information that is used in one's business and that gives one an opportunity to obtain an advantage over competitors who do not know or have it.

In 1979 the Uniform Trade Secrets Act (USTA), a set of uniform rules much like the Restatements, was adopted.[25] Since its adoption, 45 states, the District of Columbia, and the Virgin Islands have adopted a version of the USTA, making it the predominant law governing trade secrets. The purpose of the USTA was to make uniform the trade secret laws nationally, narrow the scope of the protection, strike a balance between the need to

---

[25]The American Bar Association began work on a set of rules which eventually were adopted by the National Conference of Commissioners of Uniform State Laws as the USTA.

protect business information and the need to allow employee mobility, and avoid conflict with the patent laws.

Trade secret protection in the United States is a matter of state law and contains three requirements: (1) limited availability of the secret to those outside the circle of those who need to know, (2) economic value, and (3) reasonable effort to keep the secret. Once those three requirements are met, the list of things that may qualify for trade secret protection is endless, extending from recipes to customer lists.

Trade secrets differ from the other types of intellectual property in several ways. There is no application to or registration by a government office. Trade secrets are creatures solely of state law and may continue indefinitely. Trade secret law does not prevent others from acquiring the trade secret, if done in the proper way, i.e., through reverse engineering or independent discovery of matters that form the basis of a trade secret. Protection exists only against discovery or use by improper means, such as theft, bribery, or espionage. The problem is once a trade secret is improperly acquired and widely disclosed, it is impossible to reestablish a trade secret.

EXAMPLE For instance, a business may have an employee who leaves their employ and takes a confidential client list with them that the business regards as a trade secret. Reality Check 15-13 ("Two Charged with Stealing More than Just the Towels from Hotel") demonstrates how employee theft can be devastating to a company's competitive edge and how the consequences of an injunction can disrupt plans and progress for a company.

EXAMPLE On the other hand, if, for instance, a business developed a new kind of cleaning agent for hazardous waste containers and an ex-employee experiments with different agents until finding the same combination of ingredients as discovered by the business, the business would have no cause of action for theft of trade secrets because the ex-employee did not take the formula, but instead discovered it independently through experimentation.

Unlike trademarks or patentable things, trade secrets do not require novelty or nonobviousness to be protected. Like patents and copyrights, however, mere ideas will not be protected as trade secrets; that is, a trade secret must possess concreteness or tangible form. See Take Away 15-2, "Patents v. Trade Secrets," for additional comparisons of these two options.

Misappropriation of Trade Secrets

Once a trade secret is determined to exist, the plaintiff has the burden to prove **misappropriation** of that secret. A trade secret can be misappropriated three ways: the secret

REALITY CHECK 15-13

TWO CHARGED WITH STEALING MORE THAN JUST THE TOWELS FROM HOTEL

If you think all hotel rooms basically look the same, there may be a reason for that. The Starwood Hotels has filed a complaint against the Hilton Hotels and two former Starwood executives alleging corporate espionage, theft of trade secrets, unfair competition, and computer fraud. At the heart of the dispute is the allegation that the two executives stole more than 100,000 electronic and hard copy files containing Starwood's most competitively sensitive information that the Hilton Hotels then used to create a competitor to the upscale Starwood's W hotels—the Denizen.

Included among the documents allegedly stolen are Starwood's strategic plans, property improvement plans, confidential computer files, confidential marketing and demographic studies, training modules and materials, and Starwood's brand "bibles," handbooks containing brand immersion materials and marketing plans. Also alleged is that Hilton began a relationship with the president of Starwood's luxury hotel development team, who then caused his employees to turn over massive amounts of documents to him which he downloaded on his personal computer, extracted a $600,000 severance package from Starwood, and then left and took the vice president and other employees with him, who also stole documents and trade secrets belonging to Starwood. All employees were under a confidentiality agreement with Starwood, which they are alleged to have breached.

At the moment a judge has ordered the return of all the stolen documents and has ordered the Hilton to stop development of the Denizen.

Source: Andrew L ongstreth, "Cahill Gordon Obtains Injunction in Grishamesque *Starwood v. Hilton* Case," *The American Lawyer,* April 28, 2009, http://www.americanlawyer.com.

PATENTS v. TRADE SECRETS

Occasionally a business person must decide exactly what to do with intellectual property that she might own. A trade secret may or may not meet patent requirements, but if it does, how does she decide whether to patent it? Here are some advantages and disadvantages that might be considered when making that decision.

Trade Secret	Patent
No time limit	20 year limit
No registration costs	Rather heavy registration costs
Immediate effect	No effect unless patent is granted
No information need be revealed	Must reveal all aspects of invention
May be subject to reverse engineering if revealed	Exclusive right of use or nonuse if patented
Difficult to enforce—anyone can reveal	Federal enforcement of use or nonuse
Trade secret may be patented by others if revealed	Invention cannot be patented by anyone else once patent is received

can be acquired by improper means; the secret can be disclosed after it was acquired improperly; or the secret can be disclosed after it was acquired properly. In Case 15-3, Northern Electric Co. v. Torma, the court was asked to determine whether properly-acquired information was misappropriated by a former employee.

A secret is acquired improperly if it was obtained through espionage, bribery, theft, burglary, or some other unlawful means. The meaning of improper is not limited to illegal means, however; it can be acquired through misrepresentation or it may offend commercial morality.[26] It is not improper, however, to acquire the secret through **reverse engineering** or independent discovery.

Trade secrets acquired properly may be improperly disclosed if the person acquiring the secret knew that the person who shared the secret acquired it improperly, if the person knew that the circumstances under which he received the secret gave rise to a duty to maintain its secrecy, or where the person had reason to know that the person who shared the secret with him was under a duty to maintain its secrecy. Relationships that give rise to such a duty are employer/employee, purchaser and supplier, licensor and licensee, partners and joint venturers, or any other relationship

---

[26]This was found to have occurred in the case of *E.I. DuPont v. Christopher,* 431 F.2d 1012 (5th Cir. 1970), where the defendant was charged with aerial surveillance of a plant DuPont was building.

CASE 15.3 Northern Electric Co. v. Torma

819 N.E. 2d 417 (Ind. App. 2004)

Facts: Northern Electric is a motor repair shop in South Bend, Indiana, using a specialized technique to repair electrical systems. Torma was an employee of the company and while working for Northern Electric compiled repair information on a computer disk. Torma eventually terminated his employment with Northern Electric. Northern Electric unsuccessfully sued for return of all the information Torma compiled while working for the company. The lower court ruled in favor of Torma, and Northern Electric appeals.

Issue: Whether Torma violated the trade secret act of Indiana and misappropriated the trade secrets owned by Northern Electric by compiling and taking with him the data gathered while working at Northern Electric.

Holding: Yes, the information collected by Torma was trade secrets belonging to Northern Electric, and Torma, in refusing to turn them over upon leaving the employment of Northern Electric, misappropriated the trade secrets.

Reasoning: Evidence by Torma indicates that virtually all information assembled in the data compilation was obtained during his working hours at Northern Electric. In particular, Torma testified that he gathered data from readings he took or discerned during the actual repair of the motors. He further stated that he would copy information out of manufacturers' manuals, received and maintained by Northern Electric, by using the company's copier. Torma testified that during his own time he entered all this assembled data into a word processing file, organized by manufacturer, and stored it on his home computer. He clarified that he would consult his compilation, which is the result of seven years of data collection for more than 650 servo motors, every day at work. During testimony, he not only admitted that 90 percent of his time dedicated to generating data was performed at work but also conceded that the data information compiled in the notebook belonged to Northern Electric.

The trial court found that the data was generally known or readily accessible, and that Northern Electric failed to take reasonable measures to maintain the secrecy of the servo motor data collected by Torma. On appeal, the court ruled this to be an error. The record establishes that in compiling his data, Torma used information already within the public domain, but he also used information he obtained from Northern Electric. At trial, Torma testified that he gathered the data over a period of more than seven years and devoted at least 1,892 hours to organizing the data. Furthermore, the compilation gained independent economic value by increasing Northern Electric's efficiency in repairing malfunctioning servo motors which Torma himself admitted to, which is why he refused to return the data without compensation upon resigning from Northern Electric. One witness, president of a competing servo motor repair shop, testified that if starting his business now, he would offer Torma $100,000 for the data compilation. Consequently, the court found that the data compilation was not readily accessible.

Northern Electric argued that it took reasonable efforts to maintain the secrecy of the servo motor data. Even in the absence of any specific directions by the employer, an employee is required to carry out the work in the best interest of the employer. As such, Torma, as Northern Electric's agent, is subject to a duty to act solely for the benefit of his employer. Accordingly, Torma's own efforts to protect the data compilation must be attributed to Northern Electric. When Torma left the company on his last workday and refused to give up the compilation without compensation, which is Northern Electric's property and which Torma had compiled on the company's behalf, his possession of the data became unauthorized and his acquisition improper. Accordingly, Torma misappropriated Northern Electric's trade secret.

CASE QUESTIONS

1. The court seemed to place importance on the fact that Torma gathered the information while at work and working on motors serviced by Northern Electric, and little emphasis on the fact that Torma compiled the information at his home and on his own time and without being asked to do so by Northern Electric. What do you think this message gives to employees who might want to compile information for their own benefit to help improve their skill level, but who wish to keep their work product?

2. Should the employer get the benefit of work that goes above and beyond what's required of an employee just because the extra effort turns out to be valuable?

3. Clearly, Torma kept the information almost solely within his possession during the course of his employment. What factors do you think drove the court to find that Northern Electric made the effort to keep the information secret?

of confidence. See Take Away 15-3, "Sample Non-Disclosure Agreement," for a typical form used to protect trade secrets.

 TAKE AWAY 15-3

SAMPLE NON-DISCLOSURE AGREEMENT

Sample Nondisclosure Agreement

This Nondisclosure Agreement (the "Agreement") is entered into by and between _____with its principal offices at _____ ("Disclosing Party") and _____ located at _____ ("Receiving Party") for the purpose of preventing the unauthorized disclosure of Confidential Information as defined below. The parties agree to enter into a confidential relationship with respect to the disclosure of certain proprietary and confidential information ("Confidential Information").

1. Definition of Confidential Information. For purposes of this Agreement, "Confidential Information" shall include all information or material that has or could have commercial value or other utility in the business in which Disclosing Party is engaged. If Confidential Information is in written form, the Disclosing Party shall label or stamp the materials with the word "Confidential" or some similar warning. If Confidential Information is transmitted orally, the Disclosing Party shall promptly provide a writing indicating that such oral communication constituted Confidential Information.

2. Exclusions from Confidential Information. Receiving Party's obligations under this Agreement do not extend to information that is: (a) publicly known at the time of disclosure or subsequently becomes publicly known through no fault of the Receiving Party; (b) discovered or created by the Receiving Party before disclosure by Disclosing Party; (c) learned by the Receiving Party through legitimate means other than from the Disclosing Party or Disclosing Party's representatives; or (d) is disclosed by Receiving Party with Disclosing Party's prior written approval.

3. Obligations of Receiving Party. Receiving Party shall hold and maintain the Confidential Information in strictest confidence for the sole and exclusive benefit of the Disclosing Party. Receiving Party shall carefully restrict access to Confidential Information to employees, contractors and third parties as is reasonably required and shall require those persons to sign nondisclosure restrictions at least as protective as those in this Agreement. Receiving Party shall not, without prior written approval of Disclosing Party, use for Receiving Party's own benefit, publish, copy, or otherwise disclose to others, or permit the use by others for their benefit or to the detriment of Disclosing Party, any Confidential Information. Receiving Party shall return to Disclosing Party any and all records, notes, and other written, printed, or tangible materials in its possession pertaining to Confidential Information immediately if Disclosing Party requests it in writing.

4. Time Periods. The nondisclosure provisions of this Agreement shall survive the termination of this Agreement and Receiving Party's duty to hold Confidential Information in confidence shall remain in effect until the Confidential Information no longer qualifies as a trade secret or until Disclosing Party sends Receiving Party written notice releasing Receiving Party from this Agreement, whichever occurs first.

5. Relationships. Nothing contained in this Agreement shall be deemed to constitute either party a partner, joint venturer or employee of the other party for any purpose.

6. Severability. If a court finds any provision of this Agreement invalid or unenforceable, the remainder of this Agreement shall be interpreted so as best to effect the intent of the parties.

7. Integration. This Agreement expresses the complete understanding of the parties with respect to the subject matter and supersedes all prior proposals, agreements, representations and understandings. This Agreement may not be amended except in a writing signed by both parties.

8. Waiver. The failure to exercise any right provided in this Agreement shall not be a waiver of prior or subsequent rights.

This Agreement and each party's obligations shall be binding on the representatives, assigns and successors of such party. Each party has signed this Agreement through its authorized representative.

(Signature)

(Typed or Printed Name)

Date:

(Signature)

(Typed or Printed Name)

Date:

Source: http://www.business.gov/business-law/intellectual-property/.

The Inevitable Disclosure Doctrine

One of the tensions in trade secret law concerns the employee who leaves one job and takes another in which he or she has to use trade secrets of the prior employer in order to perform his or her new job. The problem is that there is no evidence upon which a claim for misappropriation of the trade secret can be made. There has been no misappropriation, but the former employer fears such.

The **doctrine of inevitable disclosure** gives the former employer the opportunity to make the case that only by revealing trade secrets can the former employee perform the new job. This was illustrated in the case of *PepsiCo v. Redmond*.[27] In that case, a high-level executive for PepsiCo left for a very similar job at the Quaker Oats Company, the maker of Gatorade and Snapple. Even though there was no evidence of misappropriation, and Redmond fully acknowledged his obligation to keep the confidence of PepsiCo, PepsiCo was able to convince the court that there was no way for Redmond to do his job without violating the confidence of PepsiCo. The court enjoined Redmond from going to work for Quaker Oats Company for a period of five months after leaving PepsiCo.

Not all courts have adopted this doctrine. In states which value the employees' ability to be mobile between jobs, and in which promises not to compete with former employers are not valued, the doctrine does not exist.

STATE VERSUS FEDERAL REGISTRATION

Registration of goods or services not used in commerce or in a wide geographical area is protected either under the common law or by registering the trademark with the state in which the trademark is used. State systems vary from state to state, but generally require registration with the office of the secretary of state. Registration generally provides exclusive use within the jurisdiction of registration.

Intellectual Property in Cyberspace

Analysis of legal issues relating to the World Wide Web and the Internet require more than just how to use these new technologies. It requires an understanding of the power of the technology itself and how the laws that existed before the technology are compatible, or not, with resolving the disputes that arise as a result. Issues as simple as where to bring a case are perplexing when you think of the fact that both the Web and the Internet are global in scope and illusive in capture. We have previously mentioned some of these issues in discussing trademark law and cyberpiracy and cybersquatting, but here we will discuss them a bit more so you can at least see some of the important issues at stake.

DOMAIN NAMES

`LO8`

The Internet can be described as a global network of networks that facilitates communication and information transfer among the millions of computers connected to it.[28] **Domain names** are how we communicate and are similar to addresses we go to find people to talk to, things to purchase, and to pursue every other kind of information interaction imaginable. We discussed domain names earlier in the chapter in the context of trademarks, but here we discuss the rights in the domain names themselves.

---

[27]54 F.3d 1262 (7th Cir. 1995).

[28]*ACLU v. Reno*, 929 F. Supp. 824 (E.D. Pa. 1996).

DOMAIN NAMES AND THEIR PURPOSES

Below are the seven original domain names. Some are still restricted, meaning they are only available to those who qualify as falling within the category named. Others started as restricted, but were unrestricted by ICANN.

Domain Name	Purpose
.com	Commercial organizations, *now unrestricted*
.edu	Postsecondary education establishments, *restricted*
.gov	Government entities within the U.S., *restricted*
.int	International organizations established by treaty, *restricted*
.mil	The U.S. military, *restricted*
.net	Originally for network infrastructure, *now unrestricted*
.org	Originally for organizations not within other categories, *now unrestricted*

Source: ICANN, http://www.icann.org/.

Domain names are regulated by the Internet Corporation for Assigned Names and Numbers (ICANN), a nonprofit organization that has an exclusive contract with the U.S. government to maintain the domain names. At the top of the domain name pyramid are generic top-level domains (gTLDs). There were initially seven gTLDs: .com, .net, .org, .gov, .edu, .mil., and .int, with the first three being unrestricted gTLDs, meaning anyone could register a name on them. See Reality Check 15-14, "Domain Names and Their Purposes," for their general purpose and availability. Other commonly seen gTLDs are .biz for business and .pro for professionals.

EXAMPLE

The second level of domain names (SLDs), are represented by the name of the registrant. In the name google.com, for example, google is the SLD and .com is the gTLD. These individual names are registered on a first come–first served basis. Whoever gets to the gTLD with the name first gets to register that name. ICANN continues to work on adding new gTLDs for use on the Internet. It currently is focusing on adding international domain names.

CYBERSQUATTERS

In the early stages of the Internet's development, many businesses with trademarks did not realize the value associated with those marks and did not rush to register them. That allowed others not associated with the businesses to take advantage of the businesses by registering the marks and then negotiating with the businesses for the return of their marks for sizeable sums, depending on the value of the mark to the business. As discussed earlier, these people were called **cybersquatters,** because they would simply register the name, wait for the business to attempt to register the name, and then contact the business to get the business to buy the name back—or they would squat on the name.

A second type of opportunistic Internet entrepreneurs developed, and those are referred to as **cyberpirates.** These people would incorporate a trademarked name into their name and divert the hits on the website to their sites to make a profit from the online advertisers who paid per hit.

After years of unsuccessfully trying to solve the problem with traditional trademark law, Congress enacted the Anti-Cybersquatting Consumer Protection Act (ACPA) in 1999. ACPA amended the Lanham Act by outlawing the act of registering, trafficking in, or using a domain name that is identical or confusingly similar to a mark or dilutive of a famous mark with bad faith intent to profit. The elements of this act are (1) the existence of an existing mark, registered or not, including a personal name; (2) against which without regard to goods and services a corresponding domain name was registered, trafficked, or used, and (3) with a bad faith intent to profit from that activity.

One other important part of the ACPA is the ability of the mark owner to bring a cause of action even where the domain name abuser cannot be located, or the court does not have jurisdiction over the person by a procedure called *in rem* **jurisdiction.** Under this new weapon, much of the difficult litigation to protect the trademarked domain name has been moved under the easier ACPA test. ACPA applies retroactively to domain names that were registered prior to the Act; however, no money damages can be assessed for those cases. Although not brought under APCA, a case discussed in Reality Check 15-15 ("Are Domain Names Illegal Gambling Devices?") does illustrate another problem with pursuing domain name owners and registrars of those names.

REALITY CHECK 15-15

ARE DOMAIN NAMES ILLEGAL GAMBLING DEVICES?

In a case that is generating a lot of interest, a court in Kentucky has ruled that 141 domain names were illegal gambling devices under state law, and issued a forfeiture order to the registrars of the domain names, many of whom are out of state or even out of the country. The Court of Appeals disagreed, and reversed the lower court. The case is now on appeal to the Kentucky Supreme Court, who will rule on this important issue.

The case, styled *Vicsbingo.com and Internet Gaming Council v. Wingate and Kentucky,* has opponents in the form of the Internet site owners and registrars, all who claim that Kentucky's attempt to stop Internet gambling cannot be enforced through the seizure of websites that promote gambling. The proponents of the state's position argue that domain names are illegal gambling devices, and are prohibited because Internet gambling is prohibited in Kentucky.

The national and international implications are dire. How can one state official decide whether any particular website is legal or illegal, depending on its content? Morality aside, how uncertain would a business be in putting a website on the Internet? Jurisdictional issues abound. Does a state court have the authority to ban an Internet website by seizing its domain name? Constitutionally, does a state court have the authority to decide whether the site is protected free speech, or can the state censor speech this way? If the Internet is like a superhighway, can one state force the website to park when in its state?

Legally, the question may be a lot simpler: Is a domain name property, and if it is, then is the owner entitled to due process before its property can be seized? Network Solutions, LLC, one of the domain name registrars named in the suit, claims that most courts have not ruled domain names are property; rather, they entail only contract rights. In the appeal, the court focused on whether the domain names were gambling devices, and ruled that the series of numbers that constitute the domain name do not constitute a machine, mechanical, or other device designed to be used in connection with gambling.

Others have a different take on Kentucky's motives. Some argue that because Kentucky could not get to the actual owners of the domain names, they went after the middlemen—the registrars of the domain names. These are the companies with which the owners register their names. Use of the forfeiture process was a way to try to lure the owners into court to protect their property. Noting the presence of marshals in the courtroom, it was suggested that had the owners appeared, they would have been arrested, having submitted to the jurisdiction of the court by their presence.

The resolution of this case might not answer all the questions it raises, but neither side will give up without taking their fight to every state in which this issue is raised.

Source: Marcia Coyle, "Kentucky Domain Name Suit Has Web World Buzzing," February 4, 2009, http://www.law.com/jsp/ihc/PubArticleIHC.jsp?id=1202427973156.

Summary

Intellectual property is an important area of the law for businesses to be aware of. Issues in intellectual property involve liability that may be imposed upon a business for infringing on the protected rights of others. Intellectual property laws protect businesses themselves from infringement of their legitimate business rights and prerogatives. These intellectual property issues may pertain to business trademarks, patents, copyrights, service marks, and trade dress. Knowing the law and how it is evolving in the context of the Internet can help a business to grow and prosper as well as prevent the business from running into legal trouble for infringement.

Review Questions

1. Hakeem writes a story that Delilah thinks is terrific. Delilah urges Hakeem to send it out for publication. Hakeem is hesitant because he says the story is not copyrighted. Must it be in order for it to be protected? LO3

2. Gunther, an industry leader in computer technology, established early the industry standard for computer compatibility. As a part of its computer manufacturing, Gunther decides to issue a "seal of approval and compatibility" to other computer companies that request it and meet certain standards that Gunther thinks are important. The purpose is to inform consumers that the computer meets what Gunther considers to be certain minimal standards for computers. Is Gunther's idea a good one? What if another company decides to put the Gunther seal on its product without meeting Gunther's standards? Explain. LO7

3. Sula creates a new type of comfortable pants called Zamis, which can be worn by either gender. Sula registers the name Zami as a trademark. The pants are so comfortable that they quickly become a huge market hit and are known far and wide for their comfort. Within a year, the word Zami becomes a slang term for something that is supremely comfortable. For instance, someone trying on a shoe in a shoe store would say, "Oh yes, this is definitely zami" (meaning that the shoe felt wonderful). The term also starts to be used by the media, in television shows, movies, and the like. While appreciating the success of her pants, Sula does not approve of the widespread use of her trademarked name and wants to protect it. What do you advise her to do? LO6

4. Professor Bennett is gathering materials she will use in an upcoming class she is teaching. The class is new and there is currently no textbook for it on the market. Professor Bennett compiles articles from different sources, which she then takes to a local photocopying shop to have photocopied for use by her class. The photocopying shop refuses to copy the materials for Professor Bennett until she provides copyright releases from each of the authors. Professor Bennett argues that no such permission is needed. Who is correct and why? LO4

5. Yasmin is unhappy with the type of shoes currently available on the market for the active recreational life she leads. Out of frustration, she designs a running shoe for women that better distributes women's weight and is more compatible with the way women move. Yasmin decides to patent the design. When she shows the design to Julie, Julie says Yasmin will not be able to patent the idea because it is not novel in that it only takes advantage of the natural way that most women move. Does Julie's argument have any validity? LO6

6. A national grocery chain has a policy of issuing certain products under its own label. The chain determines which are the top national brands of various items, then designs its packaging to look similar to the national brand, but upon close inspection, one can tell it is the store brand. Is there anything wrong with this practice? LO3

7. A professor at a university purchases a popular computer program he thinks will be helpful for his students. He requests that each student bring in a blank disk and proceeds to copy the computer program onto each student's disk. Then he

has the students perform various assignments using the disks. When the software company discovers the professor's actions, it threatens to sue. The professor claims fair use. Who wins and why? LO4

8. You have decided to form a group to return the swastika symbol to its original Sanskrit meaning— "su" means "good," "asti" means "to be," and "ka" is a suffix. You apply to the trademark office to have the swastika registered to your group, and the office refuses, citing the Lanham Act section 2(a). Can you refute the PTO's designation of your symbol as disparaging, scandalous, or immoral? How can you convince the PTO officer that your mark is different? LO7

9. You are a filmmaker who is just starting out in business. You wish to make a movie about a boxer who rises from obscurity to reclaim the heavyweight belt from an undefeated Russian boxing champion who has never been beaten. You want to call your movie "Rocky." Your friends try to convince you that the movie has already been made, but you think you can make it better. What are the copyright issues you might face? LO3

10. You are employed by a company that has asked you to take pictures at the company party. You are a photographer by trade; it is your second job when you are not at work. You agree to take the photos at the party. Who owns the rights to the photographs you take? LO3

Ethics Issue

The Federal Circuit in D.C. hears all appeals of patent cases. It traditionally enjoins any patent infringement that has been established to have occurred. The D.C. Circuit views a patent much like real estate and always upholds property holders' right to exclude use of the patented property. That view was upheld until the plaintiff in *eBay v. MercExchange*[29] (Merc) challenged the position of the court. In that case, the U.S. Supreme Court held that just because a patent is infringed upon does not automatically warrant the issuance of an injunction. The court found that a federal court must still weigh the four factors traditionally used to determine if an injunction should issue whenever such relief is requested.

Why was this important? Look at the facts of the *eBay* case. In that case, Merc owned the patent to the "Buy It Now" feature of eBay's auction page. eBay tried to buy it from Merc, but Merc refused to sell, even though they were not themselves using the product. Remember, a patent grant gives the owner the right to exclude others from using the product, but does not require that the product be used by the owner. eBay nonetheless inserted the feature on its page. When Merc sued eBay and won on the infringement claim, it sought an injunction against eBay continuing to use the feature. The District Court refused to issue the injunction. On appeal, the Court of Appeals reversed, citing the traditional rule that requires an injunction upon a finding of infringement.

The U.S. Supreme Court reversed the Court of Appeals. However, the Supreme Court also ruled that it was improper for the District Court to refuse to enjoin eBay simply because Merc did not use its patented product itself. Rather the Supreme Court found that the rules that ordinarily apply to whether an injunction is proper should be used. Those rules require a plaintiff to demonstrate that it has suffered an irreparable injury; that remedies at law are inadequate to compensate for that injury; that a remedy in equity is warranted; and that the public interest would not be disserved by a permanent injunction. There should not be a presumption absent an application of these factors.[30]

What is really at issue here? For starters, more and more companies are producing technology in which only a small part of a complex product is the object of an infringement suit. Consider, for example, the infringement suit that threatened to turn off all BlackBerrys. That involved just such an infringement action, wherein only a small part of the device was subject to the infringement claim. With the standard of automatic injunction, the whole product is taken off the market no matter how small the infringing component. That is a big stick for a patent owner

---

[29]547 U.S. 388 (2006).

[30]In subsequent litigation, the District Court, applying the four factors, again denied an injunction to MercExchange, holding that monetary damages were a sufficient remedy. Rather than appeal this decision, eBay and MercExchange reached a settlement in which MercExchange assigned its patents to eBay for an undisclosed sum.

to swing. The infringer, no matter how small the infringement, is forced to pay astronomical amounts in settlement fees to the patent owner just to keep their product on the market.

The court may have leveled the playing field somewhat, but the question remains as to how the court should weigh the four factors? Should there be a re-evaluation of the "property" concept under patent law? In applying the four factors, how would you rule? Has the patent owner suffered an irreparable injury, or does money compensate him/her for the infringement? Or does the balance of hardship weigh in favor of the infringer in these types of cases? How about the public interest? Would the public be disserved by shutting down the BlackBerry and other technological advances? And what is to become of the patent owners promise that there is an absolute right to exclude others for a period of 20 years? Has that been diluted by the decision in *eBay*?

Group Exercise

Talk among your friends. Ask them how they obtain their music downloads and movie DVDs. Ask them if they know the law concerning copyrights. Tell them what the law is and ask if they will change their behavior now that they know the law. What do you gather from this?

Key Terms

Environmental Law and Business

Learning Objectives

After reading this chapter, you should be able to:

L01 Explain what the environment is

L02 Describe how the federal government regulates the environment

L03 Discuss the Environmental Protection Agency

L04 Explain the requirements for maintaining clean air

L05 Describe the process for maintaining clear water

L06 Explain the necessity for protecting endangered species

L07 Describe the importance of proper disposal of hazardous waste

L08 Discuss what it means to be a green business

 ## Opening Scenario

Recent closures of military bases have revealed extensive pollution on government-owned land. Radioactive contamination, leaking underground tanks, dilapidated buildings, asbestos-laden soil, and unexploded weaponry are just some of the problems. The former McClelland Air Force Base in California, closed in 1987, was placed on the EPA's Superfund list in 2007 after the EPA identified over 300 sites within the base that were contaminated with solvents, metals, and other hazardous wastes as the result of aircraft maintenance at the site.[1]

In low income neighborhoods near the former Kelly Air Force Base in San Antonio, residents have erected almost 300 purple crosses in front of homes where residents are afflicted with or have died of cancer.[2] They want the Air Force to clean up a plume of toxic chemicals in the groundwater, rather than merely preventing the plume from spreading off the base, as proposed. Several federal studies have found no link between pollution and local health problems. The residents have reported increased cancer among the population, as well as an increase in birth defects among the children born in the area. Strange childhood incidents such as cleft palates and bowed limbs have been reported as well even into the second generation. What do you think the government response should be? Do you think the government should be able to escape cleaning up the polluted areas? Can you think of a reason why the U.S. government would refuse to accept responsibility for the illnesses caused by the pollution?

---

[1]http://www.californiagreensolutions.com/cgi-bin/gt/tpl.h,content=850.
[2]http://www.healthandenvironment.org/articles/homepage/1907.

Introduction

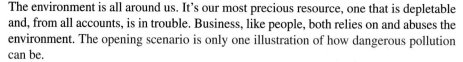

The environment is all around us. It's our most precious resource, one that is depletable and, from all accounts, is in trouble. Business, like people, both relies on and abuses the environment. The opening scenario is only one illustration of how dangerous pollution can be.

The U.S. government is charged with protecting the environment and has created the Environmental Protection Agency to guide businesses in the right direction. Awareness of the dangers of hazardous wastes, harmful chemical emissions, and discharge of pollutants into our water supply means that these things can be controlled and in some cases even eliminated. The difficulty is not just ours, it is a worldwide issue that must be addressed with global solutions. Air is ambient, and so is the pollution that gathers in it. Water flows, and so do the chemicals that pollute it. Not only is it a responsibility of business to do what it can to prevent further pollution, but in some cases it is their responsibility to clean up what they have created and left behind. That is the focus of government regulation in the United States. Starting with an overview of the EPA, below is a discussion of a few laws and regulations that exist for the protection of the environment. Reality Check 16-1, "Native Americans Police Their Tribal Lands," reminds us that Native Americans were environmentally conscious and revered the land even before settlers arrived.

Federal Regulation of the Physical Environment

The National Environmental Policy Act (NEPA) was one of the first laws ever written that establishes the broad national framework for protecting the environment. NEPA's basic policy is to assure that all branches of government give proper consideration to the environment prior to undertaking any major federal action that significantly affects the environment. It is a planning statute, not a regulatory one.

REALITY CHECK 16-1

NATIVE AMERICANS POLICE THEIR TRIBAL LANDS

Native Americans were the first environmentalists. They have continued their tradition through several organizations umbrellaed under the national tribal organizations and the EPA. Below are listed a few of the organizations that focus on environmental issues as they relate to Native Americans or their land.

Council of Energy Resource Tribes—dedicated to restructuring the federal/Indian relationship

EPA, American Indian Environmental Office—coordinates the effort to strengthen public health and environmental protection in Indian Country

First Nations Environmental Law Program—operated in conjunction with the Vermont Law School, provides environmental law fellowships for the study of Indian Country environmental law

National Tribal Environmental Council—dedicated to working with and assisting tribes in the protection and preservation of the reservation environment

Native Americans and the Environment—a nonprofit organization that educates the public on Indian environmental issues, explores the Native American environmental values and promotes conservation measures that respect Native American land

Waste Management in Indian Country—encourages solid and hazardous waste management in Indian Country

Source: National Tribal Justice Resource Center, http://www.ntjrc.org/legal/legallinks.asp?53.

NEPA requirements are invoked in four instances: (1) when federal funding is involved; (2) when a federal permit is issued; (3) when federal land, facilities, or equipment is involved; and (4) for federal rulemaking. In these four instances, NEPA requires **Environmental Assessments** (EAs) and **Environmental Impact Statements** (EISs), which are assessments of the likelihood of impacts from alternative courses of action from all federal agencies. EAs and EISs are the most visible NEPA requirements.

NEPA establishes a process that federal agencies must follow in making decisions that have the potential to have a significant impact on the environment. The process requires the agency to:

1. Identify and analyze environmental consequences of proposed action;
2. Identify and assess reasonable alternatives to the proposed action;
3. Document environmental analysis and findings; and
4. Make environmental information available to public officials and citizens before the agency makes a decision.

NEPA established the **Council on Environmental Quality** (CEQ). The CEQ is responsible for reporting to the President and Congress on the status of the environment. NEPA also requires agencies to analyze reasonably foreseeable international effects of actions proposed to occur within the U.S. NEPA can also apply to actions outside of the U.S. For example, NEPA applied to actions taken in Antarctica by the National Science Foundation.[3]

NEPA is not invoked for state government, private government, and local government actions. Many states have enacted their own NEPA-like statutes to cover state and local projects. If there is to be a cleanup of the property discussed in the chapter's opening scenario, it would most likely start with an impact statement by NEPA.

ENVIRONMENTAL ASSESSMENT (EA)

The EA is a public document that serves to provide sufficient evidence and analysis for determining whether to prepare an EIS or a Finding of No Significant Impact (FONSI). There must be enough information contained in the EA to be able to understand the basis for the decision. If there are adverse environmental impacts identified in the EA, the EA must discuss any reasonable alternative courses of action that offer less environmental risk. The EA may also discuss **mitigation measures**—measures that can be taken to reduce the harm to the environment.

ENVIRONMENTAL IMPACT STATEMENT (EIS)

If an EIS is required, the responsible agency must publish a notice of intent (NOI) in the Federal Register, indicating intent to prepare a draft environmental impact statement (DEIS) and the date and place of any **scoping meeting.** The scoping meeting is to allow any interested parties to appear and participate, and to identify the scope of the environmental impacts identified. After the meeting, the agency looks at the cumulative impact of the project and issues its DEIS. The public has 45 days to comment, after which the final EIS is reported upon. Case 16.1, *Tri-Valley Cares v. Department of Energy,* demonstrates the process of issuing an EA and an EIS and what happens if the government issues a FONSI without fully reviewing the factors necessary to determine the environmental impact.

---

[3]*Environmental Defense Fund v. Massey,* 986 F.2d 528 (D.C. Cir. 1993).

CASE 16.1 Tri-Valley Cares v. Department of Energy —

203 Fed. Appx. 105 (9th Cir. 2006)

Facts: Tri-Valley Cares, Nuclear Watch of New Mexico, appeal the lower court's order granting summary judgment in favor of defendants, the U.S. Department of Energy (DOE). Concerning the proposed building of a federal biological weapons research laboratory near San Francisco, Tri-Valley asserts that the DOE failed to comply with NEPA by issuing a finding of no significant impact after analyzing the project in an environmental assessment. According to plaintiffs, the proposed research lab may have a significant effect on the human environment and the DOE must prepare an environmental impact statement.

Issue: Whether the NEPA requirement of a full assessment of the environmental impact of its project was made by the DOE.

Decision: No.

Reasoning: If an Environmental Assessment demonstrates that substantial questions are raised about the environmental effects of a proposed agency action, a FONSI may not be issued and the agency must prepare a full Environmental Impact Statement. Plaintiffs challenge the DOE's Environmental Assessment due to its alleged failure to assess fully and correctly potentially significant effects on public health and safety (such as fire, earthquake, and terrorist attacks), uncertain effects posing substantial risks, significant precedential effects, significant cumulative effects, and public controversy.

NEPA is a procedural statute that does not mandate particular results, but simply provides the necessary process to ensure that federal agencies take a hard look at the environmental consequences of their actions. With the exception of the lack of analysis concerning the possibility of a terrorist attack, we hold that the DOE did take a hard look at the identified environmental concerns and that the DOE's decision was fully informed and well-considered.

Concerning the DOE's conclusion that consideration of the effects of a terrorist attack is not required in its Environmental Assessment, we recently held to the contrary. In *Mothers for Peace*, we held that an Environmental Assessment that does not consider the possibility of a terrorist attack is inadequate. Similarly here, we remand for the DOE to consider whether the threat of terrorist activity necessitates the preparation of an Environmental Impact Statement.

CASE QUESTIONS

1. In its opinion, the court noted that NEPA demands process, not specific results. What is meant by that phrase?

2. After 9/11, do you think that it is reasonable to impose a requirement that all federal buildings, military bases, and the like have a terrorist attack assessment?

3. In a footnote in the case, the court stated, "We note in particular the DOE's minimal assessment of earthquake risks despite the presence of known, active faults that run directly under nearby Berkeley/Alameda County, California." In spite of noting that, the court did not find that the DOE violated its requirement under NEPA to fully inform itself of the risks. What kind of standard of review does that imply the court made for this issue?

The Environmental Protection Agency

The U.S. Environmental Protection Agency (EPA), begun in 1970, is the federal agency that is responsible for protecting the natural environment—air, water, land, and endangered species. It is headed by an administrator who is appointed by the President of the United States.

The agency conducts environmental assessment, research, and education. It sets and enforces national standards under a number of environmental laws designed to address specific environmental issues. The federal EPA works closely with its state counterparts in setting standards and enforcement. It also works with industries and state governments to administer pollution prevention programs and energy conservation efforts. The EPA would be involved in the cleanup that is to be done on the former military base discussed in the opening scenario.

Many activities are covered by a variety of programs or different acts intended to deal with **pollution.** For example, an electric power plant may be covered by the acid rain program and the hazardous waste statutes. Emissions into water may be covered by both the Clean Water Act and the Endangered Species Act.

EXECUTIVE ORDERS

As we discussed in the chapter on our laws, an **executive order** is an order issued by the president or governor implementing a statute or governing operations of executive agencies. Many executive orders have been issued which address environmental concerns. For example, during the final days of President Clinton's administration, he announced new protections for nearly 60 million acres of federally controlled forest lands. During his Presidency, he also issued Executive Order 12898 addressing the federal government's environmental impact on minority and low-income populations. (See Diversity in the Law 16-1, "Environmental Justice Delayed.")

DIVERSITY IN THE LAW 16-1

ENVIRONMENTAL JUSTICE DELAYED

On February 16, 1994, then-President Bill Clinton issued Executive Order 12898, entitled Federal Actions to Address Environmental Justice in Minority Populations and Low-Income Populations. Its purpose is to focus federal attention on the environmental and human health effects on minority and low-income populations imposed by federal actions. The Executive Order directs federal agencies to identify and address the disproportionately high and adverse human health or environmental effects of their actions on minority and low-income populations, to the greatest extent possible. The order also directs each agency to develop a strategy for implementing environmental justice, to promote nondiscrimination in federal programs, as well as provide minority and low-income communities access to public information and public participation.

The EPA Administrator under President Bush removed the requirements for government agencies to take the poor and minority populations into special consideration when making changes to environmental legislation. The EPA has been criticized for its lack of progress toward environmental justice. As of 2006, there was no review of EPA programs or practices to determine compliance with the Executive Order. In addition, there were allegations that the EPA's Superfund was being administered disproportionately, skipping much of the needed cleanup work in minority areas.

Source: Sandra George O'Neal, "Superfund: Evaluating the Impact of Executive Order 12898," *Environmental Health Perspectives* 115, Issue 7, July 2007, http://www.ehponline.org/members/2007/9903/9903.pdf; and EPA at www.epa.gov.

AIR POLLUTION: CLEAN AIR ACT

Air is a difficult resource to regulate because it is not stationary. Polluted air can cross local, state, and national boundaries, and can even travel across the ocean. For this reason, regulations to control air pollution are made on every level. The EPA through the Clean Air Act establishes maximum permissible pollution emissions. Multinational, regional, and bilateral treaties are also used to govern emissions.

Due to its evolution through many amendments, the Clean Air Act (CAA) is a patchwork of federal laws that define the EPA's responsibilities for protecting and improving the nation's air quality and stratospheric ozone layer. One of the goals of the act is to set and achieve standards in every state in order to address the public health and welfare risks posed by air pollution. In order to accomplish this goal, the EPA established the National Ambient Air Quality Standard (NAAQS). NAAQS directed the states to set pollution standards and to implement plans to reach their goals. Because states had not reached the goals set by NAAQS, the CAA has been amended three times since its inception, in 1977, 1990, and 1997, to set new deadlines for achieving the desired goals. President Obama made clean air a priority by pushing for stricter emission standards and even signing off on the hugely popular "Cash for Clunkers" (later changed to Car Allowance Rebate System or CARS) program in 2009 which encouraged 700,000 consumers in a 30-day period to trade in their gas guzzlers for up to $4500 credit toward the purchase of cleaner, more fuel-efficient vehicles.[4]

The 1990 amendment to the CAA also set technology-based standards for major sources and area sources. A **major source** is defined as a stationary source or group of

---

[4]http://www.cars.gov/official-information.

stationary sources that emit 10 tons per year or more of a hazardous air pollutant. An **area source** is any stationary source that is not a major source. For major sources, the CAA requires that the EPA establish the maximum degree of reduction in emissions of hazardous air pollutants.

The CAA establishes criminal penalties for violations, including the possibility of prison terms, and authorizes the EPA to pursue civil suits for injunctions or monetary remedies. The EPA also has the authority to issue **administrative citations** for minor violations and to assess fines. For more significant violations, the EPA can initiate **administrative enforcement actions,** hold hearings, and impose more substantial financial penalties. The CAA also authorizes private rights of action by citizens against those violating the act and against agencies that fail to perform their obligations under the law.

States also have statutes that regulate clean air. States can have stronger pollution controls, but they may not have weaker controls than those imposed by the CAA.

Acid Rain Program

Acid rain, also called acid deposition, refers to a mixture of wet and dry deposited material from the atmosphere that contains higher than normal amounts of sulfur dioxide (SO_2) and nitrogen oxides (NO_x). These chemicals are from natural and man-made sources, primarily fossil fuel (mainly coal) consumption. The overall goal of the Acid Rain Program is to achieve significant environmental and public health benefits through reductions of these emissions. Reduction of emissions is achieved through the use of emission **caps**—limitations on the amount of pollution that can be used. Each source of pollution is given an "allowance" and cannot emit more than their allowance permits. When they report to the EPA, which they must do during a compliance period, they must show as many allowances as the emissions for which they are responsible.

Ozone Layer Protection and Climate Change

It is widely thought that deterioration of the ozone layer is causing climate change (global warming), skin cancers and cataracts, harm to agriculture, and damage to plant life. Ozone-destroying chemicals continue to be emitted into the stratosphere.

The U.S. banned the use of chlorofluorocarbons (CFCs) as propellants in aerosol cans in 1978. The EPA began to phase out other nonessential ozone-destroying chemicals. Consumer products are being made "user-friendly" by removing the unnecessary chemicals that harm the ozone. In 1997, a group of interested nations negotiated the Kyoto Protocol (treaty) with the goal of stabilizing greenhouse gas concentration in the atmosphere at a level that would not harm the climate. As of 2006, 140 nations had ratified the treaty, but not the U.S. Nonetheless, American scientists and members of the insurance industry are taking note of the climate change and the effects on the insurance industry, as noted in Reality Check 16-2, "Climate Change and the Insurance Industry."

WATER POLLUTION

As with air pollution, the issue of water pollution is complicated by the nature of the resource. Water exists in many forms: surface water such as lakes, ponds, and rivers, navigable or nonnavigable, or ground water that is beneath the earth. Water travels across jurisdictional lines and may be polluted by direct means such as discharge of waste into it, or indirectly, such as by acid rain. Just like air pollution, water pollution requires quality and quantity controls. The water pollution described in the opening scenario is an example of how water pollution may continue as an ongoing problem long after the original pollution occurs.

Water is also complicated by the issue of ownership. Under our common law, anyone who owns land adjacent to navigable water also owns property under the water. This

CLIMATE CHANGE AND THE INSURANCE INDUSTRY

The insurance industry has begun to experience the effects of climate change perhaps more than any other industry. Beginning with Hurricane Andrew which struck south Florida in 1992, insurers worldwide have noticed an increase in weather-related insurance losses. The Association of British Insurers (ABI), an association of insurance-risk evaluators, completed a catastrophe model to examine the effects of severe storms. By using sophisticated models, the ABI found that hurricane losses in the U.S. alone could total $100 to $150 billion in a given season. The ABI also calculated that Japanese typhoons and European windstorms could cause over 90 percent losses in insurer's capital, leading to unstable financial markets in the insurance industry. The experience with Hurricane Andrew, which caused $16 billion in insurance losses, forced 11 insurers into receivership. That $16 billion figure was approximately 50 percent more than the total amount of premiums collected in the previous 20 years in Florida. Miscalculation of catastrophic events could be very damaging for the insurance business.

What is being done now? Insurance assessors are beginning to recognize that many events are linked to climate change, and that even subtle changes in certain industries could lead to catastrophic results. For example, the farm-produce industry, tourism, energy, and transportation industries, to name a few, are very susceptible to climate changes.

Just looking at the recent past, the insurance industry sees the peril and unpredictability in climate change–related losses. Losses such as the 2003 European heat wave which led to thousands of premature deaths and the wildfires it spawned caused about $15 billion in damages; the 2004 hurricane season in Florida, with four back-to-back hurricanes, led to economic losses of $56 billion, of which $30 billion was insured. Sweden suffered a windstorm in 2005 that caused the largest-ever insurance loss in that country, with damage to commercial forestry set at $2.5 billion. South America saw it's first-ever hurricane, Catarina, which caused significant damage in Brazil. Tropical storm Vince reached the coast of Spain in October 2005, and the Canary Islands witnessed their first tropical cyclone in November of that year.

The event of 2005, however, that riveted the insurance industry was, of course, Hurricane Katrina. That event saw the correlation of many types of insurance catastrophes: health, life, and property/casualty insurance. Katrina's losses are calculated at $60 billion, in addition to the human toll of 1,500 lives lost. Total economic losses are expected to bottom out at $200 billion, in insured and uninsured losses.

This event caused even more concern for insurers, and they are now paying close attention to scientists who are linking severe storms and rising sea temperatures and increasing levels of greenhouse gases that increase the intensity of these naturally occurring events. They also noted that the number of natural disasters increased from 29 per year in the 1970s to 114 per year since 1990. There is a feeling among insurers that perhaps early scientific predictions of the effects of climate change were grossly underestimated.

Source: Gary S. Guzy, "Insurance and Climate Change," *Global Climate Change,* Michael Gerrard, ed. (ABA, Section of Environment, Energy, and Resources, 2007).

---

doctrine, called **riparian rights,** makes ownership of underwater property generally to the center of the body, and gives rights of access as well. If your ownership is of a nonflowing body of water, such as a lake, your rights are similar and said to be **littoral rights.** In some western states in the United States, the rights of ownership are said to be via the principle of **prior appropriation,** meaning whoever used the water first has a continued right to use that water. Lastly, the **public trust doctrine** allows governments to have the authority over navigable waters so that they can provide what is in the best interest of the public. The government is obligated to protect the quality of the water and to provide public access for use and recreation.

Clean Water Act

The Clean Water Act of 1972 (CWA) establishes the basic structure for regulating discharges of pollutants into the navigable waters of the U.S. and regulating quality standards for surface waters.

Under the CWA, the EPA has implemented pollution control programs such as setting wastewater standards for industry. It has also set water quality standards for all contaminants in surface waters. The CWA is implemented and enforced largely by state agencies, the EPA, and the U.S. Army Corps of Engineers. The CWA has four basic functions. It (1) authorizes water quality standards for surface waters; (2) requires permits for point source discharges of pollutants into navigable waters; (3) assists with

THE OTHER CARBON DIOXIDE PROBLEM—OCEAN ACIDIFICATION

The emission of carbon dioxide, CO_2, into the ocean has been recognized by scientists as a threat equal to global warming caused by emission of CO_2 into the atmosphere. The emission of CO_2 into the ocean causes the pH level to lower which causes the seawater to become more acidic. This, in turn, harms the marine animals' ability to form shells and skeletons needed to survive. Coastal states are required to report impaired waters, and the EPA is required to maintain or add these waters to their list of impaired ocean waters. Scientists reported that waters off the coast of Washington have had their pH lowered 0.2 units since 2000, and that seawater quality and marine ecosystems are already being affected. The Center for Biological Diversity, a nonprofit conservation organization, asked the EPA to add ocean waters off the coast of Washington to its list of impaired ocean waters because of the impact of ocean acidification. The EPA has failed to add Washington waters to its list.

As a result, the Center for Biological Diversity sued the EPA, asking that the EPA be forced to add Washington waters to its list. Adding it to its list will allow the EPA or the state to set limits on the input of pollutants into the water to prevent further degradation. Under the law, the Clean Water Act would require limits on the CO_2 emissions that contribute to ocean acidification. A spokesperson for the Center for Biological Diversity claims that ocean acidification is happening so rapidly on the west coast that Washington's waters already exceed the standard set by the EPA which triggers protection.

Source: Center for Biological Diversity, "Lawsuit Filed against Environmental Protection Agency for Failure to Combat Ocean Acidification," press release, May 14, 2009, http://www.biologicaldiversity.org/news/press_releases/2009/ocean-acidification-05-14-2009.html.

---

funding for construction of municipal sewage treatment plants; and (4) plans for control of nonpoint source pollution.

Under the CWA, it is unlawful to discharge any pollutant from a **point source** into navigable waters unless permitted by the National Pollutant Discharge Elimination System (NPDES), the EPA's permit system. Point sources are defined as discrete, identifiable sources of discharge, such as pipes, man-made ditches, or industrial or municipal systems that discharge directly into surface waters. A **nonpoint source** is pollution that comes from many sources, such as melting snow that picks up animal waste, leakage from vehicles, and pesticides. Reality Check 16-3, "The Other Carbon Dioxide Problem—Ocean Acidification," illustrates the problem our oceans face from carbon dioxide emissions in coastal waters.

Safe Drinking Water Act

The Safe Drinking Water Act of 1974 (SDWA) was established to protect the quality of drinking water and its sources: rivers, lakes, reservoirs, springs, and groundwater wells. This law focuses on all waters actually or potentially designed for drinking use, whether from above ground or underground sources. In our opening scenario, there might be pollution in the drinking water around the former military bases.

The Act authorizes the EPA to establish minimum standards to protect tap water and requires all owners or operators of public water systems to comply with these primary health-related standards. (See Take Away 16-1, "Tap v. Bottled Water: Did You Know . . . ?") Under the Act, the EPA also establishes minimum standards for state

EXAMPLE

TAP v. BOTTLED: DID YOU KNOW . . . ?

Here are a few facts you may want to think about the next time you get ready to wet your whistle by grabbing for that drink:

- A Government Accounting Office study found that the EPA's regulation of tap water under the Safe Drinking Water Act is stricter than the regulation of bottled water under the Food and Drug Administration's Food, Drug and Cosmetics Act.
- Tap water costs less than a penny per gallon; bottled water costs as much as $10 per gallon.
- Americans are the biggest bottled water consumers, accounting for 25% of the world market. In 2006, making bottles to meet America's demand for bottled water required the equivalent of more than 17 million barrels of oil and generated more than 2.5 million tons of carbon dioxide.
- Americans buy 28 billion water bottles a year. About 4 billion plastic bottles end up in the waste stream, costing cities about $70 million a year in cleanup and landfill costs.

Source: "Watersource," Athens Clarke County Public Utilities Department, quoting from http://www.tappening.com.

MUNITIONS CLEANUP BEGINS FOR MILITARY

Before the practice was banned, the military used the ocean as its dumping ground. Hawaii and other sites in the Atlantic Ocean, Gulf of Mexico, and Alaska were the sites for dumping chemical weapons. In Hawaii, these weapons were simply thrown overboard near Pearl Harbor. In an area known as Ordnance Reef off the coast of Oahu, it is believed that in addition to the munitions, the Army disposed of 16,000 M47-A2 bombs containing 598 tons of mustard gas there in 1944. The Army also believes that that area contains disposed-of chemical weapons containing blister agents lewisite and blood agents hydrogen cyanide and cyanogen chloride. There are no current plans to remove these items, but the Army is beginning to remove the munitions that were dumped there.

The Army is now under a Congressional mandate to pinpoint and determine the effects of dumping of chemical and conventional weapons in the ocean. Thus far, the Pentagon has spent over $7 million to locate and analyze the effects on the environment and to determine ways to remove the unexploded ordnance. The Army Corps of Engineers hopes to remove the munitions from Ordnance Reef using robots beginning summer 2010.

Source: Gregg K. Kakesako, "Army Is Studying Effects of Dumping Live Ammo at Sea," *Star Bulletin.com*, August 4, 2009, http://www.starbulletin.com/news/20090804_Army_is_studying_effects_of_dumping_live_ammo_in_sea.html.

programs to protect underground sources of drinking water from endangerment by underground injection of fluids.

Marine Protection, Research, and Sanctuaries Act

The Marine Protection, Research, and Sanctuaries Act of 1988 (MPRSA), also known as the Ocean Dumping Act, prohibits the transportation of material from the U.S. for the purpose of ocean dumping, or by U.S. agencies or U.S.-flagged vessels for the purpose of ocean dumping, or the dumping of material from outside of the U.S. in U.S. waters. The MPRSA provisions are administered by the National Oceanic and Atmospheric Administration.

Ocean dumping is defined as the deliberate disposal of hazardous wastes at sea from vessels, aircraft, platforms or other human-made structures. It includes ocean incineration and disposal into the seabed and sub-seabed.[5] Occasionally, attention is drawn to this issue by waste that washes up on beaches, causing closures and cleanup. Reality Check 16-4, "Munitions Cleanup Begins for Military," discusses the military's massive cleanup effort from years of polluting the oceans with military trash.

Offshore Drilling for Oil

The U.S. consumes about one-fourth of the world's oil but produces only about 10 percent off its shores. That 10 percent comes from its 1.76 billion-acre Outer Continental Shelf which extends from three to two hundred miles offshore. An area located about 175 miles from Louisiana in the Gulf of Mexico is thought to have about 3 to 15 billion barrels of oil.

EXAMPLE

There has always been vigorous debate in the United States about the benefit of offshore drilling. The events of April 20, 2010 involving the Deepwater Horizon oil spill in the Gulf of Mexico only increased the intensity of that debate. On that date, the Horizon oil rig exploded, killing 13 oil rig workers. It also began releasing oil at a rate of approximately 100,000 barrels per day, spilling an estimated 4.9 million barrels into the Gulf of Mexico by the time the flow ceased.

As this textbook goes to press, the financial fallout caused by the spill is inestimable. British Petroleum, the operator of the oil well that has been held responsible for the damage caused by the spill, spent over $350 million in the first 30 days trying to contain

---

[5]http://unstats.un.org/unsd/ENVIRONMENTGL/gesform.asp?getitem=830.

WHAT HAPPENS WHEN THINGS GO TERRIBLY WRONG

On April 20, 2010, while working on an exploratory well approximately 50 miles off the coast of Louisiana, the semi-submersible drilling rig Deepwater Horizon experienced an explosion and fire. The explosion killed 11 people and sank the rig two days later, spilling approximately 4.9 million barrels of crude oil into the Gulf of Mexico.[7] British Petroleum (BP), the operator of the rig and the developer of the oil in that region, is thought to have engaged in several irregularities during the operation of Deepwater Horizon. The exact cause of the spill is under investigation.

President Obama, who has called the Deepwater Horizon Offshore Drilling Platform accident the greatest environmental disaster in U.S. history,[8] has called for the creation of an agency to oversee offshore drilling. Until this incident, the Mineral Management Service managed offshore drilling. That agency has come under fire for alleged irregularities in its oversight and its director was fired by the President.

This disaster has caused at least one state which recently voted in favor of establishing new oil wells to reconsider its position. Florida, which in 2009 had greenlighted offshore drilling after a 19-year ban,[9] has its biggest supporters back-pedaling on that support. Both the Governor and the sponsor of the bill that reversed the 19-year ban have expressed serious reservation about going forward with Florida's plans, now that the Horizon spill threatens Florida's coasts.[10]

The ecological disaster has yet to be calculated. Hurricane season, the unknown effects of the remaining oil on the health of the region, and the fragility of the Gulf's coastline for fishing and other natural resources, will determine how much this disaster will cost both BP and the U.S. The cost will be measured in far more than dollars.

Source: See footnotes throughout the box.

---

the oil.[6] The most immediate financial impact to the region could be felt by the regions' 5.7 million commercial fishermen when fishing was suspended immediately following the spill out of public safety concerns about contaminated seafood. President Barak Obama also suspended all offshore drilling in the Gulf, essentially eliminating the two most important sources of income for its residents. In response, BP created a $20 million fund to compensate residents who lost their income as a result. Long-term impact to the ecosystem in the Gulf region will only be known over time.

Currently there is continued debate in the U.S. over whether to allow offshore drilling. In 1981, Congress imposed an offshore drilling ban. Louisiana, which has had offshore drilling since 1947, had been a staunch supporter of offshore drilling. It receives about $1.5 billion annually from its approximately 175 existing drilling rigs. That figure was expected to grow beginning in 2017 when it anticipated receiving royalties from the oil companies. There are still many Louisianans who support offshore drilling. Environmentalists on the other side of the argument point to coastal erosion caused by ports, pipelines, and petrochemical plants that are required to support the industry for their opposition to expanded offshore drilling in Louisiana. Damage by the Horizon oil spill might bolster these arguments.

California has generally opposed offshore drilling along its shores. Since the 1960s, existing California wells have produced nearly 1 billion barrels of oil and 1.5 trillion cubic feet of natural gas. Since the late 60s, however, California residents have not supported expanding drilling off its shores.

---

[6]Erwin Seba, No End in Sight to Spill as BP Costs Mount, Environmental News Network, May 10, 2010, http://www.enn.com/ecosystems/article/41304.

[7]Estimates originally varied widely, but most experts now agree that the total spillage is approximately 4.9 million barrels of crude oil.

[8]Rick Jervis and Alan Levin, "Gulf Oil Spill Now Largest in U.S. History as BP Continues Plug Effort," *USA Today,* http://www.usatoday.com/news/nation/2010-05-27-oil-spill-news_N.htmcsp=34news.

[9]Josh Hafenbrack andTonya Alanez, "Florida House Approves Offshore Drilling," *Sun-Sentinel,* April 28, 2009, http://www.sun-sentinel.com/news/local/florida/sfl-florida-oil-drilling-042709,0,210.story.

[10]Marc Caputo, Mary Ellen Klas, and Craig Pittman, "Crist Rethinks Support of Offshore Drilling," *Miami-Herald,* April 28, 2010, http://www.miamiherald.com/2010/04/28/1601349/crist-rethinks-support-of-offshore.html?utm_source=feedburner & utm_medium=feed & utm_campaign=Feed%3A+StatelineorgRss-Florida+%28Stateline.org+RSS+-+Florida%29.

Oil spills remain a primary concern among ecologists and others who study and work in the area. Massive spills, such as the 11-million-gallon Exxon *Valdez* spill in the pristine waters of the Alaskan coast, reinforce citizens and ecologists' worry about off-shore drilling. Technology has improved, which has led to a decrease in oil spills. Automatic shutoff valves and other mechanical devices are used to decrease the risk of spills. But it's clear from the Horizon incident that nothing is failsafe and the ecological risks remain.

In the U.S., the Minerals Management Service, a division of the Department of the Interior, oversees offshore drilling. However, President Barack Obama is currently calling for the creation of a new agency to oversee offshore drilling. See Reality Check 16-5, "What Happens When Things Go Terribly Wrong," for the reason why.

SPECIES PROTECTION

The Endangered Species Act (ESP) provides a program for the conservation of threatened and endangered plants and animals and the habitats in which they live. The act is administered by the National Marine Fisheries Service (NMFS), which is under the Department of Commerce, and the U.S. Fish and Wildlife Service (FWS), which is a unit of the Department of the Interior. Generally, the NMFS is responsible for species in marine environments and **anadromous** fish (those that return to rivers and streams to breed), while the FWS oversees terrestrial and freshwater species and migratory birds. The FWS maintains a worldwide list that includes all the endangered species. Endangered species include birds, insects, fish, reptiles, mammals, crustaceans, flowers, grasses, and trees. Case 16.2, Contoski v. Scarlett, discusses a case in which the FWS was challenged by a developer for keeping one of its endangered species on the list.

CASE 16.2 Contoski v. Scarlett

___ F. Supp. 2d ____, Dist. Minn., 2006 WL 2331180

Facts: Contoski owned property on Sullivan Island. While Contoski was preparing for commercial development, a bald eagle's nest was discovered. Contoski was ordered not to develop anything within 330 feet radius of the nest pursuant to the Endangered Species Act (ESA) and the Bald Eagle Protection Act (BEPA). The bald eagle was placed on the endangered species list in 1978. Since that time, the bald eagle has, in some areas, regained its population. Pursuant to that fact, the FWS, in 1999, proposed a comment period which precedes the de-listing of any endangered species. Since 1999, the FWS has not acted on their proposal. In February 2006, the FWS issued a new notice of the proposed rule to de-list, and reopened the comment period. The comment period was extended until June 19, 2006. Contoski sued Fish and Wildlife Service (FWS) claiming that they should have de-listed the bald eagle from the endangered species list. He claimed that the FWS had a proposed rule to de-list the bald eagle in 1999 and has refused to act on it. He also claims that if they were to de-list the bald eagle under the ESA, he would be able to develop his land because the

BEPA does not prohibit him from modifying the habitat like the ESA does.

Issue: Whether a party adversely impacted by an FWS designation as an endangered species that the FWS was contemplating de-listing can compel the FWS to rule on its proposed de-listing.

Decision: Yes

Reasoning: The ESA requires that a final determination be made within one year of publication of a rule proposing to determine whether a species is an endangered or threatened species, or to designate or revise critical habitat. A plaintiff may seek an administrative order compelling agency action if such action is unlawfully withheld. Here, FWS published a proposed rule in 1999 but never issued a final determination.

Under the ESA and the BEPA, a person cannot "take" an endangered species. To "take" under the ESA means to harass, harm, pursue, hunt, shoot, wound, kill, trap, capture, or collect, or to attempt to engage in any such conduct. The broadest verb is harm. Such act may include significant habitat modification or degradation where it actually kills or injures wildlife by significantly impairing essential behavior patterns, including breeding, feeding, or sheltering. Under the BEPA, the word "harm" is not found, but "take" is defined as pursue, shoot, shoot at, poison, wound, kill, capture, trap, collect, molest, or disturb. The verb "disturb" is at least as broad as the verb "harm" and both terms are broad enough to include adverse habitat modification. Therefore, the court holds that the protection against adverse habitat modification afforded the bald eagle under the BEPA is at least as protective as that provided by the ESA.

The defendants concede that they have not complied with the mandatory deadlines set forth in the ESA. The FWS has reopened its comment period, and they are asking the court to withhold relief in this case because it would be inappropriate for this court to issue a final determination before FWS has had an opportunity to examine the comments generated during this comment period. Because defendants have failed to comply with the mandatory deadlines, the court will compel the defendants to act. Therefore, the courts will allow the defendants a reasonable amount of time, but no later than February 16, 2007, unless defendants present evidence of just cause for further limited delay.

CASE QUESTIONS

1. Plaintiff thought he would be able to remove the ESA barrier by getting the bald eagle de-listed. What other barrier did the court find would be in his way?

2. Do you think it's a good idea for courts to be able to stop commercial development for the sake of one bald eagle's nest? Do you see that as injuring the land developer? What compensation, if any, does the developer get for not developing the land?

3. Once the FWS proposes to de-list the species they have a year to de-list or not, but what mechanism exists for proposing the de-listing initially? Can you think of any reason why the FWS would want to de-list a species?

The ESL protects only endangered and threatened species. Categorization depends on the degree of threat. An **endangered species** is one that is in danger of extinction throughout all or a significant portion of its range. A **threatened species** is one that is likely to become endangered in the foreseeable future.

The law requires federal agencies to ensure that actions they authorize, fund, or carry out are not likely to jeopardize the continued existence of any listed species or result in the destruction of adverse modification of designated critical habitat of such species. The law also prohibits any action that causes a taking of any listed species of endangered fish or wildlife. For example, in September 2009, two years after the grizzly bear was de-listed, a federal district judge put grizzly bears back on the endangered species list.[11] The judge found that the 2007 de-listing had not provided adequately for the survival of the bears, which live primarily in Yellowstone National Park. The judge noted that even though the bears' numbers had climbed from 200 to 600 at the time of de-listing, the Department of Interior had not made proper plans for saving their habitat or for the effects of climate change. The judge noted that warmer temperatures had caused an outbreak of mountain pine beetles, which have killed millions of acres of whitebark pine trees, whose nuts are essential in a bear's diet. The court also noted that in 2008 alone, nearly 80 grizzlies were known to have died in the Yellowstone ecosystem.

Also, the import, export, and interstate and foreign commerce of listed species is prohibited. Reality Check 16-6, "Endangered Species," provides information about how many species are threatened by the environmental carelessness exhibited in the past.

HAZARDOUS AND TOXIC WASTE DISPOSAL

The Resource Conservation and Recovery Act of 1976 (RCRA) gives the EPA the authority to control hazardous waste from "cradle-to-grave." This includes the generation, transportation, treatment, storage, and disposal of hazardous waste. RCRA also

---

[11]"Grizzlies, Back on the List," Editorial, *The New York Times,* September 27, 2009, http://www.nytimes.com/2009/09/28/opinion/28mon4.html?_r=1 & th & emc=th.

REALITY CHECK 16-6

ENDANGERED SPECIES

The U.S. Fish and Wildlife Service categorizes and keeps track of the endangered species in the United States and worldwide. As of September 2009, the following facts were available about the 1324 endangered species in the U.S.

Endangered Vertebrates (mammals, birds, reptiles, amphibians, fishes)	Endangered Invertebrates (clams, insects, arachnids, snails, crustaceans, corals)	Endangered Non-Flowering Plants (conifers, cycads, ferns, fern allies, lichens)	Endangered Flowering Plants
379	198	31	716

In addition, there are 574 endangered species outside of the U.S.; there are currently 86 proposed additional species to be placed on the list; there have been 9 species de-listed because they are extinct; and 20 species that have recovered have been de-listed.

Source: U.S. Fish and Wildlife Service, http://www.fws.gov/endangered/wildlife.html#Species.

gives a framework for dealing with nonhazardous solid wastes. The 1986 amendments to RCRA enabled the EPA to address environmental problems that could result from underground tanks storing petroleum and other hazardous substances. Love Canal, one of the most tragic of all events in the environmental history of the United States, which shows how hazardous this type of waste can be, is discussed in Reality Check 16-7, "The Tragedy of Love Canal."

How RCRA regulates waste depends on whether it is classified as solid waste or hazardous waste. All waste that is not hazardous is solid. The term **solid waste** means any garbage, refuse, sludge from a waste treatment plant, or air pollution control facility and other discarded material, including solid, semi-solid, or contained gaseous material resulting from industrial, commercial, mining, and agricultural operations, but does not include material in domestic sewage.[12] In the opening scenario, there is an allegation that there is hazardous material stored on the base that has continued to affect the nearby populations.

EXAMPLE

REALITY CHECK 16-7

THE TRAGEDY OF LOVE CANAL

"Give Me Liberty, I've Already Got Death" was a message displayed in 1978 by a resident of Love Canal. Love Canal is now a toxic ghost town, its residents evacuated in 1978 due to mismanagement of a toxic waste site. In the 1950s Hooker Chemical Company used the Love Canal as an industrial dump. After operations finished, the company covered the site and sold the land for one dollar. The working class town of Love Canal was built on this dump site. In August of 1978, corroding waste-disposal drums could be seen breaking up through the ground in backyards. The drum containers, which held 82 different compounds, 11 of them suspected carcinogens, had been decomposing and leaching their contents into the backyards and basements of 100 homes and a public school built on the banks of the canal. Trees and gardens were turning black and dying. One entire swimming pool had been popped up from its foundation, floating on a small sea of chemicals. Children returned from playing outdoors with burns on their hands and faces. This was viewed by many as the most appalling environmental tragedy in American history.

Source: http:// http://www.epa.gov/history/topics/lovecanal/01.htm.

After a material has been defined as a solid waste, then it is determined whether it is a hazardous waste. **Hazardous waste** has properties that make it dangerous or potentially harmful to human health or the environment. Hazardous waste can be liquids, solids, contained gases, or sludge. These can be by-products or discarded commercial

---

[12]Atomic Energy Act of 1954, 42 U.S.C. 6903(27).

THE MEADOWLANDS—FROM FILL TO FOOTBALL FIELD

Landfills are not dead lands. There are businesses that specialize in redeveloping closed landfills as recreational facilities such as golf courses, playing fields for team sports, and tennis courts. The redevelopment of the Meadowlands in New Jersey is an example of making productive use of what was once a useless and dangerous property.

The Meadowlands began its modern development after New Jersey expanded the New Jersey Turnpike so that the western spur ran through the center of the wetlands. Shortly thereafter, the New Jersey Sports Authority Act was passed, which had as its mission the development of a major sports center on the property. First to open was the Meadowlands Racetrack, featuring harness racing. Giants Stadium opened in 1976, and the Brendan Byrne Arena, now named the Izod Center, opened in 1981. Finally, the New Meadowlands Stadium (replacing the Giants Stadium, which was demolished in 2010) opened in 2010, and is the only stadium home to two NFL football teams, the NFC New York Giants and the AFC New York Jets. Reclamation of the wetlands continues, with a major shopping area planned for the future.

Source: Stephen Marshall, The Meadowlands Before the Commission: Three Centuries of Human Use and Alteration of the Newark and Hackensack Meadows, Urban Habitats, December 2004, http://www.urbanhabitats.org/v02n01/3centuries_full.html and http://reclaimingthemeadowlands.com/index.asp?AID=45.

products, such as cleaning fluids or pesticides. Just because property once contained a hazardous waste product does not mean the property is forever useless. Reality Check 16-8, "The Meadowlands—From Fill to Football Field," illustrates that point.

Medical Waste Tracking Act

The Medical Waste Tracking Act (MWTA) was enacted after medical waste washed up on the shores and beaches in New York and New Jersey. Public disgust and outrage prompted Congress to enact the MSTA to provide safe and uniform disposal of medical waste. Even so, as late as September 2009, medical waste, including 8-inch cotton swabs and hypodermic needles, once more washed ashore in New Jersey. Medical waste consists of infectious, hazardous, radioactive, and other general waste from doctor's offices and hospitals. The act defines medical waste as including cultures and stocks of infectious agents, pathological wastes, such as tissues, organs, and body parts, human blood and blood components, sharp instruments that have been used in patient care, animal carcasses, body parts, and bedding of animals used in testing, waste from surgery or autopsies and lab waste. The MWTA require segregation of the waste at the generator site and tracking of the waste through to the disposal facility.

The contents of medical waste are actually controlled by several statutes and agencies. RCRA governs the waste that contains mercury or other toxic substances, while waste containing radioactive isotopes or materials is covered by the National Response Center.

Toxic Substances Control Act

The Toxic Substances Control Act of 1976 (TSCA) provides the EPA with authority to require reporting, record-keeping, testing, and restrictions relating to chemical substances and/or mixtures, excluding food, drugs, cosmetics, and pesticides. The TSCA addresses the production, importation, use, and disposal of specific chemicals including polychlorinated biphenyls (PCBs), asbestos, radon, and lead-based paint.

The TSCA requires manufacturers of new chemical substances to notify the EPA before manufacture, allows testing of risky chemicals, maintains an inventory of commercially manufactured or imported chemicals, and requires importing or exporting chemicals to be reported.

Comprehensive Environmental Response, Compensation, and Liability Act

The Comprehensive Environmental Response, Compensation, and Liability Act of 1980 (CERCLA), otherwise known as the **Superfund,** provides a fund of money to clean up uncontrolled or abandoned hazardous waste sites as well as accidents, spills, and other emergency releases of pollutants and contaminants into the environment. One distinction between the other acts and CERCLA is that CERCLA is retroactive; it addresses events that have already occurred and imposes liability for actions taken before the law was enacted. Through CERCLA, the EPA was given power to seek out those parties responsible for any waste release and assure their cooperation in the cleanup. The Superfund would be one of the sources for cleaning up the military base we mentioned in the opening scenario.

CERCLA references other statutes to identify over 800 hazardous substances or potentially hazardous substances. Hazardous substances are not purely waste products. Substances that are an integral part of industry may also be designated as hazardous.

The EPA cleans up orphan sites when potentially responsible parties cannot be identified or located, or when they fail to act. Through various enforcement tools, the EPA obtains private party cleanup through orders, consent decrees, and settlements. The EPA also recovers costs from financially viable individuals and companies once an action has been completed.

The EPA operates the Superfund in all 50 states and U.S. territories. Case 16.3 illustrates how the CERCLA Superfund works.

CASE 16.3 Metropolitan Water Reclamation District of Greater Chicago v. North American Galvanizing and Coatings, Inc.

473 F.3d 824 (7th Cir. 2007)

Facts: Lake River Corporation (LRC), a wholly-owned subsidiary of North American (NA) owned about 50 acres of property which it leased to Metropolitan Water (Met), but which Met now owns. While LRC operated on the property, it constructed a facility to store, mix, and package industrial chemicals for its own use. LRC's operations involved accepting, by truck, barge, and rail, large amounts of chemicals that it held in above-ground storage tanks. The tanks were prone to leak, and it is estimated that close to 12,000 gallons of industrial chemicals leaked into the ground water and soil. These toxins were hazardous wastes as that phrase is defined in CERCLA. Met has incurred substantial expense in remedying the contaminated portions of its property. It seeks damages from LRC and NA to recoup approximately $1.8 million in damages. LRC and NA argue that they are not required to contribute to Met's costs because Met was not required by CERCLA or any other company to bear the cost of cleanup, thus their status is voluntary. Under these circumstances, Met is not entitled to a contribution from LRC or NA.

Issue: Whether under CERCLA a landowner who voluntarily cleans up hazardous waste is entitled to be reimbursed by the former owner who created the hazardous conditions?

Decision: Yes, Met is entitled to a contribution from LRC or NA.

Reasoning: Under CERCLA, Met is a "person" that has incurred "necessary costs of response," including investigation, monitoring, and cleanup costs. Because Met has neither settled any liability with the government nor has been the subject of any CERCLA suit for damages does not disqualify it for a contribution from LRC or NA. Met has not been compelled to initiate cleanup or repay the EPA, and Met's action against NA is not an action for an appropriate division of the payment one of them has been compelled to make. When Met commenced cleanup no other party had taken remedial action and there was no common liability. Therefore, Met's action is characterized more appropriately as a cost-recovery action than as a claim for contribution.

CASE QUESTIONS

1. LRC and NA argued that because Met was not required to clean up, they should not be entitled to a contribution in the cost from either of them. However, if a CERCLA action had been brought against Met requiring it to clean up the site, then, according to LRC and NA, they would have been required to contribute. What incentive would a landowner have to voluntarily clean up if the argument made by LRC and NA were to prevail?

2. Look at the structure of CERCLA. Why do you think the current landowner is required to pay

for cleanup even where they are found not to have contributed to the disposal of the waste initially?

3. CERCLA does recognize the innocent landowner exception, but restricts it to the situation where hazardous waste deposited on a landowner's property is by (1) an act of God; (2) an act of war; or (3) an act of a third party that has no contractual privity (relationship) to the defendant. None of these exceptions fit Met. Are these restrictions too narrow? Should a current landowner be responsible for cleanup if he had no notice of the presence of the waste and was not able to find out before purchasing the land? What would be the problem with a known or should have known standard here?

NOISE POLLUTION

Noise is defined as unwanted or disturbing sound.[13] Surprisingly, noise is far from being an invention of the modern world. Noise has been a problem for as long as people have been living in proximity to each other. For this reason, the law began to concern itself with noise as far back as 1876.[14] Modern science has only added new noisemakers. Airplanes, trucks, railroads, supersonic aircraft, large earthmoving devices, even boomboxes and loud car stereos all add noise to our environment.

Noise used to be strictly an urban problem, but increasingly technology and machines are bringing noise to the few remaining wild places in the world. In fact, it is thought that if it has not already occurred, the sound of human machines may be inflicted upon every square mile of the planet.[15]

At one point, the EPA enforced noise abatement through the Clean Air Act. In 1981, the EPA discontinued its enforcement efforts on the federal level and moved primary enforcement to the state and local governments. The EPA's role currently is to investigate and study noise and its effects and to evaluate the effectiveness of noise on the public's health and welfare. The EPA also retains jurisdiction to disseminate information to the public regarding noise pollution and adverse health effects.

The EPA, through other federal agencies, regulates noise sources such as rail and motor carriers, low noise emissions products, construction equipment, transport equipment, trucks, motorcycles, and the labeling of hearing protection devices. The Federal Aviation Administration has procedures to respond to the public about aircraft noise questions or complaints within the U.S. As noted in Reality Check 16-9 ("No Kidding—Noise Can Kill You"), noise is a serious problem for some individuals.

---

[13]http://www.epa.gov/air/noise.html.

[14]*Crump v. Lambert*, L.R. 3 Eq. 409 (1867).

[15]"Down with Decibels," *UNESCO Courier*, July 1967.

State Environmental Laws

Conservation has traditionally been an area left to state law. Most of the federal laws were not enacted until 1970 or after, while many state laws predate that time. At present, federal legislation preempts state law in certain areas, but states are free to regulate their environment in any area not preempted. In addition, the EPA has delegated many responsibilities for investigative activity related to, compliance with, and enforcement of federal law to the states.

For example, the Clean Air Act delegates responsibility for its enforcement and implementation to the states, with the exception of motor vehicle emissions, fuels, and aircraft emissions. The bulk of the CAA dealing with controlling air emissions from stationary sources is left to the states, upon approval of the EPA. This approval is gained by preparing a State Implementation Plan (SIP). Once approved, each SIP has the effect of federal law.

The Clean Water Act allows for similar federal–state interaction. Under the CWA, states require their point sources to obtain permits from the EPA under the National Pollution Discharge Elimination System, or states may seek permission from the EPA to set their own state permit programs. Many take advantage of the opportunity to do so.

The Safe Drinking Water Act authorizes states to implement and enforce its provisions subject to EPA approval of each state's program. RCRA continues the approach of requiring state plans subject to EPA's approval in the area of solid waste regulation. A similar pattern exists with regard to hazardous waste. Once a state has adopted an approved program, it must enforce it. States are free to issue more stringent controls than the EPA guidelines.

Some areas are totally preempted by federal law. In addition to the preemption of emissions from motor vehicles, aircraft, and fuels under the CAA, federal law preempts state regulation of aircraft noise, relabeling of pesticides under the Federal Insecticide, Fungicide, and Rodenticide Act, regulation of atomic energy under the Atomic Energy Act, and the regulation of energy conservation efforts under the Energy Policy and Conservation Act. Under federal preemption rules, even where the federal law does not occupy the entire field, a state law on the same topic is still preempted if the state law conflicts.

Reality Check 16-10 ("Corporations 'SLAPP' Back Environmental Activists") discusses an approach that was developed by corporations and developers when they met resistance to their plans by environmental activists. A preemptive lawsuit, designed solely to preoccupy and financially exhaust thinly funded environmentalists and their organizations, was filed by the developer or

REALITY CHECK 16-10

CORPORATIONS "SLAPP" BACK ENVIRONMENTAL ACTIVISTS

As environmental awareness has increased, so has environmental activism. Any proposal for a new development is likely to meet with vocal opposition by activists. Existing operations that pollute are often targeted for protests. A few years ago, the developers and businesses began to fight back.

A "strategic lawsuit against public participation," or SLAPP, is a lawsuit in which the primary goal of a corporate plaintiff is to stifle or silence a person's or a group's challenges to the corporation's actions or plans. Typically, the corporate "SLAPPer" files common law claims such as defamation, conspiracy, abuse of process, or interference with contract.

Why are SLAPPs so effective? Because a corporate executive suing the activist may have an in-house counsel department and can afford the cost of the litigation, whereas the activist usually does not. Activists can often defend themselves on First Amendment grounds, and the claims are often dismissed, but the damage has been done. As a result, some jurisdictions have enacted anti-SLAPP legislation.[16]

Source: George W. Pring and Penelope Canan, *SLAPPs: Getting Sued for Speaking Out* (Temple University Press, 1996).

---

[16]These are Arkansas, Arizona, Delaware, Florida, Georgia, Guam, Hawaii, Illinois, Indiana, Louisiana, Maine, Maryland, Massachusetts, Minnesota, Missouri, Nebraska, Nevada, New Mexico, New York, Oklahoma, Oregon, Pennsylvania, Rhode Island, Tennessee, Utah, and Washington.

corporation to discourage continued protests against proposed development. The threat of being sued chilled the protests of many. This practice was eliminated by state action that sought to protect the value of the protesters' voices.

L08

What It Means to Be a "Green" Business

Businesses have recognized that "it's not easy being green,"[17] but it may be profitable. Green business, or sustainable business, attempts to have no negative impact on the environment. A **sustainable business** is any business that participates in environmentally friendly processes, products, or activities that address environmental concerns while maintaining a profit. Sustainability has been defined as a three-legged stool—people, planet, profit.[18] The key is to balance all three through the **triple bottom line** concept: using sustainable development and sustainable distribution to impact the environment, business growth, and society.

A major focus of sustainable businesses is to reduce or eliminate the impact made on the environment by harmful chemicals, materials, and waste generated by production or service. For example, many hotels now ask if the guest wants the towels washed every day, or the linens left on the bed for more than one night. Reducing the washing load at a hotel can reduce the amount of chemicals that get disposed of into the water. More common is the effort of many businesses to go paperless. On some former military bases, the cleanup has already begun and the bases are being converted to industrial parks.

Sustainable business practices can include recycling waste and using alternative (to fossil fuels) energy sources, such as solar power. It can also include a concept called **designing for the environment** (DfE), which requires businesses to consider the potential environmental impact of a product and the process used to make that product. (Think back to Take Away 16-1 on bottled water and the amount of petroleum it takes to make the bottles and then transport them.) Working together with environmental organizations to identify and label products that protect human health and promote sustainable chemistry, the EPA DfE Safer Product Labeling Program gives the consumer the power to make safer choices by identifying products with the DfE label. Such products have reduced chemicals and provide alternative environmentally friendly products. For example, Anheuser-Busch Companies worked with aluminum can manufacturers to decrease wall thickness and lid diameter, achieving a 30 percent weight reduction in aluminum cans, and shared the design with the entire industry. Tremendous environmental and financial savings were achieved through using less material and reduced transportation costs.[19]

Upcycling is another form of sustainability. Upcycling is the process of using waste materials to provide new products.[20] It is a form of reinvestment in the environment and allows for reduction in waste and a reduction in the use of original resources for production. For example, using old bicycle innertubes for wallets, old wooden pallets for lawn furniture, and backpacks made of juice boxes are just a few upcycling ideas. On a broader scale, using rice husks as packaging material in industry can save the environment from the lifecycle of a Styrofoam peanut.[21] These and other ideas are being created by green businesses worldwide.

Social sustainability is another aspect of going green. An organization is said to be socially sustainable if it gives back to the community through employee volunteering or

---

[17]"It's not easy being green" is a phrase in a song by the same title sung by Kermit the Frog (voiced by Jim Henson) on Sesame Street during its first season in 1970.

[18]*The Brundtland Report,* UN General Assembly, 1987, http://www.un-documents.net/wced-ocf.htm.

[19]"Product Stewardship for Manufacturers," Pacific Northwest Pollution Prevention Resource Center, http://www.pprc.org/pubs/epr/dfe.cfm.

[20]Michael Braungart and William McDonough, *Cradle to Cradle: Remaking the Way We Make Things* (North Point Press, 2002).

[21]Estimates are it takes 500 years for one Styrofoam cup to dissolve, and that Styrofoam accounts for 1/4 of landfill waste; http://www.huffingtonpost.com/simran-sethi/life-cycle-styrofoam-mark_b_127456.html.

through charitable donations. Social sustainability encompasses human rights, labor rights, cultural rights, and corporate governance. The idea of social sustainability is compatible with environmental sustainability because of the belief that future generations should have the same access to social resources that the current generation has, and that there should not be depletion of those resources.

Social sustainability often manifests through **socially responsible investing** (SRI). This form of investing favors corporations that promote environmentally aware practices, consumer protection, human rights, and diversity. Some socially responsible investors avoid businesses involved in alcohol, tobacco, gambling, weapons, the military and/or abortion. Social responsibility is not new. The Quakers practiced one of the first instances of socially responsible investing in this country when they prohibited members from participating in the slave trade of buying or selling human beings in 1758. The modern SRI movement began in the 1960s with economic development projects like the Montgomery (Alabama) Bus Boycott lead by Dr. Martin Luther King Jr. in protest of Jim Crow laws against blacks in the south. On a worldwide scale, pictures of napalmed victims, skin in flames, in Vietnam generated outrage against Dow Chemical, the manufacturer of napalm, and protests against the company. From the 1970s to the 1990s, large institutions avoided investment in South Africa in protest of the institution of apartheid. As investors become more aware of their power to direct corporate involvement in the political and social fabric of countries and causes, socially responsible investing will emerge as a powerful force for change. Knowing this gives business people or those going into business awareness of hot-button issues to consider before being blind-sided by a perceived misstep.

Green businesses are on the rise. As noted in Reality Check 16-11 ("Get Your Business Certified 'Green'"), the Green Business Bureau is attempting to standardize and certify businesses that meet their definition of a green business. Reality Check 16-12 ("Travelocity Encourages Green Travel") discusses one business that has found a way to encourage other green businesses and make their products known to the clients who seek to support green travel-related businesses.

EXAMPLE

REALITY CHECK 16-11

GET YOUR BUSINESS CERTIFIED "GREEN"

The Green Business Bureau (GBB) wants to help you make your business a green business. They have produced a step-by-step guide to help any business turn green. The Bureau describes how being green can save the business money, the impact it can make on the environment, how it responds to the change in customer buying practices and requests for green services, how it improves employee morale by making employees proud, attracting the brightest employees, and providing a healthier workplace, and last but not least, how it can help businesses thrive by reaching out to the green customers that are seeking green businesses.

Once your business achieves "green," it qualifies to be "Green Business Certified" and can be awarded the GBB Seal of Approval. This seal can be displayed on your web page and in your business office. This also allows you to provide your information through the GBB to its vendors.

Source: Green Business Bureau, http://www.gbb.org/.

REALITY CHECK 16-12

TRAVELOCITY ENCOURAGES GREEN TRAVEL

Travelocity, the search engine for booking travel, is now offering its customers the option of choosing to book their travel plans with over 200 sustainability-minded hotels and suppliers through their newly created "Travel Green" website. By partnering with Energy Star, the Rainforest Alliance, the United Nations Foundation and the United Nations World Tourism Organization, Travelocity has been able to identify and rate the suppliers and hotels using a four-tier system. The system, based on the Global Sustainable Tourism Criteria Partnership, rates those businesses that are making an effort at being ecologically and culturally responsible. The criteria are based on whether the business trains their staff and management on conservation, supports the local community, works for cultural and environmental conservation, and actively reduces the carbon footprint.

Source: Janelle Nanoson, "Travelocity Goes Green," *National Geographic Traveler,* February 4, 2009, http://blogs.nationalgeographic.com/blogs/intelligenttravel/2009/02/travelocity-goes-green.html.

International Enforcement Issues

Pollution does not respect international boundaries. Because local, state, and federal efforts with respect to the environment can be undermined by pollutants from other nations, the U.S. EPA's Office of International Affairs (OIA) has entered into many agreements with the governments of other nations. The OIA focuses on issues such as marine pollution or long-range transport of pollutants that only sustained international cooperation can help.

One area that has had substantial international focus has been global climate change. This is a complicated area, however, because of the differing impact of climate change on different countries. For example, countries have various capacities to regulate greenhouse gas emissions, the largest contributor to global warming. When emerging countries are asked to regulate under the various treaties, they are skeptical about doing so because they are unsure of the industrial nations' commitment to do the same. One example supportive of this skepticism is the U.S. government's refusal to sign the Kyoto Protocol. Then-President George Bush thought it unwise to agree to caps on emission and proposed transfer policies as an alternative. In spite of the U.S.'s refusal to sign this agreement, the Kyoto Protocol has spawned international attention to this issue. In a September 2009 press release made in anticipation of the Copenhagen meeting on global climate change, the World Bank reported that a "climate smart" world is within reach in 2010.[22]

Many other agreements have focused on the environment. Agreements grew out of the United Nations Convention on the Human Environment in 1972, also known as the Earth Summit. In 1992, the UN held the Conference on Environment and Development. In 2002, there was a World Summit on Sustainable Development in South Africa.

International environmental law also involves the decisions of international courts and tribunals. Even though they have limited authority, their rulings are influential and help create awareness. The tribunals include the International Court of Justice, the European Court of Justice, and the World Trade Organization.

CORPORATE AND GLOBAL CODES OF CONDUCT

An **environmental impact statement** is an analysis of the expected effects of a development or action on the surrounding natural environment. Many organizations, businesses, and government entities create environmental impact statements. These impacts can range from the air emissions or water discharges from a manufacturing plant to the small quantities of hazardous waste or sewage generated by a school. The greater the number of impacts recorded for a project, building, or business, the more likely it is that the impacts will be managed through an **environmental management system,** or EMS.

The EMS approach developed when a number of businesses sought to manage their environmental issues more economically and efficiently than when responding on an emergency basis. Similar to financial plans, EMSs seek to plan and manage an environmental response.

EMSs provide an ability to improve, measure, control, report, and manage environmental performance. For this reason, there has been an increase in their use. EMSs are now being made a requirement for doing business with governments and large customers. Additionally, they are being used to communicate important environmental performance to local communities and financial institutions.

Executive Order 13148, dated April 22, 2000, required federal facilities covered by environmental regulations to implement EMSs by specific deadlines, with final implementation by 2005. EPA is charged with meeting EO 13148 requirements and

---

[22]http://web.worldbank.org/WBSITE/EXTERNAL/NEWS/0,contentMDK:22312494~pagePK:64257043~piPK:437376~theSitePK:4607,00.html.

overseeing implementation and assisting other agencies. Reality Check 16-13 ("The EPA Goes ISO 14001") discusses how the EPA has implemented the EMS standard utilized by many organizations, governments and firms in one branch of the EPA.

COALITION FOR ENVIRONMENTALLY RESPONSIBLE ECONOMIES

The Coalition for Environmentally Responsible Economies (Ceres) has emerged as the worldwide leader in standardized corporate environmental reporting within firms. Formed out of a partnership between large institutional investors and environmental groups, Ceres pioneered an innovative, practical approach toward encouraging greater corporate responsibility on environmental issues.

In 1989, after the Exxon *Valdez* disaster in which the freighter spilled 10.8 million gallons of crude oil in the remote salmon, bird and sea otter haven of Prince William Sound, Alaska, eventually covering 11,000,000 square miles, killing thousands of birds and animals, and in response to the public outcry about perceived corporate irresponsibility, a group of individuals announced the Valdez Principles—a 10-point code of corporate environmental conduct to be publicly endorsed by companies that strive to improve overall performance. Later renamed the Ceres Principles, they were adopted by companies that already had strong environmental commitment, such as Ben and Jerry's, The Body Shop, and Aveda. In 1993, Sunoco became the first Fortune 500 company to endorse the Ceres Principles,[23] opening the way for other large companies to join. As of 2009, more than 80 corporations are signatories to Ceres.[24] Take Away 16-2 displays "The Ceres Principles," which have been adopted by companies like Coca-Cola, eBay, Best Buy, and the GAP.

GLOBAL REPORTING INITIATIVE

The Global Reporting Initiative (GRI) is a coalition of investors, environmental groups, and social policy advocates that was launched in 1997 to promote global guidelines for enterprise-level sustainability reports. These guidelines are designed to provide a uniform method of comparing companies' performance using economic, environmental and social criteria. The GRI mission is to elevate sustainable development reporting to the level of general acceptance and practice now accorded financial reporting.

The idea of GRI is to put environmental reporting on the same footing as financial reporting by using economic and social considerations. It has attracted a variety of influential groups under its umbrella organization. Ceres, General Motors, and British Petroleum, nongovernmental organizations (NGOs), consultants, accounting firms, trade associations, academia, and others have all participated with GRI in moving its vision forward.

---

[23]http://www.ceres.org/Page.aspx?pid=416.

[24]Ibid.

THE CERES PRINCIPLES

Protection of the Biosphere

We will reduce and make continual progress toward eliminating the release of any substance that may cause environmental damage to the air, water, or the earth or its inhabitants. We will safeguard all habitats affected by our operations and will protect open spaces and wilderness, while preserving biodiversity.

Sustainable Use of Natural Resources

We will make sustainable use of renewable natural resources, such as water, soils and forests. We will conserve nonrenewable natural resources through efficient use and careful planning.

Reduction and Disposal of Wastes

We will reduce and where possible eliminate waste through source reduction and recycling. All waste will be handled and disposed of through safe and responsible methods.

Energy Conservation

We will conserve energy and improve the energy efficiency of our internal operations and of the goods and services we sell. We will make every effort to use environmentally safe and sustainable energy sources.

Risk Reduction

We will strive to minimize the environmental, health and safety risks to our employees and the communities in which we operate through safe technologies, facilities, and operating procedures, and by being prepared for emergencies.

Safe Products and Services

We will reduce and where possible eliminate the use, manufacture or sale of products and services that cause environmental damage or health or safety hazards. We will inform our customers of the environmental impacts of our products or services and try to correct unsafe use.

Environmental Restoration

We will promptly and responsibly correct conditions we have caused that endanger health, safety or the environment. To the extent feasible, we will redress injuries we have caused to persons or damage we have caused to the environment and will restore the environment.

Informing the Public

We will inform in a timely manner everyone who may be affected by conditions caused by our company that might endanger health, safety or the environment. We will regularly seek advice and counsel through dialogue with persons in communities near our facilities. We will not take any action against employees for reporting dangerous incidents or conditions to management or to appropriate authorities.

Management Commitment

We will implement these Principles and sustain a process that ensures that the Board of Directors and Chief Executive Officer are fully informed about the pertinent environmental issues and are fully responsible for environmental policy. In selecting our Board of Directors, we will consider demonstrated environmental commitment as a factor.

Audits and Reports

We will conduct an annual self-evaluation of our progress in implementing these Principles. We will support timely creation of generally accepted environmental audit procedures. We will annually complete the CERES Report, which will be made available to the public.

Source: http://www.ceres.org/Page.aspx?pid=416.

GRI hopes to produce sustainability reports from the organizations that can be used in sustainability management. Like Ceres, GRI has provided a list of guidelines to use as frameworks for its sustainability reports. The guidelines are (1) CEO statement; (2) key indicators; (3) profile of reporting entity; (4) policies, organization, and management system; (5) stakeholder relationships; (6) management performance; (7) orational performance; (8) product performance; and (9) sustainability overview. Its most recent GRI Sustainability Reporting Guideline was published in 2006.[25]

U.S. GREEN BUILDING COUNCIL

The U.S. Green Building Council (USGBC) developed an internationally recognized green building certification system called Leadership in Energy and Environmental Design (LEED). LEED is a third-party certification program that serves as a tool for buildings of all types and sizes. LEED certification verifies that a building's "green" features work as they were designed to work. LEED certification is available for all types

[25]http://www.globalreporting.org/ReportingFramework/G3Guidelines/#1.

LEED CERTIFICATION LEVELS

LEED certification can consist of points ranging from a low of 49 to over 80. The certification levels are:

Level Earned	Points Needed
Certified	40–49
Silver	50–59
Gold	60–79
Platinum	80+

Recently, New York City's One Bryant Park building, a 1,200-foot-tall, 2.1-million-square-foot, $2 billion skyscraper, achieved Platinum-level LEED certification, making it the first U.S. skyscraper to do so. Jointly owned by Bank of America and the Dunst Corporation, its features include a daylight-maximized, all-glass skin, rainwater and greywater recycling, and an advanced air filtration system.

Source: http://www.usgbc.org.

of buildings, including new construction, major renovation, commercial interiors, schools, and homes. LEED certification is a point-based system whereby projects earn points for satisfying specific green building criteria. The number of points determines the level of certification received. (See Reality Check 16-14, "LEED Certification Levels.")

LEED has been successful because it is a transparent process where the technical criteria are reviewed for approval by nearly all 20,000 USGBC members. LEED-certified buildings cost less to operate, are energy and water efficient, and are healthier for occupants.

Summary

As the opening scenario illustrates, pollution can make people sick, cause birth defects, and destroy natural resources. In the U.S., the Environmental Protection Agency is the government agency charged with addressing environmental issues. As you have seen, it is certainly not the only agency involved. There are many.

The agencies regulate businesses and their relationship with the environment; such regulation has a direct and substantial impact on business. Businesses are no longer able to dispose of hazardous waste without taking the proper precautions. Water and air pollution are similarly of concern to businesses. As we have seen, environmental concerns have also been the basis for business innovations. Some businesses, like some citizens, have become leaders in the environmental awareness movement, and for that they are awarded the label of being green businesses. Climate change, global warming, melting polar ice caps, ocean pollution and acidification, and endangered species have all increased the awareness of the global community of the importance of environmental concerns. With stiff penalties, fines, and even the possibility of prison for violating the laws, businesses would do well to know the environmental laws and abide by them.

Review Questions

1. Dewey Manufacturers thought it was a good idea to dispose of all the water that accumulated in their air conditioning units at their manufacturing plant by tunneling it into a man-made ditch and allowing it to flow into the nearby river. What violation has occurred and what damage could result from its decision? LO5

2. The county of Manchester was overrun with trash from its residents. It had two landfills and they were almost to capacity. Manchester decided to build an incinerator to burn the trash. What are the likely obstacles Manchester will encounter in trying to secure a permit for its incinerator? LO4

3. The local residents of Greene County, a small, rural, mostly minority community, have recently learned that a major oil company is putting a refinery in the county. The residents ask for an environmental impact statement and learn that one has not been done. What can they do to demand one, and what steps must be taken before the oil refinery can be built? LO2

4. Oceanliner is a 4,000-person cruise ship that boasts of state of the art facilities for its cruising customers. It has it all—nightly entertainment, a bowling alley, fitness rooms, a casino, restaurants galore—the works. Recently, the island of the Bahamas reported to the authorities that waste and debris identified as being from the Oceanliner have floated up on their beaches. What likely happened and what is Oceanliner's responsibility? LO5

5. Massive Construction Company has bought almost all the beachfront property on Luxury Island, a remote island off the coast of Florida. Massive intends to build luxury condominiums on the island along with a 5-star hotel and other facilities to attract the rich and famous. The environmental impact statement indicates that there is an endangered species living on the island, and they would not survive the commercialization of the island. The EPA has halted construction. Is there anything Massive Construction can do to remove the ban against commercializing the area? LO6

6. The local dry cleaner has to use hazardous chemicals in the dry cleaning process. The chemicals are imported into the U.S. and then sold in this market. Which law regulates the entry of that hazardous waste into the U.S. and which regulates what happens to it once it is used by the dry cleaner and disposed of by it? LO3

7. Mr. Wendell, an avid environmentalist, has decided to protest the use of plastic bags by grocery stores in his community. He began by asking the stores to remove all plastic bags from their stores, but they refused. He then began harassing each customer leaving the grocery store with a plastic bag. He has been asked to stop, but refuses. He often pickets the stores with picket signs that have the lifecycle of plastic detailed on it. While most of the customers are sympathetic, the grocery stores are not very sympathetic to Mr. Wendell. They sue him, alleging a variety of charges ranging from harassment to trespass. What is this lawsuit called and what is likely to happen when Mr. Wendell responds to it? LO7

8. Under the federal/state regulatory scheme, which level of government is likely to regulate the following:

   a. Emission testing for your automobile?

   b. Air pollutants being discharged from the local paper plant?

   c. Reports of lead in drinking water supplies in the city?

   d. A decision by the local airport to allow supersonic planes to fly overhead? LO3

9. Your business has decided to "go green." What resource is likely to be a very good place to start to learn about what steps you can take to do so? LO8

10. Your business wishes to implement an Environmental Management System. What are some of the options and what is your business trying to accomplish? LO8

Ethics Issue

In 1947, long before garbage pickup was available in this rural area, a farmer began burying his nonburnable garbage in a low spot on his land. Over the years, containers with the remnants of oven cleaner, insecticide, paint thinner, nail polish remover, antifreeze, and other hazardous wastes were thrown in the pile. In 1965, the farmer placed soil over the heap, which at this point was quite smelly, planted grass and forgot about it. About 20 years after that, the land was sold to a very wealthy homeowner who knew nothing of the garbage pit, and who constructed a multimillion-dollar home on the now-estate. As years passed, rain deteriorated the buried containers and the chemicals gradually seeped into the ground. Eventually they made their way to the water table. In 2009, local landowners learned their land wells were contaminated and were able to trace the source to the farm-now-estate. Should the neighbors be allowed to sue? Sue whom? The original farmer has long been dead and the current owner was unaware of the dump site. Should he be required to pay just because he's financially able to afford it? If not the current landowner, can they use a federal remedy? Is this a federal problem, or should the state have to address this?

Group Exercise

Calculate your footprint. Go to http://www.earthday.net/footprint/info.asp. For more information about measuring and comparing environmental footprints, visit
http://www.footprintnetwork.org/, or
http://www.sustainablesonoma.org/keyconcepts/footprints.html, or
http://www.sustainablemeasures.com/Indicators/IS_EcologicalFootprint.html, or
http://www.epa.gov/sustainability/index.htm

Key Terms

administrative citations 402

administrative enforcement actions 402

anadromous fish 407

area source 402

caps 402

Council on Environmental Quality 399

designing for the environment 414

endangered species 408

Environmental Assessment 399

Environmental Impact Statement 399

environmental management system 416

executive order 401

hazardous waste 409

littoral rights 403

major source 401

mitigation measures 399

nonpoint source 404

point source 404

pollution 401

prior appropriation 403

public trust doctrine 403

riparian rights 403

scoping meeting 399

social sustainability 414

socially responsible investing 415

solid waste 409

Superfund 410

sustainable business 414

threatened species 408

triple bottom line 414

upcycling 414

17

International Trade and Business

Learning Objectives

After reading this chapter, you should be able to:

L01 Discuss cultural implications in international business

L02 Describe the scope of international business

L03 Explain the sources of international law

L04 Describe how international trade is regulated by international organizations

L05 Explain how the U.S. regulates imports and exports

L06 Describe the corruption in the global markets

L07 Explain international business transactions

L08 Describe how international disputes are resolved

 ## Opening Scenario

The United States produces approximately 241 million tons of corn annually, which is about 41 percent of the world's output. About 47 million tons are exported. About 35 percent of all corn grown in the U.S. is genetically modified. Corn grown in the U.S. is not separated by whether it's genetically modified or not; thus, as much as 98 percent of corn products may be genetically modified.

You work in the U.S. Trade Office and the phones have been ringing off the hook all day. Your office is being asked to intervene in a decision that has caught the American farmers off guard. The European Union (EU) has just stated that it will no longer accept genetically modified goods into its markets unless it meets certain restrictions. This would reduce the exportation of corn to the EU from the 3.3 million tons that is currently exported, to just under 26,000 tons of non–genetically modified corn.[1]

The restrictions that are being placed on the corn exports are onerous to the farmers. The EU has labeled genetically modified corn as "novel," which requires extra labeling for genetically modified corn and any product made with genetically modified corn. This increased labeling will deter corn production in the U.S., severely cut the value of corn as a product for farmers in this country, and deter the continued research and development of genetically modified agricultural products in the future. Farmers expect that the EU will replace its corn imports with non–genetically produced corn from Argentina.

---

[1]Nicholas Perdikis, "EU-US Trade in Genetically Modified Goods: A Trade Dispute in the Making," in *The WTO and the Regulation of International Trade,* Nicholas Perdikis and Robert Read, eds. (Edward Elgar Publishing, 2005).

What can be done about the EU's position? What kind of impediment does this place on the farmers in the U.S.? Are there other consequences to making this kind of decision on trade between the two countries? Has Argentina violated any regional agreements with the U.S. over this trade decision? Are there any treaties that are being violated by this kind of unilateral decision? Can the U.S. retaliate against the EU? What do you tell these farmers who are asking you to do something?

Introduction

The United States is the world's largest trading nation, with exports of goods and services over $1.8 trillion in 2008.[2] Most successful U.S. businesses seek to expand their markets. If they are successful, one option is to increase profits by expanding into the international marketplace. Selling a product on the international market is more than just shipping that product to another country. Doing business globally is very different than doing business domestically; the global marketplace is largely unregulated. There are no global statutes or regulations except what is provided by treaty. A treaty is consensually enforced by each country that agrees to abide by it. Generally speaking, however, treaty enforcement is a self-regulatory process and each country gets to decide how it will implement the treaty that it signs. For example, in 1977 Congress enacted the Foreign Corrupt Practices Act (FCPA) to prohibit U.S. companies from giving or accepting bribes (more on this Act below). Beginning in 1977, the Organization for Economic Cooperation and Development (OECD), an international organization, also began drafting a treaty in an effort to rid the international community of bribery. After the U.S. signed the treaty, they amended the FCPA to reflect what they believed was required by the OECD Treaty. Each country that signed the OECD Treaty has domestic legislation which reflects what it thinks the OECD Treaty requires, but no two countries' legislation looks the same.

Cultural Implications in International Business

Cultural differences are what separate us. Not every country acts the same way because of cultural differences, and business expectations are included. Nothing illustrates this point like the issue of bribery, which has been used forever in some countries to facilitate business. While there is an international movement to outlaw bribery as a way of doing business globally, bribery is not the dirty word in some countries that it is in the United States.

Business people have a set of expectations around the role of government in business, the length and purpose of business meetings, how important issues should be communicated between parties who are in negotiations, the decision-making process, and the exchanging of gifts and personal favors, among other concerns. Various countries might have very different cultural references for these things and their codes of conduct may be very different as a result. One easy example is the exchange of business cards. In the U.S., business cards are handed out with little or no fanfare. In Japan, Japanese business people put great stock in the exchange of cards, so when you take a business card from someone, the tradition is to look at the logo, admire it, make conversation about it, and then extend your own and go though the same thing. For a group of business people, the exchange of cards can take an hour before any business is conducted. Another example

---

[2]Office of the United States Trade Representative, http://www.ustr.gov/about-us/benefits-trade.

of cultural differences is the very concept of a business meeting. For instance, business meetings in the Middle East are generally conducted in a large room with several visitors clustered in small groups. The host may go from group to group and visit with each in turn. Rounds of tea will be served, and in the course of the meeting the host may disappear for 20 minutes or more to attend to his prayers.[3]

Failure to know about and respect specific cultural differences can create embarrassment or ridicule. One such example involved a U.S. airline which had won a prestigious award. They publicized their award by placing a statement on their napkins that said, "This is not just a napkin, this is an award," and they placed the napkins on their flights between the U.S. and the U.K. Unfortunately, in the U.K. "napkin" means "sanitary napkin." For the traveler from the U.K., it was like having an embossed Kotex placed on their tray table.[4] It pays to have the cultural sensitivity training necessary to understand other cultures and to learn to operate within them. Because of increased awareness of the importance of respecting multiculturalism, U.S. businesses must also ensure that their products, salespeople, and sales techniques do not offend international buyers. In order to do this effectively, the business must be educated about both the ultimate international business environment they will deal with and their targeted consumers. In the opening scenario, part of the reason for rejecting the genetically modified corn is a cultural difference between Europe and the U.S. Europeans are said to have less faith in science as a force for good, recognizing that science can have detrimental effects.[5] This can be seen in Europe's development of the "precautionary principle,"[6] which forms the basis of Europe's legal position toward the regulation of food production and safety.[7]

L02

Defining the Scope of the International Legal Environment

International law, by definition, involves the study of many different legal systems other than our own. Those various legal systems apply a variety of mechanisms to regulate business and resolve conflicts. However, that is too wide a scope for our purposes. For this chapter, we limit our study to the sources of international law, international and U.S. regulation of world trade, methods of conducting international disputes, and remedies for unfair labor practices. Reality Check 17-1, "Legal Systems around the Globe," illustrates the kinds of different legal systems that exist around the world.

L03

Sources of International Law

Sources of international law are the rules and principles regulating the international community. The primary sources of international law include custom, treaties, agreements, and internationally accepted organization rules. Each of these has its own special considerations, which will be discussed next.

CUSTOMS

A **custom** is a principle or practice that has developed over a course of dealing; the practice is so well recognized that it becomes binding on the parties to the custom.

---

[3]Roger Extell, *The Do's and Taboos of International Trade* (John Wiley and Sons, 1989).

[4]Christina Rexrode, "Avoiding Cultural Gaffes," *Tampabay.com,* October 28, 2007, http://www.sptimes.com/2007/10/28/Business/Avoiding_cultural_gaf.shtml.

[5]Perdikis, "EU-US Trade in Genetically Modified Goods."

[6]The precautionary principle underlies all food safety and environmental issues in the EU. It is intended to prevent damage occurring from a particular action rather than letting it arise and then having to deal with the consequences.

[7]Perdikis, "EU-US Trade in Genetically Modified Goods."

LEGAL SYSTEMS AROUND THE GLOBE

The map below illustrates the incidence of different legal systems in the world.

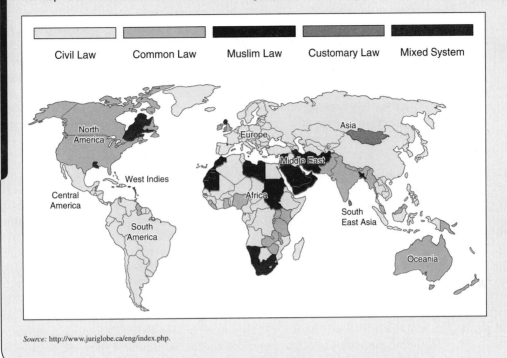

Civil Law Common Law Muslim Law Customary Law Mixed System

Source: http://www.juriglobe.ca/eng/index.php.

Article 38(1) of the 1946 Statute of the International Court of Justice defines a custom as "evidence of a general practice accepted as law." Many such customs have become the subject of treaties so the custom becomes the rule. Any practice that has not been reduced to a rule is still subject to court interpretations as to whether that practice is so well recognized that it has become a custom. For example, it's accepted as customary humanitarian law that torture tactics cannot be used on hostages of war. Because this custom preceded any treaty or convention against torture, it is seen as a custom. That means that even if the war that produces the hostage is not a war recognized by the treaty or nations who are engaged in the war, custom would still apply and torture would not be permitted. Although there may not be treaties that have reduced this custom to writing, it is accepted as binding nonetheless.

TREATIES AND OTHER AGREEMENTS

Treaties regulate a large segment of international business. A **treaty** is simply a negotiated contract between parties who happen to be nations. In addition to regulating the subject matter of the treaty, treaties often provide a structure for resolving conflicts that may arise under the treaty. For example, the General Agreement on Tariffs and Trade (GATT) (see discussion below) contains a provision that emphasizes the settlement of disagreements, rather than judgments of who is right and who is wrong. Through a series of consultations which can last for years, disagreements are urged to be settled out of court. In the dispute between the EU and U.S. about the change in rules for the exportation of corn to the EU, the GATT would require the two countries to settle their dispute amicably and to try to resolve the dispute without creating conflict or judgment.

International Trade and Business **425**

EXAMPLE

Sometimes nations are party to multiple treaties that may conflict with one another. This problem was addressed by the Vienna Convention on the Law of Treaties, adopted in 1969 (effective 1980). The convention codified the entire law of treaties, and it established rules to be applied in interpreting treaties. For example, the Vienna Convention established, among other things, every country's right to enter into a treaty, and that in the result of conflict between signatories to a treaty, each signatory would settle the dispute by peaceful means. If there arose a dispute between the U.S. and the EU or the U.S. and Argentina concerning the exporting of corn to the EU, the Vienna Convention would also be used to insist upon a peaceful resolution that is nonretaliatory.

Other types of agreements include conventions, protocols, and executive orders, none of which have the force of a treaty, but each of which may be used to further clarify sovereignty's position.

ORGANIZATIONS

International organizations are formed by agreement. There are two types of international organizations: **intergovernmental organizations** (IGOs) and **nongovernmental organizations** (NGOs). Intergovernmental organizations are made up of sovereign states called members. Such international organizations include the International Monetary Fund (IMF), the World Trade Organization (WTO), and the United Nations (UN).

Nongovernmental organizations operate internationally, are nonprofit organizations, and are separate from the government. According to the World Bank, an NGO operates as a private organization that pursues activities to relieve suffering, promote the interests of the poor, protect the environment, provide basic social services, or undertake community development.[8] The hallmark of an NGO is the fact that the organization depends on charitable contributions and voluntary service to operate. Currently there are 695 NGOs operating in Eastern Africa, 154 operating in northern Africa, 410 in Middle Africa, and 304 operating in Southern Africa.[9] Some nonprofit NGOs are the International Committee of the Red Cross, Physicians for Social Responsibility, the American Civil Liberties Union (ACLU), and Rotary International.

EXAMPLE

In addition to international organizations, there are regional organizations which consist of groups of nations whose purpose it is to regulate business within their region. Examples of such regional organizations are the Andean Common Market (ANCOM), Organization of Petroleum Exporting Countries (OPEC), Association of Southeast Asian Nations (ASEAN), and the Gulf Cooperation Council.

For an overview, see Take Away Box 17-1, "Sources of International Law."

LO4

International Regulation of World Trade

After World War II the Truman and Marshall Plans opened up the world as a marketplace for everyone. Reconstruction of much of Europe and Japan allowed for all developed nations to contribute. The increased access for U.S. businesses, plus the desire of other nations to engage in world trade, led to the creation of international agreements to promote and regulate world business.

---

[8]http://www.nonprofitexpert.com/ngo.htm.
[9]WANGO, "Connecting and Serving NGOs," Beyond Borders, http://www.wango.org/resources.aspx?section=ngodir&sub=region&regionID=18&col=BFB07D.

SOURCES OF INTERNATIONAL LAW

Source of Law	Definition
Custom	Principle or practice developed over course of dealing so well recognized that it becomes binding on parties to the custom
Treaty	A negotiated contract between parties who happen to be countries
Intergovernmental Organization	Organizations made up of sovereign states called members
Nongovernmental Organization	Nongovernment organizations separate from governments that pursue activities that promote social goals; totally dependent on contributions and volunteers

THE GENERAL AGREEMENT ON TARIFF AND TRADE (GATT) AND THE FORMATION OF THE WORLD TRADE ORGANIZATION (WTO)

After World War II, many nations were concerned with how to regulate trade as part of a larger plan for economic recovery and began to negotiate for open trading markets. The **General Agreement on Tariff and Trade (GATT)** was the outcome of these negotiations. In force since 1947, it was the only **multilateral instrument** that had agreed-upon rules for international trade. Originally the GATT had 23 **signatories,** or nations that agreed to be bound by the rules.

Occasionally the signatories to the GATT convened to negotiate new agreements. Each meeting was called a **round,** which could last for years. Most significant was the Uruguay Round, which started in September 1986, lasted until 1993 (87 months) and involved 123 countries. Out of that round came important new agreements in the areas of services, intellectual property, and goods. Most importantly, in 1994, the GATT was updated to include new obligations on its signatories, and a brand new umbrella organization was formed. The **World Trade Organization** (WTO), consisting of the 75 existing GATT members and the European Communities, became the organization under which trade agreements are now organized. Currently, there are a total of 152 member countries in the WTO. The WTO replaced GATT as an international organization, but the GATT still exists for trade in goods as updated during the Uruguay Rounds. The new GATT is known as GATT 1994 to designate the updated agreements, but most still refer to it as GATT. The WTO expanded its scope to include goods, the service sector, and intellectual rights.

The WTO has three broad principles: GATT for goods; the General Agreement on Trade in Services (GATS) for services such as tourism, banking, and construction projects or consultancies; and Trade-Related Aspects of Intellectual Property Rights (TRIPS) for addressing traditional infringement, computer piracy, and bootlegging. Within each are additional agreements entered into by individual nations. Currently, the WTO is involved in another round begun in 2001called the Doha Round, held in Doha, Qatar. It might be that the EU and U.S. would place the issue of genetically modified goods on the table for discussion during these rounds so that all nations can have input into what they are willing to allow into international commerce.

EXAMPLE

Permanent Normal Trade Relations Status

The principal objective of GATT is to liberalize international trade and place it on a secure basis, thereby contributing to the economic growth, development, and welfare of the world's peoples. GATT attempts to impose nondiscriminatory principles on its members by requiring equal treatment of all member countries. That principle, known as **permanent normal trade relations status**—formerly **most-favored-nation (MFN) status**—imposes a duty on member nations to exact the same tariffs on every country and requires that the importing country treat imported goods from member countries as though they are domestic goods. **Tariffs** are charges imposed on a product when the product is imported into a country. The higher the tariff on **imports,** the more expensive the imported goods are, and the less likely buyers are to purchase such imported goods over domestic goods that have no such tariffs imposed upon them.

Permanent normal trade relations status therefore becomes very important to a country if it wishes to have its goods readily accepted and bought in another country's markets. GATT ensures that one country's products will not have an advantage over those of another due to differences in tariffs imposed. In our opening scenario, you should anticipate that this would be the primary objection to the regulations that the EU has placed on corn imported from the U.S.

Nontariff Barriers to Trade

Nontariff barriers (NTBs) are barriers that restrict imports but are not in the form of a tariff. NTBs are criticized as a way to evade free trade rules such as those imposed by the WTO that restrict the use of tariffs. Some examples of NTBs are antidumping measures, countervailing duties, product-specific quotas, packaging and labeling conditions, product standards, and "buy national" policies. The USTR identifies each year, country by country, the nontariff barriers placed on goods, services, and intellectual property.[10] For example, reference to the 2008 report shows that Canadian requirements for foods fortified with vitamins and minerals have created a nontariff barrier. Products such as calcium-enhanced orange juice must be treated as a drug, causing a burden on manufacturers who must make separate production runs for U.S. and Canadian markets. GATT's rounds are continuously at work to remove these barriers. For instance, the U.S. would most certainly view the extra labeling of imported corn products as a nontariff barrier.

Diversity in the Law 17-1 ("WTO's Trade Policies May Deter and Defer Positive Gains for Women") illustrates how women's issues have ironically sometimes suffered at the hands of gender-neutral policies implemented by the WTO.

ORGANIZATION FOR ECONOMIC COOPERATION AND DEVELOPMENT (OECD)

The OECD is a 30-nation intergovernmental organization established in 1960 as the successor to the international body that had administered the Marshall Plan. (The Marshall Plan was the agreement made by the industrialized nations to rebuild war-torn Europe after the end of World War II.) The principal purpose of the OECD is to coordinate the key economic policies of the major industrialized countries. This would also be an avenue the U.S. could explore for resolving the dispute between it and the EU

---

[10]USTR, "Trade Estimate Report on Foreign Trade Barriers," http://www.ustr.gov/about-us/press-office/reports-and-publications/2009/2009-national-trade-estimate-report-foreign-trade.

WTO'S TRADE POLICIES MAY DETER AND DEFER POSITIVE GAINS FOR WOMEN

World trade is supposed to affect women's status positively by improved employment opportunities, social status, self-confidence, and awareness of women's rights with the over-all goal of creating greater women's autonomy. There is evidence, however, that perhaps the improvement does come with setbacks. Studies on the connection between women and trade have focused on three questions. First, does trade affect women's employment opportunities, income, and consumption? Second, what effect does trade in specific industries and geographic locations have on women? And third, does trade have noneconomic impact on women's well-being, human potential, and freedom from poverty?

The answers to these questions have given inconclusive results at best. For example, it was shown that while women have gained new jobs in the export industries, those jobs require longer hours and women are paid 20 percent to 50 percent less than men. Importation of food displaces women in the local produce and other markets and favors larger growers. This negatively affects women because they have little access to land for large-scale growing. In addition, the reduction of tariffs and export licensing indirectly affects women in that less revenue disincentivizes governments to provide services or safety nets for the most vulnerable members of society and limits the government's ability to implement policies to correct these imbalances.

The WTO's policies are thought to be gender neutral. Because of that, the WTO to date has not focused on the potential harms the policies can have on women worldwide. Women and others are calling on WTO members to respect and revitalize the UN's Beijing Platform for Action, which commits them to gender equality and mainstreaming.

Source: Geneva Women in International Trade: Gender and Trade in the Multilateral System, www.wto.org/english/tratop_E/dda_e/symp03_gwit_e.doc.

---

concerning the corn restrictions on a broader basis, for example. This same import restriction impacts Canada as well, because it also exports genetically modified corn and other products to the EU. Because all three parties are signatories to the OECD (viewing the EU as representing all of Europe), this seems an ideal forum for resolving this dispute. As illustrated in Reality Check 17-2 ("OECD Active in Strengthening International Trade and Business"), the OECD is a prime organization for implementing policies for globalizing business. For a summary of terms, see Take Away 17-2, "International Trade Regulation Terms."

OECD ACTIVE IN STRENGTHENING INTERNATIONAL TRADE AND BUSINESS

In March 2009, Israel became the 38th signatory to the OECD Anti-Bribery Convention which outlaws bribery of foreign public officials in international business transactions. Along with the Anti-Bribery Convention, the OECD has enacted several important policies designed to bring integrity, transparency, and propriety to global financial and business transactions. In the past 15 years, in addition to the Anti-Bribery Convention, the OECD has concluded:

- OECD Guidelines for Multinational Enterprises—sets out standards for business behavior in areas such as employment, industrial relations, environment, competition, and taxation.
- OECD Principles of Corporate Governance—broad rules to govern business conduct.
- OECD Financial Action Task Force—engages worldwide network to adhere to its recommendations to combat money laundering and the financing of terrorism.

In addition, the OECD has developed international tax standards for transparency and cooperation on taxation to counter tax abuse, especially in havens and countries with strict bank secrecy.

Source: "OECD's Gurria Welcomes G7 Move to Establish Set of Ethical Principles on Global Business," Organization for Economic Cooperation and Development, http://www.oecd.org/document/48/0,3343,en_2649_34487_42181872_1_1_1,00.html.

INTERNATIONAL TRADE REGULATION TERMS

GATT	Multilateral instrument that has agreed-upon rules for international trade
Round	Meetings convened to negotiate new agreements for GATT
WTO	Umbrella organization for trade agreements
PTNR	Principle that imposes same tariff on member countries as if they were domestic goods
NTB	Barriers that restrict imports but are not in the form of tariffs

L05

U.S. Regulation of World Trade

If a business decides to get into the international arena, one way it may be involved is by exporting its products. Competition for international dollars has prompted enactment of rules and regulations that attempt to ensure that only companies that meet international standards for quality can be involved in international business. If a business is to compete on the international market, those quality standards must become part of the daily operation of the business.

Exporting products into the international market requires knowledge of and compliance with export rules and regulations. Before a business can **export** products, it must apply for an export license. The type of license and the difficulty in obtaining that license is determined by the type of product it exports. Although many previously restricted technological products have been lifted from the export restriction list, certain products still require special permission to export.

BUREAU OF INDUSTRY AND SECURITY (BIS)

The Bureau of Industry and Security is responsible for implementing and enforcing the Export Administration Regulations (EAR). The BIS is charged with the development, implementation, and interpretation of U.S. **export control** policy for purely commercial commodities, **dual-use commodities,** software, and technology. A dual-use commodity is one which has commercial but also military applications. The EAR does not control all goods, services, and technologies. Other government agencies may regulate more specialized exports. For example, the U.S. Department of State has authority over defense articles and defense services. The Nuclear Proliferation Act and the Atomic Energy Act control exportation of nuclear material. The Toxic Substances Control Act controls exportation of chemical substances to foreign countries.

EXAMPLE

BIS uses a scheme of licenses to control exports from the United States depending on the type of good to be exported and the final destination. If your commodity is not listed by BIS as requiring a license, as are most commodities, then no license is required and your status is designated "No License Required" (NLR) unless its destination is to an embargoed country, to an end-user of concern, or in support of a prohibited end use. The most restricted destinations are the embargoed countries and those countries designated

BEFORE EXPORTING GOODS CHECK THE BIS LISTS

Several questions should be asked before exporting anything into a foreign country. There are strict rules which must be adhered to when exporting certain items to certain places or people. The questions are, What are you exporting, where is it going, who is getting it, and what are they using it for?

What you are exporting will determine whether you need an export license. If your item has a Department of Commerce Export Control Classification Number (ECCN) on the Commerce Control List, then you will need a license to export it. The Commerce Control List codes products into 10 general categories (such as electronics, computer, sensors and lasers, etc). Each category is further divided into five product groups. The five product groups are Systems, Equipment and Components; Test, Inspection and Production Equipment; Material; Software; and Technology. Once your product is identified, you know what type of license is needed to export it.

The next question is where is it going? Restrictions vary from country to country. The most restricted are the embargoed countries, such as Cuba, and those designated as supporting terrorist activities, such as Iran. The BIS website has a cross-referencing system to guide you in determining whether your destination is on the embargoed or terrorist list. It also lists the reason for the control of your item, ranging from Nuclear Proliferation to Crime Control.

Next you should determine who will receive your item. Some individuals and organizations are prohibited from receiving items, and others can only receive them if they are licensed. BIS identifies four categories of persons who are denied exports or who may need a license to receive them. They are *Entities*, which are organizations engaged in activities related to the proliferation of weapons of mass destruction; *Specially Designated Nationals and Blocked Persons*, for whom there is a list maintained by the Department of the Treasury containing the names of individuals who are determined to be involved in terrorism or narcotics; the *Unverified List*, which is firms for which BIS was unable to complete an end-use check who represent a red flag that exporters must inquire about before exporting to; and *Denied Persons*, a list of individuals whose export privileges have been denied.

Last, you should ask for what purpose your product is being used. Some end-users are prohibited from receiving any item no matter what your item is. You must receive specific authorization from the Department of Commerce to export items to these restricted individuals or organizations.

Source: http://www.bis.doc.gov/licensing/exportingbasics.htm.

---

as supporting terrorist activities. In addition, there are certain individuals and organizations that are prohibited from receiving exports from the U.S. The BIS website contains a list of these individuals and organizations. The exporter is required to determine if the individual or organization is on this list before exporting to them. The BIS is located within the Department of Commerce. Reality Check 17-3 ("Before Exporting Goods Check the BIS Lists") details this process.

As seen in Reality Check 17-4 ("DHL Suffers $9.4 Million Fine for Violating EAR and OFAC Regulations"), other agencies are also helpful in detecting export regulations.

U.S. REGULATION OF IMPORTS

Businesses also **import** products from foreign countries. Some products are imported directly for consumer use, but others are imported for manufacturing and other uses. In the U.S., imports to this country are governed by federal agencies, largely the U.S. Trade Representative, the International Trade Administration, U.S. Customs and Border Protection, and the International Trade Commission. Working together, these agencies regulate imports into the U.S.

DHL SUFFERS $9.4 MILLION FINE FOR VIOLATING EAR AND OFAC REGULATIONS

DHL will have to pay $9.4 million to settle a case with the BIS and Office of Foreign Assets Control (OFAC) for 90 violations it committed between May and November 2004 and eight violations between June and September 2004. DHL was charged with transporting items subject to EAR from the U.S. to Syria and Iran by failing to comply with the EAR regulations and applicable record keeping requirements. In addition to the monetary penalty, DHL will hire an expert on U.S. export controls and submit to compliance audits of all transactions between 2007 and 2009, and allow yearly audits in 2010 and 2011.

Source: BIS press release, August 6, 2009, http://www.bis.doc.gov/news/2009/bis_press08062009.html retrieved 8/29/09.

U.S. Trade Representative

The Office of the U.S. Trade Representative (USTR) is part of the executive Office of the President. Its cabinet-level office is headed by an ambassador. The USTR negotiates directly with foreign governments to create trade agreements and resolve disputes and is involved with global trade organizations. It meets with governments, business groups, and legislators to get input on trade issues. In addition to other duties, the USTR is the official U.S. representative in all activities concerning the GATT. It has headquarters in Washington D.C., Geneva, Switzerland, and Brussels, Belgium. This office would intervene in the dispute between the U.S. and the EU concerning the EU's decision to restrict the importation of corn from the U.S. into the EU and is probably the office that is fielding all the calls from irate farmers. The Ambassador would also have the President's ear, should this issue need attention.

The USTR is responsible for developing and coordinating international trade policy and oversees trade negotiations with other countries. The Ambassador serves as the vice chairman of the Oversees Private Investment Corporation (OPIC), serves as a nonvoting member of the Export-Import Bank, and is a member of the National Advisory Council on International Monetary and Financial Policies. The USTR consults with 19 other government agencies on trade matters including the Office of Homeland Security, Departments of Agriculture, Commerce, Defense, Energy, Justice, Labor, State, Treasury, and Interior, and the EPA. See Reality Check 17-5 ("The Export-Import Bank") for information about this important institution involved in the trade effort.

U.S. Customs and Border Protection

The U.S. Customs and Border Protection (CBP) is housed within the U.S. Department of Homeland Security. In terms of international business, the office is charged with the responsibility for collecting customs duties, export taxes, fees, and penalties owed for imported merchandise.

Over half of the merchandise for sale in the U.S. comes from foreign countries.[11] In 2007, the total value of all imports was more than $2 trillion. The CBP is responsible for handling these imports and for collecting the $32 billion in revenue the imports generate.[12]

International Trade Administration

The International Trade Administration (ITA) is located within the Department of Commerce. ITA promotes world trade and strengthens the position of the United States in international trade and investments. It also assists the International Trade Commission when the latter investigates charges of unfair trade practices. In our continuing example, because the U.S. farmers are calling the limitations on corn import and the restrictions unfair, this office, too, would become involved in resolving the dispute.

---

[11]http://www.cbp.gov/xp/cgov/trade/priority_trade/.
[12]Ibid.

International Trade Commission

The International Trade Commission (ITC) is an independent agency that provides trade expertise to the legislative and executive branches of government. The ITC advises the President and investigates issues such as the balance of trade between imports and exports, the economic impact in the United States of any proposed trade agreements, and effects of foreign competition on the United States. This is another office that would be involved in resolving the EU-U.S. dispute over the corn issue. The ITC also investigates charges of unfair trade practices, and it recommends appropriate action to remedy proven violations, such as dumping (see below), or patent, trademark, and copyright infringement.

The ITC protects domestic industries by determining the injury imposed on the domestic market and recommending relief to those industries, either by increasing tariffs on imports, or recommending assistance for the domestic industry. Such injuries include dumping and the sale of gray market goods in the U.S. In addition, the ITC can impose countervailing duty on products determined by the ITA to harm domestic manufacturers (see below).

Dumping Dumping occurs when a product is sold for less money in the United States or other countries into which it is imported than it is sold for in the home country. Dumping is harmful because it can undercut the competition's ability to compete in the same market. In addition, by forcing those competing companies out of business, it creates a monopoly for the importers. When competitors are injured, a tariff is imposed to make up for the advantage in price that was gained by dumping. For example, the ITC recently determined that circular welded carbon quality steel lines from China were sold at less than fair value in the U.S. market to the detriment of the domestic steel industry. The Department of Commerce then issued an antidumping order on imports of such products from China.[13]

The laws that are used to penalize those who are found to dump their products are called **antidumping** laws. The ITA is the agency that determines whether there is a lower price in the foreign market; the ITC determines whether there is injury to competing domestic companies. If both of these conditions exist, then an antidumping tariff is imposed on the importer. Reality Check 17-6 ("Who's Being Harmed by Antidumping Laws?") illustrates the point that not all agree with antidumping laws.

Countervailing Duty If a foreign government pays a subsidy to a manufacturer in that country to produce a product and that product is then imported into the U.S., then a

---

WHO'S BEING HARMED BY ANTIDUMPING LAWS?

The U.S. has done well in the global marketplace. Competition in the form of foreign products has done what it was designed to do—force U.S. industries to become more efficient in order to stay competitive. Those who do not become efficient don't stay in the market because their products become too expensive and foreign products can replace them. At least that's the idea.

What about industries that cannot streamline or don't find ways to become more efficient in producing their products? They can call on U.S. trade representatives to restrict foreign imports. The weapon at their disposal is the antidumping law. The law targets unfair trade practices, one of which is exporting products for less than production costs or selling those products below the prices charged in the domestic market. If a foreign competitor is found guilty of dumping, the WTO Antidumping Agreement and U.S. antidumping law allows duties to be imposed on them.

These duties are widespread and often used, especially in the U.S., so much so that other countries, especially nonindustrialized countries, attempted to forestall the WTO Doha Rounds unless it was understood that the U.S. antidumping laws would be repealed. In fear of such an occurrence, the U.S. Congress overwhelmingly passed a resolution ordering the U.S. Representatives at the Doha Rounds to veto *any discussion* of the antidumping laws. In settlement of this dispute, the U.S. Trade Representative allowed the issue to be placed on the table, but only to discuss negotiations aimed at clarifying the already existing antidumping laws.

The Doha Rounds are continuing, and the issue has yet to be resolved. More and more nonindustrialized countries are playing the U.S. game and imposing duties on U.S. imports, declaring that they are creating an unfair advantage over domestic products. This increase in antidumping duties on imported products is sure to bring trading to the precipice of disaster unless there is resolution of this issue.

Source: Claude Barfield, *High-Tech Protectionism: The Irrationality of Antidumping Laws* (AIE Press, 2003).

---

[13]Jiang Diqing, "New Strategy Needed in Antidumping Cases, The China Daily, May 18, 2009, http://www.chinadaily.com.cn/bizchina/2009-05/18/content_7787980.htm.

countervailing duty may be imposed on the product. A **duty** is an amount imposed upon importation of a product, much like a tariff. For example, if Japan pays a subsidy to a Japanese car manufacturer to manufacture cars and those cars are then imported into the U.S., then a countervailing duty may be imposed on the cars. This additional duty is designed to make up for the competitive edge gained by the reduction in cost to produce the item created by the subsidy. The reasoning behind the countervailing duty is that by subsidizing the manufacture of products, products can be sold for less in the foreign (U.S.) market, thus competing unfairly with unsubsidized goods in that market. Examples of government subsidies are tax rebates, loans, training and research, or tax credits.

The duty of imposing such tariffs is divided between the ITA and the ITC. The ITA determines whether a government subsidy exists and if so, how much and in what form. The ITC determines whether a domestic company is suffering because of the subsidized product. If so, then a countervailing duty is imposed.

Gray Market Goods When foreign trademark rights are given to a manufacturer by a U.S. trademark holder, there is usually a requirement made that those goods be sold only in that foreign country, and not in the United States. **Gray market goods** are goods manufactured in a country other than the United States and bearing a valid U.S. trademark, which are imported into the U.S without consent of the American trademark holder. They are distinguished from counterfeit goods in that the use of the mark is authorized by the holder of the foreign trademark. Gray market goods are subject to seizure upon entering into this country without permission. In *Davidoff SA v. CVS* (Case 17.1), the court deals with the issue of how to get gray market goods off a retailer's shelves.

CASE 17.1 Davidoff SA v. CVS Corp.

571 F.3d 238 (2d Cir. 2009)

Facts: Davidoff is a well-regarded brand for high-end luxury goods. They produce cologne for men and women called Cool Water manufactured by Coty through a license from Davidoff. As part of the quality assurance and anticounterfeit program developed by Davidoff, each box and bottle of Cool Water cologne has a UPC affixed that identifies the time and place of production, the production line, ingredients used and other important information. Davidoff uses that information, for instance, to issue rebates and recalls and to search for fakes. Davidoff, in an effort to maintain its brand, has refused to sell to CVS. Nonetheless, CVS has been able to obtain stock of Cool Water from outside of Davidoff's normal distribution channels. Davidoff's products are among CVS's top selling fragrances.

Some of CVS's Cool Water stock has been found to be counterfeit. On two other occasions, in 1998 and 2005, Davidoff sent cease-and-desist orders to CVS demanding they stop stocking Davidoff products and instructions on how to spot counterfeits. CVS assured Davidoff that they would conduct inventory review, remove counterfeit products, and source only from authorized distributors. In spite of these assurances, Davidoff discovered in 2006 that CVS continued to sell its Cool Water products. During the

course of this inspection, Davidoff discovered that the UPCs on the packages had been removed through a variety of techniques, including cutting the UPC labels off the packages, using chemicals to remove the UPC from the label, and grinding the bottom of the bottles to remove the UPC. In many instances, the packages had been opened. Davidoff sought an injunction against CVS, alleging trademark infringement by selling these gray market goods bearing the Davidoff mark. The court issued the injunction and CVS appealed.

Issue: Did Davidoff meet the requirements necessary to secure an injunction against the continued sale of its products by CVS?

Decision: Yes.

Reasoning: In cases involving claims of trademark infringement and dilution, as in other types of cases, a party seeking a preliminary injunction must demonstrate (1) the likelihood of irreparable injury in the absence of such an injunction, and (2) either (a) likelihood of success on the merits or (b) sufficiently serious questions going to the merits to make them a fair ground for litigation plus a balance of hardships tipping decidedly toward the party requesting the preliminary relief. CVS argues that Davidoff failed to establish a likelihood of success on the merits and would not suffer irreparable harm in the absence of an injunction. We disagree and affirm the district court's grant of a preliminary injunction.

CVS asserts that the goods with the codes removed are gray market goods, i.e., genuine Davidoff goods sold by Davidoff through authorized channels in other countries and subsequently imported by others into the United States. Because these goods are sold in their original packaging with the Davidoff trademarks clearly visible and unaltered, CVS contends that the removal of the codes does not negate their genuineness or constitute infringement. CVS's argument misses the point. The fact that the goods in question may be gray market goods does not furnish CVS with a valid defense. The question before us is not whether, or under what circumstances, the sale of gray market goods infringes their trademark. The injunction was justified rather on the basis that the removal of Davidoff's codes interfered unlawfully with Davidoff's trademark rights regardless of whether the goods were originally authorized by Davidoff for sale in the United States or elsewhere.

Where the alleged infringer has interfered with the trademark holder's ability to control quality, the trademark holder's claim is not defeated because of failure to show that the goods sold were defective. That is because the interference with the trademark holder's legitimate steps to control quality unreasonably subjects the trademark holder to the risk of injury to the reputation of its mark. "One of the most valuable and important protections afforded by the Lanham Act is the right to control the quality of the goods manufactured and sold under the holder's trademark." [citations omitted] In attaching its mark to its goods over time, a holder assures consumers that the goods conform to the mark holder's quality standards. Reputation for quality, whether good or bad, becomes associated with a mark in the minds of consumers. Many consumers are willing to pay more to buy goods bearing a mark which experience has taught the consumer represents an assurance of high quality. CVS argues that the presence or absence of a UPC on a particular unit of a Davidoff product does not prove the unit's authenticity or lack thereof, and as a result, cannot be considered a legitimate quality control procedure. The argument again misses the point. The code system enhances the effectiveness of Davidoff's ability to detect and prevent the sale of counterfeits. Removal of the codes makes it more difficult to detect counterfeits. Regardless of whether the presence or absence of a code on an individual unit of Davidoff product establishes the authenticity of that unit, the removal of the codes exposes Davidoff to an increased risk that any given unit sold at retail will be counterfeit. That showing was sufficient to support the court's grant of the preliminary injunction.

CASE QUESTIONS

1. CVS argues the goods were not gray market goods because they were shown to be actual Davidoff products, and not knock-offs of Davidoff's products. How did the court respond to that assertion by CVS?

2. CVS also argued that unless Davidoff could show that removal of the UPC label adulterated the product, they could not get an injunction. What was the court's response to that argument?

3. One issue not addressed by the court is the money that Davidoff loses by having its product sold into the U.S. from the black market by unauthorized sellers. Do you think that factored into the court's injunction?

In countervailing duty and antidumping investigations, the ITC works in conjunction with the ITA and U.S. Customs. The ITA determines whether the alleged subsidies or dumping are actually occurring and, if so, at what levels. The ITC determines whether the U.S. industry is materially injured by reason of the dumped or subsidized imports. If the ITC determines injury, the Commerce Department issues an order to the Customs Service to impose duties. See Take Away 17-3, "U.S. Regulation of Imports."

Corruption in the Global Market

The international community is trying to fight corruption so that companies that are trying to enter the markets of foreign countries do not have to pay a surplus in corruption fees to do so. However, graft, **bribery,** and other forms of corruption are ways of doing business in some countries and the thought of outlawing it is a difficult concept to

U.S. REGULATION OF IMPORTS

USTR	Negotiates directly with foreign governments to create trade agreements and resolve disputes and is involved with global organizations
CBP	Responsible for collecting customs duties, export taxes, fees, and penalties owed to imported merchandise
ITA	Promotes world trade and strengthens the position of the U.S. in international trade and investments
ITC	Provides trade expertise to the legislative and executive branches of government
Dumping	Occurs when a product is sold for less money in the U.S. or other country into which it is imported than it is sold for in the home country
Countervailing duty	Amount imposed upon importation of a product designed to make up for the competitive advantage gained by the subsidy given for production
Gray market goods	Goods made in a country other than the U.S. and bearing a valid U.S. trademark imported into the U.S. without consent of the trademark holder

grasp. In the U.S., antibribery statutes impose civil and criminal penalties on companies who engage in corrupt behavior. On the international level, the OECD's Antibribery Convention to prevent corrupt behavior is slowly gaining signatories. (See again Reality Check 17-2.)

THE FOREIGN CORRUPT PRACTICES ACT

The Foreign Corrupt Practices Act (FCPA) prohibits U.S. companies and citizens from bribing public officials to keep or obtain business. Passed in 1977 and amended in 1988 and 1998, the FCPA contains two main provisions: the antibribery clause and the recordkeeping and accounting provisions. The antibribery clause prohibits payoffs to foreign public officials or political parties to obtain or retain business. Payments made merely to seek an improper advantage are not outlawed.[14]

In Case 17.2 (*U.S. v. Jefferson*), the Court was asked to determine what constitutes an official act of a Congressman accused of accepting bribes in violation of the FCPA.[15]

Title 18 U.S.C. §78dd-2 applies only to issuers or domestic concerns. An **issuer** is defined as including any U.S. public company subject to SEC reporting requirements including employees and foreign agents. **Domestic concern** is defined as including any

---

[14]U.S. v. Kay, 539 F.3d 738 (5th Cir. 2004). Proscribed payments may include favorable tax or customs treatment.

[15]Jefferson was convicted on 11 of the 16 counts on August 5, 2009. The opinion included is the opinion filed in his Motion to Dismiss, which was denied.

CASE 17.2 U.S. v. Jefferson

F.Supp.2d_, 2009 WL 1491323 E.D. Va. 2009

Facts: Defendant, a sitting member of the U.S. House of Representatives, was charged with bribery in violation of the Foreign Corrupt Practices Act. Specifically, Defendant was charged with accepting money in exchange for obtaining business development assistance for business ventures by exerting his influence as a member of Congress on various U.S. and African government officials, including the Nigerian government, the Import-Export Bank, and the U.S. Trade Agency. The indictment alleged that when he solicited the bribes, he did so as a congressman and as a member of certain congressional committees relating to African trade matters. The indictment's counts describe acts Defendant undertook or agreed to undertake in exchange for things of value from individuals seeking to advance various business ventures in Africa and elsewhere. Defendant filed a motion to dismiss alleging that the government failed to allege the "official act" element of the bribery statute.

Issue: Whether the government alleged that the Defendant committed an official act when he violated the antibribery provisions of the act.

Decision: Yes, the government met its burden in establishing he was in an official act.

Reasoning: First, the act must be among the official duties or among the settled customary duties or practices of the official charged with bribery. And second, performance of the act must involve or affect a government decision or action. First, analysis of what constitutes an "official act" must begin with—and indeed, must be anchored in—the plain language of the statute defining that term. In this respect an "official act" is any decision or action on any question, matter, cause, suit, proceeding or controversy, which may at any time be pending, or which may by law be brought before any public official, in such official's official capacity, or in such official's place of trust or profit. Importantly [the statute] supplies the abstract definition of "official act" to be used in various provisions, including the bribery provision at issue here. That provision provides, in pertinent part, as follows:

> Whoever . . . being a public official or person selected to be a public official, directly or indirectly, corruptly demands, seeks, receives, accepts, or agrees to receive or accept anything of value personally or for any other person or entity, in return for . . . being influenced in the performance of any official act . . . [shall be guilty of an offense].

Thus, the plain language of [the statutes], taken together and applied to a specific case like this one, requires the government to adduce proof with respect to the "official act" element that defendant solicited a thing of value in exchange for being influenced in his performance of (i) a decision or action (ii) on a question, matter, cause, suit, proceeding or controversy (iii) which could at any time have been pending, or which could by law have been brought before him, in his official capacity, or in his place of trust or profit.

The statute clearly requires that in exchange for the alleged bribe, *defendant*—and not some third party, government or otherwise—be *influenced* in the *performance* of a decision or action. Thus, where, as here, the charged public official is a congressman, the universe of "official acts" described by the statute is not limited to so-called "legislative acts" such as voting on or introducing a piece of legislation; rather, [the statute] has been read "sufficiently broadly to encompass all of the acts normally thought to constitute a congressman's legitimate use of his office." [citation omitted]. Moreover, it is also settled that the charged public official need not have authority to make a final decision or take binding action on the "question, matter," etc., at issue. Rather, [the statute] "cover[s] any situation in which the advice or recommendation of a [public official] would be influential, irrespective of the [official]'s specific authority (or lack of same) to make a binding decision." These principles, applied here, compel the conclusion that the Indictment's "official act" allegations in this case are sufficient to withstand defendant's attempts to dismiss the bribery-related charges at this stage of the prosecution.

CASE QUESTIONS

1. Defendant argued that the government's definition of official act expanded the scope of the statute by making any act done by an official an "official act." He argued that he did not commit an "official act" when he solicited his bribes because he was not acting on any "question, matter, cause, suit, proceeding, or controversy." How did the court address this argument by the defendant?

2. The court found that whether the public official could carry out the decision did not matter and that the statute covers any situation in which the advice or recommendation would be influential. What is the intent of this part of the statute? What would be the effect if the government had to prove that the official had the power to influence, rather than he just said he did?

3. How are official acts defined? Can you define official acts based on this opinion?

CONGRESS, I THINK WE HAVE A PROBLEM

In 1973, during the Watergate investigation, the Office of the Watergate Special Prosecutor uncovered the use of unaccounted-for corporate "slush" funds used for questionable foreign payments. These unaccounted-for corporate funds were viewed as a fraud on the shareholders who invested in the corporations, and who were being lied to on the corporate disclosure filings with the SEC. The revelation of the existence of these funds resulted in the prosecution of several corporations. In one case alone, the prosecution uncovered circumstances in which the corporation had paid over $10 million to illegal political activities with funds that had not been reported on the books of the corporation—an SEC violation in and of itself. This caused the SEC to become curious about how many other corporations were engaged in this kind of activity. The SEC decided to provide an amnesty program for corporations to come forward and reveal, without penalty, their involvement in these corrupt practices. To their astonishment, more than 400 companies admitted to their wrongdoing with payouts exceeding $300 million to foreign officials, politicians, and political parties.

This was the impetus for the FCPA, which the SEC proposed to Congress and which Congress passed in 1977. This act extended the antibribery provisions from the purely domestic arena to the global arena, making it unlawful for corporations to engage in bribery regardless of where they operated in the world.

Source: Miriam F. Weisman, *Crime, Incorporated: Legal and Financial Implications of Corporate Misconduct* (ABA Publishing, 2009).

business with its principal place of business in the U.S. The FCPA applies to foreign agents of issuers or domestic concerns, but it does not apply to foreign officials. Foreign corporations are not directly subject to the act. In other words, the U.S., through the FCPA, does not exercise international jurisdiction in foreign venues.

The word **corruptly** is not defined by the act, but it is used to make clear that the offer, payment, promise, or gift must be intended to induce the recipient to misuse his official position in order to wrongfully direct business to the payor or his client, or to obtain preferential regulation. The act need not be fully completed; it is sufficient to violate the act for the offer to have been made. Nor is it a defense that the payment was demanded by the government official or first proposed by him or her. In one case, the court found corruption where the company paid for the plane tickets for a public official's honeymoon and the company won the contract shortly after the honeymoon.[16] Although not all favorable tax treatment is a violation of the act, favorable tax treatment that is made to have the effect to obtain or retain business is illegal.

EXCLUSIONS UNDER THE FCPA

The Act is strictly construed to prohibit payments to public officials for the limited purpose of obtaining or retaining business. The FCPA does not apply to private sector bribery.[17] Thus, the antibribery provisions do not apply to **grease** payments, defined as "any facilitating or expediting payment to a foreign official, political party, or party official the purpose of which is to expedite or secure the performance of routine government action by a foreign official, political party, or party official."[18] Reality Check 17-7 ("Congress, I Think We Have a Problem") shows how the famous Watergate break-in was the impetus for the enactment of the FCPA.

ENFORCEMENT OF THE FCPA AND PENALTIES

The SEC can institute civil injunctive and administrative proceedings to enforce all FCPA provisions against issuers. The DOJ can institute criminal actions against any person or company for any violation of the antibribery and recordkeeping provisions. DOJ can also institute civil injunctive action against any domestic concern for violations of the antibribery provisions.

While the FCPA is a big stick, statistics show that government has used it sparingly, if at all, until recently. The DOJ does not compile statistics publicly that shows its enforcement

---

[16]*U.S. v. Leibo,* 923 F.2d 1308 (8th Cir. 1991).

[17]These may be prosecuted under other criminal statutes or provisions, but not under the FCPA.

[18]15 U.S.C. 78dd-1(b), -2(b) (1988).

SEC AND DOJ INCREASE THEIR ENFORCEMENT EFFORTS OF FCPA VIOLATIONS

Until recently, FCPA prosecutions have been rare, which has led to lax compliance with FCPA antibribery and accounting policies by corporations that are required to have them. Because of the increased prosecution, and the high profile cases which have had compliance forced upon them as part of their settlement agreements, companies are beginning to take note of and implement compliance policies.

For example, in 2008, Baker Hughes, a technology corporation, was required to pay $44.1 million in fines to settle a corruption case. As part of the settlement, the SEC required that Baker Hughes enact detailed compliance policies under the supervision of an independent monitor. Titan Corporation, in addition to being fined $28.5 million after pleading guilty to charges surrounding a $3.5 million payment to an agent in Benin, Africa, was required to implement compliance training and policies for its personnel. Corporations did not enact these policies for one of two reasons. First, because of lax enforcement they did not associate it as a high risk behavior. Second, home offices did not always know what was happening in the field, especially in emerging markets where headquarters rely heavily on experts on the ground. Widely accepted local practices may have caused companies to rationalize the use of bribes in their own companies.

The increased prosecutions of parent companies for corruption happening in the subsidiaries through the use of the accounting provisions of the FCPA have made some companies pay more attention to what's going on. IBM, Chiquita, Bell South, ABB, and Schering-Plough have all been prosecuted recently under the accounting provisions.

Still, some companies are reluctant to invest in compliance programs. In a recent Deloitte poll, less than one-third of companies who answered their poll admitted to increasing their compliance programs. Another one-third stated that they rely on inside sources to learn of corruption that may be occurring, a source that experts admit is least effective in detecting corruption. Improper assessment of risks can cause headaches on the other end when the companies get caught.

Sources: Richard Dean, "Because Anticorruption Programs Are as Good as Required under U.S. Law, No Company Involved in International Business Should Think of Being without One," *PLI All Star Briefing,* vol. 6:28 (2008); and Lauren Mistrette, "Deloitte Poll: Less than One-Third of Companies Are Increasing Internal Controls to Prevent FCPA Violations," April 17, 2008, http://www.deloitte.com/dtt/press_release/.

of the FCPA. The SEC lists cases and investigations on its website, but there is no public case tracking system that monitors the status of cases. One source that used the SEC website statistics published by private law firms, and statistics published by the American Bar Association counted only 106 cases prosecuted between the years 1978 and 2008.[19] Her statistics also revealed that between 1978 and 2001, the SEC initiated a total of 13 cases; the DOJ only 32 criminal cases. Twenty-one companies and 26 individuals were convicted of criminal violations with corporate fines ranging from $1500 to $3.5 million, with one exception involving a $21.8 million penalty imposed by the SEC.[20] Individual fines ranged from $2,500 to $309,000. No one had been jailed as a result of these prosecutions until 1994. Under the DOJ's prosecutions, the largest case to date resulted in penalties of $44 million, but it also was settled with a nonprosecution agreement. These lax prosecutions and sparse investigations have been criticized by the international community.[21]

There is evidence, however, that the DOJ and SEC have increased their enforcement efforts to identify FCPA violations and prosecute them. See Reality Check 17-8 ("SEC and DOJ Increase Their Enforcement Efforts of FCPA Violations") for this evidence.

International Business Transactions

L07

After a business's decision to enter the international market, there remains the decision about how to market their product in another country. If a buyer has contacted the business directly, then a simple **direct sale** may be the answer. If the business has not been approached and

---

[19]Miriam Weismann, *Crime, Incorporated: Legal and Financial Implications of Corporate Misconduct* (ABA Publishing, 2009), pp. 94–95. In her report, it was revealed that of the 106 reported cases, 15 were the same investigation, 8 arose out of another single investigation, and during these years, there were 5 years in which no cases were prosecuted.

[20]Ibid.

[21]OECD, *United States Review of Implementation of the Convention and 1997 Recommendation,* 2002, http://www.oecd.org/dataoecd/16/50/2390377.pdf, as cited in ibid., pp. 102-106.

does not have the capital to venture into the market unguided, they may wish to sell their product to an export company that specializes in marketing their type of product. If their products have name recognition all their own, then the business may wish to license their products, or, conversely, they may wish to become a licensee for another company's product. Which method the business decides upon will be based upon specific considerations.

CONTRACTS

The sale of domestically manufactured goods to a foreign purchaser, or export, is the most common and direct way to conduct international trade. The manufacturer or seller is the *exporter*, and the purchaser in the *importer*. In the opening scenario, this may have been one way transactions occurred between the individual corn farmers and their buyers.

In addition to the export regulations that may affect direct sales, a common body of international sales law has developed, known as the UN Convention on the International Sale of Goods (CISG or the Vienna Convention). The CISG treaty has been adopted by over two dozen countries, including the United States in 1988. The treaty applies to the sale of goods between parties whose places of business are in different nations and who have agreed to the terms of the convention. The contracts made for the sale of corn from the U.S. to the EU would have been governed by this treaty.

The Vienna Convention regulates such items as contract formation, delivery obligations and risk of loss, buyer's and seller's remedies, and excuses for nonperformance. The convention applies only to the sale of certain goods. It does not apply to, among other things, household goods purchased for personal use. It is also applicable only between merchants doing business.

While direct sales may be the simplest way to market goods internationally, it may well be one of the riskiest. If disagreements arise between the buyer in one country and the seller in another because of contract disputes, nondelivery, delivery of nonconforming goods, nonpayment of goods, or the like, the problem may take on horrendous proportions due to the language barrier, difficulty in communication, and the inconvenience of suing. The CISG is not perfect, but it does offer some comfort to a merchant doing business with another merchant from a signatory country.

INDIRECT EXPORT SALES (DISTRIBUTION THROUGH EXPORT COMPANIES)

A business may not have been contacted directly by a potential buyer, but may still wish to enter the international market. Because of the financial risk of direct sales exporting, they may wish to export products through the use of intermediaries known as an **export trading company** (ETC) and **export management company** (EMC). Both provide the service of exporting a seller's product into an overseas market. The main difference between an ETC and EMC is size. An EMC generally is smaller and usually handles only one product or type of product; an ETC generally handles more types of goods and is larger. Another difference is that an ETC takes title to goods while the goods are still in this country, thereby providing the seller with revenue upon sale to the ETC. The seller retains title when dealing with an EMC.

Export trading companies are regulated through the Export Trading Company Act, which encourages formation of ETCs by allowing banks to be involved in setting up ETCs and by reducing an ETC's antitrust liability.

LICENSING AGREEMENTS

A **license** is an agreement (contract) that gives the licensee permission to use, produce, or distribute the licenser's product, information, or invention under the licenser's name. A licensing agreement is a document or certificate that generally states the terms of the license, including the conditions of its use, assistance the licenser may provide the licensee, compensation arrangements (royalties), the law that will govern, and the method for resolving disputes. The *licensee* is the party to whom the license is granted. The *licenser* is the party granting such permission.

Licensing is most often used when a trademark, patent, copyright, technology, or trade secret is involved. The value in licensing a product is that it creates much less financial risk compared with other forms of investment. The drawbacks in licensing are that the licenser can lose control over the product and risks the disclosure of secrets to the licenser's competitors.

Protection from such disclosures can be obtained by filing for an international trademark through the International Union for the Protection of Industrial Property (the Paris Convention), a treaty that provides for trademark protection and protects trademarks and patents from unfair use provided the country in which the goods are marketed honors the Paris Convention. See Reality Check 17-9 ("The Value of a Brand Is Worth Protecting") for a look at how important protecting your company's brand can be.

The Services Area

In addition to products, licensing is also used by service industries. A license from the owner of a trademark or trade name—in the form of an identified set of procedures for conducting a specific business or service, which permits another to sell a product or service pertaining to that trademark or trade name—is called a **franchise.** The *franchisee* is the renter or buyer or recipient of the franchise license. The *franchisor* means the grantor of the license. Franchising means conducting the business of selling or servicing franchises. Franchising operations such as McDonald's, Pizza Hut, and other fast-food chains and convenience stores use such licensing agreements.

During the past few decades, the services sector of business has become the dominant employer and producer of income in all developed and many developing countries. Although no commonly accepted definition of the services sector exists, it is generally agreed that it covers such services as transportation, communication, banking, finance, insurance, business and professional, community, social, and personal services.

This expansion prompted the GATT to establish GATS, the international trade agreement for services much like the agreements produced for trade of goods during the Uruguay Rounds. Case 17.3 describes the limitations to the reach of the GATS provisions.

CASE 17.3 U.S. v. Lombardo

2007 WL 4404641 (Dec. 13, 2007)

Facts: The defendants were charged in a 34-count indictment with violation of the RICO statutes, alleging bank fraud, transmitting wagering information in violation of the Wire Act, and money laundering. Essentially, the defendants ran an online illegal gambling operation. The defendants filed a motion to dismiss the charges, claiming their activities were protected under the General Agreement on Trade and Services (GATS) to which the U.S. had become a signatory.

Issue: Does the GATS treaty, to which the U.S. is a signatory, provide the defendants with a defense to the RICO indictment?

Decision: No

Reasoning: Pursuant to GATS, the United States has made a series of commitments to allow foreign providers of services access to certain domestic markets. The United States has also agreed to the system of dispute resolution outlined in an agreement called the Dispute Settlement Understanding, which provides for the establishment of a panel to hear disputes and render reports, which are reviewable on appeal by the WTO's Appellate Body. The decisions of the Appellate Body become final unless the WTO Dispute Settlement Board reaches consensus otherwise. Congress formally approved GATS in the Uruguay Round Agreements Act ("URAA") in 1994. In the URAA, Congress addressed the "relationship of [the Uruguay Round Agreements] to United States law" and directed that "[n]o provision of any of the Uruguay Round Agreements, nor the application of any such provision to any person or circumstance, that is inconsistent with any law of the United States shall have effect." Additionally, the URAA makes clear that "[n]o person other than the United States . . . shall have any cause of action or defense under any of the Uruguay Round Agreements or by virtue of congressional approval of such an agreement." A section of the Statement dealing with United States sovereignty states:

> The WTO will have no power to change U.S. law. If there is a conflict between U.S. law and any of the Uruguay Round agreements, section 102(a) of the implementing bill makes clear that U.S. law will take precedence. . . . Moreover, as explained in greater detail in this Statement in connection with the Dispute Settlement Understanding, WTO dispute settlement panels will not have any power to change U.S. law or order such a

change. Only Congress and the Administration can decide whether to implement a WTO panel recommendation and, if so, how to implement it.

A section of the Statement dealing with dispute resolution under the WTO states:

> It is important to note that the new WTO dispute settlement system does not give panels any power to order the United States or other countries to change their laws. If a panel finds that a country has not lived up to its commitments, all a panel may do is recommend that the country begin observing its obligations. It is then up to the disputing countries to decide how they will settle their differences.

Finally, concerning Defendants' proffered URAA interpretation, Congress explicitly stated that "[n]o provision of any of the Uruguay Round Agreements, nor the application of any such provision to any person or circumstance, that is inconsistent with any law of the United States shall have effect." Furthermore, the Statement indicates that this statutory statement "clarifies that no provision of a Uruguay Round agreement will be given effect under domestic law if it is inconsistent with federal law, including provisions of federal law enacted or amended by the [URAA]." On its face, the URAA precludes precisely the argument raised by Defendants.

CASE QUESTIONS

1. How unwieldy would it be to allow dispute resolution mechanisms to interfere with criminal prosecutions in the U.S. courts? Why would you think the U.S. would never agree to this defense?
2. What is the purpose of having a dispute resolution mechanism in place in a treaty if it could not be used by the citizens of the country that is a signatory?
3. After a case like this, would you expect the GATS Dispute Resolution Board to take up the issue of illegal gambling in the U.S. as a denial of the GATS treaty?

JOINT VENTURE

An international **joint venture** occurs between two or more companies, one of which is located in the country targeted as a market, that contribute assets for conducting the business. The usual scenario is that the business, for example, forms a joint venture with a business located in the country in which they wish to do business. This is necessary because of the complexity of setting up a joint venture and the strict rules some countries have regarding involvement by the foreign investors in the joint venture. This type of international business should not be initiated without consulting legal counsel in both jurisdictions.

However, there are substantial benefits to be considered in operating a joint venture. First, the foreign company can use its contacts, distributors, and knowledge of the foreign market. Second, the U.S. partner can decrease its risk of operation and limit its costs of doing business internationally.

Resolving International Disputes

There is no such thing as international commercial litigation as such. What does exist is litigation that takes place in the courts of a particular country, subject to its rules, which attempts to resolve disputes between litigants from different countries. Often, however, most international commercial contracts entered into between merchants contain an arbitration clause, which states that prior to or in lieu of litigation, the parties will submit their dispute to an agreed-upon arbitration board. This section of the chapter examines both arbitration and international litigation as they most commonly occur.

ARBITRATION

If the contracting parties choose to include an **arbitration clause,** the clause usually designates the arbitration board to be used. Although there are numerous boards available, one of three major boards is often selected: the International Chamber of Commerce (ICC), the American Arbitration Association (AAA), or the United Nations Commission on International Trade Law (UNCITRAL). Each of these boards has specific rules governing arbitration proceedings, but the rules are far less restrictive than court proceedings, and generally, the cost of arbitration is much less than litigation. Arbitration is the preferred method of dispute resolution for most merchants. Arbitration is unique in that it can be structured in almost any way that accommodates the needs of the parties. Should the U.S. and the EU not be able to amicably resolve their differences concerning the EU's prohibition of importing genetically modified corn, arbitration might serve as a forum to resolve the dispute. Reality Check 17-10 ("UNCITRAL's Most Famous Case Still Going After 30 Years") tells the story of a long-standing arbitration that has been involved in the relationship between Iran and the United States.

WHAT IS THE ROLE OF INTERNATIONAL LAW IN THE U.S. COURT?

In what some observers see as a growing trend in the U.S. Supreme Court, the Court has considered international law when deciding domestic cases. Is this trend a good or bad one? Some opponents see it as improper influence, and argue that a court looks at international law when it wants to express an opinion that is not supported by U.S. law. For instance, they point to the case of *Medellin v. Dretke*. Jose Medellin, a Mexican citizen, was convicted of murdering two teenage girls in Texas and was sentenced to the death penalty. Mexico learned of his sentence and appealed to the International Court of Justice at The Hague for relief using the Vienna Convention to argue that they should have been notified when Medellin was arrested. The ICJ agreed and ordered U.S. courts to review his sentence and those of 50 other Mexican citizens being held on death row. Mexico objects to the death penalty.

Of course, the U.S. always wants to know when one of its citizens is being held by a foreign country, so the position of the ICJ isn't entirely unreasonable. However, what should the remedy be? Should the U.S. take the ICJ's ruling under advisement and require the Texas courts to review the sentence of the Mexican citizens being held? The U.S. apologized and promised to do better at notifying Mexico and other countries when their nationals have been detained, but stopped short of following the ICJ's recommendation to review the sentences of Mexican citizens currently in American prisons.

Source: "Rule of (International) Law; Can Foreign Courts Tell American Ones How to Do Their Job?" February 26, 2005, http://www.opinionjournal.com/editorial/feature.html?id=110006348.

LITIGATION

If arbitration does not apply to a dispute, or the parties choose to litigate, then three scenarios generally arise. First, there is multinational litigation, which consists of concurrent proceedings in more than one jurisdiction, involving the same parties or arising out of the same factual litigation.

Second, a party can proceed in one jurisdiction on an issue that is actually ancillary to the main proceeding that is occurring in another jurisdiction, such as an action to freeze the assets of the defendant pending the outcome of the main litigation.

Third, the party may be faced with choosing the forum in which to bring action. That decision may be guided by whether the party should proceed in country X, where the opponent's assets are located, or in country Y, where litigation is quicker or may be cheaper. These choices should be left up to a trained adviser who is familiar with all the ramifications of the choice made. Litigation would seem to be an unlikely conclusion to the EU-U.S. corn debate, but if it did result in litigation, one consideration is the forum selection. In Reality Check 17-11 ("What Is the Role of International Law in the U.S. Court?"), the question of whether it is ever appropriate to use international law when resolving a purely domestic dispute is one that has constitutional scholars in debate.

EXAMPLE

INTERNATIONAL TRADE PROTECTION

The International Trade Commission (ITC) performs the task of enforcing violations of the Tariff Act of 1930 (19 U.S.C. 1337), known as "337" actions. Under this Act, the ITC conducts investigations into allegations of unfair practices in import trade. Section 337 protects intellectual property from unlawful infringement and also protects against unfair competition, such as the misappropriation of trade secrets, trade dress infringement, false advertising, and violations of the antitrust laws. The Electronic Document Information System (EDIS) is the electronic filing system used by the ITC to file a formal complaint and to start an investigation.

ANTITRUST ISSUES

Competition laws that developed in the United States, particularly around the turn of the 20th century, were also developed in foreign jurisdictions. Each country has laws governing competition within its borders. Much like the Sherman Act and others that regulate and define anticompetitive behavior in the U.S., comparable laws exist in foreign jurisdictions. In the final decade of the 20th century when the Soviet Union collapsed replacing its socialist market with a free economy one, lenders, vendors, and others insisted that the new nations that resulted adopt some form of competition laws to mirror open market principles. This was followed by adoption of free market competition models in Asia. The Asian Pacific Economic Cooperation (APEC) was formed to push the free trade agenda of the Pacific Rim nations. Africa, Latin America, and Indonesia have all adopted some model of competition law. While these laws differ in their specifics, they generally forbid certain activity universally, such as cartels, while differing on the benefit of other activity, such as remedies for violations that are imposed. The U.S. remains alone in providing the private remedy; most other nations that allow a private remedy do so on a limited basis.

The Sherman Act applies to "trade or commerce among the several states, *or with foreign nations.*"[22] Reality Check 17-12 ("U.S. Antitrust Enforcement against International Cartels") shows the damage and reach of international cartels and the DOJ's efforts to prevent and prosecute them.

However, the full scope of the Sherman Act has never been applied to international commerce. The Sherman Act reaches foreign conduct only when such conduct causes certain effects within the U.S. or on U.S. commerce. This limitation is based on the principle that the jurisdiction of a nation within its borders is absolute and exclusive. Thus, the Sherman Act would have no bearing on disputes arising in another nation. Still, there has been activity in the courts that attempted to extend the reach of the Sherman Act a number of times.

In 1982, Congress enacted the Foreign Trade Antitrust Improvements Act (FTAIA). The purpose of the Act was to limit the reach of the Sherman Act unless (1) the conduct has a direct substantial and reasonably foreseeable effect on U.S. import or export commerce, and (2) the effect gives rise to a claim under the Sherman Act. The FTAIA thus limited any actions that did not injure U.S. commerce. Under this rule, the U.S. competition rules will not interfere with the domestic competition rules of other countries. As shown in Reality Check 17-13 ("Intel Continues Battle with the European Union over Antitrust Charges"), antitrust disputes involving foreign companies can be litigated in those jurisdictions when their domestic imports are affected.

---

[22]15 U.S.C. §§1, 2 (emphasis added).

INTEL CONTINUES BATTLE WITH THE EUROPEAN UNION OVER ANTITRUST CHARGES

In a battle that has been waged since 2001, Intel has defended itself against the European Commission's (EC) charges that Intel used unfair business practices to persuade companies to buy its microprocessors. Intel's central processing units are used in four out of five of the world's 1 billion personal computers and servers. Intel is a U.S-based company.

The investigation began in 2001, when the EC began its investigation after a European company complained about Intel's practices. It is accused of abusing its dominant position with marketing and pricing practices that infringe European Union (EU) law. Specifically, Intel is charged with giving rebates to a major EU retailer on the condition that the retailer sells only Intel-based PCs. In the latest round, the EC fined Intel 1.06 billion euros and ordered it to cease illegal rebates and other practices intended to squeeze out competitors.

Source: Reuters, "Timeline—Intel's Antitrust Battle with the EU," May 13, 2009, http://www.reuters.com/article/americasRegulatoryNews/idUSLD48414920090513?pageNumber=2&virtualBrandChannel=0.

PROTECTION FOR INTELLECTUAL PROPERTY

Intellectual property protection comes primarily from the Trade Related Aspects of Intellectual Property Rights (TRIPs). TRIPs refers to the intellectual property right objectives in the GATT Uruguay Round and the successor WTO. These objectives include achieving a comprehensive agreement that would include (1) substantive standards of protection for all areas of intellectual property (patents, trademarks, copyrights); (2) effective enforcement measures (both at the border and internally); and (3) effective dispute settlement provisions.

Ethical Considerations in the International Context

Ethical considerations present the thorniest of issues in international business. What is clearly unethical in one country might be clearly ethical in another. We have already mentioned bribery as a customary way of doing business in some countries. Other ethical issues continue to gain worldwide attention. Worthy of mentioning here are food issues and child and slave labor.

FOOD PRODUCTION

EXAMPLE

In our continuing example about the U.S.-EU dispute over modified corn, we have referred to the cultural considerations Europeans have for not wanting genetically modified products imported into their countries. But there are other considerations as well. For example, it is also said that the recent experience of Europeans involving the food scares they have suffered has made them more cautious about producing and importing altered food products.[23] The question is how does the international market respond to different values in different markets? This can be illustrated clearly by looking at the labeling of food in the EU and the U.S markets.

EXAMPLE

Europe consists of several small nations all situated in close proximity to each other. This fact has generated the "precautionary principle," mentioned earlier in this chapter's discussion (refer again to footnote 6), as the underpinning of Europe's regulation of food products. Because there is no way to control the effects of the wind and the movement of birds and insects, cross-pollination becomes a real threat to food sources that a country might wish to remain organic. The regulatory policy of the EU reflects the *prevention* outlook of the precautionary principle. If no one does it, nothing will happen. Colloquially speaking, an ounce of prevention is worth a pound of cure.

Compare that concept with the U.S. regulatory policy on food. In the U.S., the agency that is responsible for ensuring the safety of genetically modified food takes the position that as long as it meets its safety criteria, it is granted the status of a nonregulated food. This allows it to enter the marketplace without restriction. The result is that in Europe, *genetically modified foods* are labeled as such, while in the U.S., *organic*

---

[23]For example, the BSE crisis, the problems with the production of Coca-Cola in Belgium, and the outbreak of foot-and-mouth disease in the U.K. are examples.

foods are labeled as such and anything not so labeled can be assumed to contain genetically modified products.

The solution is not an easy one because of the impact the divergent views may have on other areas and in other regions. For example, research and development on genetically modified food, which is a healthy industry in the U.S., might be abandoned or curtailed if the food it produces has no place in the world market. What does that do, then, for those countries that need food desperately and who depend on overproduction from industrialized nations? Less food production certainly means less food for them.

EXAMPLE

CHILD AND SLAVE LABOR

An international ethical issue that has received attention in the U.S. media is the use of child labor or slave labor to produce goods that are consumed or used in this country. While a broad discussion of these subjects is beyond the scope of this chapter, you should be aware of the ongoing effort to eradicate the use of child labor or slave labor by U.S. corporations. Some cases have been high profile, such as the revelation that Nike used child labor to produce its sneakers in Pakistan. One case of child slave labor used to produce a commodity consumed in America and elsewhere around the world involves the cocoa harvested in Africa which is then shipped to the developed nations. See Reality Check 17-14, "Slave-Free Chocolate," for a report on one country that is accused of producing chocolate with child slave labor and what is being done about it.

REALITY CHECK 17-14

SLAVE-FREE CHOCOLATE

Tucked away along the West African coast is the tiny country of Cote d'Ivoire, producer of cocoa used in one of the world's most recognized pleasures—chocolate. Cote d'Ivoire exports 43% of the cocoa used to make the world's chocolate. There are estimated to be 600,000 cocoa farms in Cote d'Ivoire, and an estimated 109,000 children working on them—15,000 of them enslaved on these cocoa plantations. Many of the country's farmers are totally dependent on the cocoa crop for their livelihoods. This, coupled with the fall in cocoa prices worldwide, has led to an increased need for cheap labor to harvest the cocoa beans. At present one-third of the economy of Cote d'Ivoire is based on cocoa production.

The presence of children in the labor market in Africa is not at all unusual; it is estimated that between 40 percent and 50 percent of children between the ages of 5 and 14 years work on the continent of Africa. Culturally, then, it is difficult for Africans to distinguish between their children working on the cocoa farms and others working on these farms. To many of them who have multiple wives and many children, children working at an early age is not unusual or undesirable. Another cultural intangible is that many African children are sent away to live with another family in order to learn a special skill. Cote d'Ivoire is typical. This makes it easy for traffickers in child slaves to lure away children from families thinking that their children are going to be cared for while learning a special skill who will then earn money enough to send back to their families. Because of their isolation and other factors, the families of these children simply are not aware of what awaits their children on the other side of the journey.

Word of the child labor market in Cote d'Ivoire made the news in the U.S. in 2001. Congressman Eliot Engel attempted to amend the 2001 Agricultural Appropriations bill to require chocolate products to carry a label confirming that slave or child laborers were not used in the cocoa production. The chocolate industry hired former U.S. Senator Bob Dole to lobby against its passage and stopped the bill. In exchange, the U.S.'s Chocolate Manufacturers Association initiated the Harkin-Engel Protocol, a voluntary, nonbinding document that established mechanisms to end child labor. By all accounts, the protocol was a failure, with the chocolate manufacturers maintaining that tracking conditions was impossible.

However, there has been significant improvement completely outside of the protocol process through the efforts of major corporations which import cocoa. Primarily, Kraft Foods' partnership with the Rainforest Alliance, Cargill, Nestle, and Mars's agreement to work with Utz Certified, and the development of new Fair Trade certified cooperatives in Cote d'Ivoire covering some 14,000 farmers all have decreased the use of child slave labor in Cote d'Ivoire. While no one of these initiatives can guarantee 100% child slave labor–free production of cocoa, all of them have done more than the protocols to help eradicate this problem in Cote d'Ivoire.

Sources: Samlanchith Chanthavong, "Chocolate and Slavery: Child Labor in Cote d'Ivoire," TED Case Studies No. 664 (2002), http://www1.american.edu/TED/chocolate-slave.htm. See also, "The Cocoa Protocol: Success or Failure?" International Labor Rights Forum, June 30, 2008, http://www.laborrights.org/sites/default/files/publications-and-resources/Cocoa%20Protocol%20Success%20or%20Failure%20June%202008.pdf.

THE ADVERSE IMPACT OF TRADE RULES ON WOMEN'S RIGHTS

After World War II, there arose two strands of international development—international humanitarian law and international trade law. Until recently, there was little thought that the two strands could be on a collision course. However, in certain areas this collision has occurred, in no place more apparently so than in Africa.

International trade law and human rights law sometimes work in contradictory directions. Because of the traditional discrimination against women, women's rights have been made the subject of humanitarian focus, most notably in the passage of the Convention on the Elimination of All Forms of Discrimination Against Women (CEDAW) and the even more powerful statement made during the 1993 World Conference on Human Rights in Vienna, which declared the human rights of women and the "girl child" inalienable, reinforced in Beijing in 1996.

However, trade rules are sometimes biased against women. For example, governments that have programs to improve the lives of women often do so through training, low-cost loans, tax breaks, and subsidies for women-owned businesses or those that employ women. The multilateral Agreement on Subsidies and Countervailing Measures (ASCM) entitles states to grant subsidies on such a limited number of grounds (narrowly defined under research and development programs and environmental aid to disadvantaged regions) that it excludes other grounds for support, such as those addressing economic or historical disadvantage. Doing so excludes government support programs for women, perpetuating the disadvantaged position of women in society.

Another area of discrimination against women is agriculture, especially in Africa. Women in Africa dominate subsistence farming aimed at household consumption and production for the local market, while men dominate cash crop production. Trade rules tend to open up the local markets to cheap imported products subsidized by other governments which displace the home grown products of women. In addition, making export a priority reduces the amount of land women use for subsistence farming. The adverse effect can be seen on the local family: no food for household consumption, no food to sustain their families. Outside work becomes necessary with low paying jobs the only jobs available, adding to the burden on women.

The human rights implications of trade rules for women are just being recognized. There cannot be a blind eye turned to these policies and their impact on women's plight. Work needs to be done to balance the need to improve the lives of all people in a region without displacing women's contributions or creating additional burdens on them.

Source: Emezat H. Mengesha, "Reconciling the Need for Advancing Women's Rights in Africa and the Dictates of International Trade Norms: The Position of the Protocol on the Rights of Women in Africa," *African Human Rights Law Journal* 6 (2006).

It should be clear that good-will efforts outside and beyond the law may be effective in solving international ethical issues that seem ill-suited for resolution in any legal arena. Nevertheless, such thorny ethical issues must continue to be addressed by the WTO, treaties between nations, organizations, businesses, and governments alike, in order that the global market be supplied with products that are both needed and wanted, while at the same time the interests of the world's people are not compromised or harmed in the process. Diversity in the Law 17-2 ("The Adverse Impact of Trade Rules on Women's Rights") revisits again how trade rules can negatively impact a segment of society because of a lack of knowledge of the history of a region, the position of women in the economy, and other cultural insensitivities.

Summary

If a business is to maximize its potential, it is highly likely that the owners or managers will decide to deal in some way with customers outside the borders of the United States, and if they do, they must be aware of the myriad rules and regulations that govern doing business internationally. The ways they choose to operate in the international arena will be based on their own individual considerations regarding the safety and political stability of the country or countries they wish to do business with, the ease with which they are able to communicate with foreign customers, language differences they encounter, the available access to litigation processes, and regulations governing the kinds of goods to be sold and how business is conducted in the other country or countries.

Once the business determines that the effort to go outside the borders of the U.S. is worthwhile economically, then becoming familiar with and understanding the culture(s) to be engaged with is a crucial factor in conducting business. Covering all the bases in understanding both the laws and as many aspects of the other culture as possible will go a long way toward ensuring their international success.

Review Questions

1. Rondon Inc. is concerned that the political situation in a Southeast Asian country to which it wishes to export its goods is so unstable that it might not be permitted to do so. What should Rondon do before exporting to this country? LO5

2. Microcorp is exporting its goods for the first time. A rather large shipment is involved, and because of cash flow considerations, the company needs to have as much cash as possible. If Microcorp decides to export its goods through an exporting company, which type should it be and why? LO5

3. Ling Tsu has a successful cartoon character that designers want to turn into a logo and place on their clothes. Several of the companies that are requesting to use her mark are located outside the U.S. Discuss what Ling Tsu's most pressing concerns are. What should be the options she considers? LO4

4. Martinez is the Chief Financial Officer for her county (in a U.S. state). She has been in talks with a major Canadian company which is looking for a place to locate its manufacturing plant and has contacted her about her county. The company has been hesitant, and Martinez learns that another county is bidding for the same plant. In an effort to persuade the Canadian company that her county is better suited, she offers the company tax breaks, guarantees that her local citizens are not interested in unionizing, and promises to pay for the roads to be paved leading from the nearby town to the plant. Are any of these a violation of the Foreign Corrupt Practices Act?

5. Consider the same scenario as in question 4, but this time Martinez offers the agent of the Canadian firm with whom she's been dealing a one-time payment authorized by the county of

$10,000 if he will recommend her county over the competitor county. Is this a violation of the Foreign Corrupt Practices Act? LO6

6. The Less-Than-A-Dollar Store wants to be able to sell a certain cosmetic, but cannot convince the distributor that its clientele is really the right market for this product, so the distributor refuses to sell to the store. In an effort to prove the distributor wrong, Less-Than-A-Dollar Store procures from a foreign agent the same product. Does this conduct violate any rules, and if so, what is likely to happen if the authorities learn of the store's conduct? LO6

7. Holland has a policy of subsidizing its domestic tulip growers because it wants to be able to claim it is the largest seller of tulips in the world. The fact is, others would be larger sellers if they could sell their tulips at a competitive price. What is likely to happen to the tulips imported into the U.S. if it is learned that Holland's subsidies are what allow their tulips to be sold at a lower price? LO5

8. While on a trip to Hong Kong, Sullivan realized that he could have his ties made there for much less than he could have them made at home in the U.S. He entered into a contract with the tie-maker to buy two dozen ties and have them shipped to his address in the U.S. What type of sale is this, and what international protection does Sullivan have if the tie-maker does not produce the ties? LO7

9. What agreement would cover a contract between a United States' firm and a foreign firm to start a tourism business in a foreign country? LO4

10. What would somebody who wishes to sell goods to a person in Lebanon have to do before shipping goods to that person? LO5

Ethics Issue

You and your classmates, local members of Killer Coke—an international campaign to make the Coca-Cola Company responsible for its acts—have been picketing and protesting for days at your university.[24] You object to the exclusive contract Coca-Cola (Coke) has to supply all outlets and vending machines with their products at your university. Your basis for objecting is that Coke has been linked with human rights violations and environmental degradation the world over. Specifically, it is alleged that Coke has looked the other way at the murders and kidnappings of union leaders at Coke's bottling plants in Colombia.

In your investigation of the exclusive contract with the university, you learn that Coke pays a lot of money to your school for exclusive pouring rights at all of the university's restaurants on campus. In addition, Coke contributes $1.75 million in sponsorship fees paid in installments of $350,000 per year, plus $15,000 for the Chancellor's Merit Scholarship and $150,000 to help complete renovations of its eating establishments. They also donated $20,000 to bring Bill Cosby to campus last year. All this in a year when the university has a $46 million deficit.

What would you do if this were your university? Can you insist that the university switch to another vendor? Should they forgo the benefit of dealing with a corporation that may or may not have committed the atrocities you complain of? Can you bring proof? Should you have to?

Group Exercise

Go to your local discount drug store or full service store (Walmart, CVS, Walgreens, Big Lots, Dollar Stores, etc). Look at the toiletries and perfume items they have for sale. Identify any gray market goods that you see. Usually, these are identifiable because they have their UPC symbols removed or altered, they may be marked Not for Individual Sale, or they may have a black mark through the item's name. Notify the manager that you think these abuses are occurring and document his or her response. Look up your local U.S. Customs and Border Protection agency and ask how to report these trade abuses. Make a report stating what you found and when.

Key Terms

[24]Source: S. P. Sullivan, "Enjoy Ethical Dilemmas," *The Collegian*, April 29, 2009, http://www.dailycollegian.com/editorial-opinion/enjoy-ethical-dilemmas-1.1739259.

THE CONSTITUTION OF THE UNITED STATES OF AMERICA

PREAMBLE

We the People of the United States, in Order to form a more perfect Union, establish Justice, insure domestic Tranquility, provide for the common defense, promote the general Welfare, and secure the Blessings of Liberty to ourselves and our Posterity, do ordain and establish this Constitution for the United States of America.

ARTICLE I

Section 1 All legislative Powers herein granted shall be vested in a Congress of the United States, which shall consist of a Senate and House of Representatives.

Section 2 The House of Representatives shall be composed of Members chosen every second Year by the People of the several States, and the Electors in each State shall have the Qualifications requisite for Electors of the most numerous Branch of the State Legislature.

No Person shall be a Representative who shall not have attained to the age of twenty five Years, and been seven Years a Citizen of the United States, and who shall not, when elected, be an Inhabitant of that State in which he shall be chosen.

Representatives and direct Taxes shall be apportioned among the several States which may be included within this Union, according to their respective Numbers, which shall be determined by adding to the whole Number of free Persons, including those bound to Service for a Term of Years, and excluding Indians not taxed, three fifths of all other Persons.[1] The actual Enumeration shall be made within three Years after the first Meeting of the Congress of the United States, and within every subsequent Term of ten Years, in such Manner as they shall by Law direct. The Number of Representatives shall not exceed one for every thirty Thousand, but each State shall have at Least one Representative, and until such enumeration shall be made, the State of New Hampshire shall be entitled to choose three, Massachusetts eight, Rhode-Island and Providence Plantations one, Connecticut five, New York six, New Jersey four,

Pennsylvania eight, Delaware one, Maryland six, Virginia ten, North Carolina five, South Carolina five, and Georgia three.

When vacancies happen in the Representation from any State, the Executive Authority thereof shall issue Writs of Election to fill such Vacancies.

The House of Representatives shall chuse their Speaker and other Officers; and shall have the sole Power of Impeachment.

Section 3 The Senate of the United States shall be composed of two Senators from each State, chosen by the Legislature thereof,[2] for six Years; and each Senator shall have one Vote.

Immediately after they shall be assembled in Consequence of the first Election, they shall be divided as equally as may be into three Classes. The Seats of the Senators of the first Class shall be vacated at the Expiration of the second Year, of the second Class at the Expiration of the fourth Year, and of the third Class at the Expiration of the sixth Year, so that one third may be chosen every second Year; and if Vacancies happen by Resignation, or otherwise, during the Recess of the Legislature of any State, the Executive thereof may make temporary Appointments until the next Meeting of the Legislature, which shall then fill such Vacancies.[3]

No Person shall be a Senator who shall not have attained to the Age of thirty Years, and been nine Years a Citizen of the United States, and who shall not, when elected, be an Inhabitant of that State for which he shall be chosen.

The Vice President of the United States shall be President of the Senate, but shall have no Vote, unless they be equally divided.

The Senate shall chuse their other Officers, and also a President pro tempore, in the Absence of the Vice President, or when he shall exercise the Office of President of the United States.

The Senate shall have the sole Power to try all Impeachments. When sitting for that Purpose, they shall be on Oath or Affirmation. When the President of the United States is tried, the Chief Justice shall preside: And no Person shall be

---

[1]Changed by the Fourteenth Amendment.

[2]Changed by the Seventeenth Amendment.
[3]Changed by the Seventeenth Amendment.

convicted without the Concurrence of two thirds of the Members present.

Judgment in Cases of Impeachment shall not extend further than to removal from Office, and disqualification to hold and enjoy any Office of honor, Trust or Profit under the United States: but the Party convicted shall nevertheless be liable and subject to Indictment, Trial, Judgment and Punishment, according to Law.

Section 4 The Times, Places and Manner of holding Elections for Senators and Representatives, shall be prescribed in each State by the Legislature thereof; but the Congress may at any time by Law make or alter such Regulations, except as to the Places of chusing Senators.

The Congress shall assemble at least once in every Year, and such Meeting shall be on the first Monday in December, unless they shall by Law appoint a different Day.[4]

Section 5 Each House shall be the Judge of the Elections, Returns and Qualifications of its own Members, and a Majority of each shall constitute a Quorum to do Business; but a smaller Number may adjourn from day to day, and may be authorized to compel the Attendance of absent Members, in such Manner, and under such Penalties as each House may provide.

Each House may determine the Rules of its Proceedings, punish its Members for disorderly Behaviour, and with the Concurrence of two thirds, expel a Member.

Each House shall keep a Journal of its Proceedings, and from time to time publish the same, excepting such Parts as may in their Judgment require Secrecy; and the Yeas and Nays of the Members of either House on any question shall, at the Desire of one fifth of those Present, be entered on the Journal.

Neither House, during the Session of Congress, shall, without the Consent of the other, adjourn for more than three days, nor to any other Place than that in which the two Houses shall be sitting.

Section 6 The Senators and Representatives shall receive a Compensation for their Services, to be ascertained by Law, and paid out of the Treasury of the United States. They shall in all Cases, except Treason, Felony and Breach of the Peace, be privileged from Arrest during their Attendance at the Session of their respective Houses, and in going to and returning from the same; and for any Speech or Debate in either House, they shall not be questioned in any other Place.

No Senator or Representative shall, during the Time for which he was elected, be appointed to any civil Office under the Authority of the United States, which shall have been created, or the Emoluments whereof shall have been encreased during such time; and no Person holding any Office under the United States, shall be a Member of either House during his Continuance in Office.

Section 7 All Bills for raising Revenue shall originate in the House of Representatives; but the Senate may propose or concur with Amendments as on other Bills.

Every Bill which shall have passed the House of Representatives and the Senate, shall, before it becomes a Law, be presented to the President of the United States; If he approves he shall sign it, but if not he shall return it, with his Objections to that House in which it shall have originated, who shall enter the Objections at large on their Journal, and proceed to reconsider it. If after such Reconsideration two thirds of that House shall agree to pass the Bill, it shall be sent, together with the Objections, to the other House, by which it shall likewise be reconsidered, and if approved by two thirds of that House, it shall become a Law. But in all such Cases the Votes of both Houses shall be determined by Yeas and Nays, and the Names of the Persons voting for and against the Bill shall be entered on the Journal of each House respectively. If any Bill shall not be returned by the President within ten Days (Sundays excepted) after it shall have been presented to him, the Same shall be a Law, in like Manner as if he had signed it, unless the Congress by their Adjournment prevent its Return, in which Case it shall not be a Law.

Every Order, Resolution, or Vote to which the Concurrence of the Senate and House of Representatives may be necessary (except on a question of Adjournment) shall be presented to the President of the United States; and before the Same shall take Effect, shall be approved by him, or being disapproved by him, shall be repassed by two thirds of the Senate and House of Representatives, according to the Rules and Limitations prescribed in the Case of a Bill.

Section 8 The Congress shall have Power To lay and collect Taxes, Duties, Imposts and Excises, to pay the Debts and provide for the common Defence and general Welfare of the United States;

---

[4]Changed by the Twentieth Amendment.

but all Duties, Imposts and Excises shall be uniform throughout the United States.

To borrow Money on the credit of the United States;

To regulate Commerce with foreign Nations, and among the several States, and with the Indian Tribes;

To establish an uniform Rule of Naturalization, and uniform Laws on the subject of Bankruptcies throughout the United States;

To coin Money, regulate the Value thereof, and of foreign Coin, and fix the Standard of Weights and Measures;

To provide for the Punishment of counterfeiting the Securities and current Coin of the United States;

To establish Post Offices and post Roads;

To promote the Progress of Science and useful Arts, by securing for limited Times to Authors and Inventors the exclusive Right to their respective Writings and Discoveries;

To constitute Tribunals inferior to the supreme Court;

To define and punish Piracies and Felonies committed on the high Seas, and Offences against the Law of Nations;

To declare War, grant Letters of Marque and Reprisal, and make Rules concerning Captures on Land and Water;

To raise and support Armies, but no Appropriation of Money to that Use shall be for a longer Term than two Years;

To provide and maintain a Navy;

To make Rules for the Government and Regulation of the land and naval Forces;

To provide for calling forth the Militia to execute the Laws of the Union, suppress Insurrections and repel Invasions;

To provide for organizing, arming, and disciplining, the Militia, and for governing such Part of them as may be employed in the Service of the United States, reserving to the States respectively, the Appointment of the Officers, and the Authority of training the Militia according to the discipline prescribed by Congress;

To exercise exclusive Legislation in all Cases whatsoever, over such District (not exceeding ten Miles square) as may, by Cession of particular States, and the Acceptance of Congress, become the Seat of the Government of the United States, and to exercise like Authority over all Places purchased by the Consent of the Legislature of the State in which the Same shall be, for the Erection of Forts, Magazines, Arsenals, dock-Yards, and other needful Buildings;—And

To make all Laws which shall be necessary and proper for carrying into Execution the foregoing Powers, and all other Powers vested by this Constitution in the Government of the United States, or in any Department or Officer thereof.

Section 9 The Migration or Importation of such Persons as any of the States now existing shall think proper to admit, shall not be prohibited by the Congress prior to the Year one thousand eight hundred and eight, but a Tax or duty may be imposed on such Importation, not exceeding ten dollars for each Person.

The Privilege of the Writ of Habeas Corpus shall not be suspended, unless when in Cases of Rebellion or Invasion the public Safety may require it.

No Bill of Attainder or ex post facto Law shall be passed.

No Capitation, or other direct, Tax shall be laid, unless in Proportion to the Census of Enumeration herein before directed to be taken.[5]

No Tax or Duty shall be laid on Articles exported from any State.

No Preference shall be given by any Regulation of Commerce or Revenue to the Ports of one State over those of another: nor shall Vessels bound to, or from, one State, be obliged to enter, clear, or pay Duties in another.

No Money shall be drawn from the Treasury, but in Consequence of Appropriations made by Law; and a regular Statement and Account of the Receipts and Expenditures of all public Money shall be published from time to time.

No Title of Nobility shall be granted by the United States: And no Person holding any Office of Profit or Trust under them, shall, without the Consent of the Congress, accept of any present, Emolument, Office, or Title, of any kind whatever, from any King, Prince, or foreign State.

Section 10 No State shall enter into any Treaty, Alliance, or Confederation; grant Letters of Marque and Reprisal; coin Money; emit Bills of Credit; make any Thing but gold and silver coin a Tender in Payment of Debts; pass any Bill of Attainder, ex post facto Law, or Law impairing the Obligation of Contracts, or grant any Title of Nobility.

[5]Changed by the Sixteenth Amendment.

No State shall, without the Consent of the Congress, lay any Imposts or Duties on Imports or Exports, except what may be absolutely necessary for executing its inspection Laws: and the net Produce of all Duties and Imposts, laid by any State on Imports or Exports, shall be for the Use of the Treasury of the United States; and all such Laws shall be subject to the Revision and Controul of the Congress.

No State shall, without the consent of Congress, lay any Duty of Tonnage, keep Troops, or Ships of War in time of Peace, enter into any Agreement or Compact with another State, or with a foreign Power, or engage in War, unless actually invaded, or in such imminent Danger as will not admit of delay.

ARTICLE II

Section 1 The executive Power shall be vested in a President of the United States of America. He shall hold his Office during the Term of four Years, and, together with the Vice President, chosen for the same Term, be elected, as follows

Each state shall appoint, in such Manner as the Legislature thereof may direct, a Number of Electors, equal to the whole Number of Senators and Representatives to which the State may be entitled in Congress: but no Senator or Representative, or Person holding an Office of Trust or Profit under the United States, shall be appointed an Elector.

The Electors shall meet in their respective States, and vote by Ballot for two Persons, of whom one at least shall not be an inhabitant of the same State with themselves. And they shall make a List of all the Persons voted for, and of the Number of Votes for each; which List they shall sign and certify, and transmit sealed to the Seat of the Government of the United States, directed to the President of the Senate. The President of the Senate shall, in the Presence of the Senate and House of Representatives, open all the Certificates, and the Votes shall then be counted. The Person having the greatest Number of Votes shall be the President, if such Number be a Majority of the whole Number of Electors appointed; and if there be more than one who have such Majority, and have an equal Number of Votes, then the House of Representatives shall immediately chuse by Ballot one of them for President; and if no Person have a Majority, then from the five highest on the List the said House shall in like Manner chuse the President. But in chusing the President, the Votes shall be taken by States, the Representation from each State having one Vote; A quorum for this purpose shall consist of a Member or Members from two thirds of the States, and a Majority of all the States shall be necessary to a Choice. In every Case, after the Choice of the President, the Person having the greatest Number of Votes of the Electors shall be the Vice President. But if there should remain two or more who have equal Votes, the Senate shall chuse from them by Ballot the Vice President.[6]

The Congress may determine the Time of chusing the Electors, and the Day on which they shall give their Votes; which Day shall be the same throughout the United States.

No Person except a natural born Citizen, or a Citizen of the United States, at the time of the Adoption of this Constitution, shall be eligible to the Office of President; neither shall any Person be eligible to that Office who shall not have attained to the Age of thirty five Years, and been fourteen Years a Resident within the United States.

In Case of the Removal of the President from Office, or of his Death, Resignation, or Inability to discharge the Powers and Duties of the said Office, the Same shall devolve on the Vice President, and the Congress may by Law provide for the Case of Removal, Death, Resignation or Inability, both of the President and Vice President, declaring what Officer shall then act as President, and such Officer shall act accordingly, until the Disability be removed, or a President shall be elected.[7]

The President shall, at stated Times, receive for his Services, a Compensation, which shall neither be encreased nor diminished during the Period for which he shall have been elected, and he shall not receive within that Period any other Emolument from the United States, or any of them.

Before he enter on the Execution of his Office, he shall take the following Oath or Affirmation:—"I do solemnly swear (or affirm) that I will faithfully execute the Office of President of the United States, and will to the best of my Ability, preserve, protect, and defend the Constitution of the United States."

Section 2 The President shall be Commander in Chief of the Army and Navy of the United States, and of the Militia of the several States, when

[6]Changed by the Twelfth Amendment.

[7]Changed by the Twenty-fifth Amendment.

called into the actual Service of the United States; he may require the Opinion, in writing, of the principal Officer in each of the executive Departments, upon any Subject relating to the Duties of their respective Offices, and he shall have Power to grant Reprieves and Pardons for Offences against the United States, except in Cases of Impeachment.

He shall have Power, by and with the Advice and Consent of the Senate, to make Treaties, provided two thirds of the Senators present concur; and he shall nominate, and by and with the Advice and Consent of the Senate, shall appoint Ambassadors, other public Ministers and Consuls, Judges of the supreme Court, and all other Officers of the United States, whose Appointments are not herein otherwise provided for, and which shall be established by Law; but the Congress may by Law vest the Appointment of such inferior Officers, as they think proper, in the President alone, in the Courts of Law, or in the Heads of Departments.

The President shall have Power to fill up all Vacancies that may happen during the Recess of the Senate, by granting Commissions which shall expire at the End of their next Session.

Section 3 He shall from time to time give to the Congress Information of the State of the Union, and recommend to their Consideration such Measures as he shall judge necessary and expedient; he may, on extraordinary Occasions, convene both Houses, or either of them, and in Case of Disagreement between them, with Respect to the Time of Adjournment, he may adjourn them to such Time as he shall think proper; he shall receive Ambassadors and other public Ministers; he shall take Care that the Laws be faithfully executed, and shall Commission all the Officers of the United States.

Section 4 The President, Vice President and all civil Officers of the United States, shall be removed from Office on Impeachment for, and Conviction of, Treason, Bribery, or other high Crimes and Misdemeanors.

ARTICLE III

Section 1 The judicial Power of the United States, shall be vested in one supreme Court, and in such inferior Courts as the Congress may from time to time ordain and establish. The Judges, both of the supreme and inferior Courts, shall hold their Offices during good Behaviour, and shall, at stated Times, receive for their Services, a Compensation, which shall not be diminished during their Continuance in Office.

Section 2 The judicial Power shall extend to all Cases, in Law and Equity, arising under this Constitution, the Laws of the United States, and Treaties made, or which shall be made, under their Authority;—to all Cases affecting Ambassadors, other public Ministers and Consuls;—to all Cases of admiralty and maritime Jurisdiction;—to Controversies to which the United States shall be a party;—to Controversies between two or more States;—between a State and Citizens of another State;[8]—between Citizens of different States;—between Citizens of the same State claiming Lands under Grants of different States, and between a State, or the Citizens thereof, and foreign States, Citizens or Subjects.

In all Cases affecting Ambassadors, other public Ministers and Consuls, and those in which a State shall be Party, the supreme Court shall have original Jurisdiction. In all the other Cases before mentioned, the supreme Court shall have appellate Jurisdiction, both as to Law and Fact, with such Exceptions, and under such Regulations as the Congress shall make.

The Trial of all Crimes, except in Cases of Impeachment, shall be by Jury: and such Trial shall be held in the State where the said Crimes shall have been committed; but when not committed within any State, the Trial shall be at such Place or Places as the Congress may by Law have directed.

Section 3 Treason against the United States, shall consist only in levying War against them, or in adhering to their Enemies, giving them Aid and Comfort. No Person shall be convicted of Treason unless on the Testimony of two Witnesses to the same overt Act, or on Confession in open Court.

The Congress shall have Power to declare the Punishment of Treason, but no Attainder of Treason shall work Corruption of Blood, or Forfeiture except during the Life of the Person attainted.

ARTICLE IV

Section 1 Full Faith and Credit shall be given in each State to the public Acts, Records, and judicial Proceedings of every other State. And the Congress may by general Laws prescribe the Manner in which such Acts, Records and Proceedings shall be proved, and the Effect thereof.

Section 2 The Citizens of each State shall be entitled to all Privileges and Immunities of Citizens in the several States.

[8]Changed by the Eleventh Amendment.

A Person charged in any State with Treason, Felony, or other Crime, who shall flee from Justice, and be found in another State, shall on Demand of the executive Authority of the State from which he fled, be delivered up, to be removed to the State having Jurisdiction of the Crime.

No Person held to Service or Labour in one State, under the Laws thereof, escaping into another, shall, in Consequence of any Law or Regulation therein, be discharged from such Service or Labour, but shall be delivered up on Claim of the Party to whom such Service or Labour may be due.[9]

Section 3 New States may be admitted by the Congress into this Union; but no new State shall be formed or erected within the Jurisdiction of any other State; nor any State be formed by the Junction of two or more States, or Parts of States, without the Consent of the Legislatures of the States concerned as well as of the Congress.

The Congress shall have Power to dispose of and make all needful Rules and Regulations respecting the Territory or other Property belonging to the United States; and nothing in this Constitution shall be so construed as to Prejudice any Claims of the United States, or of any particular State.

Section 4 The United States shall guarantee to every State in this Union a Republican Form of Government, and shall protect each of them against Invasion; and on Application of the Legislature, or of the Executive (when the Legislature cannot be convened) against domestic Violence.

ARTICLE V

The Congress, whenever two thirds of both Houses shall deem it necessary, shall propose Amendments to this Constitution, or, on the Application of the Legislatures of two thirds of the several States, shall call a Convention for proposing Amendments, which, in either Case, shall be valid to all Intents and Purposes, as Part of this Constitution, when ratified by the legislatures of three fourths of the several States, or by Conventions in three fourths thereof, as the one or the other Mode of Ratification may be proposed by the Congress; Provided that no Amendment which may be made prior to the Year One thousand eight hundred and eight shall in any Manner affect the first and fourth Clauses in the Ninth Section of the first Article; and that no State, without its Consent, shall be deprived of its equal Suffrage in the Senate.

[9]Changed by the Thirteenth Amendment.

ARTICLE VI

All Debts contracted and Engagements entered into, before the Adoption of this Constitution, shall be as valid against the United States under this Constitution, as under the Confederation.

The Constitution, and the Laws of the United States which shall be made in Pursuance thereof; and all Treaties made, or which shall be made, under the Authority of the United States, shall be the supreme Law of the Land; and the Judges in every State shall be bound thereby, any Thing in the Constitution or Laws of any State to the Contrary notwithstanding.

The Senators and Representatives before mentioned, and the Members of the several State Legislatures, and all executive and judicial Officers, both of the United States and of the several States, shall be bound by Oath or Affirmation, to support this Constitution; but no religious Test shall ever be required as a Qualification to any Office or public Trust under the United States.

ARTICLE VII

The Ratification of the Conventions of nine States, shall be sufficient for the Establishment of this Constitution between the States so ratifying the Same.

Done in Convention by the Unanimous Consent of the States present the Seventeenth Day of September in the Year of our Lord one thousand seven hundred and eighty seven and of the Independance of the United States of America the Twelfth. In witness whereof We have hereunto subscribed our Names.

AMENDMENTS

[The first 10 amendments are known as the "Bill of Rights."]

Amendment 1 (Ratified 1791) Congress shall make no law respecting an establishment of religion, or prohibiting the free exercise thereof; or abridging the freedom of speech, or of the press; or the right of the people peaceably to assemble, and to petition the Government for a redress of grievances.

Amendment 2 (Ratified 1791) A well regulated Militia, being necessary to the security of a free State, the right of the people to keep and bear Arms, shall not be infringed.

Amendment 3 (Ratified 1791) No Soldier shall, in time of peace be quartered in any house, without the consent of the Owner, nor in time of war, but in a manner to be prescribed by law.

Amendment 4 (Ratified 1791) The right of the people to be secure in their persons, houses, papers, and effects, against unreasonable searches and seizures, shall not be violated, and no Warrants shall issue, but upon probable cause, supported by Oath or affirmation, and particularly describing the place to be searched, and the persons or things to be seized.

Amendment 5 (Ratified 1791) No person shall be held to answer for a capital, or otherwise infamous crime, unless on a presentment or indictment of a Grand Jury, except in cases arising in the land or naval forces, or in the Militia, when in actual service in time of War or public danger; nor shall any person be subject for the same offence to be twice put in jeopardy of life or limb; nor shall be compelled in any criminal case to be a witness against himself, nor be deprived of life, liberty, or property, without due process of law; nor shall private property be taken for public use, without just compensation.

Amendment 6 (Ratified 1791) In all criminal prosecutions, the accused shall enjoy the right to a speedy and public trial, by an impartial jury of the State and district wherein the crime shall have been committed, which district shall have been previously ascertained by law, and to be informed of the nature and cause of the accusation; to be confronted with the witnesses against him; to have compulsory process for obtaining Witnesses in his favor, and to have assistance of counsel for his defence.

Amendment 7 (Ratified 1791) In Suits at common law, where the value in controversy shall exceed twenty dollars, the right of trial by jury shall be preserved, and no fact tried by a jury, shall be otherwise re-examined in any Court of the United States, than according to the rules of the common law.

Amendment 8 (Ratified 1791) Excessive bail shall not be required, nor excessive fines imposed, nor cruel and unusual punishments inflicted.

Amendment 9 (Ratified 1791) The enumeration in the Constitution, of certain rights, shall not be construed to deny or disparage others retained by the people.

Amendment 10 (Ratified 1791) The powers not delegated to the United States by the Constitution, nor prohibited by it to the States, are reserved to the States respectively, or to the people.

Amendment 11 (Ratified 1795) The Judicial power of the United States shall not be construed to extend to any suit in law or equity, commenced or prosecuted against one of the United States by Citizens of another State, or by Citizens or Subjects of any Foreign State.

Amendment 12 (Ratified 1804) The Electors shall meet in their respective states, and vote by ballot for President and Vice-President, one of whom, at least, shall not be an inhabitant of the same state with themselves; they shall name in their ballots the person voted for as President, and in distinct ballots the person voted for as Vice-President, and they shall make distinct lists of all persons voted for as President, and of all persons voted for as Vice-President, and of the number of votes for each, which lists they shall sign and certify, and transmit sealed to the seat of the government of the United States, directed to the President of the Senate;—The President of the Senate shall, in the presence of the Senate and House of Representatives, open all the certificates and the votes shall then be counted;—The person having the greatest number of votes for President, shall be the President, if such number be a majority of the whole number of Electors appointed; and if no person have such majority, then from the persons having the highest numbers not exceeding three on the list of those voted for as President, the House of Representatives shall choose immediately, by ballot, the President. But in choosing the President, the votes shall be taken by states, the representation from each state having one vote; a quorum for this purpose shall consist of a member or members from two-thirds of the states, and a majority of all the states shall be necessary to a choice. And if the House of Representatives shall not choose a President whenever the right of choice shall devolve upon them, before the fourth day of March next following, then the Vice-President shall act as president, as in the case of the death or other constitutional disability of the President.[10]—The person having the greatest number of votes as Vice-President, shall be the Vice-President, if such number be a majority of the whole number of Electors appointed, and if no person have a majority, then from the two highest numbers on the list, the Senate shall choose the Vice-President; a quorum for the purpose shall consist of two-thirds of the whole number of Senators, and a majority of

[10]Changed by the Twentieth Amendment.

the whole number shall be necessary to a choice. But no person constitutionally ineligible to the office of President shall be eligible to that of Vice-President of the United States.

Amendment 13 (Ratified 1865) Section 1 Neither slavery nor involuntary servitude, except as a punishment for crime whereof the party shall have been duly convicted, shall exist within the United States, or any place subject to their jurisdiction.

Section 2 Congress shall have power to enforce this article by appropriate legislation.

Amendment 14 (Ratified 1868) Section 1 All persons born or naturalized in the United States, and subject to the jurisdiction thereof, are citizens of the United States and of the State wherein they reside. No State shall make or enforce any law which shall abridge the privileges or immunities of citizens of the United States; nor shall any State deprive any person of life, liberty, or property, without due process of law; nor deny to any person within its jurisdiction the equ al protection of the laws.

Section 2 Representatives shall be apportioned among the several States according to their respective numbers, counting the whole number of persons in each State, excluding Indians not taxed. But when the right to vote at any election for the choice of electors for President and Vice President of the United States, Representatives in Congress, the Executive and Judicial officers of a State, or the members of the Legislature thereof, is denied to any of the male inhabitants of such State, being twenty-one[11] years of age, and citizens of the United States, or in any way abridged except for participation in rebellion, or other crime, the basis of representation therein shall be reduced in the proportion which the number of such male citizens shall bear to the whole number of male citizens twenty-one years of age in such State.

Section 3 No person shall be a Senator or Representative in Congress, or elector of President and Vice President, or hold any office, civil or military, under the United States, or under any State, who, having previously taken an oath, as a member of Congress, or as an officer of the United States, or as a member of any State legislature, or as an executive or judicial officer of any State, to support the Constitution of the United States, shall have engaged in insurrection or rebellion against the same, or given aid or comfort to the enemies

[11]Changed by the Twenty-sixth Amendment.

thereof. But Congress may by a vote of two-thirds of each House, remove such disability.

Section 4 The validity of the public debt of the United States, authorized by law, including debts incurred for payment of pensions and bounties for services in suppressing insurrection or rebellion, shall not be questioned. But neither the United States nor any State shall assume or pay any debt or obligation incurred in aid of insurrection or rebellion against the United States, or any claim for the loss or emancipation of any slave; but all such debts, obligations and claims shall be held illegal and void.

Section 5 The Congress shall have power to enforce, by appropriate legislation, the provisions of this article.

Amendment 15 (Ratified 1870) Section 1 The right of citizens of the United States to vote shall not be denied or abridged by the United States or by any State on account of race, color, or previous condition of servitude.

Section 2 The Congress shall have power to enforce this article by appropriate legislation.

Amendment 16 (Ratified 1913) The Congress shall have power to lay and collect taxes on incomes, from whatever source derived, without apportionment among the several States, and without regard to any census or enumeration.

Amendment 17 (Ratified 1913) The Senate of the United States shall be composed of two Senators from each State, elected by the people thereof, for six years; and each Senator shall have one vote. The electors in each State shall have the qualifications requisite for electors of the most numerous branch of the State legislatures.

When vacancies happen in the representation of any State in the Senate, the executive authority of such State shall issue writs of election to fill such vacancies: *Provided,* That the legislature of any State may empower the executive thereof to make temporary appointments until the people fill the vacancies by election as the legislature may direct.

This amendment shall not be so construed as to affect the election or term of any Senator chosen before it becomes valid as part of the Constitution.

Amendment 18 (Ratified 1919; Repealed 1933) Section 1 After one year from the ratification of this article the manufacture, sale, or transportation of intoxicating liquors within, the importation thereof into, or the exportation thereof from the United States and all territory subject to the jurisdiction thereof for beverage purposes is hereby prohibited.

Section 2 The Congress and the several States shall have concurrent power to enforce this article by appropriate legislation.

Section 3 This article shall be inoperative unless it shall have been ratified as an amendment to the Constitution by the legislatures of the several States, as provided in the Constitution, within seven years from the date of the submission hereof to the States by the Congress.[12]

Amendment 19 (Ratified 1920) The right of citizens of the United States to vote shall not be denied or abridged by the United States or by any State on account of sex.

Congress shall have power to enforce this article by appropriate legislation.

Amendment 20 (Ratified 1933) Section 1 The terms of the President and Vice President shall end at noon on the 20th day of January, and the terms of Senators and Representatives at noon on the 3d day of January, of the years in which such terms would have ended if this article had not been ratified; and the terms of their successors shall then begin.

Section 2 The Congress shall assemble at least once in every year, and such meeting shall begin at noon on the 3d day of January, unless they shall by law appoint a different day.

Section 3 If, at the time fixed for the beginning of the term of the President, the President elect shall have died, the Vice President elect shall become President. If a President shall not have been chosen before the time fixed for the beginning of his term, or if the President elect shall have failed to qualify, then the Vice President elect shall act as President until a President shall have qualified; and the Congress may by law provide for the case wherein neither a President elect nor a Vice President elect shall have qualified, declaring who shall then act as President, or the manner in which one who is to act shall be selected, and such person shall act accordingly until a President or Vice President shall have qualified.

Section 4 The Congress may by law provide for the case of the death of any of the persons from whom the House of Representatives may choose a President whenever the right of choice shall have devolved upon them, and for the case of the death of any of the persons from whom the Senate may choose a Vice President whenever the right of choice shall have devolved upon them.

Section 5 Sections 1 and 2 shall take effect on the 15th day of October following the ratification of this article.

Section 6 This article shall be inoperative unless it shall have been ratified as an amendment to the Constitution by the legislatures of three-fourths of the several States within seven years from the date of its submission.

Amendment 21 (Ratified 1933) Section 1 The eighteenth article of amendment to the Constitution of the United States is hereby repealed.

Section 2 The transportation or importation into any State, Territory, or possession of the United States for delivery or use therein of intoxicating liquors, in violation of the laws thereof, is hereby prohibited.

Section 3 This article shall be inoperative unless it shall have been ratified as an amendment to the Constitution by conventions in the several States, as provided in the Constitution, within seven years from the date of the submission hereof to the States by the Congress.

Amendment 22 (Ratified 1951) Section 1 No person shall be elected to the office of the President more than twice, and no person who has held the office of President, or acted as President, for more than two years of a term to which some other person was elected President shall be elected to the office of the President more than once. But this Article shall not apply to any person holding the office of President when this Article was proposed by the Congress, and shall not prevent any person who may be holding the office of President, or acting as President, during the term within which this Article becomes operative from holding the office of President or acting as President during the remainder of such term.

Section 2 This Article shall be inoperative unless it shall have been ratified as an amendment to the Constitution by the legislatures of three-fourths of the several States within seven years from the date of its submission to the States by the Congress.

Amendment 23 (Ratified 1961) Section 1 The District constituting the seat of Government of the United States shall appoint in such manner as the Congress may direct:

A number of electors of President and Vice President equal to the whole number of Senators and Representatives in Congress to which the District would be entitled if it were a State, but in no event more than the least populous State; they shall

---

[12]Repealed by the Twenty-first Amendment.

be in addition to those appointed by the States, but they shall be considered, for the purposes of the election of President and Vice President, to be electors appointed by a State; and they shall meet in the District and perform such duties as provided by the twelfth article of amendment.

Section 2 The Congress shall have power to enforce this article by appropriate legislation.

Amendment 24 (Ratified 1964) Section 1 The right of citizens of the United States to vote in any primary or other election for President or Vice President, for electors for President or Vice President, or for Senator or Representative in Congress, shall not be denied or abridged by the United States or any State by reason of failure to pay any poll tax or other tax.

Section 2 The Congress shall have power to enforce this article by appropriate legislation.

Amendment 25 (Ratified 1967) Section 1 In case of the removal of the President from office or of his death or resignation, the Vice President shall become President.

Section 2 Whenever there is a vacancy in the office of the Vice President, the President shall nominate a Vice President who shall take office upon confirmation by a majority vote of both Houses of Congress.

Section 3 Whenever the President transmits to the President pro tempore of the Senate and the Speaker of the House of Representatives his written declaration that he is unable to discharge the powers and duties of his office, and until he transmits to them a written declaration to the contrary, such powers and duties shall be discharged by the Vice President as Acting President.

Section 4 Whenever the Vice President and a majority of either the principal officers of the executive departments or of such other body as Congress may by law provide, transmit to the President pro tempore of the Senate and the Speaker of the House of Representatives their written declaration that the President is unable to discharge the powers and duties of his office, the Vice President shall immediately assume the powers and duties of the office as Acting President.

Thereafter, when the President transmits to the President pro tempore of the Senate and the Speaker of the House of Representatives his written declaration that no inability exists, he shall resume the powers and duties of his office unless the Vice President and a majority of either the principal officers of the executive department or of such other body as Congress may by law provide, transmit within four days to the President pro tempore of the Senate and the Speaker of the House of Representatives their written declaration that the President is unable to discharge the powers and duties of his office. Thereupon Congress shall decide the issue, assembling within forty-eight hours for that purpose if not in session. If the Congress, within twenty-one days after receipt of the latter written declaration, or, if Congress is not in session, within twenty-one days after Congress is required to assemble, determines by two-thirds vote of both Houses that the President is unable to discharge the powers and duties of his office, the Vice President shall continue to discharge the same as Acting President; otherwise, the President shall resume the powers and duties of his office.

Amendment 26 (Ratified 1971) Section 1 The right of citizens of the United States, who are eighteen years of age or older, to vote shall not be denied or abridged by the United States or by any State on account of age.

Section 2 The Congress shall have power to enforce this article by appropriate legislation.

Amendment 27 (Ratified 1992) No law, varying the compensation for the services of the Senators and Representatives, shall take effect, until an election of Representatives shall have intervened.

UNIFORM COMMERCIAL CODE

ARTICLE 2–SALES

PART 1: SHORT TITLE, GENERAL CONSTRUCTION AND SUBJECT MATTER

§ 2–101. Short Title. This Article shall be known and may be cited as Uniform Commercial Code—Sales.

§ 2–102. Scope; Certain Security and Other Transactions Excluded from This Article. Unless the context otherwise requires, this Article applies to transactions in goods; it does not apply to any transaction which although in the form of an unconditional contract to sell or present sale is intended to operate only as a security transaction nor does this Article impair or repeal any statute regulating sales to consumers, farmers or other specified classes of buyers.

§ 2–103. Definitions and Index of Definitions.

1. In this Article unless the context otherwise requires
    a. "Buyer" means a person who buys or contracts to buy goods.
    b. "Good faith" in the case of a merchant means honesty in fact and the observance of reasonable commercial standards of fair dealing in the trade.
    c. "Receipt" of goods means taking physical possession of them.
    d. "Seller" means a person who sells or contracts to sell goods.
2. Other definitions applying to this Article or to specified Parts thereof, and the sections in which they appear are:

"Acceptance"	Section 2–606.
"Banker's credit"	Section 2–325.
"Between merchants"	Section 2–104.
"Cancellation"	Section 2–106(4).
"Commercial unit"	Section 2–105.
"Confirmed credit"	Section 2–325.
"Conforming to contract"	Section 2–106.
"Contract for sale"	Section 2–106.
"Cover"	Section 2–712.
"Entrusting"	Section 2–403.
"Financing agency"	Section 2–104.
"Future goods"	Section 2–105.
"Goods"	Section 2–105.
"Identification"	Section 2–501.
"Installment contract"	Section 2–612.
"Letter of Credit"	Section 2–325.
"Lot"	Section 2–105.
"Merchant"	Section 2–104.
"Overseas"	Section 2–323.
"Person in position of seller"	Section 2–707.
"Present sale"	Section 2–106.
"Sale"	Section 2–106.
"Sale on approval"	Section 2–326.
"Sale or return"	Section 2–326.
"Termination"	Section 2–106.

3. The following definitions in other Articles apply to this Article:

"Check"	Section 3–104.
"Consignee"	Section 7–102.
"Consignor"	Section 7–102.
"Consumer goods"	Section 9–109.
"Dishonor"	Section 3–502.
"Draft"	Section 3–104.

4. In addition Article 1 contains general definitions and principles of construction and interpretation applicable throughout this Article.

As amended in 1994.

See Appendix XI for material relating to changes made in text in 1994.

§ 2–104. Definitions: "Merchant"; "Between Merchants"; "Financing Agency".

1. "Merchant" means a person who deals in goods of the kind or otherwise by his occupation holds himself out as having knowledge or skill peculiar to the practices or goods involved in the transaction or to whom such knowledge or skill may be attributed by his employment of an agent or broker or other intermediary who by his occupation holds himself out as having such knowledge or skill.
2. "Financing agency" means a bank, finance company or other person who in the ordinary course of business makes advances against goods or documents of title or who by arrangement with either the seller or the buyer

intervenes in ordinary course to make or collect payment due or claimed under the contract for sale, as by purchasing or paying the seller's draft or making advances against it or by merely taking it for collection whether or not documents of title accompany the draft. "Financing agency" includes also a bank or other person who similarly intervenes between persons who are in the position of seller and buyer in respect to the goods (Section 2–707).

3. "Between merchants" means in any transaction with respect to which both parties are chargeable with the knowledge or skill of merchants.

§ 2–105. Definitions: "Transferability"; "Goods"; "Future" Goods; "Lot"; "Commercial Unit".

1. "Goods" means all things (including specially manufactured goods) which are movable at the time of identification to the contract for sale other than the money in which the price is to be paid, investment securities (Article 8) and things in action. "Goods" also includes the unborn young of animals and growing crops and other identified things attached to realty as described in the section on goods to be severed from realty (Section 2–107).

2. Goods must be both existing and identified before any interest in them can pass. Goods which are not both existing and identified are "future" goods. A purported present sale of future goods or of any interest therein operates as a contract to sell.

3. There may be a sale of a part interest in existing identified goods.

4. An undivided share in an identified bulk of fungible goods is sufficiently identified to be sold although the quantity of the bulk is not determined. Any agreed proportion of such a bulk or any quantity thereof agreed upon by number, weight or other measure may to the extent of the seller's interest in the bulk be sold to the buyer who then becomes an owner in common.

5. "Lot" means a parcel or a single article which is the subject matter of a separate sale or delivery, whether or not it is sufficient to perform the contract.

6. "Commercial unit" means such a unit of goods as by commercial usage is a single whole for purposes of sale and division of which materially impairs its character or value on the market or in use. A commercial unit may be a single article (as a machine) or a set of articles (as a suite of furniture or an assortment of sizes) or a quantity (as a bale, gross, or carload) or any other unit treated in use or in the relevant market as a single whole.

§ 2–106. Definitions: "Contract"; "Agreement"; "Contract for Sales"; "Sale"; "Present Sale"; "Conforming" to Contract; "Termination"; "Cancellation".

1. In this Article unless the context otherwise requires "contract" and "agreement" are limited to those relating to the present or future sale of goods. "Contract for sale" includes both a present sale of goods and a contract to sell goods at a future time. A "sale" consists in the passing of title from the seller to the buyer for a price (Section 2–401). A "present sale" means a sale which is accomplished by the making of the contract.

2. Goods or conduct including any part of a performance are "conforming" or conform to the contract when they are in accordance with the obligations under the contract.

3. "Termination" occurs when either party pursuant to a power created by agreement or law puts an end to the contract otherwise than for its breach. On "termination" all obligations which are still executory on both sides are discharged but any right based on prior breach or performance survives.

4. "Cancellation" occurs when either party puts an end to the contract for breach by the other and its effect is the same as that of "termination" except that the cancelling party also retains any remedy for breach of the whole contract or any unperformed balance.

§ 2–107. Goods to Be Severed from Realty: Recording.

1. A contract for the sale of minerals or the like (including oil and gas) or a structure or its materials to be removed from realty is a contract for the sale of goods within this Article if they are to be severed by the seller but until severance a purported present sale thereof which is not effective as a transfer of an interest in land is effective only as a contract to sell.

2. A contract for the sale apart from the land of growing crops or other things attached to

realty and capable of severance without material harm thereto but not described in subsection (1) or of timber to be cut is a contract for the sale of goods within this Article whether the subject matter is to be severed by the buyer or by the seller even though it forms part of the realty at the time of contracting, and the parties can by identification effect a present sale before severance.

3. The provisions of this section are subject to any third party rights provided by the law relating to realty records, and the contract for sale may be executed and recorded as a document transferring an interest in land and shall then constitute notice to third parties of the buyer's rights under the contract for sale. As amended in 1972.

PART 2: FORM, FORMATION AND READJUSTMENT OF CONTRACT

§ 2–201. Formal Requirements; Statute of Frauds.

1. Except as otherwise provided in this section a contract for the sale of goods for the price of $500 or more is not enforceable by way of action or defense unless there is some writing sufficient to indicate that a contract for sale has been made between the parties and signed by the party against whom enforcement is sought or by his authorized agent or broker. A writing is not insufficient because it omits or incorrectly states a term agreed upon but the contract is not enforceable under this paragraph beyond the quantity of goods shown in such writing.

2. Between merchants if within a reasonable time a writing in confirmation of the contract and sufficient against the sender is received and the party receiving it has reason to know its contents, it satisfies the requirements of subsection (1) against such party unless written notice of objection to its contents is given within 10 days after it is received.

3. A contract which does not satisfy the requirements of subsection (1) but which is valid in other respects is enforceable
   a. if the goods are to be specially manufactured for the buyer and are not suitable for sale to others in the ordinary course of the seller's business and the seller, before notice of repudiation is received and under

circumstances which reasonably indicate that the goods are for the buyer, has made either a substantial beginning of their manufacture or commitments for their procurement; or
   b. if the party against whom enforcement is sought admits in his pleading, testimony or otherwise in court that a contract for sale was made, but the contract is not enforceable under this provision beyond the quantity of goods admitted; or
   c. with respect to goods for which payment has been made and accepted or which have been received and accepted (Section 2–606).

§ 2–202. Final Written Expression: Parol or Extrinsic Evidence.
Terms with respect to which the confirmatory memoranda of the parties agree or which are otherwise set forth in a writing intended by the parties as a final expression of their agreement with respect to such terms as are included therein may not be contradicted by evidence of any prior agreement or of a contemporaneous oral agreement but may be explained or supplemented
   a. by course of dealing or usage of trade (Section 1–205) or by course of performance (Section 2–208); and
   b. by evidence of consistent additional terms unless the court finds the writing to have been intended also as a complete and exclusive statement of the terms of the agreement.

§ 2–203. Seals Inoperative.
The affixing of a seal to a writing evidencing a contract for sale or an offer to buy or sell goods does not constitute the writing a sealed instrument and the law with respect to sealed instruments does not apply to such a contract or offer.

§ 2–204. Formation in General.

1. A contract for sale of goods may be made in any manner sufficient to show agreement, including conduct by both parties which recognizes the existence of such a contract.

2. An agreement sufficient to constitute a contract for sale may be found even though the moment of its making is undetermined.

3. Even though one or more terms are left open a contract for sale does not fail for indefiniteness if the parties have intended to make a contract and there is a reasonably certain basis for giving an appropriate remedy.

§ 2–205. Firm Offers. An offer by a merchant to buy or sell goods in a signed writing which by its terms gives assurance that it will be held open is not revocable, for lack of consideration, during the time stated or if no time is stated for a reasonable time, but in no event may such period of irrevocability exceed three months; but any such term of assurance on a form supplied by the offeree must be separately signed by the offeror.

§ 2–206. Offer and Acceptance in Formation of Contract.

1. Unless otherwise unambiguously indicated by the language or circumstances
    a. an offer to make a contract shall be construed as inviting acceptance in any manner and by any medium reasonable in the circumstances;
    b. an order or other offer to buy goods for prompt or current shipment shall be construed as inviting acceptance either by a prompt promise to ship or by the prompt or current shipment of conforming or non-conforming goods, but such a shipment of non-conforming goods does not constitute an acceptance if the seller seasonably notifies the buyer that the shipment is offered only as an accommodation to the buyer.
2. Where the beginning of a requested performance is a reasonable mode of acceptance an offeror who is not notified of acceptance within a reasonable time may treat the offer as having lapsed before acceptance.

§ 2–207. Additional Terms in Acceptance or Confirmation.

1. A definite and seasonable expression of acceptance or a written confirmation which is sent within a reasonable time operates as an acceptance even though it states terms additional to or different from those offered or agreed upon, unless acceptance is expressly made conditional on assent to the additional or different terms.
2. The additional terms are to be construed as proposals for addition to the contract. Between merchants such terms become part of the contract unless:
    a. the offer expressly limits acceptance to the terms of the offer;
    b. they materially alter it; or
    c. notification of objection to them has already been given or is given within a reasonable time after notice of them is received.

3. Conduct by both parties which recognizes the existence of a contract is sufficient to establish a contract for sale although the writings of the parties do not otherwise establish a contract. In such case the terms of the particular contract consist of those terms on which the writings of the parties agree, together with any supplementary terms incorporated under any other provisions of this Act.

§ 2–208. Course of Performance or Practical Construction.

1. Where the contract for sale involves repeated occasions for performance by either party with knowledge of the nature of the performance and opportunity for objection to it by the other, any course of performance accepted or acquiesced in without objection shall be relevant to determine the meaning of the agreement.
2. The express terms of the agreement and any such course of performance, as well as any course of dealing and usage of trade, shall be construed whenever reasonable as consistent with each other; but when such construction is unreasonable, express terms shall control course of performance and course of performance shall control both course of dealing and usage of trade (Section 1-205).
3. Subject to the provisions of the next section on modification and waiver, such course of performance shall be relevant to show a waiver or modification of any term inconsistent with such course of performance.

§ 2–209. Modification, Rescission and Waiver.

1. An agreement modifying a contract within this Article needs no consideration to be binding.
2. A signed agreement which excludes modification or rescission except by a signed writing cannot be otherwise modified or rescinded, but except as between merchants such a requirement on a form supplied by the merchant must be separately signed by the other party.
3. The requirements of the statute of frauds section of this Article (Section 2–201) must be satisfied if the contract as modified is within its provisions.
4. Although an attempt at modification or rescission does not satisfy the requirements of subsection (2) or (3) it can operate as a waiver.

5. A party who has made a waiver affecting an executory portion of the contract may retract the waiver by reasonable notification received by the other party that strict performance will be required of any term waived, unless the retraction would be unjust in view of a material change of position in reliance on the waiver.

§ 2–210. Delegation of Performance; Assignment of Rights.

1. A party may perform his duty through a delegate unless otherwise agreed or unless the other party has a substantial interest in having his original promisor perform or control the acts required by the contract. No delegation of performance relieves the party delegating of any duty to perform or any liability for breach.

2. Unless otherwise agreed all rights of either seller or buyer can be assigned except where the assignment would materially change the duty of the other party, or increase materially the burden or risk imposed on him by his contract, or impair materially his chance of obtaining return performance. A right to damages for breach of the whole contract or a right arising out of the assignor's due performance of his entire obligation can be assigned despite agreement otherwise.

3. Unless the circumstances indicate the contrary a prohibition of assignment of "the contract" is to be construed as barring only the delegation to the assignee of the assignor's performance.

4. An assignment of "the contract" or of "all my rights under the contract" or an assignment in similar general terms is an assignment of rights and unless the language or the circumstances (as in an assignment for security) indicate the contrary, it is a delegation of performance of the duties of the assignor and its acceptance by the assignee constitutes a promise by him to perform those duties. This promise is enforceable by either the assignor or the other party to the original contract.

5. The other party may treat any assignment which delegates performance as creating reasonable grounds for insecurity and may without prejudice to his rights against the assignor demand assurances from the assignee (Section 2–609).

PART 3: GENERAL OBLIGATION AND CONSTRUCTION OF CONTRACT

§ 2–301. General Obligations of Parties.
The obligation of the seller is to transfer and deliver and that of the buyer is to accept and pay in accordance with the contract.

§ 2–302. Unconscionable Contract or Clause.

1. If the court as a matter of law finds the contract or any clause of the contract to have been unconscionable at the time it was made the court may refuse to enforce the contract, or it may enforce the remainder of the contract without the unconscionable clause, or it may so limit the application of any unconscionable clause as to avoid any unconscionable result.

2. When it is claimed or appears to the court that the contract or any clause thereof may be unconscionable the parties shall be afforded a reasonable opportunity to present evidence as to its commercial setting, purpose and effect to aid the court in making the determination.

§ 2–303. Allocation or Division of Risks.
Where this Article allocates a risk or a burden as between the parties "unless otherwise agreed", the agreement may not only shift the allocation but may also divide the risk or burden.

§ 2–304. Price Payable in Money, Goods, Realty, or Otherwise.

1. The price can be made payable in money or otherwise. If it is payable in whole or in part in goods each party is a seller of the goods which he is to transfer.

2. Even though all or part of the price is payable in an interest in realty the transfer of the goods and the seller's obligations with reference to them are subject to this Article, but not the transfer of the interest in realty or the transferor's obligations in connection therewith.

§ 2–305. Open Price Term.

1. The parties if they so intend can conclude a contract for sale even though the price is not settled. In such a case the price is a reasonable price at the time for delivery if
   a. nothing is said as to price; or
   b. the price is left to be agreed by the parties and they fail to agree; or
   c. the price is to be fixed in terms of some agreed market or other standard as set or recorded by a third person or agency and it is not so set or recorded.

2. A price to be fixed by the seller or by the buyer means a price for him to fix in good faith.

3. When a price left to be fixed otherwise than by agreement of the parties fails to be fixed through fault of one party the other may at his option treat the contract as cancelled or himself fix a reasonable price.

4. Where, however, the parties intend not to be bound unless the price be fixed or agreed and it is not fixed or agreed there is no contract. In such a case the buyer must return any goods already received or if unable so to do must pay their reasonable value at the time of delivery and the seller must return any portion of the price paid on account.

§ 2–306. Output, Requirements and Exclusive Dealings.

1. A term which measures the quantity by the output of the seller or the requirements of the buyer means such actual output or requirements as may occur in good faith, except that no quantity unreasonably disproportionate to any stated estimate or in the absence of a stated estimate to any normal or otherwise comparable prior output or requirements may be tendered or demanded.

2. A lawful agreement by either the seller or the buyer for exclusive dealing in the kind of goods concerned imposes unless otherwise agreed an obligation by the seller to use best efforts to supply the goods and by the buyer to use best efforts to promote their sale.

§ 2–307. Delivery in Single Lot or Several Lots.
Unless otherwise agreed all goods called for by a contract for sale must be tendered in a single delivery and payment is due only on such tender but where the circumstances give either party the right to make or demand delivery in lots the price if it can be apportioned may be demanded for each lot.

§ 2–308. Absence of Specified Place for Delivery.
Unless otherwise agreed
    a. the place for delivery of goods is the seller's place of business or if he has none his residence; but
    b. in a contract for sale of identified goods which to the knowledge of the parties at the time of contracting are in some other place, that place is the place for their delivery; and

    c. documents of title may be delivered through customary banking channels.

§ 2–309. Absence of Specific Time Provisions; Notice of Termination.

1. The time for shipment or delivery or any other action under a contract if not provided in this Article or agreed upon shall be a reasonable time.

2. Where the contract provides for successive performances but is indefinite in duration it is valid for a reasonable time but unless otherwise agreed may be terminated at any time by either party.

3. Termination of a contract by one party except on the happening of an agreed event requires that reasonable notification be received by the other party and an agreement dispensing with notification is invalid if its operation would be unconscionable.

§ 2–310. Open Time for Payment or Running of Credit; Authority to Ship Under Reservation.
Unless otherwise agreed
    a. payment is due at the time and place at which the buyer is to receive the goods even though the place of shipment is the place of delivery; and
    b. if the seller is authorized to send the goods he may ship them under reservation, and may tender the documents of title, but the buyer may inspect the goods after their arrival before payment is due unless such inspection is inconsistent with the terms of the contract (Section 2–513); and
    c. if delivery is authorized and made by way of documents of title otherwise than by subsection (b) then payment is due at the time and place at which the buyer is to receive the documents regardless of where the goods are to be received; and
    d. where the seller is required or authorized to ship the goods on credit the credit period runs from the time of shipment but postdating the invoice or delaying its dispatch will correspondingly delay the starting of the credit period.

§ 2–311. Options and Cooperation Respecting Performance.

1. An agreement for sale which is otherwise sufficiently definite (subsection (3) of Section 2–204) to be a contract is not made invalid by

the fact that it leaves particulars of performance to be specified by one of the parties. Any such specification must be made in good faith and within limits set by commercial reasonableness.

2. Unless otherwise agreed specifications relating to assortment of the goods are at the buyer's option and except as otherwise provided in subsections (1)(c) and (3) of Section 2–319 specifications or arrangements relating to shipment are at the seller's option.

3. Where such specification would materially affect the other party's performance but is not seasonably made or where one party's cooperation is necessary to the agreed performance of the other but is not seasonably forthcoming, the other party in addition to all other remedies
   a. is excused for any resulting delay in his own performance; and
   b. may also either proceed to perform in any reasonable manner or after the time for a material part of his own performance treat the failure to specify or to cooperate as a breach by failure to deliver or accept the goods.

§ 2–312. Warranty of Title and Against Infringement; Buyer's Obligation Against Infringement.

1. Subject to subsection (2) there is in a contract for sale a warranty by the seller that
   a. the title conveyed shall be good, and its transfer rightful; and
   b. the goods shall be delivered free from any security interest or other lien or encumbrance of which the buyer at the time of contracting has no knowledge.

2. A warranty under subsection (1) will be excluded or modified only by specific language or by circumstances which give the buyer reason to know that the person selling does not claim title in himself or that he is purporting to sell only such right or title as he or a third person may have.

3. Unless otherwise agreed a seller who is a merchant regularly dealing in goods of the kind warrants that the goods shall be delivered free of the rightful claim of any third person by way of infringement or the like but a buyer who furnishes specifications to the seller must hold the seller harmless against any such claim which arises out of compliance with the specifications.

§ 2–313. Express Warranties by Affirmation, Promise, Description, Sample.

1. Express warranties by the seller are created as follows:
   a. Any affirmation of fact or promise made by the seller to the buyer which relates to the goods and becomes part of the basis of the bargain creates an express warranty that the goods shall conform to the affirmation or promise.
   b. Any description of the goods which is made part of the basis of the bargain creates an express warranty that the goods shall conform to the description.
   c. Any sample or model which is made part of the basis of the bargain creates an express warranty that the whole of the goods shall conform to the sample or model.

2. It is not necessary to the creation of an express warranty that the seller use formal words such as "warrant" or "guarantee" or that he have a specific intention to make a warranty, but an affirmation merely of the value of the goods or a statement purporting to be merely the seller's opinion or commendation of the goods does not create a warranty.

§ 2–314. Implied Warranty: Merchantability; Usage of Trade.

1. Unless excluded or modified (Section 2–316), a warranty that the goods shall be merchantable is implied in a contract for their sale if the seller is a merchant with respect to goods of that kind. Under this section the serving for value of food or drink to be consumed either on the premises or elsewhere is a sale.

2. Goods to be merchantable must be at least such as
   a. pass without objection in the trade under the contract description; and
   b. in the case of fungible goods, are of fair average quality within the description; and
   c. are fit for the ordinary purposes for which such goods are used; and
   d. run, within the variations permitted by the agreement, of even kind, quality and quantity within each unit and among all units involved; and
   e. are adequately contained, packaged, and labeled as the agreement may require; and

f. conform to the promise or affirmations of fact made on the container or label if any.

3. Unless excluded or modified (Section 2–316) other implied warranties may arise from course of dealing or usage of trade.

§ 2–315. Implied Warranty: Fitness for Particular Purpose. Where the seller at the time of contracting has reason to know any particular purpose for which the goods are required and that the buyer is relying on the seller's skill or judgment to select or furnish suitable goods, there is unless excluded or modified under the next section an implied warranty that the goods shall be fit for such purpose.

§ 2–316. Exclusion or Modification of Warranties.

1. Words or conduct relevant to the creation of an express warranty and words or conduct tending to negate or limit warranty shall be construed wherever reasonable as consistent with each other; but subject to the provisions of this Article on parol or extrinsic evidence (Section 2–202) negation or limitation is inoperative to the extent that such construction is unreasonable.

2. Subject to subsection (3), to exclude or modify the implied warranty of merchantability or any part of it the language must mention merchantability and in case of a writing must be conspicuous, and to exclude or modify any implied warranty of fitness the exclusion must be by a writing and conspicuous. Language to exclude all implied warranties of fitness is sufficient if it states, for example, that "There are no warranties which extend beyond the description on the face hereof."

3. Notwithstanding subsection (2)
   a. unless the circumstances indicate otherwise, all implied warranties are excluded by expressions like "as is", "with all faults" or other language which in common understanding calls the buyer's attention to the exclusion of warranties and makes plain that there is no implied warranty; and
   b. when the buyer before entering into the contract has examined the goods or the sample or model as fully as he desired or has refused to examine the goods there is no implied warranty with regard to defects which an examination ought in the circumstances to have revealed to him; and

c. an implied warranty can also be excluded or modified by course of dealing or course of performance or usage of trade.

4. Remedies for breach of warranty can be limited in accordance with the provisions of this Article on liquidation or limitation of damages and on contractual modification of remedy (Sections 2–718 and 2–719).

§ 2–317. Cumulation and Conflict of Warranties Express or Implied. Warranties whether express or implied shall be construed as consistent with each other and as cumulative, but if such construction is unreasonable the intention of the parties shall determine which warranty is dominant. In ascertaining that intention the following rules apply:

a. Exact or technical specifications displace an inconsistent sample or model or general language of description.
b. A sample from an existing bulk displaces inconsistent general language of description.
c. Express warranties displace inconsistent implied warranties other than an implied warranty of fitness for a particular purpose.

§ 2–318. Third Party Beneficiaries of Warranties Express or Implied. Note: *If this Act is introduced in the Congress of the United States this section should be omitted. (States to select one alternative.)*

Alternative A

A seller's warranty whether express or implied extends to any natural person who is in the family or household of his buyer or who is a guest in his home if it is reasonable to expect that such person may use, consume or be affected by the goods and who is injured in person by breach of the warranty. A seller may not exclude or limit the operation of this section.

Alternative B

A seller's warranty whether express or implied extends to any natural person who may reasonably be expected to use, consume or be affected by the goods and who is injured in person by breach of the warranty. A seller may not exclude or limit the operation of this section.

Alternative C

A seller's warranty whether express or implied extends to any person who may reasonably be expected to use, consume or be affected by the goods and who is injured by breach of the warranty. A seller may not exclude or limit the operation of this section with respect to injury to the person of an individual to whom the warranty extends.

As amended in 1966.

§ 2–319. F.O.B. and F.A.S. Terms.

1. Unless otherwise agreed the term F.O.B. (which means "free on board") at a named place, even though used only in connection with the stated price, is a delivery term under which

   a. when the term is F.O.B. the place of shipment, the seller must at that place ship the goods in the manner provided in this Article (Section 2–504) and bear the expense and risk of putting them into the possession of the carrier; or

   b. when the term is F.O.B. the place of destination, the seller must at his own expense and risk transport the goods to that place and there tender delivery of them in the manner provided in this Article (Section 2–503);

   c. when under either (a) or (b) the term is also F.O.B. vessel, car or other vehicle, the seller must in addition at his own expense and risk load the goods on board. If the term is F.O.B. vessel the buyer must name the vessel and in an appropriate case the seller must comply with the provisions of this Article on the form of bill of lading (Section 2–323).

2. Unless otherwise agreed the term F.A.S. vessel (which means "free alongside") at a named port, even though used only in connection with the stated price, is a delivery term under which the seller must

   a. at his own expense and risk deliver the goods alongside the vessel in the manner usual in that port or on a dock designated and provided by the buyer; and

   b. obtain and tender a receipt for the goods in exchange for which the carrier is under a duty to issue a bill of lading.

3. Unless otherwise agreed in any case falling within subsection (1)(a) or (c) or subsection (2) the buyer must seasonably give any needed instructions for making delivery, including when the term is F.A.S. or F.O.B. the loading berth of the vessel and in an appropriate case its name and sailing date. The seller may treat the failure of needed instructions as a failure of cooperation under this Article (Section 2–311). He may also at his option move the goods in any reasonable manner preparatory to delivery or shipment.

4. Under the term F.O.B. vessel or F.A.S. unless otherwise agreed the buyer must make payment against tender of the required documents and the seller may not tender nor the buyer demand delivery of the goods in substitution for the documents.

§ 2–320. C.I.F. and C. & F. Terms.

1. The term C.I.F. means that the price includes in a lump sum the cost of the goods and the insurance and freight to the named destination. The term C. & F. or C.F. means that the price so includes cost and freight to the named destination.

2. Unless otherwise agreed and even though used only in connection with the stated price and destination, the term C.I.F. destination or its equivalent requires the seller at his own expense and risk to

   a. put the goods into the possession of a carrier at the port for shipment and obtain a negotiable bill or bills of lading covering the entire transportation to the named destination; and

   b. load the goods and obtain a receipt from the carrier (which may be contained in the bill of lading) showing that the freight has been paid or provided for; and

   c. obtain a policy or certificate of insurance, including any war risk insurance, of a kind and on terms then current at the port of shipment in the usual amount, in the currency of the contract, shown to cover the same goods covered by the bill of lading and providing for payment of loss to the order of the buyer or for the account of whom it may concern; but the seller may add to the price the amount of the premium for any such war risk insurance; and

   d. prepare an invoice of the goods and procure any other documents required to effect shipment or to comply with the contract; and

   e. forward and tender with commercial promptness all the documents in due form and with any indorsement necessary to perfect the buyer's rights.

3. Unless otherwise agreed the term C. & F. or its equivalent has the same effect and imposes upon the seller the same obligations and risks as a C.I.F. term except the obligation as to insurance.

4. Under the term C.I.F. or C. & F. unless otherwise agreed the buyer must make payment against tender of the required documents and the seller may not tender nor the buyer demand delivery of the goods in substitution for the documents.

§ 2–321. C.I.F. or C. & F.: "Net Landed Weights"; "Payment on Arrival"; Warranty of Condition on Arrival. Under a contract containing a term C.I.F. or C. & F.

1. Where the price is based on or is to be adjusted according to "net landed weights", "delivered weights", "out turn" quantity or quality or the like, unless otherwise agreed the seller must reasonably estimate the price. The payment due on tender of the documents called for by the contract is the amount so estimated, but after final adjustment of the price a settlement must be made with commercial promptness.

2. An agreement described in subsection (1) or any warranty of quality or condition of the goods on arrival places upon the seller the risk of ordinary deterioration, shrinkage and the like in transportation but has no effect on the place or time of identification to the contract for sale or delivery or on the passing of the risk of loss.

3. Unless otherwise agreed where the contract provides for payment on or after arrival of the goods the seller must before payment allow such preliminary inspection as is feasible; but if the goods are lost delivery of the documents and payment are due when the goods should have arrived.

§ 2–322. Delivery "Ex-Ship".

1. Unless otherwise agreed a term for delivery of goods "ex-ship" (which means from the carrying vessel) or in equivalent language is not restricted to a particular ship and requires delivery from a ship which has reached a place at the named port of destination where goods of the kind are usually discharged.

2. Under such a term unless otherwise agreed
   a. the seller must discharge all liens arising out of the carriage and furnish the buyer with a direction which puts the carrier under a duty to deliver the goods; and

b. the risk of loss does not pass to the buyer until the goods leave the ship's tackle or are otherwise properly unloaded.

§ 2–323. Form of Bill of Lading Required in Overseas Shipment; "Overseas".

1. Where the contract contemplates overseas shipment and contains a term C.I.F. or C. & F. or F.O.B. vessel, the seller unless otherwise agreed must obtain a negotiable bill of lading stating that the goods have been loaded in board or, in the case of a term C.I.F. or C. & F., received for shipment.

2. Where in a case within subsection (1) a bill of lading has been issued in a set of parts, unless otherwise agreed if the documents are not to be sent from abroad the buyer may demand tender of the full set; otherwise only one part of the bill of lading need be tendered. Even if the agreement expressly requires a full set
   a. due tender of a single part is acceptable within the provisions of this Article on cure of improper delivery (subsection (1) of Section 2–508); and
   b. even though the full set is demanded, if the documents are sent from abroad the person tendering an incomplete set may nevertheless require payment upon furnishing an indemnity which the buyer in good faith deems adequate.

3. A shipment by water or by air or a contract contemplating such shipment is "overseas" insofar as by usage of trade or agreement it is subject to the commercial, financing or shipping practices characteristic of international deep water commerce.

§ 2–324. "No Arrival, No Sale" Term. Under a term "no arrival, no sale" or terms of like meaning, unless otherwise agreed,
   a. the seller must properly ship conforming goods and if they arrive by any means he must tender them on arrival but he assumes no obligation that the goods will arrive unless he has caused the non-arrival; and
   b. where without fault of the seller the goods are in part lost or have so deteriorated as no longer to conform to the contract or arrive after the contract time, the buyer may proceed as if there had been casualty to identified goods (Section 2–613).

§ 2–325. "Letter of Credit" Term; "Confirmed Credit".

1. Failure of the buyer seasonably to furnish an agreed letter of credit is a breach of the contract for sale.

2. The delivery to seller of a proper letter of credit suspends the buyer's obligation to pay. If the letter of credit is dishonored, the seller may on seasonable notification to the buyer require payment directly from him.

3. Unless otherwise agreed the term "letter of credit" or "banker's credit" in a contract for sale means an irrevocable credit issued by a financing agency of good repute and, where the shipment is overseas, of good international repute. The term "confirmed credit" means that the credit must also carry the direct obligation of such an agency which does business in the seller's financial market.

§ 2–326. Sale on Approval and Sale or Return; Consignment Sales and Rights of Creditors.

1. Unless otherwise agreed, if delivered goods may be returned by the buyer even though they conform to the contract, the transaction is
   a. a "sale on approval" if the goods are delivered primarily for use, and
   b. a "sale or return" if the goods are delivered primarily for resale.

2. Except as provided in subsection (3), goods held on approval are not subject to the claims of the buyer's creditors until acceptance; goods held on sale or return are subject to such claims while in the buyer's possession.

3. Where goods are delivered to a person for sale and such person maintains a place of business at which he deals in goods of the kind involved, under a name other than the name of the person making delivery, then with respect to claims of creditors of the person conducting the business the goods are deemed to be on sale or return. The provisions of this subsection are applicable even though an agreement purports to reserve title to the person making delivery until payment or resale or uses such words as "on consignment" or "on memorandum". However, this subsection is not applicable if the person making delivery
   a. complies with an applicable law providing for a consignor's interest or the like to be evidenced by a sign, or

   b. establishes that the person conducting the business is generally known by his creditors to be substantially engaged in selling the goods of others, or
   c. complies with the filing provisions of the Article on Secured Transactions (Article 9).

4. Any "or return" term of a contract for sale is to be treated as a separate contract for sale within the statute of frauds section of this Article (Section 2–201) and as contradicting the sale aspect of the contract within the provisions of this Article on parol or extrinsic evidence (Section 2–202).

§ 2–327. Special Incidents of Sale on Approval and Sale or Return.

1. Under a sale on approval unless otherwise agreed
   a. although the goods are identified to the contract the risk of loss and the title do not pass to the buyer until acceptance; and
   b. use of the goods consistent with the purpose of trial is not acceptance but failure seasonably to notify the seller of election to return the goods is acceptance, and if the goods conform to the contract acceptance of any part is acceptance of the whole; and
   c. after due notification of election to return, the return is at the seller's risk and expense but a merchant buyer must follow any reasonable instructions.

2. Under a sale or return unless otherwise agreed
   a. the option to return extends to the whole or any commercial unit of the goods while in substantially their original condition, but must be exercised seasonably; and
   b. the return is at the buyer's risk and expense.

§ 2–328. Sale by Auction.

1. In a sale by auction if goods are put up in lots each lot is the subject of a separate sale.

2. A sale by auction is complete when the auctioneer so announces by the fall of the hammer or in other customary manner. Where a bid is made while the hammer is falling in acceptance of a prior bid the auctioneer may in his discretion reopen the bidding or declare the goods sold under the bid on which the hammer was falling.

3. Such a sale is with reserve unless the goods are in explicit terms put up without reserve. In

an auction with reserve the auctioneer may withdraw the goods at any time until he announces completion of the sale. In an auction without reserve, after the auctioneer calls for bids on an article or lot, that article or lot cannot be withdrawn unless no bid is made within a reasonable time. In either case a bidder may retract his bid until the auctioneer's announcement of completion of the sale, but a bidder's retraction does not revive any previous bid.

4. If the auctioneer knowingly receives a bid on the seller's behalf or the seller makes or procures such a bid, and notice has not been given that liberty for such bidding is reserved, the buyer may at his option avoid the sale or take the goods at the price of the last good faith bid prior to the completion of the sale. This subsection shall not apply to any bid at a forced sale.

PART 4: TITLE, CREDITORS AND GOOD FAITH PURCHASERS

§ 2–401. Passing of Title; Reservation for Security; Limited Application of This Section. Each provision of this Article with regard to the rights, obligations and remedies of the seller, the buyer, purchasers or other third parties applies irrespective of title to the goods except where the provision refers to such title. Insofar as situations are not covered by the other provisions of this Article and matters concerning title become material the following rules apply:

1. Title to goods cannot pass under a contract for sale prior to their identification to the contract (Section 2–501), and unless otherwise explicitly agreed the buyer acquires by their identification a special property as limited by this Act. Any retention or reservation by the seller of the title (property) in goods shipped or delivered to the buyer is limited in effect to a reservation of a security interest. Subject to these provisions and to the provisions of the Article on Secured Transactions (Article 9), title to goods passes from the seller to the buyer in any manner and on any conditions explicitly agreed on by the parties.

2. Unless otherwise explicitly agreed title passes to the buyer at the time and place at which the seller completes his performance with reference to the physical delivery of the goods, despite any reservation of a security interest and even though a document of title is to be delivered at a different time or place; and in particular and despite any reservation of a security interest by the bill of lading

   a. if the contract requires or authorizes the seller to send the goods to the buyer but does not require him to deliver them at destination, title passes to the buyer at the time and place of shipment; but

   b. if the contract requires delivery at destination, title passes on tender there.

3. Unless otherwise explicitly agreed where delivery is to be made without moving the goods,

   a. if the seller is to deliver a document of title, title passes at the time when and the place where he delivers such documents; or

   b. if the goods are at the time of contracting already identified and no documents are to be delivered, title passes at the time and place of contracting.

4. A rejection or other refusal by the buyer to receive or retain the goods, whether or not justified, or a justified revocation of acceptance revests title to the goods in the seller. Such revesting occurs by operation of law and is not a "sale".

§ 2–402. Rights of Seller's Creditors Against Sold Goods.

1. Except as provided in subsections (2) and (3), rights of unsecured creditors of the seller with respect to goods which have been identified to a contract for sale are subject to the buyer's rights to recover the goods under this Article (Sections 2–502 and 2–716).

2. A creditor of the seller may treat a sale or an identification of goods to a contract for sale as void if as against him a retention of possession by the seller is fraudulent under any rule of law of the state where the goods are situated, except that retention of possession in good faith and current course of trade by a merchant-seller for a commercially reasonable time after a sale or identification is not fraudulent.

3. Nothing in this Article shall be deemed to impair the rights of creditors of the seller

   a. under the provisions of the Article on Secured Transactions (Article 9); or

   b. where identification to the contract or delivery is made not in current course of trade but in satisfaction of or as security for a pre-existing claim for money, security or the like and is made under circumstances which under any rule of law of the state where the goods are situated would apart from this Article constitute the transaction a fraudulent transfer or voidable preference.

§ 2–403. Power to Transfer; Good Faith Purchase of Goods; "Entrusting".

1. A purchaser of goods acquires all title which his transferor had or had power to transfer except that a purchaser of a limited interest acquires rights only to the extent of the interest purchased. A person with voidable title has power to transfer a good title to a good faith purchaser for value. When goods have been delivered under a transaction of purchase the purchaser has such power even though
   a. the transferor was deceived as to the identity of the purchaser, or
   b. the delivery was in exchange for a check which is later dishonored, or
   c. it was agreed that the transaction was to be a "cash sale", or
   d. the delivery was procured through fraud punishable as larcenous under the criminal law.

2. Any entrusting of possession of goods to a merchant who deals in goods of that kind gives him power to transfer all rights of the entruster to a buyer in ordinary course of business.

3. "Entrusting" includes any delivery and any acquiescence in retention of possession regardless of any condition expressed between the parties to the delivery or acquiescence and regardless of whether the procurement of the entrusting or the possessor's disposition of the goods have been such as to be larcenous under the criminal law.

   [*Publisher's Editorial Note: If a state adopts the repealer of Article 6—Bulk Transfers (Alternative A), subsec. (4) should read as follows:*]

4. The rights of other purchasers of goods and of lien creditors are governed by the Articles on Secured Transactions (Article 9) and Documents of Title (Article 7).

   [*Publisher's Editorial Note: If a state adopts Revised Article 6—Bulk Sales (Alternative B), subsec. (4) should read as follows:*]

5. The rights of other purchasers of goods and of lien creditors are governed by the Articles on Secured Transactions (Article 9), Bulk Sales (Article 6) and Documents of Title (Article 7).

As amended in 1988.

For material relating to the changes made in text in 1988, see section 3 of Alternative A (Repealer of Article 6—Bulk Transfers) and Conforming Amendment to Section 2–403 following end of Alternative B (Revised Article 6—Bulk Sales).

PART 5: PERFORMANCE

§ 2–501. Insurable Interest in Goods; Manner of Identification of Goods.

1. The buyer obtains a special property and an insurable interest in goods by identification of existing goods as goods to which the contract refers even though the goods so identified are non-conforming and he has an option to return or reject them. Such identification can be made at any time and in any manner explicitly agreed to by the parties. In the absence of explicit agreement identification occurs
   a. when the contract is made if it is for the sale of goods already existing and identified;
   b. if the contract is for the sale of future goods other than those described in paragraph (c), when goods are shipped, marked or otherwise designated by the seller as goods to which the contract refers;
   c. when the crops are planted or otherwise become growing crops or the young are conceived if the contract is for the sale of unborn young to be born within twelve months after contracting or for the sale of crops to be harvested within twelve months or the next normal harvest season after contracting whichever is longer.

2. The seller retains an insurable interest in goods so long as title to or any security interest in the goods remains in him and where the identification is by the seller alone he may until default or insolvency or notification to the buyer that the identification is final substitute other goods for those identified.

3. Nothing in this section impairs any insurable interest recognized under any other statute or rule of law.

§ 2–502. Buyer's Right to Goods on Seller's Insolvency.

1. Subject to subsection (2) and even though the goods have not been shipped a buyer who has paid a part or all of the price of goods in which he has a special property under the provisions of the immediately preceding section may on making and keeping good a tender of any unpaid portion of their price recover them from the seller if the seller becomes insolvent within ten days after receipt of the first installment on their price.

2. If the identification creating his special property has been made by the buyer he acquires the right to recover the goods only if they conform to the contract for sale.

§ 2–503. Manner of Seller's Tender of Delivery.

1. Tender of delivery requires that the seller put and hold conforming goods at the buyer's disposition and give the buyer any notification reasonably necessary to enable him to take delivery. The manner, time and place for tender are determined by the agreement and this Article, and in particular

    a. tender must be at a reasonable hour, and if it is of goods they must be kept available for the period reasonably necessary to enable the buyer to take possession; but

    b. unless otherwise agreed the buyer must furnish facilities reasonably suited to the receipt of the goods.

2. Where the case is within the next section respecting shipment tender requires that the seller comply with its provisions.

3. Where the seller is required to deliver at a particular destination tender requires that he comply with subsection (1) and also in any appropriate case tender documents as described in subsections (4) and (5) of this section.

4. Where goods are in the possession of a bailee and are to be delivered without being moved

    a. tender requires that the seller either tender a negotiable document of title covering such goods or procure acknowledgment by the bailee of the buyer's right to possession of the goods; but

    b. tender to the buyer of a non-negotiable document of title or of a written direction to the bailee to deliver is sufficient tender unless the buyer seasonably objects, and receipt by the bailee of notification of the buyer's rights fixes those rights as against the bailee and all third persons; but risk of loss of the goods and of any failure by the bailee to honor the non-negotiable document of title or to obey the direction remains on the seller until the buyer has had a reasonable time to present the document or direction, and a refusal by the bailee to honor the document or to obey the direction defeats the tender.

5. Where the contract requires the seller to deliver documents

    a. he must tender all such documents in correct form, except as provided in this Article with respect to bills of lading in a set (subsection (2) of Section 2–323); and

    b. tender through customary banking channels is sufficient and dishonor of a draft accompanying the documents constitutes non-acceptance or rejection.

§ 2–504. Shipment by Seller.
Where the seller is required or authorized to send the goods to the buyer and the contract does not require him to deliver them at a particular destination, then unless otherwise agreed he must

    a. put the goods in the possession of such a carrier and make such a contract for their transportation as may be reasonable having regard to the nature of the goods and other circumstances of the case; and

    b. obtain and promptly deliver or tender in due form any document necessary to enable the buyer to obtain possession of the goods or otherwise required by the agreement or by usage of trade; and

    c. promptly notify the buyer of the shipment.

Failure to notify the buyer under paragraph (c) or to make a proper contract under paragraph (a) is a ground for rejection only if material delay or loss ensues.

§ 2–505. Seller's Shipment Under Reservation.

1. Where the seller has identified goods to the contract by or before shipment:

    a. his procurement of a negotiable bill of lading to his own order or otherwise reserves in him a security interest in the goods. His procurement of the bill to the order of a financing agency or of the buyer indicates in addition only the seller's expectation of transferring that interest to the person named.

b. a non-negotiable bill of lading to himself or his nominee reserves possession of the goods as security but except in a case of conditional delivery (subsection (2) of Section 2–507) a non-negotiable bill of lading naming the buyer as consignee reserves no security interest even though the seller retains possession of the bill of lading.

2. When shipment by the seller with reservation of a security interest is in violation of the contract for sale it constitutes an improper contract for transportation within the preceding section but impairs neither the rights given to the buyer by shipment and identification of the goods to the contract nor the seller's powers as a holder of a negotiable document.

§ 2–506. Rights of Financing Agency.

1. A financing agency by paying or purchasing for value a draft which relates to a shipment of goods acquires to the extent of the payment or purchase and in addition to its own rights under the draft and any document of title securing it any rights of the shipper in the goods including the right to stop delivery and the shipper's right to have the draft honored by the buyer.

2. The right to reimbursement of a financing agency which has in good faith honored or purchased the draft under commitment to or authority from the buyer is not impaired by subsequent discovery of defects with reference to any relevant document which was apparently regular on its face.

§ 2–507. Effect of Seller's Tender; Delivery on Condition.

1. Tender of delivery is a condition to the buyer's duty to accept the goods and, unless otherwise agreed, to his duty to pay for them. Tender entitles the seller to acceptance of the goods and to payment according to the contract.

2. Where payment is due and demanded on the deliv-ery to the buyer of goods or documents of title, his right as against the seller to retain or dispose of them is conditional upon his making the payment due.

§ 2–508. Cure by Seller of Improper Tender or Delivery; Replacement.

1. Where any tender or delivery by the seller is rejected because non-conforming and the time for performance has not yet expired, the seller may seasonably notify the buyer of his intention to cure and may then within the contract time make a conforming delivery.

2. Where the buyer rejects a non-conforming tender which the seller had reasonable grounds to believe would be acceptable with or without money allowance the seller may if he seasonably notifies the buyer have a further reasonable time to substitute a conforming tender.

§ 2–509. Risk of Loss in the Absence of Breach.

1. Where the contract requires or authorizes the seller to ship the goods by carrier
   a. if it does not require him to deliver them at a particular destination, the risk of loss passes to the buyer when the goods are duly delivered to the carrier even though the shipment is under reservation (Section 2–505); but
   b. if it does require him to deliver them at a particular destination and the goods are there duly tendered while in the possession of the carrier, the risk of loss passes to the buyer when the goods are there duly so tendered as to enable the buyer to take delivery.

2. Where the goods are held by a bailee to be delivered without being moved, the risk of loss passes to the buyer
   a. on his receipt of a negotiable document of title covering the goods; or
   b. on acknowledgment by the bailee of the buyer's right to possession of the goods; or
   c. after his receipt of a non-negotiable document of title or other written direction to deliver, as provided in subsection (4)(b) of Section 2–503.

3. In any case not within subsection (1) or (2), the risk of loss passes to the buyer on his receipt of the goods if the seller is a merchant; otherwise the risk passes to the buyer on tender of delivery.

4. The provisions of this section are subject to contrary agreement of the parties and to the provisions of this Article on sale on approval (Section 2–327) and on effect of breach on risk of loss (Section 2–510).

§ 2–510. Effect of Breach on Risk of Loss.

1. Where a tender or delivery of goods so fails to conform to the contract as to give a right of

rejection the risk of their loss remains on the seller until cure or acceptance.

2. Where the buyer rightfully revokes acceptance he may to the extent of any deficiency in his effective insurance coverage treat the risk of loss as having rested on the seller from the beginning.

3. Where the buyer as to conforming goods already identified to the contract for sale repudiates or is otherwise in breach before risk of their loss has passed to him, the seller may to the extent of any deficiency in his effective insurance coverage treat the risk of loss as resting on the buyer for a commercially reasonable time.

§ 2–511. Tender of Payment by Buyer; Payment by Check.

1. Unless otherwise agreed tender of payment is a condition to the seller's duty to tender and complete any delivery.

2. Tender of payment is sufficient when made by any means or in any manner current in the ordinary course of business unless the seller demands payment in legal tender and gives any extension of time reasonably necessary to procure it.

3. Subject to the provisions of this Act on the effect of an instrument on an obligation (Section 3-310), payment by check is conditional and is defeated as between the parties by dishonor of the check on due presentment.

As amended in 1994.

See Appendix XI for material relating to changes made in text in 1994.

§ 2–512. Payment by Buyer Before Inspection.
1995 Amendments to text indicated by strikeout and underline

1. Where the contract requires payment before inspection non-conformity of the goods does not excuse the buyer from so making payment unless
   a. the non-conformity appears without inspection; or
   b. despite tender of the required documents the circumstances would justify injunction against honor under this Act (Section 5-109(b)).

2. Payment pursuant to subsection (1) does not constitute an acceptance of goods or impair the buyer's right to inspect or any of his remedies.

As amended in 1995.

See Appendix XIV for material relating to changes made in text in 1995.

§ 2–513. Buyer's Right to Inspection of Goods.

1. Unless otherwise agreed and subject to subsection (3), where goods are tendered or delivered or identified to the contract for sale, the buyer has a right before payment or acceptance to inspect them at any reasonable place and time and in any reasonable manner. When the seller is required or authorized to send the goods to the buyer, the inspection may be after their arrival.

2. Expenses of inspection must be borne by the buyer but may be recovered from the seller if the goods do not conform and are rejected.

3. Unless otherwise agreed and subject to the provisions of this Article on C.I.F. contracts (subsection (3) of Section 2–321), the buyer is not entitled to inspect the goods before payment of the price when the contract provides
   a. for delivery "C.O.D." or on other like terms; or
   b. for payment against documents of title, except where such payment is due only after the goods are to become available for inspection.

4. A place or method of inspection fixed by the parties is presumed to be exclusive but unless otherwise expressly agreed it does not postpone identification or shift the place for delivery or for passing the risk of loss. If compliance becomes impossible, inspection shall be as provided in this section unless the place or method fixed was clearly intended as an indispensable condition failure of which avoids the contract.

§ 2–514. When Documents Deliverable on Acceptance; When on Payment.
Unless otherwise agreed documents against which a draft is drawn are to be delivered to the drawee on acceptance of the draft if it is payable more than three days after presentment; otherwise, only on payment.

§ 2–515. Preserving Evidence of Goods in Dispute.
In furtherance of the adjustment of any claim or dispute
   a. either party on reasonable notification to the other and for the purpose of ascertaining the facts and preserving evidence has the right to inspect, test and sample the goods including such of them as may be in the possession or control of the other; and

b. the parties may agree to a third party inspection or survey to determine the conformity or condition of the goods and may agree that the findings shall be binding upon them in any subsequent litigation or adjustment.

PART 6: BREACH, REPUDIATION AND EXCUSE

§ 2–601. Buyer's Rights on Improper Delivery.

Subject to the provisions of this Article on breach in installment contracts (Section 2–612) and unless otherwise agreed under the sections on contractual limitations of remedy (Sections 2–718 and 2–719), if the goods or the tender of delivery fail in any respect to conform to the contract, the buyer may

    a. reject the whole; or

    b. accept the whole; or

    c. accept any commercial unit or units and reject the rest.

§ 2–602. Manner and Effect of Rightful Rejection.

1. Rejection of goods must be within a reasonable time after their delivery or tender. It is ineffective unless the buyer seasonably notifies the seller.

2. Subject to the provisions of the two following sections on rejected goods (Sections 2–603 and 2–604),

    a. after rejection any exercise of ownership by the buyer with respect to any commercial unit is wrongful as against the seller; and

    b. if the buyer has before rejection taken physical possession of goods in which he does not have a security interest under the provisions of this Article (subsection (3) of Section 2–711), he is under a duty after rejection to hold them with reasonable care at the seller's disposition for a time sufficient to permit the seller to remove them; but

    c. the buyer has no further obligations with regard to goods rightfully rejected.

3. The seller's rights with respect to goods wrongfully rejected are governed by the provisions of this Article on Seller's remedies in general (Section 2–703).

§ 2–603. Merchant Buyer's Duties as to Rightfully Rejected Goods.

1. Subject to any security interest in the buyer (subsection (3) of Section 2–711), when the seller has no agent or place of business at the market of rejection a merchant buyer is under a duty after rejection of goods in his possession or control to follow any reasonable instructions received from the seller with respect to the goods and in the absence of such instructions to make reasonable efforts to sell them for the seller's account if they are perishable or threaten to decline in value speedily. Instructions are not reasonable if on demand indemnity for expenses is not forthcoming.

2. When the buyer sells goods under subsection (1), he is entitled to reimbursement from the seller or out of the proceeds for reasonable expenses of caring for and selling them, and if the expenses include no selling commission then to such commission as is usual in the trade or if there is none to a reasonable sum not exceeding ten per cent on the gross proceeds.

3. In complying with this section the buyer is held only to good faith and good faith conduct hereunder is neither acceptance nor conversion nor the basis of an action for damages.

§ 2–604. Buyer's Options as to Salvage of Rightfully Rejected Goods.

Subject to the provisions of the immediately preceding section on perishables if the seller gives no instructions within a reasonable time after notification of rejection the buyer may store the rejected goods for the seller's account or reship them to him or resell them for the seller's account with reimbursement as provided in the preceding section. Such action is not acceptance or conversion.

§ 2–605. Waiver of Buyer's Objections by Failure to Particularize.

1. The buyer's failure to state in connection with rejection a particular defect which is ascertainable by reasonable inspection precludes him from relying on the unstated defect to justify rejection or to establish breach

    a. where the seller could have cured it if stated seasonably; or

    b. between merchants when the seller has after rejection made a request in writing for a full and final written statement of all defects on which the buyer proposes to rely.

2. Payment against documents made without reservation of rights precludes recovery of the payment for defects apparent on the face of the documents.

§ 2–606. What Constitutes Acceptance of Goods.

1. Acceptance of goods occurs when the buyer
   a. after a reasonable opportunity to inspect the goods signifies to the seller that the goods are conforming or that he will take or retain them in spite of their non-conformity; or
   b. fails to make an effective rejection (subsection (1) of Section 2–602), but such acceptance does not occur until the buyer has had a reasonable opportunity to inspect them; or
   c. does any act inconsistent with the seller's ownership; but if such act is wrongful as against the seller it is an acceptance only if ratified by him.
2. Acceptance of a part of any commercial unit is acceptance of that entire unit.

§ 2–607. Effect of Acceptance; Notice of Breach; Burden of Establishing Breach After Acceptance; Notice of Claim or Litigation to Person Answerable Over.

1. The buyer must pay at the contract rate for any goods accepted.
2. Acceptance of goods by the buyer precludes rejection of the goods accepted and if made with knowledge of a non-conformity cannot be revoked because of it unless the acceptance was on the reasonable assumption that the non-conformity would be seasonably cured but acceptance does not of itself impair any other remedy provided by this Article for non-conformity.
3. Where a tender has been accepted
   a. the buyer must within a reasonable time after he discovers or should have discovered any breach notify the seller of breach or be barred from any remedy; and
   b. if the claim is one for infringement or the like (subsection (3) of Section 2–312) and the buyer is sued as a result of such a breach he must so notify the seller within a reasonable time after he receives notice of the litigation or be barred from any remedy over for liability established by the litigation.
4. The burden is on the buyer to establish any breach with respect to the goods accepted.
5. Where the buyer is sued for breach of a warranty or other obligation for which his seller is answerable over
   a. he may give his seller written notice of the litigation. If the notice states that the seller may come in and defend and that if the seller does not do so he will be bound in any action against him by his buyer by any determination of fact common to the two litigations, then unless the seller after seasonable receipt of the notice does come in and defend he is so bound.
   b. if the claim is one for infringement or the like (subsection (3) of Section 2–312) the original seller may demand in writing that his buyer turn over to him control of the litigation including settlement or else be barred from any remedy over and if he also agrees to bear all expense and to satisfy any adverse judgment, then unless the buyer after seasonable receipt of the demand does turn over control the buyer is so barred.
6. The provisions of subsections (3), (4) and (5) apply to any obligation of a buyer to hold the seller harmless against infringement or the like (subsection (3) of Section 2–312).

§ 2–608. Revocation of Acceptance in Whole or in Part.

1. The buyer may revoke his acceptance of a lot or commercial unit whose non-conformity substantially impairs its value to him if he has accepted it
   a. on the reasonable assumption that its non-conformity would be cured and it has not been seasonably cured; or
   b. without discovery of such non-conformity if his acceptance was reasonably induced either by the difficulty of discovery before acceptance or by the seller's assurances.
2. Revocation of acceptance must occur within a reasonable time after the buyer discovers or should have discovered the ground for it and before any substantial change in condition of the goods which is not caused by their own defects. It is not effective until the buyer notifies the seller of it.
3. A buyer who so revokes has the same rights and duties with regard to the goods involved as if he had rejected them.

§ 2–609. Right to Adequate Assurance of Performance.

1. A contract for sale imposes an obligation on each party that the other's expectation of

receiving due performance will not be impaired. When reasonable grounds for insecurity arise with respect to the performance of either party the other may in writing demand adequate assurance of due performance and until he receives such assurance may if commercially reasonable suspend any performance for which he has not already received the agreed return.

2. Between merchants the reasonableness of grounds for insecurity and the adequacy of any assurance offered shall be determined according to commercial standards.

3. Acceptance of any improper delivery or payment does not prejudice the aggrieved party's right to demand adequate assurance of future performance.

4. After receipt of a justified demand failure to provide within a reasonable time not exceeding thirty days such assurance of due performance as is adequate under the circumstances of the particular case is a repudiation of the contract.

§ 2–610. Anticipatory Repudiation. When either party repudiates the contract with respect to a performance not yet due the loss of which will substantially impair the value of the contract to the other, the aggrieved party may

    a. for a commercially reasonable time await performance by the repudiating party; or

    b. resort to any remedy for breach (Section 2–703 or Section 2–711), even though he has notified the repudiating party that he would await the latter's performance and has urged retraction; and

    c. in either case suspend his own performance or proceed in accordance with the provisions of this Article on the seller's right to identify goods to the contract notwithstanding breach or to salvage unfinished goods (Section 2–704).

§ 2–611. Retraction of Anticipatory Repudiation.

1. Until the repudiating party's next performance is due he can retract his repudiation unless the aggrieved party has since the repudiation cancelled or materially changed his position or otherwise indicated that he considers the repudiation final.

2. Retraction may be by any method which clearly indicates to the aggrieved party that the repudiating party intends to perform, but must include any assurance justifiably demanded under the provisions of this Article (Section 2–609).

3. Retraction reinstates the repudiating party's rights under the contract with due excuse and allowance to the aggrieved party for any delay occasioned by the repudiation.

§ 2–612. "Installment Contract"; Breach.

1. An "installment contract" is one which requires or authorizes the delivery of goods in separate lots to be separately accepted, even though the contract contains a clause "each delivery is a separate contract" or its equivalent.

2. The buyer may reject any installment which is non-conforming if the non-conformity substantially impairs the value of that installment and cannot be cured or if the non-conformity is a defect in the required documents; but if the non-conformity does not fall within subsection (3) and the seller gives adequate assurance of its cure the buyer must accept that installment.

3. Whenever non-conformity or default with respect to one or more installments substantially impairs the value of the whole contract there is a breach of the whole. But the aggrieved party reinstates the contract if he accepts a non-conforming installment without seasonably notifying of cancellation or if he brings an action with respect only to past installments or demands performance as to future installments.

§ 2–613. Casualty to Identified Goods. Where the contract requires for its performance goods identified when the contract is made, and the goods suffer casualty without fault of either party before the risk of loss passes to the buyer, or in a proper case under a "no arrival, no sale" term (Section 2–324) then

    a. if the loss is total the contract is avoided; and

    b. if the loss is partial or the goods have so deteriorated as no longer to conform to the contract the buyer may nevertheless demand inspection and at his option either treat the contract as avoided or accept the goods with due allowance from the contract price for the deterioration or the deficiency in quantity but without further right against the seller.

§ 2–614. Substituted Performance.

1. Where without fault of either party the agreed berthing, loading, or unloading facilities fail or an agreed type of carrier becomes unavailable or the agreed manner of delivery otherwise becomes commercially impracticable but a commercially reasonable substitute is available, such substitute performance must be tendered and accepted.

2. If the agreed means or manner of payment fails because of domestic or foreign governmental regulation, the seller may withhold or stop delivery unless the buyer provides a means or manner of payment which is commercially a substantial equivalent. If delivery has already been taken, payment by the means or in the manner provided by the regulation discharges the buyer's obligation unless the regulation is discriminatory, oppressive or predatory.

§ 2–615. Excuse by Failure of Presupposed Conditions.
Except so far as a seller may have assumed a greater obligation and subject to the preceding section on substituted performance:

    a. Delay in delivery or non-delivery in whole or in part by a seller who complies with paragraphs (b) and (c) is not a breach of his duty under a contract for sale if performance as agreed has been made impracticable by the occurrence of a contingency the non-occurrence of which was a basic assumption on which the contract was made or by compliance in good faith with any applicable foreign or domestic governmental regulation or order whether or not it later proves to be invalid.

    b. Where the causes mentioned in paragraph (a) affect only a part of the seller's capacity to perform, he must allocate production and deliveries among his customers but may at his option include regular customers not then under contract as well as his own requirements for further manufacture. He may so allocate in any manner which is fair and reasonable.

    c. The seller must notify the buyer seasonably that there will be delay or non-delivery and, when allocation is required under paragraph (b), of the estimated quota thus made available for the buyer.

§ 2–616. Procedure on Notice Claiming Excuse.

1. Where the buyer receives notification of a material or indefinite delay or an allocation justified under the preceding section he may by written notification to the seller as to any delivery concerned, and where the prospective deficiency substantially impairs the value of the whole contract under the provisions of this Article relating to breach of installment contracts (Section 2–612), then also as to the whole,

    a. terminate and thereby discharge any unexecuted portion of the contract; or

    b. modify the contract by agreeing to take his available quota in substitution.

2. If after receipt of such notification from the seller the buyer fails so to modify the contract within a reasonable time not exceeding thirty days the contract lapses with respect to any deliveries affected.

3. The provisions of this section may not be negated by agreement except in so far as the seller has assumed a greater obligation under the preceding section.

PART 7: REMEDIES

§ 2–701. Remedies for Breach of Collateral Con-tracts Not Impaired.
Remedies for breach of any obligation or promise collateral or ancillary to a contract for sale are not impaired by the provisions of this Article.

§ 2–702. Seller's Remedies on Discovery of Buyer's Insolvency.

1. Where the seller discovers the buyer to be insolvent he may refuse delivery except for cash including payment for all goods theretofore delivered under the contract, and stop delivery under this Article (Section 2–705).

2. Where the seller discovers that the buyer has received goods on credit while insolvent he may reclaim the goods upon demand made within ten days after the receipt, but if misrepresentation of solvency has been made to the particular seller in writing within three months before delivery the ten day limitation does not apply. Except as provided in this subsection the seller may not base a right to reclaim goods on the buyer's fraudulent or innocent misrepresentation of solvency or of intent to pay.

3. The seller's right to reclaim under subsection (2) is subject to the rights of a buyer in

ordinary course or other good faith purchaser under this Article (Section 2–403). Successful reclamation of goods excludes all other remedies with respect to them.

As amended in 1966.

§ 2–703. Seller's Remedies in General. Where the buyer wrongfully rejects or revokes acceptance of goods or fails to make a payment due on or before delivery or repudiates with respect to a part or the whole, then with respect to any goods directly affected and, if the breach is of the whole contract (Section 2–612), then also with respect to the whole undelivered balance, the aggrieved seller may

   a. withhold delivery of such goods;

   b. stop delivery by any bailee as hereafter provided (Section 2–705);

   c. proceed under the next section respecting goods still unidentified to the contract;

   d. resell and recover damages as hereafter provided (Section 2–706);

   e. recover damages for non-acceptance (Section 2–708) or in a proper case the price (Section 2–709);

   f. cancel.

§ 2–704. Seller's Right to Identify Goods to the Contract Notwithstanding Breach or to Salvage Unfinished Goods.

1. An aggrieved seller under the preceding section may

   a. identify to the contract conforming goods not already identified if at the time he learned of the breach they are in his possession or control;

   b. treat as the subject of resale goods which have demonstrably been intended for the particular contract even though those goods are unfinished.

2. Where the goods are unfinished an aggrieved seller may in the exercise of reasonable commercial judgment for the purposes of avoiding loss and of effective realization either complete the manufacture and wholly identify the goods to the contract or cease manufacture and resell for scrap or salvage value or proceed in any other reasonable manner.

§ 2–705. Seller's Stoppage of Delivery in Transit or Otherwise.

1. The seller may stop delivery of goods in the possession of a carrier or other bailee when he discovers the buyer to be insolvent (Section 2–702) and may stop delivery of carload, truckload, planeload or larger shipments of express or freight when the buyer repudiates or fails to make a payment due before delivery or if for any other reason the seller has a right to withhold or reclaim the goods.

2. As against such buyer the seller may stop delivery until

   a. receipt of the goods by the buyer; or

   b. acknowledgment to the buyer by any bailee of the goods except a carrier that the bailee holds the goods for the buyer; or

   c. such acknowledgment to the buyer by a carrier by reshipment or as warehouseman; or

   d. negotiation to the buyer of any negotiable document of title covering the goods.

3. a. To stop delivery the seller must so notify as to enable the bailee by reasonable diligence to prevent delivery of the goods.

   b. After such notification the bailee must hold and deliver the goods according to the directions of the seller but the seller is liable to the bailee for any ensuing charges or damages.

   c. If a negotiable document of title has been issued for goods the bailee is not obliged to obey a notification to stop until surrender of the document.

   d. A carrier who has issued a non-negotiable bill of lading is not obliged to obey a notification to stop received from a person other than the consignor.

§ 2–706. Seller's Resale Including Contract for Resale.

1. Under the conditions stated in Section 2–703 on seller's remedies, the seller may resell the goods concerned or the undelivered balance thereof. Where the resale is made in good faith and in a commercially reasonable manner the seller may recover the difference between the resale price and the contract price together with any incidental damages allowed under the provisions of this Article (Section 2–710), but less expenses saved in consequence of the buyer's breach.

2. Except as otherwise provided in subsection (3) or unless otherwise agreed resale may be at public or private sale including sale by way of one or more contracts to sell or of identification to an existing contract of the seller. Sale may be as a unit or in parcels and at any time and place and on any terms but every

aspect of the sale including the method, manner, time, place and terms must be commercially reasonable. The resale must be reasonably identified as referring to the broken contract, but it is not necessary that the goods be in existence or that any or all of them have been identified to the contract before the breach.

3. Where the resale is at private sale the seller must give the buyer reasonable notification of his intention to resell.

4. Where the resale is at public sale
   a. only identified goods can be sold except where there is a recognized market for a public sale of futures in goods of the kind; and
   b. it must be made at a usual place or market for public sale if one is reasonably available and except in the case of goods which are perishable or threaten to decline in value speedily the seller must give the buyer reasonable notice of the time and place of the resale; and
   c. if the goods are not to be within the view of those attending the sale the notification of sale must state the place where the goods are located and provide for their reasonable inspection by prospective bidders; and
   d. the seller may buy.

5. A purchaser who buys in good faith at a resale takes the goods free of any rights of the original buyer even though the seller fails to comply with one or more of the requirements of this section.

6. The seller is not accountable to the buyer for any profit made on any resale. A person in the position of a seller (Section 2–707) or a buyer who has rightfully rejected or justifiably revoked acceptance must account for any excess over the amount of his security interest, as hereinafter defined (subsection (3) of Section 2–711).

§ 2–707. "Person in the Position of a Seller".

1. A "person in the position of a seller" includes as against a principal an agent who has paid or become responsible for the price of goods on behalf of his principal or anyone who otherwise holds a security interest or other right in goods similar to that of a seller.

2. A person in the position of a seller may as provided in this Article withhold or stop delivery (Section 2–705) and resell (Section 2–706) and recover incidental damages (Section 2–710).

§ 2–708. Seller's Damages for Non-acceptance or Repudiation.

1. Subject to subsection (2) and to the provisions of this Article with respect to proof of market price (Section 2–723), the measure of damages for non-acceptance or repudiation by the buyer is the difference between the market price at the time and place for tender and the unpaid contract price together with any incidental damages provided in this Article (Section 2–710), but less expenses saved in consequence of the buyer's breach.

2. If the measure of damages provided in subsection (1) is inadequate to put the seller in as good a position as performance would have done then the measure of damages is the profit (including reasonable overhead) which the seller would have made from full performance by the buyer, together with any incidental damages provided in this Article (Section 2–710), due allowance for costs reasonably incurred and due credit for payments or proceeds of resale.

§ 2–709. Action for the Price.

1. When the buyer fails to pay the price as it becomes due the seller may recover, together with any incidental damages under the next section, the price
   a. of goods accepted or of conforming goods lost or damaged within a commercially reasonable time after risk of their loss has passed to the buyer; and
   b. of goods identified to the contract if the seller is unable after reasonable effort to resell them at a reasonable price or the circumstances reasonably indicate that such effort will be unavailing.

2. Where the seller sues for the price he must hold for the buyer any goods which have been identified to the contract and are still in his control except that if resale becomes possible he may resell them at any time prior to the collection of the judgment. The net proceeds of any such resale must be credited to the buyer and payment of the judgment entitles him to any goods not resold.

3. After the buyer has wrongfully rejected or revoked acceptance of the goods or has failed to

make a payment due or has repudiated (Section 2–610), a seller who is held not entitled to the price under this section shall nevertheless be awarded damages for non-acceptance under the preceding section.

§ 2–710. Seller's Incidental Damages. Incidental damages to an aggrieved seller include any commercially reasonable charges, expenses or commissions incurred in stopping delivery, in the transportation, care and custody of goods after the buyer's breach, in connection with return or resale of the goods or otherwise resulting from the breach.

§ 2–711. Buyer's Remedies in General; Buyer's Security Interest in Rejected Goods.

1. Where the seller fails to make delivery or repudiates or the buyer rightfully rejects or justifiably revokes acceptance then with respect to any goods involved, and with respect to the whole if the breach goes to the whole contract (Section 2–612), the buyer may cancel and whether or not he has done so may in addition to recovering so much of the price as has been paid
   a. "cover" and have damages under the next section as to all the goods affected whether or not they have been identified to the contract; or
   b. recover damages for non-delivery as provided in this Article (Section 2–713).
2. Where the seller fails to deliver or repudiates the buyer may also
   a. if the goods have been identified recover them as provided in this Article (Section 2–502); or
   b. in a proper case obtain specific performance or replevy the goods as provided in this Article (Section 2–716).
3. On rightful rejection or justifiable revocation of acceptance a buyer has a security interest in goods in his possession or control for any payments made on their price and any expenses reasonably incurred in their inspection, receipt, transportation, care and custody and may hold such goods and resell them in like manner as an aggrieved seller (Section 2–706).

§ 2–712. "Cover"; Buyer's Procurement of Substitute Goods.

1. After a breach within the preceding section the buyer may "cover" by making in good faith and without unreasonable delay any reasonable purchase of or contract to purchase goods in substitution for those due from the seller.
2. The buyer may recover from the seller as damag-es the difference between the cost of cover and the contract price together with any incidental or consequential damages as hereinafter defined (Section 2–715), but less expenses saved in consequence of the seller's breach.
3. Failure of the buyer to effect cover within this section does not bar him from any other remedy.

§ 2–713. Buyer's Damages for Non-delivery or Repudiation.

1. Subject to the provisions of this Article with respect to proof of market price (Section 2–723), the measure of damages for non-delivery or repudiation by the seller is the difference between the market price at the time when the buyer learned of the breach and the contract price together with any incidental and consequential damages provided in this Article (Section 2–715), but less expenses saved in consequence of the seller's breach.
2. Market price is to be determined as of the place for tender or, in cases of rejection after arrival or revocation of acceptance, as of the place of arrival.

§ 2–714. Buyer's Damages for Breach in Regard to Accepted Goods.

1. Where the buyer has accepted goods and given notification (subsection (3) of Section 2–607) he may recover as damages for any non-conformity of tender the loss resulting in the ordinary course of events from the seller's breach as determined in any manner which is reasonable.
2. The measure of damages for breach of warranty is the difference at the time and place of acceptance between the value of the goods accepted and the value they would have had if they had been as warranted, unless special circumstances show proximate damages of a different amount.
3. In a proper case any incidental and consequential damages under the next section may also be recovered.

§ 2–715. Buyer's Incidental and Consequential Damages.

1. Incidental damages resulting from the seller's breach include expenses reasonably incurred in inspection, receipt, transportation and care and custody of goods rightfully rejected, any commercially reasonable charges, expenses or commissions in connection with effecting cover and any other reasonable expense incident to the delay or other breach.

2. Consequential damages resulting from the seller's breach include
   a. any loss resulting from general or particular requirements and needs of which the seller at the time of contracting had reason to know and which could not reasonably be prevented by cover or otherwise; and
   b. injury to person or property proximately resulting from any breach of warranty.

§ 2–716. Buyer's Right to Specific Performance or Replevin.

1. Specific performance may be decreed where the goods are unique or in other proper circumstances.

2. The decree for specific performance may include such terms and conditions as to payment of the price, damages, or other relief as the court may deem just.

3. The buyer has a right of replevin for goods identified to the contract if after reasonable effort he is unable to effect cover for such goods or the circumstances reasonably indicate that such effort will be unavailing or if the goods have been shipped under reservation and satisfaction of the security interest in them has been made or tendered.

§ 2–717. Deduction of Damages from the Price.
The buyer on notifying the seller of his intention to do so may deduct all or any part of the damages resulting from any breach of the contract from any part of the price still due under the same contract.

§ 2–718. Liquidation or Limitation of Damages; Deposits.

1. Damages for breach by either party may be liquidated in the agreement but only at an amount which is reasonable in the light of the anticipated or actual harm caused by the breach, the difficulties of proof of loss, and the inconvenience or nonfeasibility of

otherwise obtaining an adequate remedy. A term fixing unreasonably large liquidated damages is void as a penalty.

2. Where the seller justifiably withholds delivery of goods because of the buyer's breach, the buyer is entitled to restitution of any amount by which the sum of his payments exceeds
   a. the amount to which the seller is entitled by virtue of terms liquidating the seller's damages in accordance with subsection (1), or
   b. in the absence of such terms, twenty per cent of the value of the total performance for which the buyer is obligated under the contract or $500, whichever is smaller.

3. The buyer's right to restitution under subsection (2) is subject to offset to the extent that the seller establishes
   a. a right to recover damages under the provisions of this Article other than subsection (1), and
   b. the amount or value of any benefits received by the buyer directly or indirectly by reason of the contract.

4. Where a seller has received payment in goods their reasonable value or the proceeds of their resale shall be treated as payments for the purposes of subsection (2); but if the seller has notice of the buyer's breach before reselling goods received in part performance, his resale is subject to the conditions laid down in this Article on resale by an aggrieved seller (Section 2–706).

§ 2–719. Contractual Modification or Limitation of Remedy.

1. Subject to the provisions of subsections (2) and (3) of this section and of the preceding section on liquidation and limitation of damages,
   a. the agreement may provide for remedies in addition to or in substitution for those provided in this Article and may limit or alter the measure of damages recoverable under this Article, as by limiting the buyer's remedies to return of the goods and repayment of the price or to repair and replacement of non-conforming goods or parts; and
   b. resort to a remedy as provided is optional unless the remedy is expressly agreed to be exclusive, in which case it is the sole remedy.

2. Where circumstances cause an exclusive or limited remedy to fail of its essential purpose, remedy may be had as provided in this Act.

3. Consequential damages may be limited or excluded unless the limitation or exclusion is unconscionable. Limitation of consequential damages for injury to the person in the case of consumer goods is prima facie unconscionable but limitation of damages where the loss is commercial is not.

§ 2–720. Effect of "Cancellation" or "Rescission" on Claims for Antecedent Breach.

Unless the contrary intention clearly appears, expressions of "cancellation" or "rescission" of the contract or the like shall not be construed as a renunciation or discharge of any claim in damages for an antecedent breach.

§ 2–721. Remedies for Fraud.

Remedies for material misrepresentation or fraud include all remedies available under this Article for non-fraudulent breach. Neither rescission or a claim for rescission of the contract for sale nor rejection or return of the goods shall bar or be deemed inconsistent with a claim for damages or other remedy.

§ 2–722. Who Can Sue Third Parties for Injury to Goods.

Where a third party so deals with goods which have been identified to a contract for sale as to cause actionable injury to a party to that contract

a. a right of action against the third party is in either party to the contract for sale who has title to or a security interest or a special property or an insurable interest in the goods; and if the goods have been destroyed or converted a right of action is also in the party who either bore the risk of loss under the contract for sale or has since the injury assumed that risk as against the other;

b. if at the time of the injury the party plaintiff did not bear the risk of loss as against the other party to the contract for sale and there is no arrangement between them for disposition of the recovery, his suit or settlement is, subject to his own interest, as a fiduciary for the other party to the contract;

c. either party may with the consent of the other sue for the benefit of whom it may concern.

§ 2–723. Proof of Market Price: Time and Place.

1. If an action based on anticipatory repudiation comes to trial before the time for performance with respect to some or all of the goods, any damages based on market price (Section 2–708 or Section 2–713) shall be determined according to the price of such goods prevailing at the time when the aggrieved party learned of the repudiation.

2. If evidence of a price prevailing at the times or places described in this Article is not readily available the price prevailing within any reasonable time before or after the time described or at any other place which in commercial judgment or under usage of trade would serve as a reasonable substitute for the one described may be used, making any proper allowance for the cost of transporting the goods to or from such other place.

3. Evidence of a relevant price prevailing at a time or place other than the one described in this Article offered by one party is not admissible unless and until he has given the other party such notice as the court finds sufficient to prevent unfair surprise.

§ 2–724. Admissibility of Market Quotations.

Whenever the prevailing price or value of any goods regularly bought and sold in any established commodity market is in issue, reports in official publications or trade journals or in newspapers or periodicals of general circulation published as the reports of such market shall be admissible in evidence. The circumstances of the preparation of such a report may be shown to affect its weight but not its admissibility.

§ 2–725. Statute of Limitations in Contracts for Sale.

1. An action for breach of any contract for sale must be commenced within four years after the cause of action has accrued. By the original agreement the parties may reduce the period of limitation to not less than one year but may not extend it.

2. A cause of action accrues when the breach occurs, regardless of the aggrieved party's lack of knowledge of the breach. A breach of warranty occurs when tender of delivery is made, except that where a warranty explicitly extends to future performance of the goods and discovery of the breach must await the time of such performance the cause of action accrues when the breach is or should have been discovered.

3. Where an action commenced within the time limited by subsection (1) is so terminated as to leave available a remedy by another action for the same breach such other action may be commenced after the expiration of the time limited and within six months after the termination of the first action unless the termination resulted from voluntary discontinuance or from dismissal for failure or neglect to prosecute.

4. This section does not alter the law on tolling of the statute of limitations nor does it apply to causes of action which have accrued before this Act becomes effective.

"341" meeting the meeting of creditors required by section 341 of the Bankruptcy Code at which the debtor is questioned under oath by creditors, a trustee, examiner, or the U.S. trustee about his/her financial affairs (also called creditors' meeting)

80% or 4/5 Rule under employer's screening device minorities must perform at least 80% or 4/5 as well as the comparison group or there is a prima facie showing of disparate impact of the screening device

A

abandoned property property in which the owner has relinquished all interest

absolute guarantor a guarantor who places himself in the same position as a surety in his obligation to the creditor

absolute privilege privilege given to engage in certain behavior and no liability attached regardless of why the behavior is done

absolute surety a surety who agrees to pay the debts of another if the debtor does not pay; the creditor can file against the surety without being required to sue the debtor for the money first

acceptance after a prior rejection offer is initially rejected, then later accepted by the offeree

acceptance with varied terms UCC concept allowing offeree to vary the terms of the original offer without terminating it

accounting a detailed statement of the debits and credits between parties in a fiduciary relationship

accounts receivable money owed by customers to another entity in exchange for goods or services delivered or used but not yet paid for

accredited investors sophisticated investors who do not need the protection of the Securities Act in making investment decisions

actual authority authority that has been communicated to the agent either expressly or impliedly

administrative citations methods of enforcing pollution laws that do not necessitate resorting to the courts

administrative enforcement actions actions initiated by the EPA to determine pollution violations and impose penalties if needed

administrative law judge a judge employed by an agency to hear administrative disputes

Administrative Procedures Act law governing federal administrative agency conduct of business

administrative regulations formal agency dictates governing issues within its authority

administrative rules less formal agency determinations of issues within its authority

adverse possession right of one who does not own land to have a title transferred to him or her after occupying it openly and notoriously for a statutory period of time

affinity orientation which gender an individual is attracted to for primary relationships

affirmation maintain a statement or confirm conduct done by an agent

affirmative action intentional inclusion in the workplace of historically excluded groups such as women and minorities

affirmative action plan a plan developed to intentionally include minorities and females in the workplace when it is found they have been excluded

affirmative defense defense that may defeat the original claim, such as self-defense or assumption of the risk.

agency shop employee must pay the equivalent of union dues, but need not join the union

agency the agency relationship is a consensual relationship created when one person (the agent) acts on behalf of and subject to the control of another (the principal)

agent an agent is a person (which can include an entity, like a corporation, partnership, or LLC) who acts on behalf of and subject to the control of another

alternative dispute resolution (ADR) nonlitigation ways of resolving legal disputes

anadromous fish fish like salmon that return to rivers to breed

annual report report given to shareholders which contains financial and other information about the corporation; given annually preceding the annual meeting of the shareholders

answer defendant's response to plaintiff's complaint

antidumping the system of laws to reverse dumping

anti-female animus hostile, negative feelings about women

antitrust the area of law that governs trade regulation and competition in a capitalist market

apparent authority the power of an agent to bind the principal to unauthorized contracts. The power is created by

manifestations, which can be subtle and indirect, of the principal to the third party that are reasonably relied upon by the third party

appeal taking a case that has been decided by a court to the next-highest level for a review of the decision

appellant one who brings an appeal of a lower court decision

appellee one against whom an appeal is sought

appropriation of name or likeness intentionally using a picture, drawing or name of someone without his or her permission, generally for economic gain or advantage

arbitration disinterested third party hears dispute between parties and makes a decision based on the findings

arbitration clause a clause that provides for disputes to be resolved through the use of arbitration rather than litigation

area source any stationary source that is not a major source

arrest warrant issued by a judge calling for the arrest of the individual

articles of organization the formal papers that must be filed to form a limited liability company

artisan's lien the right given to a skilled person to retain possession of an item produced with his labor or materials until paid

assault intentionally putting a person in fear and/or apprehension of an immediate harmful or offensive bodily touching

assignee one who receives the transferred contract rights

assignment transferring contract rights to one not a party to the contract

assignor one who transfers the contract rights to another

assumption of the risk knowing a risk is present and deciding to take a chance anyway

attachment the point at which a security interest can be enforced against the debtor

audit committee a committee, usually consisting of members of the board of directors, that is responsible for determining whether the auditors have performed their duties under PCAOB

automatic perfection a perfection that occurs without the requirement of filing

automatic stay an injunction that automatically stops lawsuits, foreclosures, garnishments, and al collection activity against the debtor the moment bankruptcy petition is filed

avoidance powers authority given to a bankruptcy trustee to defeat a financing statement that is unperfected

award decision issued by an arbitrator

B

bail conditions, usually monetary, placed on the release of an arrestee pending trial or sentencing

bailment relationship created when the owner or legal possessor of persona property gives possession over to another for a period of time

bankruptcy a legal procedure for dealing with debt problems of individuals and businesses; specifically, a case filed under one of the bankruptcy chapters of the U.S. Code

Bankruptcy Code the informal name for title 11 of the U.S. Code; the federal bankruptcy law (11 U.S.C. §§101-1330)

bankruptcy court the bankruptcy judges in regular active service in each federal judicial district; a unit of the district court

bankruptcy judge a judicial officer of the U.S. district court who is the court official with decision-making power over federal bankruptcy cases

bankruptcy petition the document filed by the debtor (in a voluntary case) or by creditors (in an involuntary case) by which opens the bankruptcy case

bargaining unit group of employees with a community of interests who form a unit for bargaining purposes

battery intentional unpermitted or offensive touching of the body of another

bench trial a trial before a judge without a jury

bequeath disposition of property by will

beyond a reasonable doubt prosecutor's burden of proof in criminal cases

bid rigging interference with the competitive bidding for the award of a contract

bilateral contract an agreement in which both parties promise something

binding arbitration agreement in advance to be bound by the arbitrator's decision

Blue sky laws state laws that regulate securities transactions

blue sky laws state securities law that regulate the sale of securities in the state

board of directors those members of the corporation who are responsible for making the decisions for the corporation

board of directors the board of directors is responsible for making major decisions that govern the direction of the corporation

bona fide occupational qualification legalized discrimination permitted because the basis for discrimination is necessary for the employer to perform its business

bootleg illegal copies of copyrighted material sold or shown to the public

boycott the refusal to deal with either a competitor or customer to affect competition

breach if one of the parties does not perform as promised

breach of contract party to a contract not performing the contract as promised

bribe a payment resulting in the payer's receiving some right, benefit, or preference to which he has no legal right and which he would not have obtained except with the payment of the money

business agent one who represents the unions to the employer

business judgment rule a rule applied to directors that gives them the presumption of correctness in the decisions they make on behalf of the corporation

business necessity a nondiscriminatory reason for an employer's policy which seems to discriminate against a protected class

Bylaws a set of rules for governing the internal affairs of the corporation

C

capitalist markets markets that rely on free enterprise system of marketing

caps limitations on the amount of pollution that can be emitted

card check bargaining unit employees submit cards indicating whether they wish to have a union

cartel two or more individuals or firms who have colluded together to fix prices

cartel an agreement between competitors to control the market in which they compete

case or controversy two expressions used interchangeably to describe situations sufficiently defined as to be within the power of the court to decide

case of first impression a case that presents the court with issues never before decided by a court in that jurisdiction

categorical imperative decision is based on asking how the actor would want others to treat him or her

cause of action legally recognized basis for a lawsuit

certification marks used to indicate that certain goods originated in a particular area or region, or that the products are of a particular nature, quality, or characteristic

challenge objection to prospective jurors sitting on a jury

challenge for cause prospective juror does not meet statutory qualifications or is personally unfit for jury service

chapter 7 the chapter of bankruptcy code providing for liquidation , i.e., the sale o a debtor's non-exempt property and the distribution of the proceeds to creditors

chapter 9 the chapter of the bankruptcy code providing for reorganization of municipalities (which includes cities and towns as well as villages, counties, taxing districts, municipal utilities, and school districts)

chapter 11 the chapter in the bankruptcy code providing for reorganization, usually involving a corporation ro partnership

chapter 12 the chapter of the bankruptcy code providing for adjustment of debts of family farmer or a family fisherman

chapter 13 the chapter of the bankruptcy code providing for adjustment of debts of an individual with regular income

chattel paper a writing that evidences both a monetary obligation and a security interest in or a lease of specific goods

checks and balances one branch of government has the right to give input regarding decisions of the primary authority branch of government

circuit jurisdictional area of a court

civil law law governing noncriminal violations of law

clear and convincing evidence burden of proof that plaintiff must carry in more serious civil case in which there has been loss of life or heavy property damage, showing clearly that events occurred as plaintiff alleges

closed shop employee must be member of union as a condition of employment at unionized workplace and can be terminated for any reason he or she ceases to be a union member

closely held corporation a corporation whose shares are owned by individuals usually related to each other or family and whose shares are not traded publicly

closing argument argument made by lawyers at close of the evidence urging judge or jury to reach the decision each side desires

Code of Federal Regulations compilation of federal regulations issued by agencies

collateral the property subject to a security interest

collective bargaining agreement agreement reached between the employer and the union

collective mark goods or services produced by members of a collective group

collusion entering into an agreement to perform an illegal act

commercial arbitration addresses virtually all disputes to be arbitrated other than labor

community of interests employees who perform similar jobs at the workplace and have similar bargaining issues

comparable worth comparing the worth of jobs to the employer to determine the rate of pay for the job

comparative negligence comparing the plaintiff's negligence with the defendant's negligence and deducting from plaintiff's award a percentage equal to plaintiff's share of the responsibility

compensatory damages money given by defendant to plaintiff to compensate for injury

complaint initial pleading alleging a violation by a court

computer crime the intentional use of a computer to commit fraud or for other illegal purposes

conciliation parties with a dispute attempt to resolve it by communicating with each other

concurrent conditions acts on the part of each party to a contract which must take place at the same time in order for the parties' duties to perform arises

concurrent jurisdiction jurisdiction exercised simultaneously by more than one court over the same subject matter and within the same territory

condition precedent some act which must take place before the duty of a party to perform under a contract arises

condition subsequent some act, which if it takes place, ends the duty of a party to perform under a contract

conglomerate merger mergers between firms that had no prior relationship

conscious parallelism the tendency for competitors in a small market to act the same way in pricing, discounts, and marketing of their products

consent giving someone permission to do an act

consequential damages damages arising from circumstances that could have been anticipated

conspiracy an agreement by two or more persons to commit an unlawful act

contingency fee arrangement arrangement allowing plaintiff to pay attorney a certain percentage of judgment if plaintiff wins suit

contract a bargained-for legal detriment exchanged between the parties

contribution the right of a surety who has paid all of the debt owned to the creditor to have his co-sureties repay him for their proportionate amount

contributory negligence plaintiff engaging in an act of negligence which contributes to the harm arising from the negligence of another

controlling shareholder a shareholder that owns enough shares that he can effect the election

conversion seriously interfering with the personal property of another

copyright protection offered to authors, illustrators, photographers, musical composers and lyricists for their work

corruption the act of doing something with an intent to give some advantage inconsistent with official duty and the rights of others

corruptly an offer, payment, promise, or gift intended to induce the recipient to misuse his official position in order to wrongfully direct business to the payor

cost justification defense a defense to a violation of the Robinson-Patman Act which allows a seller to give discounts to a buyer if the discount represents a lower cost to the seller

Council on Environmental Quality the council that is responsible for reporting to Congress and the President the status of the environment

counterclaim lawsuit filed against the opposing party

counteroffer terminates the original offer and creates a new offer by the old offeree who now becomes the offeror

countervailing duty a duty imposed on products manufactured with the help of foreign government subsidies, which are sold for less money in the domestic market, thereby hurting the businesses that are competing in the domestic market

court of Appeal courts above the trial level that hears cases on review from lower courts

court-annexed ADR ADR done as part of a court's procedures before litigation in hopes of avoiding litigation

court-ordered dissolution the breakup of an entity ordered by a court of law rather than by agreement of the parties

craft union union organized around a specific craft, detached from a particular workplace

credit counseling the instructional course in personal financial management in chapters 7 and 13 that an individual debtor must complete before discharge is entered

creditor one to whom the debtor owes money or who claims to be owed money by the debtor

crime Violation of criminal law, which may result in incarceration and or a fine

criminal law law governing criminal matters

cross-claim lawsuit brought by one defendant against another defendant

cross-examination examination of a witness by the opposing party

custody under physical restraint by law enforcement

custom a principle or practice that has developed over time and is accepted as binding on the parties to the custom

cyberpirates those who incorporate others' similar sounding names into theirs to gain benefit from the name confusion

cybersquatters those who purchased domain names belonging to others for monetary gain

D

de minimis not substantial; just a small part of something

de novo like new

de novo review court review of agency decision as if issue had not already been litigated

debar preventing contractors from engaging in further government contracts

debt securities a type of security carried by a company that represents a debt carried by the company, usually represented by bank loans, bonds, or debentures

debtor a person who has filed a petition under the bankruptcy code; a person who owes payment or performance of an obligation

decree the decision of a court of equity

deed legal document representing ownership of real estate

deep pockets theory plaintiff suing for tort committed by an employee in the course business sues the business owner, who is thought to have more money to pay a judgment

defalcation diversion, misapplication, misappropriation, misuse, embezzlement or theft of funds by some employee, executive, or official entrusted with those funds

defamation intentionally making false statements about someone to a third person, which has the effect of lessening their reputation in the community

default debtor failing to repay a loan to creditor

default failure to act

defendant party against whom a lawsuit is filed

defendant the one who is sued in a lawsuit

definite acceptance acceptance of a UCC offer indicating assent to the offer

delegatee the one to whom such duties are delegated

delegation transferring contract duties to one not a party to the contract

delegator the one who delegates his or her duties

deposition sworn testimony of a witness or party prior to trial, given under oath before a court reporter, for later use in court

design defect product liability action based on product's being designed in such a way as its ordinary use causes harm to user or others

design patent covers any new original and ornamental design for an article of manufacture

designing for the environment businesses consider the potential environmental impact of a product and the process to make that product

direct examination first examination of one's own witness at trial

direct sale the sale of goods arranged directly between the buyer and the seller

disaffirm legal right to get out of a contract

discharge a release of a debtor from personal liability for certain dischargeable debts set forth in the bankruptcy code

dischargeable debt a debt for which the Bankruptcy Code allows the debtor's personal liability to be eliminated

disclosed principal a principal is disclosed when a third party has notice of the principal's existence and identity. Under

such circumstances, the agent acting in the transaction is not a party to the resulting contract in the absence of special facts, like guaranteeing contracts

disclosure statement a written document prepared by a Chapter 11 debtor or other plan proponent designed to provide "adequate information" to creditors to enable them to evaluate the Chapter 11 plan of reorganization

discovery procedure by which information is requested from opponent in preparation for trial

disparagement intentionally making false statements about the quality or ownership of someone's goods

disparate impact effect of facially neutral policy is deleterious for Title VII group

disparate treatment treating employee different from those similarly situated because of a prohibited Title VII factor

dissociation the withdrawal or expulsion of a partner under the Revised Uniform Partnership Act

dissolution the first step in terminating a partnership

diversity of citizenship jurisdiction jurisdiction of federal courts based on controversy between citizens of different states and amount involved

doctrine of inevitable disclosure gives a former employer an opportunity to stop a former employee from taking another job because of possible disclosure of trade secrets

document any negotiable or nonnegotiable document that is not an instrument

domain names address on the Internet or in the World Wide Web

domestic concern any business with its principal place of business in the U.S. under the FPCA

domestic corporation a corporation incorporated in the state

donee one who receives a gift

donee beneficiary one who is to receive benefits under a contract as a gift from a party to the contract

donor one who gives a gift

double jeopardy a doctrine that defendant cannot be tried twice for same crime

downstream merger merger that occurs when the supplier acquires the purchaser

dual-use commodities a commodity that can be used for commercial and military purposes

due process of law notice and an opportunity to be heard before government takes a right

dumping the sale of goods in a foreign market for a price that is lower than the price of the goods sold in the home market

duress exerting pressure on a party to influence them to enter into a contract

duty a tax levied by a government on the import, export or consumption of goods

E

eighth amendment constitutional amendment that protects against cruel and unusual punishment and ensures the right to bail

electronically stored information (ESI) information contained in electronic format

embezzlement the fraudulent taking of personal property with which one has been entrusted, especially as a fiduciary

eminent domain government's right to take property for government use, with fair market value to the owner

enabling statute statute that creates an administrative agency

enabling statute statute passed by the legislature creating an agency to which limited powers are delegated

encryption process designed to protect copyrighted works from theft

endangered species a species that is in danger of extinction

entrenchment decrease in market share caused when one firm acquires another firm that is already near monopoly size

Environmental Assessment a document that serves to provide sufficient evidence and analysis for determining whether to prepare an environmental impact statement

Environmental Impact Statement statement that details the impacts to the environment from the studied project

environmental management system an approach that plans and manages an environmental response

equitable remedies remedy beyond law, applying equitable principles

equity the area of law which goes beyond legalities and instead addresses the fairness of situations

equity security a security that represents an interest in the equity of the business – an asset. In a corporation, equity securities are usually considered to be common and preferred shares

estates (interests)　legal right to property recognized by law

estate for years　right to own property for a specified period

ethics　subjective rules to ensure that decisions are in keeping with avoidance of conflicts of interests or other factors that could cause potential harm

exclusive dealing agreement　supplier agrees to supply buyer with product only if buyer does not stock products of supplier's competitor

exclusive jurisdiction　a court's power to decide an action to the exclusion of all other courts

exclusive selling agreement　an agreement to sell only to a particular dealer in a specified territory

executed contract　one which has been performed as agreed

executive branch of government　primarily responsible for executing the laws

executive order　an order issued by the president or governor implementing a statute or governing operations of executive agencies

executory contract　a contract which has been made, but not yet performed

exempt securities　securities that are not subject to SEC filing because they are being offered to accredited investors or are small in size

exhaustion of administrative remedies　completing all requirements within agency for review of its decisions

exoneration　the right of the surety to force the debtor to pay his debt once it becomes due

export　to ship an item away from a country for sale in another country

export control　to exercise control over exports for statistical and strategic purposes

export management company　a private firm that serves as the export department for several manufacturers, soliciting and transacting export business on behalf of its clients in return for a commission, salary, or retainer plus commission

export trading company　a business organized and operated principally for the purpose of exporting goods and services to other companies

express authority　authority that has been stated to the agent orally or in writing

express contract　a contract which parties actually discuss and which may, or not, be committed to writing

express warranty　written or oral promise from seller about how a good will perform

external auditors　auditors hired by the corporation to evaluate the internal controls over financial reporting by the corporation

F

failure to adequately package goods　product liability action based on manufacturer of good failing to package goods in such a way as to prevent harm from normal use

failure to adequately warn　product liability action based on manufacturer of good failing to adequately notify purchaser or user of common potential danger in using the product

fair-use doctrine　copyright doctrine allowing material to be used as long as it meets the requirements of the doctrine

false imprisonment　intentionally confining someone to a place with no reasonable means of exit

false light　intentionally publishing something about someone which gives an incorrect impression of or about them, though the actual publication may be true

Federal Arbitration Act　applies to commercial agreements that affect interstate commerce

federal district court　court established by federal law

Federal Mediation and Conciliation Service (FMCS)　government agency that can be used by parties to conduct mediation of a dispute

federal question jurisdiction　judicial power of the United States extending to cases arising under the Constitution, the laws of the United States, and treaties.

Federal Register　official notification organ of the federal agencies

fees　an amount an employee must pay that is the equivalent of union dues, but need not belong to the union

fee simple　ownership of property without restrictions except by the government

felony　serious crimes resulting in prison time of a year or more

Fiduciary　one who acts primarily for the benefit of another

fifth amendment　constitutional amendment that protects against self-incrimination

Financial Industry Regulatory Authority (FINRA)　the organization responsible for regulatory oversight of all securities firms that do business with the public

financing statement　statement files with the clerk of the local court indicating a security interest in collateralized property

fixed image　requirement for a copyright to be issued; cannot be fleeting image

forbearance　not doing something one could legally do if one wanted to

foreclosure　the result of a firm that is acquired that formerly supplied the nonmerged firm

foreign corporation　a corporation incorporated in another state

forward looking statements　statements contained in the MD&A which are projections for future performance of the corporation

fourth amendment　constitutional amendment that protects against unreasonable searches and seizures by police or other government official

franchise　a licensed business that uses the name of the franchisor's product in the business

fraud in the execution　intentionally misrepresenting that a writing is something other than the contract it actually is

fraud in the inducement　intentionally misrepresenting material facts about a matter in order to induce a party to enter into an agreement

fraud　intentionally making untrue statements to a person in order to get him or her to enter into an agreement

free riders　bargaining unit employees covered by a collective bargaining agreement who do not belong to the union or pay the dues equivalent

fresh start　the characterization of a debtor's status after bankruptcy, i.e., free of most debts. (Giving debtors a fresh start is one purpose of the Bankruptcy Code.)

G

gap filling　UCC concept of court or parties being able to fill in blanks in a contract when UCC provides rules for such

general agent　an agent who is authorized to transact all the business of the principal of a particular kind

General Agreement on Tariff and Trade (GATT)　agreement between the United States and several other countries about trading among the nations

general intangibles　any personal property that is not an account, chattel paper, document, instrument, goods or money as identified in UCC Article 9

general jurisdiction court without limits as concerns the amount in controversy, the nature of the penalty it may adjudge, or the type of case it may consider within a broad jurisdictional area

geographic market local, regional, national, or global area in which antitrust conduct is measured as competitive or anticompetitive group boycott agreement among two or more competitors not to deal with another business or individual

gift transfer of property to another with the intent to convey title and possession with no exchange by the receiver

gift causa mortis gift given by donor to donee in contemplation of the donor's death

goods tangible personal property which is movable

goods UCC defines as tangible, movable, personal property

government corporation a corporationthat is created to administer a unit of local civil government, such as a county, city, town, village, school district, or one created by the U.S. government to conduct pubic business

grand jury the group of individuals selected to be on the panel to hear evidence presented by the prosecution in order to return, or not, an indictment

grantee one who receives an interest in property from a grantor

grantor property owner who conveys it to another

gratuitous promise promise to give someone something without receiving anything in return

gray market goods goods manufactured in a country other than the United States, bearing a valid U.S. trademark, and imported into the U.S. without the consent of the U.S. trademark holder

grease payments payments that facilitate or expedite the performance of a routine service

group boycott agreement among two or more competitors not to deal with another business or individual

guarantor person or company that agrees to be obligated for the debts of another under a separate contract with the oblige

guarantor for collection guarantor who is obligated to pay creditor only after creditor performs due diligence in trying to collect from the debtor

H

habeas corpus a writ to ask the court to review the legality of imprisoning a defendant

hacking gaining unauthorized access to a computer or computer system

hazardous waste waste that has properties that make it dangerous or potentially harmful to human's health or the environment

holding a court's determination of a matter of law pivotal to its decision

horizontal per se violation antitrust violations among and between competitors

hostile environment sexual harassment sexual harassment in which the harasser creates an offensive, hostile or intimidating environment for the harassee

hung jury in a criminal case, a jury that is unable to decide guilt or innocence of defendant

I

identity theft taking of a person's identity through theft of personal or financial information and using it for the benefit of the thief

immunity an exemption from a duty, liability, or service of process

impeach to discredit a witness

implied authority authority that an agent has a reason to belief he has been given permission to have based on words or actions by the principal

implied in fact contracts contracts gathered from the acts of the parties exhibiting an intent to contract

implied in law contracts contracts imposed by law upon the parties in an effort to prevent unjust enrichment by one party at the expense of the other

implied warranty of habitability implicit right of a tenant that the premises be minimally safe and livable

implied warranty promises arising from sale of a good that it will be fit for its normal purpose

import a foreign-produced good or service that is sold in the domestic country

import duties charges imposed on goods coming into one country from another

in rem jurisdiction process by which the court gains jurisdiction of a person whose whereabouts are out of reach or unknown

indemnify to make good a loss that someone has suffered because of another's act or default

independent contractor a person who contracts with another to do something but who is not controlled by the other with respect to his physical conduct in the performance

indictment the formal written accusation of a crime made by a grand jury and presented to a court for prosecution

indispensable paper chattel paper, instruments, and documents

industrial union union organized around particular jobs at a workplace

infringe use copyrighted or patented material in violation of the legal protection

initial public offering (IPO) the first public offering of securities by a corporation or other business that is registered under the Securities Act of 1933

injunction court order directing something to be done or not to be done

injurious falsehood another term for disparagement

inside information information of a corporation held by a person who has a relationship with the corporation that is not known to the public

insider the person who has the inside information

insider a term that refers to people having some relationship to an issuer and whose securities trading on the basis of nonpublic information may be a violation of law

insider trading the purchase or sale of a security while in possession of non-public, material information about the security

instrument any paper that evidences a right to payment of money that is not itself a security agreement

intangibles accounts that are not evidenced by chattel paper or an instrument

intellectual property concepts, information, symbols, or creative expression attributable to a person or group

intentional infliction of emotional distress intentionally doing an act which goes outside all bounds of common decency, thereby causing serious emotional distress to another

intentional interference with contractual relations intentionally interfering with either established or prospective contractual relations between two or more parties

intentional tort torts based on the intentional acts of another

inter vivos gift gift given by the donor to the donee during the donor's lifetime

intergovernmental organizations organizations made up of sovereignties who are members of the organization

international organizations organizations, either IGOs or NGOs that are involved in trade or humanitarian efforts

Internet fraud any fraudulent scheme that uses email or a website to solicit fraudulent transfers of money or information to unknown parties

interrogated the questioning of an individual by the police

interrogatories written questions about the case sent by opposing party or witness for answers and for return to sending attorney

intrusion upon seclusion intentionally coming into someone's private space, photographing them there, or tapping their phone or listening to their conversations

invasion of privacy interfering with someone's legitimate expectation of privacy through one of the four recognized means

issuer any public company subject to the SEC reporting requirements of the FCPA

issuer the corporation, government agency, local authority, or international organization that generates a security

J

Jim Crow set of legal and social policies that segregated blacks and whites from about 1865 to about 1964

joint tenant with right of survivorship multiple landowners with an undivided interest that goes to the remaining owners upon the death of an owner

joint venture a commercial enterprise organized by the participants who control and share its profits and losses

judgment judges formal determination of a controversy, which details the outcome, how the outcome was arrived at, and its consequences

judgment not withstanding verdict judgment given to side that lost by verdict

judicial branch of government primarily responsible for interpreting laws

judicial review review of an agency decision by a court of law

jurisdiction authority of a court over parties and subject matter to hear and determine legal disputes

jurisprudence the study of various theories of law

L

landlord one who owns real property and allows another to possess it for a period

law limitations imposed upon society by government to protect, govern relationships, and provide predictability and security in our persons, possessions and relationships

legal benefit obtaining a benefit to which one is not otherwise entitled in the absence of contract

legal brief written statement of facts and law supporting one side of a case and presented to the court

legal detriment a party doing something they do not have to do, or not doing something they could do if they wanted to

legal positivism legal philosophy based on the law being that which the sovereign says it is

legal realism legal philosophy which considers sociology, economics, politics or other factors in deciding the law

legislative branch of government primarily responsible for creating laws

libel written defamation

license an agreement giving the licensee permission to produce or distribute the licenser's product under the licenser's name

life estate right to own property during the duration of the measuring life to which the life estate is linked

life tenant one who owns a life estate

limited jurisdiction court limited by statute in one or more respects as to what types of cases it may handle

limited liabilitycompany a form of business that is a hybrid between a partnership and a corporation

limited partnership a partnership consisting of at least one general partner and limited partners

limited review court review of agency decision only to determine if it is unconstitutional, arbitrary, capricious or otherwise not in accordance with law

liquidated damages damages predetermined by the parties before breach

liquidation a sale of a debtor's property with the proceeds to be used for the benefit of creditors

littoral rights rights of owners of lake front property

long-arm statute a statute which gives jurisdiction over a party in a foreign jurisdiction that has minimum contacts within the state

lost property personal property accidentally allowed to leave owner or possessor's possession or control

M

Magnuson-Moss Warranty Act provides that if a manufacturer provides a warranty for goods, it must meet certain requirements to be effective to protect the manufacturer from breach of warranty claims

mail fraud an act of fraud using the U.S. Postal Service

mailbox or deposited acceptance rule once an acceptance is deposited in the system used for communication, it is a valid acceptance and creates a contract

main purpose doctrine if the main reason one acts as a surety is for his or her own personal advantage, surety contract is enforceable though oral

major source a stationary source or group of stationary sources that emit 10 tons per year or more of a hazardous air pollutant

Management's Discussion and Analysis (MD&A) a section of the annual report that discusses the corporation through the eyes of management; may contain forward looking statements that identify trends and possible occurrences

manager-managed the form of governance of a limited liability company that resembles a corporation

mandatory injunction court order that a thing be done

mandatory subjects of bargaining wages, hours and other terms or conditions of employment about which an employer must bargain

manufacturing defect product liability action based on manufacturer failing to manufacture the good well

market power when a seller can force a purchaser to buy a product which the purchaser would not normally do except for the restricted output by the seller

market share the percentage of the market owned by a specific competitor

market structure market analysis that depends on the overall competitive economic structure of the market

material information information that a reasonable person would consider important when making a decision

material statement information that a reasonable person would attach importance to in determining a course of action

means test an investigation into the financial well-being of a person to determine the person's eligibility for financial assistance or bankruptcy

mechanic's lien the right given to a skilled person to retain possession of an item produced with his labor or materials until paid

mediation disinterested third party attempts to talk to disputing parties to try to help them reach a resolution

meeting competition defense a defense to the Robinson-Patman Act that allows the seller to offer a discount to the buyer if it is done to meet prices of the competition

member-managed the form of governance of a limited liability company that resembles a partnership

merchant's firm offer merchant states in signed writing that offer will remain open for stated period, not to exceed 90 days

merger two businesses coming together to form a larger version of one of the businesses

minimum contacts a nonresident's forum-state connections, such as business activity, substantial enough to bring the defendant within the personal jurisdiction of the court

minitrial presentation of business conflict before business people to enhance chance of settlement and avoid trial

mirror image rule restatement rule requiring the offeree's acceptance not change the offer in any way

misappropriation the application of another's property or money dishonestly to one's own use

misappropriation taking of a trade secret without authority and disclosing it to the pubic

misappropriation the theory that permits a person to be prosecuted for trading on inside information when the information comes from the employer, either directly or indirectly, to the misappropriator

misdemeanor less serious crimes, resulting in jail time of less than a year or a fine

mislaid property personal property placed by the owner or possessor who has forgotten where it was placed

mitigate damages party to whom damages are due attempts to make the harm less

mitigation measures measures that can be taken to reduce the harm to the environment

mock trial pretend trial presented before group of people to see how they react to presentation of evidence before it is actually presented in court to find weaknesses

monopoly power to control prices and exclude competition

monopsony a *buyer* that has price and quantity power over goods or services, as opposed to a seller

morals personal rules of what is right and wrong for an individual

most-favored-nation (MFN) status status given to countries allowing them to enjoy impost duties no higher that those of the most favored nation

motion formal request by an attorney that a court decide a matter

motion for a new trial request to judge, made by the losing party, that new trial be granted because of error committed during trial

moving party the party that makes the motion to the court.

multilateral instrument agreement between several nations

Municipal Securities Rulemaking Board (MSRB) agency created by Congress to adopt investor protection rules governing broker-dealers, banks that underwrite, trade, or sell tax-exempt bonds, college savings plans, and other types of municipal securities

mutual assent true agreement between the parties as to the contract's terms

mutual ignorance both parties know they do not know one or more factors about the subject matter of a contract, and they enter into a contract about the subject matter anyway

mutual mistake both parties think they are agreeing to the same contract terms, but unbeknownst to them, they are agreeing to terms different from each other's

N

natural law legal philosophy in which law is based upon certain factors or morals which are universal, unchangeable and dictated by God

necessaries generally defined as food, clothing or shelter

negligence failure to meet the standard of care of a reasonable person under the circumstances

negligence per se negligence arising from violation of a statute

negotiable instrument an instrument that can be freely negotiated, i.e., bought, sold, or pledged, on the open market, including securities

no-asset case a chapter 7 case where there are no assets available to satisfy any portion of the creditors' unsecured claims

nominal damages damages awarded as acknowledgment that legal right was invaded, but little harm done

nonbinding arbitration agreement to arbitrate the conflict, but not to be bound by the arbitrator's decision

noncertificated stock stock that has no certificate issued for it and which is traded electronically

nongovernmental organizations nonprofit organizations that pursue humanitarian activities

nonobviousness requirement for receiving a patent that it not be readily apparent

nonpoint source pollution that comes from many sources

nonregistered stock that is not registered on the records of the corporation as being owned by a specific person; allows the stock to be traded by whoever is in possession of it

nontariff barriers any import quotas or quantitative restrictions, nonautomatic import licensing, customs surcharges, etc., which deny or make access difficult for goods or services

no-strike, no-lockout clause agreement prohibiting or limiting employee strikes and employer locking employees out of workplace

Not for profit corporation a corporation that is organized for a charitable, education, or scientific purpose and who does not distribute profits to its shareholders

notice of proposed rulemaking notice by agency, published in Federal Register, that agency is contemplating issuing regulations

novation agreement between obligor, assignor and assignee to allow assignor to be released from the contract and the assignee be put in the assignor's place

novelty requirement of differentness required for patent

O

obligee the person to receive another's performance under a contract

obligor the person obligated to perform under a contract

obstruction of justice interference with the orderly administration of law and justice

offeree one who receives an offer

offeror one who gives an offer

Officers those members of the corporation who are charged with managing the affairs of the corporation

oligopoly a form of competition where the products are similar and are distinguished through advertising

ombudsperson employee charged by employer with hearing and investigating potential disputes in order to avoid escalation

open shop employee need not join a union or pay the equivalent of union dues and cannot be terminated for joining union

opening statement statements by attorneys at beginning of trial outlining the case and what they expect the evidence to show

operating agreement rules in a limited liability company that are the equivalent of corporate bylaws

operation of law a status created on the facts alone, without any other formal legal action by the parties affected

option contract contract of offeror promising to keep offer open for promisee for a stated period

oral arguments verbal presentation by attorneys in court aimed at persuading a judge of their view

organizations an international body that is recognized by most countries as having rule-making capabilities to which those nations adhere

original jurisdiction jurisdiction if a appellate court to try a case

P

palming off passing off one 's, generally inferior, goods as goods of better quality

part performance exception allows an oral contract for land to be enforceable if the party moves on, makes improvements, and pays part of the consideration

Partially disclosed principal a principal is partially disclosed when the third party has notice that the agent is acting on behalf of someone but does not know the identity of the principal

partition court decree separating jointly held property into individual interests

partnership a voluntary joining together for business purposes by two or more persons of money, goods, labor and skill

past consideration the giving of something of value prior to a party agreeing to give something in return under a contract

patent protection for inventors allowing exclusive control of the invention

per se violation violation of antitrust laws which, whether reasonable or not, is illegal

peremptory strikes objections to prospective jurors made without explanation; limited to criminal cases

perfection the point at which the security interest will be valid against third parties, including a bankruptcy trustee

perjury the making of a material false or misleading statement while under oath

permanent injunction injunction granted as part of a judgment after full determination of rights of the parties

permanent normal trade relations status formerly, most-favored-nation (MFN) status, imposes a duty on member nations to exact the same tariffs on every country and requires that the importing country treat imported goods from member countries as though they are domestic goods

permissive subjects of bargaining nonmandatory workplace terms about which management may bargain with the union

Piercing the corporate veil what occurs when a shareholder of a closely held corporation loses the limited liability feature of the corporation

plaintiff the party initiating a civil legal proceeding

plant patent patents for any new and distinct variety of plant

plea bargain a negotiated agreement between a prosecutor and a criminal defendant whereby the defendant pleads guilty to a lesser offense or to one of multiple charges in exchange for some kind of lenient sentence or dismissal of the other charges

pleadings in civil cases, litigant's' written statements of their claims and responses in forms prescribed by a court

point source discrete, identifiable sources of discharge into water

political questions issues that do not present a case or controversy, but rather a dispute between two branches of government or within a single branch of government

pollution anything that, upon exposure, will or may reasonably be anticipated to cause specified harmful health effects

ponzi scheme a type of pyramid scheme where the money of later investors is used to pay dividends to early investors, but where no money is actually being invested

practical availability defense a defense to the Robinson-Patman Act which excuses violations if the discount offered the buyer is practically available to competitors of the seller

precedent previously decided cases that must be considered when similar cases arise for decision

predatory pricing selling products below costs which creates a dangerous probability of creating a successful monopoly

pre-existing contractual or legal obligation a legal requirement imposed by law or contract, which exists prior to the time a party agrees by contract to do what is already required

preliminary injunctions injunction granted after hearing before a judge in advance of trial, to last until the granting or denial of a permanent injunction

preponderance of the evidence usual burden of proof that plaintiff must bear in a civil case, showing that it was more likely than not that events occurred as plaintiff alleges

pretrial time period between filings of pleadings and trial, during which discovery is completed

price discrimination discrimination in price between different purchasers of commodities of like grade and quality

price discrimination charging different prices to buyers of the same product in the same time period

price fixing the artificial setting of prices at a certain level contrary to the workings of the free market

price fixing - an agreement by marketers of a product to set prices for a certain item

prima facie case proof of all the legal elements needed for a cause of action

principal the one for whom action is taken. The action is taken on behalf of and subject to the principal's control

prior appropriation doctrine for allocation of water rights in some states

priority the statutory ranking of unsecured claims that determines the order in which claims will be paid if there is not enough money to pay all claims in full

private law law involving rights between private citizens

privity of contract requirement that there be a contract between the injured party and the tortfeasor in order to recover for harm done by the product

probable cause a reasonable, particularized basis for believing an arrest is necessary

procedural law laws and regulations governing the exercise of substantive rights provided by law

product liability negligence action for harm caused by goods placed in the stream of commerce

product market all of the products that are available to a buyer that are similar in price, use, and quality

professional association an association which permits the practice of professions by duly licensed individuals under the corporate form

promissory estoppel court stops someone who made a promise to another, knowing it would likely be relied upon to the detriment of the relying party, when the party moves in reliance on the promise not supported by adequate consideration

promoter the person working behind the scenes to start a corporation; the promoter is in a fiduciary relationship with the future shareholders of the corporation

proposals for addition to the contract the new terms added to the original offer by offeree

prospectus a document furnished to a potential purchaser of a security that describes the security being purchased, the issuer, and the investment or risk characteristics of the security

proximate cause legal cause of negligence for which law will impose liability

proxy solicitation the process by which proxies are obtained from shareholders of publicly held corporations to voting purposes

proxy statement the document that must accompany a proxy solicitation under SEC regulations; the proxy statement provides the shareholders with enough information to make an intelligent decision

Public Company Accounting Oversight Board (PCAOB) the nonprofit company designed to oversee the auditors of public companies

Public Company Accounting Oversight Board (PCAOB) an agency created by the Sarbanes-Oxley Act that is charged with overseeing, regulating, and disciplining accounting firms when they act as auditors of corporations

public corporation a corporation operating for profit and whose shares are traded on an exchange

public domain works whose copyright has expired or never existed and whose works are freely usable by the public

public law law dealing with the government in its operations or the relationship between the government and its citizens

public trust doctrine theory that resources are held in trust for public use

publication requirement that defamatory statements be made in presence of someone other than the speaker and person spoken about

publication of private facts intentionally publishing information about someone which is a private matter

punitive damages damages awarded in civil case to punish wrongdoer

purchase exchange of property for agreed upon consideration

purchase money security interest (PMSI) an interest that automatically attaches to the purchase of consumer goods

Q

qualified privilege no liability for engaging in certain behavior as long as the behavior follows prescribed guidelines

quantum meruit payment for reasonable value of services or goods imposed by law in a transaction where one would otherwise be unjustly enriched by not being required to pay because element of valid contract is missing

quasi like, or as if

quasi contract appears to be a contract, but generally lacks mutual assent; another name for contracts implied in law

quasi-judicial agency authority to hear disputes

quasi-legislative power authority to issue regulations in prescribed areas as permitted by an agency's enabling statute

quasi-legislative administrative agency authority to issue rules and regulations

quid pro quo sexual harassment sexual harassment in which the harasser requests sexual activity from the harassee in exchange for workplace benefits

R

Racketeer Influenced and Corrupt Organizations Act (RICO) a law designed to attack organized criminal activity and preserve marketplace integrity by investigating, controlling, and prosecuting persons who participate in racketeering

Ratification a person's binding adoption of an act already completed

ratify acts or words evidencing a wish to go through with a contract despite an impediment to contracting

reciprocity occurs when one firm agrees to purchase items from another firm that agrees to purchase products from it

red herring prospectus a prospectus available to potential purchasers of an initial public offering of a company that has not yet completed registration with the SEC

redlining discriminatory business practice influenced by a customer's being located within a particular area rather than by a customer's individual characteristics

Referral Back programs agreement between EEOC and employers that EEOC will hold EEOC claim filed by employer's employee and refer it back to the employer for mediation by employer's own EEOC-approved internal mediation program

registered stock stock whose owner is registered in the records of the corporation; only the registered owner can trade or receive the benefits of registered stock

registration statement a statement filed with the SEC that contains a prospectus and additional information made available to the public before stock is placed on the market for sale

regulatory negotiation mediation between agency and interested constituents about regulations the agency is contemplating promulgating

reimbursement the right of the surety to be paid for paying the debt owed by the debtor to the creditor

rejection offeree does not accept an offer

remainder estate conveyed to one not grantor or grantee after a life estate or estate for years

remedy award of money damage or order to do or refrain from doing something

renounce give up or cast off

rent possession of the property of another for an agreed period

reply plaintiff's response to defendant's answer

report up the obligation of an attorney who discovers evidence of a material violation of the federal or state law to report to the legal officer or committee of his organization

reporting out the withdrawal of representation by an attorney whose company insists on continuing criminal activity that will injure the corporation

request for production of documents discovery tool whereby evidence is produced for examination by the opposing party

rescission contract undone by parties or court order

respondeat superior employer is held responsible for torts committed by employees in the course of employment

respondeat superior a Latin phrase that means "let the master answer." It is a shorthand expression for the doctrine that a master or employer is vicariously liable for the torts of its servants or employee committed within the scope of employment

restatement of Agency 3d reference to a series of volumes prepared and published by the American Law Institute in the area of Agency law

restatement of Contracts compilation of states' contract law into one source with suggested approaches which states can adopt if they wish, in whole or in part

restitution giving back to contract party something they gave other party under the contract

restraining order an court order prohibiting behavior or contact, or preventing the dissipation of funds or loss of property

restraint of trade behavior that limits free enterprise and free trade among competitors

retainer amount paid to an attorney to take a case

reverse discrimination majority group members feel adversely affected by affirmative action

reverse engineering a process for gleaning information about proprietary products from publicly disclosed goods or services

reversion estate that returns to the grantor after an life estate or estate for years

revocation offeror takes back an offer

right to sue letter letter from EEOC to claimant giving claimant the right to take an EEOC claim to court if the claimant is not satisfied with EEOC's disposition

right to work laws union membership or payment of union dues or their equivalent is not a condition of employment before or after hire

riparian rights rights of adjoining landowners to use a body of water

ripeness on the facts and procedurally, the case's realness and readiness for determination by the court

round meetings of the WTO are held in rounds, which are a series of meetings sometimes over a period of years in which an issue will attempt to be resolved

Rule 10b-5 the broad antifraud provision that forms the basis for most security violations involving fraudulent purchases or sales of securities

rule of reason a rule that requires only unreasonable restraints of trade to be violations of the Sherman Act

S

safe harbor rule rule that exempts forward looking statements from forming the basis of liability as long as the statements are made in good faith or with a reasonable basis

Sarbanes-Oxley Act an act passed by Congress designed to reform corporate culture that leads to abuses

Sarbanes-Oxley Act of 2002 law enacted in response to the collapse of several major corporations due to corporate misconduct; established new standards in many areas of corporate culture

scope of employment the work or service that a person is employed to do at a particular time or place

scoping meeting the meeting to allow any interested parties to appear and participate in drafting the environmental impact statement

screening device factors used to weed applicants out of the pool of potential hirees

search warrant a judge's written order authorizing a law enforcement officer to conduct a search of a specified place and to seize evidence

seasonable acceptance Acceptance of a UCC offer within either the specified time or a reasonable time

secured creditor a creditor holding a claim against the debtor who has the right to take and hold or sell certain property of the debtor in satisfaction of some or all of the claim

secured party the creditor, lender, seller or other person who owns the security interest in the collateral

secured transaction creates a debtor/creditor relationship and includes two elements – a debt to pay money and an interest of the creditor in specific property which secures the payment of the obligation

security a general term that covers shares of stock or other negotiable instruments that have the characteristics of securities

Securities Act of 1933 law enacted by Congress to regulate the introduction of securities on the market; designed to promote investor confidence

Securities Exchange Commission federal agency created by Congress to oversee the trading of stock and other securities on the private and public market

security agreement the agreement which creates or provides for a security interest

security interest an interest in personal property which secures payment or performance of an obligation

self-defense using appropriate force to protect one's self from an unpermitted touching by another

self-regulatory organizations (SRO) congressionally created agencies that enforce every aspect of the securities markets in the U.S

Sentencing Guidelines a set of standards for determining the punishment that a convicted criminal should receive

service marks mark that identifies sale or advertising of services

sexual harassment gender-based activity directed toward a harasee which either requests sexual activity of him or her or creates a hostile or intimidating environment for the harassee

shareholders those who actually own the corporation through the purchase of its shares

shares also known as stock, are a type of security that evidences ownership of a corporation owned sold in increments

shop steward a union representative who speaks to management to seek resolution for a problem in the workplace

shopkeeper's rule a shopkeeper's conditional privilege to hold someone suspected of shoplifting to investigate it, if the suspicion is reasonable, the time is reasonable and the person receives reasonable treatment

short swing profits profits made using in-an-out transactions that temporarily affect the market

signatories member nation that signs a treaty or organizational charter

signing officers officers of the corporation who must sign PCAOB and SEC filings under various reporting requirements

sixth amendment constitutional amendment that establishes your right to an attorney during the important phases of the criminal process

slander oral defamation

social sustainability an organization that gives back to the community through employee volunteering or charitable donations

socially responsible investing a form of investing that favors corporations that promote environmentally aware practices, consumer protection, human rights, and diversity

sociological theory philosophy of law in which law is a reflection of the constantly competing interests of society

sole owner one who owns property alone

sole proprietor a person who owns a business and is responsible for all its debts

solid waste any garbage, refuse, sludge, or gaseous material that results from industrial, commercial, mining and agricultural operations

special agent an agent who is authorized to conduct only a single transaction

specialized courts courts created for handling specific types of cases, e.g., United States Tax Court

specific performance equitable remedy ordering party to perform contractual obligation

standing qualification to sue or defend because of having a personal stake in the outcome

stare decisis meaning to stand by things decided; the process of ruling the same on later cases with the same facts as earlier cases with those facts

stare decisis system of looking to precedent to determine how a legal case should be decided

Statute of Frauds law requiring certain contracts to be in writing to be enforced

statutes of limitation a statute establishing a time limit for suing in a civil case

stock a type of security that evidences ownership interest in a corporation, sold in increments

stock certificate paper that is evidence of the stock of a company; usually issued in small or closely held corporations

stock market a physical or virtual location where stock is bought and sold

stolen property property illegally taken from its true owner or possessor

sublease lessee of property allowing another to lease his or her interest

sublessee one who leases property from a lessee

subrogation the right conferred upon the surety to stand in the shoes of the creditor once he pays the debt of the debtor

substantive law laws which provide rights and responsibilities, upon pain of penalty in the form of liability or criminal sanctions

summons document bringing the defendant under the court's jurisdiction when a complaint has been filed against defendant

superfund the fund of money provided by the U.S. government to help clean up hazardous waste cites

surety for collection a surety who pays only after the creditor exhausts all legal options to collect from the debtor

surety a person who promises to pay the debt of another should they default

sustainable business a business that participates in environmentally friendly processes, products, or activities that address environmental concerns while maintaining a profit

T

tangible property things that you can see, touch and feel

tariffs charges imposed on a product when imported into a country

temporary restraining order injunction granted without a hearing, usually on a showing of urgency

tenant one given possession of property

tenants by the entirety married couple owning property together

tenants in common multiple landowners with an undivided interest that can be disposed of by each of the owners

territorial restrictions agreements between competitors to carve certain markets between them

testator male who executes a will

testatrix female who executes a will

theft of trade secrets intentionally taking information which is a business secret and using it for one's own purposes

third party beneficiary contract Contract entered into between two parties for the benefit of a third person

third party creditor beneficiary One who is to receive benefits under a contract as the repayment of an obligation of a party to the contract

threatened species a species that is likely to become endangered in the foreseeable future

tippee a person who receives inside information from an insider that he knows to be confidential

title legal right to own property

tombstone ad an announcement (not an offer) of a new security for sale

tort Noncontractual, noncriminal violations of civil law

tortfeasor One who commits a tort

trade association an association that works together to inform members of beneficial information

trade dress total image of a product, including size, shape, color, texture, graphics, or technique involved

trade name name of business that identifies the producer rather than the service or product

trade secret private formula, pattern, device, or compilation used in one's business

trade secrets business information, formulas, or other secrets protected by state statute

trademark protection for goods or services identifying them as belonging to the owner of the mark

trademark infringement use of copyrighted material without the owner's permission

treaty a negotiated contract between parties who happen to be nations

treble damages antitrust damages that are three times the actual damages

trespass to personal property intentionally interfering with the personal property of another with permission of the owner or rightful possessor

trespass to real property intentionally coming onto the land of another without permission of the owner or rightful possessor

tripartite system three branches of American government: legislative, judicial, and executive

triple-bottom line using sustainable development and distribution to impact the environment, business growth, and society

trustee the representative of the bankruptcy estate who exercises statutory powers, principally for the benefit of the unsecured creditors, under the general supervision of the court and the direct supervision of the U.S. trustee or bankruptcy administrator

tying arrangement ability to obtain one good is dependent upon taking another, usually less desirable good

U

U.S. trustee an officer of the Justice Department responsible for supervising the administration of bankruptcy cases

unconscionability UCC concept of refusal of a court to give force and effect to a contract which seems grossly unfair to one of the parties

underwriter the financial firm hired to solicit potential investors in stock that is being offered through an initial public offering

undisclosed principal a principal is undisclosed when the third party is unaware that the agent is acting for a principal and thus assumes that the agent is contracting on its own behalf. Under these circumstances, the agent is a party to the contract (as the undisclosed principal)

undue influence presumption created when there is a dominant-subservient relationship, opportunity for the dominant party to influence the subservient party, and a contract which tends to favor the dominant party

unenforceable contract a contract which is not in writing as required or will not be otherwise made to be completed by the court

unfair labor practice grounds on which action is brought by labor alleging management violated the NLRA

unfair management practice management or labor can engage in an activity that breaches an agreement or labor law; parties can file to have matter resolved

Uniform Commercial Code (UCC) Compilation of state laws of contracts with a suggested approach, creating uniformity

unilateral contract an agreement in which one party promises something if the other party does an act

unilateral mistake one party makes a mistake in contracting, but the other party is not aware of it

unintended beneficiary someone who benefits by a third party contract, but was not intended to do so

union representation election an election at which employees vote for whether they want a union to represent them and which one

union security clause provision in collective bargaining agreement that employees must either become a member of the union or pay the equivalent in union dues as a condition of employment

union shop employee must join union within a certain period of hire and can be terminated for failure to pay union dues

Universal Agreements to Mediate (UAMs) agreement between EEOC and employer establishing an EEOC contact point for scheduling mediation of employee EEOC claims

unreasonable restraint of trade restraint of trade which violates law

unsecured creditor a creditor without a security interest in a debtor's property

unsecured debt debt that is not guaranteed by any collateral. Credit cards are unsecured

upcycling the process of using waste materials to provide new products

upstream merger merger that occurs when a consumer acquires a supplier

utilitarian approach decision based on what results in the greatest good for the greatest number of people

utility usefulness required to receive a patent

utility patent patent available for any new and useful process or inventions

V

valid contract one meeting the requirements of mutual assent, consideration, capacity, and legality

vertical per se violation antitrust violations among and between those in the vertical chain of commerce, i.e., seller to buyer

void contract an agreement which has no legal effect because it lacks legality or other requirement for a valid contract

voidable contract a contract which one of the parties may opt not to go through with, without fault

voir dire questioning of prospective jurors by lawyers to determine who will sit on the jury

voluntary assumption of the risk knowingly undertaking to do an act that presents an unreasonable risk of harm to the actor

W

warranty of fitness for a particular purpose promise arising from representations of seller that good will be appropriate for a particular use seller is made aware of

warranty of merchantability promise arising from sale of good that it will perform as average in the industry

white collar crime a nonviolent crime usually involving cheating or dishonesty in commercial matters

wildcat strike strike not authorized by the union

will legal document setting forth what is to be done with maker's property after death

winding up one of the steps in terminating the partnership that requires the partnership to end its business and not accept any new business

wire fraud an act of fraud using electronic communications in foreign or interstate commerce

work-for-hire doctrine employers own product created while artist employed by employer

World Trade Organization umbrella organization formed in 1994 to oversee the GATT, GATs, and TRIPs

writ of certiorari order directing a lower court to send the record of a case to an appellate court for review

yellow dog contracts contracts employers required employees to sign promising that they were not members of a union and would not become union members while working for the employer